The Complete Walt Disney World 2009

Julie and Mike Neal

coconut
press

COCONUT PRESS
Sanibel Florida

The Complete Walt Disney World® 2009

ISBN 978-0-9709-5968-3
ISSN 1547-8491
Library of Congress Control No.
2008908833

About this book

The only photo-driven guide to Walt Disney World®, this book also contains a wealth of helpful tips and practical information, including ratings and reviews of more than 700 attractions, restaurants, shops and hotels.

Planning your trip

The front of the book helps you get ready for your vacation. A brief overview introduces you to Walt Disney World, a timely What's New article addresses everything that is new or different for 2009, then two lists describe proven ways to save money and time.

A Planning Your Trip chapter offers a step-by-step approach to organizing your vacation and delves into important Practical Information on everything from what to pack to Disney's 2009 promotion that offers free admission on your birthday.

The last page of the book is a Disney World telephone directory.

Attractions

Each theme park chapter is easy to navigate. An At A Glance section contains summaries of every attraction, show and restaurant, and the locations of meet-and-greet characters. Attraction articles include storylines, histories, technological insights, Fun Finds and Hidden Mickeys, as well as:

Quality rating ★–★ ★ ★ ★ ★
Authors' choice ✔
A **specifications** list for each attraction includes ride length and capacity, "fear factor," access options for disabled guests (wheelchair, ECV access; assistive listening, handheld captioning, video captioning), height restrictions and year debuted. *FastPass* Denotes the availability of Disney's free reservation system. Typical **Fastpass return times** appear on the third page of

each theme park chapter. **Average wait times** for each attraction are listed hour-by-hour.

Restaurants

This book has restaurant and snack stand information for every Disney World theme park, water park, Downtown Disney and resort hotel. Table-service restaurant reviews include the following information:

Quality rating ★–★ ★ ★ ★ ★
Authors' choice ✔
Average price per entree
$ .... Less than $10
$$ .... $10–$15
$$$ .... $15–$20
$$$$ .... $20–$30
$$$$$ .... More than $30
Restaurant reviews include specifications such as cuisine, entree price ranges per meal, serving hours, characters (if present) and seating capacity.
Abbreviations

A	adult	C	child
B	breakfast	L	lunch
D	dinner		

Disney Signature Denotes a Disney Signature Restaurant, Disney's name for its premium eateries.

Resorts and hotels

Resort descriptions include restaurant reviews, kid-focused swimming pool details, listings of children's activities, as well as these key details:

Quality rating ★–★ ★ ★ ★ ★
Authors' choice ✔
Average nightly rate
$ .... Less than $100
$$ .... $100–$150
$$$ .... $150–$200
$$$$ .... $200–$250
$$$$$ .... More than $250
Disney resort specifications include rates; location; distance to Disney theme and water parks, Downtown Disney and ESPN Wide World of Sports; size; room particulars; amenities; transportation options; check-in and check-out times; telephone and fax numbers; street addresses; and parking fees, if any.

MICAELA NEAL

Authors Julie and Mike Neal

Abbreviations

ac	acres	biz	business
cts	courts	mi	mile
opt	optional	rm	rooms
srvc	service	tr	trail

It adds up to an entertaining, helpful and smartly organized guide that's still small enough to take with you. We hope it helps you have your best vacation ever.

About the authors

Authors Julie and Mike Neal have visited Walt Disney World more than 1,000 times. With an apartment in the adjacent Disney-developed town of Celebration, Fla., the husband and wife team still stop by Disney World at least once a week. The Neals live on Sanibel Island, Florida, with their daughter, Micaela, and lab, Bear.

Additional photos and research by Micaela Neal. Illustrations by Vince Burkhead. Unless indicated all content © 2009 Media Enterprises Inc. This book is not endorsed or sponsored by the Walt Disney Co. or Disney Destinations LLC, or connected to those companies. Walt Disney World® is a trademark of the Walt Disney Co. Walt Disney World® is officially known as the Walt Disney World Resort.® Prices as of Jan. 1, 2009.

To Amy, Mitch, Vince and Lisa, who believed in us.

Contents

The Complete Walt Disney World 2009 is published by Coconut Press, 920 Palm St., Sanibel, FL 33957. (239) 472-3985. E-mail us at info@coconutpress.com or visit our website at coconutpress.com Copyright © 2009 by Media Enterprises Inc. All Rights Reserved. Reproduction in whole or part without permission is prohibited. The publisher and authors have made every effort to ensure the information in this publication was correct at press time, but do not assume and hereby disclaim any liability to any party for any loss or damage caused by errors, omissions, misleading information, or any potential travel disruption due to labor or financial difficulty, whether such errors or omissions result from negligence, accident or any other cause. This book makes reference to various attraction dialogue and narration, characters, images, trademarks and other properties owned by the Walt Disney Co. and other parties for editorial purposes only. The publisher and authors make no commercial claim to their use. Nothing contained herein is intended to express judgment on, or affect the validity of legal status of, any character, image, term or word as a trademark, service mark or other proprietary mark. Disney characters © Disney Enterprises Inc. "A Bug's Life," "Cars," "Finding Nemo," "The Incredibles," "Monsters, Inc." and "Toy Story" characters © Disney Enterprises Inc./Pixar Animation Studios. It's Tough to be a Bug! based upon the Disney/Pixar film "A Bug's Life" © Disney/Pixar. Turtle Talk with Crush is inspired by the Walt Disney Pictures presentation of a Pixar Animation Studios film, "Finding Nemo" © Disney/Pixar. Indiana Jones" Epic Stunt Spectacular © and Star Tours © Disney/Lucasfilm Ltd. Tarzan® owned by Edgar Rice Burroughs Inc. and Disney Enterprises Inc.; all rights reserved. The Twilight Zone" is a registered trademark of CBS Inc. and is used pursuant to a license from CBS Inc. La Nouba" is a trademark of Cirque du Soleil.® American Idol® is a registered trademark of 19TV Ltd. and Freemantle Media North America Inc. Printed in the U.S.A.

Walt Disney World Resort®

1 mi
1 km

← TO TAMPA

← TO CELEBRATION

EXIT 62

Reedy Creek

■ ← MICKEY WATER TOWER

GRIFFEN RD

WORLD DR

1

ESPN
WIDE WORLD
OF SPORTS

Florida
Hospital
Celebration
Health

EXIT 64

← TO CELEBRATION

IRLO BRONSON MEMORIAL HWY

192

OSCEOLA PKWY

535

2

192

SHERBERTH RD

DISNEY'S
ANIMAL
KINGDOM

WINTER SUMMERLAND
MINIATURE GOLF

BUENA VISTA

BLIZZARD
BEACH

DISNEY'S
HOLLYWOOD
STUDIOS

OSCEOLA PKWY

VICTORY WAY

12

TYPHOON
LAGOON

Bonnet Creek

EXIT 65

INTERNATIONAL DRIVE SOUTH

536

417

TO AIRPORT →

LODGING KEY

1. Disney's All-Star Resorts
2. Disney's Animal Kingdom Lodge
3. Disney's Beach Club Resort
4. Disney's BoardWalk Inn and Villas
5. Disney's Caribbean Beach Resort
6. Disney's Contemporary Resort
7. Disney's Coronado Springs Resort
8. Disney's Fort Wilderness Resort & Campground
9. Disney's Grand Floridian Resort & Spa
10. Disney's Old Key West Resort
11. Disney's Polynesian Resort
12. Disney's Pop Century Resort
13. Disney's Port Orleans French Quarter
14. Disney's Port Orleans Riverside
15. Disney's Saratoga Springs Resort & Spa
16. Disney's Wilderness Lodge
17. Disney's Yacht Club Resort
18. Shades of Green
19. Walt Disney World Dolphin
20. Walt Disney World Swan
21. Best Western Lake Buena Vista
22. Buena Vista Palace Hotel & Spa
23. DoubleTree Guest Suites
24. Regal Sun
25. Hilton
26. Holiday Inn
27. Royal Plaza

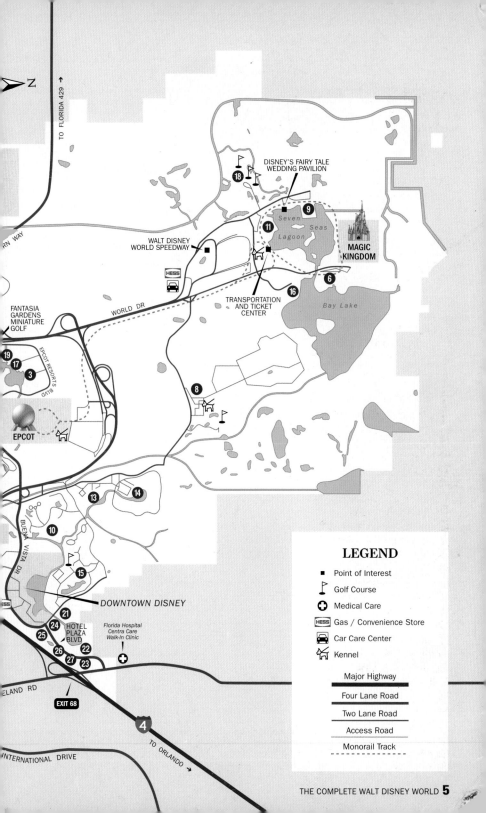

TO FLORIDA 429 →

DISNEY'S FAIRY TALE
WEDDING PAVILION

18

9

Seven
Seas
Lagoon

11

MAGIC
KINGDOM

WALT DISNEY
WORLD SPEEDWAY

HESS

6

16

Bay Lake

FANTASIA
GARDENS
MINIATURE
GOLF

WORLD DR

TRANSPORTATION
AND TICKET
CENTER

19
17
3

EPCOT RESORTS BLVD

8

EPCOT

13   14

BUENA VISTA DR

10

15

DOWNTOWN DISNEY

21

24   HOTEL
25   PLAZA
             BLVD
26
27   22
      23

Florida Hospital
Centra Care
Walk-In Clinic

ELAND RD

EXIT 68

4

TO ORLANDO →

INTERNATIONAL DRIVE

LEGEND

- ■ Point of Interest
- ⚑ Golf Course
- ✚ Medical Care
- HESS Gas / Convenience Store
- 🚗 Car Care Center
- 🐕 Kennel

| Major Highway |
| Four Lane Road |
| Two Lane Road |
| Access Road |
| - - - Monorail Track |

Tiki statues squirt water and
mist along the Adventureland
walkway in Magic Kingdom

Twice the size of Manhattan, Walt Disney World is the world's largest collection of theme parks, water parks and resorts. It's truly...

A World of its own

A trip to Walt Disney World is not just a way to spend time with your children, not just an escape from day-to-day doldrums. It's a reawakening of that free-spirited, good-natured soul who lives deep inside you—the one your spouse married, the one you want your kids to emulate. Yes it can be crowded, yes it can be expensive, yes it takes a good plan to see it all, but no other man-made vacationland so deliberately embraces creativity, optimism and a sense of wonder about the world.

Populated daily by more than 100,000 visitors as well as 54,000 employees (Disney uses the phrase "cast members"), the 47-square-mile property is the No. 1 vacation destination on the planet. It includes four theme parks, two water parks, a sports complex, a shopping and entertainment district and 19 resort hotels.

The icon of Walt Disney World, Cinderella Castle anchors its Magic Kingdom theme park

of hang gliding (Soarin') and astronaut training (Mission Space). World Showcase is highlighted by entertainment, dining and shopping.

The front of show-business-themed **Disney's Hollywood Studios** is a tribute to Old Hollywood, with re-created 1940s-era icons such as Hollywood Boulevard and Grauman's Chinese Theatre. The rear was originally a working studio, and still carries that theme. This 135-acre park includes two of Disney's World best thrill rides—the Twilight Zone Tower of Terror and the Rock 'n' Roller Coaster Starring Aerosmith. New for 2009 is the American Idol Experience, a live talent show.

Disney's Animal Kingdom theme park combines exotic live animals with high-quality attractions. Top stops include Expedition Everest, a roller coaster that travels backward into a mountain cave; Kilimanjaro Safaris, an exploration into a replicated African wildlife preserve aboard an open-sided truck; and Festival of the Lion King, a show with energetic acrobats, dancers, singers and stilt walkers. The centerpiece of the 500-acre park is the Tree of Life, a 145-foot man-made sculpture.

It's only 122 acres, 0.5 percent of Walt Disney World, but to many folks the **Magic Kingdom** *is* Walt Disney World. A more spacious version of California's Disneyland, Magic Kingdom re-imagines that park's Main Street U.S.A., Adventureland, Fantasyland, Frontierland and Tomorrowland. This family favorite has more than 40 attractions, including classics such as It's a Small World and Space Mountain. It's the most popular theme park in the world.

Sort of a permanent World's Fair, the 300-acre **Epcot** park is divided into science-themed Future World and the international pavilions of the World Showcase. Future World attractions include simulators that offer realistic sensations

On a summer morning it's hard to beat the family fun at Disney's two themed **water parks,** Blizzard Beach and Typhoon Lagoon. Disney has four championship golf courses as well as a 9-hole, two miniature golf courses and many tennis courts, and offers organized fishing, horseback riding, Segway tours, stockcar driving, surfing and water sports.

Downtown Disney is a 120-acre dining, entertainment and shopping district at the eastern edge of the property. The **ESPN Wide World of Sports** complex is 220 acres of sports facilities that host

amateur and professional competitions. It includes a baseball stadium, two fieldhouses and many outdoor fields.

Distant lands and forgotten eras are the themes at most of Disney World's 19 resorts. Accommodations range from campsites to multilevel suites.

A secret 'Project X'

In 1964, the Walt Disney company began buying up parcels of land 20 miles southwest of Orlando, using false names and dummy corporations to keep prices down. In October, 1965, the Orlando Sentinel-Star identified the buyer; a month later Walt Disney and his brother, Roy, confirmed the existence of their "Project X," a plan for a futuristic city—the Experimental Prototype Community of Tomorrow (EPCOT)—where solutions to urban problems could be explored. To help fund itself, the area would include a theme park, an East Coast version of California's Disneyland.

After Walt death in 1966, Roy decided to go ahead with idea, at least the theme-park portion, but changed its name to Walt Disney World. The largest private construction project in the history of the

Top: Stormtroopers at a Star Wars Weekend. Above: Finding Nemo—The Musical.

United States, it broke ground in 1969. Development was led by two military men. Former Army general Joe Potter had overseen operations at the Panama Canal and the 1964 World's Fair. Former Navy admiral Joe Vallor had supervised

**Top: Sisters dressed as Disney heroines.
Above: Belle performs in the musical 'Beauty
and the Beast—Live on Stage'**

the building of Disneyland. Potter, Vallor and 9,000 workers moved 8 million cubic yards of dirt and built 47 miles of canals and 22 miles of levees. They dredged the 406-acre Bay Lake and created a 172-acre "Seven Seas Lagoon." They built roads, maintenance shops, a phone company, power plant, sewage plant and tree farm.

Walt Disney World opened to the public on Oct. 1, 1971. It consisted of the Magic Kingdom, the Contemporary and Polynesian resorts and the Fort Wilderness Resort & Campground. Disney's Golf Resort (today's Shades of Green) was built in 1973. Lake Buena Vista Village (today's Downtown Disney Marketplace) opened in 1975.

The Disney company wrestled with the EPCOT idea through the early 1970s, but the vision for an experimental city just wasn't clear without its visionary. In 1976 the company announced plans for EPCOT Center, a theme park with "demonstration concepts" and an "international people-to-people exchange" located in the center of what was to be Walt Disney's city. Opened in 1982, it became the lowercase "Epcot" in 1994.

For all that Disney created in Florida during the '70s and early '80s, it has built far more since. It opened Disney-MGM Studios, Pleasure Island and Typhoon Lagoon in 1989. The Osprey Ridge and (since closed) Eagle Pines golf courses

debuted in 1992. Blizzard Beach arrived in 1995. Downtown Disney's West Side and Wide World of Sports opened in 1999.

During that same period the number of hotel rooms on Disney property grew from 2,000 to 31,000. Disney's Caribbean Beach and Grand Floridian resorts opened in 1988. Thirteen more debuted in the 1990s. They included the Yacht and Beach Club and Walt Disney World Swan and Dolphin resorts (1990), the Port Orleans French Quarter and Old Key West complexes (1991), Dixie Landings (now Port Orleans Riverside, 1992), All-Star Sports Resort and Wilderness Lodge (1994), All-Star Music and BoardWalk (1995), Coronado Springs (1997) and All-Star Movies (1999). Disney's newest hotels are Animal Kingdom Lodge (2001), Pop Century (2003) and Saratoga Springs (2004).

The southwest corner of the property was developed as a residential area with its own downtown, school and post office. Named Celebration, the planned commu-

More than 54,000 'cast members' work at Walt Disney World, including theatrical performers and street characters

nity broke ground in 1996. Today 2,700 people live there.

FUN FACTS ❯❯ Walt Disney World's employee wardrobe consists of 2,500 "costumes" (there are no "uniforms") and 1.8 million pieces. ❯❯ Disney World sells enough mouse-ear caps each year to cover the head of every man, woman and child in Portland, Oregon. ❯❯ The number of Disney World character T-shirts sold each year would clothe everyone in Chicago.

New Citizen of Hollywood
character Sparky the Electrician
at Disney's Hollywood Studios

What's new

Here's everything that's different at Disney for 2009

Something old, something new, something borrowed, something canceled, something free, something locked up and shut down. That's what you'll get this year at Walt Disney World, where changes are taking place everywhere.

A new promotion gets you in free on your birthday. New attractions include a state-of-the-art shooting gallery and a street party imported from California's Disneyland. Magic Kingdom is adding a robotic President Obama and a live meet-and-greet Tinker Bell. There are new street performers, restaurants, themed hotel rooms, even a luxury pet resort.

The big news for 2009 isn't what's opening, however, but what's shutting down. The nightclubs of Pleasure Island, Disney's adult-oriented district that once celebrated New Year's Eve every night of the year, are no more. The clubs closed for good in September, 2008.

There are other cutbacks, too. Pink slips have been given to some cherished entertainers, as well as cute little Pal Mickey. Introduced in 2003, the interactive plushie still operates in the four theme parks, but is no longer sold.

In the next few pages we'll chart most all of the Walt Disney World changes for the new year—the big and the small; the good, bad and the ugly.

Magic Kingdom

Change is coming to the **Hall of Presidents!** With the election of President Barack Obama, Disney is giving its venerable patriotic attraction (pg 65) a thorough renovation. Besides adding a robotic Obama, the company is redoing the George Washington figure so it speaks too, giving the show three talking presidents—Washington, Abraham Lincoln and Obama. Disney is also updating the show's light, mechanical, projection and sound systems. Expect the film to be more vivid and clear, and the introduction of the various presidents to be easier to follow. The new Hall opens on July 4, 2009... The other big news at Magic Kingdom: the addition of **Tinker Bell** as a live, meet-and-greet character (pg 95). The pixie star of 1953's "Peter Pan" appears along with Fawn, Iridessa, Rosetta and Silvermist, her co-stars in a new line of Disney Fairies books and DVDs... The **Disney Dreams Come True Parade** (pg 107) has a new vehicle to host its Grand Marshals. Meant to resemble a 1912 touring car, the huge convertible has Mickey Mouse (i.e., three circle) tire treads... Hey Howdy Heave Ho! Say goodbye to **Woody's Cowboy Camp** Frontierland street performance, as well as the **Main Street Family Fun Day** parade... Goofy no longer liberates your appetite at the **Liberty Tree Tavern** (pg 52). The restaurant began serving a character-free dinner in January 2009... **The Frontierland Fry Cart** has been expanded into its own building. It serves wraps and chicken nuggets as well as McDonald's fries... A new **snack stand** at the Transportation and Ticket Center sells coffee and pastries.

An Epcot Kim Possible 'Kimmunicator'

Epcot

Spaceship Earth (pg 130)—the attraction inside the geodesic sphere of the same name—has relaunched with changes finished in early 2008. It's still a time trip through the history, and future, of communications, but with a new narration, scenes, score and special effects. There's also a new post-show... Meant to be the focal point of the **IllumiNations** pyrotechnic show (pg 156), those moving images on the giant revolving Earth finally look the part. Disney installed a new LED display system on the globe in the fall of 2008... At The Land pavilion, the Nestlé Toll House **Junior Chef** experience has closed, and the **Garden Grill** restaurant (pg 124) no longer serves lunch... At **Test Track** (pg 136), the Fuel for Thought post-show exhibit has been redone.

A new high-tech scavenger hunt, the **Kim Possible World Showcase Adventure** (pg 157) sends families off through a World Showcase pavilion as secret agents fighting various comical villains and their mad inventions. It debuts in early 2009... The China pavilion's **Nine Dragons** restaurant has reopened with a refreshed decor and lighter menu, as has the adjoining fast-food spot... That

delicious gelato at the **Italian donkey cart** is no more. It's been replaced with a sweeter substitute... World Showcase entertainers no longer appearing include the legendary **Pam Brody** at the U.K. pavilion's Rose & Crown pub, **OrisiRisi** at the Outpost and **Spelmanns Gledje** in Norway... In Mexico "Three Caballeros" meet-and-greet characters **José** and **Panchito** have vamoosed, as have **Kenai** and **Koda** in Canada and **Pinocchio** and **Gepetto** in Germany.

Disney's Hollywood Studios

Known as Disney-MGM Studios until 2008, this park has added three attractions in the past year—The **American Idol Experience** talent contest (pg 175), which lets guests compete on a set modeled after the one used on the "American Idol" television series; the 3-D **Toy Story Mania** ride-through video game (pg 190); and, replacing the Stars and Motor Cars parade, **Block Party Bash** (pg 201), a street party imported from Disneyland... A new cast of puppets star in **Playhouse Disney Live on Stage** (pg 188). Appearing are characters from the shows "Mickey Mouse Clubhouse," "Handy Manny," "Little Einsteins" and "My Friends Tigger and Pooh." They debuted in Feb-

ruary 2008... The **"High School Musical 3: Right Here! Right Now!"** (pg 167) street show focuses on the "Senior Year" of that movie series... You can meet Prince Caspian at the **Journey Into Narnia: Prince Caspian** exhibit (pg 189)... Costumes along the Great Movie Ride queue now include one from 1998's "Shakespeare in Love"... **Sheriff Woody, Jessie** and other "Toy Story" characters greet guests indoors at Pixar Place, the name for the old Mickey Avenue. **Lightning McQueen** and **Mater** from the 2006 movie "Cars" appear in the Backlot at the former Al's Toy Barn, which has been re-imagined as Radiator Springs... In cutbacks, pyrotechnic show **Fantasmic!** is now held just two nights a week, and a cappella group **Four For A Dollar** no longer performs as the preshow for Beauty and the Beast — Live on Stage (pg 193).

Disney's Animal Kingdom

It's a boy! Twice! A male **baby elephant** was born in June 2008 at the park; a male **giraffe** in September. Expect to see them in the Kilimanjaro Safaris savannas (pg 226)... The live stage show **Pocahontas and Her Forest Friends** has closed... Formerly a McDonald's fries location, Dinoland U.S.A.'s PetriFries stand has a new menu and a new name: Trilobites.

Water parks

Typhoon Lagoon (pg 259) is closed until March 21, 2009 for a major makeover. Improvements include recoating the water slides and resurfacing the wave pool and children's area.

Downtown Disney

Disney has closed all of its Pleasure Island nightclubs, including **8 Trax, Adventurers Club, BET Soundstage Club, The Comedy Warehouse, Mannequins Dance Palace** and **Motion**. To make up for the loss to Disney ticket holders, the company has added complimentary tee times at its 9-hole **Oak Trail golf course** to its Water Park Fun & More ticket option and its Premium Annual Pass (pg 22).

As for Pleasure Island eateries, the Portobello Yacht Club has become simply **Portobello** (pg 270), with a third outdoor dining space and a shift in theme to that of a Tuscan country trattoria. The menu features lots of antipasti and regional dishes from Milan, Rome and Tuscany.... **Fulton's Crab House** (pg 269) will be remodeled in the spring... The **Raglan Road** restaurant and pub remains open, as do shops **Curl by Sammy Duvall, Orlando Harley-Davidson** and **Fuego by Sosa Cigars**... Unnamed at press time, a new 5,000-square-foot **Central and South American restaurant** will open in 2009 next to the old Adventurers Club. It's billed as a "high-energy, casual eatery."

At the West Side, a new **tethered balloon** attraction near Bongos will take guests 300 feet up in the air... The **Wolfgang Puck Café** (pg 268) is updating its interior and enclosing its front patio.

At the Marketplace, **T-Rex: A Prehistoric Family Adventure** (pg 270) opened in the fall of 2008. The family restaurant features huge animated dinosaurs, wooly mammoths and primitive sea life. It's loud, but fun, and the food is good... Disney's Wonderful World of Memories scrapbook shop has become Hanes-sponsored **Design-A-Tee** (pg 272)... **Goofy's Candy Company** (pg 273) has a new room for private birthday parties... A larger, covered Marketplace stage is a main venue for Disney's Magic Music Days.

Sports and recreation

Want to work on your swing? Disney's **golf lessons** (pg 278) are now given only at the Palm and Magnolia courses... **Surfing lessons** (pg 279) will not be available during the Typhoon Lagoon refurbishment (see above)... **Archery lessons** (pg 294) are now available at Disney's Fort Wilderness Resort and Campground. The 90-minute Archery Experience ($25, 407-939-7529) includes equipment and instruction. It's offered Thursday, Friday and Saturday afternoons. The resort has also added bicycle and surrey rentals... Formerly known as Disney's Wide World of Sports, the **ESPN Wide World of Sports** complex (pg 276) has more than a new name. Opened in 2008, its Jostens Center is an indoor multi-sport facility with 45,000 square feet of competition space. It can be configured as six basketball courts, 12 volleyball courts or two roller hockey rinks. A 100-lane bowling center is scheduled to open in 2010. The complex no longer offers complimentary tours.

Accommodations

Disney's Caribbean Beach Resort (pg 289) has added a pirate theme to 384 rooms within its Trinidad South Village area. Rooms have ship-themed beds, buccaneer accessories and a "swashbuckling" décor. Work should be finished by summer, with some rooms available in January. Remodeled in 2008, rooms in the Martinique section are themed to the 2003 film "Finding Nemo"... There is lots of restaurant news at **Disney's Contemporary Resort** (pg 290). In the atrium, the Concourse Steakhouse has been replaced by the Contempo Cafe, a high-tech fast-food spot where you place your order at a computer. Next door, a redone Chef Mickey's includes (finally!) a waiting area. A new table-service restaurant, The Wave, has opened downstairs behind the check-in counter... **Disney's Fort Wilderness Resort and Campground** (pg 294) has gone upscale. Well, sorta. Cabins at the rustic retreat are now classified in Disney's Moderate Resort category... Damaged during the 2004 hurricane season, the **Downtown Disney Holiday Inn** (pg 312) is scheduled for a $25 million "top-to-bottom makeover" and to reopen this year.

Three **Disney Vacation Club** properties are opening this year. The **Kidani Village** at Disney's Animal Kingdom Lodge (pg 285) debuts May 1, with reservations available for DVC members after Aug. 10. These rooms overlook the existing, now expanded, Sunset Savanna. Due to construction, animals will not be on that savanna from Jan. 15–April 15. A second phase of the Village will include its own savanna (with okapi!) and open in September. Forty-three Vacation Club rooms opened in 2008 in the lodge's original main building... The 15-story **Bay Lake Tower** DVC property opens this fall at the Contemporary Resort (pg 291). The crescent-shaped building will have 295 villas with full kitchens, separate bedrooms and dramatic views. Amenities will include flat-screen televisions, washers and dryers, granite countertops and modern artwork... The **Treehouse Villas** at Disney's Saratoga Springs Resort & Spa (pg 304) will also open late in the year. Nestled in a natural forest, the stand-alone, three-bedroom homes will use an octagonal "cabin casual" design much like the original 1975 Treehouse Villas that used to occupy the site. Each will be elevated 10 feet off the ground, have a cathedral ceiling and sleep nine...

The American Idol Experience is brand-new at Disney's Hollywood Studios

Disney has sold 298 acres of its Florida property to **Four Seasons Hotels and Resorts** for a hotel and golf course on the site of the former Eagle Pines golf course. Plans call for a 445-room Four Seasons hotel and Residence Club time shares, as well as custom single and multi-family vacation homes. The complex is scheduled to open in 2010.

And finally, a **luxury pet resort** will open on Disney World's Bonnet Creek Parkway in 2009. The high-class kennel will have pet suites with televisions and raised bedding, activities such as nature walks and playgroups, and pampering services ranging from ice cream treats to bedtime stories. It will be run by Best Friends Pet Care, the company that has

A cheerleader inspires the crowd during a 'High School Musical' street show at Disney's Hollywood Studios

been operating all Walt Disney World kennels since January 2008.

Practical information

Beginning early in 2009, Walt Disney World guests with **Verizon wireless service** will be able to access an array of real-time Disney World information on their cell phones, such as current attraction wait times, restaurant availablities, Disney character appearances and special park activities. If they like, they can also receive calls from characters... The price of **theme-park tickets** (pg 22) has gone up again. As of Oct. 1, 2008, a one-day "base" ticket—which admits its holder to one theme park each day of its use—costs $75 for adults, $63 for children ages 3–9. A weekly pass is $228 for adults, $193 for children. There are many other options... **Theme-park parking** now costs $12 per car... Extra Magic Hours (pg 283) **evening wristbands** have been discontinued. Disney resort guests now present their Key to the World cards (or applicable resort ID) to take advantage of the hours... Must be the mushrooms: In a move only a character from "Alice in Wonderland" could understand, the Disney Dining Experience restaurant discount card has been renamed **"Tables in Wonderland"** (pg 28). Cardholders save 20 percent at most Walt Disney World restaurants.

New promotion

Free on your birthday? It's true! As part of a one-year promotion called **"What Will You Celebrate?"** Walt Disney World is offering free admission to any one of its theme parks for guests who visit on their birthday during 2009. All it takes is the willingness to fill out a form, either online or in person, and a valid ID including proof of your birth date. The offer is open to any U.S. resident over age 3 (children younger than 3 already get in free). It's easy to take advantage of. Here's how you do it:

❶ First, register your birthday at the Disney web site disneyparks.com. You can sign up anytime through December 31, 2009.

❷ Print the confirmation message you receive.

❸ Bring your confirmation message and proper ID to the gate of a Disney World theme park on your birthday in 2009. You can pick up your free ticket up to seven days prior to your birthday at any designated Will Call window. If you are age 18 or older, acceptable identification is a driver's license, passport or government-issued photo ID. Those under 18 need your original birth certificate or a notarized copy of one. If you like, you can upgrade it on your birthday to a more expensive pass.

If you are an annual or seasonal Walt Disney World passholder, or already have a theme park ticket, you can still get free stuff—your choice of a Birthday Fun Card worth the amount of a one-day park ticket that's good for merchandise or activities, a special Fastpass badge that lets you skip the line on your birthday at multiple attractions, or a one-day park ticket to use any time until your next birthday.

The only catch: all of these have to be picked up in person at Walt Disney World on your birthday in 2009. If your birthday falls on February 29, Disney lets you in free on your choice of either February 28 or March 1.

By the way, you don't have to register online. You can also sign up in person at any designated Disney World Will Call window. Using the Disney web site, however, will save you time.

To accompany the offer, Disney is adding an interactive street party and retro-future Tomorrowland dance in Magic Kingdom, and decorating all its theme parks with banners, balloons and party hats.

Special events

There will be no **ABC Super Soap Weekend** in 2009. Held annually at Disney's Hollywood Studios for the past 15 years, the event has been canceled by ABC-TV bigwigs so the network's stars can tour the country instead. It may return in 2010.

Child's play? If you're organized, planning a visit to Walt Disney World doesn't have to be difficult.

Planning Your Trip

With just a little bit of preparation, it's easy to put together a terrific Walt Disney World vacation

Planning your Walt Disney World vacation takes some thought, but it isn't brain surgery. All it takes is this book, access to the Internet, a cell phone and a couple of hours of your time. You can do it at Starbucks. Ideally you should put your plan together seven months early. Here's how to do it:

Decide when to go

You can have a good time at Walt Disney World any day of the year, but if you've got the flexibility, the first two weeks of December is the **best time to go.** It's not crowded, and there's more to see and do than any other time of the year, thanks to the holiday decor and entertainment. Crowds are also light, and hotel rooms often less expensive, from the middle of January to Valentine's Day, late April to late May and the weeks between Labor Day and mid-November (but it's not all good: some attractions shut down during these periods and Magic Kingdom often closes at 6 p.m.). The least crowded week of the year is the one that starts the day after Labor Day.

The **worst times to visit?** July and early August, when crowds are thick and the air even thicker, and between Christmas and New Year's, when the crowds are incredible. In general, the parks can be packed any time schools are not in session. In fact, many families take their kids out of school to visit Disney in a less-crowded period. If you come during a peak time, you do get the benefit of the parks being open late into the evening.

For detailed **weather data** log on to weather.com, type in the ZIP code 32830 and then scroll down to the tab "Averages."

Decide how long to stay

Want to see the best of everything Walt Disney World has to offer? You'll need **at least a week**. Each theme park takes at least a day to fully enjoy, and you can easily spend a day at each water park. Diversions such as golf, fishing and horseback riding add variety to your trip. As of Oct. 1, 2008, a one-day "base" ticket—which admits its holder to one theme park each day of its use—costs $75 for adults, $63 for children ages 3–9. Longer stays cost less per day, as there's not much difference between a basic 3-day park ticket ($212 for adults) and one good for a week ($228). If you can't stay that long, **three days is enough** to get a nice dose of Disney if you have a good plan. A family of four typically spends about $450 a day on its hotel room, food and park tickets.

Decide where to stay

Disney operates 19 resorts. There are ten others on Disney World property, and **many major chains** within 10 miles. What's the difference? Disney resorts have elaborate theming and offer ben-efits such as more time in the parks, free transportation options and packaged dining and recreation plans. Rates range from $82 to $2,000 a night, though most rooms go for $100 to $300.

Disney World resort guests also get first crack at Disney restaurant reservations. They can book tables 190 days in advance, compared to 180 days for the general public. For details see our Accommodations chapter, which starts on page 282.

Choose your tickets

With park tickets you need to consider three options. The **Park Hopper** ($50) addition lets you visit more than one park a day. **Water Park Fun & More** ($50) adds visits to Blizzard Beach, Typhoon Lagoon, DisneyQuest, Disney's Wide World of Sports and/or a round of golf at Disney's 9-hole Oak Trail walking golf course. **No Expiration** ($17–$200, depending on how many days your ticket includes) means unused days never expire. You can add it anytime within 14 days of your first use. Once you buy your tickets, you can always upgrade them but can't downgrade them. For details call 407-W-DISNEY (934-7639) or log on to disneyworld.com.

Plan on visiting Disney World more than once this year? An **annual pass** provides 365 consecutive days of unlimited admission to the four theme parks, plus perks such as free theme-park parking and dining, entertainment and merchandise discounts. A Premium option adds admission to water parks, DisneyQuest and the ESPN Wide World of Sports.

For ticket **discount plans** see "Saving Money" starting on page 32.

Want a package deal?

If you're going to stay at a Disney resort, you may want to consider a **dining and recreation package**. An easy way to save on food is the **Tables in Wonderland** discount card ($60–$85 annually, formerly called the Disney Dining Experience). Both are described starting on page 28.

DISNEY WORLD WEATHER
Temperatures

■ Average daily range
■ Record monthly range

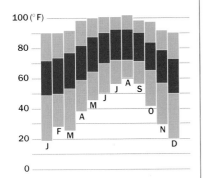

SOURCE: The Weather Channel

Though most Walt Disney World attractions are indoors, rain drives guests away from the theme parks. Most gift shops sell ponchos.

Book it!

To book tickets, a Disney-operated hotel room or a dining/recreation package go to **disneyworld.com** or call 407-W-DISNEY (934-7639) from 7 a.m. to 10 p.m. Eastern time. Other resort numbers are in our Accommodations chapter. Note: Annual passes are not sold online.

Plan your days

First, determine **what days to go to what theme parks.** Log on to disneyworld.com and click "Calendar" to find the hours, Extra Magic Hours, special events and parade and fireworks times of the parks during your stay (available six months in advance). Check pages.prodigy.net/stevesoares for Disney's live entertainment schedules. Then **make your restaurant and recreation reservations** around that schedule. Dinner shows take reservations a year in advance, restaurants 180 days early (190 days if you're staying at a Disney resort). For recreation, you can book fishing and surfing a year out, tours and stock car driving six months in advance, boat cruises and golf tee times 30 days early (90 days for Disney

resort guests) and water sports 30 days early. Other reservations to consider: Birthday parties, florist services, special events, and stroller and ECV rentals (offered with reservations from outside vendors). For phone numbers see the directory on the last page of this book.

When making your plan, keep in mind **the six most common mistakes** guests make when they visit Disney World:

❶ They don't make dining reservations before they leave home.

❷ They don't get to a theme park before it opens.

❸ They don't use Fastpass.

❹ They underestimate how long it takes to travel on Disney transportation.

❺ They go to too many parks in a day.

❻ They wear themselves out.

Grand Gatherings are unique events for groups of eight or more. They include a special breakfast at Magic Kingdom, unusual dinners at Epcot and Disney's Animal Kingdom and a Wishes fireworks cruise, all with character appearances and entertainment. For details call 407-939-7526.

Lady Tremaine greets
guests (reluctantly) at
the Fairytale Garden
Theater, Fantasyland

Birthdays

Available at theme park Guest Relations offices, free "It's My Birthday Today" **buttons** will cue cast members to recognize your celebrating family member. **Goofy will call** your Disney hotel room with a free birthday greeting; to arrange it call 407-824-2222. Many table-service restaurants can provide a 6-inch **birthday cake** ($12.50, personalized with 48 hours notice at 407-827-2253). **Birthday parties** can be held at the Winter Summerland miniature golf course, Blizzard Beach water park and Downtown Disney's Goofy's Candy Co. ($17–$20 person, inc. cake and either hot dogs or pizza). Epcot offers a birthday **fireworks cruise** (407-WDW-BDAY (939-2329)). For 2009, Disney is offering birthday guests **free admission** to any theme park. See page 19 for details.

Characters

Though some fantasy-free parents may not appreciate it, the Disney characters are real: that's not a sweaty young woman in a fur suit, it's Pluto (just ask your kids). **FACE OR FUR?** Disney has two types of characters. "Face characters," such as Cinderella, show the performer's actual face. "Fur characters," such as Winnie the Pooh, are fully costumed. Though face characters rarely intimidate, the odd, huge heads of the fur family sometimes do. To help your child feel comfortable, talk with her beforehand so she knows what to expect. For meet-and-greet lines, buy her an autograph book to give her something to focus on besides the face-to-fur encounter. Don't push her; the characters are super patient. **FINDING CHARACTERS** Besides getting a hand slap at a parade, there are only two ways to meet Disney characters: at meet-and-greet lines and character meals. Each theme park chapter of this book has a list of Character Locations in its At A Glance section. At the parks, a free Times Guide has a general overview of character locations. In addition, cast members can track down the schedule of any particular character.

Childcare

THEME PARKS Each park has a **Baby Care Center** with private nursing areas, rocking chairs and a microwave oven. Each sells supplies and over-the-counter medications. Moms can **nurse** their children anywhere on Disney property with no hassle. **RESORT CENTERS** Five Disney-owned resorts include an evening **childcare center.** Disney's Animal Kingdom Lodge, Beach Club, Grand Floridian, Polynesian and Wilderness Lodge resorts each have a secure room staffed with childcare professionals and filled with arts and crafts, books, games, toys and videos. Rates are $10 per hour per child with a 2-hour minimum charge, and include dinner from 6 to 8 p.m. Children must be toilet trained (no pull-ups) and 4 to 12 years old. Hours are 4 or 4:30 p.m. to midnight daily. For details or reservations call 407-WDW-DINE. **IN-ROOM CARE** Walt Disney World works with two in-room childcare services. **Kids Nite Out** (800-696-8105, 407-828-0920, kidsniteout.com) provides baby-sitting and childcare for kids ages 6 weeks to 12 years, including those with special needs. Caregivers arrive prepared with age-appropriate toys, activities, books, games, and arts and crafts. Rates start at $14 per hour with a 4-hour minimum charge, plus a $10 transportation fee. **All About Kids** (800-728-6506, 407-812-9300, all-about-kids.com) offers child-sitting services; services for adults, those with special needs and pets; and rents car seats, high chairs, playpens, toys and other baby and children's equipment. Childcare rates start at $13 per hour with a 4-hour minimum charge, plus a $12 transportation fee.

Getting here

BY AUTOMOBILE Two major highways border Walt Disney World. **Interstate 4** runs along the southern edge of the property, connecting it to Orlando (18 miles northeast) and Tampa (53 miles southwest). An interstate-like toll road opened in 2007, **Florida 429** runs along the western edge of Disney World, creating a shortcut for travelers coming from the north on Florida's Turnpike. It saves about a half-hour in travel time compared to taking the turnpike all the way into Orlando, and instead of congested urbania offers a pleasant, almost traffic-free drive past farms and orange groves. To use it, take the turnpike south to Exit 267A, then head southeast on Florida 429 11 miles to Exit 8, which brings you to Disney's new Western Way entrance. The toll for 429 is $1. As you travel it, after about 4 miles you can see way off to your left Cinderella Castle, Space Mountain, the Contemporary Resort, Spaceship Earth and the Walt Disney World Dolphin Resort. **FROM THE AIRPORT** Walt Disney World is 19 miles southwest of the Orlando International Airport. You can get to Disney by taxi *($40–$60, Yellow Cab: 407-699-9999)*, town car *($60–$90, Mears: 407-423-5566)*, bus or van *($18 per person, Mears: 407-423-5566)* or by renting a car *(Hertz: 800-654-3131. Avis: 800-331-1212. National: 800-227-7368.)*. **The simplest route** (25 min.): take the airport's South Exit road 4 miles to Florida 417 *($2 toll)*, go west on 417 13 miles to Osceola Parkway (Exit 3), then west again 2 miles. Guests staying at a Disney-owned resort can take a free Magical Express bus.

Guest Assistance Cards

Each Guest Relations office has complimentary Guest Assistance Cards that its cast members hand out to visitors who require special assistance. There are different cards for different disabilities. Each about the size of a Pop Tart, these cards are easy to get, but the particular one you receive depends entirely on how well you communicate your situation, and, in some cases, how well the desk attendant understands the policy.

For example, if your child is autistic, you want the card that lets your party enter attractions through their Alternate Entrances (the way to make sure you get it: when you're speaking with the Guest Relations cast member, make sure you say the word "Autism"). Known internally by many cast members, in fact, as the "Autistic Card," the Alternate Entrance Card doesn't provide front-of-the-line access, but at many attractions it lets you enter through a separate entrance which will have a shorter wait. For example, at Magic Kingdom's It's a Small World you'll board through the wheelchair entrance, and at Animal Kingdom's Kilimanjaro Safaris you'll be put in the Fastpass line. It won't help at smaller attractions such as Dumbo, or at shows, or at character greeting lines, and it won't get you seated any faster at a restaurant. It is good for a party of up to six people.

You can get a card at any Guest Relations office, which are located at the front of each theme park as well as at Downtown Disney. A card is good for the length of

your stay, or up to six months for annual passholders. And, believe it or not, you do not need a letter from a doctor. Disney simply trusts you. If you have a problem getting your card, stay polite but ask to speak to a manager or supervisor. If you're planning to get your card at a theme park, consider getting to the park one hour before it opens. The Guest Relations walk-up windows just outside the park will be open, so you'll have plenty of time to work things out while still beating the crowds.

Makeovers

A young girl can be made up as a princess, or Hannah Montana, at Disney's two Bibbidi Bobbidi Boutiques, inside Magic Kingdom's Cinderella Castle and at Downtown Disney's World of Disney store. Services include hair styling, makeup and nails. Each package comes with a sash. Boys can become "cool dudes." *$50–$190. Ages 3 and up. Reservations: 407-WDW-STYLE (939-7895).*

Money matters

There's at least one **ATM** at every theme park and resort. *Most debit and credit cards are accepted. $2–$2.50 fee per transaction.* Across from the Downtown Disney Marketplace, SunTrust Bank handles **cash advances** (Discover, MasterCard or Visa) and wire transfers. *Open 9 a.m.–4 p.m. weekdays, until 5:30 p.m. Thursdays. 407-828-6103.* In the nearby CrossRoads shopping center, Gooding's Supermarket handles **Western Union transfers.** *8 a.m.–10 p.m. daily. 407-827-1200.* All Disney charge locations accept these **credit cards:** American Express, Diner's Club, Discover, JCB, MasterCard and Visa. Character-faced **Disney Dollars** are accepted as currency at the theme parks and Disney-owned resorts and gift shops. They're sold at Guest Relations centers, Disney concierge desks and the World of Disney store at Downtown Disney. Nearly any purchase can be made with a **traveler's check.** SunTrust Bank sells AmEx traveler's checks. Guest Relations centers will **exchange foreign currency** up to $100.

Packing

Let's see. You're going to the hottest state in the country and planning to spend most of the day outside walking on pavement.

Sounds like fun! Actually, it doesn't have to be bad. Just be prepared, and dress light and comfortably. **Fundamental** are T-shirts, loose-fitting cotton tops, capris and shorts with large pockets, baseball caps and swimsuits, and broken-in walking shoes (pack two pair of shoes per person, so if it rains everyone stills has a dry pair). In the winter you'll need clothes you can layer, such as jackets, sweaters and sweatshirts, as days start off cool but warm quickly. January mornings can be below freezing at 9 a.m. but 60 degrees by noon. Temperatures at 7 p.m. will be in the 50s through March. **Other essentials** include an umbrella, sunglasses and sunscreen (sweat-proof, SPF rating at least 30). Instead of a purse, try a waist pack to keep your hands free. Don't forget tickets and confirmations. **Dress your kids** like you dress yourself, casually and comfortably, but protect them more from the sun. Wide-brimmed hats help. Bring snacks (granola bars, raisin boxes) and, for autographs, a Sharpie pen.

Pets

Five small kennels—at **Magic Kingdom** *(407-824-6568)*, **Epcot** *(407-560-6229)*, **Disney's Hollywood Studios** *(407-560-4282)*, **Disney's Animal Kingdom** *(407-938-2100)* and **Fort Wilderness Resort & Campground** *(407-824-2735)*—offer daytime and overnight caged boarding for dogs, cats, rabbits and other small creatures. At Magic Kingdom, Epcot and Fort Wilderness rates include two walks and two feedings. *Day boarding: $15 day. Overnight: $20 ($18 Disney resort guests). Reservations rec. Vaccinations req. 24-hr access. Cats, dogs must be 8 wks.).* At Disney's Hollywood Studios and Disney's Animal Kingdom kennels, guests are required to walk their pets two times a day; three times for puppies. *Day boarding: $10 day. Overnight: $15 ($13 Disney resort guests).* Fort Wilderness campers may keep their pet with them for $5 per day at select locations. Except for Fort Wilderness, only service animals are allowed in Disney resorts, theme parks, water parks or Downtown Disney.

Photos and video

Besides letting you photograph the landmarks and characters, a camera allows you to capture spontaneous moments that create treasured memories. Whatever shots you snap, take turns being the photographer. If dad takes all of the pictures, none of them will include dad. Also, consider disposable cameras for your kids, and waterproof cameras for the water parks. The results are sure to add to your memories.

CAMERA SUPPLIES Every theme park has a Camera Center which sells disposable cameras, batteries, memory cards and other supplies. Each is located just inside its park in the first building on the right. At Magic Kingdom it's in Exposition Hall on Main Street U.S.A.; at Epcot the Camera Center under Spaceship Earth; at Disney's Hollywood Studios the Darkroom on Hollywood Blvd; at Animal Kingdom it's inside Garden Gate Gifts. At the water parks, camera supplies, including waterproof disposable cameras, are sold at the main gift shops. Note: If you have your charger with you, Guest Relations offices will charge your batteries at no charge.

DIGITAL IMAGING Three Disney theme parks have **Kodak PictureMaker kiosks,** which let you create CDs of your digital files *(200 images for $11.99)* or make 4-by-6-inch prints *(69 cents).* Simplified versions of machines found in drug and grocery stores, these touch-screen kiosks accept nearly every type of storage device. You'll find them at the Camera Centers at Magic Kingdom and Disney's Hollywood Studios and in the Imageworks area inside Epcot's Imagination pavilion.

PHOTOPASS With this service Disney photographers take shots of you and your group, but you pay for only those you choose. Here's how it works: The photographers are stationed in front of each theme-park icon, at most character locations and at many other key spots. Each gives away free credit-card-like PhotoPasses, which you carry with you as an ID. Disney applies no sales pressure. You view the images at theme-park Camera Centers or at disneyphotopass.com, and decide which, if any, you want to purchase. You can order single photos and packages, CDs, custom scrapbooks and DVD slideshows. You can view your images for up to three days at any Camera Center or up to 30 days online.

Though it has its benefits, PhotoPass is not a replacement for your own camera, as the photographers shoot only posed shots at particular locations. If you use the system, write down your Photopass ID number on a sheet of paper. That way, if you lose your card you won't lose your images.

SOUVENIR RIDE PHOTOS At some attractions an automated camera takes your picture at the ride's climactic moment, then an exitway gift shop offers to sell you the shot. This happens at Splash Mountain and Buzz Lightyear's Space Ranger Spin at the Magic Kingdom, Test Track at Epcot, Rock 'n' Roller Coaster Starring Aerosmith and The Twilight Zone Tower of Terror at Disney's Hollywood Studios and Dinosaur and Expedition Everest at Animal Kingdom. The system is being updated to let you add these images into your PhotoPass account.

Restaurant policies

RESERVATIONS At Walt Disney World, having a dining reservation is often a must. The best restaurants often book to capacity far in advance, especially for the most popular dining times. During peak periods many don't accept walk-up diners, regardless of how long you're willing to wait.

Reservations can be made up to 180 days in advance (190 for Disney resort guests) at 407-WDW-DINE (407-939-3463) as well as most restaurant check-in counters and resort concierge desks. Advance reservations are required for dinner shows and Grand Gathering Experiences. Some locations require a credit-card guarantee, while others charge a cancellation fee. Reservations for parties of 13 or more always need a credit card. Most restaurants will hold your reservation 15 minutes for beyond its stated time.

The toughest reservation is Cinderella's Royal Table, located inside Cinderella Castle. It often books in full on the first day of availability. Because of that demand, its meals are charged at the time you book them. Other hot spots include California Grill and Chef Mickey's (at the Contemporary Resort), Le Cellier (Canada pavilion, Epcot) and Victoria and Albert's (Grand Floridian Resort). The toughest reservation time is 7 to 8 p.m. To eat during that hour make a reservation at least a few days early, especially for a party of six or more.

All Disney restaurants are nonsmoking and add an automatic 18 percent gratuity to the bill of parties of 8 or more.

Note: At Disney, making a reservation does not mean the restaurant holds a table for you. Instead, it books you into its system, and gives your party the next available table for its size after you arrive at the check-in desk.

KIDS MEALS At theme parks, Disney's Kids Picks meals include many tasty and nutritious entrees. Each comes with unsweetened applesauce, baby carrots or fresh fruit (your choice of two), and a beverage of low-fat milk, fruit juice or water. No more than 35 percent of a Kids Picks meal's calories come from fat, and of those calories, no more than 10 percent come from saturated fat and sugar. Fries and soft drinks can be substituted. Kids meals are also available at most resort restaurants.

DRESS CODES All Disney Signature Restaurants except Cinderella's Royal Table and the Hollywood Brown Derby have a business casual dress code. For men, that means dress slacks, jeans, trousers or dress shorts; and a shirt with a collar or T-shirt underneath. Women are required to wear dress shorts, jeans or a skirt with a blouse or sweater, or a dress. Not permitted: Cut-off shorts, men's caps or hats, swimsuits, swimsuit cover-ups, tank tops or torn clothing. Victoria & Albert's (Grand Floridian) requires jackets for men and dresses or dressy pants suits for women.

SPECIAL DIETS No-sugar, low-fat, low-sodium, vegetarian or vegan diets can be met at table-service restaurants by telling a reservation clerk, host or server. Dinner shows need 24 hours notice. With three days notice, these restaurants accommodate needs such as allergies to gluten or wheat, shellfish, soy, lactose or milk, peanuts, tree nuts, fish or eggs. At buffet restaurants, guests who have had gastric-bypass surgery pay the kids price for an adult meal. Many counter-service restaurants offer low-fat or vegetarian options. No Disney restaurant serves food with added trans fats or partially hydrogenated oils.

KOSHER MEALS Glatt kosher meals are available at most full-service restaurants with 24 hours notice at 407-WDW-DINE (939-3463). The food is prepared in Miami and flown to Disney. Kosher quick-service meals are always available at Cosmic Ray's Starlight Cafe (Magic Kingdom), Liberty Inn (Epcot), ABC Commissary (Disney's Hollywood Studios), Pizzafari (Animal Kingdom) and the food courts at the All-Star, Caribbean Beach, Pop Century and Port Orleans Riverside resorts.

TABLES IN WONDERLAND Formerly called the Disney Dining Experience, this discount card *($60–$85 annually, available to annual passholders and Florida residents, 407-566-5858, weekdays 9 a.m. to 5 p.m.)* saves its holder and up to nine guests 20 percent off food and beverages during non-holiday periods at most Disney table-service restaurants and a handful of other spots, including food courts at Value Resorts. An 18 percent gratuity is automatically added.

Transportation

You get around Disney's 47-square-mile property via a network of two- and four-lane roads (map, page 6) or by using Disney's free transportation system.

A complimentary **bus system** connects Disney resorts with all theme and water parks and Downtown Disney, and also travels between some parks. Other buses run to character breakfasts. A **monorail** track forms a giant Figure 8: the top loop connects the Transportation and Ticket Center (TTC) with Magic Kingdom and the Contemporary, Grand Floridian and Polynesian resorts; the bottom the TTC to Epcot. **Ferry boats** connect Magic Kingdom with the TTC and resorts that front Seven Seas Lagoon and Bay Lake; Epcot and Disney's Hollywood Studios with the resorts between those two parks; and Downtown Disney with the Port Orleans, Old Key West and Saratoga Springs properties. Hess **gasoline stations** sit outside the parking lot exits of Magic Kingdom, Disney's Hollywood Studios and Downtown Disney.

YOU CAN'T GET THERE FROM HERE
Despite its benefits Disney's bus system has a few flaws: ❶ Though they run from theme park to theme park, and from any theme park to Blizzard Beach, the buses do not go from any theme park to Downtown Disney or Typhoon Lagoon. ❷ There is no direct service between resorts. You can, however, take a bus from a resort to a theme park or Downtown Disney, and then transfer to different bus that goes to a second resort. (Downtown Disney buses often aren't as crowded, and run until after 1 a.m.) ❸ Buses do not run from the Epcot resorts (BoardWalk, Yacht and Beach Club, Walt Disney World Swan and Dolphin) to Epcot or to Disney's Hollywood Studios. Guests at those resorts get to those parks via ferry boat or on foot. They enter Epcot through its rear International Gateway entrance. (During thunderstorms, when the boats can't run, the buses do.) ❹ Disney buses do not serve the ESPN Wide World of Sports except from (but of course!) Disney's Hollywood Studios (8 a.m. to 8 p.m.).

Weddings and honeymoons

Up to a dozen couples tie the knot at Walt Disney World every day. And no wonder: from a practical standpoint it has unrivaled facilities for a family gathering, great year-round weather and the one-stop shopping of its Fairy Tale Weddings division. To many couples Disney World is also a home of romance, most of it fictional and childish to be sure, but still meaningful nonetheless. The average wedding costs $26,000 and includes 100 people, but prices for small affairs start at $4,500. Honeymoon packages include an online registry, which allows couples to create a wish list for the trip and have family and friends contribute toward the particulars. For details call 877-566-0969 or go online to disneyweddings.com or disneyhoneymoons.com.

ASK THE CONCIERGE
Actual questions asked at Walt Disney World resorts:
How can I learn if a theme park is filled to capacity? Call Disney at 407-939-4636.
Where can I find out about disability access? At each park's Guest Relations office. Printed guides include details on attraction access; hearing, visual and mobility services; service animals; companion restrooms; and parking issues.
I lost my digital camera two days ago. What should I do? Call Disney lost and found (407-824-4245, 9 a.m.–7 p.m.).
Where can I get a long-sleeved white men's dress shirt? Ralph Lauren styles are at the Commander's Porter shop at Disney's Grand Floridian Resort (9 a.m.–10 p.m.).
Where are XXXL Disney shirts? Typically at the World of Disney shop (Downtown Disney), the Emporium (Magic Kingdom) and MouseGear (Epcot).
Where can I buy non-Disney apparel on Disney property? At Downtown Disney, in gift shops at Disney Deluxe resorts, at Epcot's World Showcase and at water parks. Some theme-park shops sell World Wildlife Fund T-shirts.
Can I return an item bought at a Disney park to a Disney Store in a mall? Yes, with a receipt.
Where's a good outlet mall? Orlando Premium Outlet Mall is 5 minutes away (8200 Vineland Ave. at I-4 Exit 68; 407-238-7787; Mon.–Sat. 10 a.m.–10 p.m. (11 p.m. in summer), Sun. 10 a.m.–9 p.m.).

What it is

The Disney Dining Plan is a pre-paid meal program for those staying at Disney-owned resorts and Disney Vacation Club members. It's an easy way to manage your meal expenses at over 100 Disney restaurants, including those with character meals. There are five different packages available.

The **Basic Plan** *(also known as "Magic Your Way Plus Dining," about $40 per day per adult, $11 per child)* includes one table-service meal, one quick (i.e, counter) service meal and one snack per person, per night of your Disney stay.

The Disney **Deluxe Dining Plan** *(about $72 A, $21 C)* lets you eat three daily meals at table-service restaurants and comes with two snacks and a refillable drink mug for use at your resort. New for 2009, the Disney **Quick Service Plan** *(about $30 A, $9 C)* includes two counter-service meals and two snacks per day, plus a refillable mug.

If you want an active vacation but don't need much time in the parks, the Disney **Premium Plan** *(about $160 A, $110 C)* can be a great deal. It gives you unlimited use of many recreation options, including golf and water sports. Like the Deluxe plan, you get three meals a day and all can be in table-service restaurants. The package also adds vouchers to La Nouba, unlimited use of child-care facilities and unlimited theme-park tours. You need to buy at least a one-day park ticket. Book the plan six months early to cherry-pick recreation times.

The Disney **Platinum Plan** *(about $210 A, $145 C, available to guests of Disney Deluxe and Vacation Club resorts)* includes everything in the Premium Package and adds such extras as an itinerary planning service, a spa treatment, fireworks cruise and reserved seating for Fantasmic.

A **Wine and Dine option** *(about $40 A)* can be added to any of the above to include one bottle of wine each evening of your stay, redeemed at a range of table service restaurants and merchandise locations.

To purchase a plan go to disneyworld.com or call 407-W-DISNEY (934-7639) from 7 a.m. to 10 p.m. Eastern time.

How it works

You can use your meals and snacks in any combination throughout your stay. For example, you can eat all table-service meals one day, all quick-service meals the next, and nothing but snacks the day after that. If one person in your party uses up his or her plan, others can continue to use theirs.

Disney defines a breakfast meal as one single-serving of juice, one entree and one beverage; or a combo meal and a beverage or juice. Lunch and dinner are defined as one entree, one dessert and one beverage; or a combo meal, dessert and beverage.

Participating locations include just about every Disney restaurant,* and snack locations such as food carts and sweet shops. All food costs are included but not tips. You can't use the plan for alcoholic beverages or some bottled drinks, in-room mini-bars, souvenir or refillable drink mugs (except in the Deluxe and Quick-Service plans) or snacks and beverages from recreation rental counters.

The dining plans have four other major conditions: ❶ **They are sold per party, not per person.** If one person in your party buys a Dining Plan, everyone else must, too. The only exception: children under the age of 3. They can eat free from an adult's plate at no extra charge. ❷ **Children ages 3–9 must order from a kid's menu** when one is available. Likewise, those over 10 can't do so. ❸ **Some dining options charge two table-service allotments** for one meal. These include Disney Signature restaurants, dinner shows, Grand Gathering experiences, Cinderella's Royal Table at Magic Kingdom and all room-service meals at Disney Deluxe Resorts. ❹ Like Cinderella's magical accoutrements, **unused meals and snacks expire at midnight** on your check-out date.

To use the plan, you present your Key to the World card to your cashier or server. Your food usage will be tracked electronically. Each time you use your plan, your receipt will show your remaining balance of that particular meal type. Summaries of your balances are available from your hotel concierge throughout your Disney stay.

How to use it wisely

If you know how to take advantage of it, the Dining Plan will give you tremendous food and memorable meals. Handle it poorly, however, and your magical vacation can include a frustrating waste of time and money. Here are four keys to getting the most for your money:

DON'T OVERESTIMATE YOUR HUNGER
When determining which plan to purchase, keep in mind that, for most folks, it's tough

BEHIND THE SCENES

ICE CREAM

A SNEAK PEEK AT SOMETHING SWEET

to eat enough food to justify having three table-service meals a day. And though the Signature restaurants are nice, it's hard to dine at more than one a day, as each takes two or three hours to fully experience.

USE YOUR CREDITS EFFICIENTLY Except for those at Signature restaurants, nearly all table-service meals are considered equal. Believe it or not, dining with Cinderella or Lilo and Stitch at an all-you-can-eat feast takes no more table-service credits than getting a hamburger at Magic Kingdom's Plaza or a fish sandwich at Cap'n Jack's at Downtown Disney. Beware of room service: getting a meal delivered to your room at Animal Kingdom Lodge costs two meal credits, the same as a gourmet meal at Jiko.

KNOW WHERE THE DEALS ARE Though the Dining Plan charges you the same amount—one credit—for most meals, some restaurants offer better values.

Among table-service restaurants, great breakfast buffets include **Boma** at Animal Kingdom Lodge, the **'Ohana Best Friends Breakfast** at the Polynesian Resort, the **Princess Storybook Dining** in Epcot and the **Supercalifragilistic Breakfast** character meal at the Grand Floridian Resort.

For lunch, you'll get a great value at **Coral Reef** and **Le Cellier** in Epcot, **Liberty Tree Tavern** in Magic Kingdom, the **Turf Club Bar & Grill** at Saratoga Springs Resort and the **Whispering Canyon Cafe,** an entertaining barbecue restaurant at Wilderness Lodge.

The Disney Dining Plans include snacks at ice-cream stands and similar fast-food spots

For dinner, consider **Boma, Cinderella's Happily Ever After Dinner** at the Grand Floridian and **'Ohana,** an all-you-can-eat meat feast at the Polynesian Resort.

The best quick-service deals are at **The Artist's Palette** at the Saratoga Springs Resort, **Earl of Sandwich** at Downtown Disney, **Flame Tree Barbecue** and **Pizzafari** at Animal Kingdom and **Sunshine Seasons** at The Land pavilion at Epcot.

MAKE YOUR RESERVATIONS EARLY Once you purchase your plan, make your reservations as soon as possible. That way, you will be able to dine at the places that best suit your needs and give you the most for your money. An added bonus: you'll always have a place to eat.

Restaurants that do not participate in the Disney Dining Plan include Bistro de Paris, Bongos Cuban Cafe, House of Blues, Rainforest Cafe, T-Rex, the Wolfgang Puck Dining Room, Fulton's Crab House and Portobello (though the last two do accept Disney's Premium and Platinum plans). Restaurants in resorts not owned or operated by Disney also do not participate. These include the eateries of the Walt Disney World Swan and Dolphin, Shades of Green and the Downtown Disney resorts on Hotel Plaza Boulevard.

Children roast marshmallows
at Chip 'n Dale's Campfire
Sing-a-Long, a free event at the
Fort Wilderness campground

Saving Money

The average Walt Disney World vacation costs over $3,000, but you can keep expenses under control. Here are 30 ways to do it.

Theme parks

1 It's not exactly *saving* money, but you get the best value on park tickets by buying passes good for at least a week. They cost far less per day. For example, the difference between a three-day and a weekly pass is $16.

2 Check the web site **disneyworld.com** for discounts. Look for "Special Offers" on the Tickets & Reservations page.

3 Florida residents and members of the American Automobile Association (AAA) get deals (407-934-7639), as do members of the U.S. military (Shades of Green, 888-593-2242).

4 Employees of Disney World corporate sponsors such as Coca-Cola, GM and Kodak often can get discounts, too. Ask your employee benefits office.

5 Disney convention attendees often can buy tickets good only after 2 or 4 p.m., or only on days when the convention is not in session. Family discounts are sometimes available, too.

6 Old Walt Disney World tickets with unused days can be used for park admission or as credits toward new passes. Learn their value at any Disney Guest Relations office, which are located in all theme parks and at Downtown Disney.

Lodging

7 The easiest way to save money on a Disney trip is to stay at a hotel with low rates. Disney has two "Value Resort" complexes: All-Star (page 284) and Pop Century (page 301). Information on hotels outside Disney starts on page 312.

8 Room rates vary wildly by time of year. Disney divides its year into five pricing seasons: **Value** (Jan. 1–Feb. 12, Aug. 9–Oct. 1, Nov. 29–Dec. 17; room rates start at $82–$135 per night); **Regular** (Apr. 19–May 21, Oct. 2–Nov 28; rooms $105–$315); **Summer** (May 22–Aug. 8; $115–$345); **Peak** (Feb. 13–Apr. 18; $125–$365); and **Holiday** (Dec. 18–Dec 31; $135–$395).

9 Special hotel promotions often appear on the Disney World web site (disneyworld.com). Look for the "Vacation Savings" icon on the home page.

10 Ask a Disney reservations agent (407-934-7639) if there are any discounts for the dates, or resorts, you prefer. There often are, especially for Florida residents and annual passholders.

11 Some trade groups and associations offer Disney World discounts to their members. These include **airlines** (call Disney reservations for a list 407-934-7639), **AAA** (407-934-7639, members typically save 10–20 percent on Disney rates except during the Holiday Season; ther discounts include significant package savings through AAA Escapes), **AARP** (members often qualify for hotel savings of 10 percent or more), **CAA** (the Canadian Automobile Association offers deals similar to the AAA) and **nurses, teachers** and **civil employees** (at the Starwood-owned Walt Disney World Swan and Dolphin Resorts, page 306).

Finally, the **U.S. military** maintains an Armed Forces Recreation Center on Disney property, the Shades of Green resort (page 305, 888-593-2242). If Shades of Green is full, military members can stay at select Disney resorts at an "overflow" rate, not tied to rank, that's discounted up to 40 percent. Discounts are also offered at the Walt Disney World Swan and Dolphin Resorts (page 306).

12 Sign up for a complimentary Walt Disney World trip-planning DVD at disneyvacations.com. Doing so will get you on the list for Disney's marketing e-mails, which include special room rates and other discounts.

Transportation

13 Disney offers a complimentary Magical Express airport shuttle (page 283) and free monorail, bus and boat shuttles within its property.

Food

14 Bring at least a few snacks with you into a theme park. Granola bars fit easily in a fanny pack or the side pocket of a pair of cargo pants. (Disney allows food, but not alcohol.)

15 Order water to drink instead of soft drinks. Cups of ice water are free at every Disney snack stand or restaurant that serves fountain drinks.

16 Eat at fast-food spots instead of full-service restaurants. Good theme-park choices include Columbia Harbour House at Magic Kingdom (page 55), Sunshine Seasons at Epcot (page 125), Starring Rolls at Disney's Hollywood Studios (page 171) and Pizzafari at Disney's Animal Kingdom (page 217).

17 Eat at table-service restaurants for lunch, not dinner. The portions will be slightly smaller, but the check is likely to be significantly less. This strategy works especially well in the theme parks and at Downtown Disney.

18 Get a refrigerator for your room. They're available for a $5–$10 daily surcharge at Disney Value resorts, and are complimentary at all other Disney-owned resorts. Eating breakfast in your room can save time and money.

19 Most Disney resorts sell plastic soft-drink mugs ($13) that are good for free refills throughout your stay. If you plan to spend a lot of time at your resort they can be a good deal.

20 The Disney Dining Plan (page 30) has a Quick Service option ($30 per day per adult, $9 per child) for 2009. You get two fast-food meals and two snacks a day and a refillable soft-drink mug good for the length of your stay.

21 If you purchase the Disney Dining Plan and on the last day of your stay have leftover snack credits, don't let them go to waste. Use them to purchase wrapped treats that can serve as snacks as you travel back home.

22 If you plan to have a car on your trip, you'll find the best prices on snacks and soft drinks on Disney property at its three Hess convenience stores. They're located at the exits of Magic Kingdom, Disney's Hollywood Studios and Downtown Disney.

Cheap thrills

23 Disney resorts offer many complimentary or low-cost guest amenities. Depending on the resort, the list includes arcades, basketball courts, board games, children's activities, fit-

ness centers, hot tubs, ping-pong tables, playgrounds, tennis and volleyball courts and walking trails. Many resorts have bikes for rent for $8 an hour, or four-person surreys for $18 a half hour.

24 The Ft. Wilderness and Port Orleans Riverside resorts rent fishing poles and rods for less than $10 each, and sell small quantities of bait.

25 For inexpensive nightlife, consider Disney's BoardWalk Resort. Jellyrolls, a dueling-pianos bar, has a $10 cover; the Atlantic Dance nightclub has none. A short walk away is Kimonos, a cover-free karaoke sushi bar at the Walt Disney World Swan.

Free stuff

26 A monorail ride costs nothing, and can more fun for kids than many theme-park attractions. The best spot to sit is up front with the driver (just ask an attendant; if there's room the four seats are yours).

27 Want a free boat ride? Disney offers quite a few. The most enjoyable are those with outdoor seats, such as the small launches that shuttle guests

Not all Disney resorts are expensive. Rates at the Pop Century start at $82 a night.

between Magic Kingdom and the Grand Floridian and Polynesian resorts.

28 Chip 'n Dale's Campfire Sing-a-Long (page 294) is free and open to all Disney guests. Located at Disney's Ft. Wilderness Resort and Campground, it includes a 30-minute live show, then a Disney movie on an outdoor screen. Guests roast marshmallows on fire pits.

29 A dip into your resort's swimming pool can be the perfect no-extra-charge way to have fun, and relax. Many Disney World pools have fountains, slides, splash pads, waterfalls and more. The swimming pool at Disney's Animal Kingdom Lodge is open all night.

Online resources

30 Many Disney deals (and helpful news articles) can be found on independent web sites. Among the best:
- allears.net
- laughingplace.com
- magicalmountain.net
- miceage.com
- mousesavers.com
- wdwinfo.com

FASTPASS®
Return Anytime Between

11:55 AM
AND
12:55 PM

Riders must be at
least 40"(102cm)
to experience
Big Thunder Mountain

Another FASTPASS® ticket
will be available
after 11:55am

SUN JUN 22

WMK:CAS009 06/05/2008 T 12
TD2-H4

11:17

06/22/2008

**A Walt Disney World Fastpass
shows your return time for its
attraction, as well as the time
you can get another Fastpass**

Saving Time

You *could* spend your Disney vacation waiting in long lines, but you don't have to. Here's how to keep control of your time.

Use Fastpasses

WHAT IT IS You'll skip the line at Disney's top attractions by using this free automated reservation system. It allows you to use an express line, at a particular time later in the day, at particular rides that you select. To get a Fastpass, you insert your park ticket into an attraction's Fastpass machine, which is located at its entrance. The machine returns your park ticket with your Fastpass.

HOW IT WORKS When you insert your park ticket into a Fastpass machine, you get back a small card that shows your reservation time, which is always a one-hour window. When you return during that period, you show your pass and enter the ride or show through a separate entrance that has little or no wait. You can't pick your return time, but signs in front of each Fastpass-machine bank show you what it will be before you insert your park ticket. Each ticket is good for only one Fastpass at a time, but many throughout a day. The Fastpass service is free but not well understood, so only about half of all visitors use it.

HOW TO TAKE ADVANTAGE OF IT Follow this four-step plan and you'll save hours waiting in line: ❶ Designate someone in your group as your Fastpass manager. This person will hold everyone's park tickets, head off every now and then to get more Fastpasses, and keep track of when each pass is valid and when to get more (these times are printed on each Fastpass). ❷ Always hold at least one Fastpass, so you're always on the clock for at least one attraction. Pick up your first one when you get in the park, then others when possible through the day. ❸ Don't sweat it if you miss the return time. Disney doesn't enforce it. ❹ Use the service for every Fastpass attraction except those you'll be riding before 10 a.m.

Use Single Rider lines

WHAT THEY ARE Single Rider lines are for those who don't mind experiencing a ride without their family or friends. Four Walt Disney World rides have one: **Mission Space** and **Test Track** at Epcot, **Rock 'n' Roller Coaster Starring Aerosmith** at Disney's Hollywood Studios and **Expedition Everest** at Disney's Animal Kingdom. There's also a Single Rider line at the Blizzard Beach chair lift, which offers a speedy way up to that water park's main body and mat slides.

HOW IT WORKS When attraction operators can't fill a ride vehicle from guests in their regular lines without breaking up a group, they turn to their Single Rider line to fill the random seat. Waiting in this line can cut your waiting time by at least 30 minutes as compared to a regular line, especially after lunch.

Use Extra Magic Hours

WHAT THEY ARE The easiest way to avoid a long line is to simply go to a park when less people are there, and if you're staying at a Disney resort, there's an easy way to do just that. Each day one of the theme parks or water parks (or sometimes both) opens an hour early, or stays open three hours later, for guests staying at Disney-owned resorts, the Walt Disney World Swan and Dolphin, Shades of Green and the Hilton on Hotel Plaza Blvd. Not every attraction is open during the extended hours, but most major ones are. *Note: On a day when a park offers an Extra Magic Hour morning, it will be extra crowded during its regular hours.*

Use Child Swap

WHAT IT IS Disney doesn't publicize it, but this free service can save parents with young children hours of time each day. Simply put, Child Swap is a way for parents to stand in an attraction line only once, even if they both want to go on it and they have a child who is too short for its height requirement.

HOW IT WORKS Using the Child Swap system requires you to speak up. Specifically, when you want to ride an attraction with a height requirement your child doesn't meet, find the cast member standing at the ride's entrance and let him know. Regardless of whether you're using the Standby, Fastpass or Single Rider line, you'll need his consent to bring in your child, which he'll give if he understands what you're doing. You'll also need to clue in the cast member at the loading area. After that, you simply go on the ride while your spouse waits behind with your boy or girl. When you return, you and your spouse swap places and you wait with your child. It's easy. *Note: Child Swap is not available at Magic Kingdom's Tomorrowland Indy Speedway. The reason: though that attraction does require guests to be 52 inches tall to take a car out alone, it has no restrictions on simply riding in one.*

Have a touring plan

Having a specific daily plan will save you hours of time at any Disney World park, whether you want to see as many attractions as possible or just have a good time.

THIS BOOK'S 'MAGICAL DAYS' There are four touring plans in this book, one for each Walt Disney World theme park. Each plan is a relaxed, one-day schedule that includes all of its park's best attractions. You'll find these Magical Days at the beginning of each park chapter.

CUSTOM TOURING PLANS **Tour Guide Mike** (tourguidemike.com) is a respected online service that creates custom Walt Disney World itineraries based on your personal preferences. Use of its Automated Vacation Planner starts at $22.

MAKING YOUR OWN Even if you've never been to Disney before, it's easy to make your own itinerary. All you need is this simple strategy: ❶ First, skim through this book's park chapters and determine which attractions you want to see. ❷ Compare your list to our Magical Day plans, which appear at the front of each chapter. ❸ Make a custom plan by exchanging attractions evenly, based on their location and average wait times and Fastpass return times. If you can take advantage of any Extra Magic Hours, do.

Avoid morning delays

If you're staying at Disney during spring break periods, the early summer or between Christmas and New Year's Day, you can run into huge delays long before you even get to a theme park. These can happen when you try to eat breakfast, and then when you try to take one of Disney's buses to, well, anywhere.

FOOD FOR THOUGHT During peak periods Disney World restaurants can be fully booked months in advance, making the wait for walk-up patrons up to two hours. Sometimes an eatery will be so busy it will *refuse* your walk-up business,

Patience, young Padawan. Save your shopping, for items such as this Yoda action figure, for the end of the day.

no matter how long you're willing to wait. Even fast food spots can get packed; during peak mornings it can take 30 minutes just to get through one's checkout line.

Fortunately, it's easy to avoid these problems. Simply book your meals in advance. Disney takes reservations (407-939-3463) 180 days early from the general public; 190 days from Disney resort guests. If you plan to eat breakfast at a food court, get there at 7 a.m. The crowds usually don't show up until after 8.

'BEEN WAITIN' ON THE BUS ALL DAY'
Another way to ruin your Disney day, at least during a peak season, is to rely on the company's free bus service to get you around, especially in the morning.

During peak mornings the wait for a bus may take 60 minutes or more. Then, even though your destination is just a few miles away, it may take another hour to get there, as the bus may stop at other resorts or water parks along the way.

The easiest way around the bus problem is to stay within easy walking distance to the parks you most want to visit. For Magic Kingdom that's Disney's Contemporary Resort (page 290); for Epcot it's Disney's Yacht and Beach Club Resort (page 310); for Disney's Hollywood Studios it's the BoardWalk (page 287) or the Swan and Dolphin (page 306). Alas, Disney's Animal Kingdom isn't within walking distance of any hotel, but bus service from the relatively close Animal Kingdom Lodge is rarely awful.

If you stay at Disney's Contemporary, Grand Floridian, or Polynesian resorts, Magic Kingdom and Epcot are easily reached via the monorail system, which almost always runs smoothly.

Other solutions to the bus problem include renting a car (Alamo has a facility on Disney property with a free shuttle: 407-824-3470), using taxis (Mears, 407-922-2222) or simply getting up so early that you're first in line for the day's first bus.

ABOUT MAGIC KINGDOM Disney World visitors often underestimate how much time it takes to get to this theme park. If you're driving, you have to park (in the world's second largest parking lot), walk to and wait for a tram, take it to a monorail station or boat dock, then ride that to the park. The whole process takes at least 30 minutes. If you're staying at a monorail hotel, allow 25 minutes from Disney's Contemporary Resort, 15 minutes from the Polynesian, 5 minutes from the Grand Floridian. If you're staying at any other Disney resort and taking a bus to Magic Kingdom, give yourself an hour.

One of the world's most famous landmarks, Cinderella Castle sits at the end of Magic Kingdom's Main Street U.S.A.

Magic Kingdom

The world's most popular theme park

A realm that, if real, you would love to escape to, Magic Kingdom is a place straight out of your imagination, filled with barbershop quartets and hoop skirts, small towns and clean streets, charming pirates and cute little dolls, an empire where everyone is always glad to see you. The definitive theme park experience, Magic Kingdom has a universal appeal. For newcomers it's a postcard come to life. For Disney veterans it's like seeing an old friend.

Lay of the land

The park is laid out like a spoked wheel. You enter through a tunnel under a train station, where a colorful avenue leads to a hub in front of Cinderella Castle. From there paths split off to six separate lands.

You begin with a stroll through a re-created 1900s-era county seat. The past made perfect, **Main Street U.S.A.** is a world of Victorian buildings, homemade fudge, horse-drawn streetcars and horseless carriages. A central Town Square green is surrounded by the town's key civic buildings—its courthouse (or city hall), firehouse, train station and exhibition hall. In the center is a statue of the town's founding father, in this case Walt Disney's brother, Roy, who supervised the creation of Disney World after his brother's death.

Next is Main Street itself. Fronted with flowers and trees, building facades use the motion-picture technique of forced perspective to appear larger than they are—first floors are at full scale, second floors are at 80 percent of full size, third floors 80 percent of that. Upper-story windows appear to mark the offices of the street's business people, though in reality they identify key Disney alumni who have contributed to the park's success.

FASTPASS RETURN TIMES

Use the table below to help plan your Magic Kingdom day. Note that Peter Pan's Flight and Space Mountain typically run out of Fastpasses by late afternoon.

ATTRACTION	9A	10A	11A	Noon	1P	2P	3P	4P	5P	6P	7P	8P	9P
Big Thunder Mtn	10:05	10:35	11:45	12:35	1:50	2:45	3:40	4:40	5:40	6:40	7:40	8:50	9:35
Buzz Lightyear	10:20	10:45	11:50	12:40	2:15	3:10	4:00	5:15	5:45	6:50	7:50	8:45	9:35
Jungle Cruise	9:40	10:30	11:40	12:35	2:10	2:35	3:35	4:35	5:35	6:40	7:35	8:35	9:30
Peter Pan's Flight	10:10	10:40	11:50	1:15	4:10	4:45	6:40	8:30	9:25	OUT	OUT	OUT	OUT
PhilharMagic	10:05	10:40	11:40	12:40	1:40	2:40	3:40	4:40	5:40	6:40	7:40	OUT	OUT
Space Mountain	10:10	11:10	12:25	3:30	5:25	6:40	7:40	9:00	OUT	OUT	OUT	OUT	OUT
Splash Mountain	10:05	10:35	11:45	12:45	2:40	4:00	5:25	6:15	7:10	8:05	8:45	9:35	OUT
Stitch's Escape	10:10	10:40	11:45	12:40	1:40	2:50	3:45	4:40	6:00	6:50	7:50	8:40	OUT
Winnie the Pooh	10:10	10:40	11:40	12:40	1:50	3:10	4:20	5:50	6:40	7:20	8:05	9:10	9:40

Data based on surveys taken on random days during the summer of 2008

Many of the 51 facades use Cape Cod clapboarding and gingerbread trim. Some include prefabricated metalwork, an Industrial Age invention. Each has its own window framing, frieze work and cornice. The interiors include tin ceilings, brick floors and huge chandeliers.

It's a town in transition. Horse hitches are giving way to bus stops. Streetlights are changing from gas to electricity.

The sound of beating drums introduces you to **Adventureland,** a mix of African jungles, Arabian nights, Caribbean architecture and South Seas landscaping. **Liberty Square's** Federal and Georgian architecture brings back the time of the Revolutionary War. **Frontierland** looks to be a 19th-century American rural settlement, with raised wooden sidewalks, rocking chairs and lots of banjo and fiddle music twangin' from trees.

Set within the walls of Cinderella's mythical castle estate, **Fantasyland** resembles a royal courtyard during a Renaissance fair. Some buildings are designed as tournament tents; others blend styles from Great Britain and Germany.

Themed to be a rural farming exhibition, the two-acre **Mickey's Toontown Fair** also has the country homes of Mickey and Minnie Mouse. It has cartoonish "Squash and Stretch" architecture.

The theme of **Tomorrowland?** An intergalactic spaceport, a nostalgic trip back to the future as envisioned by 1930s comic books and sci-fi films. It's best appreciated at night, when the brushed-metal curves of the buildings are lit by colorful beacons, lasers and neon.

A MAGICAL DAY

8:30a	Arrive at the entrance turnstiles. Be sure to allow time for your boat, bus or monorail trip.
9:00a	Rush to Fantasyland. The crowd will be light, so you'll be able to see every major attraction in one hour. Do them in this order: Dumbo the Flying Elephant, Peter Pan's Flight, It's a Small World, Mickey's PhilharMagic.
9:55a	Get Fastpasses for The Many Adventures of Winnie the Pooh
10:00a	Mickey's Toontown Fair. Meet Mickey Mouse, then either Tinker Bell and her pixie friends or some Disney princesses.
11:15a	The Many Adventures of Winnie the Pooh.
11:45a	Get Fastpasses for Space Mountain.

The Underworld

Underneath Magic Kingdom are nine acres of warehouse-sized rooms, hallways and work space. The park's nerve center, the "utilidor" is a network of interconnected service areas, including one-and-a-half miles of color-coded tunnels that allow cast members to travel out of the view of guests.

Rooms off to the sides include an employee lounge (with lockers, ping-pong tables and video games), barber shop, cafeteria, paycheck center and wardrobe headquarters; merchandise storage areas; utility hubs; and a huge computer center that controls virtually everything in the park, from the hundreds of audio files and projection systems that support each attraction, to the water pressure needed to push the boats through It's a Small World and Pirates of the Caribbean, to all the parade operations.

Mounted on the ceiling is a fancy trash system—the park's Automated Vacuum Assisted Collection tubes. Every 15 min-

Noon	Eat lunch at Tony's Town Square restaurant, Main Street U.S.A. Make reservations ahead of time.	**2:45p**	Pirates of the Caribbean.
		3:45p	Get Fastpasses for Big Thunder Mountain Railroad.
1:00p	Get Fastpasses for Buzz Lightyear's Space Ranger Spin.	**4:45p**	Splash Mountain.
		6:00p	Have dinner with Cinderella at 1900 Park Fare at the Grand Floridian Resort.
1:05p	Space Mountain.		
1:45p	Get Fastpasses for Splash Mountain.		
2:05p	Buzz Lightyear's Space Ranger Spin.	**8:00p**	Spectromagic.
		9:00p	Wishes.
		9:30p	Big Thunder Mountain Railroad.

Magic Kingdom crowds are sparse early in the morning, even in Fantasyland

ded-seat theater that shows a 25-minute loop of classic cartoons. ❸ A Kodak display in Exposition Hall has two dozen cameras dating from 1889. ❹ Sitting on a park bench in front of Tony's Town Square restaurant, a life-size statue of Goofy says "Well, howdy!" every 30 seconds. ❺ The stars of 1955's "Lady and the Tramp" have put their paw prints in the sidewalk in front of Tony's patio. ❻ Cooks at the Confectionery make candy in view of guests until about 7 p.m. ❼ A window next to the Emporium's front door identifies its proprietor as Osh Popham, the general-store owner in 1963's "Summer Magic." ❽ Sounds of a singer and dancer come from two windows on Center Street marked "Voice and Singing Private Lessons" and "Music and Dance Lessons." ❾ Antique baseball paraphernalia lines the walls of the Casey's Corner dining area. ❿ At night many second-story Main Street windows are lit. ⓫ Tucked between the Ice Cream Parlor and Cinderella Castle, the Plaza Rose Garden includes Floribunda and Hybrid Tea prize winners. ⓬ Swan topiaries still mark the entrance to the Plaza Swan Boats, a ride that closed in 1983. ⓭ A topiary of Elliot, the star of 1977's "Pete's Dragon," swims through the grass in front of Tomorrowland. **Adventureland:** ❶ In front of the Jungle Cruise, six Tikis sync water squirts to rhythms. **Liberty Square:** ❷ Crates stacked alongside the entrance recall the Boston Tea Party. ❸ Streams of brown pavement in the walkways symbolize the sewage that often flowed down 18th-century streets. ❹ Stocks for adults and children stand in front of the boat dock. ❺ A 1987 cast of the Liberty Bell sits across from Hall of Presidents. ❻ Adjacent is the "Liberty

utes, after above-ground maintenance workers empty the park's trash cans into several backstage collection sites, the garbage is drawn through the containers at speeds up to 60 miles per hour, on its way to a giant central trash terminal behind Splash Mountain.

LANDSCAPE FUN FINDS

Main Street U.S.A: ❶ Working antique arcade games in the train station's waiting room include a mutoscope showing the adventures of "The Goddess of the Silent Screen" (and Drew Barrymore's grandmother) Dolores Costello. ❷ In the back of Exposition Hall, a Milestones in Animation exhibit includes a small pad-

Tree," a 160-year-old live oak that recalls a historic Boston elm. ❼ Two lanterns in a second-story Hall of Presidents window facing the Haunted Mansion recall the 1860 Longfellow poem "Paul Revere's Ride." ❽ A rifle sits in a window to the right, a sign the owner is home and ready to fight. ❾ A marble step beneath a blue door (No. 26) symbolizes Thomas Jefferson entering the Hall to write the Constitution. ❿ Showing four interlocking hands, a firemen's fund plaque is mounted on a set of green stable doors to the Hall's left. ⓫ The hanging sign of the Columbia Harbour House includes a U.S. shield with its eagle crying and holding arrows in its right claw—signs the country is at war on its soil. **Frontierland:** ⓬ You move literally and figuratively east to west as you travel Liberty Square and Frontierland. You start off in the Hudson Valley of the Haunted Mansion. The Columbia Harbour House is Boston; the Hall of Presidents Philadelphia. The Diamond Horseshoe represents St. Louis, Grizzly Hall is Colorado, the Pecos Bill Tall Tale Inn is Texas and Big Thunder Mountain is Utah. (Splash Mountain is Georgia, apparently washed up from the South.) **Fantasyland:** ⓭ An invisible Tinker Bell flies around the Tinker Bell's Treasures shop, spreading pixie dust on the shop's walls. Peek through the keyhole of a left vanity to see a flash of light. ⓮ Jousting lances form the canopy supports of the It's a Small World building. **Mickey's Toontown Fair:** ⓯ Donald Duck's great-great-grandfather is honored by a central statue. According to 1989 Disney comic books, Cornelius Coot founded the frontier outpost of Duckburg by popping some sweet corn to frighten away Spanish invaders. His deed was commemorated with this sculpture. **Tomorrowland:** ⓰ Standing between the entrances to the Tomorrowland Transit Authority and Astro Orbiter, a robotic Galaxy Gazette hawker talks ("Extra Extra! Read all about it! Ringleader caught on Saturn!") when you stand directly in front of him. He may insult you, with a line such as "Would you get a load of you! It's times like this I wish I didn't have X-ray vision!"

HIDDEN MICKEYS
Main Street U.S.A.: ❶ Inside Tony's Town Square restaurant, as bread loaves in a basket on a server. ❷ As a miniscule indentation in a black floor tile in front of the cappuccino machine. **Adventureland:** ❸ On the entrance bridge from Main Street U.S.A., as white flowers on the first shield on both sides of the walkway. **Liberty Square:** ❹ In the Columbia Harbour House, as circular wall maps in the room across from the order counter and ❺ as painted grapes at the top of a spice rack in the lobby, to the right of the fireplace. **Tomorrowland:** ❻ As a softball-sized impression in the concrete located between the entrances of the Tomorrowland Transit Authority and Astro Orbiter. In a wall mural inside the Mickey's Star Traders gift shop as ❼ loops of a highway, ❽ train headlights, ❾ glass domes of the building, ❿ satellite dishes, ⓫ clear domes covering a city and ⓬ Mickey Ears on top of two windows.

FUN FACTS ›› The Magic Kingdom entrance is meant to replicate the experience of going to a movie theater. The train station acts as a curtain. As it opens (i.e., as you walk through its tunnel) you see some Coming Attraction posters and smell popcorn. ›› The 850-foot-long street rises about 6 feet from the train station to the castle. ›› Much of Main Street U.S.A.'s background music is from the 1988 CD "The Whistler and His Dog" by the Paragon Ragtime Orchestra. Instrumentals of songs from American musicals such as "Put On Your Sunday Clothes" (1968's "Hello Dolly") and "Beautiful Beulah" (Disney's 1963 "Summer Magic") round out the selections. ›› The Harmony Barber Shop has 1920s barber chairs and an 1870s shoeshine chair. ›› Exposition Hall replicates the look of the 1877 Adelphi Hotel in Saratoga, N.Y. ›› The Crystal Palace combines the glass dome of San Francisco's 1879 Conservatory of Flowers with the greenhouse interior of London's 1851 Crystal Palace exhibition hall. ›› On the "Partners" statue in front of Cinderella Castle, the symbol on Walt Disney's tie tack is that of the Smoke Tree Ranch, a rustic Palm Springs, Calif., retreat where he owned a cottage.

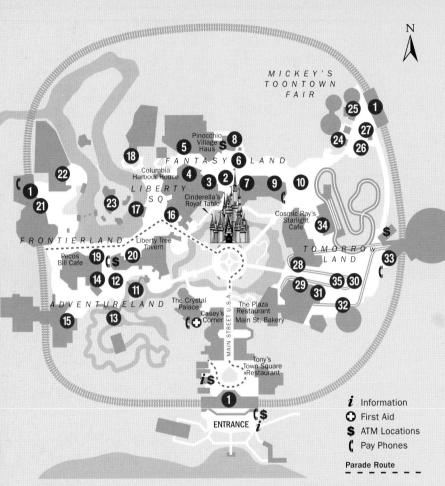

N

MICKEY'S TOONTOWN FAIR

Pinocchio Village Haus

FANTASYLAND

Columbia Harbour House

LIBERTY SQ

Cinderella's Royal Table

Cosmic Ray's Starlight Cafe

FRONTIERLAND

Liberty Tree Tavern

TOMORROWLAND

Pecos Bill Cafe

ADVENTURELAND

The Crystal Palace

Casey's Corner

The Plaza Restaurant
Main St. Bakery

MAIN STREET U.S.A.

Tony's Town Square Restaurant

ENTRANCE

i Information

✚ First Aid

$ ATM Locations

(Pay Phones

Parade Route

ATTRACTIONS

1. Walt Disney World Railroad
2. Cinderella's Golden Carrousel
3. Mickey's PhilharMagic
4. Peter Pan's Flight
5. It's a Small World
6. Dumbo the Flying Elephant
7. Snow White's Scary Adventures
8. Ariel's Grotto
9. The Many Adventures of Winnie the Pooh
10. Mad Tea Party
11. Swiss Family Treehouse
12. The Magic Carpets of Aladdin
13. Jungle Cruise
14. The Enchanted Tiki Room — Under New Management
15. Pirates of the Caribbean
16. The Hall of Presidents
17. Liberty Square Riverboat
18. The Haunted Mansion
19. Country Bear Jamboree
20. Frontierland Shootin' Arcade
21. Splash Mountain
22. Big Thunder Mountain Railroad
23. Tom Sawyer Island
24. Minnie's Country House
25. Mickey's Country House
26. The Barnstormer
27. Donald's Boat
28. Stitch's Great Escape
29. Monsters Inc. Laugh Floor
30. Astro Orbiter
31. Buzz Lightyear's Space Ranger Spin
32. Walt Disney's Carousel of Progress
33. Space Mountain
34. Tomorrowland Indy Speedway
35. Tomorrowland Transit Authority

Park resources

BABY CARE

The Baby Care Center *(next to the Crystal Palace, Main Street U.S.A.)* has changing rooms, nursing areas and a microwave; and sells diapers, formula, pacifiers and over-the-counter medications.

FIRST AID

The Magic Kingdom First Aid Center *(next to the Crystal Palace, Main Street U.S.A.)* handles minor emergencies. Registered nurses are on hand.

GUEST RELATIONS

The Guest Relations center *(outside the park turnstiles; inside the park at City Hall on Main Street U.S.A.)* has cast members trained to answer questions and solve problems in multiple languages, maps and Times Guides for all Disney World theme parks, exchanges foreign currency and stores items found in the park that day.

LOCKERS

One thousand lockers *(just inside the park entrance gate, on the right)* each rent for $5 per day plus a $5 deposit.

LOST CHILDREN

Report lost children to Guest Relations or any cast member. Kids who lose parents should tell a cast member.

MONEY MATTERS

Magic Kingdom has five ATMs—at the locker area at the entrance, at City Hall along Main Street U.S.A., in a breezeway between Adventureland and Frontierland, near the restrooms of the Pinocchio Village Haus in Fantasyland and in the Tomorrowland arcade. There is also an ATM to the right of the ticket booths at the Transportation and Ticket Center (TTC). All park cash registers take credit cards and traveler's checks.

PACKAGE PICKUP

Anything you buy can be sent to Package Pickup *(left of City Hall, Main Street U.S.A.)* for you to pick up as you leave. Purchases can also be delivered to your Disney hotel or shipped to your home.

PARKING

For day guests parking is $12 a day. Those staying at a Disney resort, and annual passholders, get free parking.

SECURITY CHECK

Security guards inspect all bags and purses at the park entrance.

STROLLERS

Single strollers ($15 per day, $13 per day length of stay) and double strollers ($31,

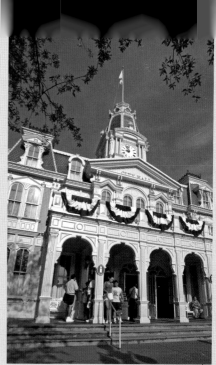

City Hall, Main Street U.S.A.

$27) are available at the Stroller Shop under the train station. If you misplace your stroller, a limited number of replacements are available in Frontierland at the Frontier Trading Post, in Fantasyland at Tinker Bell's Treasures and at the Tomorrowland arcade.

TIP BOARD

This board *(Main Street U.S.A., between Casey's Corner and Cinderella Castle)* displays waiting times for popular attractions.

TRANSPORTATION

Monorails and ferry boats arrive from the TTC. Grand Floridian and Polynesian resort guests take a monorail or boat to Magic Kingdom; Contemporary resort guests take a monorail or walk to the park; those at Fort Wilderness and Wilderness Lodge can take a boat or bus. Buses also run from Animal Kingdom, Blizzard Beach, Disney's Hollywood Studios and every other Disney hotel. The park has no direct service to Downtown Disney or Typhoon Lagoon.

WHEELCHAIRS, ECVS

The Stroller Shop rents wheelchairs ($10 per day, $8 per day length of stay) and Electric Convenience Vehicles ($45 per day plus a $20 deposit). ECVs book quickly; many are used by overweight guests.

Jungle Cruise skipper, Adventureland

Attractions

Main Street U.S.A.

MAIN STREET VEHICLES
★★★★ ✓ 3 min. No wait. Mornings only. Pg 59
Horse trolleys, antique-style vehicles
shuttle passengers to Cinderella Castle.

WALT DISNEY WORLD RAILROAD
★★★ 20 min. (round trip). No wait. Pg 58
Steam trains circle park. Wooded route.

Adventureland

THE ENCHANTED TIKI ROOM
— UNDER NEW MANAGEMENT
★★ 9 min. Avg wait 5 min. Scary Tiki goddess,
realistic thunderstorm. Pg 61
Iago ("Aladdin"), Zazu ("The Lion King")
take over Disney's robotic-bird revue.

JUNGLE CRUISE
★★★ ✓ 10 min. Avg wait 25 min. FastPass Pg 62
Shady outdoor boat ride was designed to
be serious, now played for laughs.

MAGIC CARPETS OF ALADDIN
★★★ 2 min. Avg wait 15 min. Pg 60
Four-seat hub-and-spoke ride.

PIRATES OF THE CARIBBEAN
★★★★★ ✓ 9 min. Avg wait 20 min. Short dark
drop, realistic cannon fire. Pg 64
Indoor dark boat ride travels through
elaborate settings with robotic pirates.

SWISS FAMILY TREEHOUSE
★★ Allow 15 min. No wait. Pg 60
Climb-through makeshift home.

Liberty Square

THE HALL OF PRESIDENTS
★★★★★ ✓ 20 min. Avg wait 12 min. Pg 67
Widescreen film followed by robotic display
of every U.S. president, including Obama.

THE HAUNTED MANSION
★★★★ ✓ 11 min. Avg. wait: 10 min. Ominous
atmosphere, some screams, pop-up heads. Pg 69
Dark ride tours ghostly retirement home.

LIBERTY SQUARE RIVERBOAT
★★★ 13 min. Avg. wait: 20 min. Pg 68
Paddle wheeler circles Tom Sawyer Island.

Frontierland

BIG THUNDER MOUNTAIN RAILROAD
★★★★★ ✓ 4 min. Avg wait 25 min. Height
restriction 40 in. Fast turns, dips. FastPass Pg 76
Roller coaster twists, turns through
mountain landscapes, mining town.

COUNTRY BEAR JAMBOREE
★★ 16 min. Avg wait 10 min. Pg 73
Lowbrow musical revue stars robotic bears.

FRONTIERLAND SHOOTIN' ARCADE
★★★ Unlimited. Extra charge. Pg 78
Old-fashioned arcade has infrared rifles.

SPLASH MOUNTAIN
★★★★★ ✓ 12 min. Avg wait 35 min. Steep drop,
most riders get wet. FastPass Pg 74
Soggy flume ride through robotic scenes
tells tale of Brer Rabbit, drops 52 feet.

TOM SAWYER ISLAND
★★★ Allow 45 min. Young children can get
temporarily lost in the cave. Pg 78
Wooded island has cave, mine, other small
adventures. Adjacent isle has calvary fort.

Fantasyland

ARIEL'S GROTTO
★★ 1 min. Avg wait 45 min.
Meet the Little Mermaid, tail and all, at
the end of a slow-moving outdoor line.

CINDERELLA'S GOLDEN CARROUSEL
★★★★ 2 min. Avg wait 8 min. Pg 82
Canopy-covered antique merry-go-round.

DREAM ALONG WITH MICKEY
★★★ 20 min. No seats, no shade. Pg 81
Stage show with Mickey, Minnie, Donald,
Goofy, princesses, "Peter Pan" characters.
Held in front of Cinderella Castle.

DUMBO THE FLYING ELEPHANT
★★★★ ✔ 2 min. Avg wait 25 min. Pg 89
Gentle hub-and-spoke ride.

IT'S A SMALL WORLD
★★★★★ ✔ 11 min. Avg wait 15 min. Pg 86
Dark indoor boat ride through fantasy
world of singing dolls, whimsical animals
and abstract settings.

MAD TEA PARTY
★★★ 2 min. Avg wait 15 min. You'll get dizzy. Pg 93
Canopy-covered spinning teacups.

**THE MANY ADVENTURES OF
WINNIE THE POOH**
★★★★ ✔ 4 min. Avg wait 20 min. FastPass Pg 92
Charming storybook ride recalls the
Blustery Day. Lots of special effects.

MICKEY'S PHILHARMAGIC
★★★★★ ✔ 12 min. Avg wait 15 min. Some
sudden images. Briefly totally dark. FastPass Pg 83
Donald Duck travels through Disney's
best animated musicals in 3-D. Delightful.

PETER PAN'S FLIGHT
★★★ 3 min. Avg wait 25 min. FastPass Pg 85
Vintage dark ride offers classic aerial
views of London and Never Land.

SNOW WHITE'S SCARY ADVENTURES
★★★ 3 min. Avg wait 15 min. Threatening scenes,
loud screams. Pg 90
Vintage spook-house ride portrays the
most frightening moments of the 1937
film "Snow White and the Seven Dwarfs."

STORYTIME WITH BELLE
★★★ 15 min. Arrive 15 min. early. Pg 81
Intimate, cute stage show has "Beauty and
the Beast" heroine bring children onstage
to help tell her story.

Mickey's Toontown Fair

THE BARNSTORMER
★★★★ ✔ 1 min. Avg wait 25 min. Height restriction
35 in. Intense for some preschoolers. Pg 96
Kiddie roller coaster offers brief thrills.

DONALD'S BOAT
★★★ No wait. Pg 97
Kiddie water-play area has cartoon tugboat.

MICKEY'S COUNTRY HOUSE
★★★ Avg wait to meet Mickey 40 min. Pg 95
Walk-through home leads to meet-and-
greet session with Mickey Mouse.

MINNIE'S COUNTRY HOUSE
★★★ Allow 15 min. Pg 94
Walk-through home has detailed
furnishings, hands-on activities.

TOONTOWN HALL OF FAME
★★★★ 2 min. Avg wait 40 min. Pg 97
Air-conditioned area leads to chatty
princesses Aurora, Belle and Cinderella
for meet-and-greet session. Second room
has Tinker Bell and her fairy friends.

Tomorrowland

ASTRO ORBITER
★★★ 2 min. Avg wait 35 min. Scary angle. Pg 102
Elevated rockets circle at 45-degree angle.

BUZZ LIGHTYEAR'S SPACE RANGER SPIN
★★★★ ✔ 5 min. Avg wait 13 min. FastPass Pg 100
Ride-through shooting gallery uses lasers.

CAROUSEL OF PROGRESS
★★★★ ✔ 21 min. Avg wait 13 min. Pg 104
Robotic characters show how electricity
has improved family life. Rotating theater.

MONSTERS INC. LAUGH FLOOR
★★★ 15–20 min. Avg wait 30 min. Pg 99
Live comedy show has animated
characters interact with audience.

SPACE MOUNTAIN
★★★★★ ✔ 18 min. Avg wait 30 min. Height
restriction 44 in. Dark drops, turns. FastPass Pg 106
Dark roller coaster simulates space trip.

STITCH'S GREAT ESCAPE
★ 18 min. Avg wait 15 min. Height restriction 40 in.
Restrictive harness, dark periods. FastPass Pg 98
Dark theatrical show creates illusion of
Experiment 626 skittering around you.

TOMORROWLAND INDY SPEEDWAY
★★ 5 min. Avg wait 0 min. Height restriction 52
in. to take car out alone. Pg 108
Freewheeling race cars for kids go 7 mph.

TOMORROWLAND TRANSIT AUTHORITY
★★★ ✔ 10 min. No wait. Pg 103
Elevated tour of Tomorrowland.

Parades

DISNEY DREAMS COME TRUE PARADE
★★★ 15 min. Arrive 30 min early. Pg 109
Character floats travel Adventureland,
Liberty Square, then Main Street U.S.A.

SPECTROMAGIC
★★★★★ ✔ 20 min. Arrive 30 min early. Chernabog
float has spooky music, animated monster. Pg 110
Evening light parade based on vintage
animation. Travels Main Street U.S.A.,
then Liberty Square, Adventureland.

Fireworks

WISHES
★★★★★ ✔ 12 min. Loud explosions. Pg 112
Fireworks show synchronizes explosions
with dialogue, music, life lesson.

Alice and the Mad Hatter greet guests at the Mad Tea Party, Fantasyland

Character locations

The Fab Five

MICKEY MOUSE
❋ Judge's Tent at Mickey's Country House, Mickey's Toontown Fair.

MINNIE MOUSE
❋ Judge's Tent at Mickey's Country House, Mickey's Toontown Fair.

DONALD DUCK
Across from the Frontierland Shootin' Gallery, Frontierland.*

GOOFY
To the left of Splash Mountain, Frontierland.*

PLUTO
Town Square, Main Street U.S.A.*

Princesses

ARIEL Star of 1989's "The Little Mermaid."
Ariel's Grotto, Fantasyland.

AURORA Star of 1959's "Sleeping Beauty."
❋ Toontown Hall of Fame, Mickey's Toontown Fair; ❋ Cinderella's Royal Table (B, L; often), Cinderella Castle.

BELLE Star of 1991's "Beauty and the Beast."
❋ Toontown Hall of Fame, Mickey's Toontown Fair; after "Storytime with Belle" performances at Fairytale Garden, Fantasyland; ❋ Cinderella's Royal Table (B, L; often), Cinderella Castle.

CINDERELLA Star of 1950's "Cinderella."
❋ Toontown Hall of Fame, Mickey's Toontown Fair; ❋ Cinderella's Royal Table queue line (B, L), Cinderella Castle.

JASMINE Co-star of 1992's "Aladdin."
Magic Carpets of Aladdin, Adventureland; ❋ Cinderella's Royal Table (B, L; often), Cinderella Castle.

SNOW WHITE Star of 1937's "Snow White and the Seven Dwarfs."
Town Square**, Main Street U.S.A.; ❋ Toontown Hall of Fame, Mickey's Toontown Fair; ❋ Cinderella's Royal Table (B, L; often), Cinderella Castle.

Other characters

ALADDIN Star of 1992's "Aladdin."
Magic Carpets of Aladdin, Adventureland.

ALICE, MAD HATTER Star, tea party host of 1951's "Alice in Wonderland."
Mad Tea Party, Fantasyland.

BUZZ LIGHTYEAR Deluded Space Ranger toy in 1995's "Toy Story," 1999's "Toy Story 2."
Carousel of Progress, Tomorrowland.

CAPTAIN HOOK, MR. SMEE Head pirate, comical first mate in 1953's "Peter Pan."
Pirates of the Caribbean, Adventureland.

CHIP 'N DALE Mischievous chipmunk stars in 1940s, 1950s Disney cartoons.
Town Square, Main Street U.S.A.

DAISY DUCK Donald Duck's girlfriend.
Town Square, Main Street U.S.A.

DOPEY Dim-witted dwarf in 1937's "Snow White and the Seven Dwarfs."
Town Square, Main Street U.S.A.

FAIRY GODMOTHER From 1950's "Cinderella."
Cinderella Castle (back left corner), Fantasyland; ❋ Cinderella's Royal Table (D), Cinderella Castle.

GUS, JACQUES Lead mice in 1950's "Cinderella."
❋ Cinderella's Royal Table (D), Cinderella Castle.

LADY TREMAINE, ANASTASIA, DRIZELLA Stepmother, stepsisters in 1950's "Cinderella."
Fairytale Garden, Fantasyland.

MARY POPPINS Star of 1964's "Mary Poppins."
Town Square, Main Street U.S.A.

PENGUINS Waiters in 1964's "Mary Poppins."
Town Square, Main Street U.S.A. (sporadically, with Mary).

PETER PAN, WENDY Stars of 1953's "Peter Pan."
Pirates of the Caribbean, Adventureland.

PINOCCHIO Star of 1940's "Pinocchio."
Town Square**, Main Street U.S.A.

POOH, TIGGER, EEYORE, PIGLET Bear, tiger, donkey and piglet from 1977's "The Many Adventures of Winnie the Pooh."
Pooh's Playful Spot playground, Fantasyland; ❋ Crystal Palace (B, L, D), Main Street U.S.A.

RAFIKI, TIMON Baboon, meerkat from 1994's "The Lion King."
Veranda at Adventureland main entrance

STITCH Mischievous alien creature, star of 2002's "Lilo & Stitch."
Galaxy Palace Theater, Tomorrowland.

TINKER BELL Pixie in 1953's "Peter Pan."
❋ Toontown Hall of Fame, Mickey's Toontown Fair (appears with either Fawn, Iridessa, Rosetta or Silvermist, all fairies in the new series of Tinker Bell books, movies and toys).*

Additional characters, such as Marie, the white kitten from 1970's "The Aristocats," greet guests "secretly" in Mickey's Toontown Fair on Thursday and Saturday mornings, between Mickey's Country House and the train tracks of the Walt Disney World Railroad.

* Scheduled for 2009. Details may change.
** Moves inside Exposition Hall in inclement weather.

❋ **Air-conditioned waiting line**

The Main Street Trolley Parade

Street performers

Park entrance

MAGIC KINGDOM WELCOME SHOW
8 min. 8:48am (7:55am on Extra Magic Hour mornings). Behind the Mickey Mouse floral just inside the park turnstiles.

A Citizen of Main Street (see below) welcomes Mickey Mouse and other Disney characters, who arrive on the Disney World show train to open the park. Helping out are Gay '90s couples from the Trolley Parade (see below) and a guest family. Songs include "Good Morning" (best known from the 1952 film "Singin' in the Rain"), "Casey Junior" (from 1941's "Dumbo") and "Zip-A-Dee-Doo-Dah" (from the 1946 movie "Song of the South").

Main Street U.S.A.

CASEY'S CORNER PIANIST
20 min. Hourly 11am–6:20pm. Casey's Corner patio.
An old-time entertainer bangs out honky tonk, rag and requests.

CITIZENS OF MAIN STREET
20 min. Hourly 10am–2pm most days. In the streets, shops and restaurants.
This troupe of improvisational actors portrays the boulevard's living, breathing townsfolk. Characters include the town mayor, fire chief, news reporter, voice teacher and assorted socialites. They chat, dance, joke, sing and pose for pictures with guests. Nearly all partici-

pate in the song-and-dance Mayoral Campaign Rally (9:45, 10:45 a.m. Tuesdays, Wednesdays, some Thursdays).

DAPPER DANS
20 min. Hourly 9am–4pm (9am show often on trolley), most days.
This barbershop quartet mixes its harmonically perfect repertoire with chimes, tap dancing and corny humor. They'll do "Happy Birthday" on request.

FLAG RETREAT
20 min. 5pm. Town Square.
Magic Kingdom's Security Color Guard lowers the U.S. flag that flies over Town Square, usually with the help of a guest military veteran. With the Dapper Dans and the Main Street Philharmonic.

MAIN STREET PHILHARMONIC
20 min. Hourly noon–5pm except parade hour.
This 12-piece brass band performs a comedic revue of Americana favorites. Hang around until the finale to see a perky female guest "volunteer" to honk a horn as the band plays "Hold That Tiger."

MAIN STREET SAXOPHONE FOUR
20 min. 10–11am Mon.–Thr.
This sax quartet harmonizes deftly on ragtime, jazz and Disney tunes. The same group appears in the afternoon as the Fantasyland Woodwind Society.

MAIN STREET TROLLEY PARADE
Three 5 min. shows hourly 9:20–11:20am.
Gay '90s couples hop off the horse trolley to perform a soft-shoe pantomime as they lip-sync "The Trolley Song" (from the

1944 movie "Meet Me in St. Louis") and a service number ("We're Walking Right Down the Middle of Main Street U.S.A.") that exalts Magic Kingdom ("The place was made with a magical plan! And just around the corner is a Fantasyland!"). So strange, but so very Disney.

Adventureland

CAPTAIN JACK SPARROW'S PIRATE TUTORIAL

20 min. Hourly 10am–5pm. On the left side of the Pirates of the Caribbean entrance.

A comical Capt. Jack Sparrow and his first mate Mack teach volunteer children how to be rescued from a deserted island, use a swordplay trick to flee from an enemy and sing the classic Disney tune "Yo Ho (A Pirate's Life for Me)." To give your kids a good chance to be picked, arrive 15 min. early and stand right up next to the rope that Mack lays out.

Frontierland

FRONTIERLAND HOEDOWN

20 min. 4:45 pm daily except Tue., Fri. Some days have additional later shows. In front of the Prairie Outpost and Supply Shop.

Volunteers of all ages learn to square

Top left: Main Street citizen Miss Inga DaPointe.
Top: The Notorious Banjo Brothers and Bob.
Above: Captain Jack Sparrow with a new recruit.

dance and do the hokey pokey in this down-home street show, led by seven country couples dressed in gingham dresses and blue jeans. Percussion comes from the Country Bears, who roam through the crowd with a washboard and spoons. Brer Rabbit greets guests, too.

THE NOTORIOUS BANJO BROTHERS AND BOB

20 min. Hourly 11am–5pm Tue.–Sat. (1st Wed. show at 3:30pm).

Two banjo pickers and a tuba player perform Disney tunes, bluegrass songs and cowboy melodies such as "Back in the Saddle Again."

Fantasyland

FANTASYLAND WOODWIND SOCIETY

20 min. Hourly noon–3pm Sun.–Thr. (1st Sun. show typically at 1pm).

This sax quartet plays whimsical Disney tunes. The group appears in the mornings as the Main Street Saxophone Four.

Performers, schedules subject to change.

Cinderella's Royal Table, Cinderella Castle

Restaurants
Full service restaurants

CINDERELLA'S ROYAL TABLE ★ Character meals $$$$$ **B:** Cinderella, Fairy Godmother, other princesses; $35 A, $24 C, 8–11:15am. **L:** Cinderella, Fairy Godmother, other princesses; $38 A, $25 C, 12–3pm. **D:** Fairy Godmother, Gus, Jacques; $43 A, $27 C, 4pm–park close. Seats 184. *Disney Signature*
This pre-plated meal can be disappointing—you only meet Cinderella briefly, if at all, and you're rushed through your meal. Prices include a cheap toy and photo with Cinderella, who appears only in the foyer. Guests are subtly urged to get out within an hour. Meals are always fully booked far in advance; make reservations (407-WDW-DINE, 407-939-3463) 190 days early if you'll be staying at a Disney resort (180 days if not). Reservations must be guaranteed. The Gothic hall overlooks Fantasyland.

CRYSTAL PALACE ★★ Character buffets $$$$ Winnie the Pooh, Tigger, Eeyore, Piglet. **B:** $19 A, $11 C, 8–10:30am. **L:** $21 A, $12 C, 11:30am–2:45pm. **D:** $29 A, $14 C, 3:45pm–park close. Seats 400. Main Street U.S.A.
The characters are irresistible, but during peak times it's hard to hear yourself think at this busy cafeteria. Cursed with a wood ceiling that amplifies every sound, the Crystal Palace can be one of Disney's least enjoyable character experiences. Best times to dine are 8:05 a.m. (the first breakfast seating), 10:30 a.m. (the last breakfast seating, when the crowd lessens and the characters can spend more time with you) and 3:15 p.m. (the first dinner seating). The food is uneven—good carved-to-order flank steak (lunch) and prime rib (dinner), OK eggs, salty soups and vegetables. Dinner includes peel-and-eat shrimp. The pretty dining room has marble tabletops, wrought iron chairs, a raised central ceiling and rows of cathedral windows.

LIBERTY TREE TAVERN ★★★★ ✔ American $$$$ **L:** $9–$17, 11:30am–2:45pm. **D:** $17–$28, 4pm–park close. Seats 250. Liberty Square.
Despite its name, this Magic Kingdom institution is not a bar and does not serve alcohol. Instead, you'll find a hearty New England menu and six dining rooms, each themed to a Colonial American figure. At lunch, the crab cakes are smooth, the pot roast tender. Dinner is a family-style Thanksgiving feast which, in a change for 2009, no longer has characters. Window-side tables of the Paul Revere and John Paul Jones rooms offer views of evening parades; for the quietest experience ask for the smaller Betsy Ross room.

THE PLAZA ★★★ ✔ American $$ Sandwiches. $9–$12, 11am–park close. Seats 94. Main Street U.S.A.
The crowd is calm, the food good at this easy-to-overlook Victorian cafe. Its menu is limited to salads and sandwiches, but everything is a touch above any quick-service alternative. Best bets are the hamburger and the creamy tomato soup, though the legendary German potato salad is gone. Desserts, which come from the Plaza Ice Cream Parlor next door, include hand-dipped shakes, splits and sundaes. They're all good. The pleasant decor features marble-like tabletops, a carpeted floor and wrought iron chairs with padded seats. Restrooms, however, are next door at the Tomorrowland Terrace Noodle Station.

TONY'S TOWN SQUARE ★★★ ✔ Italian $$$$ **L:** $11–$17, 11:30am–2:45pm. **D:** $17–$28, 4:30pm–park close. Seats 286. Main Street U.S.A.
A new chef and upgraded kitchen have made this comfortable spot better than

ever. Lunch offers flatbreads, pasta, salads and sandwiches; dinner has chicken, fish, pasta, seafood and steak. Marble tables and a tile floor keep things cool even during summer months. Located at the front of the park, Tony's is over-looked by Disney neophytes. Walk-up seating is usually available for lunch, especially at 11:30 a.m. Meant to be the cafe of 1955's "Lady and the Tramp," Tony's has a window in the back right corner that secretly looks into that movie's alley. Many booths. Restrooms are tiny; women get three stalls, men just one.

Patriotic shortcake, Liberty Tree Tavern

Counter-service cafes

CASEY'S CORNER Hot dogs. Seats 123 inc. 43 inside. Main Street U.S.A.
Worn atmosphere, usually crowded.
COLUMBIA HARBOUR HOUSE ✓ Veggie chili, sandwiches. Seats 593. Liberty Sq.
Sit upstairs for a peaceful atmosphere.
COSMIC RAY'S STARLIGHT CAFE Chicken, burgers, ribs. Seats 1,162. Tomorrowland.
Robotic lounge singer; nice condiment bar. Amusement-park crowd.
MAIN STREET BAKERY ✓ Bagels, pastry, yogurt parfaits, quiche. Seats 29. Main Street U.S.A.
Mornings are crowded; afternoons nice.
PECOS BILL CAFE Burgers, wraps, salads. Seats 1,107. Frontierland.
Rooms at the far right stay quiet.
PINOCCHIO VILLAGE HAUS Pizza, chicken, salads. Seats 400. Fantasyland.
Crowded by noon. Many screaming kids.
PLAZA ICE CREAM PARLOR ✓ Hand-dipped treats. Main Street U.S.A.

Outdoor counter cafes

AUNT POLLY'S DOCKSIDE INN Desserts. Seats 44. Tom Sawyer Island, Frontierland.
AUNTIE GRAVITY'S GALACTIC GOODIES Soft-serve ice cream, smoothies. Seats 12. Tomorrowland.
EL PIRATA Y EL PERICO RESTAURANTE ✓ Tacos, taco salads. Shares seats with Pecos Bill

Cafe. Adventureland.
ENCHANTED GROVE Swirls, slushes, orange juice. Seats 28. Fantasyland.
LIBERTY SQUARE MARKET ✓ Corn on the cob, baked potatoes, fresh fruit. Seats 22. Liberty Sq.
THE LUNCHING PAD Turkey legs, pretzels, frozen drinks. Seats 83. Tomorrowland.
MRS. POTTS' CUPBOARD Soft-serve ice cream, desserts. Seats 53. Fantasyland. (You, too, can look like a teapot!)
SCUTTLE'S LANDING ✓ Muffins, pretzels, coffee. Seats 80. Fantasyland.
SLEEPY HOLLOW Funnel cakes, caramel corn, soft-serve ice cream. Seats 51. Liberty Sq.
SUNSHINE TREE TERRACE ✓ Frozen orange juice swirled with vanilla soft-serve ice cream, slushes, floats. Seats 46. Adventureland.
TOMORROWLAND TERRACE NOODLE STATION ✓ Chicken with steamed rice, noodle bowls, teas. Dinner only. Seats 500. Tomorrowland.
VILLAGE FRY SHOPPE Hot dogs, fries. Shares seats with Mrs. Potts. Fantasyland.

Snack stands

ALOHA ISLE ✓ Pineapple/vanilla soft-serve. Juice, pineapple spears, floats. Adventureland.
EGG ROLL WAGON ✓ Egg rolls, corn dogs. Adventureland.
FRONTIERLAND FRIES McDonald's chicken nuggets, fries. Frontierland.
PLUTO'S DOGGONE GOOD DOGS Hot dogs. Mickey's Toontown Fair.
TOONTOWN FARMER'S MARKET ✓ Yogurt, fresh fruit. Mickey's Toontown Fair.
WESTWOOD HO REFRESHMENTS Muffins, hot dogs. Frontierland.

A wall of plushies at the Emporium gift shop

Shopping

You'll find the same mix of Disney souvenirs at many park shops. The two largest are the Emporium *(Main Street U.S.A.)* and County Bounty *(Mickey's Toontown Fair)*. Many items, however, are concentrated in particular locations:

Apparel

CAPS AND HATS
General: County Bounty *(Mickey's Toontown Fair)*. **Monogrammed Mickey ears:** The Chapeau *(Main Street U.S.A., creates custom mouse ears)*; Sir Mickey's *(next to Cinderella Castle, Fantasyland)*.

CHARACTER COSTUMES
Princess and Tinker Bell: The Emporium *(Main Street U.S.A.)*; Tinker Bell's Treasures *(next to Cinderella Castle, Fantasyland)*; County Bounty *(Mickey's Toontown Fair)*. **Pirate:** Pirate's Bazaar *(Pirates of the Caribbean, Adventureland)*. **Snow White:** Seven Dwarfs Mine *(Snow White's Scary Adventures, Fantasyland)*.

CHILDREN'S WEAR
Disney Clothiers, The Emporium *(Main Street U.S.A.)*; County Bounty *(Mickey's Toontown Fair)*; Fantasy Faire *(Mickey's PhilharMagic, Fantasyland)*.

FASHION
Disney Clothiers *(Main Street U.S.A.)*; Island Supply *(across from Swiss Family Treehouse, Adventureland, has brands such as Roxy, Quiksilver)*; Pirate's Bazaar *(Pirates of the Caribbean, Adventureland)*.

SANDALS
Disney Clothiers and the Emporium *(both Main Street U.S.A.)*; Island Supply *(across from Swiss Family Treehouse, Adventureland)*; Sir Mickey's *(adjacent to Cinderella Castle, Fantasyland)*.

SPORTS APPAREL
Disney Clothiers *(Main Street U.S.A.)*.

T-SHIRTS
General: The Emporium *(Main Street U.S.A.)*. **Attraction:** Briar Patch *(Splash Mountain, Frontierland)*; Buzz Star Command *(Buzz Lightyear's Space Ranger Spin, Tomorrowland)*; Fantasy Faire *(Mickey's PhilharMagic, Fantasyland)*; Space Mountain shop *(Tomorrowland)*.

Other merchandise

ART
Traditional: The Art of Disney *(Main Street Cinema, Main Street U.S.A.)* has quality lithographs, posters, prints and two-foot-tall Disney character figurines. **China figurines:** Uptown Jewelers *(Main Street U.S.A.)*. **Ceramics, crystal, glass:** Crystal Arts *(Main Street U.S.A., formerly Market House, also has decorative swords)*; La Princesa de Cristal *(Caribbean Plaza, Adventureland)*. **African woodcarvings:** The Agrabah Bazaar *(Magic Carpets of Aladdin, Adventureland)*.

BOOKS
Disney titles: The Emporium *(Main Street U.S.A.)*; County Bounty *(Mickey's Toontown Fair)*; Fantasy Faire *(Mickey's PhilharMagic, Fantasyland)*. **Brer Rabbit, Uncle Remus:** The Briar Patch *(Splash Mountain, Frontierland)*. **U.S. history:** Heritage House *(Hall of Presidents, Liberty Square)*. **Winnie the Pooh:** Pooh's Thotful Shop *(The Many Adventures of Winnie the Pooh, Fantasyland)*.

CANDY
The Main Street Confectionery *(Main Street U.S.A.)* makes its own fudge, Rice Krispy treats, candy and caramel apples, cotton candy and peanut brittle, all within view of guests. Treats are also sold at County Bounty and Prairie Outpost & Supply *(Frontierland)*.

Monogrammed **Mickey ears** are a Disney classic

CHRISTMAS ITEMS
Ye Olde Christmas Shoppe *(Liberty Square)*.

HOUSEWARES
The Emporium *(Main Street U.S.A.)*;
Yankee Trader *(Liberty Square)*; County
Bounty *(Mickey's Toontown Fair)*.

JEWELRY
Fine: Uptown Jewelers *(Main Street
U.S.A.)*. **Costume:** The Emporium *(Main
Street U.S.A.)*; Island Supply *(across from
Swiss Family Treehouse, Adventureland)*;
Bwana Bob's cart *(at Adventureland's
main entrance)*; Pirate's Bazaar *(Pirates
of the Caribbean, Adventureland)*.

MUSICAL INSTRUMENTS
Authentic African musical instruments
are sold at the Agrabah Bazaar *(Magic
Carpets of Aladdin, Adventureland)*.

PET PRODUCTS
Firehouse Gift Station *(Engine Co. 71,
Main Street U.S.A.)*.

PINS
Pin central: Frontier Trading Post
(Frontierland). **General:** Exposition Hall,
Uptown Jewelers *(Main Street U.S.A.)*.

TOYS
General: The Emporium *(Main Street
U.S.A.)*; County Bounty *(Mickey's
Toontown Fair, includes a make-your-own
Mr. Potato Head station)*.

WATCHES
General: Uptown Jewelers, Disney
Clothiers *(Main Street U.S.A.)*. **Custom:**
Artists at Uptown Jewelers personalize
sketches of Disney characters and reduce
them onto watch dials.

Specialty shops

BUZZ LIGHTYEAR
Buzz Star Command *(Buzz Lightyear's
Space Ranger Spin, Tomorrowland)*.

DONALD DUCK
Fantasy Faire *(Mickey's PhilharMagic,
Fantasyland)*.

FIREFIGHTERS AND POLICE
Firehouse Gift Station *(Engine Co. 71,
Main Street U.S.A.)*.

PATRIOTISM AND PRESIDENTS
Heritage House *(Hall of Presidents,
Liberty Square)*.

PIRATES OF THE CARIBBEAN
Pirate's Bazaar *(Pirates of the Caribbean,
Adventureland)*.

PRINCESSES
Tinker Bell's Treasures *(adjacent to
Cinderella Castle, Fantasyland)*.

SNOW WHITE & THE SEVEN DWARFS
Seven Dwarfs Mine *(Snow White's Scary
Adventures, Fantasyland)*.

STAR WARS
Merchant of Venus *(Stitch's Great
Escape, Tomorrowland)*.

STITCH
Merchant of Venus *(Stitch's Great
Escape, Tomorrowland)*.

TINKER BELL
Tinker Bell's Treasures *(adjacent to
Cinderella Castle, Fantasyland)*.

WINNIE THE POOH
Pooh's Thotful Shop *(The Many Adventures
of Winnie the Pooh, Fantasyland)*.

Built in 1925, the 10-wheel Roger E. Broggie steam locomotive is one of four in Disney's fleet

Walt Disney World Railroad

★★★ 20 min. round trip (1.5 miles). Capacity: 360. Fear factor: None. No eating, drinking or smoking. Idle during parades, fireworks or thunderstorms. Folding strollers OK, no Disney rental strollers allowed. Access: Must be ambulatory. Handheld captioning available. Debuted: 1971.

Chugging around the outside of the park, these full-size trains stop at Main Street U.S.A., Frontierland and Mickey's Toontown Fair. Pulled by authentic steam locomotives, the open passenger cars look like Industrial Age street trolleys. Though a folksy narrator warns "Be on the lookout!" there are no surprises. Ironically, the ride does not show much of the park. You only glimpse three attractions—Splash Mountain, Big Thunder Mountain Railroad and the Tomorrowland Indy Speedway. You do pass two small Indian encampments and some wildlife figures, including two "snapping" alligators. Most of the trip is heavily wooded.

Average Wait	
9am	5 min
10am	5
11am	5
Noon	5
1pm	5
2pm	5
3pm	closed
4pm	5
5pm	5
6pm	5
7pm	5
8pm	5
9pm	closed

Disney acquired the four steam engines from the United Railway of the Yucatan. Built by Philadelphia's Baldwin Locomotive Works between 1916 and 1928, they hauled passengers, jute, sisal and sugar cane through Mexico for decades. Disney had the engines restored at the Tampa Shipbuilding and Dry Dock Company in 1971.

The Main Street station replicates an old American depot. Its lobby has mutoscopes and other antique amusements. The lower level has vintage railway maps and placards that detail the engines' histories.

FUN FACTS ›› The trains go 10 to 12 mph. ›› The steel bridge just past Frontierland is half of an original two-track bridge from the Florida Flagler route. ›› Some trees past the Indian village have charred trunks, the result of falling Wishes fireworks. ›› The engines take on water every third time they stop at Mickey's Toontown Fair. ›› Every few hours a "pit crew" at that station gives each engine a quick service. ›› There are four sets of passenger cars—red, yellow, blue and green. ›› The green cars appear only during the park's opening ceremony. In order for performers to exit that train's left side, those cars are missing their left safety rails.

▶ **The best views are on the right, though live alligators sometimes swim in a canal on the left.**

Main Street Vehicles

★★★★ ✔ Apx. 3 min., depending on traffic (and, with trolleys, the horse). No horse petting. Fear factor: None. Access: Must be ambulatory. Debuted: 1971.

These old-fashioned vehicles shuttle passengers between Town Square and Cinderella Castle. The rides are free, and there's never a line. The vehicles are only out in the mornings. The fleet consists of:

■ **Horse trolleys.** There are four of these open-air vehicles, which run on a track embedded in the center of the street. Passengers are often joined by the Dapper Dans barbershop quartet. Each trolley seats 22.

■ **A double-decker bus.** A replica of buses used in New York City in the 1920s, this International Harvester-built vehicle has a loud "ah-ooo-gah" horn to keep pedestrians out of its way. The 6-cylinder engine gives the bus the ability to top out at 50 mph, though around guests it never gets out of first gear. It seats 40.

■ **A miniature fire truck.** Complete with a giant spotlight and a ladder and fire hose strapped to its sides, this bright red vehicle seats eight.

■ **Horseless carriages.** Each literally a "surrey with the fringe on the top," these self-powered canopied carriages are based on luxury Franklin-brand automobiles built between 1903 and 1907. There are three vehicles, one blue, one red and one yellow. Each has two benches and seats six.

■ **Jitneys.** These two topless paddy wagons look like the small buses that once shuttled tourists along the Atlantic City, N.J., boardwalk. Each seats eight.

The trolley horses are all former workhorses. The

A Main Street trolley pulled by the Clydesdale known among Disney cast members as "Queasy"

team is made up of three Percherons (Charlie, Dave and Lucky), two Belgians (Fritz and Drummer) and one flashy Clydesdale (Qes, nicknamed, for phonetic reasons only, "Queasy.") Formerly a lawnmower horse in Amish country, laid-back Fritz has been pulling the trolley for 10 years. All geldings, the horses are stabled at Fort Wilderness. An infant Clydesdale, Jacob, is being groomed to join the group in a few years.

The motorized vehicles have been operating at Walt Disney World since the park opened in 1971. They run on natural gas.

FUN FACT » The motorized vehicles' license plates are dated 1915, the first year Florida issued vehicle plates.

Average Wait	
9am	0 min
10am	0
11am	0
Noon	0
1pm	n/a
2pm	n/a
3pm	n/a
4pm	n/a
5pm	n/a
6pm	n/a
7pm	n/a
8pm	n/a
9pm	n/a

▶ The horse trolleys stay on the street until 11:30 a.m. The other vehicles go in about noon.

Surrounded by tropical vegetation, the Swiss Family Treehouse is 60 feet tall and 90 feet wide

The bouncy, low-sided Magic Carpets can be a fun diversion for all ages, even teenagers

Swiss Family Treehouse

★★ Allow 15 min. Capacity: 300. Fear factor: None. Access: Must be ambulatory. Debuted: 1971 (Disneyland 1962).

Based on the 1960 movie "Swiss Family Robinson," this climb-through treehouse re-creates the makeshift home of a ship-wrecked family. A narrow stairway leads past a dining room, kitchen and two bedrooms. The house is filled with ideas on how to live in the wild, from vine hand-rails to an ingenious water system that uses pulleys and bamboo buckets. The dining room's pull-stop organ is a real antique.

Unfortunately, the tree shows its age. Designed in 1962, it has no interactive elements, and its 62-step climb can exhaust guests who aren't that fit. The house seems the most realistic at night.

Average Wait

9am	0 min
10am	0
11am	0
Noon	0
1pm	0
2pm	0
3pm	0
4pm	0
5pm	0
6pm	0
7pm	0
8pm	0
9pm	0

Magic Carpets of Aladdin

★★★ 90 sec. Capacity: 64. Fear factor: None. Access: ECV users must transfer to a wheelchair. Debuted: 2001.

This breezy hub-and-spoke ride can be more fun than Dumbo the Flying Elephant. The line is shorter, each low-sided vehicle seats four instead of two, and it's a tad more exciting. Riders use an amulet to control their height and pitch, and can be "spit on" by a golden statue of a camel. (Want to get hit? Fly about halfway high.)

The ride is based on the 1992 movie "Aladdin." As you fly on Prince Ali's carpet, you circle Genie's bottle and hear instrumental versions of songs from the film.

HIDDEN MICKEY
Set in pavement behind the camel facing the ride, as a design on two yellow stones of a four-piece bracelet.

Average Wait

9am	0 min
10am	5
11am	10
Noon	15
1pm	10
2pm	10
3pm	5
4pm	5
5pm	5
6pm	5
7pm	10
8pm	10
9pm	0

▶ **Rafiki, Timon, Aladdin and Jasmine often greet guests along the Adventureland walkway.**

The Enchanted Tiki Room — Under New Management

★★ 9 min. Capacity: 250. Opens 10am. Fear factor: A threatening goddess, thunderstorm effects. Access: Guests may remain in wheelchairs, ECVs. Assistive listening; handheld captioning. Debuted: 1998; original version 1971 (Disneyland 1963).

When Iago (from 1992's "Aladdin") and Zazu (from 1994's "The Lion King") take over this creaky musical revue of robotic birds and flowers, Iago wants to toss it for something more current. But when he insults the Tiki gods he learns that "you cannot toy with the Enchanted Tiki Room." Songs include "Hot Hot Hot," "Conga," and, from the mouths of wooden Tiki poles, "In the Still of the Night." A preshow stars bickering talent-agent parrots voiced by Don Rickles and the late Phil Hartman.

The original show was the first Disney robotic attraction. After a barker bird out front enticed guests to

Average Wait

9am	closed
10am	5 min
11am	5
Noon	5
1pm	5
2pm	5
3pm	5
4pm	5
5pm	5
6pm	5
7pm	5
8pm	5
9pm	5

Originally known as the Tropical Serenade, the Tiki Room was redone with a new story in 1998

"Come to the Tiki Room," everyone would sing along to 18 minutes of tunes such as "Let's All Sing Like the Birdies Sing."

FUN FINDS ❶ As cockatoos start to sing "Conga," José says "I wonder what happened to Rosita," an original tiki bird no longer in the show. ❷ "Boy, I'm tired," Iago says just before the exit doors close. "I think I'll head over to the Hall of Presidents and take a nap."

HIDDEN MICKEYS ❶ On the entrance doors, as 2-inch berries on a stem underneath a bird's tail, 4 feet off the ground. ❷ On the bottom of Iago's perch, where a small carved face is wearing Mickey ears.

FUN FACTS ❯❯ Unchanged over the years, the show's bird calls and whistles were all voiced by one man. A. Purvis Pullen was also the voice of Cheetah in the 1930s Johnny Weissmuller Tarzan films and Bonzo the chimp in the 1951 Ronald Reagan flick "Bedtime for Bonzo." ❯❯ Does Pierre sound like Lumiere, the candelabrum in 1991's "Beauty and the Beast"? Both are Jerry Orbach, Det. Briscoe on TV's "Law & Order."

▶ Sit on the left side of the theater and you'll face the Tiki goddess.

Lush tropical vegetation forms a canopy over the Jungle Cruise waterway

Jungle Cruise

★★★ ✔ 10 min. Capacity: 310. *FastPass* Fear factor: A trip through a dark temple gets close to unrealistic snakes. Access: Guests may remain in wheelchairs, ECVs. Assistive listening; handheld captioning available. Debuted: 1971 (Disneyland 1955).

This tongue-in-cheek boat ride takes you through the jungles of the world. Your skipper tells non-stop corny jokes and puns as your canopied craft passes scenes that, though designed to be serious, are now played for laughs. Exploring the Amazon, Congo, Nile and Mekong rivers (all so narrow!) you learn such facts as "the Nile River goes for Niles and Niles and Niles. If you don't believe me, then you're in de-Nile." The sights include dancing headhunters, a crashed plane and, in a flooded temple, a golden monkey shrine guarded by pythons.

To a child the ride offers a lot. Its cartoonish scenes include one of gorillas sacking a camp that was re-created in 1999's "Tarzan." Rising hippo heads and squirting elephant trunks create some kid-friendly thrills.

Average Wait	
9am	0 min
10am	15
11am	30
Noon	30
1pm	30
2pm	35
3pm	40
4pm	45
5pm	30
6pm	30
7pm	20
8pm	20
9pm	10

Designed in the 1950s, the attraction isn't exactly modern. Many of its animals don't move, and the ones that do never change expression. The cultural stuff is often mixed up (the designs on the Congo canoes are Polynesian) and the colonialistic theme of it all is, if taken seriously, almost racist.

The ride makes more sense if you look at it from the personal perspective of Walt Disney: a Missouri farm boy's wide-eyed interpretation of the mysterious Third World. Disney wasn't looking down on these people and places, he—like the rest of America—just didn't know much about them. In fact, the ride's only buffoons are the British, the colonialists themselves. These hapless boobs don't know what they're doing, and end up being forced up a tree by a rhino.

Premiering at Disneyland shortly after that park's opening in 1955, the Jungle Cruise was originally a serious attraction, an educational tour of regions most Americans had never seen, even in pictures. The humor began in the 1960s, with the addition of the playful bathing elephant grotto (1962) and the treed safari party (1964). By the time the Florida version opened the entire thing was meant to be a joke. In 1994 the ride's queue area got its radio broadcast and some new props. In 1998 its boats were redone in

▶ **Ask nicely and your child may be able to join the real pilot in the wheelhouse.**

their current vintage design, a look that includes cooking gear hanging from a roof net.

With all that in mind, the trip can be a jolly good time. Its best quips come at the end. "After five years of college you too can become a Jungle Cruise skipper!" guides tell guests. "My parents are so proud."

FUN FINDS

❶ A sign along the queue honors the cruise company's latest Employee of the Month: E.L. O'Fevre. ❷ Toward the end of the queue, a cage holds a giant tarantula. It jerks and rears up. Next to it are crates labeled "arachnid sedative." ❸ A chalkboard on the dock lists the crew's weekly lunch menu as fricassee of giant stag beetle, BBQ'd 3-toed skink, consomme of river basin slug and fillet of rock python. ❹ The headhunters include the line "I love disco!" in their chant. It's often drowned out by the skipper's spiel. ❺ Next to the exit, a list of missing persons includes "Ilene Dover" followed by "Ann Fellen." ❻ Two crates just outside the exit were once part of the Swiss Family Treehouse landscape. One is addressed to "Thomas Kirk Esq." and "M. Jones" on the island of "Bora Danno," references to Tommy Kirk (a star of the 1960 film "Swiss Family Robinson" and the title character of the 1964's "The Misadventures of Merlin Jones") and James MacArthur (a "Swiss" star who went on to play "Danno" Williams in the 1968–1980 television series "Hawaii Five-O"). The other is addressed to "Swiss" director Kenneth Annakin.

HIDDEN MICKEYS

❶ The queue-area radio plays Cole Porter's 1935 hit "You're the Top," including the lyrics *"you're a Bendel bonnet, a Shakespeare*

Smiling elephants bathe beside a waterfall along the Jungle Cruise

sonnet, you're Mickey Mouse!" ❷ On the side of the crashed plane, between and below the windows. ❸ As yellow spots on the back of a giant spider in the temple, on your right just past the snakes. ❹ In the framing of the temple, directly above each of the statues on your left (nearly impossible to see because of the darkness). Some of these are said to be Hidden Minnies, as they have bows (three smaller circles) on their heads.

FUN FACTS ❯❯ The river is only 3 feet deep. ❯❯ The water is dyed its dark, murky color. ❯❯ Walt Disney wanted the trip to have live animals. The robotic versions were Plan B. ❯❯ The boats are on a track. Skippers control their speed, but not their course.

SHRUNKEN NED'S JUNIOR JUNGLE BOATS
You steer a miniature Jungle Cruise boat through obstacles at this diversion at the ride entrance. The boats are hard to control. If you play, pick one that's already in a fun spot and not stuck behind something. Rely on your forward gear. $2 for 2 minutes.

▶ Consider a night cruise. The line will be short and the boat's spotlight adds to the fun.

Pirates of the Caribbean

★★★★★ ✓ 9 min. Capacity: 330 (15 per boat). Fear factor: Darkness, cannon fire may scare toddlers. Access: ECV and wheelchair users must transfer. Handheld captioning available. Debuted: 1973, revised 2006 (Disneyland 1967).

A rowdy, rum-soaked version of It's a Small World, this dark indoor boat ride takes you on a slow-moving cruise through stage sets filled with robotic characters. But instead of clean, cute little dolls singing a clean, cute little song, here you get hairy, scruffy, drunken life-size pirates who, as the attraction's jaunty theme "Yo Ho (A Pirate's Life For Me)" says, *"pillage and plunder... rifle and loot... kidnap and ravage and don't give a hoot."*

The inspiration for the recent series of "Pirates of the Caribbean" motion pictures, the ride keeps a lightweight tone. Its Audio-Animatronics villains have such caricatured features they seem straight out of a cartoon. Updated in 2006 to include characters from the recent movies, the ride includes the characters of Davy Jones, Capt. Hector Barbossa and Capt. Jack Sparrow. The Sparrow robot looks just like Johnny Depp. Special effects simulate fire, lightning, wind and splashing cannon fire. There's one dark fall, but it's short and not too steep.

AYE, A STORY THERE BE!

Pirates of the Caribbean has a storyline, though it's tough to grasp without repeat visits. Revised in 2006 to tie in with the Disney movies, it now tells the tale of Capt. Barbossa's sacking of a Spanish port in the Caribbean as he searches for Capt. Jack. Barbossa's men loot the village, capture its women and set fire to its buildings. Meanwhile, the sneaky Sparrow nabs the town's treasure.

The ride tells its story in flashback form. It begins with the present—a watery grotto lined with the skeletons of dead pirates—then takes you back to the past, to the golden age of piracy. You take the time trip despite the warnings of Davy Jones, the octopus-faced ocean ruler who appears in the fog.

Literally falling into the waters of an old Caribbean port, you sail between the guns of Barbossa's ship and those of a Spanish fortress. As shots splash close to your boat, Barbossa yells "It's Capt. Jack we're after, and a fortune in gold!" Attempting to literally shiver Barbossa's timbers, the Spanish respond *en español:* "¡Apenten! ¡Disparen! ¡Fuego!" ("Ready! Aim! Fire!")

Rounding a bend, you come upon more of Barbossa's crew in a courtyard, interrogating the mayor by dunking him in a well. "Where be Capt. Jack Sparrow and the treasure, ya bilge rat?" one demands. Actually Jack is just a few feet away, peering out from behind some dressmaker forms.

Next you sail through a bridal auction, where a band of buccaneers are selling off the town's maidens to raucous hecklers.

Another turn sends you deeper into the village. As an old pirate with a treasure map rambles on ("What I wouldn't give to see the look on Capt. Jack Sparrow's face when he hears tell 'tis only me that gots the goods..."), Sparrow himself pops up out of a barrel, sneaking a peek at the old salt's map before ducking back out of sight. Behind them, some matrons chase looting pirates in endless circles.

Other scenes show pirates setting fire to the town and trying to escape from its jail by luring a dog that holds keys. In the finale a giddy Sparrow has found the village treasure room. Lolling on an ornate rocking chair, leg draped over one of its arms, he sings, slurs, and chats with a parrot.

HISTORIC IT BE

The last Disney attraction personally developed by Walt Disney, Pirates of the Caribbean combines a Missouri farm boy's view of high-seas adventure with a Hollywood showman's use of theatrics. "Walt came from a world of movies," explains Disney Imagineer Jason Surrell. "He wanted rides

IT'S A GREAT BIG BEAUTIFUL SMALL SCURVY WORLD. Originally conceived as a wax museum, Pirates became an Audio-Animatronics flume ride after the success of two Disney technologies that debuted at the 1964 World's Fair: The robotics used at Carousel of Progress and the propulsion system of It's a Small World.

Average Wait	
9am	0 min
10am	5
11am	5
Noon	15
1pm	20
2pm	20
3pm	15
4pm	10
5pm	5
6pm	5
7pm	5
8pm	5
9pm	5

LYRICS © WONDERLAND MUSIC COMPANY INC.

▶ **The right queue has the most fun detail, including some chess-playing skeletons.**

that use lighting and back-drops, establishing shots and lots of characters—up-close ones who are most important, and faraway characters who are less so."

Premiering at California's Disneyland in the 1960s, the attraction was not part of Walt Disney World when it opened in 1971. Disney officials figured the ride wouldn't be popular in Florida since the actual Caribbean is close by. They changed their minds almost immediately, and debuted this version in 1973, just two years later.

Additional 2006 improvements include a revamped soundtrack featuring the new films' rousing instrumental theme, a new sound system that adds a "whumph" to each cannon shot, and remastered vintage tracks that make it easier to understand what the pirates are saying. An upgraded lighting system makes everything easier to see.

PC IT BE NOT

The attraction's story is all in good fun, but even the most carefree parent may wonder if scenes showing torture, heavy drinking and the selling of women are sending the best messages to a wide-eyed child. "There is nothing politically correct about Pirates of the Caribbean," admits Imagineer Eric Jacobson. "Much of it is patently offensive."

In fairness, the ride does imply the results of such behavior. As the first scene illustrates, the pirates end up murdered, their skeletons left behind in a deserted cave.

It *is* more sensitive than it used to be. That barrel that now holds Capt. Jack? Originally it hid an embarrassed young woman, nearly naked. As the pirate in front held her slip in his hand, he spoke of his desire to "hoist me colors on the likes of that shy little wench." Then, believe it or not, this Disney character added: "I be willin' to share, I be!"

To most, the ride is a hoot. As we heard some college girls sing as they waited in line (to the tune of "It's a Small World"):

A skeleton mans the crows nest of a makeshift mast at the entrance to Pirates of the Caribbean

"It's a world of fog and a world of caves.
It's a world of torture and of sex slaves.
But there's gold, and there's rum!
Johnny Depp? He's no bum!
It's the Disney pirates ride!"

FUN FINDS

Entrance: ❶ Alongside the right entrance queue, visible through some windows on the right, two chess-playing pirates in a dungeon apparently reached a stalemate some time ago. Their skeletons still stare at the board. **Caverns:** ❷ A crab on your left rears up as it moves its eyes, claws and pinchers. **Harbor attack:** ❸ A sign on the ship's stern reveals its name: the Wicked Wench. ❹ Capt. Barbossa orders his men to "Strike yer colors, ye bloomin' cock-

▶ Captain Hook and Mr. Smee often greet guests across from the ride entrance.

Two pirates loot and set fire to a Spanish port in a scene from Pirates of the Caribbean

the window "Don't tell him Carlos! Don't be chicken!" Carlos responds "I am no chicken! I will not talk!" ❼ Jack's hands rest on the derrieres of the female forms around him. **Bridal auction:** ❽ A crate on your left is filled with bobbing, clucking chickens. ❾ The first woman in line is beaming, happy to be sold. ❿ The auctioneer refers to the first woman's portly body as "stout-hearted and cornfed" and asks her to "shift yer cargo, dearie. Show 'em yer larboard side." ⓫ Impatient to be next, a buxom redhead pulls up her skirt to show her leg. ⓬ The auctioneer instructs the redhead to "Strike yer colors you brazen wench! No need to expose yer superstructure!" ⓭ The second to last woman is crying. **Chasing scene:** ⓮ At the end of the scene, a drunken pirate to your right invites two gray cats to join him in "a little ol' tot of rum." **Burning town:** ⓯ On your left, a dog barks along to the cantina band. ⓰ On the right a snoring pirate lolls in the mud with three intoxicated pigs. His chest heaves. ⓱ As you leave the scene, the hairy leg of a pirate above dangles toward your face. ⓲ A parrot with him squawks "A parrot's life for me!" **Dungeon:** ⓳ Frustrated that the dog in front of the jail won't respond, a prisoner demands "Hit him with the soup bone!" ⓴ As the dog looks at you, another captive says "Rover, it's us what needs yer ruddy help, not them blasted lubbers." **Treasure room:** ㉑ Jack says the loot is "my reward for a life of villainy, larceny, skullduggery and persnickety." ㉒ After Capt. Jack sings the "Yo, Ho" lyric *"maraud and embezzle and even hijack"* his parrot interrupts with "Hi Jack! Hi Jack!" ㉓ Jack refers to the colorful bird as "my chromatic winged beast." **Exit area:** ㉔ Painted on the exit ramp's moving walkway, "shoeprints" that indicate where to step consist of a normal right shoe and peg-leg left mark.

roaches!" **Interrogation:** ❺ The captain has a hook for a hand. ❻ When the pirates ask the mayor where Jack is, his wife calls from

FUN FACTS › The Davy Jones fog screen is made of water droplets so small you stay dry as you pass through them. It's held in place by columns of air. **›** The fall drops 14 feet. **›** The voices of Davy Jones and Capts. Barbossa and Sparrow are those of Bill Nighey, Geoffrey Rush and Johnny Depp. **›** The auctioneer is Paul Frees, the Haunted Mansion's ghost host. **›** In reality, the redhead is little more than a pole from the waist down. **›** The ride has 125 Audio-Animatronics characters: 65 people and 60 animals. **›** The exterior facade, the "Castillo del Morro," is based on the 16th-century El Morro fortress in San Juan, P.R.

›› How much does a pirate pay for corn on the cob? A buck an ear. **›› What's a pirate's favorite cookie?** Ships Ahoy. **›› What type of socks does a pirate wear?** Aaaaarrrrgyle.

▶ Peter Pan and Wendy often greet guests across from the ride exit.

Abraham Lincoln speaks at the Hall of Presidents

The Hall of Presidents

★★★★★ ✓ 20 min. Capacity: 740. Shows every 30 min. Fear factor: None. Access: Guests may stay in wheelchairs, ECVs. Assistive listening; reflective captioning. Debuted: 1971, updated 2009.

Reopening July 4, 2009, after a nine-month refurbishment, this patriotic theatrical presentation combines a short film with a robotic stage show. Still highlighted by the introduction of every U.S. president (improved to be easier to follow), it now has three talking figures—George Washington, Abraham Lincoln and Barack Obama. Light, sound and projection systems have also been made current.

As before, the show focuses on the role slavery has played in our history. The film, shown on a 180-degree screen, counts how early leaders debated slavery, from the Constitutional Convention to the Lincoln-Douglas debates.

The presidents act human. They nod at the audience, fidget, shift their weight, look around, even whisper to one another. A Disney publicist used to tell visiting reporters that some of the presidents were real people—that since there were always a few robots out for repairs, each show had at least one human stand-in. When he once asked Walter Cronkite to spot the live actor, the veteran newsman just laughed. A minute later he turned back and said, "Jefferson?"

Some paintings used in the film hang in the foyer and at the Town Square City Hall.

LINCOLN 2.0
The Lincoln figure is a simplified remake of Disney's original Honest Abe, a problematic robot that debuted at the 1964 World's Fair. With any spike in current, Disney's first Lincoln would flail its arms, hit itself repeatedly in the head and then slam itself back down in its chair. The malfunction inspired a scene in a 1993 episode of "The Simpsons." In "Selma's Choice," Aunt Selma takes Bart and Lisa to the Disney World-like Duff Gardens, where every attraction is themed to Duff Beer. At the Duff Hall of Presidents, Lincoln holds up a Duff can and takes a swig, then mindlessly smashes it onto his head.

HIDDEN MICKEY
In a painting in the lobby just to the right of the theater entrance, at the tip of George Washington's sword.

Average Wait

9am	closed
10am	15 min
11am	15
Noon	15
1pm	15
2pm	15
3pm	15
4pm	15
5pm	15
6pm	15
7pm	15
8pm	15
9pm	15

▶ **The Hall of Presidents will be closed during the first half of 2009.**

A large paddle wheel drives Walt Disney World's Liberty Square Riverboat

Liberty Square Riverboat

★★★ 13 min. Capacity: 400. Open 10am—dusk, with rides every half hour on the half hour. Fear factor: None. Access: Guests may remain in wheelchairs, ECVs. Debuted: 1971, updated 2007.

You relive the glory days of riverboats on this cruise around Tom Sawyer Island. Riding on a real steamboat, you pass scenes that recall life on the Mississippi and other American rivers during the time of Mark Twain. The boat's pilot, Sam Clemens himself, narrates the journey.

Though the sights along the riverbank aren't that special—a burning cabin, an old fisherman, an Indian village, a sacred burial ground and a few remarkably stoic animals—the boat is pretty cool. A three-tiered vessel, it has a functioning boiler room, steam engine and paddle wheel on its lower deck. The second floor has a small stateroom. Up on top there's a working smokestack and a steam whistle. The boat was built by Disney at a backstage shop; its boiler and steam engine were purchased at a Tampa shipyard. It rides on a rail.

You also hear Capt. Horace Bixby, in real life the boat pilot who mentored Clemens. "Steady as she goes!" he commands.

On hot days the best places to stand are on the shady second-floor bow. The best views, of course, are from the top deck.

Now known as the Liberty Belle, the boat was named the Richard F. Irvine until 1996. It once had a twin, the Admiral Joe Fowler, until that vessel was dropped by a crane during a 1980 refurbishment. Irvine helped design Magic Kingdom. Fowler was in charge of the original Walt Disney World construction. Today, the names Irvine and Fowler are used by ferrys in the Seven Seas Lagoon, the man-made lake in front of the park.

FUN FACTS ›› River water is pumped into the boiler before each trip. ›› The boiler is kept at 700 degrees. It uses diesel fuel. ›› The steam engine powers everything on the boat, including its lights and sound system. ›› The leadsman is exaggerating when he calls out "Mark Twain!" indicating the water is two fathoms (12 feet) deep. These "Rivers of America" run 9 feet.

Average Wait

9am	closed
10am	15 min
11am	15
Noon	15
1pm	15
2pm	15
3pm	15
4pm	15
5pm	15
6pm	15
7pm	closed
8pm	closed
9pm	closed

▶ **Don't miss seeing the engine. It's on the lower deck, just in front of the paddle wheel.**

The Haunted Mansion

★★★★ ✓ 11 min. Capacity: 320. Fear factor: None. Access: Must be ambulatory. Handheld captioning. Debuted: 1971, revised 2007.

Loaded with detail and special effects but never truly scary, this dark indoor tour of a ghostly retirement home is a spooky treat for any age. Refurbished in 2007, it now includes a room of converging staircases that's based on the work of artist M.C. Escher, a floating crystal ball and a completely new attic. Disney World veterans will notice new paintings in the portrait corridor, more movement in a suit of armor and a lot of new moving, blinking eyes in the mansion's bat-eyed wallpaper.

'ANY VOLUNTEERS?'

The show starts outside. As you near the home, its grounds are unkempt. An old hearse is parked out in front but its horse is gone. A distant wolf howls.

A walkway leads to a side foyer. Once you're let in, a spooky voice—your "ghost host"—informs you that spirits are present, "practicing their terror with ghoulish delight." Their first trick: transforming the portrait above the room's mantelpiece from a young man to a corpse.

Next up: a portrait chamber, where again the ghosts pull pranks. The door disappears, the walls stretch, the lights go out and the ceiling suddenly reveals a hanging body above your head. Once you escape, you board a bench-seat "doom buggy" for the rest of your tour.

Soon you learn the spirits' true purpose: they want you to join them. "We have 999 happy haunts here," your host tells you as you move through the mansion, "but there's room for a thousand. Any volunteers?" In the library, busts in the shelves look you over as you pass.

You pass some of the ghosts' earlier attempts to land a new resident. A man is trapped in a casket in a conservatory; locked door handles in a hallway twist and turn as knocks behind them grow desperate. One of the doors flexes so much it seems to breathe.

Average Wait	
9am	0 min
10am	5
11am	5
Noon	15
1pm	20
2pm	20
3pm	15
4pm	10
5pm	5
6pm	5
7pm	5
8pm	5
9pm	5

A ghostly bride in the attic joyfully holds an ax

The hall leads to a seance, where a spiritualist—a disembodied head in a floating ball—beckons the ghosts to materialize.

Then, they do. You see the mansion's residents in the ballroom, where they've gathered for a rollicking "death-day" party, and pass many more in the graveyard and a crypt. One joins you in your vehicle.

Near the exit a tiny bride appears and urges you to come again. "Hurry back... hurry back..." she coos, standing on a ledge above you, a dead bouquet in her arms, her veil blowing in the breeze.

As you leave, the ghosts promote the benefits of joining them one last time. *"Mortals pay a token fee,"* the spirits sing, faintly. *"Rest in peace, the haunting's free. So hurry back, we would like your company."*

Your tour also includes a music room where a spirit plays a piano, an endless hall with a floating chandelier and a trip through the attic, a room with its own storyline, of a woman who spent her life marrying wealthy men then chopping off their heads to collect their fortunes. You pass each of her wedding portraits, each transforming to show its groom losing his head.

▶ **Is Haunted Mansion scary? Only for some children. The ride is spooky, but not threatening.**

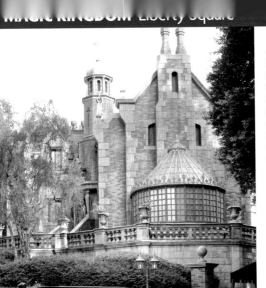

The Haunted Mansion exterior recalls 19th-century homes in New York's Hudson River valley

The bride stands at the end of the room. Holding an ax, she sarcastically recites wedding vows ("in sickness and in health" becomes "in sickness and in wealth"). Fully animated, she looks real, though she's actually a video projection on a three-dimensional figure.

SPIRITED INSPIRATIONS

Many Haunted Mansion moments are inspired by classic films and literature. A tapping, thumping corridor of doors, including one that breathes, appears in the 1963 horror movie **"The Haunting."** Human statues follow guests with their gazes and wall sconces are held by human arms in the 1946 French film **"La Belle et la Bete,"** a version of the Beauty and the Beast fairy tale. Os-

car Wilde's 1890 novel **"The Picture of Dorian Gray"** includes a transforming portrait in which a young man becomes old and disfigured, a change that reflects his damaged soul. Edgar Allen Poe fans will find Mansion allusions to the 1845 poem **"The Raven"** as well as the 1846 novel **"The Cask of Amontillado,"** in which a man is entombed alive in a brick crypt.

FAMOUS VOICES

Many of the Haunted Mansion voices were supplied by famous Hollywood talents.

The ghost host is **Paul Frees,** who voiced Boris Badenov in the 1959–1964 television series "The Adventures of Rocky and Bullwinkle." At the Pirates of the Caribbean he's the auctioneer, Carlos, as well as the concertina player and nearby dog, even the bridge parrot.

The spiritualist is actress **Eleanor Audley,** who provided the voice of Lady Tremaine in Disney's 1950 "Cinderella" and Maleficent in 1959's "Sleeping Beauty." She played Eunice, the mother of Oliver Douglas, in the 1960s television series "Green Acres."

The group singing "Grim Grinning Ghosts" is the **Mellomen,** a quartet who performed on Rosemary Clooney's 1954 "Mambo Italiano" and were Elvis Presley's backup singers in the movies "It Happened at the World's Fair" (1963), "Roustabout" (1964) and "Paradise Hawaiian Style" (1966).

The graveyard's singing busts feature Mellomen lead singer **Thurl Ravenscroft** (second from the left). The voice of Country Bear Jamboree buffalo head Buff and the Enchanted Tiki Room's Fritz the parrot, he sang "You're A Mean One, Mr. Grinch" in the 1966 television special "How the Grinch Stole Christmas!" and was the longtime voice of Tony the Tiger for Kellogg's Frosted Flakes cereal.

The graveyard's singing executioner is **Candy Candido,** the man who played the angry apple tree in 1939's "The Wizard of

▶ **For the shortest wait, take your tour of the mansion before 10:30 a.m. or late at night.**

Oz" ("Are you hinting my apples aren't what they ought to be?"), the Indian chief in 1953's "Peter Pan" and a goon in 1959's "Sleeping Beauty."

FUN FINDS

Entrance: ❶ Horseshoe and wheel tracks lead from a barn to a hearse. ❷ Dead roses lie inside it. ❸ Madame Leota's eyes open and close on her tombstone face, which tilts toward you. **Foyer:** ❹ The fireplace grate forms a cross-eyed, arrow-tongued face. **Stretching Room:** ❺ Grates along the bottom of the walls form monstrous faces. **Loading Area:** ❻ The chain stanchions are toothy brass bats. **Portrait Corridor:** ❼ A woman in a transforming painting turns into Medusa. **Library:** ❽ Bat faces are carved into the paneling between the busts. **Music Room:** ❾ The window frame is decorated with coffins. **Endless hallway:** ❿ Fang-baring serpents extend from the hall's frame molding. **Conservatory:** ⓫ Coffin handles are bats. **Corridor of Doors:** ⓬ The grandfather clock is a demon. The casing forms its hair and eyes; the clockface its mouth, the pendulum a tail. **Grand Dining Hall:** ⓭ On the mantle, a ghost in a top hat has his arm around a bust. ⓮ The fireplace grate includes the silhouettes of two black cats. ⓯ In front of the fireplace, an old woman knits in a rocking chair. ⓰ Five ghosts float in from a coffin, which has fallen out of a hearse that has pulled up to an outside door. ⓱ Mr. Pickwick, from the 1836 Dickens novel "The Pickwick Papers," swings out from the chandelier. ⓲ Marc Antony and Cleopatra sit next to Mr. Pickwick. ⓳ Julius Caesar sits at the left end of the table. ⓴ The sheet-music stand is a leering bat. **Graveyard:** ㉑ A medieval minstrel band includes a flutist emerging from his tomb, ㉒ a drummer tapping out a beat on bones lying on the flutist's crypt cover, ㉓ a bagpiper in a kilt, ㉔ a soldier playing a small harp, ㉕ and a trumpeter wearing pajamas and a stocking cap. ㉖ When the

Graves border the Haunted Mansion entranceway

trumpeter rears back, so do two owls perched above him. ㉗ Sitting on a tomb, five cats yowl and hiss to the band's beat. ㉘ A skeletal dog howls on a hill. ㉙ A ghostly king and queen ride on a makeshift seesaw: a board balanced on a tombstone. ㉚ Swinging from the branch of a tree, a princess sips tea behind them. ㉛ A British duke and duchess toast themselves at a candlelit table. ㉜ Behind them, four ghosts ride bicycles in a circle. ㉝ Wearing hoop earrings, a pirate near you raises his teacup, and sometimes his head, from behind a grave. ㉞ Floating by itself in the air, a teapot pours tea into a cup. ㉟ Tracks from a hearse veer off from your path. ㊱ The driver of the hearse chats with a duchess, who sits atop the hearse sipping tea. ㊲ A ghost sits up from the hearse's coffin, which has fallen

▶ Each Haunted Mansion 'doom buggy' seats two comfortably. Three children can ride together.

Each of the 20 occupants of the Haunted Mansion mausoleum has a pun for a name

crypt. **Crypt:** ㊼ Human arms hold up the wall sconces in the crypt (as well as in the unload area). **Outside the exit:** ㊽ Each of 20 mausoleum occupants has a pun for a name. They include "Hal Lusinashun," "I. Emma Spook" and "Wee G. Bord." ㊾ Dogs and snakes appear in the side frames of benches in front of a hillside pet cemetery. ㊿ Mr. Toad is buried in the pet cemetery.*

HIDDEN MICKEYS

❶ The foyer and two stretching rooms form the three-circle shape. ❷ As the leftmost place setting on the near side of the ballroom banquet table. ❸ As a silhouette in the final scene of the graveyard, at the end of the uplifted arm of the Grim Reaper (visible on your far right just after your doom buggy turns away from the tea party). ❹ On the right side of the souvenir cart, on the index finger of a painted hand beneath the word "Parlour."

* J. Thaddeus Toad is "dead" because his attraction, Mr. Toad's Wild Ride, is no longer at Magic Kingdom. An original park attraction, it was replaced by The Many Adventures of Winnie the Pooh in 1998.

out of the back. ㊳ He's chatting with a sea captain. ㊴ A dog sniffs an Egyptian sarcophagus. ㊵ Its mummy is sitting up, stirring his tea, mumbling through his bandages. ㊶ "What's that? Louder! I can't hear you! Eh?" says an old bearded man to the mummy, holding a horn to his ear. ㊷ The Grim Reaper floats inside a crypt to your extreme far right. His beady eyes stare at you from inside his hood. ㊸ Dressed in Viking gear, a male and female opera singer each belt out an exaggerated solo. ㊹ Holding his severed head in his hand, a knight cheerfully sings a duet with his gravelly voiced executioner. ㊺ Shackled with a ball and chain, a pint-sized prisoner harmonizes with them. ㊻ Sensing the party's over, an arm of a ghost trowels itself back into a

FUN FACTS 》 Built during the Civil War, the hearse appeared in the 1965 John Wayne film "The Sons of Katie Elder." 》 The mansion's interior design comes from the 1874 Harry Packer home in Jim Thorpe, Penn. 》 The song "Grim Grinning Ghosts" is performed in eight styles, including a dirge that plays as you enter. 》 The "dust" is made from fuller's earth, an ingredient in kitty litter. 》 Except for a few books, the library bookcase is a flat painted backdrop. 》 So is the back wall of the ballroom, including its molding and woodwork. 》 The spiritualist is known as "Madame Leota," a reference to Disney modelmaker Leota Toombs whose face she shares. Toombs also appears as, and voices, the crypt bride. 》 You never go in the home. The entire 960-foot ride takes place in a nondescript building behind the facade.

▶ At the Haunted Mansion exit, Madame Leota's cart sells "DOOM BGY" license plates.

Big Al performs an off-key version of the Tex Ritter classic "Blood on the Saddle" during the Country Bear Jamboree

Country Bear Jamboree

★★ 16 min. Capacity: 380. Opens 10am. Fear factor: None. Access: Guests may remain in wheelchairs, ECVs. Assistive listening; reflective captioning. Debuted: 1971.

Goofy-faced mechanical bears perform in this cornpone musical revue. Set in an 1880s lumber-camp union hall, the show features 18 life-sized performers singing snippets of 14 country and cowboy songs.

Tutu-clad Trixie warbles the 1966 Wanda Jackson hit, "Tears Will Be the Chaser for my Wine." Temptress Teddi Barra sings "Heart, We Did All That We Could," a 1967 Jean Shepard tune. "Ya'll come up and see me sometime!" she coos at the end, channeling Mae West. Replies the emcee: "As soon as I can find a ladder!" The best bear is sad-eyed, tone-deaf Big Al. He butchers the 1960 Tex Ritter dirge "Blood on the Saddle." Ritter himself provides the voice.

Mounted up on the side wall, talking trophy heads Buff (a buffalo), Max (a deer) and Melvin (a moose) bicker and banter.

Full of personality, the exaggerated faces are funny, as are some song titles (Tex Ritter's 1950 "My Woman Ain't Pretty (But She Don't Swear None)," Homer & Jethro's 1964 "Mama Don't Whip Little Buford (I Think You Should Shoot Him Instead)"). But unless you're a fan, the concept wears thin. Worse, the show's sound system is poor. The lo-fi soundtrack plays through speakers situated only on and behind the stage.

Designed in the 1960s, the Country Bear Jamboree was intended for Disney's Mineral King Ski Resort, a development planned for a historic valley in California's High Sierra mountains. Instead, the land became part of the Sequoia National Forest. Though he never saw it finished, the show was said to be one of Walt Disney's favorites.

FUN FACTS » Henry's phrase "'cause we've got a lot to give" refers to the 1970s slogan of the show's first sponsor: "You've got a lot to live, and Pepsi's got a lot to give." » Sung here by The Five Bear Rugs, "Devilish Mary" was the first country song recorded by a woman. Roba Stanley sang it in 1924.

Average Wait	
9am	closed
10am	0 min
11am	10
Noon	10
1pm	10
2pm	10
3pm	10
4pm	10
5pm	10
6pm	10
7pm	10
8pm	10
9pm	10

▶ Sit in the front of the theater. Guests in back rows have a hard time hearing the show.

Splash Mountain

★★★★★ ✔ 12 min. Capacity: 440. *FastPass* Fear factor: One small drop is completely dark. The big drop can scare adults. Chicken exit. Access: Must be ambulatory. Height restriction: 40 in. Debuted: 1992 (Disneyland 1989).

This flume ride in, out, around and down a mountain is the most "satisfactual," but least understood, ride in Magic Kingdom. Lined with 68 robotic creatures in cartoon-like musical scenes, the half-mile trip takes you through bayous, swamps, a cave and a flooded mine shaft. The ride includes five short drops and a five-story plummet.

Based on scenes from Disney's 1946 film "Song of the South," themselves based on a series of folk tales popular with slaves in the antebellum South, Splash Mountain has a story that's impossible to follow if you don't already know it, but fascinating if you do.

You're in it from the start. Climbing through some barns in rural Georgia, you come upon a secret passageway that leads to Critter Cave, the home of wise old story-teller Brer Frog. "Mark my words," he tells two grandkids, in a shadow diorama on your left. "Brer Rabbit gonna put his foot in Brer Fox's mouth one of these days."

Once in your log (hollowed out by beavers, the story goes), you travel past the crafty rabbit's briar patch playground and up Chick-A-Pin Hill, home to the tenacious but gullible Brer Fox and strong but stupid Brer Bear. You float into the mountain and down a magnolia bayou, where you come upon Brer Rabbit packing to leave. *"I've had enough of this old briar patch,"* he sings. *"I'm lookin' for a little more adventure."*

Overhearing, Brer Fox and Brer Bear scheme to catch the hare and cook him for dinner. First the fox traps the rabbit with a rope, but then the hare tricks the bear into switching places. (Though not shown on the ride, in the film the rabbit tells the bear that he's a scarecrow making $1 a minute. "You'd make a mighty fine scare-crow, Brer Bear. How'd you like to have this job?")

Average Wait	
9am	0 min
10am	5
11am	30
Noon	40
1pm	50
2pm	60
3pm	50
4pm	55
5pm	70
6pm	45
7pm	70
8pm	45
9pm	30

Right: Splash Mountain includes a 52-foot drop into a briar patch

▶ For the driest drop, duck down before the splash and stay down until after the slosh.

Then, saying he's headed to a "laughin' place," the rabbit leads the others into a hollow, fallen tree, which leads to a flooded mine filled with bees. "I don't see no laughing place, just bees" the bear says. "I didn't say it was *your* laughin' place," laughs the rabbit. "I said it was *my* laughin' place!"

Brer Fox slams a beehive over the rabbit and ties him up at a cooking pot. "Well Brer Rabbit, it looks like I'm gonna have to cook ya!*" the fox says. "Do what you will," Brer Rabbit responds, "but whatever you do, please don't fling me in that briar patch!"

Of course, that's what Brer Bear does.

A singing showboat welcomes the bunny back home, but Brer Bear and Brer Fox are in the patch, too. Stuck in the thorns, the dim-witted bear sings "Zip-A-Dee-Doo-Dah" with the rabbit's friends. "This is all your fault Brer Bear!" Brer Fox says, trying to pull the bear free while fighting off an alligator. "You flung us here. So stop that singing!"

The moral? On the surface, there's no place like home. On a subversive level, that if they're crafty, the weak can do "pretty good sure as you're born" against the strong.

FUN FINDS

❶ "Fleas, flat feet and furballs" are all cured by the "Critter Elixir" trumpeted on a wagon past the second lift hill. ❷ Around a corner, Brer Bear snores in his house. ❸ Just before the drop, vultures above you warn "Time to be turning around... if only you could. If you've finally found your laughing place, how come you aren't laughing?"

HIDDEN MICKEYS

❶ As stacked barrels on your right along the second lift. ❷ As a three-orbed fishing bobber on your left (left of a picnic basket, inside the mountain just past Brer Frog toe-

* Alternates with "hang ya!" "roast ya!" and "skin ya!"

FUN FACTS ❯❯ The logs reach 40 mph on the final drop, making it the fastest Magic Kingdom moment. ❯❯ The ride uses 956,000 gallons of water. It's recycled every four minutes. ❯❯ In 1993, Great Britain's princes William and Harry, then ages 11 and 8, visited Disney World with their mother, Princess Diana. Splash Mountain was William's favorite ride, so they rode it three times. ❯❯ Because of the film's racial overtones, Disney does not market "Song of the South" on DVD. ❯❯ "Brer" is slang for "Brother."

Brer Fox captures Brer Bear with a beehive in a mine-shaft scene in Splash Mountain

fishing on top of Brer Gator). ❸ As a hanging rope in the flooded cavern (on your right, behind a lantern, past a turtle on a geyser). ❹ After the big drop, reclining as a full figure in the sky to the right of the riverboat, as the upper outline of a cloud. Mickey's head is to the right.

PUBLISHED IN "The Complete Tales of Uncle Remus," an 1895 compilation of 185 African-American folk tales by Joel Chandler Harris, a columnist for the Atlanta Journal-Constitution, the stories "How Mr. Rabbit Was Too Sharp For Mr. Fox," "Mr. Rabbit and Mr. Bear" and "Brother Rabbit's Laughing-Place," rival the best European folk tales for charm and meaning. Walt Disney loved "their rich and tolerant humor; their homely philosophy and cheerfulness." Harris, though, has been scorned. In his forward, the white Harris described his narrator, a fictional freed slave named Uncle Remus, as having "nothing but pleasant memories of the discipline of slavery." Disney's film ignored that premise but was still associated with it. The 1987 book "The Tales of Uncle Remus" by Julius Lester offers most of the folk tales in a more unadulterated state.

▶ **The front seat gets the wettest. The back seat usually stays relatively dry.**

All curves all the time, Big Thunder Mountain Railroad is fun for all ages

Big Thunder Mountain Railroad

★ ★ ★ ★ ★ ✓ 4 min. Capacity: 150. *FastPass* Fear factor: Jerky, violent turns toss you around in your seat. Many sharp hills and sudden dips. Access: Must be ambulatory. Height restriction: 40 in. Debuted: 1980 (Disneyland 1979).

All curves all of the time, this roller coaster is exciting but never scary. Meant to be a trip through Utah's Monument Valley, the track takes you around and through a realistic mountain that's filled with detail. Sights include a cave with swarming bats, hot springs, a flooded town, a collapsing mine shaft, even the remains of a dinosaur.

Scattered around the attraction are hundreds of pieces of authentic mining gear, which Disney scoured from ghost towns during the 1970s. The rusty equipment includes buckets, cogwheels and ore carts. There are also nearly 20 fairly realistic animals, including big-horned sheep, bobcats and javelinas. Live cactus dots the landscape.

Average Wait	
9am	0 min
10am	20
11am	30
Noon	35
1pm	40
2pm	45
3pm	50
4pm	45
5pm	40
6pm	40
7pm	40
8pm	35
9pm	30

Technically, this "wildest ride in the wilderness" consists of three lift hills and three series of hairpin turns. There are many small hills and sudden dips, but no big drops and you never go upside down. Top speed is 36 mph. Like vehicles of most conventional coasters, the trains run faster late in the day, after the track grease melts.

GODS AND GREED
Unlike most roller coasters, Big Thunder Mountain Railroad tells a story, a tale of a Gold Rush mining town whose relentless pursuit of riches upsets the spirits of nature. Here's the storyline:

During the height of the Gold Rush, men in the desert town of Tumbleweed were searching for the precious metal on a

FUN FACTS >> The train names are I.B. Hearty, I.M. Brave, I.M. Fearless, U.B. Bold, U.R. Courageous and U.R. Daring. **>>** The "Howdy partners!" announcer is Dallas McKennon, the voice of Ben Franklin at Epcot's American Adventure. A longtime Hollywood voice talent, he also voiced the 1960s television versions of Gumby and Archie Andrews, and the Rice Krispies characters Snap, Crackle and Pop.

▶ **For the wildest ride ask for the back seat. It's faster on the drop and turns.**

nearby mountain, which was also a Native American burial ground. Though the ridge rumbled whenever any mining took place—the Indians called it Big Thunder Mountain—the gold diggers were persistent. Determined to strike it rich, they took their ore trains deep into the mountain's cavern, and dynamited new shafts.

Adding insult to injury, the miners partied hearty at night. They entertained themselves with poker games, parlor girls and crates of whiskey.

Eventually, the spirits had enough. One day an engineer noticed that bats in the cave seemed spooked. Then his train spun out of control, flying around the mountain like a bat out of hell. Moments later a flash flood hit the town, then an earthquake. Some miners were too drunk to notice.

No gold was ever found.

In reality, the mountain is a painted cement and wire-mesh skin over a concrete-and-steel frame. Inside are the attraction's computers, electronics and water pumps.

FUN FINDS

❶ The lights continuously flicker and dim. ❷ A box to the right of the entrance walkway reads "Lytum & Hyde Explosives Co." ❸ As you walk down into the boarding area a crate above you holds whiskey. ❹ On the ride, as you arrive in Tumbleweed a prospector on your right has washed into town still in his bathtub. ❺ Immediately on your left rainmaker Professor Cumulus Isobar bails himself out. ❻ The proprietors of the dry goods store are D. Hydrate and U. Wither. ❼ Inside the Gold Dust Saloon, a whiskey-fueled game of poker has been flooded out. ❽ After the (actual) sun sets, drunks and dance-hall dames party on the saloon's second floor. ❾ Around a bend on your left, a "Flood-ometer" reads "Flooded Out." ❿ If you exit the ride from the left track, you walk alongside the office of the railroad's telegraph manager, Morris Code. ⓫ The right exitway has a canary in a cage (he's not moving!)

The landscape of Big Thunder Mountain Railroad is based on Utah's Monument Valley

and, above a "Blasting in Progress" sign, a plunger. It's pushed in.

HIDDEN MICKEY

The three-circle shape appears toward the end of the ride as three rusty gears laying on the ground on your right, after you go under the dinosaur rib cage.

DURING THE MID-1800s, a discovery of gold in a remote mountain area would often bring in a feverish migration of prospectors, who would search stream beds and canyon walls hoping to instantly find their fortune. Later a commercial company often arrived to mine for gold ore, chunks of rock with deposits of the precious metal.

▶ The ride is especially fun at night, when the landscape is lit but the track is not.

Tom Sawyer Island

★★★ Allow 45 min. Capacity: 400. Closes at dusk. Fear factor: The cave has side niches where young children can get temporarily lost. Access: Must be ambulatory. Debuted: 1973.

Accessible only by a powered raft, this wooded island sits within the waterway used by the Liberty Square Riverboat. Lined with paved trails, it offers a variety of small adventures.

Cranny filled Injun Joe's Cave has a hidden scary face inside. Old Scratch's Mystery Mine is a creepy, twisting shaft with wailing winds and glowing crystals. Other fun spots include a climb-through grist mill, a barrel bridge and windmill. Atop a hill is a brook, a duck pond, a playground with a tiny rope swing and two picnic tables.

Along the shore is Aunt Polly's Place, a shady snack bar (open seasonally).

A suspension footbridge leads to Fort Langhorne, a calvary outpost with a snoring sentry, robotic horses and a clearly marked "secret" escape tunnel along the back wall. Watchtowers have electronic rifles kids can play with free of charge.

Barrels of fun. A bouncy bridge extends over the water on Tom Sawyer Island.

Average Wait	
9am	0 min
10am	5
11am	5
Noon	15
1pm	20
2pm	20
3pm	15
4pm	10
5pm	5
6pm	5
7pm	5
8pm	closed
9pm	closed

FUN FINDS

❶ Games of checkers are often set up on a landing down the left trail from the raft dock. ❷ The mill's various creaks and groans subtly create the tune "Down By The Old Mill Stream." ❸ The bird that's trapped in the mill's cogs re-creates a scene from the landmark 1937 cartoon "The Old Mill." ❹ The women's restroom at Fort Langhorne is labeled "Powder Room."

Frontierland Shootin' Arcade

★★★ Allow 5 min. Capacity: 16. Fear factor: None. Access: Guests may remain in wheelchairs, ECVs. Debuted: 1971. $1 for 25 shots.

Surprisingly fun, this old-fashioned arcade is filled with more than 50 silly targets. Direct hits trigger sight and sound gags—a prisoner escapes from a jail, an ore car comes out of its mine, a grave-digging skeleton pops out of a hole.

Ideal for children, the targets are easy to hit and the infrared rifles easy to hold. Guns mounted in the center of the arcade have the best view of the most targets.

▶ The guns of the Shootin' Arcade are each loaded with a secret free round each morning.

Cinderella Castle

One of the world's most photographed buildings, Cinderella Castle has its picture taken 30,000 times a day. And no wonder. It's not only a world-famous landmark, but also quite a piece of fantasy architecture.

Its design combines the looks of a medieval fortress and Renaissance castle. Heavy lower walls have saw-toothed battlements like those that hid artillery atop 11th-century stone forts. The top has the turrets, spires and Gothic trim of French castles of the 14th, 15th and 16th centuries. Accents include 13 winged gargoyles and a portcullis. An iron grate over the entrance appears ready to drop at a moment's notice.

Though the castle appears to be a 300-foot-tall stone fortress, it is actually a 189-foot steel frame covered in fiberglass. The building was designed to be seen from a mile away, so guests arriving on ferries and monorails can spot it with anticipation.

The interior includes a restaurant and gift shop, security rooms, three elevators and a fourth-floor apartment. Though planned for the use of the Disney family, the apartment space was left unfinished for decades. It was used as a radio room, switchboard center and dressing room until 2006, when it was finished off as the Cinderella Castle Suite.*

WAR AND PIECES

Also inside is a terrific piece of art. Created out of 500,000 bits of glass in 500 colors, the five-panel mosaic tells the Cinderella story. The 15- by 10-foot arches were crafted by a

Cinderella Castle combines the looks of a medieval fortress and a Renaissance castle

team led by Hanns-Joachim Scharff, based on a design by Disney's Dorothea Redmond.

The mosaic took two years to create. First, Redmond's paintings were redrawn to larger proportions on heavyweight brown craft paper. These images were cut up into 50 or so jigsaw-puzzle-like pieces. Scharff used both smooth and uneven glass. Many pieces were hand-cut and shaped with a power grindstone; a third were fused with silver and gold. Thin glass strips outlined hands and faces. Multihued rods were chopped crosswise for other effects.

Scharff was a fascinating man in his own right. Born in Germany in 1907, he became a Luftwaffe interrogator of captured U.S. Air Force fighter pilots during World War II. One of the best interrogators in the history

---

* Often offered to guests, the suite includes a foyer, salon, bedroom and bath. The bedchamber includes a 17th-century desk with inlaid computer hookups. Bath sinks resemble wash basins; faucets look like hand pumps. A cut-stone floor recalls the castle mosaic. Guests access the suite through a door in the breezeway. An elevator leads to a foyer decorated with original "Cinderella" concept art by artist Mary Blair and a display case holding a glass slipper.

▶ Cinderella's Fairy Godmother often greets guests across from Tinker Bell's Treasures gift shop.

Top: The castle mosaic. **Above:** In a family snapshot from 1971, mosaic artist Hanns Scharff compares a reference painting to his working art at his California studio.

of armed combat, he treated his prisoners with kindness and respect, which led them to unwittingly reveal pieces of information which fit into a bigger strategic picture. Scharff saved six Americans from execution by proving their innocence to the Gestapo. He himself was investigated by the Gestapo for collaboration with the enemy because of his unusual treatment of prisoners.

After the war Scharff befriended many of his former prisoners in the United States. He moved to New York, where out of a pre-war hobby he started a mosaic studio. A Neiman Marcus order of 5,000 tables gave the artist the funds to move to California and set up a new mosaic studio, where he was credited with introducing the smooth-surface Venetian glass form of mosaic art to this country in 1952. Scharff died in 1992, but his studio continues under the stewardship of his daughter-in-law, Monika. She started her mosaic apprenticeship by working on these five Cinderella murals, and later led the team that created the mosaics at The Land pavilion at Epcot.

Hanns-Joachim Scharff is widely respected today, especially by U.S. military veterans who argue against the torture of terrorist suspects.

FUN FINDS

❶ In the castle mosaic, stepsister Drusilla's face is green with envy, while Anastasia's is red with anger. ❷ Two of the faces in the mosaic are those of Disney Imagineers. The page holding Cinderella's slipper has the profile of castle designer Herb Ryman. His assistant is Walt Disney World master planner John Hench. ❸ The columns alongside the mosaic are topped with molded sculptures of Cinderella's animal friends. ❹ Her wishing well sits to the right of the castle, along the walkway that connects the back of Fantasyland to Tomorrowland. ❺ Her fountain is behind the castle to the left. Thanks to a wall sketch behind it, toddlers who stand in front of the fountain see the princess wearing her crown.

▶ Cinderella's stepmother and stepsisters often greets guests at the Fairytale Garden theater.

Cinderella is among many princesses who appear in the stage show Dream Along with Mickey

"Marry me, Belle!" orders a young Gaston in Storytime with Belle

Dream Along with Mickey

★★★ 20 min. No seats, no shade. Fear factor: None. Access: Guests may stay in wheelchairs, ECVs. Best ages: 3–10. Debuted: 2006.

Mickey and Minnie Mouse prove dreams come true in this song-and-dance revue, held on the castle forecourt stage. It's highlighted by the evil fairy Maleficent, whose dream is to turn the Magic Kingdom "into a place where nightmares come true." Flame pots, fireworks and other special effects add extra spark.

Other characters include Donald Duck, Goofy, various Disney princesses and stars of "Peter Pan." The eyes and mouths of the fur characters move. Songs include "A Dream is a Wish Your Heart Makes," "So This is Love," "Some Day My Prince Will Come" and "A Pirate's Life." All vocals are prerecorded.

Average Wait	
9am	0 min
10am	0
11am	0
Noon	0
1pm	0
2pm	0
3pm	0
4pm	0
5pm	0
6pm	0
7pm	0
8pm	n/a
9pm	n/a

Storytime with Belle

★★★★ 15 min. Capacity: Apx. 75 seats, plus standing room. Fear factor: None. Access: Guests may stay in wheelchairs, ECVs. Debuted: 1999.

The heroine from 1991's "Beauty and the Beast" is just a few feet from you in this cozy show. Tucked into the tiny Fairytale Garden theater, a shady alcove between Main Street and the Mad Tea Party, her stage sits just off the ground, in front of only four rows of benches. Six children and one dad join Belle onstage to act out her story.

To help your child be selected, sit to the left, in front of the stage steps, and have your child shout out the answers when Belle asks some early questions ("Who did I live with in my quiet little village?"). Sit at the far right to be among the first in line for an autograph when the show ends.

To get the best seats arrive 30 minutes ahead of time. To get a good seat get here 15 minutes early.

Average Wait	
9am	n/a
10am	n/a
11am	15 min
Noon	15
1pm	15
2pm	15
3pm	15
4pm	15
5pm	15
6pm	n/a
7pm	n/a
8pm	n/a
9pm	n/a

▶ **"Dream Along with Mickey" is best after dark, when spotlights add a theatrical flair.**

Cinderella's Golden Carrousel

★ ★ ★ ★ 2 min. (4 revolutions). Capacity: 91 (87 horses, four-seat chariot). Fear factor: None. All horses have safety belts. Access: Must be ambulatory. Debuted: 1971.

Every horse gallops on this large, antique merry-go-round. Designed to fit every member of the family, five sizes of ponies move to calliope-style Disney music.

The carrousel has an interesting history. It was built in 1917 by the Philadelphia Toboggan Co., a roller coaster manufacturer that also sold hand-carved merry-go-rounds. (The use of the word "toboggan" in the name comes from the fact that roller coasters evolved from actual toboggan rides down the mountains of Russia.) One of only four five-row units the shop ever built, this patriotic "Liberty" model originally had 77 maple horses as well as a cresting and six chariots adorned with Miss Liberty, a regal blonde in a robe and sandals.

Average Wait	
9am	0 min
10am	5
11am	5
Noon	5
1pm	10
2pm	10
3pm	15
4pm	15
5pm	10
6pm	10
7pm	5
8pm	5
9pm	5

Top: Toronto's Elise Meiers, 2, rides with her mom, Terri. **Above:** Miss Liberty decorates the chariot.

The ride debuted at Michigan's Detroit Palace Garden Park. It later moved to Olympic Park in Maplewood, N.J. In 1967 the Disney company bought it to install at Walt Disney World, which had just broken ground. To fulfill Walt Disney's belief that every carrousel rider should feel like a hero, workers repainted the horses white, repositioned their legs so they cantered instead of pranced, and removed the chariots to add more horses. To give the ride a feminine Cinderella theme, Disney painted its trim pieces blue, gold, pink and purple—even Miss Liberty's red-white-and-blue duds.

Today's horses are fiberglass replicas, but one original wooden chariot has returned. Reinstalled in 1997, it offers the carrousel's only truly antique seats.

Because of the ride's wide diameter, its outside horses move twice as fast (7 mph) as those on its inner rim (3.5 mph).

▶ Accented by hundreds of tiny white light bulbs, the carrousel is most beautiful at night.

Donald Duck searches for the Sorcerer's Hat in the "Beauty and the Beast" dining hall

© DISNEY

Mickey's PhilharMagic

★★★★★ ✓ 12 min. Capacity: 450. *FastPass* Fear factor: Sudden images, briefly totally dark. Access: Viewers may stay in wheelchairs, ECVs. Assistive listening, reflective captioning. Debuted: 2003.

This 3-D film uses a panoramic screen and surprising in-theater effects to immerse you into signature moments from some of Disney's best animated musicals. Action packed yet never scary, it's great for any age. You don 3-D glasses to watch it.

The plot? When maestro Mickey Mouse runs late for a performance of his wily musician-free orchestra, Donald Duck attempts to replace him. But when the duck loses the secret to controlling the ensemble—Mickey's magical Sorcerer's Hat—the result is a madcap adventure that everyone can enjoy, as Donald gets swept into the worlds of "Beauty and the Beast," "Fantasia," "The Little Mermaid," "The Lion King," "Peter Pan" and "Aladdin."

Hidden odorizers, air guns and misters let you smell a fresh-baked pie, feel popping champagne corks and get spritzed with water. The sound system includes nine hidden speaker clusters that wrap around the audience. An innovative lighting system is synchronized with the show. Positioned above the audience, it includes miniature spotlights and strobes that emphasize the film's 3-D effects. Smoke effects make the beams of the lights visible. Everything unfolds on a 150-foot-wide screen.

Some of the 3-D objects, such as Ariel's collection of "thingamabobs," appear to leave the screen and hang in front of you. Others, like Donald himself, seem to fly right over your head. The sequence for "The Lion King" song "I Just Can't Wait to be King" features the film's kaleidoscope of flat 2-D cutouts, but here they twist and turn over the audience.

Created by Walt Disney Feature Animation—the company's feature film division that rarely gets involved in park attractions—the basic animation is delightful. The best parts are the scene transitions. The "Be Our Guest" feast falls into "The Sorcerer's Apprentice" workshop; that room's water washes into Ariel's "Part of Your World" grotto; the shimmer of sunlight above that underwater cave turns into the African sun of "The Lion King."

Average Wait

9am	0 min
10am	10
11am	10
Noon	10
1pm	15
2pm	20
3pm	20
4pm	20
5pm	20
6pm	10
7pm	10
8pm	10
9pm	10

▶ The best seats are in the middle rear of the theater, in front of the main projector.

FUN FINDS

❶ There's a murmur in the theater crowd even when there's no one there. Faint audience noise plays from the loudspeakers. ❷ As Goofy walks behind the crowd, he hums the "Mickey Mouse March" and steps on a cat ("Sorry little feller!"). ❸ The instruments gasp when Donald grabs the flute, they watch as he throws it into the audience and they laugh when it whops him on the head. ❹ When Lumiere rolls out toward you he's on a tomato that wasn't there a moment earlier. It arrived when Donald briefly blocked your view to ask, "Where's my hat?" ❺ Ariel giggles as she swims onscreen. ❻ Strobes in the ceiling flash when Donald kisses the eel. ❼ When a crocodile sends Donald flying during "I Just Can't Wait to be King" (on the line "Everybody look right!") you hear the duck circle behind you before he returns to the spotlight. ❽ When Simba sings that he's "in the spotlight," so are some members of the audience. ❾ When a pull chain then falls into view, Zazu pulls it to turn Simba's light off and respond, "Not yet!" ❿ Jasmine waves to an audience guest as she starts to sing "A Whole New World." ⓫ When she and Aladdin wave goodbye to Donald, so does their carpet. ⓬ Once Mickey regains control of his orchestra, the flute wakes up the tuba and then trips Donald into the tuba. ⓭ As you leave the theater and exit past the gift shop, Goofy says goodbye to you in five languages ("Sigh-a-NAIR-ee!").

HIDDEN MICKEYS

❶ In the lobby mural, as seven 1-inch-wide white paint splotches. From the right, they appear between the third and fourth bass violin, between the second and third clarinet, above the second trumpet, below the second trumpet, to the left of the fourth trumpet, and twice to the left of the sixth clarinet (one's a stretch). ❷ On the theater's right stage column, in the tubing of the French horn. ❸ In the film's "Be Our Guest" scene, as brief shadows on the dining table, visible as Lumiere sings the word "it's" in "Try the gray stuff, it's delicious!" Lumiere's hands cast Mickey's ears; his base Mickey's face. ❹ As a hole made in a cloud as Aladdin's carpet flies through it. ❺ When the carpets dive toward Agrabah, as three domes atop a left tower. ❻ In the gift shop, as music stands along the top of the walls.

Déjà Donald

With just a few exceptions (such as the humming of the song "Be Our Guest"), Donald Duck's lines in Mickey's PhilharMagic come from cartoons of the 1930s and 1940s, as recorded by the original voice of Donald, Clarence "Ducky" Nash.

DONALD'S LINE...	COMES FROM...
"OH BOY OH BOY!," said when he realizes Mickey has left the Sorcerer's Hat unattended...	**1942'S "SKY TROOPER,"** said when he realizes he can train to be a pilot if he peels some potatoes.
"ATTEN... TION!," said to the PhilharMagic Orchestra as he begins to conduct it...	**1940'S "FIRE CHIEF,"** said to nephews Huey, Dewey and Louie as he teaches them to be firemen.
"I'LL SHOW YOU WHO'S BOSS!," shouted at an unruly flute before he tosses it into the audience...	**1941'S "EARLY TO BED,"** shouted at a noisy alarm clock before he tosses it across his bedroom.
"WHO DID THAT?," said after the flute returns from its flight and hits Donald on the head...	**1941'S "ORPHAN'S BENEFIT,"** said after a boy blows his nose during Donald's recitation of "Little Boy Blue."
"BLIBA-BLIBA-BLIBA," blubbered after the Sorcerer's brooms throw buckets of water on him...	**1937'S "DON DONALD,"** blubbered after early girlfriend Donna Duck pushes him into a fountain.
"YOO-HOO!," yelled up to Ariel so the mermaid will slow down and wait up for him...	**1940'S "WINDOW CLEANERS,"** yelled down to Pluto so the dog will wake up and help him wash windows.
"NOTHIN' TO IT!," said after Peter Pan sprinkles Tinker Bell's pixie dust on him, allowing him to fly...	**1944'S "COMMANDO DUCK,"** said after Donald learns to bend his knees when he lands, so he can parachute.
"FASTER! FASTER!," said to his magic carpet while flying it through the narrow streets of Agrabah...	**1937'S "DON DONALD,"** said by Donna Duck (later known as Daisy) to Donald while riding in his car.
"AH, PHOOEY," said at the end of the show, after he falls through the back wall of the theater...	**1942'S "DONALD GETS DRAFTED,"** said at the draft board, after he learns he has to pass a physical.

▶ **The Fantasy Faire gift shop offers a wide range of Donald Duck merchandise.**

Peter Pan's Flight

★ ★ ★ 3 min. Capacity: 60. *FastPass* Fear factor: None. Access: Must be ambulatory. Handheld captioning. Debuted: 1971 (Disneyland 1955).

Suspended from a ceiling-mounted track, a two-person pirate ship takes you above and through the story of Disney's 1953 movie "Peter Pan" in this old-fashioned dark ride. You feel like you're flying as you get a bird's-eye view of nighttime London and swoop and sway through Never Land.

The ride's technology is way past its prime. The glow from a volcano comes from clearly visible sheets of aluminum foil.

You start off in the nursery of the Darling home, where Peter beckons the children—and you—to fly off with him to Never Land. Along the way you soar over London, where the roads are filled with moving automobiles. Arriving at Never Land, you pass the Lost Boys, mermaids, the Indian Encampment and, finally, Skull Rock. (One mermaid is a dead ringer for Ariel, star of 1989's "The Little Mermaid.")

Average Wait

Time	Wait
9am	0 min
10am	5
11am	20
Noon	40
1pm	45
2pm	55
3pm	30
4pm	65
5pm	60
6pm	45
7pm	40
8pm	60
9pm	60

Peter Pan's Flight guests fly miniature pirate galleons over London and off to Never Land

Next you sail to Capt. Hook's ship, where the pirate has kidnapped the kids. As Peter duels Hook on the mainsail, Hook's crew has Wendy walk the plank. A ticking crocodile hints that Hook's time is up, and soon Peter stands triumphantly at the helm with Wendy and her brothers. Hook, meanwhile, is in the water. "Help me Mr. Smee! Help me!" he calls, straddling the croc's jaws.

HIDDEN MICKEY

As scars on the fourth painted tree trunk on your left as you face the turnstile, 4 feet off the ground.

FLIGHTS, FIGHTS AND TIGHTS Based on a 1904 play by English author James Matthew Barrie, Disney's 1953 movie "Peter Pan" follows the adventures of a boy who refuses to grow up. One night he arrives at the London home of the Darling family and convinces daughter Wendy and her brothers John (who wears a top hat) and Michael to fly off with him to Never Land, a remote island where children don't age. Sprinkled with magic dust from moody pixie Tinker Bell, the kids join Peter's gang of Lost Boys (each lost by his parents when he fell out of his pram) for a series of adventures.

▶ **Go first thing in the morning or use a Fastpass. The afternoon wait can be more than an hour.**

So much that we share. It's a Small World dolls wear different costumes but have identical faces.

it's a small world

★★★★★ ✔ 11 min. Capacity: 600. Fear factor: None. Access: ECV users must transfer to a wheelchair; handheld captioning. Debuted: 1971, renovated 2006 (New York World's Fair 1964, Disneyland 1966).

This indoor boat ride promotes international brotherhood as it takes you on a colorful trip around the world. Singing dolls, whimsical animals and abstract settings fill your field of vision as you float through six huge dioramas, each representing the cultural history of a particular area. Though there's too much to see with just one visit, the ride can be appreciated on at least three levels:

Average Wait

9am	0 min
10am	5
11am	10
Noon	10
1pm	20
2pm	20
3pm	**40**
4pm	**30**
5pm	20
6pm	20
7pm	10
8pm	5
9pm	5

As a children's ride. To infants It's a Small World is the cruise of their dreams, a wide-eyed journey filled with happy faces, funny animals, gentle music and the largest crib mobiles they've ever seen. To preschoolers it's a place to bond with their parents, as there's no narration and lots of time to chat ("Where are we now, mom?" "Hawaii!").

As a political statement. It's a Small World argues that you can honor diversity while still celebrating the commonality of mankind—or, as the dolls sing, that "it's time we're aware there's so much that we share." Though each doll wears a costume unique to its culture and has skin tone unique to its race, the doll's faces are nearly identical. And though they speak different languages, they sing the same song.

"It's a Small World portrays the world as we would like it to be," explains Disney Imagineer Jason Surrell. "It's a childlike view, yes, one which is pure and innocent and optimistic."

As a piece of art. Just like a painting in an art museum, the attraction has a sophisticated sensibility that is often overlooked. As created by illustrator Mary Blair — she did the backgrounds of the Disney movies "Cinderella" (1950) and "Alice in Wonderland" (1951)—the modernist sets form a stylized pop-art collage, and have a conceptual playfulness that is remarkably pleasing to the eye. They use both organic and geometric shapes, and are finished in ways that combine the impulsiveness of childhood with the classic motifs of various cultures. As for color, Blair left no hue unused and

▶ **Ask to sit in the front row of a boat. You'll see more details and have more legroom.**

used no shading within one, yet managed to have everything blend together.

Each doll costume is a mix of embroidery, feathers, lace, satin, sequins and ribbons. There's nearly every type of hat and shoe known to man.

WHERE YOU SAIL

Though the ride is billed as "the happiest cruise that ever sailed," it never clearly states where you go. Here's a guide:

You start off in **Europe,** a two-minute sensory overload of dozens of dancing, marching, singing, swinging, unicycling, even yodeling dolls and creatures. Then you cross **Asia,** an orange and yellow land of belly dancers, lute players and snake charmers. Above you are flying carpets and kites. Cool blues and greens surround you in **Africa,** a hip jungle of wild animals diggin' a Dixieland band. Chilean penguins lead you to an orange **Latin America.** Rio's Carnivale is on your left; Mexico's Day of the Dead on your right. A blue-green Brazilian rainforest is a world of twirly-headed birds. As the rain falls (as the plastic strips hang), a crocodile and jaguar bring out umbrellas.

Polynesian percussion welcomes you to a green and purple **South Pacific,** then you're back in Europe, at Copenhagen's **Tivoli Gardens,** where all the world's children come together to celebrate the "world that we share" by dressing in white and singing in unison. The world's oldest amusement park, Tivoli Gardens was Walt Disney's inspiration for the look of California's Disneyland.

BLAME IT ON RIO

The history of It's a Small World dates back to 1941. Working in Brazil, illustrator Blair created dozens of collage-style paintings, which had a vibrancy unseen in commercial art at the time. "Brazil is really a very colorful country," she said. "The jungle... the costumes and native folk art are really bright and happy." Her ideas would be used in the 1944 film "The Three Caballeros."

Pixie dusted. Tinker Bell animator Marc Davis also designed the animals in It's a Small World.

Though she had left Disney in 1953, Blair returned a decade later, when Walt Disney wanted her to help design the ride for the UNICEF pavilion at the 1964 World's Fair. For background ideas, she created collages of

SECOND VERSE, SAME AS THE FIRST

Yep, it's mighty repetitive, but on the ride the song "It's a Small World" isn't nearly as annoying as its reputation suggests. Though the roundelay plays constantly, it's usually as an instrumental, and sometimes just a rhythm track. When the dolls do sing, half the time they're doing so in Italian, Japanese, Spanish or Swedish. In fact, on average you hear the words "small world" only about once every 30 seconds.

▶ The ride includes 289 human dolls and 210 anthropomorphic animals and toys.

Organic and geometric shapes mix together in the settings of It's a Small World

To move guests through the scenes, Disney developed a first-of-its-kind flume system. It used tiny water jets to propel free-floating, open-topped boats.

The ride was a smash hit. Though the Fair had more than 50 pavilions that charged a fee, It's a Small World accounted for 20 percent of paid admissions. It also inspired some political merchandise: The Women's International League for Peace and Freedom sold It's a Small World dolls, with proceeds funding protests against the Vietnam War.

FUN FINDS

❶ In the loading area, a giant clock comes to life every 15 minutes. ❷ In Europe, a pink poodle ogles the cancan girls. ❸ A Mary Blair doll is under the Eiffel Tower. ❹ A Bobby guards the Tower of London with a cork gun. ❺ Crazy-eyed Don Quixote tilts at a windmill while Sancho Panza looks on. ❻ One flying carpet has a steering wheel. ❼ Cleopatra winks at you from a barge. ❽ The eyes of three tongue-wagging African frogs spring out of their sockets. ❾ Singers include an ax-wielding yodeler (Europe); a horse, cow and three basket people (Mexico); and a ball-necked yellow, orange and turquoise ostrich (Brazil). ❿ Musicians include a bagpiper (Europe) and guitar-playing saguaro cactus (Mexico).

HIDDEN MICKEYS

❶ The three circles appear as 6-inch purple flower petals in Africa, on a vine between the giraffes on your left.

wallpaper cuttings, cellophane and acrylic paint. For the dolls, she made three-dimensional versions of the "Mary Blair kid," a child with a large head and simple, smiling face that she had used in the 1942 "Caballeros" prequel "Saludos Amigos" and in 1950s advertising and package art for Meadow Gold Ice Cream and Dutch Boy Paint.

'Anything But That!'

Since it debuted, It's a Small World has been a popular subject for parody. In "Selma's Choice," a 1993 episode of **"The Simpsons,"** Aunt Selma takes Bart and Lisa to Duff Gardens, a theme park where every attraction is themed to Duff Beer. On the boat ride Little Land of Duff, they find hundreds of dolls singing a one-verse song: *"Duff Beer for me, Duff Beer for you, I'll have a Duff, You have one, too!"* "I want to get off!" Bart yells. "You can't," says Selma. "We have five more continents to visit!" After Lisa takes a drink of the water, she hallucinates that the dolls are coming after her. "They're all around me!" she screams. "There's no way out!"

Even Disney cracks jokes. Here at Walt Disney World, some **Jungle Cruise** skippers tell guests that any children left on board will be taken to It's a Small World, have their feet glued to the floor and be forced to sing the theme song "over and over for the rest of their lives." At Disney's Hollywood Studios, Small World dolls help destroy the theater in the finale of **Jim Henson's MuppetVision 3-D.** The song is also dissed in the 1994 film **"The Lion King."** After evil lion Scar becomes king, hornbill Zazu begins to sing "Nobody Knows the Trouble I've Seen." When Scar demands something more upbeat, the bird chirps *"It's a small world after all; It's a small world after all..."* "No, no, no!" cries Scar. "Anything but that!"

▶ **The U.S. is represented by cowboy, Hawaiian, Inuit and Native American dolls.**

Above: All ages enjoy Dumbo the Flying Elephant. **Below:** A puzzle post along the queue.

Dumbo the Flying Elephant

★ ★ ★ ★ ✓ 2 min. Capacity: 32. Fear factor: None. Access: Must be ambulatory. Debuted: 1971, revised 1993 (Disneyland 1955).

This gentle hub-and-spoke ride features vehicles in the shape of baby pachyderms. Offering a gentle way for toddlers to fly, its 16 elephants stay level as they climb and circle. Riders control height with a lever.

Cynics who dismiss it as just another carnival ride need to wake up and smell the elephant. As anyone with an inner child knows, *this is Dumbo,* the sympathetic star of the 1941 Disney classic. His story is so sweet, his face so cute, he transforms the ride into something special.

But Dumbo or not, this is no midway ride. It's clean, free from grease and grime. The view is not of trash and weeds but of flowers, trees, a carrousel and castle. In fact, that's the best part. Flying around with your child, gazing down upon Fantasyland, you realize that you're finally here, on vacation, at the epicenter of the Disney experience.

The ride itself looks like a giant windup toy. Topped with a spinning key, its hub is decorated in gilt and pinwheels. Swinging picture frames re-create the film's opening sequence of a stork delivering the baby to a Central Florida circus. Timothy Mouse stands on top on his hot-air balloon, holding Dumbo's magic feather.

A 1993 replacement for Disney World's original 1971 Dumbo ride, the Jules Verne-style contraption was initially intended for Disneyland Paris.

JUMBO JR. When a stork delivers a baby to circus elephant Mrs. Jumbo in 1941's "Dumbo," she names him Jumbo Jr., but his huge ears soon earn him the nickname Dumbo. At first he fails as a performer, but when a mouse convinces him that holding a feather will let him fly, Dumbo becomes a star. Later he discovers he can fly whenever he wants, magic feather or not.

Average Wait	
9am	0 min
10am	20
11am	20
Noon	20
1pm	20
2pm	30
3pm	30
4pm	50
5pm	40
6pm	30
7pm	30
8pm	30
9pm	20

▶ Bring a camera with you to ride Dumbo. The attraction has no PhotoPass photographers.

Figures of Snow White were added to Snow White's Scary Adventures in 1994

Snow White's Scary Adventures

★ ★ ★ 2 min, 30 sec. Capacity: 66. Fear factor: Scares many young children. Nearly every scene is threatening; there are some loud screams. Access: Must be ambulatory. Handheld captioning. Debuted: 1971, revised 1994 (Disneyland 1955).

Designed in 1954, this classic dark ride is a Disney take on a carnival spook house. Guided by a rail, a wheeled vehicle twists and turns through a series of scenes that depict a vain old woman trying to kill her stepdaughter, the fairytale story of Disney's 1937 movie "Snow White and the Seven Dwarfs."

Though the creepy vibe scares many toddlers and preschoolers, older riders can find a lot to like.

The attraction's creative depth is often under-appreciated. In its forest scene, Snow White's emotions are brought to life visually, from her point of view. The young girl's terror at being left alone turns the trees into predators with scowling faces and limbs that reach out to grab her, logs into alligators that chase after her, and every glint of moonlight into a glaring eye. As she calms down the forest gets friendly, and its eyes become those of small happy creatures.

The ride has an attention to detail few Disney attractions have ever matched. For example, the list of ingredients in the poisoned-apple potion include Black of Night, Old Hag's Cackle, Scream of Fright and Mummy Dust. In the dwarfs' cottage, animals are carved into the woodwork in so many places—such as candlestick bases and organ pipes—you can't possibly notice them all. As Snow White takes the poisoned apple, the water pipe to her side fears for her.

Though much of its technology is way past its prime—the mouths of the "talking" characters don't even move—one illusion, an ingenious transformation of the Queen into the old witch, still seems real.

The ride begins outside the castle, as Snow White scrubs steps while her stepmother spies on her from a window. The next scene is the throne room, where the Magic Mirror declares that Snow White is the fairest of them all. As the Queen yells "Never!" she turns herself into a witch.

Entering the castle dungeon, you pass a skeleton then see the witch mixing a potion

Average Wait

9am	0 min
10am	10
11am	15
Noon	15
1pm	20
2pm	20
3pm	30
4pm	20
5pm	20
6pm	25
7pm	25
8pm	25
9pm	25

▶ **Ask to sit in the front seat. Many scenes take place directly in front of you.**

HIDDEN MICKEYS ❶ A mischievous mural painter has converted hearts on a pair of boxer shorts (right) in the loading area to the three-circle shape. ❷ The silhouette appears on the cottage chimney directly under two flowers (above) and ❸ in the ride's first dark scene, on top of the magic mirror. ❹ On the lower right of the entrance to the dwarfs' mine, a full-figure dwarf-nosed Mickey wears dwarf clothes and has a shovel.

to make a poisoned apple. After you travel through the woods you come upon the seven dwarfs' cottage, where model figures portray the witch giving her apple to Snow White ("That's right dearie, take a bite…").

A trip through the dwarfs' mine cumulates with the seven short guys chasing the witch before she falls to her death.

The final scene shows Snow White apparently dead, lying on a funeral bier, about to be kissed by the prince. Just before the exit, a painted mural shows the smiling couple riding off to live happily ever after.

Originally the attraction had guests playing the role of Snow White throughout the ride. The princess didn't appear until the last scene, lying on the casket. Oddly, the ride didn't tell its guests they were Snow White, so children unfamiliar with the story thought it ended with the young girl dead. Disney redid things in 1994, adding in images of Snow White as well as the figure of the prince.

ONE BITE, LONG NIGHT When a young girl's father dies, she's forced to contend with her evil stepmother, the Queen, and is relegated to doing menial chores such as scrubbing steps in Disney's 1937 film, "Snow White and the Seven Dwarfs." Obsessed with her looks, the Queen gets jealous when a magic mirror says her stepdaughter has become "the fairest one of all." The Queen orders a huntsman to take Snow White to a forest and kill her, but he has a change of heart and lets her escape. The girl takes refuge in the cottage of the Seven Dwarfs, a group of men who work in a diamond mine. Meanwhile, the Queen transforms herself into a witch, tracks down Snow White and gives her a poisoned apple, which makes the girl faint and appear to be dead. After the witch falls to her death while trying to crush the dwarfs with a boulder, the heartbroken men plan to bury the girl. Just in time, a prince arrives and gives Snow White "love's first kiss," breaking the spell.

▶ **T-shirts at a stand at the ride exit feature sayings such as "I'm Grumpy Because You're Dopey."**

Tigger warns Pooh of heffalumps and woozles just before the bear falls asleep during The Many Adventures of Winnie the Pooh

The Many Adventures of Winnie the Pooh

★★★★ ✔ 3 min, 30 sec. Capacity: 48. *FastPass* Fear factor: Some sudden, though mild, effects. The nightmare scene can be disorienting for toddlers. Access: ECV users must transfer to a wheelchair. Debuted: 1999.

Retelling the story of "Winnie the Pooh and the Blustery Day," this storybook-style adventure combines the cute style of the Pooh films with imaginative visuals and effects. Riding in a four-person Hunny Pot, you travel through the pages of a book to witness the tale's windstorm, thunderstorm and flood. Hidden behind swinging doors, each scene comes as a surprise. Your vehicle travels through each scene by itself, which makes the experience more personal.

A liberal dose of special effects adds to the fun. Shaky walls and beams make it appear that Owl's treehouse is falling in as you travel through it. A simple light trick allows the dreaming Pooh to float in the air, while fiber-optic rain ripples in the Floody Place. Your vehicle jerks through the treehouse, bounces with Tigger and sways as you float through the flood. There are also wind, smoke and temperature effects.

Across the walkway from the attraction, **Pooh's Playful Spot** is a shady, soft-floored playground designed for children ages 2–5. It includes slides, tunnels and a splash-pad pond. It's anchored by a toddler-sized, walk-in version of Mr. Sanders house.

MR. TOAD'S WILD FANS
You get drunk, steal a car, mouth off to a cop... then go to hell! That was the story told by this building's former attraction, Mr. Toad's Wild Ride, a ride based on Disney's 1949 compilation movie, "The Adventures of Ichabod and Mr. Toad." The loud, action-packed adventure had ardent fans. When Disney announced the ride's closing in 1997, some fans picketed next to its entrance.

FUN FINDS
❶ A boarding-area mirror makes it appear that the Hunny Pots disappear into the storybook. ❷ The words blow off the ride's first storybook page. ❸ Along the side of the first diorama, Pooh grips a balloon string to

Average Wait
9am	0 min
10am	10
11am	20
Noon	30
1pm	30
2pm	25
3pm	30
4pm	20
5pm	40
6pm	35
7pm	40
8pm	30
9pm	30

▶ Pooh, Tigger, Eeyore and Piglet often greet guests in front of Pooh's Playful Spot.

float up to a beehive, a scene from the 1966 featurette "Winnie the Pooh and the Honey Tree." ❹ Perched on a rafter, Owl drones on about the big wind of '67—or was it '76? ❺ A framed photo of Mr. Toad handing Owl the deed to the space hangs on the left wall of Owl's house. ❻ Another picture, of Toad's friend Mole bowing to Pooh, lays on the right floor. ❼ The air chills as you enter the Floody Place. ❽ Words wash off the Floody Place storybook. ❾ On the treehouse of Pooh's Playful Spot, above the main door's indoor frame, is an indentation of a submarine, a reference to the former attraction on that spot, 20,000 Leagues Under the Sea: Submarine Voyage.

HIDDEN MICKEYS

❶ On the radish marker in Rabbit's garden. ❷ At Pooh's Playful Spot treehouse, on the transom of the front door.

BACK TO THE DAYS... The childhood of Christopher Robin Milne inspired his father, A.A. Milne, to create a series of books and poems featuring the boy's toys. Born in England in 1920, Christopher spent much of his young life at his family's country home in Ashdown Forest, Sussex, which was surrounded by a 500-acre wood. He received a toy stuffed bear for his first birthday. At the London Zoo, Christopher's favorite animal was Winnipeg, a black bear presented to the zoo by World War I troops from Winnipeg, Canada. Near the country home was a lake with a swan called Pooh. The boy eventually named his bear Winnie the Pooh after those animals. Christopher Robin Milne died in 1996, at age 75.

The 1968 Disney featurette "Winnie the Pooh and the Blustery Day" tells of the toys' thunderstorm adventure. Pooh's pals include excavation expert Gopher (a Disney invention), timid Piglet, fastidious gardener Rabbit, motherly Kanga and adventurous son Roo, gloomy donkey Eeyore, self-important Owl and ebullient tiger Tigger, who loves to bounce. Pooh's enemies, so he thinks, are heffalumps and woozles, the elephants and weasles who Tigger claims steal honey. Pooh has never seen one, but in his nightmares the crazy beasts blow smoke rings and morph into hot-air balloons and watering cans. The video was included in the 1977 feature film "The Many Adventures of Winnie the Pooh."

Raise your arms in the air on the Mad Tea Party and you'll slide right into each other

Mad Tea Party

★ ★ ★ 2 min. Capacity: 72 (18 4-seat cups). Fear factor: None. Access: Must be ambulatory. Debuted: 1971 (Disneyland 1955).

You spin around in a giant teacup on this old-fashioned carnival ride. Covered by a huge canopy, it's one of the few outdoor Disney attractions that runs in any weather.

Though kids and teens usually love it, the ride makes most guests dizzy, some nauseous. Your spinning cup sits on a spinning disk, which circles around a hub. You control your cup's spinning by turning a central wheel. (To avoid getting dizzy, stare at the wheel.)

The ride is themed to 1951's "Alice in Wonderland," in which a prim and proper Alice attends an Unbirthday Party, a nonsensical tea time that leaves her dazed and confused. The party's Japanese tea lanterns hang overhead; the hub has the film's soused mouse and teapot.

Average Wait	
9am	0 min
10am	5
11am	15
Noon	15
1pm	20
2pm	15
3pm	15
4pm	15
5pm	15
6pm	15
7pm	10
8pm	10
9pm	10

▶ **Alice and the Mad Hatter often greet guests alongside the Mad Tea Party.**

Rounded and out of proportion, Minnie's house (and Mickey's, right) looks drawn by hand

Minnie's Country House

★ ★ ★ Allow 15 min. Capacity: 125. Fear factor: None. Access: Guests may remain in wheelchairs, ECVs. Debuted: 1996.

Minnie Mouse lives in this walk-through bungalow. It's filled with everything from her furniture to her family heirlooms. Areas include Minnie's living room, hobby room, kitchen and flower-filled sun porch.

There's a lot for kids to do. A button on the answering machine plays messages from Mickey Mouse and other characters. In the kitchen, kids can open the refrigerator to see what Minnie eats (lots of cheese), pretend to bake a cake or microwave some popcorn, or try to grab an illusory cookie.

With no straight lines, the house looks like it was drawn by hand, like something right out of a cartoon. In fact, nearly every visual element—the walls, windows, roof, even the chimney—bulges. It's an architectural style Disney calls "squash and stretch." The home is painted pink and purple instead of Minnie's trademark red and white.

Average Wait

9am	0 min
10am	0
11am	0
Noon	0
1pm	0
2pm	0
3pm	0
4pm	0
5pm	0
6pm	0
7pm	0
8pm	0
9pm	0

FUN FINDS

❶ The book "Famous Mice in History" sits on the living room coffee table. Subjects include Attila the Mouse, a misunderstood invader who "merely came to taste the local cheeses," and Leonardo da Moussi, the inventor of the microwave cheese pizza. Minnie wrote it. ❷ A photo on the wall is of her great-grandparents, Milo and Mabeline. ❸ In the hobby room sits her half-finished painting of Wiseacre Farm, the scene that is visible out her window. ❹ Earlier Minnie completed her take on Norman Rockwell's "Triple Self Portrait." ❺ The answering machine plays a series of messages from Goofy, who each time has called only to say he forgot why he called. ❻ The kitchen spice rack holds Thyme, Good Thyme, Bad Thyme and Out of Thyme. ❼ Sun-porch "Pun Plants" include buttercups (teacups, each with a pat of butter) and palms (with hands for fronds). ❽ "Clarabelle's Big Book of Pun Plants" sits on the room's wicker table.

HIDDEN MICKEY
The three-circle shape appears as a hanging kitchen skillet and pots.

FUN FACT » The house has no bedroom.

▶ **The loveseat and chairs in the house are the only indoor spots to sit in all of Toontown.**

With its picket fence, workshop garage and wooded yard, Mickey's Country House is an archetypical 1940s American home

Mickey's Country House

★★★ Capacity: 125. Fear factor: None. Access: Guests may stay in wheelchairs, ECVs. Debuted: 1988.

This walk-through attraction is also the best place to meet Mickey Mouse. First you tour his cartoon home. Out back you inspect his collection of appropriately shaped produce. Finally you meet him, in his Judge's Tent.

The house offers many details about Mickey's life. The television is on in the living room, where he, Donald Duck and Goofy have been watching football. In the bedroom hang many copies of Mickey's red-and-black tuxedo. The den has just seen Mickey beat his pals in ping pong. The kitchen is in the middle of a very messy Donald-and-Goofy renovation. You look into each area from a central hall.

In the tent you watch cartoons as you wait in an air-conditioned line, then enter a small room with about 15 or so other guests, where Mickey patiently greets, signs an autograph and poses for a picture with each one. A Photopass photographer is on hand.

Average Wait to meet Mickey	
9am	closed
10am	0 min
11am	20
Noon	20
1pm	20
2pm	25
3pm	35
4pm	30
5pm	25
6pm	25
7pm	15
8pm	15
9pm	10

FUN FINDS
❶ A foyer photo shows Donald, Goofy and Mickey building the house. ❷ The bedroom has photos of Mickey as a baby, with Santa and as a Boy Scout. ❸ It reveals that Mickey wears glasses. ❹ Mail includes letters from Buzz Lightyear and Ariel. ❺ The kitchen plans are from the "Chinny Chin Chin Construction Co.; General Contractor Practical Pig," a reference to the 1933 cartoon "The Three Little Pigs." ❻ The blueprints include a garbage disposal that is simply a pig under the sink. ❼ Scales on the plans read "16 parts = 8.9 parcels," "7 pinches = 2 dollops" and "1 smidgen = 4 oodges." ❽ A birdhouse version of the home sits on a garage workbench. ❾ Garage books include "The Auto Biography of Susie the Blue Coupe," star of the 1952 short "Susie the Little Blue Coupe."

HIDDEN MICKEYS
In the garage, as ❶ hubcaps, ❷ paint stains on an apron and ❸ a tiny bale of hay.

FUN FACT » The queue lines for Mickey and the princesses next door move faster than those at any other character location. How? Notice all the doors in the final hall.

▶ If you don't have time to meet Mickey, you can tour the home and leave through the garage.

*Goofy's **Barnstormer** crashes through a barn*

The Barnstormer

★★★★ ✔1 min. Capacity: 32. Fear factor: Intense for some preschoolers. Access: Must be ambulatory. Height restriction: 35 in. Debuted: 1996.

With a short steep drop and a tiny tight spiral, this child-friendly roller coaster offers real thrills, but they're condensed into 19 seconds of high-speed action. (Though the total ride time is about a minute, most of that is spent leaving the boarding area and climbing the lift hill.) Taking off in Goofy's handbuilt and cleverly named Multiflex Octoplane cropduster, you immediately veer off course and soon crash through a barn.

Dale running on a hamster wheel. ❺ Just outside the barn, a closet door labeled "Electrical Main" has been altered to read "Electrical Main Street Parade," a reference to the park's former evening procession, the Main Street Electrical Parade. ❻ A Goofy scarecrow stands in the garden. ❼ Real garden crops often include beets, cabbage, corn, kohlrabi, squash and tomatoes. ❽ Cartoon crops include "bell" peppers, popcorn, and squash that's been squashed by Goofy's feet. ❾ Cartoon jelly-jar lamps light the queue.

HIDDEN MICKEY
In the barn, on a helicopter seatback above Goofy's drafting table.

FUN FACTS ›› The coaster was built by Vekoma, the company that created the Rock 'n' Roller Coaster Starring Aerosmith at Disney's Hollywood Studios. **››** The ride is based on the 1940 cartoon "Goofy's Glider." **››** The chickens once roosted inside Epcot's World of Motion (1982–1996). **››** The first Toontown attraction on this site was Grandma Duck's Farm (1988–1995) a petting zoo with live pigs as well as Minnie Moo, a cow with Mickey-shaped spots. The pigs were retired to the Fort Wilderness Campground. Ms. Moo, alas, moos no more.

Average Wait	
9am	closed
10am	0 min
11am	10
Noon	10
1pm	20
2pm	25
3pm	30
4pm	20
5pm	15
6pm	20
7pm	30
8pm	20
9pm	10

FUN FINDS
❶ Goofy's pants fly like a flag above the silo. ❷ The chickens roosting in the barn squawk after each plane passes. ❸ Behind them is a "chicken exit," the slang term for the special exits at Disney's thrill rides for those who chicken out before boarding. ❹ Plans on Goofy's drafting table (located in the barn and the boarding area) show that the plane is powered by

▶ For the wildest ride ask for the back seat. It's faster on the drop and turns.

Belle of "Beauty of the Beast" poses with Sara Feitz, age 8, of Huntington Beach, Calif.

Anchoring a water-play area, Donald's Boat looks like it came straight out of a cartoon

Toontown Hall of Fame

★★★★ 5 min. Capacity: 45. Fear factor: None. Access: Guests may remain in wheelchairs, ECVs. Debuted: 1996.

A variety of characters await you at this meet-and-greet center, which is located inside the County Bounty gift shop. One line leads to Disney princesses Aurora (Sleeping Beauty), Belle and Cinderella; the other goes to Tinker Bell and a rotating group of Fairy Friends who include Fawn, Iridessa, Rosetta and Silvermist.

All of the girls can be quite chatty, especially if there's not a big crowd waiting behind you. Tinker Bell usually has just the right sassy attitude.

Waits can be more than an hour, but the lines are air conditioned. There are no lines right at 10 a.m., when this section of Magic Kingdom first opens. Lines are shorter on Sundays.

Autograph books are sold in the shop.

Average Wait	
9am	closed
10am	0 min
11am	30
Noon	60
1pm	60
2pm	75
3pm	50
4pm	60
5pm	75
6pm	75
7pm	60
8pm	60
9pm	60

Donald's Boat

★★★ Unlimited. Capacity: 60. Fear factor: None. Access: Guests may remain in wheelchairs, ECVs. Debuted: 1996. Note: The water is often turned off.

This water-play area is anchored by the S.S. Miss Daisy, a huge cartoon tugboat. The leaky vessel features a walk-in control room where pint-sized seafarers can clang a loud bell or secretly squirt water on others who have just gone out the back door.

The ship sits in a spongy duck pond, an elaborate splash pad where lily pads spout streams and spray without warning. Bring a swimsuit, or perhaps a change of clothes, so your child can drench himself with abandon. Some parents just strip their kids down and let 'em romp.

The two-story ship looks like it came straight out of a cartoon. Its color scheme mimics Donald's sailor uniform and bill. The roof of the bridge resembles his signature blue cap.

Average Wait	
9am	closed
10am	0 min
11am	0
Noon	0
1pm	0
2pm	0
3pm	0
4pm	0
5pm	0
6pm	0
7pm	0
8pm	0
9pm	0

▶ **The nearby Pete's Garage restroom makes a good changing spot for Donald's Boat.**

© DISNEY

Experiment 626 isn't happy with his detainment at Planet Turo's Prisoner Teleport Center

Stitch's Great Escape!

★ 18 min. Capacity: 240 (2 120-seat theaters). *FastPass* Fear factor: Restrictive harnesses, dark periods scare some children. Access: ECV users must transfer. Handheld captions, assistive listening. Height restriction: 40 in. Debuted: 2004.

A low-budget makeover of the attraction that preceded it (The ExtraTERRORestrial Alien Encounter), this in-the-round theatrical show is geared to those familiar with the early moments of the 2002 movie "Lilo & Stitch." It includes a cool Experiment 626 robot, but spends most of its time showing uninspired animated videos. Sit in the back for the best view. The character sits high off the floor.

The story takes place before the film. When 626 is held at a Planet Turo jail, he's guarded by cannons that track genetic signatures. Then the creature spits on the floor, the power shorts out and he escapes. Thanks to some hidden devices in your seat harness, it sounds, feels and smells as if 626 lingers near you.

Eventually making his way to Earth, the monster attempts to hook up with a very famous Florida female. He's rejected.

The use of Audio-Animatronics technology is impressive. A preshow sergeant shifts his weight from foot to foot and counts down on his fingers. The 39-inch 626 has 48 functions. His ears have multiple, simultaneous movements just like those of a dog, and his eyes, arms, fingers and spine move fluidly.

CREATURE FEATURE In "Lilo & Stitch," a mad scientist on Planet Turo uses the genes of ferocious beasts to create his tiny Experiment 626. Programmed to destroy everything it touches, the six-limbed monster can see in the dark and think faster than a supercomputer. When the Grand Councilwoman asks it to "show us there is something inside you that is good," it defiantly responds "Meega, nala kweesta!" As it licks its holding glass, the monster is exiled to an asteroid, then guarded by robotic cannons that track genetic signatures. But when the ingenious creature coughs on the floor the guns stalk the spit and 626 breaks loose, knocking out a power grid and escaping to Earth. Landing in Hawaii, the creature is adopted and named "Stitch" by Lilo, a 7-year-old misfit.

Average Wait

9am	0 min
10am	5
11am	10
Noon	20
1pm	20
2pm	30
3pm	20
4pm	10
5pm	10
6pm	10
7pm	10
8pm	5
9pm	5

▶ **Stitch often appears in front of the Galaxy Palace Theater, next to the Carousel of Progress.**

Lines for Monsters, Inc. Laugh Floor rarely extend outside the theater

Monsters, Inc. Laugh Floor

★ ★ ★ 15–20 min. Capacity: 400. Bench seats. Fear factor: None. Access: Guests may stay in wheelchairs, ECVs. Reflective captioning, assistive listening. Debuted: 2007.

Projected animated characters interact with the audience at this improvisational comedy show. Three large video screens front a comedy-club-style theater, where characters from the world of the 2001 film "Monsters, Inc." chat with, tease and joke with the audience. The attraction pulls off its magic thanks to hidden cameras, real-time animation technology and backstage actors using video-game style equipment.

Average Wait	
9am	0 min
10am	10
11am	10
Noon	10
1pm	10
2pm	10
3pm	10
4pm	10
5pm	10
6pm	10
7pm	10
8pm	10
9pm	10

As you wait, you can text-message jokes to the comedians to use during the show. The attraction is hosted by Mike Wazowski, a prerecorded character who is trying to generate electricity by gathering laughter in bulk.

Every performance is different, as the characters base some of their jokes on guests in the audience. The best shows are those with a full house, which are typically in the middle of the day.

FUN FINDS
❶ In the second queue room, a vending machine immediately to your left offers such treats as Same Old Raccoon Bar as well as a Polyvinyl Chloride candy bar, which small print on its wrapper notes is artificially flavored. ❷ In the video shown in the second queue room, the first child Mike makes laugh has a poster on his bedroom wall of Tomorrowland. ❸ The newspaper Roz is reading in that video—a tabloid called The Daily Glob with the headline "Baby Born With Five Heads; Parents Thrilled"—also appeared in the movie.

IN THE PIXAR FILM, Monsters, Inc. is a utility company that generates energy from the screams of human children. Its "scare floor" employs monsters, including eyeball-on-legs Mike Wazowski, to frighten kids and collect their reactions. As the film ends, however, they discover that laughter is ten times more powerful than screams. Other characters include Roz, a surly secretary.

▶ To increase your odds of having a character speak to you, wear a colorful shirt or a big hat.

Evil Emperor Zurg controls his secret weapon with stolen "crystallic fusion power cells"

Buzz Lightyear's Space Ranger Spin

★★★★ ✓ 5 min. Capacity: 201. *FastPass* Fear factor: None. Access: ECV users must transfer to a wheelchair. Handheld captioning. Debuted: 1998.

This interactive indoor ride turns the idea of a shooting gallery inside out: here the targets stay in one place while you move on a track. Traveling in an egg-shaped "space cruiser," you fire a laser gun at more than a hundred targets, many of which move, make noise or light up as you rack up points. You can rotate your vehicle to access more targets. A dashboard display tracks your score. At the end of the ride you get rated based on how you did.

BUZZ VS. ZURG

Themed to the two "Toy Story" films, the attraction is presented as a battle between Buzz Lightyear and the Evil Emperor Zurg.

The queue area is Star Command Headquarters, where Buzz mistakes you for a new recruit in his Galactic Alliance. And you're just in time. In order to power his new secret-weapon space scooter, Zurg's robotic henchmen are stealing all "crystallic fusion power cells" (batteries, in Buzz-speak) from the world's toys. To fight back, Buzz orders the Little Green Men to recapture the batteries, and you to destroy the robots.

Flying into space in your XP-37 space cruiser, you and a partner first battle past two huge guards (room 1). Landing on Zurg's volcanic home of Planet Z (room 2), you fight off his monsters, then sneak into his ship (room 3) and face him head-on. Fortunately his weapon won't fire; his inept aides have knocked the batteries loose.

You chase Zurg out into space (room 4), where he and his scooter reappear, this time as a video image. "Prepare for total destruction!" he roars, darting in front of you. You fire (whether you pull the trigger or not) and send Zurg spinning right to the Little Green Men (room 5). They capture him and leave him hanging—from a claw.

The entire ride takes place in a world of toys. Buzz gets his information from a Viewmaster; Zurg's lead henchman looks like a Rock 'Em Sock 'Em Robot. Your space cruiser gets its power from a backpack of batteries; its remote control sits to your right as you cruise in to the exit area.

Average Wait	
9am	0 min
10am	10
11am	15
Noon	25
1pm	35
2pm	45
3pm	30
4pm	40
5pm	40
6pm	30
7pm	30
8pm	35
9pm	30

▶ **Buzz Lightyear often greets guests in front of the entrance to the Carousel of Progress.**

The Buzz Lightyear figure in the queue is remarkably lifelike. It combines Disney's Audio-Animatronics technology with a rear-projection video system for Buzz's face.

HOW TO GET A HIGH SCORE
The maximum points possible on the ride is 999,999. Here's how your score can get close to that: ❶ Call dibs on the joystick. You'll keep your vehicle aimed at the right targets. ❷ Sit on the right side of your vehicle. That side has two-thirds of the targets. ❸ Once your gun is activated, pull the trigger and hold it in for the entire ride. The flashing laser beam will help you track your aim. It will fire about once a second. ❹ Aim only at targets with big payoffs: As you enter Room 1, aim for the left arm of the left robot (each hit is 100,000 points). As you pass the robot, turn your vehicle to the left and hit the other side of that same arm (25,000). As you leave the first room, turn backwards and aim at the overhead claw of the other robot (100,000). As you enter Room 2, aim at the top and bottom targets of the large volcano (25,000). As soon as you see Zurg, hit the bottom target of his space scooter (100,000) by firing early and late; you can't aim low enough to hit it straight on. As you go into Room 3, aim about six feet to either side of the exit to hit a target in the middle of a rectangular plate (25,000). ❺ If the ride stops, keep your blaster fixed on a high-value target and keep firing. You'll rack up points.

IF YOU HAD WINGS
Disney veterans will note that the track layout is unchanged from the ride's days as If You Had Wings.* A 1970s Eastern Airlines attraction, it took passengers through a series of sets, each with video screens that portrayed Caribbean or Latin American destinations. One area (room 4) created the sensation of speed by combining a slight breeze with wraparound clips of high-speed sports shown from the participants' point of view.

Zurg's lead henchman confronts you on Buzz Lightyear's Space Ranger Spin

HIDDEN MICKEYS
❶ In the queue room, a Mickey Mouse profile appears on a poster as a green land mass on the planet Pollost Prime. The planet and its mass also appear three more times—to the left of the Viewmaster in the queue, on the right as you battle the video Zurg and in the final battle scene (room 5) on the left. ❷ Another Mickey profile appears on your left as you enter Zurg's spaceship, behind the battery-delivering robot and under the words "Initiate Battery Unload." ❸ The three-circle shape appears across from the souvenir-photo monitors as an image on a painted video monitor on a mural. ❹ Also in that room, on a painted window to the left of the full-size pink character Booster, as a cluster of three stars at the top center of a star field. ❺ As a second star cluster at the bottom right of that field.

▶ Souvenir space cruisers are sold at the gift kiosk in front of the attraction.

Retro rockets. Astro Orbiter's Art Deco vehicles soar within a ring of twirling planets and moons.

Astro Orbiter

★★★ 2 min. Capacity: 32. Runs during light rains; grounded by downpours and lightning. Fear factor: The height and steep angle bother even some adults. Access: Must be ambulatory. Debuted: 1971, updated 1994 (Disneyland 1955).

The most thrilling of Disney's four hub-and-spoke rides, Astro Orbiter is fast, high and a little scary. With its loading area three stories off the ground, the attraction lifts its one-person-wide rockets 55 feet off the ground. It's located atop the boarding station of the Tomorrowland Transit Authority, which itself is the roof of a large snack stand. You ride an elevator to reach it.

But there's more to this ride than just height. Your tandem-seat rocket flies in a banked circle, tilted at 45 degrees. Top speed is 20 mph—plenty zippy when you're circling, especially when you feel like you're about to fall out.

There's a lot to look at. You circle within a few feet of a huge kinetic model of rings, planets and moons. One moon even has its own moon. In the distance you can see everything from the Enchanted Tiki Room in Adventureland to the various tents and houses of Mickey's Toontown Fair. You can even spot the Twilight Zone Tower of Terror, five miles away at Disney's Hollywood Studios.

A typical trip makes about 20 revolutions. That's a mile of sky-high orbits.

Restyled in 1994 as part of a retro re-theming of Tomorrowland, Astro Orbiter's highly stylized look recalls a 1920s machine-age view of the future. The look works best at night. While neon circles of blue, red and then pink pulse on the huge central antenna, the rockets glow green from their nose cones and red from their exhaust fires.

Unchanged from the ride's original incarnation as space-age Star Jets, the ride's green, steel-mesh elevator recalls the rocket gantries that were used in early launches at nearby Cape Canaveral, Fla.

Unfortunately, the waiting line for Astro Orbiter is usually awful. The ride loads as slowly as Dumbo, and the elevator delay just makes things worse. First thing in the morning, however, there's usually no one here. In fact, if you rush here immediately when the park opens you can often ride twice, maybe three times in a row without getting off.

Average Wait

9am	5 min
10am	10
11am	20
Noon	25
1pm	25
2pm	35
3pm	20
4pm	45
5pm	40
6pm	45
7pm	45
8pm	45
9pm	30

▶ **Time it right and Astro Orbiter offers a terrific way to view the Wishes fireworks display.**

"**TTA**" offers an elevated tour of Tomorrowland

Tomorrowland Transit Authority

★★★ ✓ 10 min. Capacity: 900. Fear factor: None. Access: Must be ambulatory. Handheld captioning available. Debuted: 1975, revised 1996.

A nice way to get off your feet, this elevated tour of Tomorrowland takes you alongside and often through the area's four buildings. At night, the track glows red. Presented as a mass-transit system of a silly retro-future world, the ride passes one piece of real future past: the center section of Walt Disney's working model of his proposed EPCOT city.

Average Wait	
9am	0 min
10am	0
11am	0
Noon	0
1pm	0
2pm	0
3pm	0
4pm	0
5pm	0
6pm	0
7pm	0
8pm	0
9pm	0

TRAIN IN VAIN
The concept of the ride began life as a sketch drawn by Walt Disney in the 1960s. Planning EPCOT, Disney thought a system of small electric trains would provide residents an efficient way to run errands or get to work, as it would snake alongside or circle over convenience stores, offices and mass-transit stations without creating pollution or traffic problems.

Clean, efficient and easy to maintain, the power system has no moving parts except for its wheels. Every six feet or so a coil embedded in a shoebox-size rectangle in the track pulses with electricity, turning on to pull the next car to it (each car has a steel plate in its floor) then turning off to let that vehicle roll past. These bursts continue around the track, moving the trains in a silent glide of linear induction. Loading is fast, as each train slows but never stops. The concept won a design achievement award from the National Endowment for the Arts and the U.S. Dept. of Transportation.

The Disney company believed in the system so much it formed a separate division, called Community Transportation Services, to sell it to municipalities. Originally called the WEDway People Mover, this ride was the concept demonstrator.

But without Walt, the dream died. EPCOT the city was abandoned, and CTS sold only one train, in 1981, to what is today the George Bush Intercontinental Airport in Houston. It's still running, unmarked and unappreciated, under the main terminal.

HIDDEN MICKEY
On a belt buckle in a beauty salon, on your right just after you enter the building that holds Buzz Lightyear's Space Ranger Spin.

▶ When Space Mountain is closed, hop on TTA to see that dark ride with its work lights on.

Walt Disney's Carousel of Progress

★★★★ ✔ 21 min. Capacity: 1,440. Fear factor: None. Access: Guests may remain in wheelchairs, ECVs. Assistive listening; handheld and activated video captioning. Debuted: 1975, revised 1994 (same unit: NY World's Fair 1964, Disneyland 1967).

A robotic family demonstrates how electricity has made life better in this vintage theatrical show. Guests sit in a rotating theater to follow a dad, mom, son and daughter through four scenes depicting life in the 1900s, 1920s, 1940s and 1990s. Personally developed by Walt Disney, the show still has a wide-eyed charm, though cynics will find plenty to ridicule. Regardless of their reasons, most guests walk out with a smile.

'DON'T BARK AT HIM, ROVER'

Carousel of Progress debuted at the 1964 New York World's Fair, as part of a General Electric pavilion called Progressland. Starring Disney's first Audio-Animatronics humans, the show was hosted by the father of a typical American family. Four acts demonstrated how electricity—and specifically GE appliances—had improved family life. The sponsor's name was woven throughout the script. "Don't bark at him, Rover," the dad told the family dog when it barked at a stranger. "He might be a good customer of General Electric."

Walt Disney wrote much of the dialogue, and insisted his characters perform not only basic movements but also "business"–small supplemental actions that made them more real. For a 1920s scene, for example, Walt decided that visiting Cousin Orville should not only relax in a bathtub, but also wiggle his toes.

Set in a 1960s all-electric home, a Christmastime finale included "a GE push-button kitchen that all but runs itself."

To bridge the acts, songwriters Robert and Richard Sherman (best known for "It's a Small World") wrote "There's a Great Big Beautiful Tomorrow." The tune's lyrics perfectly captured the fair's blind optimism: *"There's a great big beautiful tomorrow, shining at the end of every day. There's a great big beautiful tomorrow, just a dream away!"*

After the fair closed Disney relocated the theater to California's Disneyland, where it opened in 1967. A revamped finale featured a home videocassette recorder, a product that wouldn't appear in stores for more than a decade.

THAT '70S SHOW

When the show moved to Walt Disney World in 1975, a new script tied it into the women's movement. Though her father warned "It's a man's world out there," the 1920s daughter searched Help Wanted ads. The 1940s wife demanded "equal pay" for wallpapering the rumpus room, rhetorically asking her husband "If you hired a man to do this, wouldn't you pay him?"* A new finale made dad the cook.

To meet GE's demand that the show focus on the present, the Sherman Brothers wrote a new theme song, "Now is the Time." Dissing the future as *"still but a dream,"* it proclaimed *"Now is the time! Now is the best time! Now is the best time of your life!"*

Though the show had rotated clockwise, it switched directions in its new Florida theater. The 1975 show also returned to using human-hair wigs. Nylon versions had been used at Disneyland, but over time klieg lights above the father had melted his hair into a sticky pile of goo.

TODAY'S CAROUSEL

Disney created the current version of the show in 1994. Embracing the past even more than its predecessors, it's peppered with old-fashioned sayings. The wife "gets to the core of the apple." The husband knows it won't rain because "my lumbago isn't acting up." Peering into his dad's stereoscope, the son exclaims "Ooh la la! So that's Little Egypt doing the hoochie-koochie!"

Today's finale takes place in the great big beautiful tomorrow of, well, 1994. While Grandma enjoys a virtual reality helmet, mom's programming of a "voice activation system" ends up burning the turkey. Early scenes take place on specific holidays— Valentine's Day, 1904; Independence Day, 1927; and Halloween, 1949.

*After the husband responded "Well, we might negotiate something later on, dear," a bird in a nearby cuckoo clock popped out and chirped "Now is the time! Now is the best time!"

Average Wait

9am	5 min
10am	5
11am	5
Noon	5
1pm	5
2pm	5
3pm	5
4pm	5
5pm	5
6pm	5
7pm	5
8pm	5
9pm	5

▶ Kids will enjoy watching the family dog, who often glances at the audience.

Voices include Jean Shepherd (the narrator of the 1983 movie "A Christmas Story") as the father, Debi Derryberry (the voice of Nickelodeon's Jimmy Neutron) as the daughter, Mel Blanc (the longtime voice of Bugs Bunny and other Warner Bros. cartoon characters) as Cousin Orville, Rex Allen (1950s singing cowboy) as the Christmas Grandpa, and Janet Waldo (daughter Judy in the 1960s cartoon series "The Jetsons" and Josie in the 1970s "Josie and the Pussycats") as the Christmas grandma.

No longer sponsored by General Electric, today's Carousel doesn't mention the company, though antique GE appliances still appear.

'BIGGER THAN TOAD!'

In the fall of 2001, ironically less than a month after Walt Disney World started a 15-month celebration of Walt Disney's 100th birthday, it closed his beloved Carousel of Progress and took it off park maps. The reason: dwindling attendance, caused in part by the Sept. 11 attacks. Within days, fans of the show organized an Internet protest. "Let's make this bigger than Toad!" wrote one blogger, referring to an earlier, failed attempt to save the Disney World Fantasyland attraction Mr. Toad's Wild Ride. This time, however, the protest worked. Disney reopened the Carousel a few months later.

Still, it cries out for a major refurbishment. As time has passed it by, the show now ignores the entire second half of the 20th century—the only time most of us have lived through. Imagine how fun it would be to see the daughter as a 1960s hippie chick with a stack of LPs, a 1970s 'droid daddy playing Pong, or a 1984 son writing "Hello" on his newfangled Macintosh. As for the future scene, it's just a Steve Jobs dream away.

HIDDEN MICKEYS

❶ In Act 3, the sorcerer's hat Mickey wore in the 1940 movie "Fantasia" sits on a stool

I, Robot. Built in 1964, the Carousel of Progress dad was Disney's first Audio-Animatronics human.

to the right of the exercise machine. Mickey items in the finale include ❷ a nutcracker on the mantel, ❸ a plushie under the Christmas tree, ❹ a white salt shaker on the bar ❺ and an abstract painting of the Sorcerer's Apprentice on the wall to the right of the dining table. ❻ During the first moments of the virtual-reality video game, the three circles appear on the television as engines of a spaceship.

FUN FACTS ❯❯ The first grandma also rocks in front of the fireplace in the Haunted Mansion ballroom. ❯❯ The six auditoriums rotate at 2 feet per second on large steel wheels and tracks, just like a train on a railroad. Altogether they weigh 375 tons.

▶ Nicely air-conditioned, Carousel of Progress offers a good way to beat the heat.

Space Mountain

★ ★ ★ ★ ★ ✔ **2 min, 30 sec. Capacity: 180.** *FastPass*
Fear factor: Dark drops and turns, but you don't go upside down. Access: Must be ambulatory. Height restriction: 44 in. Debuted: 1975.

"I want to go again! I want to go again! I want to go again!" said the 8-year-old boy to his parents. "That! Was! Cool!" said the 18-year-old college dude, here on Spring Break. "I rode it daddy! I rode it!" said a fully gowned Cinderella, age 6. Where are these people? At the exit dock of Space Mountain, climbing out of their rockets after a trip on this roller coaster in the dark.

Now *this* is the happiest place on earth.

The world's first indoor roller coaster, this rocket-in-a-planetarium is a series of constant surprises. You never know where you are going, and rarely know where you are. Projected onto the underside of a smooth dome, twinkling stars and shooting comets have no beginning and no end. Pinpoint projectors and hidden mirror balls put some stars right in your

Space Mountain gets its shape from Japan's Mt. Fuji. Inside is a roller coaster in the dark.

path. In fact, you have no reference points at all, not even the sides of your rocket. It's all sensation, no thought required.

Half the fun is the vehicle itself. Only slightly wider than you are, your rocket sits only waist-high, thigh-high for taller folks.

A FUTURISTIC SPACE FLIGHT

The ride's story begins as you walk into the building, a futuristic spaceport and repair center that's orbiting above the earth. Passing the departure board, you walk to the launching platform, an open-air loading zone with its own control tower.

Once you climb into your rocket, a sign flashes "All Systems Go." This activates the rocket transporter, which takes you through the energizing portal, a flashing blue tunnel of ever-louder "whoops" that powers your machine and ignites your engine.

Climbing the launch tower (the chain lift), you pass under robotic arms that secure a ship that has come in for service. As two mechanics work on its engines, two control-room operators monitor their progress.

Then you blast off, on a journey through, according to an early press release, "the void of the universe." Zooming through space, "you become engulfed in a spectacular spiral nebula with flashing comets and a

Average Wait

9am	0 min
10am	20
11am	40
Noon	50
1pm	60
2pm	60
3pm	50
4pm	50
5pm	60
6pm	70
7pm	60
8pm	60
9pm	45

▶ **Ask for the front row. You'll fly through the air with a breeze on your knees.**

whirling galaxy." Apparently you lose your bearings, as you also fly back through the launch bay. When you return you trigger a sonic boom in a red de-energizing tunnel.

Much of the attraction is a subtle tribute to the 1968 film, "2001: A Space Odyssey." The entranceway's eerie music recalls that of the movie's early scenes of a moon transport shuttle. The hallway's angled plastic clapboard walls duplicate those of the movie's transport interior.

The movie's Discovery One spacecraft shows up three times. In the ride's boarding area, the spool-like corners the rockets pass by look just like the axle of Discovery One's rotating living quarters. The blue strobe tunnel recalls its hexagonal corridor that leads to its EVA pods. On the lift hill, the docked ship has the craft's unique head-spine-and-hip shape. The docked ship also appears outside an entranceway window.

'WHERE'S MR. SMEE?'
With its first passengers NASA astronauts Scott Carpenter, Gordon Cooper and Jim Irwin, Space Mountain opened with an elaborate ceremony on January 15, 1975. Disney officials declared it "the nation's most breathtaking thrill ride." But not everyone got the message. As park guests walked in, many expected something along the lines of Peter Pan's Flight, since at the time Disney didn't do roller coasters.

A few seconds later, up came their lunches and out flew their hats, purses, eyeglasses and, on more than one occasion, false teeth. Disney's response included posing two of the rockets in a dive up on an entrance tower, putting a video in the queue in which Cooper told guests it was A-OK with him if they would rather head for the exit ramp, and discreetly ironing out some of the ride's most violent jerks and jolts.

Though it opened during a recession, Space Mountain was an instant smash. When summer came, families with teenagers, many of whom would have never considered a Disney vacation before, began crowding Magic Kingdom turnstiles early each morning, running straight to Space Mountain as soon as the park opened.

Three decades later the only real difference in the attraction is its postshow along the exit ramp. Originally it was the elaborate RCA Home of Future Living, as dioramas showed a dad teleconferencing from a patio chair while kids inside watched vid-

eodiscs. In 1985 the area became the RYCA-1 Dream of a New World, as robots built a pod city on a "hostile planet." A silly Federal Express FX-1 Teleport took over from 1993 to 1998, as "teleportation units" digitized and transported alien fossils back to earth (remnants of these scenes remain today). The FedEx years also had a preshow. Monitors in the boarding area aired the futuristically wacky "SMTV" network. Commercials featured Crazy Larry selling used spaceships, while a space newscast featured ditzy weather girl Wendy Beryllium: "Our extended forecast: giant comet. Wow, scary!"

The robotic boy and dog have been around since the beginning. Known as Billy, the then-human boy used to film guests for their TV appearances on the Speedramp.

FUN FINDS
❶ Just inside the building, destinations on the departure board include Star Sirius, Real Sirius, World Ceres and Beta Beleevit.
❷ As you move down the corridor the music changes from a light melody to an ethereal mix of harmonics, chimes and pings.

FUN FACTS 》 The left track is a little darker, has a longer first drop and covers a slightly greater distance: 3,196 feet compared to the right track's 3,186. The final drop of both tracks is 35 feet. 》 The meteorites projected on the ceiling are not pictures of chocolate-chip cookies. They just look that way. 》 The energizing portal has a practical function: its flashing blue strobes shrink your pupils, which makes your space flight seem darker than it really is. 》 Why do the docked ship's engine nozzles look like the plastic caps of spray-paint cans? Because they are! Used by an artist on a pre-production model, they were mistakenly reproduced as-is on the full-scale prop. 》 Your rocket's top speed is only 28 mph. 》 The "sonic boom" in the red re-entry tunnel is the reversed sound of a jet engine starting up. 》 There are 30 rockets, numbered 1 through 31. There is no rocket 13. 》 The building is 183 feet tall with a 300-foot diameter. It covers about two acres. Each of its 72 exterior concrete "ribs" weighs 74 tons, is 117 feet long and narrows from 13 feet wide at its base to 4 feet wide at its top. 》 The building gets its sweeping-pillar look from Israel's Kennedy Memorial. Its shape comes from Japan's Mt. Fuji.

▶ **For the wildest ride ask for a back seat. It's faster on the drop and turns.**

Tomorrowland Indy Speedway

★★ 5 min. Capacity: 292 (146 2-seat vehicles). Fear factor: None. Access: Must be ambulatory. Height restriction: 52 in. to take a car out alone. Debuted: 1971 (Disneyland 1955). Revised 1996.

This winding, wooded "race" track puts your little boy or girl at the controls of a 5-year-old's dream machine—a small-scale race car with a rough ride and a rumbly, smelly engine. The winding half-mile course takes you around five turns, down one short straightaway and under and over a bridge.

For what you get, the waiting line is one of the worst in the park. There's shade but no air conditioning, and on peak days wait times can exceed an hour. There's no wait, however, first thing in the morning, or sometimes late at night.

There's never much of a race, as top speed is only 7.5 mph and you can't pass—a rail underneath your car keeps it in its lane. However, if your family takes up more than one car, you should know that the heaviest car is always the slowest. Once when my daughter got a car of her own and I crammed into a second one, she left me behind while automobiles behind me continuously smacked my bumper! My daughter thought it was funnier than I did.

Why is the ride in Tomorrowland? For a reason that could only make sense to Disney. When it was built in 1971, the track was an update of the Disneyland attraction Autopia, which, when that ride premiered in 1955, was a simulation of the exciting limited-access highways destined for that era's future.

A year-2000 sponsorship by the Indianapolis Motor Speedway and a 1994 re-theming of Tomorrowland as an alien world confused things further. Though its cars still have 1970s bodies, signs along the ride's queue area now present it as a wacky space race, with a history that parallels that of the real race in Indiana.

FUN FINDS
❶ Speakers around the track feature famed Indy announcer Tom Carnegie calling your "race." ❷ A brick from the 1909 pavement of the Indianapolis Motor Speedway is embedded in the "starting line" between lanes 2 and 3, close to the elevated exit walkway.

Average Wait

9am	0 min
10am	15
11am	20
Noon	20
1pm	30
2pm	30
3pm	30
4pm	40
5pm	30
6pm	30
7pm	30
8pm	30
9pm	20

▶ Take your spin early in the morning or late at night to avoid a long wait.

Piglet greets parade guests on Main Street U.S.A.

Disney Dreams Come True Parade

★★★ 15 min. 3pm. Starts in Frontierland; travels to Liberty Sq. (arrives 3:07pm), Cinderella Castle (3:15) and down Main Street U.S.A. to Town Sq. (3:25). Arrive 30 min. early for good seats. Fear factor: None. Access: Special viewing areas for those in wheelchairs, ECVs. Debuted: 2001, revised 2006.

This seven-float parade features dozens of Disney's classic animated characters. Some wave to guests from floats while others dance on the street and greet the crowd in person. The floats feature princesses, villains and the stars of "Aladdin" (1992), "Alice in Wonderland" (1951), "Mary Poppins" (1964), "Peter Pan" (1953), "Pinocchio" (1940), "Snow White and the Seven Dwarfs" (1937), "Song of the South" (1946) and "The Many Adventures of Winnie the Pooh" (1974). Also on hand: Minnie Mouse, Donald Duck, Goofy, Pluto and the ever-present Chip 'n Dale. (Boo loudly at the villains. They will often respond.)

Unfortunately, the parade does not contain any familiar Disney music. Instead, the characters dance to a service number which plays in a continuous loop.

The best viewing spot is anywhere along the shady western side of Main Street

U.S.A. Curb seats get taken about 2:30 p.m. As guests wait, cast members keep children entertained with hula hoops, jump ropes and games such as Red Light Green Light.

The procession is an update of the Share a Dream Come True parade (2001–2006), a rolling tribute to Walt Disney. The first character, in fact, is Walt himself. Surrounded by ink-and-paint girls on bicycles, a performer portrays the young animator as he looked in the 1920s, drawing Mickey Mouse.

The first float, It Was All Started By a Mouse, features Mickey Mouse. The live character is surrounded by 11 sculpted figures of himself, showing how he evolved from a gloveless black-and-white imp in 1928's "Plane Crazy" to a colorful cherub in 1983's "Mickey's Christmas Carol." Walking alongside the float are the magical brooms from the 1940 film, "Fantasia."

OVERHEARD: Four-year-old boy and his mom waiting for parade: **Boy:** When do they put on their suits? **Mom:** Who? **Boy:** The characters. **Mom:** What suits? **Boy:** (Thinking) **Mom:** You mean they put on special suits for the parade? **Boy:** (long pause) Yeah. **Mom:** Who's going to be in the parade? **Boy:** Piglet. **Mom:** Piglet? **Boy:** Both Piglets. Piglet and his brother, Piglet Pan.

▶ **The best viewing spot: On the curb on the shady western side of Main Street U.S.A.**

Cinderella's pumpkin transforms into a white carriage as part of the finale of SpectroMagic

SpectroMagic

★★★★★ ✓ 20 min. Arrive 30 min. early for a good seat, an hour early for the best spots. Route: Starts on Main Street U.S.A. between the Town Square firehouse and car barn. Continues to the castle hub, through Liberty Square and Frontierland. Fear factor: The Chernabog float has spooky music and a 30-foot-tall animated monster. Access: Special viewing areas for guests in wheelchairs and ECVs. Debuted: 1991. Revised: 2001, 2008.

Viewing this evening light parade is like gazing at a Christmas tree in a dark living room: just the sight of it makes you feel good. A cavalcade of colorful floats and costumes, it's a moving gallery of synchronized light patterns. And though everything is lit, it's all against a pitch-black backdrop. Nearly all the light is emitted internally, from rope lights and fiber optics. Disney turns out its park lights just before the parade begins.

Set to a symphonic score and filled with things that normally would be figments of your imagination (twirling butterfly girls, spinning fish, dancing ostriches), the parade is also like a hallucinatory dream: you can't understand it, but it sure is interesting.

Based on heritage Disney animation, SpectroMagic features more than 80 characters, 90 percent of them from cartoons and animated musicals released before 1960.

FLOAT SEGMENTS

SpectroMen. The procession is led through the park by this exuberant group of trumpeters, whirlyball riders and other odd fellows who, according to Disney, are keepers of light and just a little bit shy. They come from a land where everything is filled with bursts of color, and are here to share their mystical rays with you.

Mickey Mouse. Wearing a grand magician's cape that extends 17 feet above his head, the Mouse stands majestically on a float all his own. Powering the parade through his Electro-ball, he controls the light of the SpectroMen, altering the colors, effects and luminosity of floats near him. A confetti of light sparkles around Mickey, created by reflections from mirror balls.

Vintage cartoons. This three-float symphony includes the bass violins from the 1935 Silly Symphony "Music Land," the Golden Harp from 1947's "Mickey and the Beanstalk" (from the film "Fun and Fancy Free"), Goofy on the timpani and, dressed in Liberace capes, Chip 'n Dale on a grand piano. The conductor is Genie, of "Aladdin."

Sleeping Beauty. Shimmering lights create a giant peacock at the front of this three-float caravan based on the 1959 movie. Fairies Fauna (in green), Flora (blue) and

▶ Running late? Good seats are often still available in front of the Town Square firehouse.

Merriweather (pink) ride within a flower garden that changes from a multicolor day to a blue-and-green night. Dancing around them are human butterfly and dragonfly girls, their wings electroluminescent panels.

The Little Mermaid. This 10-piece unit combines twirling giant fish with a float that hosts the stars of Disney's 1989 musical. On board are Ariel, Sebastian and King Triton. A freewheeling Ursula spins past, too.

Fantasia. Six floats are themed to Disney's 1940 experiment in animating classical music. First up, a tribute to the film's "Dance of the Hours" operetta, as dancing ostriches entertain Bacchus, the god of wine. From the film's take on "The Pastoral Symphony," flying horse Pegasus and his family ride by on three floats above some dry-ice clouds. Then Chernobog, the monstrous bat-winged demon from the movie's "A Night on Bald Mountain" segment arrives, unfurling his wings dramatically to create a 38-foot span.

Finale. A seven-float convoy features the stars of the 1932 Silly Symphony short "The Little Pigs," 1937's "Snow White," 1940's "Pinocchio," 1950's "Cinderella," 1951's "Alice in Wonderland" and 1953's "Peter Pan." It includes Cinderella's coach, Captain Hook's ship and a full-size rotating merry-go-round. Poised in front is Practical Pig, who flicks a paint brush to change the lights behind him—on every float and every costume—from white to a rainbow of hues.

The parade was updated in late 2007. The SpectroMen are now face characters. Instead of giant plastic heads, their faces are highlighted by silver makeup and blue and purple eye shadow, topped with LED wigs and whimsical straw hats. The butterfly and dragonfly girls also have new costumes.

WHERE TO SIT

A good viewing spot for SpectroMagic is in front of Tony's Town Square Restaurant along Main Street U.S.A. You'll get a good view of the front and side of every float, and be right next to the park exit.

FUN FINDS

❶ The SpectroMen's horns light up when they're played. ❷ When he touches it, Mickey's Electro-ball sizzles and adds rays to his cape. ❸ Other cape lights are synchronized to the soundtrack. ❹ The bass violins pluck themselves. ❺ Notes project on the ground around the violins. ❻ A sun changes to a moon on the first "Sleeping Beauty"

float. ❼ A waterfall cascades down the back of the last garden float. ❽ The butterfly and dragonfly girls have painted faces. ❾ Each pair of eyes in "The Little Mermaid" fish school moves in a different way. ❿ Bubbles come from three of the freewheeling fish in that unit. ⓫ Ursula stops to chat with some guests ("Hello handsome!"). ⓬ Ariel does the breast stroke. ⓭ The spinning fish wink. ⓮ The ostriches wear heavy eyeliner and tuxedo jackets. ⓯ They often peck, kick and slap each other. ⓰ Lightning strikes under the horses and on Bald Mountain. ⓱ The pink-lined Bald Mountain turns into a red-lit Chernabog. ⓲ Two buzzards guard him. ⓳ The Three Little Pigs taunt the Big Bad Wolf, who walks in front of them. ⓴ A crown spins above Cinderella. ㉑ Her coach transforms from a pumpkin to a carriage. ㉒ An image of Tinker Bell appears in Cinderella's castle windows and flies out of them. ㉓ Two mechanical "Alice in Wonderland" playing cards paint their roses red. ㉔ An image of Cheshire Cat disappears except for his mouth and eyes. ㉕ Mary Poppins' umbrella lights up with her jacket. ㉖ Dumbo is a carrousel animal. ㉗ The stars of the 1945 movie "The Three Caballeros" appear on the ride's top rear panel. ㉘ Capt. Hook's hook lights up. ㉙ His cannons fire dry-ice smoke in time to the music. ㉚ Hook's Jolly Roger flag has glowing red eyes. ㉛ Riding with the captain, Snow White's Evil Queen has her magic mirror. ㉜ Peter Pan has been known to sneak up and kick Mr. Smee. ㉝ Tink appears again inside the Evil Queen's castle. ㉞ Pinocchio's teapot steams. ㉟ Lights circle the ground around Minnie Mouse and Donald Duck, who ride on the final float. ㊱ Facing backward, Jiminy Cricket appears on the last float, waving "So long! See ya later!"

FUN FACTS » The floats are covered in scrim, a transparent black gauze. **»** The drivers' faces hide behind mesh screens. **»** The parade uses 2,000 car batteries. Walking performers wear battery packs. **»** There are 600,000 miniature lights; 100 miles of fiber-optic cable. **»** Soundtrack composer John Debney created the scores for the movies "Elf," "Bruce Almighty," "The Passion of the Christ" and "Swing Vote." **»** It is the only Disney parade theme ever recorded in 3/4 time, which means it's the only one you can waltz to. **»** Roger Rabbit was the parade's symphony conductor during its original run.

▶ **A bad spot to sit: In Frontierland, facing the Rivers of America. A spotlight shines in your face.**

Dozens of rockets and nearly 700 explosions light up the sky during the Wishes fireworks show

Wishes

★★★★★ ✔ 12 min. Fear factor: Loud explosions. Access: Special viewing areas for wheelchair and ECV guests. Debuted: 2003.

Every! Other! Fire! Works! Show! Emphasizes! Every! Explosion!

Not this one. Disney's signature fireworks show is artistic, even subtle. Though it explodes 683 different pieces of pyro in just 12 minutes, Wishes paints delicate strokes as well as bold. Sometimes the sky sparkles, sometimes it flashes. Some explosions form stars, hearts, even a face. Some bursts dribble away, others disappear. Comets shoot off by themselves and by the dozen.

But that's just the half of it. Synchronizing its visuals to a symphonic score, Wishes packs an emotional punch. Narrated by Jiminy Cricket with help from the Blue Fairy (both from the classic 1940 Disney movie "Pinocchio"), it teaches a heart-tugging lesson about believing in yourself.

The show starts without fanfare, as a quiet chord grows louder and the castle begins to glow and sparkle. Then you hear the Blue Fairy: "When stars are born they possess a gift or two... They have the power to make a wish come true." Right on cue a lone star arcs across the sky. *"Starlight, star bright, first star I see tonight,"* a chorus of little girls sings. *"I wish I may I wish I might, have the wish I wish tonight..."* Blue stars—not bursts but actual five-pointed stars—explode above Cinderella Castle.

"I'll bet a lot of you folks don't believe that, about a wish coming true, do ya?" Jiminy asks. "Well I didn't either. But lemme tell you: the most fantastic, magical things can happen, and it all starts with a wish!"

And with that, the spectacle begins.

First Tinker Bell (a real person) steps off the top turret of Cinderella Castle and glides over the crowd to Tomorrowland. Major explosions fill the air as the voices of Cinderella, Ariel, Pinocchio and other Disney stars recall their wishes, then medleys of fireworks (each in its own color palette) express courage and love.

IN 1940'S "PINOCCHIO," the Blue Fairy, a symbol of patient wisdom, appoints Jiminy Cricket to serve as the boy's conscience.

"STARLIGHT, STAR BRIGHT" is a 19th-century American nursery rhyme. It's based on the notion that if you see the first star of the night sky before any others have appeared, any wish you make will come true. In reality, an evening's first visible "star" is often the planet Venus.

▶ Watch the show from in front of the castle. Main Street doesn't fill until showtime.

"Fate is kind," a choir sings, as the tune switches to the bridge of "When You Wish Upon a Star," the "Pinocchio" theme song. *"She brings to those who love... the sweet fulfillment of... their secret longing."*

A fan of comets wipes the sky clean, then Roman candles dance to "The Sorcerer's Apprentice." A villains segment has crackling bursts, some as bright as strobes.

"Wishes *can* come true," the cricket says. "And the best part is, you'll never run out. They're shining deep down inside of you."

WHERE TO WATCH IT

With fireworks that launch directly behind Cinderella Castle as well as symmetrically alongside, **Wishes is best seen from in front of the castle,** anywhere on Main Street U.S.A. The perfect spot is right on the crest of the Main Street bridge, between the Tip Board and the castle hub. From there you'll be close enough to see all the castle effects, but still far enough away to see all the pyrotechnics. There's always room to stand in this area, as cast members don't let guests out onto the street until just minutes before showtime.

Avoid Town Square (the lights stay on) and especially the Main Street U.S.A. train station balcony (there's no audio). Want to dash out of the park as soon as the show ends? Stand in front of the Emporium, the closest dark spot to the exit.

But why fight the crowd? Instead, why not embrace the magical mood you'll be in to get an ice cream and relax. Your kids will be happy; why not talk with them? Ask about their dreams and wishes. Tell them yours.

FUN FINDS

❶ Blue stars appear above Cinderella Castle during the opening verse, just after the lines *"When you wish upon a star..."* *"makes no difference who you are..."* and *"anything your heart desires will come to you..."* ❷ Tinker Bell starts her flight from the castle just after Jiminy Cricket says "...and it all starts with a wish!" ❸ As each Disney character says their wish, the accompanying fireworks are the color of his or her famous wardrobe (for example, Cinderella's are blue, Ariel's are green). ❹ After Aladdin tells Genie "I wish for your freedom!" a shout of "Wishes!" brings out another blue star. ❺ Red hearts appear above the castle at the end of the song "Beauty and the Beast." ❻ More blue stars explode as Jiminy

Disney presents special fireworks displays for its 4th of July, Halloween and Christmas events

sings "...when you wish upon a star, your dreams... come true!" ❼ "Whoa!" Genie says as his fireworks appear. "Ten thousand years can give ya such a crick in the neck!" ❽ During the "Sorcerer's Apprentice" sequence, the castle turns into the blue Sorcerer's Hat, complete with its white stars and moons. ❾ A red explosion introduces the villains. ❿ Images of the Evil Queen's mirror appear on the castle as she commands "Slaves in the magic mirror, come from the farthest space..." ⓫ A frowning face appears in the sky, and the castle mirrors become faces, when the queen commands "Let me see thy face!" ⓬ Meanwhile the castle glows in dark greens, oranges and purples and is flashed with lightning. ⓭ It turns blue again as the Blue Fairy returns.

FUN FACTS 》 The fireworks launch from 11 locations. 》 Tinker Bell is sometimes a man. The role's physical requirements are only that the performer weigh no more than 105 pounds and be no taller than 5 feet 3 inches. 》 Wishes replaced Fantasy in the Sky, the park's fireworks show from 1976 to 1993. Though only five minutes longer, Wishes uses almost three times the explosions.

▶ **Keep an eye on the castle. It sparkles, flashes and changes colors as part of the show.**

The symbol of Epcot, Spaceship Earth is a 180-foot-tall geodesic sphere covered in 11,000 triangular facets

Epcot

A permanent world's fair

Where can you talk with a sea turtle, crash through test barriers, soar over California, take a rocket ride to Mars, be chosen King of England, buy some exclusive French perfume and feast at a German Oktoberfest? At Epcot, a unique theme park that puts a Disney spin on the science expositions, national pavilions and large, iconic structures of a classic world's fair—all of it set in a relaxing, if huge, musical garden.

Two parks in one

The world's fair theme kicks off in Future World, a science-and-technology zone themed to subjects such as agriculture, automotive safety and geography. Sound dull? It isn't. Each of those topics is the subject of a ride—a greenhouse boat cruise (Living with the Land), a spin around a General Motors proving ground (Test Track), a hang-gliding flight over California (Soarin'). Other highlights: the interactive "Turtle Talk with Crush" and the realistic Mission Space.

You'll travel around the world, and stop only in friendly countries, when you take the 1.3-mile trek around Epcot's World Showcase. Circling a 40-acre lagoon, 11 pavilions are filled with native entertainment, food and merchandise. Most offer an attraction or small museum. Each is staffed by chatty young natives of its country.

Located throughout the park, a series of Kidcot activity tables lets children create custom cardboard masks using markers, stamps and hanging paper cutouts representing the host pavilion.

History

Epcot opened on Oct. 1, 1982. Four pavilions were added during the park's first decade—Morocco (1984), The Living Seas (1986, now The Seas with Nemo & Friends), Norway (1988) and Wonders of Life (1989, now closed). Its biggest change came in 2000, when its futuristic Horizons pavilion was demolished to make way for Mission Space.

FASTPASS RETURN TIMES

Use the table below to help plan your Epcot day. Note that Soarin' and Test Track typically run out of Fastpasses by mid-afternoon.

ATTRACTION	9A	10A	11A	Noon	1P	2P	3P	4P	5P	6P	7P	8P	9P
Honey, I Shrunk...	10:00	11:00	12:00	1:00	2:00	3:00	4:00	5:00	6:00	N/A	N/A	N/A	N/A
Living with Land	N/A	N/A	11:40	12:40	1:40	2:40	3:40	4:40	5:40	6:40	N/A	N/A	N/A
Maelstrom	N/A	N/A	11:50	1:05	1:40	2:40	3:50	5:00	N/A	N/A	N/A	N/A	N/A
Mission Space	9:40	10:40	11:40	12:55	2:50	3:50	4:50	5:50	7:10	8:10	8:20	N/A	N/A
Soarin'	9:40	12:00	1:50	3:40	5:40	7:00	OUT	OUT	OUT	OUT	OUT	OUT	OUT
Test Track	9:50	12:00	1:45	4:05	6:50	7:50	OUT	OUT	OUT	OUT	OUT	OUT	OUT

Data based on surveys taken on random days in the summer of 2008

Originally an acronym, the word "Epcot" comes from the Experimental Prototype Community of Tomorrow, an actual city Walt Disney planned to be centered on this site. After his death the company considered building it, but eventually took two of Walt's EPCOT ideas—a science center that would show ways to improve existing communities and an expo that would showcase the culture, history and goals of other nations—and reworked them into a theme park.

With nearly two dozen pavilions spread out over 260 acres, Epcot takes two days to fully enjoy. As shown below, an easy plan is to spend one day in Future World and another at World Showcase. The two areas keep separate hours. Future World opens at 9 a.m. and closes at 7 p.m. except for its major attractions; World Showcase opens at 11 a.m. and closes at 9 p.m.

LANDSCAPE FUN FINDS

❶ The layout of Future World mimics the left-right division of the human brain. As you enter the park, pavilions on your left are themed to analytical, linear or engineering issues (i.e., energy, space travel, automobile) and sit within a landscape of straight-lined walkways. Those on the right cover more natural topics (seas, land, imagination) and rest in a hilly, meandering, watery landscape. ❷ Three drinking fountains imitate submarine sounds, sing opera and offer wisecracks such as "Hey, save some for the fish!" when water hits their drains. One is east of the Innoventions fountain in front of the MouseGear shop, a second is near the play fountain between Future World and World Showcase, the third is close to the restrooms behind Innoventions West. ❸ Voices inside a trash can talk to you inside the Electric Umbrella restaurant. Swing

TWO MAGICAL DAYS

Day 1	**Future World**		the 10:45 a.m. marine biology presentation.
8:30a	Arrive at the entrance turnstiles. Be sure to have already booked your dinner reservation, and to allow time for your boat, bus or monorail trip.	**Noon**	The Land. Buy tickets to the 2 p.m. Behind the Seeds tour, ride Soarin', then have lunch at Sunshine Seasons food court.
9:00a	Test Track.	**3:00p**	Mission Space.
9:30a	Get Fastpasses for Soarin'.	**4:30p**	Innoventions.
9:45a	The Seas with Nemo & Friends. See Turtle Talk with Crush, then	**6:00p**	Spaceship Earth.
		7:00p	Dinner at Coral Reef.

© DISNEY

World Showcase consists of 11 international pavilions that circle a 40-acre lagoon

open the lid of the receptacle marked "Waste Please" (next to the topping bar to the left of the order counter) and you may hear a surfer dude complain "Like, your trash just knocked off my shades!" or a Frenchman exclaim "Zis ees my lucky day! French fries!" ❹ Fiber-optic lights are embedded in the sidewalks in front of the Innoventions buildings. Pinpoints of shimmering stars hide in dozens of small squares. Larger, colorful changing patterns appear in three 6-foot squares in front of Innoventions West. The lights are on all day, but most no-

ticeable at night. ❺ Thirty-eight discoveries and inventions are honored in the Epcot Inventor's Circle, five concentric rings embedded into the walkway that leads from Innoventions Plaza to The Land pavilion.

LANDSCAPE HIDDEN MICKEYS

❶ As wall gauges behind the main cash registers of MouseGear. ❷ As snowflake crystals on the food trays of The Land pavilion's Sunshine Seasons food court.

Day 2	World Showcase		
10:30a	Arrive at the park.	3:15p	Germany pavilion. See the miniature train village.
11:00a	U.K. pavilion. Stay for the first World Showcase Players show.	3:45p	China pavilion. See the Tomb Warriors exhibit, then the Dragon Legend Acrobats.
Noon	France pavilion. Watch Impressions de France.	5:30p	Norway pavilion. Ride Maelstrom.
12:40p	Lunch at the Japan pavilion's Tokyo Dining restaurant. See Miyuki, the candy artist.	6:30p	Back to the China pavilion for dinner, at Nine Dragons.
2:30p	See the American Adventure.	8:30p	Illuminations.

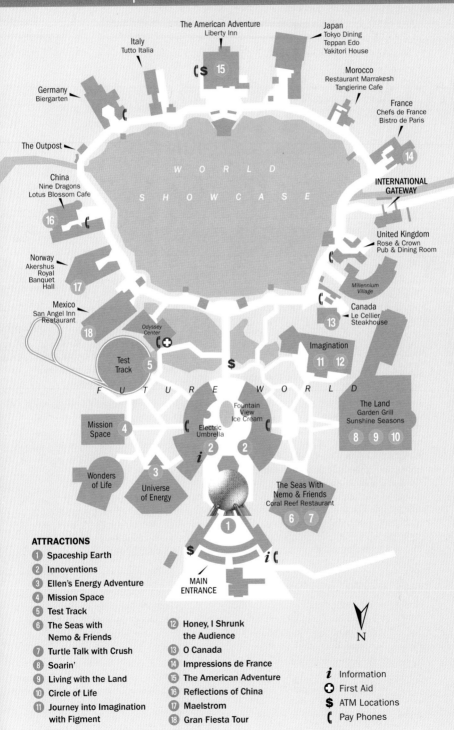

The American Adventure
Liberty Inn

Italy
Tutto Italia

Japan
Tokyo Dining
Teppan Edo
Yakitori House

Morocco
Restaurant Marrakesh
Tangierine Cafe

Germany
Biergarten

France
Chefs de France
Bistro de Paris

The Outpost

INTERNATIONAL GATEWAY

China
Nine Dragons
Lotus Blossom Cafe

WORLD SHOWCASE

United Kingdom
Rose & Crown
Pub & Dining Room

Norway
Akershus
Royal
Banquet
Hall

Millennium
Village

Mexico
San Angel Inn
Restaurant

Canada
Le Cellier
Steakhouse

Odyssey
Center

Imagination

Test Track

FUTURE WORLD

Fountain
View
Ice Cream

The Land
Garden Grill
Sunshine Seasons

Mission Space

Electric
Umbrella

Wonders of Life

Universe of Energy

The Seas With Nemo & Friends
Coral Reef Restaurant

MAIN ENTRANCE

ATTRACTIONS

1. Spaceship Earth
2. Innoventions
3. Ellen's Energy Adventure
4. Mission Space
5. Test Track
6. The Seas with Nemo & Friends
7. Turtle Talk with Crush
8. Soarin'
9. Living with the Land
10. Circle of Life
11. Journey into Imagination with Figment
12. Honey, I Shrunk the Audience
13. O Canada
14. Impressions de France
15. The American Adventure
16. Reflections of China
17. Maelstrom
18. Gran Fiesta Tour

i Information
First Aid
$ ATM Locations
Pay Phones

N

Park resources

BABY CARE
A Baby Care Center *(inside Future World's Odyssey Center)* has changing rooms, nursing areas and a microwave; and sells diapers, formula, pacifiers and over-the-counter medications.

FIRST AID
A First Aid Center *(inside Future World's Odyssey Center)* handles minor emergencies. Registered nurses are on hand.

GUEST RELATIONS
Two Guest Relations offices *(outside the park at the far right of the park entrance; inside the park to the left of Spaceship Earth)* have cast members trained to answer questions and solve problems in multiple languages, maps and Times Guides for all Disney World theme parks, exchanges foreign currency and stores items found in the park that day.

LOCKERS
Lockers rent at the Camera Center *(under Spaceship Earth)* for $5 per day plus a $5 deposit. The lockers themselves are to the right of Spaceship Earth.

LOST CHILDREN
Report lost children to Guest Relations or any cast member. Kids who lose parents should tell a cast member.

MONEY MATTERS
Epcot has three ATMs—near the park entrance on the left near the kennel, at the bridge between World Showcase and Future World near a Disney Vacation Club kiosk and at American Adventure by the restrooms. All cash registers take credit cards and traveler's checks.

PACKAGE PICKUP
Anything you buy can be sent to Package Pickup *(park entrance or International Gateway)* to pick up as you leave. Purchases can also be delivered to your Disney hotel or shipped to your home.

PARKING
For day guests parking is $12 a day. Those staying at a Disney resort, and annual passholders, get free parking.

SECURITY CHECK
Security guards inspect all bags and purses at the park entrance.

STROLLERS
Single strollers *($15 per day, $13 per day length of stay)* and double strollers *($31, $27)* are available at the east side of the entrance plaza, and at the International Gateway. If you misplace your stroller, a limited number of replacements are available in the Germany pavilion at the Glas und Porzellan shop.

TIP BOARDS
Electronic boards in Future World display waiting times for popular attractions.

TRANSPORTATION
Boats and walkways lead to Disney's Hollywood Studios and the BoardWalk, Yacht and Beach Club and Swan and Dolphin resorts. A monorail connects through the Transportation and Ticket Center to the Contemporary, Grand Floridian and Polynesian resorts and Magic Kingdom. Buses run from every other Disney resort, Animal Kingdom, Blizzard Beach and Disney's Hollywood Studios. There is no direct service from Downtown Disney or Typhoon Lagoon.

WHEELCHAIRS, ECVS
Available for rent at the east side of the entrance plaza and at the International Gateway *(wheelchairs $10 per day, $8 per day length of stay, Electric Convenience Vehicles $45 per day plus a $20 deposit)*. ECVs book quickly; many are used by overweight guests.

Attractions
Future World

CIRCLE OF LIFE
★★★ 13 min. Avg wait 10 min. Pg 141
Film with stars of 1994's "The Lion King" teaches environmental protection.

ELLEN'S ENERGY ADVENTURE
★★★ 45 min. Avg wait 10 min. Intense for preschoolers; the Big Bang is loud. Pg 133
Ellen DeGeneres hosts a series of widescreen films and a slow-moving ride that teach an oil-company view of energy.

HONEY, I SHRUNK THE AUDIENCE
★★★ 15 min. Avg wait 10 min. Some children will be terrified by the effects. *FastPass* Pg 142
Funny 3-D film based on 1989's "Honey, I Shrunk the Kids."

INNOVENTIONS
★★★★ ✓ Presentations avg 20 min. Allow 2–3 hrs if you stop at every exhibit. Wait times vary by exhibit, expect crowds in poor weather. Pg 132
Sponsored exhibits showcase interesting innovations and new technologies.

JOURNEY INTO IMAGINATION... WITH FIGMENT
★★ 6 min. Typically no wait. Loud noises, a skunk smell, a sudden flash. Pg 143
Mischievous Figment interrupts host Eric Idle's tour of a stuffy Imagination Institute.

LIVING WITH THE LAND
★★★ 14 min. Avg wait 15 min. *FastPass* Pg 141
Indoor boat ride through greenhouses full of amazing plants, aquaculture tanks.

MISSION SPACE
★★★★ ✓ 6 min. Avg wait 20 min. Height restriction 44 in. Intense; can cause disorientation, nausea. Take the warnings seriously: don't ride if you have any serious health issues or a head cold. *FastPass* Pg 134
Space-flight-simulator ride; one version spins for realistic sensations, one doesn't.

THE SEAS WITH NEMO AND FRIENDS
★★★★ Unlimited. Avg wait 10 min. Pg 137
Calm dark ride retells story of 2003 film "Finding Nemo"; leads to marine exhibits and aquariums with dolphins, manatees.

SOARIN'
★★★★★ ✓ 5 min. Avg wait 65 min. Height restriction 40 in. *FastPass* Pg 140
Simulated hang-glider tour of the best sights of California.

SPACESHIP EARTH
★★★★ ✓ 14 min. Avg wait 20 min. Pg 130
Slow-moving dark ride uses Audio-Animatronics characters to teach the history of communications.

TEST TRACK
★★★★★ ✓ 5 min. Avg wait 70 min. Height restriction 40 in. Intense for those scared by high speeds or sharp turns. *FastPass* Pg 136
GM test vehicles zip through an indoor-outdoor proving ground, reach 65 mph.

TURTLE TALK WITH CRUSH
★★★★★ ✓ 12 min. Avg wait 15 min. Pg 137
Interactive theatrical show features real-time conversations with animated sea turtle from the 2003 film "Finding Nemo."

World Showcase

THE AMERICAN ADVENTURE
★★★★★ ✓ 30 min. Pg 149
Film and Audio-Animatronics figures tell story of the United States.

GRAN FIESTA TOUR
★★★ 8 min. Typically no wait. Pg 155
Dark indoor boat tour through the cultural history of Mexico stars Donald Duck and his compatriots from the 1944 film "The Three Caballeros."

IMPRESSIONS DE FRANCE
★★★★ 18 min. Avg wait 9 min. Pg 146
Film celebrating the landscape, music and art of France.

KIM POSSIBLE WORLD SHOWCASE ADVENTURE
★★★★ ✓ Allow 45–60 min per adventure; game can be played at up to seven pavilions. Pg 157
Interactive scavenger hunt using a cell-phone-like "Kimmunicator."

MAELSTROM
★★★ 15 min. Avg wait 30 min. Dark; scary faces. *FastPass* Pg 154
Indoor boat ride, 5-minute travelogue celebrate the Spirit of Norway.

O CANADA!
★★★ 14 min. Avg wait 10 min. Pg 144
Comedian Martin Short hosts humorous CircleVision 360 film about Canada.

REFLECTIONS OF CHINA
★★★★ 20 min. Avg wait 10 min. Pg 153
CircleVision 360 film celebrates Chinese culture, geography and history.

ILLUMINATIONS
★★★★ ✓ 15 min. Loud explosions, fire. Pg 156
Nightly fireworks and laser show portrays an abstract history of the world.

Character locations

ALADDIN, GENIE From 1992's "Aladdin."
Morocco pavilion (location varies).
ALICE Star of 1951's "Alice in Wonderland."
The Toy Soldier, U.K. pavilion; also among the characters who appear at ❋ Akershus Royal Banquet Hall, Norway.
ARIEL Star of 1989's "The Little Mermaid."
Among the characters who appear at ❋ Akershus Royal Banquet Hall, Norway.
AURORA Star of 1959's "Sleeping Beauty."
France pavilion (location varies); also among the characters who appear at ❋ Akershus Royal Banquet Hall, Norway.
BELLE Star of 1991's "Beauty and the Beast."
France (location varies, often appears with the Beast); also among the characters who appear at ❋ Akershus Royal Banquet Hall, Norway.
CHIP 'N DALE Chipmunks in 1940s, 1950s cartoons.
❋ Garden Grill, The Land pavilion.
CINDERELLA Star of 1950's "Cinderella."
Among the characters who appear at ❋ Akershus Royal Banquet Hall, Norway.
DONALD DUCK
❋ To the right of the Mexico pavilion, World Showcase (in garb from the 1944 movie "The Three Caballeros").
DOPEY Dim-witted dwarf in 1937's "Snow White and the Seven Dwarfs."
To the left of the Germany pavilion.
ESMERELDA Gypsy in the 1996 movie "The Hunchback of Notre Dame."
Among the characters who appear at ❋ Akershus Royal Banquet Hall, Norway.

❋ Air-conditioned waiting line

GOOFY
❋ Epcot Character Spot, Future World.
JASMINE Co-star of 1992's "Aladdin."
Morocco pavilion (location varies); also among the characters who appear at ❋ Akershus Royal Banquet Hall, Norway.
MARY POPPINS Star of 1964's "Mary Poppins."
The Toy Soldier, U.K. pavilion.
MICKEY MOUSE
❋ Epcot Character Spot, Future World;
❋ Garden Grill, The Land pavilion.
MINNIE MOUSE
❋ Epcot Character Spot, Future World.
MULAN, MUSHU Co-stars of 1998's "Mulan."
China pavilion (location varies); also among the characters who appear at ❋ Akershus Royal Banquet Hall, Norway.
PLUTO
❋ Epcot Character Spot, Future World;
❋ Garden Grill, The Land pavilion.
SNOW WHITE Star of 1937's "Snow White and the Seven Dwarfs."
To the left of the Germany pavilion; also among the characters who appear at ❋ Akershus Royal Banquet Hall, Norway.
WINNIE THE POOH, TIGGER From 1977's "The Many Adventures of Winnie the Pooh."
The Toy Soldier, U.K. pavilion.

Street performers
Future World
JAMMITORS
When break time comes, this trio of roving janitors transforms into a percussion group using trash cans as drums **(20 min shows)**.

World Showcase
CANADA
Quirky kilt-wearing Celtic rock band Off Kilter **(20 min shows, promenade stage)** combines electric guitars, a bagpipe and a sense of humor into a fun show. At many performances at least a few guests get up and twirl with Deadhead joy.
UNITED KINGDOM
The improvisational World Showcase Players **(20 min shows, on the promenade and on Tudor Street)** butcher classic literature with street skits that star audience volunteers. Each set from Beatles tribute band The British Invasion **(20 min shows, on the back green)** consists of spot-on impressions of Fab Four hits. The former resident musician at Pleasure Island's Comedy Warehouse, "Hat Lady" Carol Stein is the new piano

Italian juggler Sergio puts children in his show

entertainer at The Rose & Crown Pub **(20 min sets, 5:40–9pm, 12 seats with a direct view)**. Songs include Irish anthems, Cockney show tunes.
FRANCE
A Serveur Amusant ("amusing server") **(20 min shows, in front of Chefs de France)** and his chef mime a balancing act that gets progressively complex. What starts off as simple tray balancing and handstands grows to a finale involving a table, five chairs and five bottles of champagne.
MOROCCO
Fronted by a robed belly dancer, Mo'Rockin **(20 min shows, promenade bandstand)** blends Moroccan rhythms with world music melodies. Its mix of a violin, keyboards, darbouka drum, electronic Zendrum and passionate vocals create a hypnotic sound.
JAPAN
Arrive early for candy artist Miyuki **(20 min, at the Mitsukoshi entrance)**, who makes free sweets for lucky children who stand right in front of her. Grabbing a taffy-like ribbon of rice dough, the Tokyo native quickly snips out a child's choice of colorful animals, each with amazing detail. The intense Matsuriza Taiko Drummers **(20 min, on the base of the pagoda)** pound out propulsive beats on hand-made instruments. Also

Japanese candy artist Miyuki

CHINA

The Dragon Legend Acrobats (20 min, just beyond the entrance gate or inside the Hall during inclement weather) are a group of Chinese teenagers who perform individual and group balancing acts. Each show includes three of the troupe's ten routines. Modern background music includes an instrumental version of the Carl Douglas 1974 novelty hit, "Kung Fu Fighting." Shows during calm winds include more challenging numbers. Qin zitherist Si Xian (20 min, inside the Hall, before most screenings of "Reflections of China") plays silk-music folk tunes. A rectangular sound box with a curved surface with tight strings, her instrument produces a multiple of echoing sounds.

MEXICO

Led by trumpets, violins and confident vocals and backed by harmonizing guitars, the 11-piece Mariachi Cobre (20 min, most shows inside the pavilion) is Epcot's best live band. Formed in Tucson in 1971, the group has played with Linda Ronstadt.

geared to children, friendly storyteller Honobono Minwa (20 min, courtyard) retells some of Japan's most famous folk tales with wide-eyed enthusiasm. She begins by introducing her audience to the Japanese language, teaching guests how to pronounce a few words and numbers.

AMERICAN ADVENTURE

Led by a town crier, the dramatic Spirit of America Fife & Drum Corps (10 min, promenade) performs "Battle Hymn of the Republic," "God Bless America" and similar tunes. Children join in to recite the Pledge of Allegiance. Harmonizing on "Amazing Grace," "Ol' Man River" and "This Land Is Your Land," spirited a cappella group The Voices of Liberty (20 min, rotunda, before most performances of the theatrical show) breathes life into aspects of American history that are too often ignored. The open-air American Gardens Amphitheater hosts free concerts sporadically throughout the year.

ITALY

The World Showcase Players (20 min, central plaza) perform "Romeo and Edna," a botched version of "Romeo and Juliet," with help from audience "volunteers." Humorous juggler Sergio (20 min, central plaza) puts children into his act.

Restaurants

Full service restaurants

AKERSHUS ROYAL BANQUET HALL ★★★

Character meals $$$$ American breakfast, Norwegian lunch and dinner. Five characters rotate among Alice in Wonderland, Ariel, Aurora ("Sleeping Beauty"), Belle, Cinderella, Esmerelda, Jasmine, Mary Poppins and Mulan. B: $23 A, $13 C, 8:30–10:45am. L: $25 A, $14 C, 11:10am–4pm. D: $30 A, $15 C, 4:15–8:40pm. Seats 255. Norway.

Five female characters come to your table at this bustling "Princess Storybook Dining experience." Breakfast is traditional American, served family-style at your table. Lunch and dinner are three-course Norwegian buffets. Appetizers such as sliced peppered mackerel (i.e., fish jerky) are acquired tastes, but the lamb stew and kjottkake will be familiar to anyone raised on hearty American standards. Kids can choose from hot dogs, pasta, pizza and grilled chicken. The room is noisy. Reservations should be made at least a week early, though the last lunch and dinner seatings often have tables available. Optional photo package.

BIERGARTEN ★★★★ ✔ German buffet with band $$$$

L: $20 A, $11 C, 11am–3:45pm. D: $27 A, $13 C, 4–9pm (last show 8:05pm). Seats 400. Germany.

As you get down with schnitzel and spaetzle, a live band rolls out a barrel full

© DISNEY

Coral Reef, Future World

of polkas and waltzes at this Octoberfest-style buffet, stopping occasionally to lead toasts or demonstrate some strange instrument. Unless you're a party of eight you'll share your table with others. Led by the band, you'll toast your new friends at least once or twice, and, since the tables are small, share conversations whether you want to or not.

All ages have a good time. At our most recent visit, a 9-year-old next to us couldn't have been giddier as she raised her mug of Sprite to join in a shout of "Tiki toki tiki toki! Hoy! Hoy! Hoy!"

Best bets on the hearty 40-item buffet include potato leek soup, beef rouladen and pork schnitzel (the last two at dinner only). Pass on the seafood. Beer choices include a light and dark Spaten, Becks and Franziskaner Hefe-Weisse.

The dining room simulates an evening in a medieval Rothernberg courtyard. Wrapped by three-dimensional building facades, the three-tiered eating area is lit by a moon in the sky. The band plays a 20- to 25-minute set about once an hour. The waitresses don't exactly dress like St. Pauli Girls, but the young waiters wear the goofiest outfits in all of World Showcase—green lederhosen shorts, white shirts, green suspenders, little black hats and teeny weeny little ties. Traditional Bavarian tracht wear, in Germany it's mainly worn at festivals by older men.

BISTRO DE PARIS ★★★★ Gourmet French $$$$
D: $30–$53, 5–9pm. Seats 120. France.

This intimate, second-floor dining room overlooks the World Showcase promenade. Gourmet seafood (fish, lobster, scallops) and meats (duck, beef, lamb, venison, veal) highlight an ever-changing menu. Appetizers are outstanding. Ask for a window table.
CHEFS DE FRANCE ★★★★ ✓ French $$$$ **L: $12–$20, Noon–3pm. D: $19–$34, 5–9pm. Seats 266. France.**
Generous with its cream and cheese, this sophisticated dining spot offers a wide-ranging menu that includes salads and sandwiches for lunch, duck and lamb for dinner, and beef, chicken, crepes, fish, pasta and seafood anytime. Good appetizers include Lobster Bisque. Big kids will love the regular menu's macaroni and cheese (lunch only), made with cream and gruyere. The decor includes tile floors and tin ceilings; nice to look at but noisy.
CORAL REEF ★★★★★ ✓ Seafood $$$ **L: $12–$26, 11:30am–3:30pm. D: $17–$32, 4–8:50pm. Seats 275. The Seas with Nemo & Friends pavilion.**
You eat fish while you watch fish at this dimly lit hidden treasure, which looks into The Seas with Nemo & Friends aquarium. As you dine, you watch angelfish, rays, sea turtles and sharks swim by. The signature appetizer is creamy lobster soup. Like spicy food? Try the blackened catfish—my husband's favorite fish dish in all of Disney. You eat on brushed-metal tables trimmed in light woods. Arrive right at 11 a.m. and you may walk right in, otherwise book lunch

© DISNEY

Aurora and Snow White meet fans at Norway's Akershus Royal Banquet Hall

two weeks early, dinner 60 to 90 days out. When you arrive, ask for a window-front table or a booth near the tank.

GARDEN GRILL ★★★★ ✓ Character buffet $$$$ **D:** $29 A, $14 C, 4:30–8pm. Seats 150. Land pavilion. This country-style meal is served family style—all-you-can-eat but brought to your table. As you dine, farmer Mickey, Pluto and Chip 'n Dale mosey up to say hi and, if you invite them, sit for a spell. Thanks to the restaurant's small size you see the characters often, at least three times each if you stay an hour. The circular restaurant is built like a merry-go-round— the kitchen is the hub, while the seating area rotates, circling completely every two hours. An open balcony, the outside rim overlooks the dioramas of the Living with the Land attraction. Ask to sit on the outside of the ring and your booth's high-backed seats will make every character visit a sudden, delightful surprise.

LE CELLIER ★★★★★ ✓ Steakhouse $$$$ **L:** $13–$30, 11:30am–3pm. **D:** $21–$37, 4–9pm. Seats 156. Canada. The toughest World Showcase reservation, this low-ceilinged, stone-walled eatery resembles a chateau wine cellar. Alberta-beef steaks are aged 28 days; the best is the filet mignon (dinner only). Made with Moosehead beer, a cheddar-cheese soup makes a great dip for complimentary soft breadsticks. Other options include salmon, seafood, chicken, entree salads and sandwiches. The young staff is friendly. Reserve your table months in advance.

NINE DRAGONS ★★★★ ✓ Chinese $$$$ **L:** $14–$21, Noon–3:45pm. **D:** $16–$27, 4–9pm. Seats 300. China.

A 2008 refurbishment at this China Company restaurant has brightened its decor, inspired its youthful staff and livened up its menu with modern dishes. New entrees are light and savory instead of salty and heavy. Direct from China's National Guest House, the small cucumber stack appetizer is a light indulgence. Holdovers include honey-sesame and stir-fried Kung Pao chicken. A serene decor is highlighted by greens, yellows and blues. Servers are helpful and humble. Window tables make for good people-watching. Good teas; bizarre Banana Cheesecake Egg Roll dessert.

RESTAURANT MARRAKESH ★★★★ ✓ Moroccan $$$$ **L:** $15–$22, Noon–3:30pm. **D:** $21–$28, 3:30–8:45pm. Seats 255. Morocco. Although it may sound exotic, there is nothing scary about this food. Ingredients are the same used in American cooking, flavors are uniformly mild and it's all pretty good. The lamb shank couscous is like your mom's pot roast tossed in rice, complete with roasted carrots and meat that falls off the bone. Menus also include beef and fish dishes; dinner adds large sampler platters. Of course, mom's meals probably didn't include a belly dancer. Here, one shimmies on a dance floor (on the hour 1pm–8pm except at 4pm), her moves more graceful than sexy. Children can join her. The spacious restaurant has intricately decorated ceilings and walls covered in colorful tiny tiles. Since Moroccan food is unfamiliar to many Americans, this is the least popular Epcot eatery. Usually you can walk right in. Ask to sit by the dance floor to get an up-close view of the show.

ROSE & CROWN DINING ROOM ★★★★ ✓ British $$$$ **L:** $13–$19, Noon–3:30pm. **D:** $13–$25, 4–9pm. Seats 242, inc 40 on covered porch. U.K. It's not the fanciest food in Epcot and probably a little too hearty for our own good, but every time we eat here we want to come back. Maybe it's the menu, which hides some of the most deliciously creamy potato soup we've ever had. Maybe it's the servers, a young, pretension-free bunch who exude a classic British charm. Maybe it's the little covered patio, which on a nice day is one of Disney's best outdoor dining spots. Maybe it's just the cheese plate. The menu includes a split pea soup that will warm your soul, British entrees such as bangers and mash (good) and shepherds pie (better), even a few Indian dishes.

SAN ANGEL INN ★★★★ ✔ Mexican $$$$ **L: $15–$22, 11:30am–4pm. D: $24–$34, 4:30–9pm. Seats 156. Mexico.**

¡Aye carumba! Prices have skyrocketed in the past year at this relaxing dining spot, though the food is as flavorful as ever. Good choices include signature tortilla soup and a steak that tastes like it's straight off a backyard grill. Worth the indulgence is the premium margarita ($12). Sitting on padded chairs and benches around a lantern-lit table, you dine in what appears to be a moonlit courtyard. Off in the distance is a rumbling volcano that, depending on your margarita intake, may appear to be the most realistic effect Disney has ever created. The restaurant is run by the Debler family, the proprietors of the namesake restaurant in Mexico City.

TEPPAN EDO ★★★★ ✔ Teppanyaki (Hibachi) $$$$ **L, D: A: $16–$30, C: $12. Noon–9pm. Seats 192. Japan.**

An entertaining tableside chef may juggle knives or make a "smoking Mickey train" out of onion stacks at this completely refurbished collection of dining rooms, which now have a stunning red and black color scheme. Using a grill set into your table, the chef's hands fly fast as they slice, dice and stir-fry your choice of beef, seafood or chicken. You share your table with other guests.

TOKYO DINING ★★★★ ✔ Japanese, sushi $$$$ **L, D: $15–$28, Noon–9pm. Seats 116. Japan.**

A combination of good food, great atmosphere and obsessive service, this is what a World Showcase restaurant is supposed to be—a non-threatening way to experience the cuisine of a foreign culture. A mix of traditional Japanese entrees, the menu includes a tender beef teriyaki and nice shrimp tempura. The sushi and sashimi menu has 49 selections, highlighted by a "volcano" California roll that's stacked and coated with a creamy hot chili sauce. For dessert, the green tea pudding melts in your mouth. The peaceful decor has diffused lighting. Dark tables sit on a tile floor. What tops everything are the bows. Hostesses and servers bow to you as you enter, every time they come to your table and as you leave.

TUTTO ITALIA ★★★★★ Italian $$$$$ **L: $15–$30, 11:30am–3:30pm. D: $24–$36, 3:30–8:45pm. Seats 300. Italy.**

Every bit as good as the meals we used to love back on the Hill in south St. Louis, the meals at this new eatery are built on imported pastas and delicate sauces. Meat and fish entrees are tempting, too, though side dishes are $10 each. Entree salads use ingredients such as asparagus, curly endive and fava beans. As you arrive, don't let the formal maître'd fool you; the young Italian wait staff is friendly. An elegant decor has dark woods. Tutto Italia is one of a handful of World Showcase restaurants not run by Disney. The others are in the China, Japan and Mexico pavilions.

Counter service cafes

ELECTRIC UMBRELLA Burgers, chicken, salads, sandwiches. 11am–9pm. Seats 426. Innoventions East. Good veggie chili.

FOUNTAINVIEW ICE CREAM SHOP ✔ Ice cream. 10:30am–9pm. Seats 108, inc. 68 outside. Innoventions West. Hand-dipped Edy's ice-cream sandwiches are especially good.

LIBERTY INN Burgers, chicken, salads. Kosher meal. 11:30am–9pm. Seats 710. American Adventure.

LOTUS BLOSSOM CAFE Egg rolls, chicken, stir-fry, specialty drinks. 11am–9pm. Seats 100. China.

SUNSHINE SEASONS ✔ Quality salads, soups, sandwiches, noodle dishes, grilled meats, bakery items. Breakfast egg dishes, oatmeal, cold cereals. B: 9–11am. L: 11am–9pm. Seats 707. The Land.

TANGIERINE CAFE ✔ Chicken, lamb platters; sandwiches. Pastries, tea, liqueur coffees, beer. 11:30am–9pm. Seats 101. Morocco.

YAKITORI HOUSE ✔ Beef, chicken, good noodles, packaged sushi. Miso soup. Salads. Beer, wine. Garden setting. 11:30am–9pm. Seats 94 inc. 36 outside. Japan.

Outdoor counter cafes

BOULANGERIE PATISSERIE ✔ Pastries, quiche, cheese plates. Seats 24. France.

CANTINA DE SAN ANGEL Tacos, churros, margaritas, beer. Seats 150. Mexico.

FIFE & DRUM Turkey legs, hot dogs, smoothies, beer. American Adventure.

KRINGLA BAKERI OG KAFE ✔ Sandwiches, pastries. Seats 51. Norway.

LOTUS BLOSSOM CAFE Chinese standards. Seats 107. China.

PROMENADE REFRESHMENTS Turkey legs, hot dogs, smoothies, beer. Showcase Plaza.

SOMMERFEST ✔ Bratwurst, frankfurters, pretzels, desserts, beer. Seats 24 under a covered patio. Germany.

YORKSHIRE COUNTY FISH SHOP Fish and chips, Bass ale. Seats 31. United Kingdom.

Snack stands

BIERLINE, DAS KAUFHAUS CART
Pretzels, beer, wine. Germany.

COOL WASH
Soft drinks, chips. Test Track.

CREPES DES CHEFS DE FRANCE
Crepes, waffle cones, beers, coffees. France.

DONKEY CART
Gelato, ices. Italy.

FUNNEL CAKE KIOSK
✔ American Adventure.

JOFFREY'S COFFEE
Coffees, baked goods, smoothies, tea. Between Innoventions East and Universe of Energy; Showcase Plaza; between Canada and U.K.; at American Adventure.

JOY OF TEA
Hot and iced tea. China.

KAKI GORI
✔ Shaved ice, beer. Japan.

LES VINS DES CHEFS DE FRANCE
Champagne, wine, cheese. France.

MARGARITA KIOSK
Frozen margaritas. Mexico.

OASIS
Baklava, mint tea, slushies, beer. Morocco.

PIZZA CART
Test Track.

REFRESHMENT COOL POST
Soft-serve ice cream, hot dogs, coffee, beer. Outpost.

REFRESHMENT PORT
McDonald's. Near Canada.

TUTTO ITALIA STAND
Desserts, coffee, beer, wine. Italy.

Bar

ROSE & CROWN PUB
✔ Beer, mixed drinks, appetizers, sandwiches. Evening entertainment. Seats 20. United Kingdom.

Shopping

Future World

ENTRANCE AREA
Outside the park turnstiles on the extreme right, the Package Pickup gift shop carries general Disney merchandise and sundries such as candy, disposable cameras, hats, pins, totes and toys. To the extreme left of the entrance plaza, the Stroller rental gift shop is a covered outdoor counter carrying a small selection of candy, disposable cameras, hats, pins, sandals, tennis shoes, totes and toys. Offering Disney souvenirs, hats, toys and T-shirts, Gateway Gifts is on the east side of the entrance plaza, underneath Spaceship Earth. Stocking cameras and photo gear, the Epcot Camera Center sits under the west side of Spaceship Earth. The classy Art of Disney gallery showcases original animation art including framed paintings, production cels and character figurines, as well as delicate sculptures by artist Giuseppe Armani. Some works include Swarovski crystals.

IMAGINATION PAVILION
The photography-themed ImageWorks gift shop is at the exit to the Journey into Imagination with Figment ride. It sells cameras, camera supplies, frames, photo albums and scrapbooks. Photographs can be turned into puzzles, posters, applied to coffee mugs or etched into crystal cubes. "Picture Yourself" photo booths offer prints or stickers. Figment plushies and T-shirts are also available.

INNOVENTIONS PLAZA
A one-stop shop for everything Disney, MouseGear is on the east side of Future World, just past Spaceship Earth. Here you'll find a huge variety of apparel for all ages, books, costumes, Christmas items, DVDs, food, housewares, jewelry, pet products, pins, photo albums, scrapbooks and toys. This is the best spot to buy Epcot-themed merchandise. It's the largest shop in any of the four Disney theme parks. Located to the right of the Innoventions Plaza fountain, Club Cool offers free self-service samples of eight Coca-Cola Company soft drinks from around the world. China's watermelon-flavored Smart and Mexico's fruity Lift are pretty good; Italy's bitter Beverly is awful. The store also sells—surprise!—Coke merchandise. Loud pop music fills the air.

MISSION SPACE
Cargo Bay has an impressive array of space-themed apparel and merchandise, including freeze-dried astronaut food, Mission Space X2 spacecraft and "Star Wars"-themed Disney-character plushies. Goofy as Jar Jar Binks is a hoot.

THE SEAS WITH NEMO & FRIENDS
The small Seas gift shop offers "Finding Nemo" and sea-life-themed products such

as coffee mugs, costume jewelry, plushies, toys and T-shirts.

TEST TRACK

Inside Track has all sorts of automobile-themed merchandise, from items themed to the 2006 movie "Cars" to fuzzy dice to die-cast metal toy cars. At the counter you can purchase the souvenir photo shot on the attraction. A photo booth lets you create a Test Track "driver's license."

THE LAND

Plant lovers, take note. At the Soarin' counter next to Soarin' you'll find seed packets, gardening supplies and Mickey's Mini-Gardens plant tissues, which are essentially living clones of plants you can take home and grow yourself. Also available are Soarin' T-shirts.

World Showcase

At World Showcase Plaza, Showcase Station West Port is an upscale shop geared to adults, while East Port is a youth-oriented store with clothing, candy, plushies and toys. Next to the back entrance to Epcot, World Traveler sells upscale Disney merchandise as well as bottles of wine.

CANADA PAVILION

Left of the totems, Northwest Mercantile is the place to pick up NHL jerseys, books about Canada and apparel. The Hatley boutique has amusing cartoon bear and moose aprons, shirts and sleepwear. Pure maple syrup, maple candy and cookies will tempt you next door at the Trading Post, which also carries dreamcatchers and plushies of Canadian animals such as huskies, bear, beaver and moose. On the promenade, the Canada wood cart offers personalized leather items, Off Kilter CDs and a plushie depicting Goofy as a lumberjack.

UNITED KINGDOM PAVILION

Look up the history of your family name and purchase your coat of arms at The Crown & Crest. Also found here: Beatles items. The Magic of Wales sells lovely Tartan scarves and sweaters and silver jewelry. You'll want to step in The Queen's Table just for its heavenly aroma. Perfume, lotions and other toiletries come from brands such as Bronnley, Burberry, Miller Harris and Taylor of London. British sports fans come to the Sportsman's Shoppe for the soccer and rugby apparel, Adidas tennis shoes, balls

and books. Treats offered include outstanding Cadbury dairy milk caramel candy bars. Explicitly for tea lovers, the cozy Tea Caddy stocks fine bone china by Dunoon and Royal Albert, many varieties of Twinings tea (loose and in bags), biscuits and candy. The Toy Soldier sells kids books, costumes including hard-to-find Alice in Wonderland outfits, dolls and plush. Merchandise features Alice in Wonderland, Peter Pan, Thomas the Tank Engine and Winnie the Pooh characters. Finds at a promenade wood cart include authentic pub coasters and a plushie of Minnie Mouse as a London bobbie.

FRANCE PAVILION

France is known for exquisite fragrances. Case in point: the imported perfumes sold at Plume et Palette. Brands include Annick Goutal, Chanel, Dior and Givenchy. Women who *love* perfume will find Guerlain Paris irresistible. Formerly La Signature, the classy shop offers limited-edition and exclusive fragrances, including some in the company's classic sculpted bee bottles. You can have Guerlain cosmetics applied on the spot. L' Esprit de la Provence channels a homey kitchen in a small French village.

A marionette from the China wood cart

Marketplace in the Medina, Morocco

Mostly kitchen goods, items come from the Provencal region of France. Cookbooks are especially tempting. The cozy **Les Vins de France** has wine by the bottle or glass. Formerly called Galerie des Halles, **Souvenirs de France** offers authentic French berets and a plushie of Minnie Mouse as a beret-clad Parisienne. Meanwhile, artisans at **promenade stands** create personalized parasols and portraits.

MOROCCO PAVILION

Half brass shop, half food store, **The Brass Bazaar** has detailed handmade brass plates and platters, packages of couscous and Moroccan spices, ceramic and wooden kitchenware and rosewater bottles. Don't miss the aromatic bowls and boxes made of thuya, a burled-root wood grown only in Morocco. A tiny connected room, **Medina Arts** offers pottery and ceramics. Inside the Medina, **Casablanca Carpets** has Moroccan rugs, incense holders, lamps that filter their light through henna-dyed camel skin and colorful sequined pillows. The **Marketplace in the Medina** is an open-air alley with belly-dancer kits, bargain-priced seagrass baskets, ceramic-topped furniture, scarves and two strange drums: ceramic tam-tams covered in stretched camel skin and open-top darboukas with bottoms of flounder skin. Tucked alongside, **Tangier Traders** is a clothing store with traditional caftans, gandouras and other robes and wraps, as well as handmade leather slippers and jewelry.

Out front, the open-air **Souk-Al-Magreb** sells a mixture of merchandise from the other Moroccan shops. The name means "The Flea Market of Northern Africa."

JAPAN PAVILION

A 10,000-square-foot department store, **Mitsukoshi** is divided into four sections. Inspired by the Kyoto's Nishiki Food Market, Festivity stocks chopsticks, cooking gear, porcelain dishes, teas and sweets. A sake tasting bar offers five microbrews. The zen-themed Silence area offers apparel and home items such as bonsai trees, draperies, lanterns, rice paper, small tables and tatami mats. Clothing includes embossed jackets, tenugui head coverings and silk kimonos. The store's Harmony zone bridges Japanese and Western cultures with handbags, glass-bead jewelry, sandals, shirts and silver. Stunning Mikimoto pearl jewelry is displayed in its own room. Bowls of water in each case keep pearls moist. Mitsukoshi's largest area, Interest has a Pick-A-Pearl (from an oyster) bar, kitschy Lucky Cats, trans-forming Rhythm and Seiko clocks, Hello Kitty merchandise and quirky toys. Outside, a walk-in **Mitsukoshi kiosk** sells candy and inexpensive souvenirs.

THE AMERICAN ADVENTURE

The uninspired **Heritage Manor Gifts** has pa-triotic apparel and educational items with a history theme. Too bad most of the merchandise has a "Made in China" sticker. Out front, the American Adventure wood cart offers patriotic T-shirts and pins.

ITALY PAVILION

An eclectic collection of Murano glass, jewelry, Bulgari and Ferragamo perfumes highlight the wares at Il Bel Cristallo. Also on hand: Puma sportswear and soccer books. Handmade in the cozy La Bottega shop, the exquisite papier-mâché and fabric Carnivale masks are works of art. Also available are books about Italy, Perugina candy, housewares, wines and wine samplings. Look for the cute gondolier Mickey Mouse plushie.

GERMANY PAVILION

Makers of famous M.I. Hummel glass and porcelain figurines, German company Goebel sponsors the Glas und Porzellan shop. Based on the artistic style of German nun Maria Innocentia Hummel, these pieces are collected worldwide. A Goebel artist is often onsite painting and finishing. The lovely Volkskunst has traditional wares such as Schneider cuckoo clocks (large and small), beer steins and glassware, pewter ware and Troika watches. Check out egg artist Jutta Levasseur, who often works in the corner. A $1200 ostrich egg is on display. Der Teddybar offers expensive Steiff teddy bears and detailed, customized Engle-Puppen dolls. Pick out the parts you want and watch while your doll is made. Kunstarbeit in Kristall is the spot to find jewelry, including Swarovski crystal pins and Arribas Brothers glassware and collectibles. Glassware can be personalized while you wait. A wonderfully tempting confectionery shop, Sussigkeiten offers fresh baked pastries and snacks, and imported treats including Haribo gummies. There's a small but good selection of cookbooks. An open-air promenade stand, Glaskunst has glass items an artisan will personalize for you on the spot: glassware, steins, frames, figures. Germany's Christmas shop, Die Weihnachts Ecke has unusual imported items including pickle ornaments and handmade Steinback nutcrackers. Hundreds of varieties of wines and schnapps are offered at Weinkeller by the bottle or glass. The sports-themed merchandise at Das Kaufhaus includes backpacks, balls and Adidas apparel.

OUTPOST

Unified families with intertwined arms are the signature sculptures of Village Traders wood and soapstone sculptor Andrew Mutiso. He also creates lovely animals, busts, canes and masks. Guests can commission art, too.

CHINA PAVILION

The sprawling Yong Feng Shangdian department store is packed with imported goods. Weave between antiques, apparel, silk fans, food, fountains, furniture, housewares, jewelry, prints, silk rugs, tea sets and jade sculptures. The prices range from a dollar or so for trinkets to thousands of dollars for intricately carved furniture and jade antiques. Elaborate marionettes and personalized parasols are among the wares at the promenade China wood cart.

NORWAY PAVILION

The quality apparel at The Puffin's Roost includes stylish, pricey Helly Hansen items and thick woolen sweaters from Dale of Norway. Other Norwegian wares include Christmas ornaments, Geir Ness perfume, toys and plastic trolls. Don't miss the Viking Donald Duck plushie, or the silly plastic Viking helmets, all with horns, some with braids.

MEXICO PAVILION

Wild styles dominate painted copal-wood sculptures at Animalés Fantásticos: Spirits in Wood, a collection of folk-art animals, humans and mythical creatures carved with machetes and pocketknives then painted with brushes, cactus spines and syringes. Artisans work on the spot. For a scene that suggests a bustling Mexican market, check out the indoor Plaza de los Amigos. You'll not only find blankets, glassware, musical instruments, paper flowers, piñatas, ponchos, salsa, sombreros and toys, but it's also a fun place to souvenir shop for everything from hand-painted piggy banks to tequila. Many items are inexpensive. Off the Plaza, the small La Familia Fashions spotlights Mexican jewelry and leather accessories. Handcrafted silver pieces from Taxco are especially beautiful. Delicate Arribas Brothers crystal is on display in another side room, La Princesa Cristal. A small promenade shop, El Ranchito del Norte sells a sampling of everything found elsewhere in the pavilion.

You enter the Spaceship Earth attraction from underneath the giant sphere

Spaceship Earth

★★★★ ✓ 14 min. Allow up to 45 min. for postshow activities. Capacity: 308. Fear factor: None. Access: Must be ambulatory. The ride stops intermittently to load mobility impaired guests. Vehicles offer a choice of narration languages: English, French, German, Japanese, Portuguese and Spanish. Debuted: 1982, revised 1994, 2008.

For years ridiculed as one of Disney's more boring experiences, Future World's onetime showcase attraction is once again one of its most entertaining. Though the ride is still a Smithsonian-serious trip through a 56-robot history of communications, a 2008 refurbishment has made it more fun. New scenes depict a 1960s IBM computer room where two programmers maintain a gigantic reel-to-reel mainframe and a 1977 California garage where a young man creates the first PC.

The ride's 19 other dioramas depict communication advances from the days of cave dwellers. They include new costumes, lighting and set pieces. A new narration by Dame Judi Dench emphasizes the roots of tech-

Average Wait

9am	10 min
10am	20
11am	20
Noon	20
1pm	30
2pm	30
3pm	30
4pm	20
5pm	20
6pm	15
7pm	10
8pm	5
9pm	0

nology, while a new score features a 62-piece orchestra and 24-voice choir.

As the ride nears its finish, a new touchscreen in your ride vehicle lights up with a series of questions, asking how you'd like to live or work in the future. Then you're treated to a cartoon view of yourself a few decades from now, complete with your face superimposed onto an animated character.

When you get off the ride you head into Project Tomorrow: Inventing the World of Tomorrow, a new post-show area that features four interactive video exhibits, all of which subtly showcase the attraction's new sponsor, Siemens. You learn about automotive accident-avoidance systems on a driving simulator, urban energy management by playing a group shuffleboard game, remote surgery technologies on a digital human body and home medical diagnostic systems through a series of memory, handeye coordination and reflex exercises.

A giant globe in the room pinpoints the hometowns of all of that day's Spaceship Earth passengers, while video screens include your face as it appeared in your video. You can e-mail the image free of charge.

On one of our recent visits the exitway was filled with smiling faces. A preschooler refused to get off, demanding to go again.

▶ Hop on after 5 p.m. when the line is short. After dark there's often no line at all.

Jumping out of his ride vehicle, a school-age boy shouted "That was awesome, dad! Let's go again!" Entering the post-show, a group of teenaged girls giggled as one glanced up at the ceiling and yelled "There I am!"

If only school was this much fun.

BUILDING THE BALL

A 180-foot-high geodesic sphere, Spaceship Earth took 26 months to build, from August 1980 to September 1982. It was created without scaffolding or temporary supports.

First, a foundation team pounded over 100 steel pilings into the ground, to depths of 150 feet. Three pairs of angled legs were placed on top, themselves topped with a six-sided platform about 45 feet off the ground. Secured on that platform, adjustable cranes built a circular frame around themselves, using hundreds of metal-strut triangles.

After an outside crane hoisted the pre-constructed, 50-foot-wide dome, workers built the bottom, a separate piece that is not load-bearing. Rubber-coated panels were secured onto the triangles, creating a giant waterproof black ball. A separate, decorative outer sphere was then added, set off two feet from the core by 4-inch aluminum pipes.

The outer sphere is made up of 11,324 triangles of Alucobond, a rustproof material made of polyethylene plastic bonded to two layers of anodized aluminum. First used in 1978, it today covers more than 50,000 buildings, including many Honda dealerships.

Spaceship Earth does not drip water: a 1-inch gap between each panel allows the triangles to expand and contract in the Florida heat and lets rainwater flow into two interior gutters that drain through the building's support legs into canals that run alongside the park.

Disney got the idea for the structure from the icons of the New York World's Fairs of 1939 and 1964, both held in Flushing Meadows, N.Y. The 1939 event featured the 180-foot-tall Perisphere, a sphere which held a slow-moving, educational ride (it portrayed Democracity, a "perfectly integrated garden city" from the year 2068). The icon of the 1964 fair was the Unisphere, a 140-foot open-grid Earth that symbolized global interdependence. It's still standing.

The attraction can also trace its parentage to the 1940s geodesic domes designed by engineer R. Buckminster Fuller. Billed as homes of tomorrow, his futuristic half-circles were composed of self-bracing triangles. The houses had no internal supports and could be built in one day. The "Bucky balls" caught on as weather stations and airport radar shelters, but never got beyond a cult following as private homes (one reason: they leaked water).

Fuller coined the phrase "Spaceship Earth." His 1963 treatise, "An Operating Manual for Spaceship Earth," argued that all the world's peoples must work together as a crew to guide our planet's future.

FUN FINDS

❶ The radio station's call letters "WDI" refer to Walt Disney Imagineering. ❷ A desk placard on the right side of the computer room includes the word "Think," the slogan of IBM founder Thomas J. Watson Sr. It later spawned the 1990s Apple slogan, "Think Different." ❸ Nearby lies a manual for the System 360 Job Control Language used on 1964 IBM mainframes. ❹ On the right is an IBM Selectric typewriter, an icon of the 1970s office. ❺ The snapshot on the garage wall resembles a classic Microsoft photo.

HIDDEN MICKEYS

❶ As blots made by the sleeping monk on the top right of a piece of parchment. ❷ As bottle rings on the table of the first Renaissance painter.

FUN FACTS ›› Science-fiction author Ray Bradbury helped design the attraction, along with consultants from the Smithsonian Institution, the University of Southern California and the University of Chicago. ›› The caveman is speaking a Cro-Magnon language. The cave drawings are based on images found in the Salon-Niaux cave in Ariège, France. ›› The Egyptian hieroglyphics reproduce actual Middle Eastern drawings. The pharaoh's words come from a real letter. ›› The refocused script has changed the meaning of a few scenes. The former Greek thespians are now teaching math. The burning of Rome is now a fire at the Library of Alexandria. And though they were once "debating ideas," Disney's medieval scholars are now "watching over... books to save our dreams of the future." ›› Touchscreen "Work" futures predict "a great big, beautiful tomorrow"—the title of the theme song to Magic Kingdom's Carousel of Progress. ›› The building weighs 16 million pounds. That's 158 million golf balls.

▶ Many guests assume that, since it's in Future World, the ride closes at 7pm. It closes at 9pm.

Innoventions Fountain offers a five-minute show choreographed to music every 30 minutes

Innoventions

★★★★ ✔ Presentations avg. 20 min. Allow 2–3 hrs. if you stop at each exhibit. Fear factor: None. Access: Guests may stay in wheelchairs, ECVs. Assistive listening. Debuted 1994; revised often.

Many of the exhibits are brand new in these two large buildings, which house interactive presentations from outside sponsors. Each building also has a nice Kidcot area.

INNOVENTIONS EAST

Waste Management's **Don't Waste It** game gives you a mini "garbage truck" cart filled with virtual trash, which you take to a sorting station, incinerator and landfill as you create electricity. Children love to push the cart, which beeps when you back it up. The **House of Innoventions** tour includes an overhead oven that descends for loading, a dining table made of corrugated cardboard and a miniature talking robot. The Federal Alliance for Safe Homes' **Storm Struck** combines a theatrical show with a display about how two differently built Punta Gorda, Fla., homes fared during 2004's Hurricane Charley. Back for a return engagement, Cornell University's **It's a Nano World** is a child-focused look at things too small to see. It first came here in 2004. A holdover exhibit is Underwriters Laboratories' **Test the Limits Lab,** where you can swing a hammer at a TV, smash a 55-gallon drum onto a helmet and cause other havoc. An **Environmentality Corner** display lets you make paper.

INNOVENTIONS WEST

What's Your Problem is a wacky game show from The Velcro Companies in which live hosts Liza Loopy and Hank Hook choose contestants to solve "Seemingly Insurmountable Problems." Returning exhibits include Liberty Mutual's **Where's the Fire?,** where guests use "safety lights" to find hazards on interactive walls that represent rooms of a home. A companion tour teaches fire safety to kids. **Segway Central** offers test drives on the Segway Human Transporter, a single-axle gyroscopic electric scooter (1–7 p.m., riders must be at least 16 years old. Those under 18 require legal consent). Also still here: a free **PlayStation arcade.** Debuting in 2009: A reconfigured **IBM Thinkplace** and **When Pigs Fly,** a T. Rowe Price look at financial planning.

Average Wait

Time	Wait
9am	0 min
10am	0
11am	0
Noon	0
1pm	0
2pm	0
3pm	0
4pm	0
5pm	0
6pm	0
7pm	closed
8pm	closed
9pm	closed

▶ The Innoventions exhibits get crowded when the weather is cold or rainy.

Disney's Universe of Energy pavilion, home to Ellen's Energy Adventure

Ellen's Energy Adventure

★ ★ ★ 45 min. (new shows begin every 17 min.) Capacity: 582. Fear factor: The Big Bang portrayal is loud. Access: ECV guests must transfer. Assistive listening; handheld captioning. Debuted: 1996.

This 45-minute multimedia presentation about the history and future of energy combines three theatrical films with a tram ride past Audio-Animatronics dinosaurs.

Watching a series of video screens, you meet star Ellen DeGeneres in her apartment as Bill Nye* stops by to ask for some aluminum foil, a clothes pin and a candle (Ellen replies "Another hot date, huh?"). Then she falls asleep watching her old roommate (Jamie Lee Curtis) compete on the game show "Jeopardy!"

Dreaming she's a contestant on that show, Ellen learns that all of the categories deal with one thing she knows nothing about: energy. When she asks Nye for help, he takes the comedienne back in time for a crash course in Energy 101.

Average Wait	
9am	0 min
10am	10
11am	10
Noon	10
1pm	10
2pm	10
3pm	10
4pm	10
5pm	10
6pm	10
7pm	closed
8pm	closed
9pm	closed

Moving into a large theater, you watch as three huge screens dramatically display the Big Bang and the creation of the Earth: billions of years compressed into one stunning minute. Then the seating area breaks apart into ride vehicles and you travel to the Mesozoic Era—a swamp filled with dinosaurs—to get a close-up look at the beginning of fossil fuels. Arriving in a third theater, you're brought back to the present through a series of radio broadcasts, then watch as Ellen learns about man's energy use. Finally you return to the first theater, where you watch Ellen become a "Jeopardy" champion.

Produced when the average price of a gallon of gasoline was $1.30, the show ignores the problems of fossil fuels. There's no mention of the Middle East, no talk of global warming or fuel efficiency. The show was created in conjunction with Exxon-Mobil, its sponsor until 2004.

FUN FINDS

❶ After Trebek says to Ellen, "Your first correct response!" her lips don't move when she yells "Freeze!" ❷ Nye's lips stay shut when, in front of a solar mirror, he says "all right."

* A one-time mechanical engineer, Nye hosted "Bill Nye the Science Guy," a 1992-1998 PBS preteen program which Disney later sold as a video series.

▶ Sit in the theater's back right corner. You'll spend more time with the dinosaurs.

Mission Space

★ ★ ★ ★ ✓ 6 min. Capacity: 160. *FastPass* Height restriction: 44 in. Fear factor: Intense, can cause disorientation, headaches, nausea. Take the warnings seriously: don't ride if you have any serious health issues or a head cold. Access: ECV and wheelchair guests must transfer. Activated video captioning. Debuted: 2003.

So intense it includes motion-sickness bags, this flight simulator offers realistic sensations of space travel. Developed with NASA, it's Disney's most advanced attraction ever.

Why do riders get sick? Because you spin. You can't tell it when you're in your vehicle, but the ride is a centrifuge, a circular machine with a series of rapidly rotating containers on its spokes. As it spins, it applies centrifugal force to its contents (that's you) that mimic the G-forces of a rocket launch and then the weightlessness of space. The spinning creates forces up to 2 Gs, or twice that of the Earth's gravity. That may not sound like much—it's actually less than many roller coasters—but this force is sustained; you feel it continually throughout the ride. It's one of the ways NASA trained astronauts for decades.

Many adults have no problem with the ride, and children often fare better than their parents. Still, the side effects have landed some riders in the hospital. A few guests have died, though in each of those cases the rider had existing health problems and ignored the warning signs. The most common troubles are dizziness and a lingering headache. To avoid getting sick, continually stare straight at your monitor and do not close your eyes. Don't eat or drink alcohol before you go. If you do feel bad afterward, get lots of fresh air, take it easy and have some saltine crackers or a soda.

BYE BYE BYE!

The story begins as soon as you enter the building. You're in the year 2036 at the International Space Training Center, where astronaut hopefuls come to see if they have the right stuff. You're there to train for an upcoming mission to Mars. (Robots, you soon learn, have already been established on the Red Planet. You are training to be one of the first humans.)

The first queue room is the Space Simulation Lab. Alongside you is a 35-foot model of a Gravity Wheel, a slowly rotating prop from the 2000 film "Mission to Mars" that's

Average Wait

9am	0 min
10am	30
11am	30
Noon	30
1pm	40
2pm	25
3pm	15
4pm	20
5pm	25
6pm	10
7pm	10
8pm	15
9pm	0

▶ **Disney also offers a mild version of the ride, in which the centrifuge does not spin.**

The steely facade of Mission Space has no straight lines. Spheres symbolize Earth, Jupiter, Mars and the moon.

PHOTO © DISNEY

complete with exercise rooms, offices, work areas and sleeping cubicles. Nearby is a real Lunar Roving Vehicle display unit, on loan from the National Air and Space Museum in Washington, D.C.

After the voice of Mission Control ("CSI" actor Gary Sinise, also known for his roles in 1995's "Apollo 13" and 2000's "Mission to Mars") introduces you to your vehicle, you climb in your trainer and buckle in.

Once a cast member seals the door, an elaborate control panel pivots into place. As you angle into launch position, you look out into a beautiful blue (video) sky complete with birds passing overhead. Then the engines power up and the countdown begins.

"3... 2... 1... Zero!" The earth begins to rumble and in a moment that seems absolutely real, you take off. As the G-forces push your body back into the seat, it truly feels like you're on your way to Mars.

Soon Mission Control breaks in with instructions. "Initiate first stage separation, now!" Sinise tells the mission commander. The others get similar orders.

You head past the space station, are slingshot around the moon, feel weightless for a moment, then go into hypersleep. But then alarms wake you up! Not only are you in a meteor storm, but your autopilot has broken and Mars is coming up fast! Still, your team performs with flying colors, and you land on Mars safely.

MISSIONS FOR ALL

With entrances from both the exit area and the gift shop, the Advanced Training Lab post-show area is a series of calm, interactive experiences designed for every age group, even toddlers. **Mission Space Race** is a group video game where two teams (each with up to 25 guests) race spaceships from Mars back to Earth. **Space Base** is a preschooler climbing area with a crawl-through rocket, some zany mirrors and a lookout tower. The **Expedition: Mars** video game lets you test your joystick skills as you navigate through dust devils, polar ice and quicksand to rescue fellow astronauts. Everyone will get a kick out of **Postcards from Space,** a video booth which puts your animated face into an alien abduction, saucer invasion or other goofy space scenes and e-mails the results anywhere you choose.

HIDDEN MICKEYS

❶ As overlapping craters on the moon sphere in the courtyard, above and to the left of the Luna 8 impact site. ❷ As tiny round tiles in the courtyard patio, 40 feet from the Fastpass entrance. The ears are blue; the head black. ❸ Along the queue a notepad on a left desk reads "Mickey and Goofy are scheduled to launch at exactly 3 p.m." ❹ As craters on Mars on the far left and ❺ right monitors above the desks. ❻ As part of the grid on a circuit board to the upper left and right of the joystick consoles for the post-show game Expedition Mars. ❼ As black craters in the mural behind the gift shop cash registers, under Minnie's foot. ❽ A profile of Mickey appears in the reddish dust in the photos of space on the gift shop ceiling, above a Spaceman Mickey statue. ❾ As three electrical boxes on the gift shop walls. One is a Mickey profile.

FUN FACTS ›› The logo for Horizons, the previous attraction at this site, appears on the hub of the Gravity Wheel. ›› The ride's music was composed by Trevor Rabin, who, as a member of the band Yes wrote 1983's "Owner of a Lonely Heart." ›› Centrifuges are also used to separate fluids of different densities, such as cream from milk.

▶ The Mission Space Cargo Bay gift shop sells freeze-dried astronaut food.

© DISNEY

The fastest ride at Walt Disney World, Test Track reaches speeds up to 65 mph

Test Track

★★★★★ ✔ 5 min. Capacity: 192. *FastPass* **Fear factor: Intense for those scared by speed. Access: Must be ambulatory. Assistive listening; activated captioning. Height restriction: 40 in. Debuted: 1999.**

Think of it as Snow White's Scary Adventures with a $60 million budget. Themed to an automobile proving ground, Test Track is a big-bucks take on a classic dark ride—sitting in a small vehicle, you speed around corners and through barriers. With 34 turns but no falls or loops, the mile-long course is perfect for those who like excitement but hate roller coasters.

Average Wait	
9am	0 min
10am	30
11am	50
Noon	60
1pm	100
2pm	100
3pm	100
4pm	110
5pm	90
6pm	60
7pm	55
8pm	50
9pm	45

A rhythmic mechanical soundtrack fills the queue, a display of 22 testing demonstrations. Next, a Briefing Room introduces you to engineers Bill and Sherry, who appear on a video link. As he determines your test schedule, she programs it into a computer. "And depending on how you and your vehicle hold up," Bill adds, "we'll even throw a few surprise tests in there."

"Surprise tests?" Sherry asks. "Yeah. Pick one."

With a grin, Sherry chooses the Barrier Test, which slams its car into a wall. Before you can protest, you board your vehicle and off you go. Heading to the (indoor) testing grounds, you rumble over some blocks, skid through some cones and twist up a hill.

Then things go wrong. Did Sherry forget to turn off those Environmental Test robots? Oh no! You get sprayed with acid! Miss that sign that said to turn on your headlights? Oh no! Here comes a truck! And remember that surprise test? Oh no! You're heading right into the...

FUN FINDS

❶ The left anticorrosion robot is labeled "CRUS-T." ❷ The right one is marked "RUS-T." ❸ In the post show, a house of mirrors re-creates GM's truck plant in Shreveport, La. Can you spot the real walls?

HIDDEN MICKEYS

❶ As washers on the left side of a desk near queue area 7b. ❷ As fender stains on the left side of the Corrosion Chamber. ❸ As stains on a car door on that chamber's right side. ❹ As crash-test stickers on an open gas-tank filler door on a car to your left in the Barrier Test area. ❺ As a coil of hoses on that floor, just before the wall.

▶ **The adjacent gift shop offers a unique souvenir: a remote-control Test Track car.**

The Seas with Nemo & Friends

★★★★ ✔ Allow 60 min. Fear factor: None.
Access: Guests may remain in wheelchairs, ECVs.
Reflective captioning, assistive listening. Debuted:
1982, 2007

There's a lot to like in this revamped pavilion, which is themed to the 2003 Disney/Pixar film "Finding Nemo." Quality attractions combine with live marine-life aquariums, exhibits and demonstrations.

First, there's a ride. Once you enter the building, a long walkway takes you under the sea and eventually to a "clam-mobile," a vehicle similar to a Haunted Mansion Doom Buggy. It takes you past animated dioramas and synchronized, see-through video screens that re-create scenes from the movie. In the finale, the animated fish appear to swim with the real ones in the pavilion's huge aquarium.

You exit on the first floor of the two-story pavilion, which includes some interesting sea life exhibits, a

Average Wait	
9am	0 min
10am	10
11am	15
Noon	20
1pm	20
2pm	30
3pm	20
4pm	20
5pm	10
6pm	10
7pm	0
8pm	0
9pm	0

The entrance sign to The Seas with Nemo & Friends pavilion portrays waves crashing onto a rocky shoreline

stunning theatrical show and some fascinating demonstrations.

DOWNSTAIRS

"That was cool!" said the 60-year-old man to his wife, as the couple exited **Turtle Talk with Crush** (★★★★★ ✔ 12 min. Avg wait 15 min). He's right. The pavilion's headline attraction, this theatrical show amazes even the most worldly adult. Appearing on a huge video screen that appears to be a window into the sea, the sea-turtle star of the 2003 film "Finding Nemo" interacts with guests in real-time conversations. He addresses guests individually ("Elizabeth, your polka-dot shell is totally cool!"), asks specific questions ("Is that your female parental unit in the fourth row? She's a total babe!") and reacts to their responses. His facial expressions are priceless. The reptile works in some turtle trivia and welcomes blue tang Dory, who can speak whale perhaps a little too well. Crush mostly talks to kids who sit down front, but sometimes seeks out guests along the theater's center aisle. The show's queue area holds jellyfish, stingrays, and fish from the Great Barrier Reef.

Also downstairs, a **Nemo & Friends** room displays live versions of many of the

▶ To have Crush talk with your child, have her sit down front and wear a funny hat.

A bottlenose dolphin interacts with a young guest in the Seas pavilion's aquarium

movie's stars. Walk-around tubes hold clownfish (Nemo), regal blue tangs (Dory) and Moorish idols (Gill), as well as sea horses, eels, camouflaged frogfish and venomous lionfish and scorpionfish. In a recreation of the film's sunken submarine, **Bruce's Shark World** has kid-friendly interactive displays and photo props.

UPSTAIRS

On the second floor, a huge **saltwater aquarium** simulates a Caribbean coral reef. It's filled with blacknose, brown and sand tiger sharks; some angelfish, cobia, snapper and tarpon; schools of lookdown; a Goliath grouper; sea turtles; and a few rays. An observation tunnel extends into it. There are three daily **fish feedings**, at 10 a.m., 1 p.m. and 3:30 p.m. A diver unloads his pouch in front of you while a narrator adds educational trivia. A side area holds a bachelor herd of **dolphins**—Rainer (born in 1986), Calvin and Kyber (1997) and Malabar (2001). Stop by at 10:45 a.m., 2:15 p.m. or 4:15 p.m. to see a **dolphin training session**, which can include identity-matching, rhythm-identification or echolocation lessons. Huge bars keep the dolphins in their area; otherwise they'd hassle the fish.

A **manatee aquarium** holds two Florida sea cows. You can watch them from above the surface or through an underwater win-

dow on the first floor. Five-minute talks are given at 15 and 45 minutes after each hour.

A **mariculture room** displays how commercial farming can prevent overfishing of clownfish, queen conchs, bamboo sharks and giant clams. There's an exhibit on coral reef propagation. The pavilion's **Kidcot table** is upstairs, too, next to the main aquarium.

FUN FINDS

❶ The Audio-Animatronics gulls on the rocks outside the pavilion squawk "Mine! Mine! Mine!" ❷ "Hey wait! Take me with you!" says sea star Peach as your clam-mobile leaves the aquarium, as the animated fish continue to sing "Big Blue World." "It's a nice song but they just never stop! Never, never, ever, ever, ever!" ❸ Rub Bruce's sandpapery skin in Bruce's Shark World and he'll say "Oooooooo! That's good!"

FUN FACTS ›› The aquarium's 3,500 inhabitants represent 65 species. ›› The observation area has 61 acrylic windows that are 4 to 8 inches thick. Each 24-foot central panel weighs 9,000 pounds. ›› Since the parrotfish naturally eat coral, Disney plants synthetic coral (dental plaster) into the artificial reef.

▶ The pavilion's daily dolphin training sessions are at 10:45am, 2:15pm and 4:15pm.

The animated sea turtle star of "Finding Nemo" interacts with guests in real-time at Turtle Talk with Crush

Soarin' flies you high, virtually, over the Golden Gate Bridge and many other sights of California

Soarin'

★★★★★ ✔ 5 min. Capacity: 174. The Land pavilion. *FastPass* Fear factor: Troubling for some who fear heights. Access: ECV and wheelchair users must transfer. Handheld captioning. Height restriction: 40 in. Debuted: 2005 (Disneyland 2001).

This one may take you by surprise: it really does give you the feeling of flight. More than just a 5-minute film, Soarin' uses an innovative theater to immerse you in its experience. Exhilarating but not scary, it's a smooth, fun fantasy everyone will love.

After you board a multi-seat "hang glider," you lift up to 40 feet into an 80-foot projection dome. From all sides your vision is filled with the beauty of California. You get the impractical delight of gliding over the Golden Gate Bridge and El Capitan, an aircraft carrier and the evening traffic of Los Angeles. Your glider tilts as its travels, your legs dangling free underneath.

The seating device is equipped with special effects. Hidden fans put wind in your hair, odorizers let you smell pines and or-

anges, surround-sound speakers re-create a crashing surf and thunderous waterfall.

The entranceway, waiting area and theater resemble an airport. Cast members dress as uniformed airline employees. The gift stand looks like a ticket counter; the ride's walkway is a concourse; its boarding areas gates. The theater has runway lights; the gliders navigation lights.

HIDDEN MICKEYS

❶ As a blue balloon at the beginning of the Palm Springs scene, held by a man behind a golf cart at the far lower left. ❷ As a small silhouette on the golf ball that flies toward you. Flinch and you'll miss it. ❸ In the second burst of Disneyland fireworks, in the center of the screen.

FUN FACTS ❯❯ Cast members may refer to your flight as "number 5-5-0-5," a sly reference to the ride's opening date of May 5, 2005. ❯❯ Film locations include Redwood Creek, Napa Valley, the Sierra Mountains, the PGA West golf complex in La Quinta and the USS Stennis aircraft carrier off San Diego. ❯❯ The hang glider you see over Yosemite is computer generated. So is that errant golf ball.

Average Wait	
9am	0 min
10am	30
11am	60
Noon	65
1pm	65
2pm	75
3pm	85
4pm	90
5pm	85
6pm	70
7pm	70
8pm	60
9pm	45

▶ **The best Soarin' seats are top-row center. Ask the gate attendant for Row 1, Gate B.**

Living with the Land's quonset hut uses red light to keep its animals calm and reduce algae growth

Living with the Land

★★★ 14 min. Capacity: 20 per boat. The Land pavilion. *FastPass* Access: ECV users must transfer to a wheelchair. Handheld captioning. Debuted: 1982 (as Listen to the Land); revised 1993.

This indoor boat ride takes a subject usually thought of as dull as dirt—agricultural science—and presents it as entertainment. A trip through four working greenhouses, it's filled with plants most Americans never see, and some odd growing techniques. Your boat meanders so close to the plants that you can often smell the leaves and fruit.

Crops include banana palms, papayas, 2-foot jackfruit, 3-foot winter melons and 500-pound Atlantic giant pumpkins. The Creative Greenhouse always has a Mickey-shaped cucumber, pumpkin or watermelon. Many plants hang from strings or trellises, roots in the air. Some grow on overhead conveyor belts.

An aquaculture hut has catfish, sturgeon, shrimp, eels, even young alligators.

The ride begins with a trip through a rainforest, desert and farm.

Average Wait	
9am	0 min
10am	0
11am	0
Noon	0
1pm	0
2pm	0
3pm	0
4pm	0
5pm	0
6pm	0
7pm	0
8pm	0
9pm	0

HIDDEN MICKEYS
❶ As bubbles in the waiting area mural (under the word "nature," a Mickey profile). ❷ In the mural behind the loading area, one green and two blue circles form an angled Mickey (about 7 feet from the right wall, a half-foot off the floor). ❸ As trays of red-leaf lettuce surrounded by trays of green. ❹ In the final greenhouse, as green test-tube caps behind the lab windows.

Circle of Life: An Environmental Fable

★★★ 13 min. Capacity: 482. Avg wait 7 min. Access: Guests may stay in wheelchairs, ECVs. Handheld, reflective captioning; assistive listening. Debuted: 1995.

This movie uses the stars of 1994's "The Lion King" to teach environmental protection. When Timon and Pumbaa start to clear their savanna to build a tourist resort, Simba tells them about a creature who first lived in harmony with nature, but now often forgets that everything is connected in the great circle of life. Live-action sequences show smokestacks, clogged highways and an oil-soaked cormorant, but also wind turbines, electric cars and recycling efforts.

▶ A Behind The Seeds tour ($14, 45 min) offers an informative backstage view of the greenhouses.

A dog greets "shrunken" guests during Honey I Shrunk the Audience. *Photo illustration.*

Honey, I Shrunk the Audience

★★★ 15 min. Preshow: 5 min. Kodak slide show. Capacity: 570. *FastPass* Fear factor: Some children will be terrified by the 3-D animals. In the film, two loud flashes will jolt those of any age. Access: Guests may remain in wheelchairs, ECVs. Assistive listening; reflective captioning. Debuted: 1994.

"Everybody either hates the mice or hates the snake." That's what one cast member says about the 3-D movie Honey, I Shrunk the Audience. Featuring the realistic sensations of mice crawling at your ankles, wild cats in your face and a gigantic snake that tries to bite you, it's the only Epcot attraction that routinely reduces toddlers to shrieking, sobbing lumps. In fact, it seems to be created by someone who takes glee in scaring children. "Here dearie," we can hear some evil Imagineer cackling, "take a seat..."

The film is murky and a little out of focus from most seating locations, and its dialogue is hard to hear.

Average Wait	
9am	10 min
10am	10
11am	10
Noon	10
1pm	10
2pm	10
3pm	10
4pm	10
5pm	10
6pm	10
7pm	closed
8pm	closed
9pm	closed

The story sounds innocent. You're in the auditorium of the Imagination Institute, on hand to watch Professor Wayne Szalinski (Rick Moranis, reprising his role from 1989's "Honey, I Shrunk the Kids") accept the Inventor of the Year Award.

But when the bumbling nerd gets lost in the wings, everything goes wrong. Before you know it the auditorium fills with scurrying rodents (actually prerecorded sounds coupled with some convincing special effects under your seat), a sharp-toothed lynx and ferocious lion pop out of the screen right at your face, then a snake slides into the theater and opens its fangs.

Soon Szalinski fixes things and everyone is safe. But wait—Szalinski blew up the dog, a curious canine who looks in at you, sniffs and sneezes. It's about the only effect where you don't hear crying afterward.

FUN FINDS
❶ An upside-down waterfall propels water up and into a pool in front of the Imagination pavilion. ❷ A single splash of water seems to hop from pad to pad at the Leap Frog Fountain, directly in front of the attraction. ❸ Jelly-like blobs of water hang in midair after they break off from the streams of the nearby Jellyfish Fountain.

▶ The screen has the best focus if you sit in the center rear of the theater.

Journey into Imagination... with Figment

★★ 6 min. Capacity: 224. Fear factor: A dark room has the loud clamor of an oncoming train; a blast of air smells like a skunk; the last room has a sudden flash. Access: Guests may remain in wheelchairs, ECVs. Handheld captioning. Debuted: 1983, revised 1998, 2002.

A tongue-in-cheek open-house tour of the stuffy—and, of course, fictional—Imagination Institute, this slow-moving dark ride is constantly interrupted by Figment, a mischievous (some say bratty) dragon. The ride stops at various labs, where ever-practical Institute director Dr. Nigel Channing (Monty Python alum Eric Idle) attempts to demonstrate how his outfit is studying the human senses in an attempt to "capture and control" human imagination. The free-thinking Figment, however, believes the imagination works best not when it's controlled, but rather when it's set free.

The trip includes a tour of Figment's house, which is upside-down to show how your imagination can really come "home" when you look at things from a new perspective. By the end, Figment's impish antics convince Dr. Channing how much fun a free imagination can be.

Though the ride appeals to many young children, it's a long way from Disney's best and, ironically, one of the company's least imaginative attractions. There is, however, one great effect: in a cage past the Sight Lab, a huge butterfly appears to disappear as you go by. Post-show activities include a chance to conduct music by waving your arms.

The attraction's theme song "One Little Spark," was written by Richard and Robert Sherman, perhaps best known for the infamous "It's a Small World."

FUN FINDS

Lining the entrance hall are office doors of **❶** Professor Wayne Szalinski, the subject of the attraction Honey, I Shrunk the Audience, **❷** 1997's "Flubber" in-

Mischievous dragon Figment takes a call during Journey into Imagination... with Figment

ventor Dr. Phillip Brainard and **❸** Dean Higgins, the principal in 1969's "The Computer Wore Tennis Shoes." **❹** There's a page for Merlin Jones ("Your monkey is on the loose"), the chimp teacher in 1965's "The Monkey's Uncle." **❺** A look-through door lets you see into Dimension Hall, a corridor that seems much longer than it really is. To see the room's actual size look into it from the opposite window, an unmarked pane in the ImageWorks lab just left of the "Magic Photo Studio." **❻** Red tennis shoes sit outside the ride's computer room, a second reference to the 1969 film. **❼** As you enter Figment's house you pass under a real Chevrolet S-10 pickup.

HIDDEN MICKEYS

❶ A Mickey-eared headphone sits in the Sight Lab, on top of the left wheeled table. **❷** As two small circular carpets and a flowered toilet seat in Figment's bathroom. **❸** Between the letters "I" and "M" in the ImageWorks logo. **❹** In place of a letter in the eyechart in the Kodak demonstration area at the entrance to ImageWorks.

Average Wait	
9am	0 min
10am	0
11am	0
Noon	0
1pm	0
2pm	0
3pm	0
4pm	0
5pm	0
6pm	0
7pm	closed
8pm	closed
9pm	closed

▶ A color chart hangs on a wall just past the Sight Lab. Reading it out loud is nearly impossible.

Disney's Hotel du Canada facade recalls Ottawa's Chateau Laurier

of rustic villages, ornate cities, the Scottish influence of the Maritimes and the ruggedness of the Canadian west.

It's dominated by a three-dimensional French Gothic "Hotel du Canada" facade. Based on Ottawa's Chateau Laurier, it sits behind a flower garden inspired by Victoria's Butchart Gardens. Alongside an entrance courtyard, a log cabin, trading post and 30-foot totems represent a Native village. Carved by a Tsimshian Indian in 1998, the leftmost totem (the only real one) shows the Raven folkbird releasing the sun, moon and stars from a carved cedar chest. Up the steps, a stone building reflects British styles of the east coast.

The back of the pavilion recalls the Canadian Rockies. A flowered path leads to a small canyon, where a 30-foot waterfall flows into a stream. Pine-studded slopes surround a shaft opening to what Disney calls Maple Leaf Mine (the entrance to the theater), which is trimmed with shoring and Klondike equipment.

Canada

A funny film, an offbeat rock band and a good restaurant highlight this 3-acre salute to our northern neighbor. The first pavilion you come to if, like most folks, you tour World Showcase in a counterclockwise pattern, Disney's Canadian pavilion is not its most elaborate but often its most crowded.

Unfortunately, exploring this miniature Canada can seem almost as exhausting as hiking the real thing. It's a decent walk back to the theater, and there's no way to get off your feet unless you eat at the restaurant or sit on a sun-baked bench.

All ages will find the movie funny, but overall there's little for kids. A Kidcot table sits next to the restaurant's front door.

For many, the best part of the pavilion is its landscaping and architecture, a mixture

O Canada!

★★★ 14 min. Capacity: 600. No seats. Fear factor: None. Access: Guests may remain in wheelchairs, ECVs. Assistive listening, reflective captioning. Debuted: 1982, revised 2007.

Projected on a wraparound screen in a stand-up theater, this travelogue surrounds you with the people and places of Canada. An update of a film that played here until 2007, it dumps its previous devotion to the outdoors for a joke-filled journey that equally focuses on urban centers. As explained by host Martin Short, the movie wants to correct the misconception

Average Wait	
9am	closed
10am	closed
11am	10 min
Noon	10
1pm	10
2pm	10
3pm	10
4pm	10
5pm	10
6pm	10
7pm	10
8pm	10

▶ Canadian sweet treat: Pure maple sugar candy ($10 per 15-piece box). It melts in your mouth.

The U.K. pavilion's architecture re-creates historic facades. The Sportsman's Shoppe (above right) mimics the white-stone Abbotsford on its left, Henry VIII's red-brick Hampton Court on its right.

that Canada is nothing more than a Great White North. Stand in the center of the theater for the best experience.

The film mixes scenes of mountains and redwoods with stops in Montreal, Quebec City, Toronto, Vancouver and Victoria. The old New Brunswick video is still present, but you no longer hear from that area's heavily accented locals. The Mounties that used to circle around you to start the show now kick off its conclusion. As for music, lumberjack ballads have been replaced by orchestral tracks. The theme song ("Canada, You're a Lifetime Journey") is now sung by 2006 "Canadian Idol" winner Eva Avila.

Unfortunately, whereas the old movie made it appear *you* were riding a dogsled or racing a toboggan, the new one makes Short the participant. None of the new footage wraps around you, the unique feature of these CircleVision 360 presentations. Instead, new segments simply encircle you with multiple versions of the same image.

Developed in the 1950s by Disney video engineer (and original Mickey Mouse animator) Ub Iwerks, the technique uses nine projectors to display synchronized video on screens that wrap around its audience. Filming is done by a nine-lens camera. (Why nine? Because the concept only works with an odd number. Each projector sits in a gap between two screens, yet lines up with one

screen directly across from it.) Once a major type of Disney attraction, CircleVision 360 theaters now exist only at Epcot. The other one is in the China pavilion.

HIDDEN MICKEYS
❶ On both sides of the left totem underneath the top set of hands. ❷ As wine-rack bottles behind Le Cellier's check-in counter.

United Kingdom

Though it doesn't have an attraction, this pavilion has so much to see and do you can spend hours here. You can stop in for a brew at a British pub, relax in a green to a Beatles tribute band, or take in a rowdy street show. The area includes two nice gardens.

Getting around is easy. Buildings line both sides of the promenade, and most all of the stores are interconnected. Kids will enjoy watching the street performers, browsing the toy shop, stopping at the Kidcot table there, and meeting characters Winnie the Pooh, Tigger, Mary Poppins and Alice (from "Alice in Wonderland"). Cast members often chalk out a promenade hopscotch game at 11 a.m.

▶ **U.K. sweet treat:** Cadbury dairy milk caramel candy bar ($3), filled with flowing caramel.

The France pavilion recalls the Paris of a hundred years ago

France

A good spot to get off your feet even if you're not hungry, this pavilion offers a nice film in a cozy theater, a tempting array of pastries and some good dining experiences. A couple of small shops stock fine perfume and wine. The perfume shop is worth walking in just for its aroma.

For children, Belle and the Beast, Princess Aurora and sometimes Marie (from 1970's "The AristoCats") pose for pictures and sign autographs. A Kidcot table sits in the Souvenirs de France gift shop.

You approach the pavilion on a replica of the Pont des Arts footbridge, then gaze upon the Paris of La Belle Époque, "the beautiful time" from 1870 to 1910. Three-story facades have copper and slate mansard roofs, many with chimney pots. A rear shop is based on the Les Halles fruit and vegetable market, an 1850 iron-and-glass-ceilinged Parisian structure. Towering behind it all is the Eiffel Tower, complete with its period-correct tawny finish. Disney built the one-tenth-scale replica using Gustave Eiffel's blueprints.

Each building represents a different historical period. The brick turrets and medieval crenulation of the Sportsman's Shoppe mimic Henry VIII's 16th-century Hampton Court. Its white-stone side is Abbotsford, the 19th-century Scottish estate where Sir Walter Scott wrote novels. Across a street is the 16th-century thatched-roofed cottage of Anne Hathaway, the wife of William Shakespeare. Further down the street sits a half-timbered 15th-century Tudor leaning with age, a plaster 17th-century pre-Georgian, a stone 18th-century Palladian and a home built of angled bricks. Bordering the World Showcase lagoon, the Rose & Crown Pub is divided vertically into three styles— a medieval rural cottage, a 15th-century Tudor tavern and an 1890s Victorian bar.

Impressions de France

★★★★ 18 min. Capacity: 325. Fear factor: None. Access: Guests may remain in wheelchairs, ECVs. Assistive listening, reflective captions. Debuted: 1982.

Set to an ethereal classical score, this movie fills your field of vision with the fairy-tale grandeur of the French landscape. The 200-degree screen packs 40 scenes in 18 minutes. Starting off over the cliffs of Normandy, your trip includes stops at four chateaus, a church, market, vineyard, the gardens of Versailles, a rural bicycle

Average Wait	
9am	closed
10am	closed
11am	10 min
Noon	10
1pm	10
2pm	10
3pm	10
4pm	10
5pm	10
6pm	10
7pm	10
8pm	10

▶ French sweet treat: Strawberry tart ($4) with berries, creamy filling; Boulangerie Pàtisserie.

A Moroccan cast member plays a darbouka drum while waiting out a thunderstorm

tour and an antique Bugatti race through Cannes. And that's just the first five minutes. Still to come are hot-air balloons, fishing boats, a train, Notre Dame and a flight above the Alps.

The only sour note comes early, when the stuffy narrator intones "My Frahnce awakens with the early dawn." Well, duh!

Based on Napoleon III's elegant royal theater in Fontainebleau, the intimate auditorium has padded, if petite, seats.

Morocco

This exotic pavilion features food, merchandise and music that is little-known in the West. It includes some small shops, table-service and fast-food restaurants and an exhibit. A smart layout makes the pavilion easy to visit. Alongside the promenade is a cafe with a tiny sweet shop; a handful of small stores connect to it from behind. The smell of incense in the air will remind some baby boomers of a head shop. Created by the Kingdom of Morocco, the pavilion is managed independently of Disney.

Kids can meet Aladdin, Princess Jasmine and Genie in a room behind the shops. A Kidcot table sits in an open-air market.

Meant to evoke a desert city, buildings are made of brick, tan plaster and reddish sandstone. Like most Moroccan cities, it's divided into two sections, the Ville Nouvelle (new city) and the medina (old town). The new city fronts the promenade. Anchored by two sandstone towers topped with fortress-like crenelation, a fountain courtyard and two buildings recall Casablanca and Marrakesh. Towering over the courtyard is a large prayer tower, a replica of the Koutoubia Minaret in Marrakesh.

The medina of Fez (Morocco's religious and cultural center) lies in back, behind the 8th-century Bab Boujouloud Gate. On the left is the Fez House, a replica of a central courtyard of a traditional Moroccan home, complete with the sounds of the family. On the right is an open-air market, its bamboo roof loosely lashed to thick beams. Restaurant Marrakesh is a Southern Moroccan fortress. Past the restaurant stands a reproduction of the Nejjarine Fountain in Fez. Rising above the old city is a replica of the Chellah Minaret, a 14th-century necropolis found in Morocco's capital city of Rabat.

Landscaping represents Morocco's agriculture—date, olive and sour orange trees; mint and ornamental cabbage plants. Along the shoreline is a working replica of an ancient waterwheel, an ingenious contraption that shuttles water from the lagoon to a grid of nearby desert gardens. The wheel lifts

▶ Moroccan sweet treat: Flakey, honey-drenched baklava ($3); Tangierine Cafe, Oasis snack stand.

The rear of the Japan pavilion resembles the country's historic Nijo and Shirasagijo castles

HIDDEN MICKEYS
❶ As brass plates on a green door of the Souk-Al-Magreb shop. ❷ As a dome window in a minaret on the photo backdrop in Aladdin's indoor meet-and-greet area. Mickey's in the upper right-hand segment, next to a small ladder.

Japan

Though you can't tell it as you walk by, this pavilion includes a full-size department store, two restaurants and an exhibit gallery. No characters appear, but children will enjoy watching candy artist Miyuki and listening to a storyteller. Japan's Kidcot table is located in a small exhibit hall. The pavilion is run by the Mitsukoshi company, Japan's oldest retail business. It was founded in 1673.

Graceful architecture and landscaping symbolize aspects of Japanese culture.

Elements on the left side of the complex represent culture and religion. An 83-foot pagoda that recalls the 8th-century Horyuji Temple in Nara. Its five stories represent the elements from which Buddhists believe all things are created—earth, water, fire, wind and sky. A hill garden's evergreens symbolize eternal life, its rocks the long life of the earth and its koi-filled water the brief life of animals and man. Within the garden, the rustic Yakitori House is modeled on Kyoto's 16th-century Katsura Imperial Villa.

Housing the store and two restaurants, the building on the right represents commerce. Though it may look bland to Western eyes, the structure recalls the ceremonial Shishinden Hall of the 8th-century Gosho Imperial Palace at Kyoto.

The rear of the complex symbolizes Japan's political history. Once you pass through a (very thin) 17th-century wood and stone Nijo castle with its sculptures of mounted samurai warriors, you cross a moat to enter what appears to be the Shirasagijo (White Heron) castle, a 14th-century feudal fortress which, in real life,

water in compartments inside it, then releases it into a series of wooden troughs.

Moroccan artists created the pavilion's detailed tiles from nine tons of ceramic pieces. Deliberate imperfections in the work reflect the Muslim belief that only Allah creates perfection.

Gallery of Arts and History

Used in possession rituals, a guitar-like gimbri is among the antique musical instruments and other artifacts on display in this small three-room hall. The gallery itself is a piece of art, heavily tiled and molded, with an intricate raised ceiling that's a work of art unto itself. Easy to overlook, it sits to the left of the front courtyard.

▶ Japanese sweet treat: Botan rice candy ($1). Each piece has a melt-in-your-mouth wrapper.

Robotic figures of Benjamin Franklin and Mark Twain host the American Adventure attraction

still overlooks the city of Himeji. Its curved stone walls protect white-plaster buildings topped with blue-tile roofs.

Tin Toy Stories

What do robots, astronauts, Godzilla and Mickey Mouse have in common? They were all tin toys, a 1950s Japanese creation. With video narration by "Toy Story" director John Lasseter (also the chief creative officer of Pixar and Disney Animation Studios), this exhibit showcases dozens of these period pieces. It's located at the left rear of the pavilion, in the Bijutsu-kan Gallery.

HIDDEN MICKEYS
❶ In the metal tree grates in the courtyard.
❷ As the center of a koi-pond drain cover, near a bamboo fence.

The American Adventure

The focus of this U.S. pavilion is its attraction, an theatrical history lesson that uses many Audio-Animatronics figures. Plan to spend up to an hour here—30 minutes for the show and up to another 30 in the worthwhile small exhibit of historical artifacts. A Kidcot table is outside, by the gift shop.

The colonial (English Georgian) building uses 110,000 hand-formed bricks, laid with an old-fashioned one-then-a-half technique. The structure uses reversed forced perspective to appear just three stories tall, though it rises more than 70 feet. The illusion only works from a distance; up close the second-story windows look huge.

The American Adventure

★★★★★ ✔ 30 min. Capacity: 1,024. Fear factor: None. Access: Guests may remain in wheelchairs, ECVs. Assistive listening, reflective captioning available. Debuted: 1982; revised 1993, 2007.

Combining film footage with Audio-Animatronics versions of dozens of historic figures, this impressive theatrical attraction is better than any museum presentation in Washington D.C. It's moving as well as educational.

The only World Showcase attraction that is critical of this country, the show embraces the triumphs of America and the optimism of its people, but doesn't

Average Wait	
9am	closed
10am	closed
11am	20 min
Noon	20
1pm	20
2pm	20
3pm	20
4pm	20
5pm	20
6pm	20
7pm	20
8pm	20

▶ **U.S. sweet treat:** Flat, sugary funnel cakes ($6, $8 with ice cream), at the Funnel Cake kiosk.

The Italy pavilion re-creates the Doge's Palace of Venice. Plaster columns resemble veined marble.

twitches and pulls of a real animal. The film, a combination of real and re-created images, pans across paintings and photos in a style later made famous by documentarian Ken Burns.

The show includes both proud and ugly episodes of the American story. Chatting with Franklin after the Revolutionary War, Twain says "You Founding Fathers gave us a pretty good start... [but then] a whole bunch of folks found out that 'We the People' didn't yet mean all the people." Subsequent scenes cover slavery and Native Americans.

A photomontage finale covers events of the past 50 years. Images added in 2007 include that of Apple founder Steve Jobs with the first Macintosh computer and Muhammad Ali lighting the torch at the 1996 Atlanta Olympics.

Twelve statues along the sides of the auditorium represent the Spirits of America.

Hidden from view, the staging system is a mechanical marvel. Just beneath the sight line of the audience is a mass of wiring and hydraulic cables which give movement to the figures. Underneath sits a 175-ton scene changer—a steel frame 65 feet long, 35 feet wide and 14 feet high. It wheels in 13 sets horizontally, raising them into view on telescoping hydraulic supports. Other devices bring in side elements. Behind all that is a 155-foot rear-projection screen that shows a 70mm film. The show uses 35 Audio-Animatronics characters, including three Ben Franklins and three Mark Twains.

National Treasures

This small group of artifacts from famous Americans is worth wandering through. Pieces include one of Abraham Lincoln's stovepipe hats (with frayed edges), a kinetoscope, kinetophone and tinfoil phonograph of Thomas Edison, a microscope used by George Washington Carver, chairs from the homes of Benjamin Franklin and

shy away from our country's flaws and challenges. Ben Franklin and Mark Twain tell the American story, leading you from the time of the Pilgrims through World War II, with help from everyone from George Washington and Thomas Jefferson to Will Rogers and Rosie the Riveter.

At the end, Franklin quotes Thomas Wolfe: "So, then, to every man his chance... the right to live, to work, to be himself, and to become whatever thing his manhood and his vision can combine to make him."

The robots move convincingly. For a moment Franklin appears to walk; Frederick Douglas sways on a rocking raft. Some movements are subtle. Braving Valley Forge, Washington shifts his weight in his saddle, and his horse has the indistinct

▶ Best U.S. beer: Samuel Adams draft ($6), sold at the Fife & Drum Tavern promenade stand.

The outdoor plaza of the Germany pavilion

George Washington and a pool cue from the den of Mark Twain. The exhibit is in the American Heritage Gallery, off on the left side of the lobby.

Italy

Except for watching its street performers, this pavilion offers little to do but spend money. The restaurant is expensive, and there's nothing for kids but a Kidcot table, located behind the La Bottega gift shop.

Ironically, the entrance area is one of the most attractive in the World Showcase. It's designed to look like Venice.

A town square resembles the Piazza San Marco. The two freestanding columns mimic the square's two 12th-century monuments, one topped by the city's guardian, the winged lion of St. Mark the Evangelist, the other crowned by St. Theodore, the city's former patron saint. He's shown killing the dragon that threatened the city of Euchaita, an act that gave him the courage to declare himself a Christian. The 10th-century Campanile (bell tower) dominates the skyline, though this version is just 100 feet tall, less than a third the height of the original. Gold-leafed ringlets decorate an angel on top.

On the left of the square is a replica of the 14th-century Doge's (leader's) Palace. Its facade replicates many details of the original. The first two stories rest on realistic marble columns that front leaded-glass windows. The third floor is tiled and topped by marble sculptures, statues, reliefs and filigree. Adjoining the palace, a stairway and portico reflect Verona.

With the World Showcase lagoon doubling as the Adriatic Sea, a waterfront area includes replicas of the city's bridges, gondolas and striped pilings.

On the right side of the pavilion, the La Bottega gift shop resembles a Tuscany homestead. A sculpture behind it of Neptune and his dolphins recalls Bernini's 1642 fountain in Florence.

Germany

Like its Italian pavilion, Disney's miniature Germany is little more than shops and food. But in this case, it's worth a stop. Not only can you sample the foods at an outdoor cafe (with tables tucked into a recessed patio), the restaurant is the most fun place to eat in the World Showcase. Still, there's no entertainment except in the restaurant.

If you've got children, make sure you stop at the miniature outdoor train village, located to the right of the main pavilion. A walkway leads over track tunnels and alongside the little town, which has its own

▶ Italian sweet treat: A Baci Perugina hazelnut chocolate fortune ball (71¢), sold at La Bottega.

An army of half-size reproductions of ancient "tomb warriors" is displayed in the China pavilion

ond story recall the rule of the Hapsburg emperors. The rear facade combines the looks of two 12th-century castles, the Eltz and the Stahleck.

HIDDEN MICKEYS

❶ In the center of the crown of the left-most Hapsburg emperor statue on the second story of Das Kaufhaus. ❷ A three-dimensional Mickey Mouse is often hiding in the train village. Usually he's a plastic figure standing in a window of a hilltop castle.

China

This pavilion includes a good exhibit, Disney's best remaining CircleVision 360 movie, memorable entertainers, a department store and some good food. For children, Mulan and Mushu from Disney's 1998 film "Mulan" appear. A Kidcot table sits at the rear of the large gift shop.

The China pavilion was refurbished in 2008. Its restaurant and counter-service cafe have new menus and decor.

A Suzhou-style garden and reflecting ponds symbolize the order and discipline of nature. Keeping with Chinese custom, it appears old and in a natural state. Alongside the lagoon, large pockmarked boulders demonstrate a tradition of designing surprising views in landscapes by creating holes in waterside rock formations.

The pavilion is anchored by a triple-arched gate. Behind it sits a miniature Hall of Prayer for Good Harvests, the circular main building of Beijing's 1420 Temple of Heaven, a summer retreat for emperors. Its rotunda alludes to the cycles of nature. Twelve outer columns represent the months of the year and the years in a cycle of the Chinese calendar. Four central columns denote the seasons, a central beam represents earth, a topping beam heaven. A floor stone is cut into nine pieces, reflecting the Chinese belief that nine is a lucky number.

Architecture also includes facades of an elegant home, a school house and shop

wee little live landscape. Four working trains roam out over the rivers and through the woods, each on its own track. Snow White and Dopey appear to the left of the pavilion. Germany's Kidcot table sits inside a teddy bear shop. The village was refurbished in 2008.

As for architecture, an outdoor plaza has some interesting detailing. Its centerpiece is a sculpture of the patron saint of soldiers, St. George, slaying a dragon during a trip to the Middle East. A clock comes to life at the top of each hour with a 3-minute animated display. On the right side of the plaza, the facade of the Das Kaufhaus shop was inspired by the Kaufhaus, a 16th-century merchants' hall in the Black Forest town of Freiburg. Three statues on its sec-

▶ German best beer: Spaten Oktoberfest draft ($8), medium-dark with a roasted nut flavor.

Gift shop facades recall coastal cottages at Disney's Norway pavilion

fronts reflecting European influences. The gallery has a formal saddle-ridge roof line.

Reflections of China

★★★★ 20 min. Capacity: 200. Fear factor: None. Access: Guests may stay in wheelchairs, ECVs. Assistive listening; reflective captioning. Debuted: 1982, updated 2003.

You stand up to watch this poetic travelogue. It includes 30 vistas that wrap around you, which provides a sense that you are actually at the various locations. Sights include everything from the Great Wall and the Forbidden City to the modern cityscapes of Hong Kong and Shanghai to rural areas that include Tibet and Inner Mongolia. One scene was filmed by a camera hanging from a banking helicopter. The host portrays 8th-century Chinese poet Li Bai. The movie's mages are crisp; its sound clear.

Developed in the 1950s by Disney video engineer Ub Iwerks (the original animator of Mickey Mouse), the movie uses nine projectors to synchronize video onto nine screens arranged above its audience. Dubbed CircleVision 360, it places projectors into the gaps between its screens so that everything lines up. Filming is done by a nine-lens camera. Originally a major type of Disney attraction, CircleVision 360 theaters now exist only here and at Epcot's Canada pavilion.

Average Wait	
9am	closed
10am	closed
11am	15 min
Noon	15
1pm	15
2pm	15
3pm	15
4pm	15
5pm	15
6pm	15
7pm	15
8pm	15

Tomb Warriors — Guardian Spirits of Ancient China

The focus of this exhibit is the terra cotta "spirit army" found in the tomb of China's first emperor Qin Shi Huang (259–210 BC). The largest archeological find in the world, the 22-square-mile site contains 8,000 full-size statues arranged in military formations. None of those figures are here, but an army of 200 half-size reproductions offers a sense of the real thing. A side display shows how the site is being excavated. The exhibit also includes two dozen tomb artifacts from the Han, Six, Sui and Tang Dynasties (through 906 AD). They're small, but real. The exhibit is in the Gallery of the Whispering Willow, in the rear center of the pavilion.

Norway

Welcome to Norway, where men are menn and women are kvinner and meatballs are

▶ Chinese sweet treat: A tasty cup of ginger ice cream ($3) from the promenade snack stand.

kjottkakers and all in all there are just way too many consonants. Pronunciation differences aside, the beautiful country is the basis of one of Epcot's best pavilions.

The big attraction is the restaurant, where a gaggle of Disney princesses host every meal. It also has another bevy of beauties: a group of perfectly toned Norwegian natives that greet you at every cash register. The guys look good, too.

On the downside, there's no live entertainment, and if you don't want to dine with the dames no indoor place to eat.

A Kidcot table sits inside the shop.

The grounds combine a variety of architectural styles. Standing at the entrance is a replica of the 13th-century Gol Church of Hallingdal, one of Norway's stave churches that played a key role in the country's movement to Christianity. Next door, a bakery has a sod roof, a traditional way to insulate homes in Norway's mountains. Gift shop facades recall coastal cottages. The restaurant and rear facade re-create Akershus, a 14th-century Oslo fortress.

Maelstrom

★★★ 15 min. (5 min ride, 5 min wait, 5 min film). Capacity: 192. *FastPass* Fear factor: Often dark, with a few scary faces. In the film, two loud flashes will jolt those of any age. Access: Wheelchair, ECV users must transfer. Assistive listening; handheld and reflective captioning. Debuted: 1988.

Themed to Norway's rich seafaring heritage, this indoor boat ride has a quirky appeal. After you set sail in a dragon-headed longboat, you head up a dark chainlift, where a god above urges you to "seek the spirit of Norway." Your search starts off peacefully but becomes a confused chaos (a "maelstrom") after trolls commandeer your ship. Falling into the North Sea, you make landfall at a fishing village.

Average Wait	
9am	closed
10am	closed
11am	5 min
Noon	10
1pm	10
2pm	20
3pm	30
4pm	35
5pm	40
6pm	30
7pm	30
8pm	30

The second half is optional. After you climb out of your boat, you head in to a small theater where you can stay for a short film. "The Spirit of Norway" portrays the daydreams of a young boy. As he examines an old Viking ship, he imagines many types of successful Norwegians. The point? "The spirit of Norway... is in its people!" Cynics will note that, based on the gender of the actors, the spirit of Norway is apparently mostly in its men.

Vikings: Conquerors of the Seas

Axe in hand, a lifesize Rögnvald the Raider stares you down in this five-case exhibit inside the Stave Church Gallery. The displays also include figures of Erik the Red and King Olaf, a detailed scale model of the 9th century Viking ship and authentic swords, arrows and axe blades, some of which date back more than 1,000 years.

HIDDEN MICKEYS

Mickey appears three times in the mural behind the Maelstrom loading area: ❶ As Mickey ears on a Viking in the middle of a ship toward the left, ❷ as shadows on a cruise-line worker's blouse (her right pocket is Mickey's head, her clipboard ring is his nose) and ❸ at the far right on the watch of a bearded construction worker wearing a hardhat. ❹ As black circles on King Olaf II's tunic embroidery in the Stave Church.

Mexico

Great entertainment, good shopping and a mutant freak of an attraction make this pavilion an interesting diversion. Housed in what appears to be an ancient pyramid, its cool, dark marketplace, restaurant and boat ride are all great ways to get out of the sun.

A Kidcot table is in the Casa Mexicana room. Donald Duck signs autographs and poses for pictures in his garb from Disney's surreal 1944 film "The Three Caballeros."

The pyramid facade is modeled on the Aztec temple of serpent god Quetzalcoatl in the ancient city of Teotihuacan. Traditionally the god of the morning and evening star, Quetzalcoatl later became known as the patron of priests, inventor of books and of the calendar, and as the symbol of death and resurrection. His worship involved human sacrifice. Quetzalcoatl himself is depicted by heads along Disney's priests' steps.

Inside the building (actually a large rectangle), the entry portico to the "outdoor" market resembles a Mexican mayor's mansion. Surrounding facades represent the 16th-century silver mining town of Taxco.

Back outside, the Cantina de San Angel cafe looks similar to the 17th-century San Angel Inn in Mexico City.

▶ Norwegian sweet treat: A Daim candy bar ($2), milk chocolate with an almond caramel center.

Gran Fiesta Tour

★★★ 8 min. Capacity: 250. Fear factor: None. Access: ECV users must transfer. Handheld captioning. Debuted: 1982, revised 2007.

An update of the old El Rio Del Tiempo attraction, this dark boat ride is still a tour through the cultural history of Mexico, but now its video screens tell a story based on Disney's 1945 movie "The Three Caballeros." After ladies man Donald Duck, suave Brazilian parrot José Carioca and hyper Mexican cowboy rooster Panchito plan to reunite for a concert in Mexico City, Donald disappears to take in the sights and his feathered friends try to find him.

It's a strange trip. In Acapulco, Donald's bathing suit falls off. At night, he heads to a bar to smooch human señoritas.

As for history, you start off in the 1st century, sailing through a rainforest before passing a Mayan pyramid and drifting into a temple. A Small World-style celebration includes the Day of the Dead. In modern Mexico you pass Acapulco's cliffs and grottos, then travel Mexico City's Reforma Boulevard.

Average Wait	
9am	closed
10am	closed
11am	0 min
Noon	0
1pm	0
2pm	0
3pm	0
4pm	0
5pm	0
6pm	0
7pm	0
8pm	0

The facade of the Mexico pavilion is modeled on the Aztec temple of serpent god Quetzalcoatl

Casa Mexicana

A series of push-button displays promotes the art, food, music and regions of Mexico inside this side room off the courtyard.

'Come here, my little enchilada!' The most bizarre movie in the Disney canon, 1945's "The Three Caballeros" combines psychedelic animation with a storyline that makes Donald Duck a libidinous wolf. Its point? The charms of Latin America. The film's plot is mirrored in the Gran Fiesta attraction. When Donald has a birthday, his presents are pop-up books that include Brazilian playboy parrot José Carioca and Mexican six-gun-shooting cowboy rooster Panchito. The rooster tosses sombreros to his friends, proclaims the trio "three gay caballeros" and takes them on a flying-serape tour of his country. On Acapulco Beach, Donald goes ga-ga for dozens of live-action bathing beauties ("Come to Papa! Come here, my little enchilada!") and keeps losing his swimming suit. At night the duck can't stay away from the clubs, where he dances with still more real-life señoritas. Bizarre animation includes illogical color changes and an overdose of morphing gags.

▶ Best Mexican drink: The premium rocks margarita ($12) available only in the restaurant.

IllumiNations' lasers and fireworks light up the sky over the World Showcase Lagoon

IllumiNations: Reflections of Earth

★★★★ ✓ 15 min. Guests may remain in wheelchairs, ECVs. Preshow: 30 min. of instrumental music from Japan, South America, Scandinavia and Spain. Fear factor: Loud, bright explosions and fire can be intense for toddlers, some preschoolers. World Showcase Lagoon. Debuted: 1988; revised 1997, 1999.

The lights go dark, then a fireball explodes over the stage as thousands stare in awe. As the music begins, fireworks erupt and lasers shoot out from backstage.

Baby boomers may think it's a Pink Floyd concert, but it's actually the beginning of this spectacle of "Wow, man!" effects that concludes every Epcot day. Synchronized to a symphonic world-music score, the extravaganza uses the entire World Showcase as its stage, as strobe lights flash on, and laser beams shoot from the various international pavilions. A rotating Earth moves across the water and shows moving images on its continents, eventually unfolding to reveal a giant torch.

Though there's no narration, the show tells the history of the world in three acts: "Chaos," "Order" and "Celebration."

"Chaos" begins with the dawn of time—the Big Bang and the creation of Earth—symbolized by a lone shooting star that explodes into a fiery "ballet of chaos."

"Order" brings the planet under control. Scenes on the globe depict primal seas and forests; the development of cultural landmarks including the Sphinx, the Easter Island statues and Mount Rushmore; and historical figures such as the Dalai Lama, Martin Luther King Jr., Mother Teresa and, if you look closely, Walt Disney. The coolest image: a video of a running horse that transforms into a cave painting.

The third act, "Celebration," begins as the globe unfurls into a lotus flower and a 40-foot torch rises from its heart. Celebrating both human diversity and the unified spirit of mankind, a fireworks finale heralds a new age of man—the 21st century.

IllumiNations ends with a loud crackle, sending you off to embrace the future. As you leave, the exit song is "We Go On."

WHERE TO WATCH IT
The symmetrical show is directed to the front of the park, at Spaceship Earth. The best viewing spot is the World Showcase Plaza, where you'll see everything as the

▶ Pick out a viewing spot for IllumiNations at least 30 minutes early to get a good view.

designers intended it. The photo on the opposite page was taken there. An added plus: the plaza is the closest viewing spot to Epcot's main exit, so you'll be ahead of the masses when the show ends.

Many locations have a fine view of all the effects, but watching IllumiNations from another location is like sitting at the side, or rear, of a concert stage: It may be interesting, but you don't get the full show.

If you can't make it to the plaza, better spots include the Canadian waterfront; waterside tables at the U.K. pavilion's Rose and Crown (notoriously tough to snare, as you can't reserve one) and the bridge between the U.K. and France. Other decent spots include the balcony above Japan's Mitsukoshi department store; the bridge between China and Germany; and the Cantina de San Angel cafe at Mexico, where you can munch nachos while you watch.

The music can be heard throughout World Showcase. Speakers line the lagoon.

FUN FACTS)) The 2,800 fireworks launch from 34 locations that house 750 mortar tubes. Some ring the shore, just a few feet from unsuspecting guests.)) The four fountain barges pump 5,000 gallons of water per minute.)) The 150,000-pound "inferno barge" has 37 propane nozzles.)) The 28-foot steel globe rotates on a 350-ton barge that houses six computers, 258 strobe lights and an infrared guidance system. Wrapped in more than 180,000 light-emitting diodes, the globe is the world's first spherical video display.)) The performance uses 67 computers in 40 locations.)) The pavilions are outlined in more than 26,000 feet of lights—nearly 5 miles worth.)) The Morocco pavilion does not participate in the show.)) The music supervisor was Hans Zimmer, the composer for the 1994 Disney movie "The Lion King.")) The songs "The Promise" and "We Go On" are performed by country singer Kellie Coffey.)) There are 19 torches around the lagoon, symbolizing the first 19 centuries of modern history. The 20th torch, in the globe, represents the Millennium.)) Disney occasionally tests some effects, or releases leftover fireworks or propane, after midnight. Stay up late at the BoardWalk, Swan and Dolphin or Yacht and Beach Club resort and you may see, or at least hear, an unannounced piece or two of pyro.

Kim Possible World Showcase Adventure

★★★★ ✔ Allow 45–60 min. Recruitment Stations open 9am–7pm; Field Stations 11am–9pm. Fear factor: None. Access: Guests may remain in wheelchairs and ECVs. Debuted: 2009.

A cell-phone-like "Kimmunicator" helps you trigger hidden effects at the World Showcase pavilion in this secret-agent scavenger hunt. Your mission? To save the world, by helping Kim Possible and her friends vanquish a silly villain. You make a reservation to play it.

You get started at one of three Recruitment Stations, which are located in Future World's Innoventions buildings as well as on the bridge between Future World and World Showcase. Here, you swipe your park ticket to receive a Mission Pass, a Fastpass-style reservation ticket for use later in the day. One pass is good for up to three "Kimmunicator" handsets.

When your time comes, you report to your assigned Field Station (located at the International Gateway, Italy or Norway) to get your handset and receive your mission.

Then it's simple: Just follow the instructions on the device. Focused on one particular pavilion (the U.K., France, Japan, Germany, China, Norway or Mexico), you search for clues and eventually capture your bad guy. When you're done, you return the handset to a drop box.

The experience is fun even if you've never heard of Kim Possible. The best parts are the hidden effects. With the touch of a button you can make a jade monkey appear in China, a chimney smoke in Norway, a beer stein yodel in Germany, a waterfall emerge in Japan, a volcano erupt in Mexico. Ever get the urge to turn the tiny townsfolk in Germany's miniature train village into red-eyed zombies? This is your chance.

ON THE ANIMATED TELEVISION SERIES
"Kim Possible," Kim is a redheaded high school cheerleader who saves the world from comic super villains in her spare time—an easier job that dealing with the everyday challenges of being a teenager. She's helped by best friend and crush Ron Stoppable and his pet naked mole rat Rufus, as well as computer genius Wade.

▶ The best IllumiNations viewing spot is World Showcase Plaza. The show plays to that direction.

Disney's
Hollywood
Studios

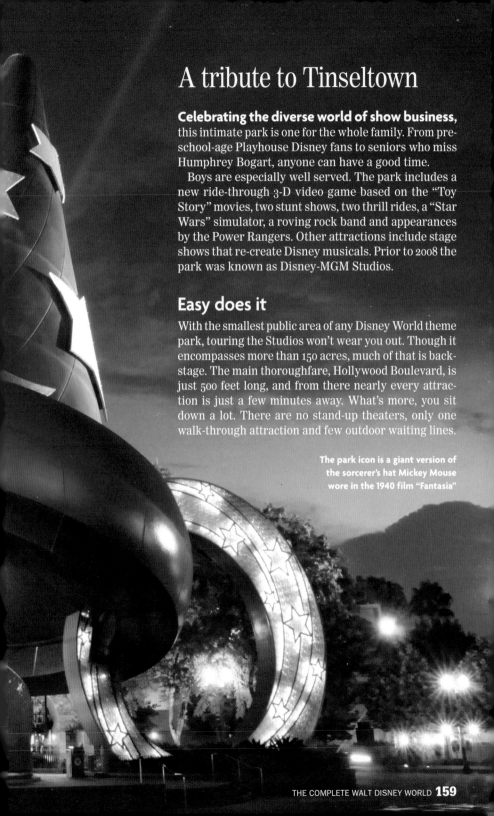

A tribute to Tinseltown

Celebrating the diverse world of show business, this intimate park is one for the whole family. From pre-school-age Playhouse Disney fans to seniors who miss Humphrey Bogart, anyone can have a good time.

Boys are especially well served. The park includes a new ride-through 3-D video game based on the "Toy Story" movies, two stunt shows, two thrill rides, a "Star Wars" simulator, a roving rock band and appearances by the Power Rangers. Other attractions include stage shows that re-create Disney musicals. Prior to 2008 the park was known as Disney-MGM Studios.

Easy does it

With the smallest public area of any Disney World theme park, touring the Studios won't wear you out. Though it encompasses more than 150 acres, much of that is back-stage. The main thoroughfare, Hollywood Boulevard, is just 500 feet long, and from there nearly every attraction is just a few minutes away. What's more, you sit down a lot. There are no stand-up theaters, only one walk-through attraction and few outdoor waiting lines.

The park icon is a giant version of the sorcerer's hat Mickey Mouse wore in the 1940 film "Fantasia"

FASTPASS RETURN TIMES

Use the table below to help plan your Hollywood Studios day. Note that an entire day's worth of Fastpasses for Toy Story Mania typically runs out by noon.

ATTRACTION	9A	10A	11A	Noon	1P	2P	3P	4P	5P	6P	7P	8P	9P
Indiana Jones	*	*	*	*	*	*	*	*	*	*	CLSD	CLSD	CLSD
LMA	*	*	*	*	*	*	*	*	*	*	CLSD	CLSD	CLSD
Little Mermaid	10:10	11:10	12:10	1:20	2:20	4:00	5:00	6:20	7:20	8:20	9:00	OUT	OUT
R'n'R Coaster	10:10	11:30	12:40	2:50	4:50	6:50	8:20	9:20	OUT	OUT	OUT	OUT	OUT
Star Tours	10:05	11:05	12:05	1:05	1:40	2:40	3:40	4:40	5:40	6:20	7:20	8:20	OUT
Tower of Terror	10:10	10:40	11:40	1:20	2:20	4:45	6:40	8:30	9:25	OUT	OUT	OUT	OUT
Toy Story Mania	10:10	4:35	8:10	OUT	OUT	OUT	OUT	OUT	OUT	OUT	OUT	OUT	OUT

* During our survey period, Fastpasses for the Indiana Jones Stunt Spectacular and Lights Motors Action were always good for the next scheduled show. Data based on surveys taken on random days during the summer of 2008.

The park is divided into two sections. The front is Old Hollywood. This 1940s world features period architecture, signs and stoplights. The rear resembles a production center and backlot. Its entrance arch is modeled on the Paramount Studio gate; side streets have faux security gates. Its "Streets of America" faux studio set is dominated by New York Street, a 500-foot Beaux Arts thoroughfare based on the Big Apple's West 40th St. A crossing street recalls San Francisco. Details include graffiti, soot stains and a stairway that appears to lead to a subway station.

Architecture

The front of the park re-creates the look of Los Angeles during the mid-20th century. The turquoise entrance structures and their white-ringed pylons reflect 1935's art deco Pan Pacific Auditorium, a sports and music hall.

Hollywood Boulevard is a dreamlike, 500-foot version of the iconic Tinseltown thoroughfare. Its 15 facades are modeled on actual structures in Los Angeles. A Crossroads of the World gift kiosk is a replica of a Streamline Moderne stand at the 1937 Crossroads of the World shopping center. Sid Cahuenga's is a tribute to 1930s and 1940s Craftsman bungalows that became Hollywood tourist shops. The Disney & Co. store brings back a Hollywood veterinary clinic and the black-marble-and-gilt Security Pacific Bank building, itself a copy of L.A.'s Richfield Oil Building, whose black and gold trim represented the "Black Gold" of the oil industry. Keystone Clothiers includes facades of Hollywood's Max Factor Building and Jullian Medical Building.

A MAGICAL DAY

8:15a	As you wait for the gates to open (usually at 8:45 a.m.), visit the adjacent Guest Relations window to pick up a Times Guide and confirm the 11 a.m. Beauty and the Beast show time. If you haven't already, make meal reservations. When the gate opens, be among the first at the Sunset Boulevard rope barrier.	**9:00a**	Get Fastpasses for Toy Story Mania.
		9:10a	The Twilight Zone Tower of Terror.
		9:40a	The Great Movie Ride.
		10:30a	Beauty and the Beast — Live on Stage. Sit in the center of one of the first non-handicapped rows.
		Noon	Lunch at the Hollywood Brown Derby. On your way to the

A cheerleader collects screams from the crowd during Disney's Block Party Bash

The right side of the street is equally inspired. The photo center is a clone of The Darkroom, a 1938 Hollywood photo shop known for its front window trim that looked like a giant camera. Celebrity 5 & 10 evokes an Art Deco building that once housed a J.J. Newberry five and dime. Next door, Adrian and Edith's Head to Toe and the adjacent L.A. Cinema Storage recall a two-block Spanish Colonial Revival area.

Finally, the Hollywood Brown Derby is modeled from the 1929 second location of the famous restaurant, a legendary din-ing spot for hundreds of movie stars. Inside the buildings is a ceiling lover's paradise. Cover Story's film-roll theme recalls Frank Lloyd Wright. The tiny Head to Toe foyer towers 30 feet.

At the end of the road is a full-scale model of Grauman's Chinese Theatre. The front is designed from the same blueprints as the 1927 building and has essentially all the original's trim pieces and detailing. The only real difference: this one has its ticket booth off to the side.

	restaurant, send one person to the Rock 'n' Roller Coaster for Fastpasses. While you eat, check your Times Guide for Indiana Jones show times then fine-tune the following plan:	**6:00p**	Dinner at '50s Prime Time Cafe. Share s'mores for dessert.
		7:30p	Muppetvision 3-D.
		8:30p	Fantasmic (if scheduled). You should get there in time to get good seats for the 10 p.m. show.
2:00p	Indiana Jones Stunt Spectacular.		
2:45p	Block Party Bash.	**Note**	Those with young children may want to substitute Playhouse Disney—Live on Stage for one of the choices above.
4:00p	Rock 'n' Roller Coaster.		
5:00p	Toy Story Mania.		

Echo Lake recalls downtown L.A.'s Echo Lake Park, where 1920's silent-movie czar Mack Sennett shot many of his Keystone Comedies.

Two snack stands re-create that era's programmatic architecture. Appearing to be a tramp steamer is Min & Bill's Dockside Diner. What appears to be an apatosaurus is Dinosaur Gertie's Ice Cream of Extinction. This tribute to 1914 cartoon star Gertie the Dinosaur includes footprints in the sidewalk. Nearby, the Hollywood & Vine restaurant evokes a cafeteria that once stood on North Vine, near the actual Hollywood Blvd.

Sunset Boulevard begins with a replica of the 1940 Mulholland Fountain in Griffith Park. On your left, the Colony Sunset shop is New York City's Colony Theatre as it appeared in 1928, when it premiered the first Mickey Mouse sound cartoon, "Steamboat Willie." The Sunset Ranch Market recalls the 1934 Los Angeles Farmers Market.

On your right, the Legends of Hollywood store has the facade and spiral corkscrew tower of the 1938 Academy Theater. The Once Upon a Time shop is a dead ringer for the 1926 Carthay Circle Theatre, which hosted the premiere of "Snow White and the Seven Dwarfs" in 1937. Next up, the Theater of the Stars is an homage to the 1922 Hollywood Bowl.

The entrance to Fantasmic's Hollywood Hills Amphitheater draws its design from the Los Angeles Ford Amphitheater nestled in the Hollywood Hills. The stone entranceway to The Twilight Zone Tower of Terror is a nearly exact replica of the Hollywood Gates, the 1923 entrance to the Hollywoodland real-estate development. The Hollywood Tower Hotel recalls the Spanish Revival look of the 1902 Mission Inn in Riverside, Calif.

In the rear of the park, buildings were inspired by the Walt Disney Studios in

---

BY THE NUMBERS 》》 **122:** Height, in feet, of the Sorcerer's Hat. **350:** How tall, in feet, Mickey Mouse would have to be to wear it. 》》 **300,000:** Gallons of water that will fit in the water tower. **0:** Gallons of water in the tower, which is a prop.

California. Pixar Place is styled after the Pixar headquarters in Emeryville, Calif.

History

The park opened as a production facility in 1988 and to the public on May 1, 1989. A Hollywood-style gala, the Grand Opening featured legends Lauren Bacall, George Burns, Audrey Hepburn and Bob Hope. "Welcome to the Hollywood that never was and always will be," then-CEO Michael Eisner said.

Originally the park's soundstages and backlot streets were used for real movie and television work. A young Christina Aguilera, Britney Spears and Justin Timberlake starred in Disney Channel's "New Mickey Mouse Club," which was filmed inside today's Toy Story Mania building from 1989 to 1994. The animation building produced cartoons and feature films such as 2002's "Lilo & Stitch."

LANDSCAPE FUN FINDS

Hollywood Boulevard: Second-story offices include those of ❶ tailor Justin Stitches and ❷ Allen Smythee Productions* above a second entrance to Keystone Clothiers. **Echo Lake:** Offices to the right of the pond include ❶ an acting-and-voice studio run by thespian Ewell M. Pressum, voice coach Singer B. Flatt and account executive Bill Moore, ❷ a dentistry run by C. Howie Pullum, Ruth Canal and Les Payne, ❸ Holly-Vermont Realty, a real business that in 1923 rented its back room to Walt and Roy Disney to use as their first office. ❹ Above, from 1988's "Who Framed Roger Rabbit," a billboard promotes Roger Rabbit employer Maroon Studios. ❺ The office of that film's grumpy gumshoe Eddie Valiant sits above the Hollywood & Vine restaurant. Roger has crashed through a window. Crates left of Min & Bill's snack stand refer to classic films: ❻ One to "Charles Foster Kane, Xanadu Compound, Gulf Coast, Florida, to the Rosebud Sled Co." refers to 1941's "Citizen Kane." ❼ A crate from "Curtiz Wine & Spirits Ltd. to Rick Blaine" references 1942's "Casablanca." ❽ One marked

At left, Hollywood's Carthay Circle Theatre in 1927. Above, Disney's tribute.

"From Fleming Fashions Ltd., Atlanta to Scarlett O'Hara, Tara Plantation, 121539 Mitchell Lane, Jonesboro County, Georgia," alludes to the director, premiere city, lead character, main setting, premiere date, novelist and inspiration (Jonesboro, Ga.) of 1939's "Gone With the Wind." ❾ A crate from "Wainwright Enterprises to George Bailey of Bedford Falls" recalls the 1946 film "It's a Wonderful Life." ❿ A fifth crate is addressed to fictional producer Max Bialystock of 1968's "The Producers." ⓫ On Sunset Blvd., an office above Villains in Vogue is home to the International Brotherhood of Second Assistant Directors (IBSAD, say it carefully), a union with the motto "We're standing behind you."**

HIDDEN MICKEYS
Hollywood Boulevard: ❶ A pattern of Mickey ears is in the black molding beneath the second-floor windows of Cover Story. **Echo Lake:** ❶ As washers used to secure coffee-table tops in the Tune-In Lounge. ❷ As napkin and utensil holders at 50s Prime Time Cafe. **Sunset Blvd.:**

❶ Small impressions along the curbs read "Mortimer & Co. Contractors 1928," a reference to Walt's original name for his 1928 cartoon mouse. ❷ In Rosie's All-American Cafe, as gauges on a welding torch behind the counter. **Backlot:** At Toy Story Pizza Planet ❶ in a mural above the cash registers, as star clusters left of the spaceship near the pizza-slice constellation and ❷ as craters in the moon in a large mural above the arcade (a three-quarter Mickey profile). At Mama Melrose's Ristorante Italiano ❸ as a spot on the right shoulder of a dalmation in a lobby statue, and ❹ as a leaf on a vine to the right of that eatery's check-in podium, at the bottom right of a lattice fence. ❺ At the Writer's Stop, as yellow stickers on ceiling stage lights.

* "Allen Smythee" was an official pseudonym-credit used by film, television and music-video directors between 1968 and 1999 when they did not want to be associated with a production. ** During the Great Depression, "Second Assistant Director" was a mercy title given to studio go-fers, who were often told to "Get coffee and stand behind me."

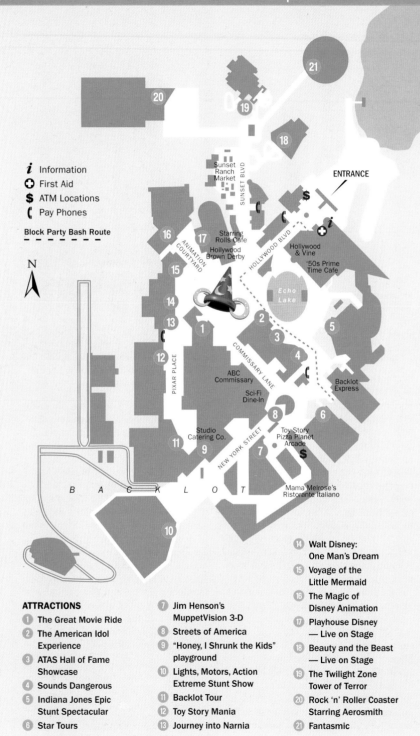

i Information

✚ First Aid

$ ATM Locations

(Pay Phones

- - - Block Party Bash Route

N

Sunset Ranch Market

SUNSET BLVD

ENTRANCE

Starring Rolls Cafe

Hollywood Brown Derby

ANIMATION COURTYARD

HOLLYWOOD BLVD

Hollywood & Vine

'50s Prime Time Cafe

Echo Lake

PIXAR PLACE

ABC Commissary

COMMISSARY LANE

Sci-Fi Dine-In

Backlot Express

Studio Catering Co.

Toy Story Pizza Planet Arcade

NEW YORK STREET

Mama Melrose's Ristorante Italiano

B A C K L O T

ATTRACTIONS

1. The Great Movie Ride
2. The American Idol Experience
3. ATAS Hall of Fame Showcase
4. Sounds Dangerous
5. Indiana Jones Epic Stunt Spectacular
6. Star Tours
7. Jim Henson's MuppetVision 3-D
8. Streets of America
9. "Honey, I Shrunk the Kids" playground
10. Lights, Motors, Action Extreme Stunt Show
11. Backlot Tour
12. Toy Story Mania
13. Journey into Narnia
14. Walt Disney: One Man's Dream
15. Voyage of the Little Mermaid
16. The Magic of Disney Animation
17. Playhouse Disney — Live on Stage
18. Beauty and the Beast — Live on Stage
19. The Twilight Zone Tower of Terror
20. Rock 'n' Roller Coaster Starring Aerosmith
21. Fantasmic

Park resources

BABY CARE

The Baby Care Center *(inside Guest Relations, which is located just inside the park entrance)* has changing rooms, nursing areas and a microwave. It sells diapers, formula, pacifiers and over-the-counter medications.

FIRST AID

The First Aid Center *(next to Guest Relations just inside the park entrance)* handles minor emergencies. Registered nurses are on hand.

GUEST RELATIONS

The Guest Relations center *(just inside the park entrance)* has cast members trained to answer questions and solve problems in multiple languages, maps and Times Guides for all Disney World theme parks, exchanges foreign currency and stores items found in the park that day.

LOCKERS

The Crossroads of the World kiosk *(Hollywood Blvd., just inside the park entrance)* rents lockers (at Oscar's Super Service) for $5 per day plus a $5 deposit.

LOST CHILDREN

Report lost children to Guest Relations or any cast member. Kids who lose parents should tell a cast member.

MONEY MATTERS

Disney's Hollywood Studios has ATMs beside the package pickup window at the park entrance and inside the Toy Story Pizza Planet counter-service cafe. All park cash registers take credit cards and traveler's checks.

PACKAGE PICKUP

Anything you buy can be sent to Package Pickup *(at Oscar's Super Service just inside the park entrance)* for you to pick up as you leave. Purchases can also be delivered to your Disney hotel or shipped to your home.

PARKING

For day guests parking is $12 a day. Those staying at a Disney resort, and annual passholders, get free parking.

SECURITY CHECK

Security guards inspect all bags and purses at the park entrance.

STROLLERS

Single strollers *($15 per day, $13 per day length of stay)* and double strollers *($31 per day, $27 per day length of stay)* are available at Oscar's Super Service station, just inside the park entrance on the right. If you misplace your stroller, a limited

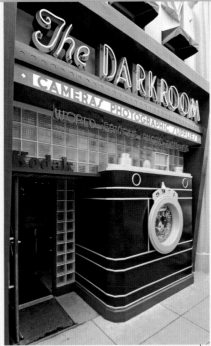

The Darkroom shop (Hollywood Blvd.) is the park's camera and PhotoPass center

number of replacements are available at Tatooine Traders next to Star Tours.

TIP BOARD

This board *(Hollywood Blvd. at Sunset Blvd.)* displays waiting times for popular attractions.

TRANSPORTATION

Boats and walkways lead to Disney's Hollywood Studios and the BoardWalk, Yacht and Beach Club and Swan and Dolphin resorts. Buses run from all other Disney resorts, Animal Kingdom, Blizzard Beach, Epcot and Disney's Wide World of Sports. Magic Kingdom guests arrive by taking a monorail to the Transportation and Ticket Center then a bus to the park. There is no direct service from the theme park to Downtown Disney or Typhoon Lagoon.

WHEELCHAIRS, ECVS

Oscar's Super Service, just inside the park entrance, rents wheelchairs *($10 per day, $8 per day length of stay)* and Electric Convenience Vehicles *($45 per day plus a $20 deposit)*. Replacement wheelchairs are available at the In Character gift shop in the Animation Courtyard. ECVs book quickly; many are used by overweight guests.

Attractions

Hollywood Boulevard

THE GREAT MOVIE RIDE
★★★★ ✓ 22 min. Avg wait 20 min. "Alien" creature moves toward you. Pg 172
Indoor tram tours classic film scenes.

Echo Lake

THE AMERICAN IDOL EXPERIENCE
★★★★ ✓ 20–25 min. Finale 45 min. Pg 175
Talent contest features amateur singers.

INDIANA JONES EPIC STUNT SPECTACULAR
★★★★ 30 min. Avg wait 10 min. *FastPass* Pg 176
Physical stunt show reenacts film scenes.

SOUNDS DANGEROUS
★★ 12 min. Avg wait 7 min. Some scary sounds. Pg 175
Dark sound-effects show uses headphones.

Backlot

"HONEY, I SHRUNK THE KIDS' PLAYGROUND
★★★ Unlimited. No wait. Pg 185
Playground has larger-than-life props.

JIM HENSON'S MUPPETVISION 3-D
★★★★ ✓ 25 min. Avg wait 15 min. Pg 180
3-D movie has classic Muppet wit.

LIGHTS, MOTORS, ACTION EXTREME STUNT SHOW
★★★ 33 min. Avg wait 20 min. *FastPass* Pg 183
Outdoor car, motorcycle stunt show.

STAR TOURS
★★★ 7 min. Avg wait 25 min. Height restriction 40 in. Can cause motion sickness. *FastPass* Pg 178
A "Star Wars" trip in a motion simulator.

STUDIO BACKLOT TOUR
★★ 30–40 min. Avg wait 20 min. Water demo uses fire; canyon scene simulates disasters. Pg 184
Walking/tram tour shows movie secrets.

Animation Courtyard

JOURNEY INTO NARNIA: PRINCE CASPIAN
★ 15 min. Avg wait 8 min. Violent movie clips. Pg 189
Guests stand to watch glorified trailer.

THE MAGIC OF DISNEY ANIMATION
★★★★ ✓ 10 min film, 10 min Animation Academy, rest self-guided. Avg wait 20 min. Pg 186
Short film, computer games, character meet-and-greet, exhibits, drawing lesson.

PLAYHOUSE DISNEY—LIVE ON STAGE
★★★★★ 22 min. Avg wait 25 min. Pg 188
A puppet show for preschoolers.

VOYAGE OF THE LITTLE MERMAID
★★★★ 17 min. Avg wait 25 min. Giant villain Ursula makes some toddlers cry. *FastPass* Pg 187
Musical stage show tells Ariel's story with puppets, live singer, special effects.

WALT DISNEY: ONE MAN'S DREAM
★★★ ✓ Allow 35 min; includes 16 min film. No wait. Pg 189
Memorabilia, short biographical film.

Pixar Place

TOY STORY MANIA
★★★★★ ✓ 4 min. Avg wait 80 min. *FastPass* Pg 190
Ride-through series of 3-D video games.

Sunset Boulevard

BEAUTY AND THE BEAST—LIVE ON STAGE
★★★★★ ✓ 25 min. Gaston stabs the Beast. Pg 193
Stage musical retells "tale old as time."

ROCK 'N' ROLLER COASTER STARRING AEROSMITH
★★★★ 1 min 22 sec. Avg wait 80 min. Height restriction 48 in. Very fast start. *FastPass* Pg 194
Dark roller coaster loops, blares rock tunes.

THE TWILIGHT ZONE TOWER OF TERROR
★★★★★ ✓ 25 min. Avg wait 50 min. Height restriction 40 in. Sudden, swift drops and lifts in the dark; creepy atmosphere. *FastPass* Pg 196
Out-of-control elevator ride falls 13 stories.

Street Party

DISNEY'S BLOCK PARTY BASH
★★★★★ ✓ 22 min. Arrive 30 min early. Pg 201
Interactive street party with Pixar stars.

Fireworks

FANTASMIC
★★★★ 25 min. Arrive 90 min early. Loud noises, bright flashes, fire, villains. Pg 203
Evening outdoor extravaganza has lasers, dancing fountains, water screens.

Character locations

ANNIE, JUNE, LEO, QUINCY "Little Einsteins."
Animation Courtyard; June, Leo also at ❄ Play 'N Dine character meals, Echo Lake.

BELLE Star of 1991's "Beauty and the Beast."
Sorcerer's Hat, Hollywood Blvd.

CHIP 'N DALE Chipmunks in 1940s, 1950s cartoons.
Sorcerer's Hat, Hollywood Blvd.

DAISY DUCK Donald Duck's girlfriend.
Sorcerer's Hat, Hollywood Blvd.

DONALD DUCK
Sorcerer's Hat, Hollywood Blvd.

❄ **Air-conditioned waiting line**

GEPPETTO Woodcarver in 1940's "Pinocchio." Sorcerer's Hat, Hollywood Blvd.

GREEN ARMY MEN From 1995's "Toy Story." Pixar Place, roaming the street.

GOOFY Sorcerer's Hat, Hollywood Blvd.

HANDY MANNY From TV series "Handy Manny." Animation Courtyard.

MR. AND MRS. INCREDIBLE, FROZONE From 2004's "The Incredibles." ❋ The Magic of Disney Animation, Animation Courtyard

JOJO AND GOLIATH From TV series "JoJo's Circus." Animation Courtyard; also at ❋ Play 'N Dine character meals, Echo Lake.

KIM POSSIBLE, RON STOPPABLE Stars of the TV series "Kim Possible." Streets of America.

LIGHTNING MCQUEEN, 'MATER Stars of 2006's "Cars." Luigi's Garage, Streets of America.

LILO, STITCH Stars of 2002's "Lilo & Stitch." Sorcerer's Hat, Hollywood Blvd.

MARY POPPINS, PENGUINS From 1964's "Mary Poppins." Sorcerer's Hat, Hollywood Blvd.

MICKEY MOUSE ❋ The Magic of Disney Animation, Animation Courtyard; Sorcerer's Hat, Hollywood Blvd.

MIKE, SULLEY Stars of 2001's "Monsters, Inc." Backlot, at exit to Backlot Tour.

MINNIE MOUSE Sorcerer's Hat, Hollywood Blvd.

PINOCCHIO Star of 1940's "Pinocchio." Sorcerer's Hat, Hollywood Blvd.

PLUTO Sorcerer's Hat, Hollywood Blvd.

POCAHONTAS, GOV. RADCLIFF From 1995's "Pocahontas." Sorcerer's Hat, Hollywood Blvd.

POWER RANGERS From various TV series. Backlot, in front of Lights, Motors, Action.

PRINCE CASPIAN Star of 2008's "The Chronicles of Narnia: Prince Caspian." ❋ Journey Into Narnia: Prince Caspian, Animation Courtyard.

FRIAR TUCK, LITTLE JOHN Merry men in 1973's "Robin Hood." Sorcerer's Hat, Hollywood Blvd.

QUEEN OF HEARTS, TWEEDLEDEE, TWEEDLEDUM From 1951's "Alice in Wonderland." Sorcerer's Hat, Hollywood Blvd.

SNOW WHITE, EVIL QUEEN From 1937's "Snow White and the Seven Dwarfs." Sorcerer's Hat, Hollywood Blvd.

WOODY, BUZZ LIGHTYEAR Stars of 1995's "Toy Story," 1999's "Toy Story 2." ❋ Picture Shootin Corral, Pixar Place.

The Power Rangers greet guests along the Streets of America, near Lights Motors Action

Street performers

CITIZENS OF HOLLYWOOD
30 min. Hourly 10am–2:30pm. 4:15, 5:15. Various spots on Hollywood Blvd. and Sunset Blvd.
This improvisational troupe roams the park's Olde Hollywood section portraying the residents of a 1940s Tinseltown. The oddball characters include directors, divas, has-beens, wanna-bes and public works employees. Audience-participation skits include a dating game and celebrity spelling bee. (If you see her, tell script girl Paige Turner the Neals said hi.)

HIGH SCHOOL MUSICAL 3: RIGHT HERE! RIGHT NOW!
20 min. Hourly 10am–1pm, 4:35pm, 5:35pm. Sorcerer's Hat, Hollywood Blvd.
Fourteen young entertainers perform lively choreographed routines to songs from the "High School Musical" movie series. Children join in.

JEDI TRAINING ACADEMY
20 min. Hourly 10am–5pm. To the left of Star Tours, Backlot.
Kids learn lightsaber techniques then duel Darth Vader. Arrive 15 minutes early to give your child a good chance at participating.

Melvin Macheezmo, Citizens of Hollywood

MULCH, SWEAT AND SHEARS
25 min. 11am, noon, 1pm, 4, 5 Tues, Thurs–Sat; 1pm, 4, 5 Wed. Streets of America.
Humorous landscape-crew-turned-rock band invites audience members to play cow bells, air guitars.

Shopping
Though you'll find a generic mix of Disney souvenirs at many park shops— the largest is Mickey's of Hollywood (*Hollywood Blvd.*)—many items are concentrated in particular locations:

Apparel
CAPS AND HATS
General: Mouse About Town and Sunset Ranch Souvenirs (*both Sunset Blvd.*).
Monogrammed Mickey ears: Adrian & Edith's Head to Toe (*Hollywood Blvd.*).
CHARACTER COSTUMES
Princess and Tinker Bell: In Character (*Animation Ctyrd.*). **Minnie Mouse:** The Studio Store (*Animation Ctyrd.*).
CHILDREN'S WEAR
L.A. Cinema Storage (*Hollywood Blvd.*), Stage 1 Co. Store (*next to MuppetVision 3-D, Backlot*).
FASHION
Keystone Clothiers (*Hollywood Blvd.*).
SANDALS
Keystone Clothiers (*Hollywood Blvd.*), Mickey's of Hollywood (*Hollywood Blvd.*).

SPORTS APPAREL
Mouse About Town (*Sunset Blvd.*), Youse Guys Moychendise (*Backlot*).
T-SHIRTS
General: Keystone Clothiers and Mickey's of Hollywood (*Hollywood Blvd.*), Stage 1 Co. Store (*next to MuppetVision 3-D, Backlot*). **Attraction:** Indiana Jones Adventure Outpost and Indiana Jones souvenir carts (*Echo Lake*); Playhouse Disney stand (*Animation Ctyrd.*); Rock Around the Shop (*Sunset Blvd.*); Tatooine Traders (*Star Tours exit, Echo Lake*); Tower Gifts (*Sunset Blvd.*).

Other merchandise
ART
Traditional: Animation Gallery (*Animation Ctyrd.*) has lithographs, posters and two-foot-tall character figurines. Once Upon a Time and Sunset Club Couture (*Sunset Blvd.*) artists personalize character sketches. **Movie posters:** American Film Institute Showcase (*Studio Backlot Tour exit, Backlot*); Sid Cahuenga's One-Of-A-Kind (*Hollywood Blvd.*).
BOOKS
Disney titles: Animation Gallery (*Animation Ctyrd.*); The Writer's Stop (*Backlot*). **Bestsellers, novels:** The Writer's Stop (*Backlot*). **Movie and television:** American Film Institute Showcase (*Studio Backlot Tour exit, Backlot*); Sid Cahuenga's One-Of-A-Kind

(Hollywood Blvd.). **Star Wars:** Tatooine Traders *(Star Tours exit, Echo Lake).* **Twilight Zone:** Tower Gifts *(Twilight Zone Tower of Terror exit, Sunset Blvd.).*

CANDY
Sweet Spells *(Sunset Blvd.)* makes its own caramel and candy apples, chocolate-covered strawberries, cotton candy and fudge while you watch.

CHRISTMAS ITEMS
It's a Wonderful Shop *(Backlot),* Mouse About Town *(Sunset Blvd.).*

HOUSEWARES
Celebrity 5 and 10 *(Hollywood Blvd.),* Once Upon a Time *(Sunset Blvd.),* The Writer's Stop *(Backlot).*

JEWELRY
Fine: Sunset Club Couture *(Sunset Blvd.).* **Costume:** Indiana Jones souvenir carts *(Echo Lake),* Keystone Clothiers *(Hollywood Blvd.),* Mouse About Town and Sunset Ranch Souvenirs *(Sunset Blvd.).*

PET PRODUCTS
The Writer's Stop *(Backlot).*

PINS
Pin central: The open-air shop underneath the Sorcerer's Hat *(Hollywood Blvd.).* **General:** The Hollywood Junction kiosk *(Hollywood Blvd. at Sunset Blvd.).*

TOYS
Celebrity 5 and 10 *(Hollywood Blvd.),* Golden Age Souvenirs *(Echo Lake),* L.A. Cinema Storage *(Hollywood Blvd.),* The Stage 1 Co. Store *(at MuppetVision 3-D, Backlot),* Studio Prop Shop *(Backlot),* Tatooine Traders *(Star Tours exit, Echo Lake).*

WATCHES
General: Mouse About Town and Sunset Ranch Souvenirs *(Sunset Blvd.).* **Custom:** Artists at Sunset Club Couture *(Sunset Blvd.)* personalize character sketches and reduce them onto watch dials.

Specialty shops

HANNAH MONTANA
Legends of Hollywood *(Sunset Blvd.).*

HIGH SCHOOL MUSICAL
Legends of Hollywood *(Sunset Blvd.).*

INDIANA JONES
Indiana Jones Adventure Outpost and Indiana Jones souvenir carts *(Echo Lake).*

MINNIE MOUSE
The Studio Store *(Animation Ctyrd.).*

MOVIES AND TELEVISION
American Film Institute Showcase *(Studio Backlot Tour exit, Backlot),* Sid Cahuenga's One-Of-A-Kind *(Hollywood Blvd.).*

The Adventure Outpost sells Indiana Jones items

MUPPETS
Stage 1 Co. Store *(next to MuppetVision 3-D, Backlot).*

NIGHTMARE BEFORE CHRISTMAS
American Film Institute Showcase *(Studio Backlot Tour exit, Backlot),* Villains in Vogue *(Sunset Blvd.).*

PLANET HOLLYWOOD
Planet Hollywood Super Store *(Sunset Blvd.).*

PLAYHOUSE DISNEY
Playhouse Disney stand *(Animation Ctyrd.).*

PRINCESSES
In Character *(Animation Ctyrd.).*

ROCK AND ROLL MUSIC
Rock Around the Shop *(Rock 'n' Roller Coaster exit, Sunset Blvd.).*

STAR WARS
Tatooine Traders *(Star Tours exit, Echo Lake).*

TINKER BELL
In Character *(Animation Ctyrd.).*

TOY STORY
Story Dept. stand *(Pixar Place).*

TWILIGHT ZONE
Tower Gifts *(Twilight Zone Tower of Terror exit, Sunset Blvd.).*

VILLAINS
Villains in Vogue *(Sunset Blvd.).*

Original Cobb salad, Hollywood Brown Derby

Restaurants

Full service restaurants

50'S PRIME TIME CAFE ★★★★ ✔ American $$$
L: $12–17, 11am–4pm. D: $15–21, 4pm–park close. Seats 225. Echo Lake.
Expect trouble if you put your elbows on the table, or don't eat your vegetables, at this surreal spot. Your server plays your mom, aunt or uncle. Formica tables, sparkly vinyl chairs and period knick-knacks re-create 1950s dinettes. Ask for a TV table and you'll sit next to a black-and-white TV playing clips from old sitcoms. Fried chicken, meatloaf and (modern) pot roast—it's all good. Desserts include s'mores and PB&J milkshakes.

HOLLYWOOD & VINE Breakfast, lunch:
★★★★ ✔ Character buffet $$$$ **June and Leo from "Little Einsteins," JoJo and Goliath from "JoJo's Circus." B: A $23, C $12 8am–11:20am. L: A $24, C $13, 11:40am–2:20pm. Dinner: ★★** American buffet $$$$
3:30pm–30 min before park close. A: $26, C: $13. Seats 468. Echo Lake.
Morning and lunch buffets offer the most character interaction of any Disney restaurant. Sparse crowds let the stars spend lots of time at every table. Every 20 minutes they lead kids in singing and dancing. Breakfast has Mickey-shaped waffles and a build-your-own burrito station; lunch offers good salads, salmon and spoon bread. A character-free dinner adds prime rib, but overall is bland.

THE HOLLYWOOD BROWN DERBY
★★★★★ ✔ American $$$$ **L: $15–26, 11:30am–2:40pm. D: $22–29, 3:30pm–park close. Seats 224. Hollywood Boulevard.** *Disney Signature*

A sincere homage to the Tinseltown landmark, the Derby brings back the heydey of Old Hollywood. Over 1,000 celebrity caricatures line the walls, which surround a narrow terrace and sunken dining room. Heart-healthy dishes highlight a menu of meats, noodle bowls, pasta and seafood. Two classic Derby items also appear: the original chopped Cobb salad (tossed at your table) and tart grapefruit cake. Soft lighting, inlaid-wood tables. California wines. Another throwback: tableside phone service. Arrange it with the hostess and your child (of any age) will get a call from Goofy. Gawrsh!

MAMA MELROSE'S RISTORANTE ITALIANO
★★★★ ✔ California Italian $$$ **L: $12–20, Noon–3:30pm. D: $12–$22, 3:30–8pm. Seats 250. Backlot.**
Mama's offers quality meals at moderate prices. The menu has flatbreads, meats, pasta, salads and seafood, as well as an eggplant dish. Best bets include the wood-fired seafoods and the seafood pasta. All sauces and soups are made from scratch; the house-made desserts are smooth and packed with flavor. Artisan breads. The decor is that of a converted warehouse. White Christmas lights hang from an open ceiling; walls are covered with Californian and Italian pop-culture memorabilia. Wood tables, chairs and floors.

SCI-FI DINE-IN THEATER RESTAURANT
★★★ American $$$ **L: $12–20, 11am–4pm. D: $12–23, 4pm–park closing. Seats 252. Commissary Lane.**
It's all about atmosphere, not food, at this time trip to the past. Nearly dark, a large star-lit dining room re-creates the look of a 1950s drive-in movie theater. You sit in a replica of a classic convertible, and face a large screen which shows trailers from such kitschy classics as "Catwomen of the Moon" and "Devil Girl From Mars," as well as News of the Future newsreels, intermission bumpers, even some space-age cartoons. Sound comes from authentic drive-in speakers; some servers are on roller skates. Though the menu offers meats, pasta, salads, sandwiches, soups

Tune-In Lounge, 50's Prime Time Cafe

and tofu, the best bet is the Oreo cookie milkshake. Relatively quiet. Can be chilly. Ask for a bench seat in a car when you make your reservation; otherwise you may end up at a conventional table in back.

Counter service cafes

ABC COMMISSARY ✔ Cuban sandwiches, burgers. B: 9–10:30am. L&D: 10:30am–8:30pm. Seats 562. Commissary Lane.
Comfortable carpeted cafe with cushioned booths and chairs. Good Cuban sandwich; decent burgers, fried fish, Asian salad. Thick crowds and slow service at peak periods. Breakfast offers uninspired bagel sandwiches, pastries.
BACKLOT EXPRESS Burgers, hot dogs, grilled sandwiches. 11:30am–8pm. Seats 600. Echo Lake.
Themed as crafts shop, filled with real down-and-dirty clutter, including the Toon Patrol truck and Bennie the Cab stunt car from the 1988 movie "Who Framed Roger Rabbit."
TOY STORY PIZZA PLANET Individual pizzas, salads. 11am–7:30pm. Seats 584.
Noisy arcade looks nothing like the one in 1995's "Toy Story." Tables are upstairs. An open floor plan amplifies the racket.

Outdoor counter cafes

MIN AND BILL'S DOCKSIDE DINER Shakes, pretzels, beer, frozen lemonade. 10am–6pm. Seats 140. Appears to be a boat. Echo Lake.
STARRING ROLLS CAFE ✔ Pastries,

sandwiches, coffee. Uses Brown Derby kitchens. 9am–4pm. Seats 40. Sunset Blvd.
STUDIO CATERING CO. Sandwiches, salads, desserts. 11:30am–5:30pm. Seats 498. Backlot.
SUNSET RANCH MARKET Six-station outdoor food court with burgers, fresh fruit, hot dogs, pizza, sandwiches, turkey legs, hand-dipped ice cream. 10:30am–park close. Seats 400. Sunset Blvd.

Snack stands

BACKLOT CATERING Whole fruit, fruit cups, vegetables. Backlot.
DINOSAUR GERTIE'S Soft ice cream, waffle cones. Echo Lake.
DIP SITE Pretzels, popcorn, caramel corn. 50 seats. Echo Lake.
HERBIE'S DRIVE-IN Pretzels, chips, slushie-style drinks. Backlot, at Lights Motors Action.
HEY HOWDY HEY TAKE AWAY Slushie-style treats, ice cream, snacks. Pixar Place.
KRNR THE ROCK STATION Frozen lemonade, smoothies, soft ice cream. Sunset Blvd., at Rock 'n' Roller Coaster.
PEEVY'S POLAR PIPELINE ✔ Slushie-style frozen treats. Echo Lake.
THE WRITER'S STOP ✔ Bagels, coffee, cookies, pastries. Two-person table, chair, sofa. Backlot.

Bars

HIGH OCTANE REFRESHMENTS Outside. Backlot, next to Studio Catering Co.
TUNE-IN LOUNGE ✔ Full menu from adjacent 50's Prime Time Cafe. 14 barstools. Echo Lake.

Off to see the Wizard, Dorothy and her pals chat in a Great Movie Ride diorama

The Great Movie Ride

★ ★ ★ ★ ✓ 22 min. Capacity: 560. Fear factor: Intense for preschoolers. The "Alien" creature moves toward you from the ceiling and then appears suddenly out of the right wall. The Wicked Witch looks real. Access: ECV users must transfer. Assistive listening, handheld captioning. Debuted: 1989.

The Studio's original showcase attraction creates a dreamlike tribute to the Golden Age of Hollywood. A guided indoor tram travels through 16 classic film scenes, each one brought to life on a soundstage set that is filled with Audio-Animatronics characters and special effects.

Average Wait

9am	0 min
10am	10
11am	15
Noon	20
1pm	25
2pm	20
3pm	20
4pm	20
5pm	15
6pm	20
7pm	20
8pm	20
9pm	30

Your tram passes Gene Kelly "Singin' in the Rain" (1952) and "Public Enemy" James Cagney (1931), gets stuck in gangster and Old West shootouts, encounters the stalking "Alien" (1979) on the Nostromo spaceship of Sigourney Weaver and travels to Munchkinland to confront the Wicked Witch of the West from "The Wizard of Oz" (1939). Other sets portray the Fountain of Beauty from "Footlight Parade" (1933), the jungle of "Tarzan and His Mate" (1934), the airport of "Casablanca" (1942), the rooftops of "Mary Poppins" (1964) and the Well of Souls of "Raiders of the Lost Ark" (1981). Robotic characters also depict Clint Eastwood and John Wayne. There's a clip from "Fantasia" (1940). Altogether the ride showcases nearly every movie genre.

Comedy comes from the tram operator, a self-absorbed projectionist who introduces herself by proclaiming "Let's talk about me!" and "I love movies!" Inspired by Buster Keaton's character in the 1923 comedy "Sherlock Jr.," she uses the tram to magically take you into some of her favorite films. Along the way a second live performer (a gangster or Old West outlaw) steps out of a set (a reference to Jeff Daniels in 1985's "The Purple Rose of Cairo") and hijacks your vehicle.

The ride concludes in a theater, with a three-minute montage of film clips.

The best character is the Wicked Witch, Disney's most realistic human robot. Flexing her backbone, swiveling her hips and pointing her finger, the green-skinned villain has a lifelike face as she confronts your guide: "I'll get you my pretty…"

For the best experience, ask a cast member at the boarding area to let you sit in the

▶ Costumes displayed in the queue line now include one from 1998's "Shakespeare in Love."

first seats in either the first or second row, so you'll be right next to the guide. Not only will the spiel make more sense (you'll always be viewing the same scene), you'll get an up-close view of the hijacker, who may direct a few scripted lines your way or talk with you off mic.

The ride's entrance facade and lobby are full-size re-creations of Grauman's Chinese Theatre, a 1927 Hollywood landmark.

Disney's Imagineers look back on their Great Movie Ride work with fondness. "It's really dear to my heart," says show producer Eric Jacobson, "not only because of all the effects, but also because of all the work we did. Getting the rights to those movies was not a simple task."

CELEBRITY HANDPRINTS

More than 100 Hollywood celebrities have placed their hands and feet into the concrete courtyard of Disney's Chinese Theatre. Front and center is the work of Warren Beatty, who stopped by as part of the premiere of the 1990 movie "Dick Tracy," which was held at Downtown Disney. Nearby are the marks of Bob Hope, Jim Henson (who brought Kermit) and Dustin Hoffman and Robin Williams (who both brought their kids). Others on hand: George Burns, Tony Curtis and George Lucas.

Most of the prints are from the early 1990s, made at ceremonies during the park's old "Star of the Day" events. All are authentic except the impressions of Judy Garland's ruby slippers from "The Wizard of Oz," which are replicas of those in the concrete slab at the California theater.

During Charlton Heston's 1995 ceremony, a photographer yelled "Charlton!" just as the Hollywood legend was drawing out the "R" in his first name, causing him to look up. When the then-72-year-old star got back to work, he accidentally skipped the next letter of his name, creating a signature that reads "Charton" Heston.

FUN FINDS

❶ Window displays outside the attraction include photographs from the actual Chi-

"Maybe nobody will get hoit." Live character Mugsy the gangster fights off a mob ambush.

nese Theatre premieres of "Mary Poppins" and "The Jungle Book." ❷ Lobby props include Julie Andrews' "Mary Poppins" carousel horse, which also appears in a queue-line trailer. ❸ The actual Chinese Theatre is shown in the "Singin' in the Rain" trailer. ❹ The boarding area is lined with real soundstage equipment. ❺ That area's lights, including those on its Hollywood mural and neon marquee, synchronize to the ride's opening music. ❻ As your tram pulls into Gangster Alley, an argument takes place in the flat above Patrick J. Ryan's Bar. One man has a gun. ❼ In the Western town, a Sheriff's Office sign swings when it gets hit by an illusionary bullet. ❽ Along the Nostromo spaceship's left floor, inside jokes

* Walt Disney Imagineering has its headquarters in Glendale, Calif.

▶ Ask to sit up front. You can see better, and the narration will be in sync with the scenes.

Petite prints. A young girl compares her hands with those of screen legend Audrey Hepburn.

rock. ❹ A full-figure Mickey pharoah appears on the Well's left wall, just past the second statue of Anubis. An Egyptian Donald Duck is serving him some cheese.

OTHER HIDDEN CHARACTERS

❶ Minnie Mouse hides in the center of the mural in the boarding area. Facing left, her profile is just above and to the right of a tile roof, tucked under some palm fronds. ❷ On the left wall of the Well of Souls, a center carving two blocks up from the floor shows a pharoah holding "Star Wars" character R2-D2 while C-3PO repairs him with a screwdriver (the carving also appears on the same wall in the "Raiders of the Lost Ark" movie).

FUN FACTS ›› Replicas of statues at the real Chinese Theatre (themselves replicas of statues in the Forbidden City), two Fu Dogs guard the central entrance doors. Fu Dogs were used in early China to ward off evil spirits. ›› Filling 95,000 square feet, the ride has more than 60 Audio-Animatronics characters and nearly 3,000 effects. ›› The Cagney robot wears one of the star's actual tuxedos, donated by his family. ›› Gangster Alley buildings and signs refer to classic movies. Ryan's Bar, J.L. Altmeyer & Sons Novelty Manufacturing, the Red Oaks Social Club and Western Chemical Co. are settings in "The Public Enemy." The signs "Dead End" and "Society for Juvenile Delinquents" refer to the 1937 Bogart film "Dead End." ›› In the Western town, a "Ransom Stoddard" placard alludes to the attorney Jimmy Stewart played in 1962's "The Man Who Shot Liberty Valence." ›› Historical references include a "021-429" license plate on a gangsters' 1931 Chrysler (the Feb. 14, 1929, St. Valentine's Day massacre) and the Western town's Monarch Saloon (the Leadville, Colo., home of outlaw gambler Doc Holliday) and Cochise County Courthouse (the site of Tombstone, Ariz.'s gunfight at the O.K. Corral). ›› The "No Help Wanted" and "Sheriff's Office" signs are real movie props from the MGM backlot. ›› The attraction was built to portray three "Wizard of Oz" scenes. The "Fantasia" room was to be Dorothy's tornado (note its sepia-toned funnel). In the final theater, you were to be told to "pay no attention to that man behind the curtain." Last-minute copyright snags forced the cutback. ›› Not all of Disney's handprints are on display. Among those stored backstage: Johnny Depp's.

on the first video screen include the ride's "estimated time till next special effects failure" and ❾ a "welcome to all aliens visiting from the Glendale galaxy."* ❿ The third screen lists an astronaut as "still programming the witch." ⓫ Once it captures its victim, the eyes of the dog-like Anubis statue glow red. ⓬ Along the left wall of the skeleton room, a snake squirms out of a sarcophagus eye and ⓭ a pharoah pets a mummified cat. ⓮ A Munchkin pops out of a manhole next to the start of the yellow brick road at the beginning of the song "Ding Dong the Witch is Dead," just as in the movie. ⓯ After the Wicked Witch warns "Just try to stay out of my way, just try," a Munchkin hiding behind her peeks out for a moment.

HIDDEN MICKEYS

❶ As a silhouetted profile in the second-story windows of the Western Chemical Co. building, on your left side as you enter Gangster Alley. ❷ Mickey's tail and one of his shoes are visible on a poster underneath the one for "The Public Enemy" on the alley's left wall. ❸ As a profile on a piece of broken stone below the Ark of the Covenant in the Well of Souls. Facing left, a light-gray Mickey hides in plain sight on a dark-gray

▶ **Want the outlaw? Tell the cast member at the entrance to the boarding area.**

The American Idol Experience

★★★★ ✓ 20–25 min. Showtimes at 11a, Noon, 1p, 2p, 4p, 5p, 6p. Finale (showtime 7p) 45 min. Capacity: 1040. Fear factor: None. Access: Guests may remain in wheelchairs, ECVs. Assistive listening. Debuted: Feb. 14, 2009.

Held in the park's former ABC Theater, this live talent show lets audience members select its winners. As selected park guests perform on an "American Idol" stage, the crowd votes for its favorite using electronic keypads on the side of each seat. Each day, seven competitions lead to a championship round.

Like the television series, the show features an entertaining host and a three-judge panel that offers its opinions. The cynical judge isn't nearly as mean as Simon Cowell.

The stage has dozens of video monitors, "neon" (actually LED) lights that change color from red to blue to purple and spiral-staircase catwalks. Thanks to a small transmitter each performer wears, spotlights automatically track them as they move around the stage.

Anyone 14 or older can try out. Aspiring contestants first sing an a cappella song in front of a backstage screener. Those making the cut audition again to their choice of pre-selected tunes and arrangements. Three singers are chosen for each show. Winners advance to a nightly finale to compete for a regional audition with a producer for the "American Idol" series.

In front of the show, the **ATAS Hall of Fame Showcase** is a small plaza with 15 bronze busts of television stars, all members of the Academy of Television Arts and Sciences Hall of Fame. Included are Lucille Ball, Andy Griffith and Mary Tyler Moore. Plaques on a back wall list all the inductees for each year. Disney stopped adding busts and plaques in 1996.

An outdoor video screen lets passing park guests view the nightly American Idol Experience finale

Average Wait	
9am	n/a
10am	n/a
11am	20 min
Noon	20
1pm	20
2pm	20
3pm	20
4pm	20
5pm	20
6pm	20
7pm	20
8pm	n/a
9pm	n/a

Sounds Dangerous

★★ 12 min. Capacity: 240. No wait. Fear factor: Some scary sounds. Access: Guests may stay in wheelchairs, ECVs. Assistive listening. Debuted: 1999.

When incognito TV investigator Drew Carey shorts out his spy cam, the theater of his test audience—that's you—goes completely dark. You're at the mercy of your imagination when he opens a jar of bees, gets a shave and bumps an elephant. Guests wear headphones to get the full effect.

The postshow, **SoundWorks** ✓, lets you dub your voice to cartoon and movie characters and create sound effects with help from, via video, the late sound wiz Jimmy MacDonald. Walls are lined with gadgets he used for 20 classic films. The SoundWorks entrance is the Sounds Dangerous exit.

▶ For details on auditioning for The American Idol Experience log onto disneyworld.com

Indiana Jones punches a sword-wielding assassin in the Indiana Jones Epic Stunt Spectacular

Indiana Jones Epic Stunt Spectacular

★ ★ ★ ★ 30 min. Capacity: 2,000. *FastPass* Fear factor: None unless kids think the action is real. Access: Guests may remain in wheelchairs, ECVs. Assistive listening; handheld captioning. Debuted: 1989, revised 2000.

Seventeen live performers re-create physical stunts from 1981's "Raiders of the Lost Ark" in this outdoor stage show.

First you relive the opening scene, as an actor playing Indiana drops, literally, into a Mayan ruin. Pursuing a golden idol, he dodges spears, hatchet-slamming statues and a giant rolling boulder. Next, Indy and Marion take on a village of Cairo bad guys. Indy fights 'em off with his bullwhip and gun, many folks fall off building facades and Marion makes a death-defying escape out of a flipping, flaming truck.

For the finale, our heroes are at a North African Nazi airfield. When a Flying Wing comes in for fuel, Indy and Marion try again to escape. They fight Nazis in, on and around the spinning plane, fleeing to safety just as leaking fuel sparks a huge explosion.

MEAT, WITH CHEESE

Basically the same since 1989, the show hasn't lost its appeal. Most of its stunts look real, there's always something to watch and there's plenty of humor. Audience volunteers are ridiculed throughout the show, as are some of the cast. Cartoonish sound effects add to the fun. Between scenes you see how sets can be quickly dismantled, how heavy-looking props can be featherlight and see how to fake a punch.

For flavor, Disney pretends the show is a real film shoot. Mock cameramen peer through mock cameras; a pretend director barks out pretend directions. When the "Assistant Director of the Second Unit" decides "We're going to shoot 36 instead of 24 frames per second," his boss declares "I like it!"

The show's creation was overseen by George Lucas. "Raiders of the Lost Ark" stunt coordinator Glenn Randall personally designed the stunts.

The first performance of the day usually has the smallest crowd. The last show is often the best looking, as the darker sky makes the explosions more dramatic.

Average Wait

9am	n/a
10am	10 min
11am	10
Noon	10
1pm	10
2pm	10
3pm	10
4pm	10
5pm	10
6pm	10
7pm	10
8pm	n/a
9pm	n/a

▶ Arrive early to sit in the first few rows. You'll get a closer view and feel heat from the fires.

FUN FINDS

Out front: ❶ Just to the left of the Fastpass machines, a British archeologist has dug a hole and lowered himself down to the bottom of it. Pull on his rope and he'll become irritated and talk to you ("I say! Stop mucking about up there!"). **Preshow:** ❶ One of the audience volunteers is actually a professional stuntman. Can you spot him first? **Cairo scene:** ❶ Indy says the signature Lucas line "I have a bad feeling about this" during the street scene. ❷ In reality the truck of Marion's kidnappers stops behind its building. A second empty truck finishes the circle. Attached to the building by a pole, it "flips" by rotating over. Though Marion appears to run out of that truck, she actually returns through a small gray crate just to its right. **Airfield scene:** ❶ The sidecar motorcycle is a duplicate of the one Harrison Ford commandeered in the 1989 movie "Indiana Jones and the Last Crusade." It even has the same front-fender license number: WH38475. ❷ In reality, the Flying Wing mechanic falls through an easily visible trapdoor. **Left exit area:** ❶ Behind the Outpost gift shop sit three vehicles used in the filming of "Indiana Jones and the Last Crusade," in the scenes where Indy and the Nazis are racing to find the Holy Grail. Just off the sidewalk you'll find the Nazi staff car and truck, as well as the "Steel Beast" tank (its side gun barrel is still "exploded"

Indy and Marion escape a Nazi excavation camp in Disney's Indiana Jones Epic Stunt Spectacular

from when Indy stuffed it with a rock). Each vehicle still displays the symbol of the film's version of the Republic of Hatay.

A CLASSIC ADVENTURE, 1981's "Raiders of the Lost Ark" starts its story in 1936. Archaeology professor Dr. Henry "Indiana" Jones Jr. has just returned from the jungles of Peru, where he has failed to recover an idol from the Temple of the Chachapoyan Warriors. Then the Army calls, with news that Nazi Germany has plans to find and possess the Ark of the Covenant, the casket used by ancient Hebrews to hold the Ten Commandments. Its supernatural powers, legends say, can wipe out entire armies. Uncle Sam wants to find it first. So off Dr. Jones goes, first to reunite with gutsy old girlfriend Marion Ravenwood, then to Cairo, where the Nazis have recruited henchmen to kidnap Marion and steal her medallion, which can reveal the ark's location. As Indy fights off a gang of assassins, Marion knocks one out with a handy frying pan, but soon she is taken away in a truck, which explodes. At first Indy thinks she's dead, but then finds her captive at an excavation camp where Nazis are about to load the Ark on a Flying Wing bound for Germany. The couple tracks down the plane and, while it's fueling, takes it over. Marion shoots Nazis from the cockpit while Indy's fight with a mechanic ends when the bad guy is shredded by a propeller. When leaking fuel catches fire, Indy and Marion run to safety just before everything blows up.

▶ To be in the show, jump and scream wildly when the casting director asks for volunteers.

Star Tours

★ ★ ★ 7 min. Capacity: 240. *FastPass* Fear factor: The vehicle's unpredictable sways and dives can cause motion sickness in guests of any age. Access: ECV guests must transfer to wheelchairs. Guest-activated captioning. Height restriction: 40 in. Debuted: 1989 (Disneyland 1987).

You journey into space in this elaborate "Star Wars"motion simulator.* For a Lucas project it's surprisingly unrestored, but it does have the same mix of wit and action of the early "Star Wars" films.

The story begins as you enter the building. You're in deep space, inside a spaceport during a time after the 1983 movie "Return of the Jedi." Darth Vader is dead and the Republic and its rebels (the good guys) have a tentative hold on the galaxy. R2-D2 and C-3PO are working for intergalactic airline Star Tours. You're there to board a tourist shuttle to the Ewoks' moon of Endor.

The queue first weaves through a maintenance bay, where C-3PO and R2-D2 are repairing a Star Tours shuttle. Then you step into a "Droidnostics Center," as a robotic mechanic assembles the company's pilots and navigators.

Finally you board your shuttle, known as a StarSpeeder 3000. R2 is its navigator but its pilot is a rookie, RX-24. "Rex" is sitting in front of you, at the controls.

Rex makes mistakes right away, sending your ship off its docking ledge and down a repair bay, barely missing a swinging crane before flying out a side door—then past Endor into a field of ice crystals. You tunnel through the biggest crystal and smash your way out. But an enemy destroyer is nearby, and is pulling you toward it.

"Oh no! We're caught in a tractor beam!" Rex yells. A rebel fighter pilot breaks in on your video monitor. "Star Tours?!? What are you doing here? This is a combat zone!"

You pull free but then get hit, and fall toward a

Average Wait

9am	0 min
10am	5
11am	30
Noon	20
1pm	20
2pm	50
3pm	30
4pm	20
5pm	20
6pm	30
7pm	10
8pm	30
9pm	20

* Used by airlines and militaries to train pilots, these enclosed, garbage-truck-sized machines create a sensation of flight by synchronizing their tilts, dives and other movements to films that simulate the view out of windshields.

Death Star. Fortunately, R2-D2 repairs your ship just in time, and you escape.

But your adventure is not over.

"I've always wanted to do this!" Rex says as he dives toward the Death Star. "We're going in!" You swoop along the surface, zooming under bridges and into a trench, blasting bad guys along the way. You watch as the lead fighter drops two torpedoes down the Star's exhaust port, and rocket away just as it explodes.

Despite nearly skidding into a fuel tanker on the way in, you return to your Star Tours hangar shaken but sound.

Choose a middle row for a fun ride that won't make you sick, the back seats for lots of rock 'n' roll. The front row is the most calm. Perfect for photos, a climb-on replica of a Speeder Bike (the woods-weaving vehicle of "Return of the Jedi") sits across from the ride entrance.

FUN FINDS

❶ The entrance area is a "stage set" of a village of Ewoks, the teddy-bear creatures that helped save the day in 1983's "Return of the Jedi." Redwood, sequoia and pine "props" are just tall enough for a film scene. At night you can hear the Ewoks in their tree huts, talking and drumming. The set features a captured, 35-foot-tall Imperial Walker, a woodland path (the brown sidewalk) and, just inside, the directors chairs of C-3PO and R2-D2. ❷ "Don't insult me, you overgrown scrap pile!" 3PO snaps to R2 in the maintenance bay. ❸ Pages call "Egroeg Sacul" ("George Lucas" backward), Dr. Tom Morrow (host of 1970s Magic Kingdom attraction Flight to the Moon) and the owner of a vehicle with the ID THX-1138 (the title of the first George Lucas movie, from 1971). ❹ Little red men chase each other across the bottom of the large video screen. ❺ A watermelon-sized robot circles around the left floor of the Droidnostics Center. ❻ The mechanic asks for your help ("Could you tell me where this goes?") and gets offended by your attention ("Take a picture, it will last longer"). ❼ A wiggling hand and foot hide in a pile of robotic junk on your right. ❽ "Ex-

FUN FACTS ❯❯ Anthony Daniels provided the voice of C-3PO and the alien voice in the maintenance bay. ❯❯ In the Droidnostics Center, two droids behind G2-9T appeared in the first "Star Wars" film.

▶ For the calmest ride, sit in the front of the theater. The back row is the bumpiest.

cuse me but you'll have to check the excess baggage," the gate attendant tells you. "Oh, I'm sorry, I didn't realize that was your husband." **9** As you leave the Center, two robotic hawks above you tend their nests. **10** Inside your shuttle, a red plastic strip attached to Rex reads "Remove Before Flight." **11** "I have a bad feeling about this!" Rex yells as you fly into the crystals, repeating a line used in nearly every Lucas film. **12** As you re-enter the maintenance bay Lucas himself appears as a control-room operator. He's standing in an office in front of you. **13** After you leave the simulator, just before the gift shop, a glass case on your right displays character sketches and a page of the script from 1999's "Star Wars Episode 1: The Phantom Menace."

HIDDEN MICKEY
An Ewok child holds a Mickey doll in the pre-boarding video.

It's got legs. You enter Star Tours by walking underneath an All-Terrain Armored Transport.

A SPACE FANTASY that takes place "a long time ago, far, far away," the "Star Wars" movies tell a timeless tale of good versus evil. Combining a space-opera plot similar to those of the Buck Rogers serials of the 1930s and '40s with the use of special effects and modeling inspired by the 1968 film "2001—A Space Odyssey," the films' mix of wit, mythology and simulated reality has entranced audiences worldwide for more than three decades.

Some classic "Star Wars" vehicles and weapons play key roles in your Star Tours flight. You become caught in an Imperial Star Destroyer's tractor beam, an invisible force field that can capture and redirect rebel ships. Rebel forces fly the X-Wing starfighter. The symbol of the rebel fleet, its double-layered wings separate into an "X" formation during combat. Luke Skywalker flew one in the first "Star Wars" trilogy. The bad guys use the TIE starfighter, named for its twin ion engines. These bare-bolts machines lack hyperdrives and deflector shields. The Empire's most horrific weapons are its Death Stars. Powered by a fusion reactor in its center, each of these moon-sized space stations is staffed with over a million troops. Its main weapon is a superlaser housed in a crater-like cannon well.

There have been three Death Stars in "Star Wars" history. The first destroyed Princess Leia's home planet of Alderaan in 1977's "Star Wars," then fell victim to Luke Skywalker when he dropped a pair of proton torpedoes into its exhaust port. The second was never finished; the rebels destroyed it in 1983's "Return of the Jedi." The third appears during your flight. It's destroyed by the X-Wing in front of you.

▶ The Tatooine Traders gift shop often carries Darth Tater, a special Mr. Potato Head.

A poster along the entranceway shows the cast of Jim Henson's MuppetVision 3-D

Jim Henson's MuppetVision 3-D

★★★★ ✓ 25 min. including preshow. Capacity: 584. Fear factor: None. Access: Guests may remain in wheelchairs, ECVs. Assistive listening; reflective, activated video captioning. Debuted: 1991.

Built around a 3-D film, this inspired show mixes vaudeville humor with silly special effects. As you sit in the red-velvet theater from the 1970s television series "The Muppet Show," you watch a typical Muppet misadventure. Nicki Napoleon and his Emperor Penguins perform in the orchestra pit, while cranky curmudgeons Statler and Waldorf watch with you from the balcony.

The Muppets have retrofitted the auditorium to debut a new film technology. The Swedish Chef readies the haphazardly assembled projection equipment. As the movie begins, Kermit takes you to the lab of Dr. Bunsen Honeydew, creator of the devilish Waldo, a "living, breathing 3-D effect."

Everything goes wrong. Inept lab assistant Beaker gets caught in the machinery, then nearly sucks up the theater with a VacuuMuppet. Miss Piggy storms off after her song's special effects are revealed as nothing more than plastic butterflies on sticks.

The finale nearly destroys the theater. When Sam Eagle is forced to condense his patriotic "three-hour extravaganza" into 90 seconds, all the performers end up onstage at once. The result is a chaos of falling, tripping, shooting and, in one case, stripping.

The effects look their age, but the show's timeless wit keeps it entertaining. Despite Kermit's assurance that "at no time will we be stooping to cheap 3-D tricks," his cast does exactly that. Don't miss the preshow, 12 minutes of general confusion that plays out over synchronized video monitors. The rarely-used outdoor queue area is also worth a look. Wrapping around the rear of the building, the covered walkway is lined with zany drawings and posters.

The attraction was the last major project of Muppet creator Jim Henson, who died just before it debuted. His gifted touch is everywhere, from queue-line and theater details to plot points such as the title of Sam Eagle's presentation—"A Salute to All Nations But Mostly America." That's also him voicing Kermit and the Swedish Chef.

Average Wait

9am	0 min
10am	0
11am	0
Noon	0
1pm	0
2pm	0
3pm	0
4pm	0
5pm	0
6pm	0
7pm	0
8pm	0
9pm	0

▶ Head here in the afternoon. There's rarely a long wait, and the queue is air conditioned.

FUN FINDS

Courtyard: **①** In a fountain, Gonzo and Fozzie are filming a brassy Miss Piggy. Clad in a gown and sandals, she's re-creating her Statue of Liberty role in the film's finale. She stands on a half shell, an homage to William Bouguereau's 1879 painting "The Birth of Venus." **②** Underneath are three rats in the fountain: Rizzo and two friends snorkeling for coins and fishing for dollars. **③** A side staircase leads to the projection room, where the Swedish Chef runs a combination editing and catering business. Its slogan: "Frøöm Qüick Cüts tø Cöld Cüts." **④** A grayscale Gonzo hangs from a clock tower in tribute to the 1923 Harold Lloyd black-and-white film "Safety Last!" **⑤** An Acme anvil honors Warner Bros. cartoons. **⑥** Atop a side wall, two large round planters hold ice cream sundaes. One is half-eaten. **Outdoor queue:** **①** Posters along a rarely used rear walkway promote such faux films as "Beach Blanket Beaker" and "Kürmet the Amphibian" ("So Mean He's Green").
② MuppetLabs placards help you get from "here" to "there" (an eight-step process), perform experiments such as "How to Stick Out Your Tongue and Touch Your Ear" and understand the surprisingly complex 3-D glasses. **Entryway:** **①** The sign at the Security Office saying "Key Under Mat" isn't lying. **②** Inside the office is a wanted poster for Fozzie (for impersonating a comic) and a Piggy cheesecake calendar. **③** The directory case includes listings for Statler and Waldorf's Institute of Heckling and Browbeating and Gonzo's Dept. of Poultry and Mold Cultivation. **④** A sign above the 8-foot archway reads "You must be shorter than this to enter." A chip at the top indicates someone didn't see it. **⑤** A hall door leading to the MuppetLabs' Dept. of Artificial Reality reads "This is not a door." **Queue room:** **①** Hanging from the ceiling is a net full of Jell-O, a reference to 1950s Mouseketeer Annette Funicello. **②** Next to it is a bird cage with a perch—a fish, not a pole. **③** Down

A twirling brass fountain features Miss Piggy as "Ms. Liberty." She's holding a box of chocolates.

front a "2-D Fruities" crate holds flat cutouts of a banana, cherry and lemon. **④** A box sent to the Swedish Chef from Oompah, Sweden's "Sven & Ingmar's Kooking Kollection" include "Der Noodle Frooper." **⑤** Catwalks hold the SwineTrek spaceship used in "Pigs in Space" TV skits as well as some wooden soldiers and frontiersmen used in the 3-D film's finale. **⑥** Up front is a hydraulic tube from the film's MuppetVision machine. **⑦** Along the walls are large reprints of "Kermitage Collection" portraits issued as a calendar in 1984. They include parodies of Henri Rousseau ("The Sleepy Zootsy") and Hans Holbein ("Jester at the Court of Henry VIII,"), a painting of Fozzie holding a banana to his ear which includes the Latin phrase *Bananum In Avre Habeo* ("I'm holding a banana in my ear."). **⑧** A photo hanging from the ceiling shows a banjo-holding Henson-like Muppet, a character in a "Muppet Show"

▶ The film is in its best focus from seats in the center rear of the theater.

A pipe above the outdoor waiting area helps recall an NBC Studios closet Jim Henson, Frank Oz and others surreptitiously decorated in 1963

band. ❾ Up front, a box of Gonzo's stunt props holds "mold, fungus, helmets, helmets covered with fungus and mold, helmets with mold—no fungus" and "fungus and mold—no helmets." ❿ A crate of "emergency tuxedos" for the penguins is stamped "Open in the event of an event." ⓫ The birds' food has arrived in a box from Long Island Sound and Seafood Supplies ("Everything from Hearing to Herring"). ⓬ A sarcophagus peers through a pair of 3-D glasses. **Theater:** ❶ As the show begins, the Swedish Chef mans the projection room and reassures Kermit that "der machinen is goin' der floomy floomy." Later, when the penguins fire their cannon at the projector, he yells "Schtupid crazy birds!" ❷ The penguin orchestra cackles at Statler and Waldorf's barbs (especially when Waldorf says the birds "probably took the job for the halibut") and coughs when it get squirted by Fozzie's boutonniere. One gets sucked up by Beaker's VacuuMuppet. ❸ Statler and Waldorf gape in amazement at the MuppetVision machine, nod as Waldo bounces off people's heads, duck from the VacuuMuppet and hide when the Chef brings out his cannon. ❹ As you leave, the eight holes created by the cannon fire dis-

appear. Changes in lighting expose, then conceal, the holes. **Movie:** ❶ A chicken wanders behind Kermit as the frog begins the tour of MuppetLabs. Later, another flies off its perch. ❷ The lab's Beethoven bust wears a pair of 3-D glasses on its head. ❸ Two goldfish eventually swim in a beaker above the Chinese takeout boxes. ❹ When Kermit returns, Scooter and Janis bicycle behind him. ❺ After Kermit says "This way, folks," a brass bald eagle wears the glasses. ❻ Miss Piggy loses her head as she is pulled into the lake. It falls backward. ❼ Some marching band members aren't wearing pants. **Exitway:** ❶ Posters include ads for penguin outfitter Frankie ("Large formalwear for the hard-to-fit. Small formalwear for the hard-to-find.") and a Rowlf record album ("the critics are howling!"). **Stage 1 Company Store:** ❶ The Muppet lockers and Happiness Hotel registration area from 1981's "The Great Muppet Caper" form a back corner. ❷ Nearly two dozen silly signs include one over a doorway that reads "Absolutely no point beyond this point."

HIDDEN MICKEYS

❶ On Gonzo's inflatable ring float in the courtyard fountain. ❷ In a small sketch of a DNA model in the "5 Reasons" poster along the back outdoor queue area. ❸ As a test pattern in the early moments of the preshow video. ❹ In the film's final scene, park guests behind the fire truck hold Mickey Mouse balloons. ❺ Outside the Stage 1 Company Store, as purple paint drips on a recessed light under a bronze lion head. ❻ As green drips on a shelf of a wood bureau along a side wall. ❼ Mickey's red shorts hang above the hotel desk.

FUN FACTS » The outdoor waiting area and covered bus shelter are a salute to a closet Henson, Frank Oz and others decorated in 1963, when the Muppets were booked on "The Jack Paar Program" at the NBC Studios in New York. Mistakenly arriving six hours early, they killed time by decorating their dressing room's utility closet with some Muppet touch-up paint, covering the walls with loopy designs and faces, incorporating pipes as noses. » When Sweetums walks on screen and, for no reason, starts knocking a paddle ball into the audience, he's channeling a famously pointless scene from the 1953 Vincent Price film, "House of Wax."

▶ The queue room is filled with real Muppet memorabilia. Plan time to look through it.

Hot hatch. An Opel Corsa leaps through fire in the finale of Lights, Motors, Action

Lights, Motors, Action Extreme Stunt Show

★ ★ ★ 40 min. Arrive 30 min. early for a good seat. Capacity: 5,000. *FastPass* Fear factor: None. All the action is far away from the seating area. Access: Guests may remain in wheelchairs, ECVs. Assistive listening. Debuted: 2005.

Cars and motorcycles fly through the air, and barely miss each other as they skid and spin on the ground in this outdooor stage show, as skilled stunt drivers demonstrate how chase scenes are created for modern action-adventure films. The premise is the filming of a European spy thriller, with a working crew on a live set.

There are four scenes. First, six Opel Corsas race around in a choreographed chase. The cars return to jump over a blockade of produce stands and trucks (one car jumps backward). Then three motorcycles arrive, one jumping through what appears to be a plate-glass window as the cars drive on two wheels and, for a moment, two guys end up on Jet Skis. This scene ends as a motorcyclist falls and, thanks to a special jumpsuit, catches fire. For the finale, a car jumps directly at the audience as 40-foot fireballs billow in the air.

After each scene, an enthusiastic director ("That was awesome!") appears to combine the shots into a completed scene.

There's also a car that breaks in half.

The set resembles a seaside village marketplace in southern France (one shop is the Café Fracas, the "restaurant of the noisy rumpus"). The show debuted at Disneyland Paris, hence the French connection.

HIDDEN MICKEYS

❶ A vintage full-figure Mickey appears in the window of the Antiquites Brocante ("Secondhand Antiques") shop. ❷ As a gear and two circular belts in the top right corner of the motorcycle shop window.

FUN FACTS » Each car has a 2-stroke, 150-hp engine with four forward and four reverse gears, which lets it reach the same speed in either direction. **»** Each car weighs 1,300 pounds, less than half that of a similar production vehicle. **»** The "live" video was filmed before the show opened in 2005.

Average Wait	
9am	n/a
10am	20
11am	20
Noon	20
1pm	20
2pm	20
3pm	20
4pm	20
5pm	20
6pm	20
7pm	20
8pm	n/a
9pm	n/a

▶ Sit low in the stands for the most exciting view. Sit on the left to exit past a glimpse backstage.

A tram appears to have crashed through the entrance facade of the Studio Backlot Tour

Studio Backlot Tour

★★ 30–40 min. Capacity: 1,000. Fear factor: Simulated disasters. Access: Guests may remain in wheelchairs, ECVs. Handheld and activated video captioning. Debuted: 1989, revised 2004.

Disney shut down its working backlot years ago. So what's left of this tour? A water-effects demo, a staged prop room, a peek into costume and set shops (now used for park work) and a stop at a fancy faux disaster set.

It begins with a demonstration of how water cannons and fire bursts can simulate torpedo and bombing attacks, as volunteers get splashed on a PT boat. A small prop room leads to a tram tour, which rumbles past shops then heads to Catastrophe Canyon, a Mojave Desert effects area that simulates an earthquake, fire and flood. As you head back you pass some movie vehicles and Walt Disney's 1960s jet.

You exit through a walk-through exhibit, an American Film Institute (AFI) Showcase of movie-villain costumes. A display case holds ten antique film cameras and projectors.

Average Wait

9am	closed
10am	15 min
11am	10
Noon	20
1pm	20
2pm	20
3pm	20
4pm	10
5pm	10
6pm	20
7pm	10
8pm	closed
9pm	closed

FUN FINDS

Queue: Displays include ❶ the Black Pearl figurehead from 2003's "Pirates of the Caribbean: Curse of the Black Pearl" and ❷ a model USS Oklahoma from 2001's "Pearl Harbor." **Prop Warehouse:** Real props include ❶ cans of eyeballs and glue from 1988's "Who Framed Roger Rabbit," ❷ the shrinking machine and a giant shoe from 1992's "Honey, I Blew Up The Kid," ❸ the Austin of England taxi from 1984's "The Muppets Take Manhattan," ❹ an 18-foot Holy Temple statue from 1989's "Indiana Jones and the Last Crusade" and ❺ furniture from 1990s TV show "Dinosaurs." ❻ A hang glider and balloon basket (with pilot and chicken) is from Epcot's old World of Motion attraction.

HIDDEN MICKEYS

❶ As a blue-sky cutout in the white clouds of the "Harbor Attack" backdrop. ❷ In the prop room, on the yellow "Marvin's Room" refrigerator door and as cannon balls hanging from the ceiling. ❸ At Catastrophe Canyon, as gauges on your right on top of the third barrel from the exit. ❹ A full-figure Mickey hides in a mural to your right just as you enter the AFI exhibit. He stands on top of a gravestone about halfway up the right third of the scene.

▶ Want to volunteer for the Harbor Attack demonstration? Ask an entranceway cast member.

Girls race around a giant can of Play-doh at the 'Honey, I Shrunk the Kids' movie set playground

'Honey, I Shrunk the Kids' Movie Set Adventure Playground

★★★ Unlimited. Capacity: 240, including parents. Fear factor: None. Access: Guests may remain in wheelchairs, ECVs. Debuted: 1990.

This soft-floored outdoor playground lets children pretend they're the size of bugs, lost in a suburban backyard. Topped by towering blades of grass, it's a small area but filled with things to do. There are many small nooks and crannies to explore, including a series of dimly lit "ant tunnels," large climb-on spider web and a slide that's a roll of film.

Oversized props include an Oreo cookie, a Super Soaker water gun and a climb-on ant. (Cynics will note that the props' scale varies wildly. The ant is larger than the film roll. The Super Soaker is the same size as the cookie.)

Children love every inch, of course, but parents can get cranky. Cramped into a small triangular area surrounded by tall walls, the playground is usually stuffy and sometimes very humid. It's often crowded, but offers almost no place for parents to sit.

Also, it's easy to lose sight of your children, though there's only one exit—the entrance—and it's narrow and always monitored by a Disney cast member.

The playground is most fun early in the day, when it's cloudy, or late in the afternoon. It's located between the park's Streets of America area and the Studio Catering Company outdoor counter cafe.

The area is based on the 1989 movie "Honey, I Shrunk the Kids," in which an inventor mistakenly shrinks his children who then get lost in their own yard.

FUN FINDS

The playground has three hidden interactive features. ❶ As you enter, look to your left for a leaky garden hose, which squirts water on unsuspecting heads. In-ground squirters are nearby. ❷ Walk up to the top of the back wall to find the nose of a huge dog. He sniffs you, then sneezes. ❸ Look behind the entranceway, to the right of the dried bubble gum, to discover the Sound Steps, three-inch-high cut grass stalks that make noise when you step on them.

Average Wait	
9am	0 min
10am	0
11am	0
Noon	0
1pm	0
2pm	0
3pm	0
4pm	0
5pm	0
6pm	0
7pm	0
8pm	0
9pm	0

▶ Bring a camera. The oversized props make good photo backgrounds.

THE MAGIC OF

Disney

ANIMATION

The Magic of Disney Animation sits in a building that was once a working animation studio

The Magic of Disney Animation

★ ★ ★ ★ ✔ Unlimited (Film: 10 min. Animation Academy: 10 min. Rest self-guided.) Capacity: Theater: 150; Animation Academy: 50. Fear factor: None. Access: Guests may remain in wheelchairs, ECVs; lap boards available for drawing. Reflective, video captioning. Debuted: 1989, revised 2004.

This lightweight attraction consists of a short film, a hands-on drawing lesson, some computer games, an air-conditioned chance to meet characters and some exhibits.

A short film, "Drawn to Animation," shows how Disney created Mushu, the dragon sidekick in 1998's "Mulan." An open area has preschooler-friendly computer games. Nearby, Mickey Mouse and characters from recent Disney movies greet guests and pose for pictures.

You learn how to draw a Disney character at the superb Animation Academy. A classroom setting has you sit at a drafting table and follow step-by-step instructions from a live instructor to create a Disney character. You keep your sketch.

The final area is the Animation Gallery, a few small rooms filled with conceptual models and drawings, including Tinker Bell as a redhead and Buzz Lightyear with a pompadour. A glass case holds a dozen actual Oscar statuettes won by the Disney company. The one for the short "It's Tough to be a Bird" is the actual award from the 1970 ceremony.

The building the attraction sits in is the former East Coast home of Disney Feature Animation. Artists here created the Roger Rabbit cartoons "Tummy Trouble" and "Roller Coaster Rabbit;" painted cels for "The Little Mermaid;" produced segments of "Beauty and the Beast," "Aladdin" and "The Lion King;" and created the movies "Mulan," "Lilo & Stitch," "Brother Bear" and "Home on the Range" in their entireties. At its peak the animation studio had a staff of 350. Disney closed the studio in 2004.

FUN FIND

Take too long to make your choices at the Soundstage computer screens and Ursula, the sea witch from 1989's "Little Mermaid," will shout "Hurry and make a choice! I have fish sticks in the oven!"

Average Wait

Time	Wait
9am	0 min
10am	10
11am	10
Noon	15
1pm	15
2pm	20
3pm	20
4pm	20
5pm	20
6pm	0
7pm	0
8pm	0
9pm	0

▶ There's typically no wait after the characters leave, which is usually about 5:30 p.m.

Voyage of the Little Mermaid

★ ★ ★ ★ 17 min. Capacity: 600. *FastPass* **Fear factor:** Real. Ursula causes some toddlers to cry. **Access:** Guests may remain in wheelchairs, ECVs. Assistive listening, reflective captioning. Debuted: 1992.

Black-light puppets, live actors and imaginative effects retell the story of Ariel in this condensed version of the 1989 movie, "The Little Mermaid."

As a water curtain opens across the stage, the show begins with a rousing blacklight puppet version of "Under the Sea." Then you meet Ariel (she wants legs, and Prince Eric) who belts out "Part of Your World" like a Broadway star. The evil Ursula the Sea Witch—a parade-float-sized robotic octopus—slithers in to trick Ariel out of her voice, singing "Poor Unfortunate Soul." Video clips advance the plot to the finale, where the live actress grows her gams and hugs her honey.

The Howard Ashman lyrics alone make the show worthwhile. *"Out in the sun they slave away,"* the puppet Sebastian the crab sings, *"while we devotin' full time to floatin'."* The theater's high-backed cloth seats, dark ambiance and cool breezes make it a great place to relax.

She wants more. Gadgets and gizmos aplenty aren't enough for Ariel, the Little Mermaid.

Average Wait

9am	0 min
10am	20
11am	20
Noon	20
1pm	20
2pm	30
3pm	20
4pm	30
5pm	20
6pm	10
7pm	30
8pm	20
9pm	10

FUN FIND

Hanging over the right entrance door to the seating area is a Disney-fied replica of P.T. Barnum's 1842 FeJee Mermaid. On a tour of the United States, the infamous huckster displayed what he billed as a real mermaid caught off the Fiji Islands. In truth it was simply the shriveled body of a monkey stitched to the dried tail of a large fish.

REBEL REBEL The 1989 film "The Little Mermaid" broke new ground for a Disney heroine: Ariel's dream comes true because she takes control. Her problem: She wants legs, and the human Prince Eric. Ursula the Sea Witch offers to make the girl human—if Ariel will give up her voice and agree to get it back only if she kisses Eric within three days. Ursula transforms herself into a rival beauty with Ariel's voice, and nearly marries the prince herself. A singing crab and a friendly fish help Ariel land her man. The movie leaves out some grim moments of Hans Christian Andersen's original 1836 fable. In that version, the Sea Witch takes the teen's voice by cutting out her tongue, and the prince dumps her for the girl next door.

▶ The best seats are in the middle of the theater. The front row sits too low to see on the stage.

SONG LYRICS © WONDERLAND MUSIC COMPANY INC.

Handy Manny and Mr. Pat the hammer fix a bubble machine in Playhouse Disney—Live on Stage

Playhouse Disney — Live on Stage

★★★★★ 22 min. Capacity: 600. Fear factor: None. Access: Guests may remain in wheelchairs and ECVs. Assistive listening, reflective and activated captions. Debuted: 2001, updated 2008.

Characters from the Playhouse Disney television programs "Mickey Mouse Clubhouse," "Handy Manny," "Little Einsteins" and "My Friends Tigger and Pooh" star in this elaborate puppet show. Four short stories include plenty of opportunities for kids to bounce, cheer, clap, dance, shout and catch bubbles, leaves and streamers. The audience sits on a carpeted floor.

The life-like puppets blink their eyes and open their mouths. The sound is crisp, and nearly a hundred spotlights provide professional theatrical lighting.

The plot? Mickey Mouse wants to throw Minnie a surprise party, but none of his pals can figure out how to pull it off. The stories teach gentle lessons about working together.

Average Wait

9am	n/a
10am	20 min
11am	20
Noon	20
1pm	20
2pm	20
3pm	20
4pm	20
5pm	20
6pm	n/a
7pm	n/a
8pm	n/a
9pm	n/a

FUN FINDS

❶ When the live host stands to the side of the stage, he (or she) sometimes "chats" with the puppets who aren't in the spotlight. ❷ When Casey asks Goofy what he learned from the "Little Einsteins" story, for a moment the dippy dog can't think of anything.

DON'T KNOW YOUR MEESKA FROM YOUR MOOSKA? You're not alone. Here's a primer: Mickey Mouse and his pals help viewers solve problems on **"Mickey Mouse Clubhouse."** When they need help they shout "Oh Tootles!," which brings forth a magical flying machine equipped with "mouse-ka-tools." A clubhouse appears when the characters call "Meeska, Mooska, Mickey Mouse!" **"Handy Manny"** features the adventures of bilingual handyman Manny Garcia and his talking tools. **"Little Einsteins"** uses classical music to urge preschoolers to interact with four smart children who travel the world on various missions. Along with Darby, a redheaded 6-year-old, Disney's Winnie the Pooh characters solve mysteries on **"My Friends Tigger & Pooh,"** though impatient Tigger often needs Darby to remind him to "think, think, think."

▶ Have your children sit along an inner aisle to interact with Casey, the live host.

Early bird. A 1960s Audio Animatronic parrot on display at Walt Disney: One Man's Dream.

Walt Disney: One Man's Dream

★ ★ ★ ✔ **Allow 35 min. Capacity: 200. Fear factor: None. Access: Guests may remain in wheelchairs, ECVs. Assistive listening, handheld and reflective captioning available. Located on the walkway between Pixar Place and the Animation Courtyard. Debuted: 2001.**

A salute to the life of Walt Disney, this exhibit combines memorabilia exhibits with a short film. It includes the school desk Disney used as a Missouri second-grader, his studio desk from the 1930s and his (re-created) 1960s office.

Walt Disney's role in theme-park history is well represented. Hand-built by Disney himself in 1949, a wooden diorama displays early ideas for dark rides such as Peter Pan's Flight. The "Dancing Man" electronic marionette tested techniques that led to Audio-Animatronics robots. A simulated TV studio shows Disney filming a video to interest investors in his ultimate dream: the Experimental Prototype Community of Tomorrow (EPCOT). The back room has two Audio-Animatronics creatures you can control yourself: a robotic man and Tiki bird.

A 200-seat theater shows a moving biographical film. Narrated by Walt Disney himself through vintage audio clips, the 16-minute film explores Disney's never-ending drive and the hardships he overcame.

Average Wait	
9am	0 min
10am	0
11am	0
Noon	0
1pm	0
2pm	0
3pm	0
4pm	0
5pm	0
6pm	0
7pm	0
8pm	0
9pm	0

Journey Into Narnia: Prince Caspian

★ This 15-minute walk-through promotional display for the 2008 movie "The Chronicles of Narnia: Prince Caspian" consists of the viewing of a making-of video and a few props and costumes used in the film. The exhibit area resembles the movie's vault where the lion Aslan sacrificed himself. In front of the exhibit entrance, Prince Caspian himself poses for photos in front of a backdrop of the movie's Dancing Lawn. The video has violent scenes. *Access: Guests may remain in wheelchairs and ECVs. Assistive listening; reflective and activated captions.*

▶ One Man's Dream is a great spot to duck out of a rainstorm. You can stay as long as you like.

Mr. Potato Head, a talking Audio-Animatronics figure, interacts with guests at Toy Story Mania

Toy Story Mania

★★★★★ ✔ 7 min. (game play 5 min.) Capacity: 108. *FastPass* Fear factor: None. Vehicles move from game to game in a jerky, funhouse fashion. Access: Offline loading area for disabled guests, into vehicles that have shooting guns with buttons as well as pull strings. ECV users must transfer. All ride vehicles offer closed captioning. Debuted: 2008.

This high-tech ride is a series of 3-D video shooting galleries. Climbing into a vehicle that pairs you up with another person, you don 3-D glasses and enter a sequence of five dark corridors that are lined with large video screens. You stop at each one, where you play a virtual midway game. But instead of tossing real objects with your hand, you shoot virtual ones out of an old-fashioned spring-action cannon mounted in front of you.

The action seems real. As you play, you actually see the objects you launch leave your gun and travel into the screens, which appear to have remarkable depth. For some targets, timely sprays of water let you feel it when they explode. For others, blasts of air enhance the sense that they are popping out of the screen and flying past your head. Designed to appeal to all ages and skill levels, the games are easy to play but offer many hidden challenges. Toy Story Mania is located on the former Mickey Avenue, in the building that most recently hosted Who Wants to Be a Millionaire—Play It.

Unfortunately, the biggest challenge is avoiding a long line. On a typical day when the park opens at 9 a.m., the standby wait for Toy Story Mania will be 30 minutes by 9:05 a.m., at least an hour by 10 a.m., and up to two hours by noon. As for Fastpasses, the entire supply for a day is typically distributed before noon.

Once you do make it in, each of the five games you play will be hosted by a different "Toy Story" character. Hamm invites you to shoot virtual plastic eggs at barnyard targets. Bo Peep has you aim darts at a landscape full of balloon sheep, trees and clouds. The Green Army Men sergeant orders you to break plates with baseballs, then the Little Green Aliens pop up in a ring-toss game hosted by Buzz Lightyear. For the finale, you launch suction-cup darts at Woody's Wild West scenes, then again at some mine carts controlled by the mis-

Average Wait

9am	30 min
10am	60
11am	60
Noon	70
1pm	70
2pm	130
3pm	150
4pm	65
5pm	80
6pm	85
7pm	80
8pm	80
9pm	70

▶ To avoid a long wait, get here within 5 minutes of the park opening or get a Fastpass.

You've Got a Friend in... your partner

BY MICAELA NEAL There are three keys to getting a high score on Toy Story Mania. The first two are obvious: shoot constantly (your cannon can fire up to six objects per second) and know where the high-value targets are. The third key is teamwork. To get a top score, you have to work together with the person sitting next to you. That way, you can hit multiple targets simultaneously, which in turn will reveal hidden levels of the game.

GAME BOOTH	HIGH-VALUE INITIAL TARGETS	HOW TO REVEAL BONUS TARGETS
HAMM AND EGGS	❶ In the doorway of the barn is a 500-point horse. ❷ The green ducks in the lake are also 500 points. ❸ A 500-point squirrel runs up both the left and right edges of the screen. ❹ Three gophers repeatedly pop up along the bottom. The brown gophers are worth 500 points; the gray ones 1000 points. ❺ The animals in the tree are 1000 points each. A 1000-point goat peers out of the barn window. A 1000-point mouse skitters along the barn's roof.	❶ Hit the mouse (see Tip No. 5 at left) and the barn will rotate to reveal its interior, which is filled with 2000-point rats. Hit every barn rat and more rats appear in the grass as 1000-point targets. ❷ Hit the fox on top of the henhouse (in the bottom left corner of the screen) and three hens will scurry out. The first is worth 1000 points; the second is worth 2000 points; the third 1000 points. ❸ Hit the 500-point donkey that walks along the hills and the animal will turn and run the other way as a 2000-point target.
BO PEEP'S BAAA-LOON POP	❶ Each of the reoccurring pink three-headed sheep balloons are worth 1000 points. ❷ The balloons on the clouds are worth 500 points each. ❸ 2000-point hot-air balloons occasionally float in the sky. ❹ Sheep balloons at the bottom of the screen are worth 500 points each.	❶ Hit a pink flower balloon to have a 500-point bee balloon fly out and float toward you. ❷ Hit all the balloons on the left cloud to have blue 500-point balloons rain down. ❸ Hit all the balloons on the right cloud to make the sun come out, which brings with it yellow 500-point balloons. ❹ **Team up with your partner** to simultaneously hit all the balloons on both clouds to create a rainbow, which causes many 2000-point multicolored balloons to fall from the sky. Note: this only works if the two final balloons are popped within the same second.
GREEN ARMY MEN SHOOT CAMP	❶ Helicopters hover with plates worth 1000 points. Other 1000-point plates appear within the mass of plates, while more are carried by trucks along the bottom. ❷ Planes in the sky tow plates worth 2000 points. Other 2000-point plates are tossed up from both sides of the mountain.	❶ **Team up with your partner** to simultaneously hit the two 2000-point plates that are tossed up from the sides of the mountain (see left) at the same time. Doing so will open the mountain and reveal a tank that shoots plates toward you worth 5000 points each.
BUZZ LIGHTYEAR'S FLYING TOSSERS	❶ Meteors near the sides of the screen are 500 points. ❷ Rockets are 1000 points. ❸ Aliens with jetpacks are worth 2000 points. ❹ Aliens at the top corners of the screen are 5000 points.	❶ **Team up with your partner** to simultaneously hoop all of the aliens in the large central rocket to launch it and reveal a huge robot. When the robot's mouth opens, toss rings into it to score—if you reveal the robot early enough—up to 2000 points per toss.
WOODY'S ROOTIN' TOOTIN' SHOOTIN' GALLERY	All initial targets are worth 100 points each.	❶ Each 100-point target triggers a series of bonus targets worth up to 1000 points each. ❷ As your vehicle moves from the first screen to the second (or from the second to the Woody's Bonus Roundup screen), hit two 100-point or 500-point targets close together to reveal a 2000-point target.
WOODY'S BONUS ROUNDUP	❶ The second-to-last mine cart on each track is always worth 2000 points.	❶ Hit the 1000-point targets by the bats that appear above the carts to wake them up and reveal 5000-point targets. ❷ Hit all of the carts on a track and the last one will be worth 5000 points. ❸ The final target increases its point value up to 2000 if you hit it often enough.

chievous Stinky Pete. One last super target lets you really pile up the points.

The ride starts at a practice booth, where you toss virtual cream pies at targets held by Buzz, Jessie, Rex and Woody.

Your score is tallied as you play. At the end of the ride, you learn how you've done against your partner, as well as the best players of the day and month.

The ride takes its inspiration from the fact that Andy's toys spring to life whenever he is away. In this case, Andy has received a "Midway Games Play Set" for his latest birthday, and the toys have opened the box and set up the game booths and carnival trams in his absence.

The air-conditioned queue room is decorated with huge versions of classic board games as well as giant crayons, playing cards, toys, even Andy's cardboard playsets from the 1995 film. Two ViewMaster reels are each nearly 4 feet across.

The waiting area features a 5-foot 2-inch Audio-Animatronics version of Mr. Potato Head, a robot who acts as the ride's carnival barker. Thanks to a library of audio clips recorded by comedian Don Rickles, the character says more lines of dialogue than any other Disney robot, and can even chat with guests one-on-one. His eyes can look directly at the guest he's speaking with, and his mouth moves fluidly, so that it actually appears to form vowel sounds and words. He occasionally takes off his ear; sometimes his hat. Disney spent more time programming the state-of-the-art character than any other robotic figure in its history.

The attraction's loading area is meant to be Andy's bedroom. A giant Tinkertoy roof has rods that are 4 inches around and connectors 2 feet wide.

FUN FINDS

Exterior: ❶ Across the Pixar Place walkway, some of Andy's toys are sending messages to its riders. A Green Army Man has hung a Mr. Spell off the side of the building across from the Fastpass machines. Its messages include "Toy Story Midway Mania... More fun than a barrel of monkeys... Sorry monkeys." Other Army Men have hung a Scrabble board across from the ride's entrance. Spelling out the message "You've got a friend in me," it hints at the teamwork the ride requires to get a high score (see previous page). Andy has left a note on the door of the back of the Pixar Place entrance gate

that explains the setup: Mr. Spell is a "signal corps communicator;" the Scrabble board is a "top secret message decoder." **Queue room, first area:** ❶ A pink crayon is the only one in the room unused. Why? "It's Andy's room," an Imagineer tells us. "He's a boy." **Queue room, third area:** ❶ The Pixar star ball and Luxo Jr. lamp sit on either side of Mr. Potato Head. ❷ Toy blocks under him show the letters "P" and "H." ❸ Near the end of the standby queue, Andy has painted a rough version of Nemo from 2003's "Finding Nemo." **Loading area:** ❶ The books on the wall murals that portray Andy's room are the same as those in his room in the "Toy Story" film. **Bo Peep's Baaa-Loon Pop:** ❶ Pop a water balloon to be sprayed with water. ❷ On the right cloud, pop the second balloon from the left to have it fly toward you. **Green Army Men Shoot Camp:** ❶ Hit either of the two yellow plates to have an adjacent cannon fire a shot at you. **Buzz Lightyear's Flying Tossers:** ❶ Hoop one of the aliens wearing a jetpack to have it fly over your head. ❷ Hoop one of the rockets to have it shoot toward you. ❸ As your vehicle moves to Woody's Rootin' Tootin' Shootin' Gallery, a wall mural of a carnival includes Toy Story Mania as one of its attractions. **Woody's Rootin' Tootin' Shootin' Gallery:** ❶ A bank-robbing squirrel pops out of the bank when you hit the target next to it. ❷ Hitting the target by the bird nest causes the bird sitting on it to pop up in the air. Sequential targets make baby birds fly away. ❸ A beaver pops up when you hit the target on the dam. Sequential targets make the beaver squeak. **Prize booth:** ❶ Confetti will pop out of your gun. ❷ On some screens, Bo kisses Woody as the curtain closes. **Exit area:** ❶ Two blocks facing the exit walkway show the letters "C" and "U." ❷ As you leave, you pass a "Tin Toy" Little Golden Book that has jammed Andy's bedroom door closed—so that the toys can play with his new game indefinitely.

HIDDEN MICKEYS

❶ Near the end of the standby queue, upside down, as a paint splotch under the tail of a Nemo-like clownfish. ❷ In the boarding area mural, as frames around Bullseye, Mr. Potato Head and Slinky Dog on the Toy Story Midway Games Playset box. ❸ Toward the end of the ride, on a mural to your right as you rotate into position for the screen that tallies your score, as the dot in the exclamation point of the phrase "Circus Fun!"

▶ **All Toy Story Mania Fastpasses for a day are usually distributed before noon.**

Swaying dancers are persuaded to "Kill the Beast!" during "The Mob Song"

Beauty and the Beast — Live on Stage

★★★★★ ✔ 25 min. Capacity: 1,500. Fear factor: During "The Mob Song" Gaston stabs the Beast, but you don't see the wound. Access: Guests may remain in wheelchairs and ECVs. Assistive listening. Debuted: 1991, revised 2001.

This uplifting show re-creates the spirit of Disney's 1991 animated film by focusing on its music. "Belle," "Gaston," "Be Our Guest," "Something There," "The Mob Song," "Beauty and the Beast"—they're all here. Most lead vocals are sung live.

Average Wait	
9am	n/a
10am	20 min
11am	20
Noon	20
1pm	20
2pm	20
3pm	20
4pm	20
5pm	20
6pm	20
7pm	n/a
8pm	n/a
9pm	n/a

The supporting cast is outstanding. When Gaston struts on stage the village girls fight over him with flirty passion; when he chooses Belle instead they stalk off in a huff. The "Be Our Guest" maids squeal in delight when Lumiere announces dinner. Two tickle Belle with their feather dusters; later two whisper to each other, leave the stage and return with a giant sundae that transforms into a warbling diva.

Colorful costumes and creative lighting effects add to the theatrical feel. In the first scene the supporting dancers wear six different hues. In the ballroom scene Belle's gold gown is offset by vivid pink dresses. The Hollywood Bowl-like stage arch flashes during "Be Our Guest;" dappled lights color "The Mob Song." The open-air theater is covered with a roof.

CELEBRITY HANDPRINTS
Thirty television stars have left impressions outside the theater, in a small plaza next to the rear bleachers. "Star Trek's" Scotty, James Doohon, added "Beam Me Up." "Jeopardy" host Alex Trebek wrote "Who is Alex Trebek?" Also here: Morey Amsterdam, Imogene Coca, Bob Denver, June Lockhart, George Wendt, even journeyman Martin Mull.

FUN FINDS
❶ The show begins with a pun: a ringing bell. ❷ "The Mob Song" includes a quote from Shakespeare. "Screw your courage to the sticking place" Gaston says as he rallies the villagers to kill the Beast, the same phrase Lady Macbeth uses to urge her husband to kill Duncan. ❸ As Gaston incites the mob, a few villagers remain skeptical.

▶ For a full experience, get in line 45 minutes before showtime and sit down front.

Max axe. A 40-foot guitar graces the entrance. Its neck transforms into a simulated coaster track.

Rock 'n' Roller Coaster Starring Aerosmith

★★★★ 1 min, 22 sec. Capacity: 120 (5 24-seat vehicles). *FastPass* Fear factor: Anticipating the launch scares even adults. Access: ECV users must transfer. Height restriction: 48 in. Debuted: 1999.

This popular thrill ride has a lot going for it—a launch that blasts you to 57 mph in 2.8 seconds, two loops, a tight corkscrew, rock music and a fun theme.

The grins begin as you enter the building, the headquarters of G-Force Records. Step through the lobby (mimicking guitar necks, its columns are complete with fret boards and strings) and you're off on a time-warp to the 1970s. You pass displays of real vintage recording and playback gear. Soon you enter Studio C, where you find the band Aerosmith mixing the rhythm tracks to their 1975 hit "Walk This Way."

Suddenly the guys have to leave; they're late for a show. When the band offers you backstage passes, their manager phones for a limo to take you there. "We're going to need a stretch," she says, counting the crowd. "In fact, make it a super stretch."

"The show is all the way across town," she tells you, "but I got you a really fast car."

You're then ushered into a grimy back alley, where up pulls a baby-blue 1959 Caddy convertible. Soon you rocket into the Los Angeles night, with Aerosmith blasting on the stereo. You zoom through the famous HOLLYWOOD sign, through a billboard doughnut, through a half-mile of twists and turns.

Plenty thrilling for most folks, the ride gets mixed reviews from coaster freaks. The launch is exhilarating, but everything after that is rather mild. You slow down dramatically after the first couple of turns, and average just 28 miles per hour.

The smooth ride has no steep drops and you're not jerked around in your seat. But the turns are tight, the tunes rock and it's all in the dark. In other words, you won't get sick, but your palms will sweat.

FUN FINDS

❶ Equipment in the first display case includes a disc cutter. In the days of vinyl, it etched sounds from a mixing console onto a master disc, creating the phrase "cutting a record." Nearby is a 1958 Gibson Les Paul

Average Wait

9am	0 min
10am	40
11am	50
Noon	65
1pm	80
2pm	70
3pm	60
4pm	80
5pm	70
6pm	75
7pm	75
8pm	90
9pm	100

▶ For the most tense launch, ask to sit in the front seat. You'll have little clue it's coming.

Standard guitar. ❷ The second case holds vintage record players, from a 1904 external-horn Edison Fireside to a 1970s "Disc-O-Kid." ❸ Put your ear to the doors marked "Studio A" or "Studio B" and you will hear Aerosmith rehearsing. ❹ Wall-mounted concert posters include one for a 1973 show from Aerosmith's first national tour, as the opening act for the New York Dolls. It's midway down on the right. ❺ Alley puns include signs on the rear of the G-Force building indicating work has been done by Sam Andreas and Sons Structural Restoration, ❻ the garage is run by Lock 'n' Roll Parking Systems, ❼ its dumpster is owned by the Rock 'n' Rollaway Disposal Co. and ❽ a glass case with rates for Wash This Way Auto Detail. ❾ Each limo license plate sports an apt message such as 2FAST4U and UGOBABE. ❿ Once you arrive at the show, a concert video shows Tyler screaming "Rock 'n' Roller Coaster!!!"

HIDDEN MICKEYS
Twice on the building's sign: ❶ Tyler's shirt has Mickey silhouettes and ❷ the boy wears mouse ears. ❸ As three pieces in a beige section of the foyer's floor mosaic, just before you leave the room. ❹ As a distorted carpet pattern in the first display room. ❺ As cables on the recording studio floor. ❻ On the registration sticker on each of the limousines' rear license plates. ❼ As the "O" in the phrase "Box #15" on a trunk along the ride exit walkway.

FUN FACTS ❯❯ The manager is actress Illeana Douglas, perhaps best known as Angela on the HBO series "Six Feet Under." ❯❯ The car radio's DJ is voiced by longtime L.A. rock jock Uncle Joe Benson. ❯❯ The squeal you hear as each limo peels out is prerecorded. It comes from barely visible speakers under the driveway. ❯❯ Most of the ride takes place inside "Stage 15," the structure behind the G-Force building.

Your Rock 'n' Roll limo loops just after launch

PHOTO © DISNEY

ALL-AMERICAN ROCK 'N' ROLL Known for its driving riffs and suggestive lyrics, Aerosmith formed in Boston in 1970. Its raunchy swagger, highlighted by singer Steven Tyler's prancing stage antics, drew comparisons to the Rolling Stones. Tyler and Stones singer Mick Jagger even looked similar. Early hits included 1975's "Walk This Way," which, like the Stones' earlier "Satisfaction," used a groove so strong the words didn't matter. Aerosmith also created rock music's first power ballad, adding strings to 1973's piano-based "Dream On." Plagued by drugs in the late 1970s, the band got back on track in 1986, when Tyler and lead guitarist Joe Perry appeared on rap group Run D.M.C.'s cover of "Walk This Way." The video became an MTV staple.

▶ Long legs? Ask for an odd-numbered row. They have far more legroom.

The side of Disney's Hollywood Tower Hotel shows its ornate Mission Revival architecture

The Twilight Zone Tower of Terror

★★★★★ ✔ 4 min. Capacity: 84. *FastPass* Fear factor: Mighty frighty. The drops are smooth, but the mind games start as soon as you pass the gate. Access: ECV guests must transfer to a wheelchair. Activated captioning. Height restriction: 40 in. Debuted: 1994; revised 1996, 1999, 2002.

Loaded with effects and detail, this superb attraction is designed to freak you out. Checking in to a deserted hotel, you climb into a freight elevator as souls of earlier guests beckon you to join them. Then you enter a supernatural dimension, where you fall up to 130 feet though it's never the same ride twice. Meant to recall the peculiar style of the television series "The Twilight Zone," the trip is even more fun if you know its story.

According to Disney, the luxurious 12-story Hollywood Tower Hotel opened in 1917. Known for its service, it became a gathering place for the Tinseltown elite. Fast forward to Oct. 31, 1939. As the hotel hosts a Halloween party in its rooftop lounge, many guests check in for the night. But then a thunderstorm sweeps in and, at precisely 8:05 p.m., a huge lightning bolt hits the hotel. Its force dematerializes two wings of the building, including two elevator shafts. Among the victims are five people in an elevator—a child actress with her nanny, a couple of young rising stars and a hotel bellhop. The remaining guests run out in horror, leaving their luggage and other belongings behind.

The Hollywood Tower Hotel stands deserted for more than 50 years, but mysteriously reopens in 1994. Strangely, the staff from that fateful night is still on hand, unaged, with no memory of the disaster.

As you walk through the entrance gate, you're a guest of the reopened hotel and are arriving to check in. But something is wrong—a misty garden is lush but overgrown, a fountain has no water, the lobby is covered in dust and cobwebs.

A bellhop prepares to take you to your room, but since the lobby elevators aren't working (behind an "Out of Order" sign, their doors hang crooked in their tracks), he asks you to wait in the library.

Then things get freaky. The library power goes out, but then its TV set comes on. It's a

Average Wait

9am	0 min
10am	40
11am	40
Noon	45
1pm	50
2pm	80
3pm	40
4pm	60
5pm	80
6pm	20
7pm	60
8pm	80
9pm	60

▶ Glance around at the library detail quickly. The lights go out almost immediately.

black-and-white model circa 1959. Rod Serling appears, describing "tonight's story on 'The Twilight Zone'," a "somewhat unique" fable about a maintenance service elevator. The screen shows those five guests, boarding their elevator car just before the flash. When it hits, they disappear.

"We invite you if you dare to step aboard," Serling says, "because in tonight's episode, you are the star."

You're directed into a back boiler room, an industrial area of the hotel clearly not meant for visitors. You board a rusty service elevator, but as the doors close you discover it clearly has a mind of its own.

First the lights go out. Then you're whisked to the fourth floor, where the doors open. Do Not Disturb signs hang on most of the room doors, shoes and wine bottles sit outside them. As lightning flashes in the window, those five elevator guests flicker into view again. Still back in 1939, they beckon you to follow them down the hall, until, wrapped in a crackling net of electricity, they again become invisible. The walls disappear, revealing a night sky. The hall window floats, and shatters.

You've entered the Twilight Zone.

The ominious Hollywood Tower Hotel contains The Twilight Zone Tower of Terror attraction

The doors close and up you go again, this time to the hotel's 13th floor—a level that doesn't exist. The doors open, and you hear Serling speak again: "One stormy night long ago, five people stepped through the door of an elevator and into a nightmare. That door is opening once again, and this time it's opening for you."

Your cabin moves forward in the dark, out of its shaft and alongside the glowing, moving silhouettes of that spooky quintet. Ahead of you is a star field, but it too moves, forming a line which then separates with a bright flash. Those lines become the edge of another opening door—into one of those elevator shafts that no longer exists.

You move into the space. The doors slam shut. It's completely dark. Silent. Tense.

Then your entire elevator car is tossed—violently— up, down—down, up—up, up, down. Occasionally elevator doors in front of you open, revealing the open sky of the theme park. You may see those five figures again, or hear rain fall, or smell something.

After about a minute the madness stops. Your car arrives calmly in the basement.

"The next time you check into a deserted hotel..." Serling says, "make sure you know just what kind of vacancy you're filling. Or you may find yourself a permanent resident of... 'The Twilight Zone.'"

THE SCIENCE OF SPOOKY

Hidden behind all the theming is a unique mix of innovative engineering, classic special effects and modern math. Combining

▶ Hang onto your stuff! Anything loose will go flying during your fall.

A cautionary notice at the ride entrance

three distinct ride systems, the mechanics of the attraction represent a novel achievement of applied science. Its "elevator" goes up, moves forward, then plummets down and soars up a second shaft, all in one seamless experience.

The first system is obvious: an elevator. When you leave the boiler room, you're in a standard, 50-foot elevator shaft, with sliding doors and two stops. The second system kicks in at the top of the shaft. As your car (an independent vehicle, which rode up the shaft in a cage) moves forward, it's using the technology of a self-guided palette driver, an automated machine used by companies such as Anheuser-Busch to move inventory through large warehouses. Controlled by an unseen computer, it rolls on wheels and gets its power from an on-board battery.

The third system is Disney's own. Once your cabin enters the drop shaft, it's silently locked into a second cage that is tightly suspended on a looped steel cable. Pulled by high-speed winches and motors, the cage "falls" faster than the pull of gravity (you reach 37 mph in just 1.5 seconds, about a quarter of a second faster than if you were falling freely) and shoots up with similar speed. The result: though you never actually fall and are never truly free of the ride's grasp, you feel completely out of control.

Though often stunningly realistic, most of the elevator effects are created by simple, time-tested methods.

At your first stop, a long corridor filled with translucent people, disappearing windows and sudden star fields is really a shallow area filled with transparent screens, which show images from hidden projectors. Though it looks far away and 8 feet tall, the end of the hall is actually just a few feet in front of you, and only 4 feet high.

Once your elevator moves forward, mirrors on the floor and ceiling make it seem those planes have disappeared. The characters to your side are simply independently moving plastic cutouts, split down the middle to make them look warped. In front of you, the changing star field comes from synchronized fiber-optic lights built into the doors to the final drop zone.

Each ride is different, as a computer system chooses the particulars of your fall using a random-number generator based on modulo functions—calculations that search for two numbers that, when divided by a third number, have the same remainder.

A HAUNTED HISTORY

While planning the attraction Disney considered a variety of themes. At first it was to be housed in a real resort, the Haunted Hollywood Hotel. One idea featured actor Mel Brooks as a madman hotel owner who chased guests into an elevator. Another had actors filming a horror movie, with a walk-through segment narrated by Vincent Price.

▶ Your fall is over when you see the turning spiral from "The Twilight Zone."

The attraction has a reprogrammable ride system, which has made it possible for Disney to update it three times so far.

At first the ride was one plummet of about 100 feet. A 1996 revision added three falls, adding a half drop and a false fall. Three years later Disney debuted a seven-fall experience that brought faster acceleration, more weightlessness and more shaking.

Finally, on New Year's Eve 2002, the company introduced "Tower of Terror 4," the current mix of random drops enhanced with physical, sound and visual effects. "We can reinvent the experience as often as we want," says Imagineer Theron Skees. "We can add effects, change timing sequences and alter the way the elevator moves."

FUN FINDS

Lobby: ❶ To the right of the reception desk, an American Automobile Association plaque honors the hotel's "13-diamond" status. A real award, it was presented by the AAA when the ride opened in 1994. **❷** Abandoned items at the desk include a fedora, topcoat, folded newspaper, open registration book, alligator-skin luggage and mail-slot mail and messages. **❸** A bag, cane and white fedora lean against the concierge desk. **❹** A poster at the concierge desk promotes a show by Anthony Freemont, the name of a 6-year-old boy in a 1961 "Twilight Zone" episode ("It's a Good Life") who uses telepathic powers to terrorize his neighbors. **❺** A diamond ring, white glove and two glasses rest on a table on the left. Next to it is a champagne bucket. **❻** A mah-jongg game is in progress on a nearby table. "One of our designers actually learned to play mah-jongg," Imagineer Eric Jacobson says, "so he could make sure the game pieces would be in a proper position." **❼** Tea has just been served to the players; a cart holds cups ready for pouring, roses and a newspaper. **❽** Another teacup rests on the end table in front of a fireplace; a goblet and small plate sit on a table to the right. **Library: ❶** The footage of Serling has been altered to remove a cigarette from his right hand. **❷** The little girl sings the nursery rhyme "It's Raining, It's Pouring" on the video and on the fourth floor. The bookcases hold such items as **❸** the devil-headed, "Ask Me a Yes or No Question" fortune-telling machine from the 1960 episode "Nick of Time" (a story of a man unable to make decisions for himself) and **❹** the tiny silver robot featured in the 1961 episode "The Invaders" (a tale of a farm woman who kills what appear to be small invading aliens). **Boiler room: ❶** Though the service elevators' tracking dials only go to "12," their arrows go to an unmarked "13." **Elevator: ❶** As your doors close, a hint at your destination—a "1" on the left door and a "3" on the right—disguises itself as a "B," the elevator's letter. **❷** The small inspection certificate on the interior wall of the elevator is signed by "Cadwallader," a jovial character in the 1959 episode "Escape Clause" who secretly is the devil. Dated Oct. 31, 1939, the certificate has the number 10259, a reference to the date the TV program premiered: Oct. 2, 1959. When your elevator stops to unload, you sit next to a basement storage area that includes **❸** a "Special Jackpot $10,000" slot machine from the 1960 episode "The Fever" (a story of a talking slot that drives a tightwad crazy) and **❹** two ventriloquist dummies used in 1962's "The Dummy"(a dummy switches places with his human owner) as well as 1964's "Caesar and Me" (a ventriloquist

---

TRANSCENDENTAL TV "There is a fifth dimension beyond that which is known to man... a middle ground between light and shadow, between science and superstition... it is an area which we call The Twilight Zone." Along with a four-note theme song ("do-do-do-do, do-do-do-do..."), those classic words welcomed viewers to "The Twilight Zone," an imaginative CBS television anthology that aired from 1959 to 1964. Placing ordinary people into extraordinary situations, the episodes often had mind-bending twists, with confused characters in unfamiliar, sometimes supernatural surroundings. Host Rod Serling created the show after getting fed up with censorship hassles at his job as a writer of the dramatic series "Playhouse 90." Though "The Twilight Zone" was as popular as today's "American Idol" (each episode was watched by about one in 10 Americans) Serling had to fight hard to keep it on the air. In the pre-cable world of the 1960s, an audience that size was considered pitiful. Though the show made him a giant in the TV industry, Serling stood only 5-foot-5 and weighed just 137 pounds. A chronic smoker, he died from complications of heart surgery in 1975, at age 50.

▶ The gift shop offers thick, comfortable "Hollywood Tower Hotel" bathrobes.

Reputedly untouched since 1939, the Hollywood Tower Hotel lobby is covered in dust and cobwebs

form Mickey's face, the eye rims make his ears). ❷ 1932's "What! No Mickey Mouse?" is the song featured on some sheet music in the left library, on a bookcase directly in front of the entrance door. ❸ The little girl in the TV video is holding a 1930s Mickey Mouse doll. ❹ As large, round ash doors beneath a fire box on a brick furnace in the boiler room (on your right just after you've entered the basement). ❺ As water stains just to the left of a fuse box on the boiler room's left wall, just past the spot where the queue divides. ❻ On the 13th floor, in the center of the star field as it comes together to form a pinpoint.

FUN FACTS ⟩⟩ When Serling speaks on the television, you're actually watching him introduce the 1961 "Twilight Zone" episode, "It's a Good Life." He originally said "This, as you may recognize, is a map of the United States," though on the video the camera cuts away as he pronounces the word "map" and you hear him say "maintenance service elevator." Since Serling died in 1975, and there was never a "Twilight Zone" episode about a Hollywood Tower Hotel, Serling's lines are voiced by impersonator Mark Silverman. ⟩⟩ The lobby in the video is not the one at the attraction. Disney filmed it on a California soundstage with a similar set. ⟩⟩ The elevators have four loading areas but only two exits. The initial four shafts merge into two paths on the top floor. ⟩⟩ The cast members' break room is between the drop shafts. When you scream, they hear you. "It's very difficult to relax," one tells us. ⟩⟩ The ride's engines are at the top and bottom of the shafts. Each develops 110,000 foot-pounds of torque, uses regeneration for deceleration control and is 35 feet long, 7 feet wide, 12 feet tall and weighs 132,000 pounds. ⟩⟩ The Tower is 199 feet high, just short enough to not require aircraft warning lights. ⟩⟩ In 1993, as the Tower was being built, it was struck by lightning.

uses his cigar-smoking dummy to commit crimes). **Basement:** ❶ The clock in the basement office is stuck on the time 8:05, the moment of the lightning strike. ❷ Up in the far top left corner of the office is a small silver spaceship, the home to the library's "Invaders" robot. ❸ The bulletin-board notes to the right of the basement office (the "Picture If You Will" souvenir-photo area) seek finders of items such as "Pocket watch, sentimental value, broken crystal" a reference to the 1963 episode "A Kind of Stopwatch" (in which a bank robber stops time forever when he breaks an unusual timepiece). **Gift shop:** ❶ The outdoor display windows are still decorated for the Halloween of 1939.

HIDDEN MICKEYS
❶ In the lobby, as a pair of folded wire-rim glasses on the concierge desk (the temples

▶ A cool hidden resting spot: a stone bench to the right as you exit the gift shop.

Dancin' in the street. Sheriff Woody and Bo Peep "get down and get funky" during a performance of Disney's Block Party Bash.

Block Party Bash

★★★★★ ✔ 22 min. (5-min staged and scored setup, 12-min show, 5-min departure; times may be reduced during summer). Arrive 15 min early for a good seat, 30 min early for best spots. First show on Hollywood Blvd; second on walkway in front of The American Idol Experience and Sounds Dangerous. Fear factor: None. Access: Special viewing areas for ECV and wheelchair guests. Debuted: 2008 (Disneyland 2005).

Imagine a line of nearly a hundred cheerleaders that stretches down the length of a football field, from one goal post to the other. Dressed as everything from cowgirls to ladybugs, they dance to a driving beat of disco, rock and Motown classics. Joining them are a troupe of acrobats and jumping stilt-walkers, as well as 15 cartoon characters.

Next year's Super Bowl half-time show? No, this year's Block Party Bash, a Pixar street party held every afternoon.

Park guests toss beach balls back and forth to the cheerleaders, compete with one another in a scream contest, and join performers in the street to dance to tunes such as "Macarena," "(Shake, Shake, Shake) Shake Your Booty" and "Y.M.C.A."

Unlike a parade, Block Party Bash is not a continuously moving procession. It's a staged street performance that rolls out and stops, once on Hollywood Blvd. and once on the walkway that leads from the Sorcerer's Hat to Sounds Dangerous.

The 500-foot-long show includes three floats representing the Pixar films "A Bug's Life" (1998), "Monsters, Inc." (2001) and "Toy Story" (1995) and "Toy Story 2" (1999). Between them are elevated stages and trampolines. Standing above the action, "Toy Story" Green Army Men order the crowd to "get down, get funky and be all you can be!"

Dancing characters include Mr. Potato Head, Bo Peep and Jessie the cowgirl from the "Toy Story" films; Mike, Sulley, janitors Needleman and Smitty, scarer George Sanderson and little girl Boo from "Monsters, Inc."; and Flik, Atta, Heimlich the caterpillar, Gypsy the moth and Slim the walking stick from "A Bug's Life." The finale has appearances by Mr. and Mrs. Incredible and Frozone from 2004's "The Incredibles."

RECOMMENDED VIEWING SPOTS
The show stops on Hollywood Boulevard and then alongside Echo Lake. Shady spots are snared 30 minutes early. Park benches on Hollywood Boulevard are snagged even earlier than that. The best viewing spots for the first show are directly in front of the Hot

▶ Little rubber souvenir balls are often tossed out to the audience at the end of each show.

A "Toy Story" cowgirl dances during the Block Party Bash at Disney's Hollywood Studios

and Fresh popcorn stand for "Toy Story" characters, the intersection of Hollywood Blvd. and Vine St. for the stars of "Monsters, Inc." and in front of the Cover Story shop for the performers from "A Bug's Life." The best spots for the Echo Lake show are at the ATAS Showcase ("Toy Story"), in front of The American Idol Experience ("Monsters, Inc.") and from there to the Sorcerer's Hat ("A Bug's Life").

FUN FINDS

"Toy Story" float: ❶ The brand name of Mike the tape recorder reads "Oldskool." ❷ The crayon brand is "Pixola." ❸ On that float's side, the eyes of Lenny the pair of binoculars move as they watch guests. **"Monsters, Inc." float:** ❶ From his point of view, Sulley's control panel reads "071555," a reference to the July 15, 1955, opening of California's Disneyland Resort. (Debuting at Disneyland, the Bash was created in conjunction with that park's 50th anniversary.) ❷ A sign on that float indicates it has had "4 Accident-Free Days." ❸ Its rear license plate expires in May 2005, the month the Block Party Bash debuted at Disneyland. **"A Bug's Life" float:** ❶ The nutrition facts of the Casey Jr. box of animal crackers indicate it has 15,000 calories, including "Calories from fat: 14,999." ❷ It also lists zero percent of vitamin "A113," a term that appears in every Pixar film. A113 is the license plate number of Andy's mom's minivan in the "Toy Story" films, the model of the scuba diver's camera in 2003's "Finding Nemo" and the code for Auto's directive in 2008's "WALL-E." It's also the license plate number of every earth vehicle in the 2002 movie "Lilo & Stitch." The term sometimes appears in the television series "The Simpsons." In reality, A113 is a room at the California Institute of the Arts used to teach character animation. ❸ Underneath the nutrition facts, the crackers' ingredient list includes "essence of low-fat butterfly," "caterpillar of salt," "evaporated bug juice," "natural vanilla, minimally natural vanilla, I-can't-believe-it's-not-vanilla, you-could-call-it-vanilla-if-you-wanted-to vanilla," "lions, tigers and bears, oh my!," "vita-veta-vegamins" and "a pinch of P. T. Flea's Famous Flaming Death."

FUN FACT ❯❯ Each Block Party Bash has 114 live performers and a support crew of 30.

Fantasmic!

★★★★ 25 min. Capacity: 9,900 (6,900 seats). Arrive 90 min early for the best seats. Snack bar. Fear factor: Loud noises and bright flashes frighten some children. Access: Guests may remain in wheelchairs, ECVs. Assistive listening; reflective captioning. Debuted: 1998 (Disneyland 1992).

The kitchen sink of Disney's evening extravaganzas, this outdoor theatrical show takes place in a lagoon dominated by a large island with a 60-foot mountain. The plot: Mickey Mouse has a nightmare.

Dressed as the Sorcerer's Apprentice, the dreaming mouse conducts water fountains like instruments in an orchestra, creating water screens that show scenes from 1940's "Fantasia." As his powers increase, Mickey shoots fireworks from his fingers and imagines flowers and animals who perform a surreal version of "I Just Can't Wait to be King."

As more images appear, Monstro the whale (from 1940's "Pinocchio") lunges at the audience. "Hey!" Mickey yells as things go dark. "What's going on?"

Bang! The thunder of a cannon transforms the set into the 17th-century Virginia of Disney's 1995 film "Pocahontas." As Native Americans paddle by in torch-lit canoes, prissy Gov. Ratcliffe claims the land. As they burn down trees, dig up land and shoot Indians, Englishmen sing "Mine Mine Mine." Eventually, Pocahontas puts a stop to it.

After a romantic boat parade of Ariel, Belle and Snow White, the Evil Queen arrives and morphs into the old hag. "Now I'll turn that little mouse's dream into a nightmare Fantasmic!" she cackles, summoning up Disney villains including Jafar, who transforms into a live-action snake, and Maleficent, who becomes a 40-foot dragon and ignites the waterway with her breath.

But Mickey fights back. "You may think you're so powerful," he tells the dragon, "well, this is *my* dream!" All ends well.

For the finale a showboat arrives filled with characters, piloted by the black-and-white Mickey from the 1928 cartoon "Steamboat Willie." To end the show there's a burst of fireworks and a delightful now-you-see-him, now-you-don't farewell from your host. The show has 50 performers.

HIDDEN MICKEY

Pinocchio's water-screen bubble forms Mickey's head; two others form his ears.

▶ At Fantasmic, two-person gaps in front-center rows often exist 30 minutes before showtime.

A "party animal" in
Mickey's Jammin' Jungle
Parade at Disney's
Animal Kingdom

Disney's
Animal
Kingdom

Creativity gone wild

Though it's not as famous as Magic Kingdom, in many ways Disney's Animal Kingdom is much more magical. Set in 500 acres of botanical wonder, Disney's largest theme park features a real safari through a 110-acre African wilderness, two Broadway-style shows, a thrilling roller coaster, and up-close encounters with what seems like every strange creature on the planet. The park's mission: to make it easy—and fun—to appreciate the beauty, magnificence and importance of the animal world.

The intrinsic value of nature

The park's zoological operations are respected worldwide, but are fully hidden behind man-made hills, rivers and rocks. Scientists are breeding endangered species, and on-site researchers are studying animal behaviors, but you barely hear about it. The park is a member of the acclaimed Association of Zoos and Aquariums, but the AZA logo appears only on a flag out front.

Why? Because Disney wants you to see the real world of animals, not the artificial world of zoos. "Disney is all about storytelling, and here real live animals help tell them," executive designer Joe Rohde tells us. The park's stories "tend to propose conflicts—mostly conflicts with no full resolution—that get you to think about the intrinsic value of nature. You are free to engage in our stories at any level you want, including saying 'I'm not really interested, I'm just here to have fun.'"

"We want people to get a little tug on their heartstrings," adds Animal Kingdom vice president Dr. Beth Stevens, "and get people to care about animals."

FASTPASS RETURN TIMES

Use the table below to help plan your Animal Kingdom day. Note that all attractions typically have Fastpasses available until at least 4 p.m.

ATTRACTION	9A	10A	11A	Noon	1P	2P	3P	4P	5P	6P	7P	8P	9P
Dinosaur	10:10	10:45	11:45	12:45	1:45	2:45	3:45	4:45	OUT	OUT	OUT	CLSD	CLSD
Expdtn. Everest	10:10	11:45	12:50	2:30	4:00	5:00	6:00	6:30	7:00	OUT	OUT	CLSD	CLSD
Kali River Rapids	10:10	11:20	11:50	1:20	2:40	4:00	5:15	6:30	OUT	OUT	OUT	CLSD	CLSD
Kilimanjaro Safaris	10:10	11:10	12:20	1:20	2:20	3:20	4:20	5:20	6:20	OUT	OUT	CLSD	CLSD
Primeval Whirl	10:10	10:45	11:45	12:45	1:45	2:45	3:45	4:45	OUT	OUT	OUT	CLSD	CLSD
Tough To Be a Bug	10:10	11:15	11:35	12:35	1:35	2:45	3:45	4:45	5:45	OUT	OUT	CLSD	CLSD

Data based on surveys taken on random days during the summer of 2008.

Laid out in a classic hub-and-spoke style, this celebration of nature welcomes you with an entranceway free from even a single gift shop. Instead, you meander through the aptly named Oasis, a tropical jungle. Your path leads to the centrally located Discovery Island. From there five lands radiate outward.

How many days?

Though some say Animal Kingdom is just a half-day experience, that's only if you have no interest in wildlife. Actually, it can take four days to see everything.

Each of the animal habitats can take up to an hour to fully experience, and each is most rewarding before 11 a.m. Likewise, Conservation Station's public animal-care procedures take place only in the morning, and require a separate train trip to get to. The park has just nine major rides and shows, but they're all worthwhile. The parade is one of Disney's most creative processions. And the nature of the atmosphere itself—the first-class street performers, the stunning landscaping, the detailed interiors, the museum-like theming—makes you want to slow down and take it all in.

Though its animal attractions close at dusk, the park is sometimes open until 9 or 10 p.m. It's one of Disney's nicest night spots. Lit from within the trunk, the upper branches and leaves of the Tree of Life appear to glow. Strings of light bulbs line the paths of Asia, while flashing bulbs add cheesy charm to the Dino-Rama carnival at DinoLand U.S.A. The dining area of the Flame Tree Barbecue outdoor cafe is especially pretty.

Adventureland 2

Critics have often praised Walt Disney World as an example of how functional

A MAGICAL DAY

8:30a	Arrive at the park. As you wait for the gates to open (typically at 8:50 a.m.), pick up a Times Guide from the Guest Relations window at your left.
9:05a	Get Fastpasses for the Expedition Everest roller coaster.
9:10a	Maharajah Jungle Trek. The giant bats will be at their most lively.
9:45a	Kilimanjaro Safaris.
10:30a	Pangani Forest Trail. The gorillas and meerkats should be active.
11:30a	Expedition Everest. Ask for the front row for the best views, the back seat for the biggest thrill.
12:30a	Lunch. Air-conditioned Pizzafari has good counter-service food and a terrific decor. Close to Everest, the outdoor Flame Tree BBQ offers good food and nice

urban design can entertain with its form. The company has a knack for creating pedestrian walkways that also function as fully realized immersive environments.

Animal Kingdom takes the concept to a new level. Whereas Disney's other parks create visual cues from familiar Western icons such as European castles, this one develops them from nonspecific buildings whose designs come from developing countries, with architectural styles and building methods that are virtually unknown in the West.

The buildings and snack stands of **Discovery Island** are the company's most colorful, and best-looking, ever. Exteriors are bright, patterned and soulful, a combination of styles best described as Mexican Wedding Dress meets No Worries Caribbean. Each structure is lined in whimsical Balinese animal wood carvings, some 1,500 pieces in all. Interiors are just as attractive, with fanciful animals adorning the ceilings, columns, shelves and walls. Floors mix textured concrete with inlaid stone and broken-tile mosaics.

Each store has its own theme. Migrating and working animals highlight the primary gift shop, Island Mercantile.

Performance artist DiVine appears in Asia

Main rooms of Disney Outfitters are embellished with animals from the four compass directions of North, South, East and West. The right room has animals of the ground; the left has those of the air (a mural has animal constellations). Next

	views. While you eat, check your Times Guide to confirm your afternoon's show and parade times. *Note: Dining at Tusker House or Yak & Yeti will take too much of your time to see the 2 p.m. "Lion King" show.*	**3:00p**	Get Fastpasses for Kali River Rapids.
		3:30p	See Finding Nemo—The Musical. A show usually starts at 4 p.m.
1:20p	Festival of the Lion King. Get in line to see the 2 p.m. show. You'll get a great seat.	**4:30p**	Kali River Rapids. Who cares if you get soaked. You're done! (Don't want to get wet? Check out the character greeting trails at Camp Minnie-Mickey. Lines will be short, or nonexistent.)

The mythical African town of Harambe appears weathered by sand storms

tice that every structure has its own motif. Elsewhere, the carvings and paintings on each snack stand relate to the product sold there. Safari Coffee is adorned with hyper critters such as kangaroo rats. Safari Popcorn's creatures snack on clusters of flies, mice and minnows. The popcorn cart has anhingas snacking on lizards and shrimp. Safari Pretzel is decorated with eels, octopus, ostriches and other animals that can contort themselves into strange shapes.

The largest section of Animal Kingdom is **Africa**, which includes the mythical East African port town of Harambe. Appearing worn and weathered by decades of rain and sand storms, the village represents an old gold and ivory trading post trying to establish a new economy based on tourism.

Typical of Swahili construction techniques, the buildings appear to have coral-rock substructures that, for the most part, are covered with plaster and topped with corrugated-metal or reed-thatch roofs.

door, Beastly Bazaar is decorated with crabs, fish and other water creatures, as well as the animals that catch them. On the pathway to Africa, Creature Comforts features striped and spotted animals. Street lamps in front are topped with large ladybugs that light up at night.

Bright murals cover the Pizzafari restaurant. Each of the four rooms portrays a different type of animal — those that carry their homes, camouflage themselves, hang upside down or are nocturnal. Bugs rule the porch in back. Hanging from the walls and ceiling are 570 carved animals from Oaxaca, Mexico.

The concept of predators and prey is the theme of the Flame Tree Barbecue outdoor cafe. Look closely and you'll no-

Foundations of former buildings are still visible in the main streets, while lampposts bear the phrase "Harambe 1961," a reference to the year the village supposedly gained independence from Great Britain. Spread throughout the village are vintage tin signs (mostly real) and Kenyan-English advertising posters (mostly fake). Interiors are dotted with authentic East African canned goods, cots and camping paraphernalia. Harambe's research camp and conservation school (located on the Pangani Forest Exploration Trail) are scattered with letters, notes and journals of field workers and the head researcher.

In **Asia**, the mythical kingdom of Anandapur is a collage of architectural and landscaping themes that portray another community trying to save its environment. In this Asian story, locals have turned an ancient royal forest and crumbling hunting lodge into a wildlife preserve and bird sanctuary. Nearby, a river-rafting business fights with loggers for control of a once-pristine turbulent river.

Two monument areas, one Thai and one Nepalese, provide homes for hooting gibbons. Supposedly built in 637 A.D., the temples are covered in bamboo scaffolding as cash-starved villagers restore them. Nearby, a crumbling Indian tiger shrine has scarf and garland offerings and bells that celebrate answered prayers. Meanwhile, two entrepreneurs are offering mountain climbers a shortcut to Mount Everest, ignoring warnings from concerned villagers about a Yeti.

Like Africa, Asia's best details include many rusted signs and aged murals. They're not authentic, but look to be.

With the most peculiar theming of any Disney land, **DinoLand U.S.A.** embraces America's fascination with all things dinosaur. Simultaneously, it parodies the stuffiness of scientists and the tackiness of roadside tourist traps and traveling carnivals.

The story begins in 1947, when an amateur fossil-hunter named Chester discovered some dinosaur bones outside his Diggs County gas station. Realizing the importance of the find, the bone-hunter contacted some scientist friends. They banded together to buy the site. In 1949 the scientists transformed its old fishing lodge into the Dino Institute, a non-profit organization dedicated to the Exploration, Excavation and Exultation of dinosaur fossils. For nearly six decades, the site has been inhabited by scientists and graduate students.

During the 1970s the Institute received a large grant from McDonald's (yes, product placement even in a fictitious story), which allowed it to build a formal museum and new research center, and develop a new archeological technique: time travel. The old building's museum became the student cafeteria; its adja-

Advisories from 'locals' try to convince you to cancel your Expedition Everest trip

cent buildings a dorm and garage. Soon the entire area was opened to the public as DinoLand U.S.A., a "dinosaur discovery park." Tourists poured in.

But when the crowds arrived, so did Chester's newfound interest: money. Teaming up with his wife, Hester, he turned his gas station into a souvenir stand: the gaudy Chester & Hester's Dinosaur Treasures (an "Emporium of Extinction") that sold trinkets of little value, but high profit margin.

As the couple's fortunes grew, the embarrassed Dino Institute pressured Chester and Hester to sell. But the couple refused, and retaliated by turning their parking lot into a cheap carnival ("Dino-Rama," a play on "diorama") that mocks the scientists. The couple's cousins run the attractions, while two Institute interns moonlight in Hester's homemade dinosaur outfits. An additional story about the three grad students is told by a paper trail of notes and scribbles throughout and around the Boneyard and Restaurantosaurus.

Finally, there's **Camp Minnie-Mickey.** This area portrays a summer camp where Mickey Mouse and his friends have gone on vacation. Its T-shaped walkway is lined with birch and cedar trees and hand-hewn benches.

FUN FACTS 〉〉 150 different animal species have been bred by the park. 〉〉 2.6 million gallons of water cycles through the park's treated-water system five times a day. It's used in the streams, waterfalls and other water features that come in contact with the live animals. 〉〉 The park has plants from every continent except Antarctica. There are 40 types of palms, 260 grasses and 2,000 kinds of shrubs. DinoLand U.S.A. has many ancient species, including 20 types of magnolia and more than 3,000 palm-like (but cone-bearing) cycads. 〉〉 Originally the Camp Minnie-Mickey pathway was to connect Discovery Island with the Beastly Kingdom, a never-built area of the park themed to mythical creatures. 〉〉 The word "Harambe" means "coming together" in Swahili. Tamu Tamu means "sweet sweet," Dawa means "strong medicine." 〉〉 Africa's seven thatch huts were built on-site by 13 Zulu craftsmen visiting from Kwazulu-Natal, South Africa, using 15 semi-truck loads of Berg grass harvested by relatives back home. 〉〉 Harambe's "coral" rock is volcanic rock from California. 〉〉 Sanskrit for "place of delight," Anandapur is also the name of an actual East Indian town of 35,000 people. 〉〉 Asia's rusty Asian bicycles were purchased at garage sales. 〉〉 The apatosaurus skeleton that straddles the entrance to DinoLand U.S.A. is a cast of a real 52-foot fossil found in Colorado in 1900. The original is in Chicago's Field Museum. 〉〉 The name of the DinoLand highway (U.S. 498) refers to the month the Animal Kingdom opened: April, 1998. 〉〉 The Restaurantosaurus Airstream once belonged to an Imagineer's grandmother.

Secrets in the scenery

FUN FINDS

DISCOVERY ISLAND Landscape: ❶ Mushroom shades cap the lights along the main walkways. ❷ The digestive tracks of alligators, eagles and turtles are portrayed by the gaps in the two-piece backrests of multicolored plastic benches. ❸ "Ancient" animal-themed statues and large clay pots sit in the foliage in front of the shops and restaurants. ❹ Collages of carved creatures form six windsock poles along the pathway to Camp Minnie-Mickey. **Pizzafari murals:** UPSIDE-DOWN ROOM: ❶ The front room murals include only one animal that is right side up. Toward the back, a small blue bug stands upright under a purple bird, painted on a header that frames the rearmost seating area. ❷ On the opposite side of that header, an opossum tail without a body appears between the second and third opossums from the right. ❸ Dozens of carved wooden bats hang from the ceiling. HOME ROOM: Located on the left side of the main hall, this room has ❹ hundreds of carved snails and turtles crawling on its ceiling. NOCTURNAL ROOM: To the right of the hall, this room has murals with scurrying red mice. On the back wall, ❺ nine white stars join three mice to rush away from a spraying skunk. CAMOUFLAGE ROOM: Dozens of animals hide in the murals in this large rear room. They include (from the left, as you enter): ❻ two bitterns standing in the reeds under the orange fox, ❼ a frog, resting on the tree trunk under the brown leopard ❽ and a stickbug, posing on a leaf at the top of a plant to the left of the orange tiger.

CAMP MINNIE-MICKEY Landscape: ❶ As the entranceway crosses the Discovery River, a stone dragon lies along the right bank. What starts in the woods as scattered slabs of stone forms into its head. ❷ Further along that side of the walkway, a figure of Daisy Duck leads Donald's nephews Huey, Dewey and Louie on a hike. ❸ Mickey Mouse and his pals are fishing to the left of a bridge that leads to the Festival of the Lion King Theater and Character Greeting Trails. Donald Duck has caught a boot. Goofy has fallen asleep.

AFRICA Landscape: ❶ A cacophony of murmuring voices, clattering pots and pans and a radio sometimes can be heard from a kitchen behind the back door of Harambe's Dawa Bar. The sounds are meant to be from the residents of the hotel above. Sometimes there's knocking on a door: a landlady trying to collect back rent. ❷ A sly tribute to Animal Kingdom's chief design executive appears in the "open-air market" (the indoor reception area) of the Tusker House restaurant. Looking down on you from the market's second floor, the Jorodi Masks & Beads shop is an homage to famed Disney Imagineer Joe Rohde. The store's "earings" (sic) sign is a reference to Rohde's distinctive lobal adornments. Posters for the shop are plastered throughout Harambe Village.

ASIA Landscape: ❶ The "dried mud" pathways include bicycle tracks and footprints made by barefoot Disney cast members and their children. ❷ Each Anandapur business displays a tax license featuring the fictional kingdom's king and queen. The bigger the license, the more taxes that business pays. ❸ On a side trail along the walkway to Africa, visible seams in an authentic Indian marble pavilion reveal where Disney cut the structure apart to ship it to the United States. ❹ Walls and drain covers shoot water at a small play area between Kali River Rapids and the Maharajah Jungle Trek. ❺ Inside one of the siamang temples is an air-conditioned kitchen. Its door is protected by an electrified vine that emits a noticeable slow clicking.

DINOLAND U.S.A. Landscape: ❶ Two baby dinosaurs hide underneath the adjacent "concretosaurus" folk-art sculpture. One is hatching. ❷ "Lost—My Tail" reads one of the notes on the bulletin board across from the Boneyard entrance. It's from the nearby aptosaurus cast, which has a disconnected tailbone. ❸ DinoLand U.S.A.'s original layout, which included a real fossil prep area and cast display room on the site of today's Dino-Rama, is shown on a map pinned to the board. **Restaurantosurus:** Archeological and dinosaur references abound. Among the best: ❶ the shapes formed by greasy hand prints on the walls of the quonset hut; ❷ the cans of Sinclair Litholine Multi-Purpose Grease and Dynoil ("keep your old dinosaur running") on the shelves of that room; ❸ the reproductions of four dino sketches for the "The Rite of Spring" sequence in Disney's 1930s film project "Concert Feature" that became the 1940 movie "Fantasia;" ❹ the titles in the Hip Joint rec room juke box (e.g., "Dust in the Wind"); ❺ the posters in that room for Dinosaur Jr. and T Rex; and the ambient music, which includes ❻ the 1988 Was Not Was hit "Walk the Dinosaur" and obscure tunes such as ❼ proto-punk icon Jonathan Richman's "I'm a Little Dinosaur" as well as ❽ "Ugga

Bugga," ❾ Bruce Springsteen-like tune by one-time child star Bill Mumy. ❿ Chester and Hester appear in a photo in the main dining hall. ⓫ The letters A-I-R-S-T-R-E-A-M on the front of the restaurant's travel trailer have been rearranged to spell the phrase I ARE SMART. **Dinosaur Treasures:** ❶ Four hanging signs above the entrance to the shop read "Rough scaly skin... Making you groan?... Don't despair... Use Fossil Foam" from one direction, "When in Florida... Be sure to... Visit... Epcot" from the other. ❷ The price of gas is 29.9 cents a gallon on Chester's rusty old gas pump alongside the building, as well as on a painted-over sign on the rear roof. ❸ Tiny plastic dinosaurs ride trains, snow ski and flee lava flows above the gift shop's main room. ❹ Boxes above Chester's garage floors include "Chester's dig '47," "Chester's pet rocks 1966" and "Train Parts." ❺ An oil funnel and gas-pump nozzle are among the items that have been turned into dinosaurs on the shop's walls. ❻ Fictitious entrepreneurs Chester and Hester appear in a photo on one of the shop's walls. ❼ Heard in the adjacent restrooms, the bone-themed country songs played on radio station "W-BONE" include "I Like Bananas Because They Have No Bones," an actual 1935 ditty by the Hoosier Hot Shots.

HIDDEN MICKEYS

Pizzafari: ❶ As an orange firefly in the nocturnal room, to the left of a large tiger, behind a frog. **Camp Minnie-Mickey:** ❷ A profile appears as the hole of a birdhouse that hangs in the courtyard. ❸ In the carved woodwork of the ice cream stand, as sideways accents. **Harambe Village:** ❹ As a large shape of gray pavement on the walkway in front of Harambe School, behind the Fruit Market. A bench may be sitting on it. ❺ As a drain cover with the letter "D" on it and two round pebble groupings, just left of the main entrance to Mombasa Marketplace, across from Tusker House. ❻ As another drain cover (this one with the letter "S") and two round pebble groupings in front of Tamu Tamu Refreshments, facing Discovery Island. **DinoLand U.S.A.:** ❼ As cracks in the asphalt in the parking area next to the Cementosaurus, to the left of Dinosaur Treasures. ❽ On a Steamboat Willie cast member pin on the right of the fourth hump on the back of the Cementosaurus. ❾ As three small, black scales on the back of the red and green hadrosaurus at the start of the Cretaceous Trail.

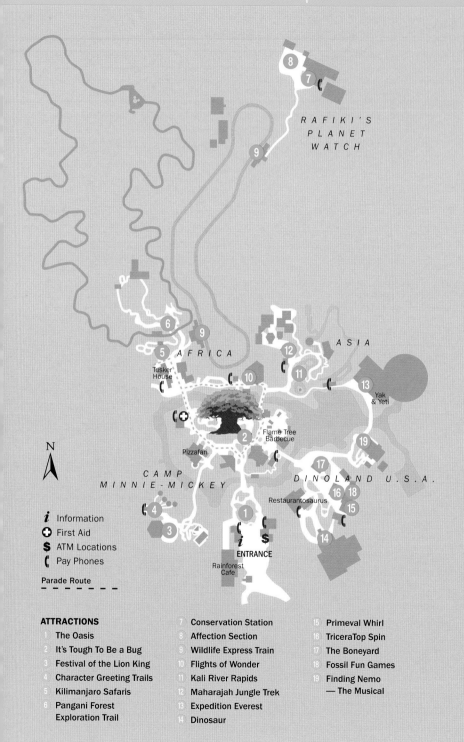

RAFIKI'S
PLANET
WATCH

ASIA

AFRICA

Tusker
House

Yak
& Yeti

Flame Tree
Barbecue

Pizzafari

CAMP
MINNIE-MICKEY

DINOLAND U.S.A.

Restaurantosaurus

N

i Information

✚ First Aid

$ ATM Locations

(Pay Phones

Parade Route — — — —

ENTRANCE

Rainforest
Cafe

ATTRACTIONS

1 The Oasis
2 It's Tough To Be a Bug
3 Festival of the Lion King
4 Character Greeting Trails
5 Kilimanjaro Safaris
6 Pangani Forest
   Exploration Trail

7 Conservation Station
8 Affection Section
9 Wildlife Express Train
10 Flights of Wonder
11 Kali River Rapids
12 Maharajah Jungle Trek
13 Expedition Everest
14 Dinosaur

15 Primeval Whirl
16 TriceraTop Spin
17 The Boneyard
18 Fossil Fun Games
19 Finding Nemo
   — The Musical

Park resources

BABY CARE

The Baby Care Center *(behind Creature Comforts, Discovery Island)* has changing rooms, nursing areas, a microwave and playroom. It sells diapers, formula, pacifiers, over-the-counter medications.

FIRST AID

The First Aid Center *(behind Creature Comforts, Discovery Island)* handles minor emergencies. Registered nurses are on hand.

GUEST RELATIONS

The Guest Relations center *(entrance plaza; walk-up window outside gate, office inside)* has multilingual cast members trained to answer questions and solve problems, and maps and Times Guides for all Disney World theme parks. It exchanges foreign currency and stores items found in the park that day.

LOCKERS

Daily rate: $5 plus a $5 deposit *(entrance plaza, next to Guest Relations)*.

LOST CHILDREN

Report lost children to Guest Relations or any cast member. Children who lose parents should tell a cast member.

MONEY MATTERS

The park has one ATM *(entrance plaza, on the right)*. All cash registers accept credit cards and traveler's checks.

PACKAGE PICKUP

Anything you buy in the park can be sent to Package Pickup *(Garden Gate Gifts, entrance plaza)* for you to pick up as you leave or delivered to your Disney hotel (both free) or shipped to your home.

PARKING

Daily rate for automobiles: $12. Those staying at a Disney resort, and annual passholders, get free parking.

SECURITY CHECK

Security guards inspect all bags and purses at the park entrance.

STROLLERS

Single strollers *($15 per day, $13 per day length of stay)* and double strollers *($31, $27)* are available *(Garden Gate Gifts, entrance plaza)*. If you misplace yours, a limited number of replacements are at Mombasa Marketplace in Africa.

TIP BOARD

This board *(Discovery Island)* displays waiting times for popular attractions.

TRANSPORTATION

Disney buses run to Animal Kingdom from all Walt Disney World resorts, Epcot, Disney's Hollywood Studios and Blizzard Beach. Magic Kingdom guests take a monorail to the Transportation and Ticket Center, then a bus to Animal Kingdom. The park has no direct service to Downtown Disney or Typhoon Lagoon.

WHEELCHAIRS, ECVS

Wheelchairs *($10 per day, $8 per day length of stay)* and Electric Convenience Vehicles (four-wheeled, single-seat scooters) *($45 per day plus $20 deposit)* are available at Garden Gate Gifts at the entrance plaza. ECVs book quickly, as many are used by overweight guests.

Attractions

Oasis

OASIS EXHIBITS

★★★★ ✓ Allow 15 min. No wait. Pg 220
Shady walkways lead from the park entrance to its hub, meandering through a lush garden filled with exotic animals.

Discovery Island

DISCOVERY ISLAND TRAILS

★★★★ ✓ Allow 20 min. No wait. Pg 222
Walkways wind through expansive tropical garden, passing wildlife including small monkeys, kangaroos, "carved" roots of Tree of Life.

IT'S TOUGH TO BE A BUG

★★★★ 8 min. Avg wait 8 min. Intense for preschoolers. *FastPass* Pg 223
Funny 3-D theatrical show displays survival behaviors of insects. Stars characters from 1998's "A Bug's Life."

TREE OF LIFE

★★★ Allow 15 min. No wait. Pg 221
Towering park icon has "carved" animals.

Camp Minnie-Mickey

FESTIVAL OF THE LION KING

★★★★★ ✓ 28 min. Avg wait 25 min. Pg 224
Rousing in-the-round musical revue includes stilt walkers, acrobats, fire-baton twirler. Based on 1994's "The Lion King."

Africa

KILIMANJARO SAFARIS

★★★★★ ✓ 22 min. Avg wait 20 min. Preshow video shows killed animals. *FastPass* Pg 226
Bouncy open-air truck ride through 100-acre African forest and savanna.

Finding Nemo—The Musical, DinoLand U.S.A.

encounters live elephants, giraffes, lions, rhinos and other wild creatures.

PANGANI FOREST EXPLORATION TRAIL
★★★★★ ✔ Allow 30 min. No wait Pg 228
Walkway rambles past exotic African animals, through aviary, indoor "research center," gorilla habitat.

Rafiki's Planet Watch

AFFECTION SECTION
★★★ ✔ Allow 15 min. No wait. Pg 229
Outdoor petting zoo.

CONSERVATION STATION
★★★★ ✔ Allow 30 min. No wait. Pg 229
Actual research and veterinary facility has viewable medical procedures, exhibits and presentations.

Asia

EXPEDITION EVEREST
★★★★ ✔ 3 min. Avg wait 45 min. Height restriction 44 in. High lift, dark backwards travel, one steep, turning drop. *FastPass* Pg 234
Smooth roller coaster speeds into and out of a mountain, goes backward, finds Yeti.

FLIGHTS OF WONDER
★★★★ ✔ 25 min. Avg wait 5 min. Pg 231
Conservation-themed free-flying bird show displays natural behaviors.

KALI RIVER RAPIDS
★★★★ ✔ 6 min. Avg wait 45 min. Height restriction 38 in. Jerky, wet. *FastPass* Pg 232
Whitewater raft ride in rainforest river being destroyed by loggers.

MAHARAJAH JUNGLE TREK
★★★★★ ✔ Allow 30 min. No wait. Pg 233
Walking trail around crumbling palace has exotic Asian animals, aviary.

DinoLand U.S.A.

THE BONEYARD
★★★★ ✔ Allow 15–30 min. No wait. Pg 241
Dig-site playground has climbing zone, slides, tunnels, much more.

DINOSAUR
★★★★ ✔ 3 min, 30 sec. Avg wait 20 min. Height restriction 40 in. Dark, intense. *FastPass* Pg 236
Jerky thrill ride goes back in time to search for dinosaurs.

FINDING NEMO—THE MUSICAL
★★★★★ ✔ 35 min. Avg wait 30 min for best seats. Pg 242
Theatrical spectacle retells story of 2003's "Finding Nemo" with huge imaginative puppets, live singers.

FOSSIL FUN GAMES
★★★ ✔ Allow 15 min. No wait. Extra cost. Pg 240
Carnival-style midway games.

PRIMEVAL WHIRL
★★★★ ✔ 2 min, 30 sec. Avg wait: 20 min. Height restriction 48 in. One steep drop. Tough on those with inner-ear problems. *FastPass* Pg 239
Wild-mouse-style spinning roller coaster has kitschy time-travel theme.

TRICERATOP SPIN
★★★ ✔ 1 min, 30 sec. Avg wait 9 min. Pg 239
Four-seat hub-and-spoke ride has cartoon-dinosaur ride vehicles.

Parade

MICKEY'S JAMMIN' JUNGLE PARADE
★★★★★ ✓ **15 min. Arrive 30 min. early.** Pg 243
Huge mechanical puppets and humorous
character SUVs highlight safari-themed
procession that circles Discovery Island.
Starts, and ends, in Africa.

Character locations

BALOO, KING LOUIE Bear, orangutan from
1967's "Jungle Book."
Beside Tamu Tamu, Africa; Oasis.
CHIP 'N DALE Chipmunks in 1940s, 1950s cartoons.
Character greeting trails, Camp Minnie-
Mickey; Oasis.
DONALD DUCK, DAISY DUCK
Character greeting trails, Camp Minnie-
Mickey; ✳ Donald's Safari Breakfast,
Tusker House, Africa.
FLIK Ant star of 1998's "A Bug's Life."
Oasis.
GOOFY
Character greeting trails, Camp Minnie-
Mickey; DinoLand U.S.A.; ✳ Donald's
Safari Breakfast, Tusker House, Africa.
JIMINY CRICKET From 1940's "Pinocchio."
✳ Conservation Station, Rafiki's Planet
Watch; Oasis.
KODA, KENAI Stars of 2003's "Brother Bear."
Character greeting trails, Camp Minnie-
Mickey; Oasis.
LILO, STITCH Stars of 2002's "Lilo & Stitch."
Outside Island Mercantile, Discovery
Island.
MICKEY MOUSE
Character greeting trails, Camp Minnie-
Mickey; ✳ Donald's Safari Breakfast,
Tusker House, Africa.
MINNIE MOUSE
Character greeting trails, Camp Minnie-
Mickey.
PLUTO
DinoLand U.S.A.; Oasis.
POCAHONTAS Star of 1995's "Pocahontas."
✳ Conservation Station, Rafiki's Planet
Watch; Character greeting trails, Camp
Minnie-Mickey.
RAFIKI Baboon from 1994's The Lion King."
✳ Conservation Station, Rafiki's Planet
Watch; Oasis.
TIMON Meerkat from 1994's The Lion King."
Oasis.
TURK Girl gorilla from 1999's "Tarzan."
Across from Pizzafari, Discovery Island.

✳ **Air-conditioned waiting line**

Lilo appears outside the Island Mercantile shop

**WINNIE THE POOH, EEYORE, PIGLET,
TIGGER** From 1977's "The Many Adventures of
Winnie the Pooh."
Character boat landing across from
Flame Tree BBQ, Discovery Island.

Street performers
Discovery Island

VILLAGE BEATNIKS
20 min. Hourly 10:35am–2:45pm.
Musicians use five drum sets, a zendrum
and a cow bell to create syncopated
cadences. Guests shake rhythm tubes.

Africa

THE HARAMBE SCHOOL
**20 min. 10am, 11:30am, 2pm. Live animal
presentation 30 min. before each presentation.**
Botswanans, Namibians and South
Africans talk about their homelands at
this three-bench open-air classroom.
MOR THIAM
20 min. Hourly 9am–noon.
So unaffected you'd never guess he's a
living legend, Djembe drum master Mor

Street performers
Tam Tams of Congo
perform in the
park's Africa area

Thiam ("Chahm") has been called Africa's greatest percussionist. He's played with American artists such as B.B. King, and is the father of R&B artist Akon.

TAM TAMS OF CONGO
20 min. Hourly 10:45am–2:45pm. Dawa Bar.
A crowd favorite, this rousing native quintet brings guests of all ages up for quick lessons in West African dances.

Rafiki's Planet Watch

PIPA THE TALKING RECYCLING BIN
20 min. Hourly 11:30am–2:40pm.
Roving real trash can jokes with guests.

Asia

DIVINE
45 min. Hourly 10am–1pm. On the walkway between Africa and Asia.
Covered in a foliage costume, this slow-moving, stilt-walking performance artist blends into the landscape.

DinoLand U.S.A.

SMEAR, SPLAT & DIP
20 min. Hourly 10am–3:30pm Sun–Thr. DinoLand U.S.A.
Three dippy painters become a balance and juggling troupe.

TROPICALS
20 min. Hourly 11am–4pm. DinoLand U.S.A.
Steel-drum band often plays Disney tunes.

Camp Minnie-Mickey

GI-TAR DAN
20 min. Hourly 10am–3:30pm Mon–Fri. Camp Minnie-Mickey.
Funnyman acoustic guitarist sings about animals, invites children to join in.

Restaurants
Full service restaurants

RAINFOREST CAFE ★★★ American $$$$ **B: $9–$14, 8:30am–10am. L, D: $11–$40, 10am–park close. Participates in Disney Dining Premium, Platinum plans only. Annual passholders save 10% off up to four entrees. Direct reservations: 407-938-9100. Seats 1,057 inc. 72 at bar. Entrance plaza.**
You dine in an elaborate three-dimensional jungle of plants, trees and waterfalls at this non-Disney restaurant. Robotic elephants, gorillas and other creatures come to life as a thunderstorm strikes every 20 minutes. Rear areas have saltwater aquariums; one has a huge statue of Atlas. Breakfast usually has no wait, lunch and dinner menus offer dozens and dozens of choices.

TUSKER HOUSE Donald's Safari Breakfast:
★★★★ Character buffet $$$ **Donald Duck, Daisy Duck, Mickey Mouse, Goofy. A $19, C $11 (opt. photo package), 8am–10:30am. Lunch, dinner:** ★★★★
African/American buffet $$$$ **L: A $20, C $11, 11:30am–3:30pm. D: A $27, C $13, 4 pm–park close. Seats 1,206. Africa.**
African flavors spice up the menu at this buffet restaurant. Characters at breakfast invite guests to grab a noisemaker and join them as they sing and dance around the room. Lunch and dinner have good spiced sirloin and many vegetarian items. Dinner adds salmon and prime rib.

YAK & YETI ★★★★ Pan-Asian $$$$ ✔ **$17–25, L: 11am–3:45pm. D: 4:30pm–park close. Participates in Disney Dining Premium, Platinum plans only. Annual passholders save 10% off up to four entrees. Direct reservations: 407-824-YETI. Seats 250. Asia.**
This two-story eatery is run by Landry's Restaurants, the company that operates Rainforest Cafe. The menu has many good choices. Our favorite is the mahi mahi, which is doused in a hot garlic peanut-butter sauce. The strangest dish is Pho, a Vietnamese shrimp noodle bowl. You flavor it by adding in basil, cilantro, bean sprouts and, if you're daring, a spoonful or two of a sauce made from pressed anchovy filets. Each the size of a huge tamale, the marvelous pork egg rolls are mild yet so full of flavor they don't need the included chili-plum dipping sauce (the secret is in the wrapper). For dessert, a sorbet sampler is so tangy you can devour it only in small bites; the yummy mango pie is a thick yellow slab with the consistency of cheesecake. Good mango daiquiri, Asian beers. The restaurant is meant to be a converted hotel and former home. Dining areas are lined with hundreds of artifacts.

Counter service cafes

PIZZAFARI ✔ **Individual pizzas, salads, sandwiches. B: 9–10:30am. L, D: 10:30am–park close. Seats 680. Discovery Island.**
Beautiful murals, floor mosaics, ceiling art add to a relaxing feel. Clean and cool.

RESTAURANTOSAURUS Burgers, chicken nuggets, hot dogs. 10:30am–park close. Seats 750. DinoLand U.S.A.
Lavishly wacko theme (dorm for

excavation students was former dinosaur institute, fishing lodge). Right-corner Hip Joint room stays peaceful, cool.

Outdoor counter cafes

FLAME TREE BBQ ✔ BBQ, baked beans, corn on the cob. Seats 500. Discovery Island.
Good food, shady gardens, waterside pavilions.
YAK & YETI LOCAL FOOD CAFES ✔ Asian. Seats 350. Asia.

Snack stands

ANANDAPUR ICE CREAM TRUCK
Soft serve. Asia.
DINO-BITE
Churros, pastries, hand-dipped ice cream, yogurt. Seats 50. DinoLand U.S.A.
DINO DINER
Hot dogs, popcorn, slushies. Seats 30. DinoLand U.S.A.
DRINKWALLA
Fruit cups, whole fruit, chips. Asia.
HARAMBE FRUIT MARKET
✔ Whole fruit, soft pretzels. Africa. Seats 8.
HARAMBE POPCORN
Popcorn, churros. Africa.
HOT DOG STANDS
Asia, Camp Minnie-Mickey, Rafiki's Planet Watch.
ICE CREAM STAND
Soft-serve. Camp Minnie-Mickey.
JOFFREY'S COFFEE
Coffees, teas, pastries, fruit, smoothies. Entrance plaza.
KUSAFIRI COFFEE SHOP AND BAKERY
✔ Coffees, teas, pastries, fruit. Africa.
MR. KAMAL'S
Chicken breast nuggets, corn dog nuggets. Asia.
ROYAL ANANDAPUR TEA CO.
✔ Specialty teas, pastries. Asia. Seats 12.
SAFARI COFFEE
✔ Shade-grown, specialty coffee; pastries; fruit; yogurt. Discovery Island.
SAFARI POPCORN
Popcorn, lemonade, punch. Discovery Island.
SAFARI PRETZEL
Soft pretzels. Discovery Island.
SAFARI SANDWICH
Discovery Island.
SAFARI TURKEY
Turkey legs, chicken wings. Discovery Island.
SLUSH
Frozen lemonade, pretzels. Asia. Seats 16.
TAMU TAMU
Sandwiches. Africa.
TRILOBITES
DinoLand U.S.A.

Bars

DAWA BAR
African beer, liquor, specialty drinks. Shaded outdoor patio. Africa. Seats 256.
TUKI'S TIKI BAR
Specialty drinks, draft beer, smoothies. In outdoor garden of Rainforest Cafe. Entrance plaza. Seats 30.
YAK & YETI QUALITY BEVERAGES
Specialty drinks, Asian beers. Asia. Shares seats with Local Food Cafes.

Shopping

The park's main shop is Island Mercantile *(Discovery Island)*. Many goods, however, are concentrated in other locations:

Apparel

CAPS AND HATS
Chester and Hester's Dinosaur Treasures *(DinoLand U.S.A.)*, Mombasa Marketplace and Ziwani Traders *(Africa)*, Outpost shop *(entrance plaza)*.
CHARACTER COSTUMES
Minnie Mouse: Creature Comforts *(Discovery Island)*. **Pocahontas:** Out of the Wild *(Rafiki's Planet Watch)*.
CHILDREN'S WEAR
Creature Comforts *(Discovery Island)*, Disney Outfitters *(Discovery Island)*, Mombasa Marketplace and Ziwani Traders *(Africa)*, Rainforest Cafe Gift Shop *(entrance plaza)*.
FASHION
Disney Outfitters *(Discovery Island)*.
SANDALS
Bhaktapur Market *(Asia)*, Dino Institute gift shop *(at exit to Dinosaur, DinoLand U.S.A.)*, Kali cart *(outside Kali River Rapids, Asia)*, Rainforest Cafe Gift Shop *(entrance plaza)*.
SPORTS APPAREL
Disney Outfitters *(Discovery Island)*.
T-SHIRTS
General: Island Mercantile *(Discovery Island)*. **Wildlife-themed:** Mombasa Marketplace and Ziwani Traders *(Africa)*, Out of the Wild *(Rafiki's Planet Watch)*, Rainforest Cafe gift shop *(entrance plaza)*. Attraction: Dino Institute gift shop *(at exit to Dinosaur, DinoLand U.S.A.)*, Kali cart *(outside Kali River Rapids, Asia)*, Mombasa Marketplace and Ziwani Traders *(Kilimanjaro Safaris, Africa)*, Serka Zong Bazaar *(at exit to Expedition Everest, Asia)*.

Anandapur ice cream truck, Asia

Other merchandise

ART

Traditional: The Art of Disney boutique at Disney Outfitters *(Discovery Island)* stocks quality lithographs, oils, Lenox porcelain items, 2-foot-tall character figurines and painted ostrich eggs. **Beaded figures:** Mombasa Marketplace and Ziwani Traders *(Africa)*. **African pottery and woodcarvings:** Mombasa Marketplace and Ziwani Traders *(Africa)*.

BOOKS

Disney titles: Creature Comforts *(Discovery Island)*. **Africa:** Mombasa Marketplace and Ziwani Traders *(Africa)*. **Wildlife:** Out of the Wild *(Rafiki's Planet Watch)*, Rainforest Cafe Gift Shop *(entrance plaza)*. **Asia:** Bhaktapur Market *(Asia)*. **Dinosaur:** Dino Institute gift shop *(at exit to Dinosaur, DinoLand U.S.A.)*. **Mt. Everest:** Serka Zong Bazaar *(at exit to Expedition Everest, Asia)*.

CANDY

Beastly Bazaar *(Discovery Island)* has chocolates, cookies, gummies, jelly beans, lollipops, chocolate-covered pretzels, taffy.

CHRISTMAS ITEMS

Beastly Bazaar *(Discovery Island)*.

HOUSEWARES

Beastly Bazaar *(Discovery Island)*, Outpost shop *(entrance plaza)*.

JEWELRY

Fine: Disney Outfitters *(Discovery Island)*. **Costume:** Creature Comforts *(Discovery Island)*, Mandala Gifts *(Asia)*, Mombasa Marketplace and Ziwani Traders *(Africa)*.

MUSICAL INSTRUMENTS

Mombasa Marketplace and Ziwani Traders *(Africa)*.

PET PRODUCTS

Beastly Bazaar *(Discovery Island)*, Island Mercantile *(Discovery Island)*.

PINS

Pin central: Island Mercantile cart *(Discovery Island)*. **General:** Mombasa Marketplace and Ziwani Traders *(Africa)*.

TOYS

The two best selections are at Island Mercantile *(Discovery Island)* and Chester and Hester's Dinosaur Treasures *(DinoLand U.S.A.)*. Other toy areas: Creature Comforts *(Discovery Island)*, Dino Institute gift shop *(at exit to Dinosaur, DinoLand U.S.A.)*, Mombasa Marketplace and Ziwani Traders *(Africa)*, Rainforest Cafe gift shop *(entrance plaza)*, Serka Zong Bazaar *(at exit to Expedition Everest, Asia)*.

WATCHES

Beastly Bazaar *(Discovery Island)*, Disney Outfitters *(Discovery Island)*.

Specialty shops

DINOSAURS

Dino Institute gift shop *(at exit to Dinosaur, DinoLand U.S.A.)*.

MT. EVEREST, YETI

Serka Zong Bazaar *(at exit to Expedition Everest, Asia)*.

The Oasis

★ ★ ★ ★ ✔ Allow 15 min. 3 trails (1200 ft), 13 viewing areas, 18 species. Fear factor: None. Access: Guests may stay in wheelchairs, ECVs. Debuted: 1998.

The thematic entrance to the park, this "A"-shaped grouping of walkways connects Animal Kingdom's turnstiles and guest services area with Discovery Island. Tucked under a canopy of bamboo, eucalyptus and palms, a man-made haven of pools, streams and waterfalls is, in essence, its own small zoo. Displayed in natural habitats, exotic animals include a babirusa, swamp wallaby, spoonbills and black swans.

Top: An Oasis walkway. **Above:** College interns are on hand each morning until about 11 a.m., displaying skulls and insects.

Average Wait

9am	0 min
10am	0
11am	0
Noon	0
1pm	0
2pm	0
3pm	0
4pm	0
5pm	0
6pm	0
7pm	0
8pm	0
9pm	0

FUN FINDS ❶ You can see, and touch, the back of the waterfall from within a small cave where the paths converge. ❷ A swaying rope bridge runs alongside the final few feet of the left walkway. It leads into the cave. Water bubbles up from the rocks underneath it. ❸ The Animal Kingdom dedication plaque sits near a lamppost in front of the black swans.

FUN FACT ›› Continually used for bathing, feeding and, yes, pooping by dozens of ducks and wading birds, the water in the ponds, streams and waterfalls is discreetly cleaned and recirculated five times per day. Pipes run under the walkways.

▶ Park animals are most active first thing in the morning and late in the day.

Tree of Life

Symbolic of the interconnected nature of plants and animals, this man-made park centerpiece has a tapestry of 325 animals sculpted into its gnarled roots, trunk and thick branches. Pathways take you through the root system and up to the trunk. The structure resembles an Africa baobab tree.

The tree took 18 months to build. An oil-rig-style frame hosts 12 main branches, each of which is encircled in a giant expansion joint which lets the branch sway in the wind. Disney created the trunk outside the park, then cut it into a dozen segments and flew it to a construction site near its final location. A crane hoisted the pieces up to assemble.

"We want our visitors to wander up to the tree, to recognize some animals and then seek out others," says chief sculptor Zsolt Hormay. "Finding the balance between the animal forms and the wood textures was a challenge."

Animal Kingdom Executive Designer Joe Rohde calls the Tree of Life "the most impressive artistic and engineering feat we

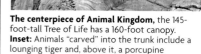

The centerpiece of Animal Kingdom, the 145-foot-tall Tree of Life has a 160-foot canopy. **Inset:** Animals "carved" into the trunk include a lounging tiger and, above it, a porcupine

have achieved since Sleeping Beauty Castle at Disneyland."

HIDDEN MICKEYS

❶ Facing the Oasis, as moss on the trunk, to the left of a buffalo, near a tiger. ❷ On the side of the trunk that faces the walkway from Asia to Africa, upside down, above a hippo's eye.

FUN FACTS » The concrete trunk is 50 feet wide at its middle, 170 feet at its base. It has 8,000 fiberglass branches and 103,000 leaves. » Designer Hormay also created the rockwork at Magic Kingdom's Big Thunder Mountain Railroad and the snow and rockwork at Blizzard Beach.

Average Wait	
9am	0 min
10am	0
11am	0
Noon	0
1pm	0
2pm	0
3pm	0
4pm	0
5pm	0
6pm	0
7pm	0
8pm	0
9pm	0

▶ A main branch resembles the upturned trunk of an elephant. It's to the left of a bald eagle.

Discovery Island Trails

★★★★ ✔ Allow 20 min. 2 trails (1680 ft), 9 viewing areas, 15 species. Fear factor: None. Access: Guests may stay in wheelchairs, ECVs. Debuted: 1998.

Live animals—including flamingos, kangaroos and small primates—surround the Tree of Life, in the park's largest tropical habitat, a lush few acres filled with pools, waterfalls and some hidden winding walkways.

The trails aren't marked, so they're tough to find but never crowded. Most of the area is shady, a blessing on a hot day.

Crested cranes, exotic deer, lemurs and tamarins roam within the Tree of Life Garden, a lush area directly in front of the tree. To its right are cotton-top tamarins. To its left, a series of connected ponds holds flamingos, otters and cute little whistling ducks. The otter pond features an underwater viewing area, which holds tambaqui fish.

To the left of the ponds, a small trail often has its entrance partially blocked by a gift cart or character greeting line. It leads to a gray- and red-kangaroo ex-

Top: A flamingo rests in the Tree of Life garden.
Above: A macaw perches by the Discovery River.

hibit and eventually to a ring-tailed-lemur habitat that's behind the Fastpass machines for the attraction "It's Tough to be a Bug."

A second trail runs behind the tree along the Discovery River, from the gate to the park's Africa section to the gate for Asia. This path is home to macaws, crested porcupines, storks and Galapagos tortoises.

Average Wait

9am	0 min
10am	0
11am	0
Noon	0
1pm	0
2pm	0
3pm	0
4pm	0
5pm	0
6pm	0
7pm	0
8pm	0
9pm	0

▶ Watch the tambaqui fish. It sometimes sucks up pebbles then spits them out.

It's Tough To Be a Bug

★★★★ 8 min. Capacity: 430. *FastPass* Fear factor: Intense for preschoolers. Access: Guests may remain in wheelchairs, ECVs. Assistive listening, reflective captioning. Debuted: 1999.

Kids and adults scream with delight at this cartoonish theatrical attraction. It combines a 3-D movie with startling theater effects. Hosted by Flik, the mild-mannered ant of 1998's "A Bug's Life," it has a cute charm and a wicked sense of humor.

"Take it from an ant. It's tough to be a bug," Flik says. "That's why we've developed some amazing survival techniques." Soon a tarantula shoots poison quills, a soldier termite sprays acid and a stink bug, well, stinks.

Then Hopper crashes the show. What bugs him? People.

"You guys only see us as monsters!" the grasshopper roars at the audience. "Maybe it's time you got a taste of your own medicine!" That cues an attack on the theater by a giant fly swatter, a can of bug spray and some angry spiders and hornets. A musical finale recalls a Busby Berkeley production number.

For the best focus sit in the middle, toward the back. Lean back in your seat to feel all the special effects.

An Audio-Animatronics Hopper confronts the audience during It's Tough To Be a Bug

Average Wait

9am	0 min
10am	5
11am	10
Noon	20
1pm	10
2pm	10
3pm	5
4pm	5
5pm	5
6pm	5
7pm	5
8pm	5
9pm	5

FUN FINDS

❶ Just outside the holding room, a wall plaque honors Dr. Jane Goodall's commitment to chimpanzees. It's next to a carving of David Graybeard, one of her subjects. ❷ Lobby posters promote past theater shows such as "Beauty and the Bees" and "Little Shop of Hoppers." ❸ A lobby display features a giant dung ball from "The Dung and I." ❹ The lobby music consists of songs from those shows. ❺ The auditorium looks like it's inside an anthill. ❻ The projection booth is a wasp nest. ❼ The pre-show announcer reports that "the stinkbug will be played by Claire DeRoom." ❽ After Claire performs, Flik tells her "Hey, lay off the churros!" ❾ As the performance ends, fireflies swarm to the exit signs.

HIDDEN MICKEYS

❶ As spots on a root in the lobby, left of the theater's handicapped entrance.

FUN FACTS » Voices include Dave Foley (Flik), Cheech Marin (Chili the tarantula) and Kevin Spacey (Hopper).

▶ The best time to see the show is the last half-hour of the day. There's no line.

Dressed as animals, dancers perform a choreographed routine

Festival of the Lion King

★★★★★ ✓ 28 min. Capacity: 1,375. Fear factor: None. Access: ECV, wheelchair accessible. Assistive listening, handheld captioning. Debuted: 1998.

A spectacular revue of the best songs from the 1994 film, "The Lion King," this in-the-round theatrical show combines the pageantry of a parade with the excitement of a tribal festival. Live singers, circus acts, stilt walkers, giant puppets and dancers dressed as animals fill your entire field of vision as they celebrate the joy of life.

The show opens just like the movie, with the dramatic African chant from "The Circle of Life." This time instead of watching a cartoon sunrise you see a live-action one, performed by interpretive dancers.

After the introductions of four lead singers dressed in tribal robes, a catchy chorus of "I Just Can't Wait to be King" brings in nearly four dozen additional performers as well as four parade floats.

On one float is Simba, a 12-foot animated figure sitting atop Pride Rock. An-

Average Wait	
9am	10 min
10am	20
11am	20
Noon	20
1pm	30
2pm	30
3pm	30
4pm	30
5pm	30
6pm	n/a
7pm	n/a
8pm	n/a
9pm	n/a

other float includes Pumbaa. Timon, meanwhile, is the wisecracking emcee.

After Timon leads the crowd in "Hakuna Matata," he introduces the Tumble Monkeys, a troupe of silly, costumed acrobats who flip, flop and fly across the stage, bounce on a trampoline and perform on still rings, bars and a flying trapeze set.

A fire-baton twirler performs to "Be Prepared," as stilt walkers stage an abstract battle. A touching "Can You Feel the Love Tonight" duet features a ballet dancer who, costumed as a bird, soars into the air. Next is a spirited version of "The Circle of Life."

Timon returns to lead an audience sing-along to "The Lion Sleeps Tonight." As sections of the crowd compete against each other, dancers select children from the first few rows to join them in an instrumental parade around the stage.

A rousing finale includes a gospel-like reprise of the songs synchronized to a moving kaleidoscope of dancers, lighting and kites. A literal circle of life, it has four singers circle on the stage, dancers circle around them and at times form circles themselves. Lights, kites and eventually that flying bird twirl overhead.

Dancers' costumes are imaginative. Each combines cuffs, a headpiece, leotard, leg-

▶ Get to the theater 40 minutes before showtime to grab the best seats.

gings, makeup, a skirt and yoke to become a colorful abstract animal.

The best shows are those with a full house, as the performers are more energetic when a huge crowd cheers them on. The first show of the day, however, is the easiest to get into. Typically held at 9:40 a.m., it's often less than half full. Usually, you can show up at the last second and still choose your seat.

Where to sit? As you enter the theater you'll find four seating areas, two on your left and two on your right. To see the show the way it's intended, sit in the quadrant at the back right. Timon will face you during his "Hakuna Matata" number and you'll sit between the Pumbaa and Simba float puppets, which will make them easy to hear.

FUN FINDS

❶ As Timon's float enters the theater and heads to a corner, the Catskills-comic meerkat looks at the dancer holding the float's remote-control device and says "Slow down! I'm supposed to be center stage!" ❷ The monkeys pick bugs off of audience members and each other. ❸ Their music includes a Tarzan yell, a cow moo, a gargled version of Duke Ellington's 1937 "Caravan" and a snippet of the 1923 ditty "Yes, We Have No Bananas." ❹ Timon is a show all by himself. He cracks up watching the monkeys, trembles during "Be Prepared" and swoons throughout "Can You Feel the Love To-

Sitting in a backstage dressing room, singer Nicola Lambo prepares for her role as Princess Kibibi

night?" ❺ The giraffe often mouths the words to the songs. ❻ As you exit, Timon says "Could somebody hose down those Tumble Monkeys? They're starting to smell a little gamey."

FUN FACTS ❯❯ The floats are from a 1990s parade at California's Disneyland. ❯❯ Tarzan yells and other odd sounds in the Tumble Monkeys music are cues for the acrobats. ❯❯ There are puppeteers inside the parade floats, and they can see out. If the floats are still present as you leave the theater, stand in front of Simba, Pumbaa, the elephant or giraffe and wave or say hi. They may nod back.

LION CUB SIMBA finds his place in nature's circle of life in Disney's 1994 film "The Lion King." After his father is killed by his uncle Scar, Simba thinks he caused it and flees into exile. Befriended by the warmhearted (and often pungent) warthog Pumbaa and freewheeling meerkat Timon, Simba adopts the duo's "hakuna matata" (no worries) attitude as he grows up. When childhood sweetheart Nala re-enters his life, the adult Simba takes his place as king.

▶ Watch the movie first. The show's more fun after you refresh your memory of the film.

An African lion watches ostriches in the savanna area of Kilimanjaro Safaris

Kilimanjaro Safaris

★★★★★ ✔ 22 min. Capacity: 1,344. *FastPass* Fear factor: None. Access: ECV users must transfer. Assistive listening; handheld and activated captioning. Debuted: 1998.

One of the best zoological attractions in the United States, this jerky, jolty open-air tour takes you through a near-perfect 100-acre re-creation of African jungles and savannas. You'll splash through rivers, cross bridges, climb hills, pass free-roaming elephants, giraffes, rhinoceros and other exotic creatures, including some of the world's rarest species. Though the most dangerous creatures are kept distant by unseen barriers, other animals can come right up to your vehicle. Visit at the right time (such as first thing in the morning, or during a rain) and you may get within inches of a curious wildebeest, or find yourself in a staring contest with a stubborn ostrich.

In fact, no matter how many times you ride you never know exactly what you'll see. Bongos, man-drills, okapi, warthogs… they're all here, feeding, fighting, running, even nursing in what appear to be wide-open forests, rivers, grasslands, hills and streams. It can't be completely authentic—if it was the animals would be eating each other—but it so clearly seems to be.

Not everything you see is real. There's a reason your driver says the termite mounds are "as hard as concrete." A pile of ostrich eggs is equally tough to crack. Tusk marks in the red clay pits are also man-made.

How does the savanna appear to go on forever? Because the horizon is actually Disney World's 300-acre tree farm, an area not accessible to guests.

'POACHERS MAY BE INVOLVED'
Every Disney World ride has a story, and this tale is one of the company's most relevant and, at times, grim. Supposedly an effort by the nearby village of Harambe to replace its timbering economy with eco-tourism, Kilimanjaro Safaris takes you on a "two-week" trip through the "800-square-mile" Harambe Wildlife Preserve. The storyline begins in the queue, as overhead monitors introduce you to the refuge and show you its main problem: its creatures are being killed by poachers. In a jolting dose of real-

Average Wait

9am	0 min
10am	**30**
11am	20
Noon	20
1pm	20
2pm	20
3pm	10
4pm	20
5pm	20
6pm	20
7pm	10
8pm	closed
9pm	closed

▶ The best trips are early in the day or during a light rain, when the animals are lively.

A Kilimanjaro Safaris truck roams through the realistic 110-acre wildlife habitat

ity, the video shows slaughtered animals. On that jolly note, you climb into your truck, meant to be a flatbed logging vehicle retrofitted with bench seats and a canvas top.

Once underway, your guide establishes radio contact with the preserve's warden, Wilson Matuah. He flies above you in his spotter plane, watching for poachers and occasionally giving your driver directions to various roaming herds. After about 20 minutes, Matuah radios with an urgent plea for help: he's spotted two poaching trucks, one with a baby elephant in back, and he needs your help to stop them. Cutting short your safari, your driver leaves the preserve through a broken gate, chasing the poachers through a flooded gorge and into a clearing where the warden catches them. Mission accomplished, you head to Matuah's office, the ride exit.

Redone in 2007, the radio transmissions are a condensed version of a previous storyline ("They've shot Big Red!") that played a much larger role in the experience.

FUN FINDS

❶ When the phone rings in the safari office (just inside the standby queue), a machine answers it with "Harambe Wildlife Preserve… When it comes to safaris, we go wild!" ❷ The deflated hot-air balloon of the Kinga balloon-safari business (advertised on Harambe posters) is stored in the rafters above the queue. ❸ A grouping of black-faced royal ibis and East African crowned cranes wander a small habitat tucked in between the ride's Fastpass machines and the standby queue. ❹ "Prehistoric" tribal drawings are visible on the gate just past the flamingos and on rocks to your right as you pass the lions. ❺ While chasing the poachers you pass their camp, where a fire is still smoldering and tusks are scattered about.

HIDDEN MICKEY

As the flamingo island.

FUN FACTS ❭❭ Disney created the rutted road by coloring concrete to look like soil, then rolling tires through it and tossing in dirt, stones and twigs. ❭❭ The acacias are really Southern live oaks with close-cropped crew cuts. ❭❭ Hidden animal boundaries include fences, moats and trenches. ❭❭ The safari has the largest collections of Nile hippos and African elephants in North America. ❭❭ The animals respond to sound cues to come in at night. Elephants hear drums. ❭❭ The trucks run on propane. ❭❭ Kilimanjaro Safaris is the largest Disney attraction in the world.

▶ Taking photos is tough. The bouncy ride makes it hard to keep your camera still.

A gorilla watches guests photograph him in a habitat of the Pangani Forest Trail

Pangani Forest Trail

★★★★★ ✓ Allow 30 min. 1 trail (2055 ft), 9 viewing areas, 28 species plus aviary. Fear factor: None. Access: Guests may stay in wheelchairs, ECVs. Debuted: 1998.

Streams and gentle waterfalls weave through the lush grounds of this self-guided tour of fascinating African animals. It's divided into eight areas.

An outdoor hut (the "Endangered Animal Rehabilitation Centre") offers a good view of black-and-white colobus monkeys and of a yellow-backed duiker. Few Americans have ever seen an okapi, but you will at an observation blind that also has Stanley cranes.

Two colonies of naked mole rats crawl from room to room among "study burrows" in a huge wall display inside the replica research station. Other creatures there include cute spiny mice, a pancake tortoise and a fire skink. You can open some cabinet drawers to find collections of preserved butterflies, feathers, shells, small skulls (including those of bush pigs

and dwarf crocodiles), even giant beetles, scorpions and tarantulas.

You won't notice it when you enter an aviary, a screened-in area with a waterfall and pond. Two dozen species of exotic birds fly above you, rest in the trees and scurry on the ground. Don't miss the gigantic nest of the hammercop stork or the hanging homes of taveta golden weavers. A fish-viewing area has a 4-foot-long lungfish.

A 40-foot glass wall lets you view hippos underwater. It's best early, when the 100,000-gallon tank is clear. Stay quiet and the hippos may come up to the window.

Meerkats stand guard and dig burrows at a savanna overlook. Gerenuk roam nearby. Next is a gorilla blind, then a suspension bridge leads to a walkway that runs between two gorilla habitats. One side has a family (a silverback, two moms and three kids); the other a bachelor troupe. The gorillas are most active early, when they eat, drink, slap heads and chase each other.

The word "pangani" is Swahili for "place of enchantment."

HIDDEN MICKEYS

❶ In the research station, as a small shape on a backpack to the left of the naked mole rat exhibit.

Average Wait

9am	0 min
10am	0
11am	0
Noon	0
1pm	0
2pm	0
3pm	0
4pm	0
5pm	0
6pm	0
7pm	0
8pm	0
9pm	0

▶ The fish on display often suck up small pebbles and spit them out. Kids love it.

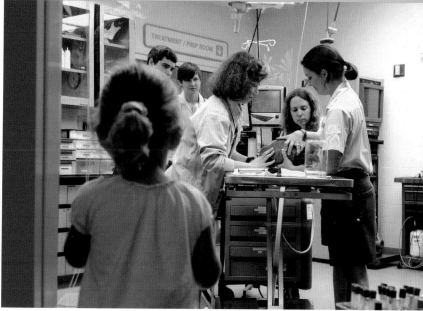

A young girl peers through a window to watch a gopher tortoise exam at Conservation Station

Conservation Station

★★★★ ✔ Allow 45 min. 49 species. Fear factor: None. Access: Guests may stay in wheelchairs, ECVs. Debuted: 1998.

Visiting this animal-care area can be exhausting. To see it means walking to a train station, waiting for a train, taking it to another station and then trekking down a long path. Once you reach the main building, you stay on your feet. To leave, you hike back.

Still, it's one of the few places at Disney where you enter a world that's totally real.

Named after the shaman mandrill in the 1994 film "The Lion King," the area features Conservation Station, a serious science center with a lot to see. In the mornings, observation windows let you look in on medical procedures on animals up to 500 pounds—expect to see anything from a bandage change on a goat to a root canal on a gorilla. Vets explain what's going on. Usually about three animals are brought in each morning.

Other windows peer in on researchers studying elephant vocalizations and

Average Wait	
9am	closed
10am	0 min
11am	5
Noon	5
1pm	5
2pm	5
3pm	5
4pm	5
5pm	5
6pm	closed
7pm	closed
8pm	closed
9pm	closed

tracking a sea turtle off the Florida coast. Adjacent exhibits include a butterfly room, a food preparation area and arachnid, insect and reptile displays.

You can zoom in on the park's primates, elephants, giraffes and other animals with remote-control Animal Cams. You'll hear rain, booming thunder and buzzing insects in the Song of the Rainforest exhibit, a group of cool, dark, family-sized audio booths. Eco Hero kiosks let you "speak" with Dr. Jane Goodall or George Schaller of the Tibet Wildlife Reserve. A Caring for the Wild exhibit has a telescope used by Dr. Goodall's and notebooks of Dian Fossey. A short film offers a look at endangered creatures. Cast members bring out lizards, owls, parrots and snakes. Meet-and-greet characters include Pocahontas, Rafiki and Stanley.

An adjacent petting zoo, **Affection Section** has domestic animals. Roaming free are African pygmy, San Clemente and Nigerian dwarf goats and Gulf Coast native and Tunis sheep. Behind a fence is a Dexter cow, a llama, two rare Guinea hogs and two Sicilian miniature donkeys. The largest goat, a brownish-gray fella named Luke, will steal stuff right out of your pockets.

To get to the area, you take a train from the Harambe Village station in the park's

▶ Take the first train of the day and you'll probably see an exam-room procedure.

Pleased to meet you. A goat nuzzles the authors' daughter at Affection Section.

a spider's abdomen (above a white owl chick), ⓫ in the pupil of an opossum, ⓬ as black spots on the yellow wings of a butterfly above an arm of a praying mantis. Middle wall, right to left: ⓭ As the pupil of an ostrich, ⓮ scales on the back of a green snake, ⓯ a sucker on the bottom of a starfish (a profile), ⓰ on the top of a butterfly body (a detailed and smiling Mickey face), ⓱ as spots on the wings of a butterfly (under a monkey) and ⓲ on a silver frog's left pupil (a profile). Many Mickeys hide in the Song of the Rainforest area. Left to right: ⓳ As the petals of a yellow flower, ⓴ as a white spot on a fly above a flower, ㉑ as a shadow on a tree in front of the rainforest doors (a profile), ㉒ as a white spot on a tree to the left of "The Accidental Florist" sign, ㉓ as a spot on the tree bark, across from a fly, about 4 feet off the ground, ㉔ as an impression in tree bark in the "Song of the Rainforest" sign to the lower right of Grandmother Willow's face (a profile), ㉕ as a nearby painted hole in a leaf, ㉖ as spots on a wooden cockroach inside a tree in the front of the rainforest area, ㉗ as three dark green spots on the side of a chameleon above the "Giant Cockroach" sign at the right of the rainforest area, ㉘ as and three round petri dishes in the far left window of the reptile display room. **Affection Section:** ㉙ As a pattern on a sheared sheep. ㉚ As orange spots on a stage wall, right of a lizard door.

Africa section. Called the **Wildlife Express,** it runs past Disney's "Jurassic Park"-style animal-care facilities. A long walkway, **Habitat Habit** is highlighted by a display of cotton-top tamarins.

FUN FINDS

Harambe train station: ❶ Plastered with posters, the Harambe station walls are stenciled "Affixing of Advertisements is Forbidden." **Wildlife Express Train:** ❷ Ankole cattle skulls are strapped on the front of the locomotives. **Landscape:** ❸ Impressions of a bird, fish, insect, human, shell, snail, reptile, Simba and the Tree of Life in the walkway under the Habitat Habit pavilions come together in a Circle of Life as you reach Conservation Station. **Conservation Station:** ❹ In the restrooms, placards give you The Scoop on Poop and offer a Whiz Quiz.

HIDDEN MICKEYS

Planet Watch train station: ❶ As blue circles in the rafter's cross beams. **Landscape:** ❷ As overlapping circles in the grates of Affection Section trees and in the Conservation Station lobby. **Conservation Station:** On the left wall of the inside entrance mural, left to right: ❸ As a pupil of a squirrel, ❹ wrinkles on a hippo's chin (a profile), ❺ a scale behind the eye of a crocodile, ❻ a shadow on a walrus's neck to the right of his tusks, ❼ an owl's pupils, ❽ a spot on a yellow fish (obscured by an octopus), ❾ black spots on a butterfly's left wing (above a bat). On the right wall, right to left: ❿ As a pink spot on

---

FUN FACTS ›› Complete with a corrugated-metal water tank, the train's African depot is patterned after British structures built in East Africa during the early 1900s. Next to the formal station is a local plaster-and-thatch addition. ›› Why such a fancy train? Because its track was originally meant to be a safari of its own, before the care facilities grew larger than anticipated. ›› The thatched-roof huts along the train track were made by hand in Indonesia.

▶ Have questions? Cast members will cheerfully discuss animal nutrition and health care.

A parrot appears to answer math problems in a demonstration of training techniques

Flights of Wonder

★★★★ ✔ 25 min. Capacity: 1,150. ECV and wheelchair accessible. Assistive listening. Bird species change periodically. Debuted: 1998.

The birds fly just inches above the audience in this inspirational live presentation, which demonstrates the natural behaviors of many different species.

Though the subject is serious—the need to understand wildlife on its own terms, and to value the survival of endangered and threatened species—the presentation is anything but. Just as the show gets started, it's interrupted by a loony lost tour guide, who wanders up on stage, tour flag in hand, in search of his group. You soon learn that he suffers from FOB— "fear of birds." As he faces his fears, you witness up-close-and-personal flight demonstrations from various birds of prey.

In fact, the presentation has many fun moments. After the host throws a grape in the air for a hornbill to catch, he asks for a child to come down and try it. "I'll toss the grape," he says, "you fly up and get it." Later, another child gets to challenge a parrot in math skills.

Want your child to be picked? You'll increase the odds if you sit front row center and have him or her wave wildly when the trainer ask for volunteers.

Altogether you'll see about 20 birds, including a Harris hawk, an Eastern crowned crane and a bald eagle. The eagle doesn't fly. You'll also see proof that the show's rat problem "is behind us."

When the show's over, handlers bring out a bird or two to the edge of stage for a brief meet-and-greet session. A similar preshow usually takes place in front of the theater, about 15 minutes before showtime.

Shows take place in a shaded outdoor theater, and are held rain or shine. During a significant shower the regular show is scrapped, and trainers simply walk through the audience with birds on their wrists.

The grassy natural stage features a backdrop of a crumbling stone building sitting in a shady grove. The area is said—fictionally, of course—to have been the gathering place of long-gone, animal-loving maharajahs, and is being used now by the natives of Anandapur, Disney's fictional Asian country, to acquaint others with the birds of their area.

Average Wait	
9am	n/a
10am	5 min
11am	5
Noon	5
1pm	5
2pm	5
3pm	5
4pm	5
5pm	5
6pm	n/a
7pm	n/a
8pm	n/a
9pm	n/a

▶ To have birds fly over you during Flights of Wonder, sit front and center or along an aisle.

Kali River Rapids

★★★★ ✔ 6 min. Capacity: 240 (20 12-person rafts). *FastPass* ECV users must transfer. Height restriction: 38 in. Debuted: 1999.

Habitat destruction has never been so fun! Set within realistic scenes of a pristine jungle being clear-cut and burned, this twisty trip through a whitewater obstacle course is so much fun you'll hardly remember its message. There's a chance you'll get soaked as you take a round, 12-person raft down a splashy river filled with powerful geysers, an abrupt waterfall, overhead water jugs and mischievous elephant statues.

Average Wait

9am	0 min
10am	20
11am	40
Noon	60
1pm	90
2pm	60
3pm	50
4pm	50
5pm	30
6pm	30
7pm	10
8pm	closed
9pm	closed

FUN FINDS ❶ In the queue area, Mr. Panika's Shop sells "Antiks Made to Order." ❷ Michael Jackson and a Nike logo appear on the murals in the last queue room. The King of Pop rides a raft named the Sherpa Surfer; the Nike swoosh icon appears on a girl's white shirt on the raft Khatmandoozy. The murals were created in Nepal, India, by a fan of Jackson and the shoe company.

Top: Rafts splash through turbulent waters.
Above: Guests watching the river can spray water on unsuspecting riders.

FUN FACTS ›› Raft names include Baloo Me Away, Delhi Donut, Khatmandoozy, Papa-Do-Ron-Rani and So Sari. ›› The river is the Chakranadi, Sanskrit for "the river that runs in circles." ›› Kali is the Hindu goddess of destruction.

▶ Take your river trip at the end of the day. If you get soaked, it won't matter.

Maharajah Jungle Trek

★★★★★ ✔ Allow 30 min. 1 trail (1500 ft), 7 viewing areas, 14 species plus aviary. Fear factor: None. Access: Guests may stay in wheelchairs, ECVs. Debuted: 1998.

This series of Asian animal exhibits is set in a re-creation of a decaying hunting lodge turned conservation station. The trail passes a Komodo dragon, tapir and tiger habitats and wanders through a fruit bat pavilion and a lush garden aviary. Don't miss the tigers. They're often climbing hills, ducking under bushes or scanning the landscape for prey, behaviors you don't see in a regular zoo.

An **Asian tiger** roams the ruins of an ancient royal hunting lodge at the Maharajah Jungle Trek

FUN FINDS

❶ The buildings and surroundings tell a story of a king and his three sons. As shown in murals at the second tiger area, one was an architect, the second a nature lover, the third a tiger hunter. ❷ Just past the footbridge, an environmental history of man is shown in a sequence of carvings on a wall to your right. Man emerges out of the water; comes to a paradise rich with wildlife; chops down its tree; faces floods, death and chaos; and finally gains happiness when he learns to respect nature. ❸ Next you enter a mythical tomb of Anantah, the first ruler of Disney's Anandapur kingdom. His ashes are said to be in the large fertility urn in the middle of the room.

HIDDEN MICKEYS

❶ At the second tiger viewing area, as swirls of water under a tiger in the first mural to your right. ❷ As a golden earring and ❸ three small bushes in the first mural to your left. ❹ As rocks in a mountain range above a flying dove in the second mural to your left. ❺ As swirls in a cloud formation in the second painting to your right. ❻ Past the tigers, as a leaf in a mural to your left, about 9 feet off the ground. ❼ In the top right of a mural left of the Elds Deer habitat, an orange flower and two leaves form a detailed Mickey face and waving arm. ❽ As necklace beads in the middle stone carving, just before the aviary.

FUN FACTS ❱❱ The tiger pool is kept at 70 degrees, and includes fish for the tigers to catch. ❱❱ The bridge over the tiger habitat is actually a wall separating the cats from an area of barred geese. ❱❱ The aviary weeds are frayed by hand for a consistent look.

Average Wait	
9am	0 min
10am	0
11am	0
Noon	0
1pm	0
2pm	0
3pm	0
4pm	0
5pm	0
6pm	0
7pm	0
8pm	0
9pm	0

▶ Bats feed first thing in the morning; tigers often play in the water at closing time.

The Expedition Everest roller coaster climbs into, and falls out of, a snowy mountain range

Expedition Everest

★★★★ ✔ 3 min. Capacity: 170. *FastPass* **Fear factor:** The lift rises high over the ground, you travel backwards in darkness 10 sec.; one turning drop. **Access:** ECV and wheelchair users must transfer. **Height restriction:** 44 in. **Debuted:** 2006.

A modern Disney megaride, Expedition Everest combines sly Disney mind games with coaster-like thrills and the excitement of a close encounter of the hairy kind. Aboard an out-of-control railcar that races forward and backward, you swoop into the mysterious world of the Yeti, the mythical Himalayan creature also known as the Abominable Snowman.

It's the mental tricks that psych you out. As one 8-year-old girl put it, "That monster was like 100 feet tall!" Actually, he's only 18.

What begins as a peaceful trip through a forest turns into a tense chase through mountain caves. Though it doesn't go upside-down, your 4,000-foot journey climbs 200 feet, stops twice, goes backward, takes an 80-foot drop and hits a top speed of 50 mph.

Average Wait	
9am	0 min
10am	40
11am	50
Noon	45
1pm	50
2pm	45
3pm	45
4pm	40
5pm	30
6pm	45
7pm	40
8pm	20
9pm	0

A MONSTER MYTH

To deepen your experience Disney has created a full back story—a tale of a mythical creature, weird accidents, wise villagers and clueless entrepreneurs.

"The Legend of the Forbidden Mountain" begins in the 1920s, a time when tea plantations flourished in the mountains of the imaginary Asian kingdom of Anandapur. Private rail lines carried the tea to villages, where it was shipped to distant markets. The Royal Anandapur Tea Co. used one such route extensively through the early 1930s, sending "steam-donkey" trains through the mysterious mountains to the village of Serka Zong.

Starting in 1933, however, the railroad was plagued with accidents. Some residents drew a connection between the mishaps and increasing British expeditionary attempts to reach the summit of nearby Mt. Everest, invoking the spirit of the Yeti, the fabled, monstrous creature that guards the sacred area. By 1934, equipment breakdowns and strange track snaps caused the tea company to pull up stakes.

The legend of a guardian beast continued to circulate among locals. It came to a head in 1982, with the tragic disappearance of the Forbidden Mountain Expedition.

▶ Sit in the back for the wildest ride. You'll get whipped harder and fall faster.

Cut to today. Bob, a bohemian American, grooves to the village's Hare Krishna vibe but doesn't believe in the Yeti. To earn a living, he's teamed up with a local entrepreneur, Norbu, and restored the old railroad to create Himalayan Escapes Tours and Expeditions, a business designed to make it easy for trekkers get to Everest quickly. Instead of hiking for two weeks through the foothills and over the smaller ranges, now climbers can arrive at the foot of Everest in just a few hours, riding safely on a quaint old steam train through a scenic mountain range.

THREE MOUNTAINS IN ONE

In reality, Disney's mountain range combines three free-standing structures. One is the ride, a dynamic system with internal framing that extends down to the foundation. The second is the building, with its beams and columns. The third is the Yeti, which has its own independent supports. Though intertwined like spaghetti, the three structures don't touch. If they did, the mountain's plaster and stucco would flake off. "In some cases we ran building beams down the middle of A-frame ride columns," says project manager Mike Lentz.

FUN FINDS

❶ Plaster on the Fastpass building and gift shop simulates the Himalayan building material of dried yak dung. ❷ A bulletin board note on the wall of Gupta's Gear (left of the main village) reads "Billy—It's a small world after all! Met your brother on the trail... Mikey." ❸ Steam escapes from the train's boiler after it pulls into the boarding area. ❹ It pulls out with a "toot-toot!" ❺ The Yeti's claw marks and footprints appear in the snow to your right at your first stop. ❻ When you stop in the cave, watch the track in front of you. It flips over.

HIDDEN MICKEYS

❶ In the queue, as a tiny Mickey hat worn by a Yeti doll in Tashi's Trek and Tongba Shop, on the top shelf of a cupboard to the right. ❷ As black water bottle caps in a display of patches in the same shop. ❸ As a dent and two holes in a tea kettle that's part of the wreckage of a camp in the Yeti museum. ❹ On the left wall after the museum, a Mickey with eyes, a nose, and a Sorcerer's hat appears as wood stains in a photograph that shows a woman with a walkie-talkie.

An 80-foot drop highlights your trip aboard the Expedition Everest tea train

---

FUN FACTS ⟩⟩ The mountain has 1,800 tons of steel, 18.7 million pounds of concrete, 2,000 gallons of stain and paint and 200,000 square feet of rock work. ⟩⟩ The Yeti has a potential thrust of 260,000 pounds of force—more than a 747 airliner. It's Disney's most advanced Audio-Animatronics creature. ⟩⟩ Much of the queue-line woodwork, including the entire Yeti temple, was handcrafted by Himalayan artists. ⟩⟩ The Buddha statues, Nepalese Coke bottles, desk phone and pot-bellied stoves are among 8,000 items Disney imported from Asia. ⟩⟩ The 6-acre area has 900 bamboo plants and 100 types of bushes. ⟩⟩ The buildings were aged with blowtorches, chainsaws and hammers. ⟩⟩ "Serka Zong" is Tibetan for "fortress of the chasm."

▶ If you can, ride it at night. The mountain is lit in orange and purple, but the track stays dark.

© DISNEY

Too close for comfort. An angry carnotaurus threatens guests riding a Dinosaur Time Rover.

Dinosaur!

★ ★ ★ ★ ✔ 3 min, 30 sec. Capacity: 144. *FastPass* Fear factor: Intense. Access: ECV and wheelchair users must transfer. Assisted listening, video captioning. Height restriction: 40 in. Debuted: 1998 (as "Countdown to Extinction").

You'll remember the last second of this dark indoor ride for days: a dinosaur gets right in your face and lets loose with an unearthly roar. The rest is almost as tense.

You start off in the Dino Institute Discovery Center, a parody of the Smithsonian's National Museum of Natural History. As you pass earnest murals and displays, a multimedia show explains how an asteroid wiped out the dinosaurs long ago.

In the Orientation Room you meet Director Helen Marsh (Phylicia Rashad) via a video hookup. She shows you the Time Rover, a vehicle that will take you back on a peaceful visit to the Age of the Dinosaurs.

But her assistant has a different plan. Once Marsh leaves the room, Dr. Grant Seeker (Wallace Langham, of television's "CSI") se-

Average Wait	
9am	0 min
10am	20
11am	30
Noon	20
1pm	20
2pm	30
3pm	30
4pm	20
5pm	20
6pm	15
7pm	10
8pm	5
9pm	0

cretly reprograms her computer to send you to a time just before the asteroid strikes, to bring an iguanodon to the present.

Soon a flashing, smoky tunnel sends you 65 million years back in time, to a dark forest. As you careen forward you see many dinosaurs, including an alioramus swallowing its dinner. Suddenly a huge carnotaurus starts chasing you. Then it gets worse—your power starts to fail. As a massive meteor destroys your trail, it appears that you, too, are about to become extinct.

In a final burst of speed, you find your iguanodon, narrowly miss the last lunge of the carnotaurus and crash back to the present. Security monitors show you did indeed pick up the iguanodon.

DINO-SUE

A cast of the largest, most complete Tyrannosaurus rex fossil ever found (Sue, uncovered in South Dakota in 1990) stands in front of the Dinosaur attraction. Named after paleontologist Sue Hendrickson, the 67-million-year-old creature is estimated to have been 45 feet long and 14 feet tall. Much of the real fossil's bonework (now at Chicago's Field Museum) was done in the late 1990s in front of Disney guests, where today's Dino-Rama carnival sits.

▶ Sit on the far right side of your Time Rover for the closest encounter with the carnotaurus.

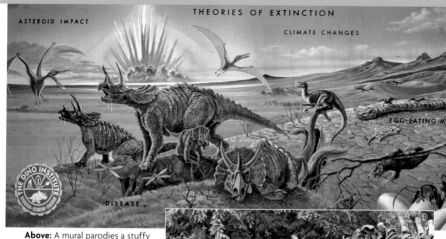

THEORIES OF EXTINCTION

ASTEROID IMPACT

CLIMATE CHANGES

EGG-EATING M

THE DINO INSTITUTE

DISEASE

Above: A mural parodies a stuffy museum. **Right:** A cast of a T-Rex skull. **Below:** A McDonald's sign shows a scene from the ride.

CRETACEOUS TRAIL

This shady path meanders through a garden that uses ancient plant species to replicate a dinosaur-era jungle. The greenery includes conifers, ferns, mosses, more than 20 magnolia species and the third largest cycad collection in North America. Dinosaur sounds and statues add a lightweight touch. The trail is wheelchair and ECV accessible.

FUN FINDS

❶ An entrance dedication plaque is dated April 22, 1978—exactly 20 years before the attraction opened. ❷ Smithsonian allusions include a cheap lobby diorama with a plastic rat glued to a plastic tree, beneath which swim plastic fish in a plastic pond. ❸ Dr. Seeker claims flash photography "interferes with the homing signal and that's not good." ❹ Actually an above-ground warehouse, the "underground research facility" where the ride begins is cooler than the earlier rooms, and has flickering lights. ❺ Gift-shop monitors show the iguanodon continuing to wander the building. ❻ A cast of an ancient sea turtle hangs over the gift shop.

FUN FACT ❯❯ An "enhanced motion vehicle," your Time Rover gets its movements from 3,000 PSI of hydraulic pressure. On-board tanks hold 100 gallons of fluid.

Have you had a Crocodilian today?

▶ A climb-on dinosaur on the Cretaceous trail makes a good photo prop.

Out for a spin. Primeval Whirl riders start to spin as they head down the ride's big drop.

Dumbo XL. Unlike its famous cousin, TriceraTop Spin has room for four.

Primeval Whirl

★★★★ 2 min, 30 sec. Capacity: 52 on each of two tracks. *FastPass* Fear factor: One steep drop. The spinning can affect those with inner-ear issues. Access: ECV and wheelchair users must transfer. Height restriction: 48 in. Debuted: 2002.

A spoof of the nearby Dinosaur attraction, this spinning roller coaster also takes you back to the age of hitchhiking dinosaurs, but this time in a tongue-in-cheek vehicle equipped with a kitchen timer, clock radio and alarm clock, candy-colored and stylistically cued like a 1950s automobile. Scenery combines comic dinosaur and meteor cutouts with cartoon clocks and vortexes. A time portal alongside the queue area is decorated with egg beaters and hubcaps.

The ride itself is a wild trip. An updated take on an old Wild Mouse carnival coaster, it picks up speed slowly down a switchback track. Once the meteors hit, your car starts to spin.

HIDDEN MICKEY

As meteor craters that appear throughout the ride.

Average Wait	
9am	0 min
10am	30
11am	20
Noon	20
1pm	20
2pm	30
3pm	20
4pm	20
5pm	20
6pm	10
7pm	20
8pm	10
9pm	0

TriceraTop Spin

★★★ 1 min, 30 sec. Capacity: 64. Access: ECV users must transfer. Debuted: 2001.

This carnival-style attraction is Disney's most elaborate hub-and-spoke ride. Circling around a giant spinning top that has playful dinosaurs popping out of its rim, you ride in a chubby triceratops that climbs, dips and dives at your command. The vehicles circle the top once every 13 seconds, the same speed as Magic Kingdom's similar Dumbo the Flying Elephant.

Though the ride doesn't offer the charm of the Dumbo ride, it is easier to enjoy. There's rarely a long line, and a large covered queue includes fans to keep you cool as you wait. Each vehicle seats four, so small families can ride together.

Manic banjo and fiddle music adds corny charm, while vivid colors help give the ride the look of a toy—the top itself is orange, blue and red. Extra eye candy includes flying cartoon comets on the hub and, at night, white light bulbs lining the hub and spokes.

Average Wait	
9am	0 min
10am	5
11am	5
Noon	5
1pm	10
2pm	20
3pm	10
4pm	10
5pm	10
6pm	5
7pm	10
8pm	5
9pm	0

▶ To avoid getting dizzy on Primeval Whirl, stare at the orange radio in front of you.

A dino double! The authors' daughter with some Fossil Fun Games winnings.

Fossil Fun Games

★ ★ ★ ✔ Allow 15 min. Capacity: 1–10 per game. Fear factor: None. Access: Guests may remain in wheelchairs and ECVs. Debuted: 2002.

The centerpiece of Disney's tongue-in-cheek roadside carnival (the purposely tacky Chester and Hester's Dino-Rama) these six colorful midway games have silly dinosaur themes. Three are designed for children, three for adults. Each costs $2 to play, and awards cartoonish stuffed dinosaurs to its winners. Unlike many real carnivals, the games aren't rigged and their prizes, though small, are often easy to win.

For children, the midway offers an easy water-squirt game (Fossil Fueler), a ball-rolling racing derby (Mammoth Marathon) and a mallet-strike contest (Whac-A-Pachycephalosaur).

Each requires only two players and always awards a prize. In other words, if one of these three games has no one waiting to play it—a common situation, especially in the early morning—you and a child can spend a total of $4 and one of you will absolutely win a small stuffed dinosaur worth at least that much. (Smart parents discreetly find a way to lose.)

Our daughter, who has played the three games for years, offers these tips on how to win at them:

Fossil Fueler: For the most accurate shooting, use your free hand to cradle the front of your gun.

Mammoth Marathon: Roll the balls gently. If you use too much force a ball will go into a hole with a lesser value and your mammoth will move slowly. To get the hang of it ask the attendant for a practice ball before your race starts.

Whacky Packy: Wait until you see a head pop up before you try to hit it.

Three other games require serious skill to win anything, and some luck— a ball toss (Comet Crasher), basketball throw (Bronto Score) and a classic strongman mallet strike that sends a weight up a pole to ring a bell (Dino-Whamma, which these days is rarely open). Prizes for these latter three games are not guaranteed, regardless of how many people compete.

For all games, smaller prizes can be saved up and traded in for larger ones. Prizes can be sent to package pickup free of charge, so you don't have to carry them with you.

Average Wait	
9am	0 min
10am	0
11am	0
Noon	0
1pm	0
2pm	0
3pm	0
4pm	0
5pm	0
6pm	0
7pm	0
8pm	0
9pm	0

▶ Whac-A-Pachycephalosaur ("Whacky Packy") is the easiest game for kids.

A **1970s Jeep** sits "stuck in the mud" of The Boneyard playground

The Boneyard

★★★★ ✔ Allow 15–30 min. Capacity: 500. Fear factor: None. Access: Guests may remain in wheelchairs, ECVs. Debuted 1998.

This realistic paleontological dig site is filled with opportunities for kids to burn off energy. Two distinct areas connected by an overhead footbridge, it features a three-story tower of nets and slides and a sandy pit that hides bones of a woolly mammoth.

Extras include a maze of tunnels, its walls embedded with bones of a Triceratops and gaping jaws of a T-Rex, and a few waterfalls sized just right to drench a young head. An abundance of hidden nooks and crannies makes it easy to lose sight of your child, but there's only one exit, and its shut gate is monitored.

Average Wait

9am	0 min
10am	0
11am	0
Noon	0
1pm	0
2pm	0
3pm	0
4pm	0
5pm	0
6pm	0
7pm	0
8pm	0
9pm	0

FUN FINDS

❶ Though it looks like a stegosaurus shoulder bone, the Boneyard marquee is in the original shape of the theme park, before the addition of Asia. An "N" points north. ❷ Notes sound when kids bang a "xylobone" by the Jeep. ❸ Across from a whiteboard along the top back wall, dinosaur tracks trigger roars when kids step on them. ❹ On the whiteboard itself, three fictional grad students and their professors have posted their findings and work schedules. ❺ Their personal possessions and notes to each other are scattered throughout the playground, on the bulletin board at the DinoLand U.S.A. entrance as well as in the nearby Restaurantosaurus, where the students supposedly live in the rafters. ❻ Scientific debates about dinosaurs appear on signs throughout the playground. ❼ Ambient music (pirate radio station W-DINO) includes the Move's 1970 U.K. hit, "Brontosaurus."

HIDDEN MICKEYS

❶ As a water stain under the drinking fountain near the entrance. ❷ As a quarter and two pennies on a table behind a fenced-in area, on the second level by the slides in the back. ❸ As a fan and two hardhats in a fenced-off area at the back of the woolly mammoth excavation.

FUN FACT ≫ The woolly mammoth was not a dinosaur. It lived just 10,000 years ago. Dinosaurs died off 65 million years earlier.

▶ The Boneyard offers plenty of shady spots for parents to get off their feet.

'Haven't you seen Jaws?' Marlin (left) confronts his son in Finding Nemo—The Musical.

Finding Nemo — The Musical

★★★★★ ✔ 35 min. Capacity: 1,700. Fear factor: None Access: ECV, wheelchair accessible. Reflective captioning. Debuted: 2007.

Singers who somersault as they "swim" above the stage... giant jellyfish that billow through the theater... a chorus line of shimmying sharks. The creativity never ends in this musical retelling of the 2003 movie, "Finding Nemo." A spectacle of color, movement and imagination, it redefines the meaning of the term "puppet show."

Costumed live singers act out the roles of Nemo, Dory and other characters as they simultaneously operate larger-than-life puppet versions. Peripheral characters are brought to life by Japanese *bunraku*, in which one huge puppet is operated by multiple puppeteers. The puppets were created by Michael Curry, who did the park's parade floats and the puppets in the Broadway production of "The Lion King."

Average Wait	
9am	n/a
10am	30 min
11am	30
Noon	30
1pm	30
2pm	30
3pm	30
4pm	30
5pm	n/a
6pm	n/a
7pm	n/a
8pm	n/a
9pm	n/a

The songs are accessible and seamlessly fit into the story. The show also includes acrobats, dancers, animated backdrops and terrifically abstract props, like a fish net comprised simply of six bowed ladders.

The production takes place in the Theater in the Wild, located along the walkway between DinoLand U.S.A. and Asia. Sit in the middle to see the full spectacle, along the catwalk to be immersed in it.

As you leave, the movie's "Mine! Mine!" sea gulls bid you "Bye! Bye!" They're voiced by Andrew Stanton, the film's director.

HIDDEN MICKEYS

❶ As three blue bubbles, two lit and one drawn, at the bottom left of the stage wall.

IN THE 2003 FILM "Finding Nemo," curious clownfish Nemo defies his overprotective father, Marlin, and swims out to a boat, only to be captured by a diver hunting for aquarium fish. Determined to find his son, Marlin encounters Dory, an absentminded blue tang, as well as sharks, jellyfish and sea turtles. Meanwhile, Nemo, relocated to a fish tank in Sydney, makes new friends who teach him that he's stronger than he thinks, and help him reunite with his dad.

▶ The last show of the day is usually the least crowded.

The view from one of the guest floats in
Mickey's Jammin' Jungle Parade

Mickey's Jammin' Jungle Parade

★★★★★ ✓ 15 min. Circles around Discovery Island. Starts, and exits, in Africa. Access: Special viewing locations for those in wheelchairs and ECVs. Assistive listening. Debuted: 2001.

Towering mechanical animal puppets, whimsical stilt-walkers, colorful Jeeps and Land Rovers, dozens of dancers and infectious music combine to celebrate the harmony between man and animals in this lively procession, which winds along shady pathways that are often just 12 feet wide.

Handcrafted in a leafy motif from what appears to be natural materials, the abstract puppets move like real creatures: a chameleon sticks out its tongue; a frog jumps.

Dancing alongside are safari guides, creature-costumed stilt-walkers and characters including Pluto, Chip 'n Dale, Timon from Disney's 1994 "The Lion King," Terk from 1999's "Tarzan," Baloo and King Louie from 1967's "The Jungle Book" and Brer Bear and Brer Rabbit from the 1946 "Song of the South."

A whimsical back story ties it all together. The parade is simply Mickey Mouse and Rafiki (the mandrill from "The Lion King") taking the other characters camping.

Minnie Mouse, Donald Duck and Goofy travel in their own personalized safari truck, though none appear to know how to pack. Donald totes a leaky boat. Minnie brings a bathtub. Goofy's the worst: he's brought everything from his bowling trophy to, literally, his kitchen sink.

A catchy soundtrack features Disney versions of the 1954 New Orleans standard "Iko Iko," South African legend Miriam Makeba's 1960s dance classic "Pata Pata" and "Mas Que Nada," the 1966 signature tune of Brazil's Sergio Mendes.

Selected at random each day, up to 25 park guests ride in the parade.

FUN FINDS

❶ Minnie's bathtub blows bubbles. ❷ It also has a Donald Duck rubber ducky. ❸ Goofy's hood ornament, a bowling trophy, topples over as his engine overheats. ❹ Strapped onto Goofy's hood is Aladdin's lamp and carpet. ❺ His vehicle carries a Donald Duck life preserver. ❻ Timon's backpack is full of bugs. ❼ The driver of the hippo rickshaw is the animal's pic-pic bird. ❽ The kangaroo float has a spring for a tail. Its drummer sits in the mechanical marsupial's pouch. ❾ Brooms create the mane and tail of the zebra stilt-walker.

▶ The parade passes through Africa on its way out and back. Crowds are light for the return trip.

Gerenuk, Pangani Forest Trail

ANTEATER

A walking vacuum cleaner, the Latin American **giant anteater** *(The Oasis)* sucks up ants and termites with its toothless snout. It can flick its 2-foot tongue 150 times a minute, eat 30,000 insects a day, yet sleep 15 hours a day. Growing up to 9 feet long, a giant anteater has the largest claws of any mammal and the longest tongue of any mammal for its size. To protect its claws, an anteater walks on its front knuckles. It uses its tail as a blanket when it sleeps. Though fed a prescribed diet, Disney's anteater still digs for insects.

ANTELOPE

The beautiful **bongo** *(Kilimanjaro Safaris)* has white stripes on a chestnut coat. Called the Ghost of the Forest, the shy creature is the largest forest antelope, weighing up to 600 pounds. The delicate **gerenuk** *(Pangani Forest Exploration Trail)* stands up to feed on tree leaves. Its hip joints swivel to let its

backbone line up with its hind legs. The most agile antelope, the **impala** *(Kilimanjaro Safaris)* can leap 10 feet in the air and turn in mid-flight. It can run 40 mph and take bounds of almost 40 feet. A male attracts females (and scares off other males) by repeatedly sticking out his tongue. The world's largest antelope, the **Patterson's eland** *(Kilimanjaro Safaris)* can stand 6 feet tall and weigh 1,500 pounds. The aggressive **sable antelope** *(Kilimanjaro Safaris)* drops to its knees to engage foes with its horns. At rest, a group will lie in a circle with its heads facing out, protecting young that lie in the middle. The tiny **Thomson's gazelle** *(Kilimanjaro Safaris)* stands only 2 or 3 feet tall, but can run 50 mph. Still, it is the favorite prey of the cheetah. The **white-bearded wildebeest** *(Kilimanjaro Safaris)* is also known as the gnu, the sound of its call. A gregarious animal, it sleeps in rows, gives birth in groups and migrates annually in a herd of up to 1.5 million—the world's single largest wildlife movement. Named for its habit of diving into underbrush when frightened, the chunky **yellow-backed duiker** ("diver" in Afrikaans) *(Kilimanjaro Safaris)* is the world's largest duiker, growing up to 3 feet. *Permanently attached, antelope horns are not shed.*

APES

The largest and loudest gibbon, the 3-foot-tall **siamang** *(Asia, at the monument towers between Flights of Wonder and Kali River Rapids)* inflates a throat sac to produce a hoot that can reach 113 decibels, nearly as noisy as a jet aircraft at 100 yards. A family's adult female will start a group morning call that can last 30 minutes. Monogamous mates sing duets to express affection. Family members groom each other and usually don't venture more than 30 feet apart. The father shares in raising a baby and takes over care after an infant's first year. A siamang's arms are longer than its legs, which lets it swing through tree branches 30 feet apart.

A crescendo of siren-like whoops is the territorial call of the smaller **white-cheeked gibbon** *(Asia, near the exit to Kali River Rapids)*. It travels up to a mile each day, farther than any other forest ape or

Western lowland gorilla, Pangani Forest Trail

monkey. That agility makes it virtually invulnerable to predators, though human activities (rainforest farming, logging, wars) have destroyed most of its habitat. It lives in southern China, Laos and North Vietnam. Males and juveniles are black with white cheeks. Females and newborns are blond.

The **western lowland gorilla** *(Pangani Forest Exploration Trail)* is the most populous gorilla subspecies, with about 94,000 wild animals. The world's largest and most powerful primate, a gorilla is also the least aggressive; its iconic chest-beating is just a display. The ape lives in a group of five to 30 animals, of which the most mature male serves as the benevolent dictator. Identified by the silver hair on his back, this "silverback" will baby-sit an infant while its mom looks for food.

Like humans, gorillas have fingerprints, 32 teeth, can stand upright, have the same sexual cycle (females menstruate about every 28 days, births happen at 9 months, juveniles mature at around 11 or 12 years), use tools and can learn sign language. Disney World has a family of six gorillas (one silverback, two adult females, three juveniles) as well as three bachelors.

BABIRUSA

With a face only a mother could love, the freakish **babirusa** *(The Oasis)* looks like a giant pig with a dental problem. In males, huge upper tusks extend through the

snout. Like a macaw, a babirusa eats clay to cleanse its system. Though its name means "pig-deer," a babirusa is more closely related to a hippo. It lives in Indonesia.

BATS

The largest bat in the world, the **Malayan flying fox** *(Maharajah Jungle Trek)* has a wingspan so massive (up to 6 feet) it can't take off from the ground. The **Rodrigues fruit bat** *(Maharajah Jungle Trek)* has a 3-foot span. *Bats are the only flying mammals. These two species are vegetarians. The Disney bats cling to their hanging food with their claws and eat it upside down. They groom and lick each other to express affection, often nuzzling snouts. They turn rightside-up to relieve themselves. Bats can sense rain. Just before a shower begins, Disney's bats will fold up, just as they do when it's too hot or sunny.*

CAVY

The world's second largest rodent, the **Patagonian cavy** *(The Oasis)* can weigh 25 pounds. Related to a guinea pig, it uses its long legs to run up to 28 mph and leap up to 6 feet. It lives around the Andes mountains of South America.

CHEETAH

Using its long tail for balance, the **cheetah** *(Kilimanjaro Safaris)* can accelerate from 0

Rodrigues fruit bat, Maharajah Jungle Trek

CROCODILES

Much larger than its alligator cousin, the brawny **American crocodile** *(DinoLand U.S.A.)* can grow up to 15 feet long and weigh 2,000 pounds. It can go up to two years between meals, using its tail fat for nourishment. Only about 500 are left in the United States, all in southern Florida. Disney's creature often lies with its mouth wide open to keep cool (a croc has no sweat glands). Reaching up to 20 feet long, the aggressive **Nile crocodile** *(Kilimanjaro Safaris)* will run onto land to snatch prey. Life starts off sweet: hatchlings call to their mother from inside their eggs when ready to hatch, then both parents roll the eggs in their mouths to crack the shells. The mom carries her foot-long newborns in her jaws to water, then guards them for up to six months. *Disney's crocs are trained to come in at night. Keepers ring a bell and dangle food in front of an enclosure.*

DEER

Almost constantly rutting, a male **Axis deer** *(Discovery Island)* will make loud bugle-like bellows. Females fight. Like boxing kangaroos, they paw at one another while standing on their hind legs. The most endangered deer, the **Elds deer** *(Maharajah Jungle Trek)* lives only in a 15-square-mile marsh around Loktak Lake in Eastern India. Its antlers curve out then up and sport at least six points. The **Reeves muntjac** *(The Oasis)* is called the barking deer due to the sound it makes when alarmed. A male grows large canine teeth that curl from its lips, like tusks.

DUCKS

One of the smallest diving ducks in the world, the **bufflehead** *(The Oasis)* is less than a foot long. It was originally called the Buffalo Head, a reference to the male's large noggin. To attract females, a male will puff up its crest, bob its head and show off its diving skills. The endangered **white-backed duck** *(Pangani Forest Exploration Trail)* can stay under the water for 30 seconds. With a

to 70 mph in three seconds. The fastest land animal, it can outrun any other creature but only for a short distance. Adapted for traction, its claws are only slightly curved and only partially retract. As the cats naturally hunt in daylight, safari guests see them eyeing intended prey.

CRANES

The **East African crowned crane** *(Discovery Island)* has a brush-like crest of golden feathers: camouflage for the tall grass of its wetland habitat. It's the only crane that roosts in trees. Listen for its honking trumpets. Standing 6 feet high, the **sarus crane** *(Maharajah Jungle Trek)* is the tallest flying bird. Its wingspan is 8 feet. *In courtship, a pair will bow toward each other; hop, jump, strut and flap wings as they circle each other, and perform a series of coordinated honks and squawks.*

Komodo dragon, Maharajah Jungle Trek

high-pitched three-note whistle, the **white-faced whistling duck** *(Discovery Island)* sounds like a squeak toy. It lives in Africa, the Caribbean and Latin America. Nearly extinct, the **white-winged wood duck** *(Maharajah Jungle Trek)* once thrived in Southeast Asian rainforests. Today most of its habitat is gone.

ELEPHANT

The largest land mammal, the **African elephant** *(Kilimanjaro Safaris)* can weigh 11,000 pounds. It has few natural enemies but has been relentlessly hunted for its tusks, a prize that is actually made of the same stuff as human teeth: ivory dentine.

An elephant's trunk combines a long nose with an upper lip. It can hold up to 3 gallons of water. Two finger-like projections at the tip can pluck grasses and manipulate small objects. The trunk has 40,000 muscles, more than in a human body. An elephant's skin is so sensitive it can feel a fly landing on it. An African elephant can make a variety of vocal sounds, including low frequency rumbles that are below the human range of hearing, but can be heard by other elephants up to 5 miles away.

Females can breed for three to six days every four years. Bulls find mates by listening for female tummy rumbles that can be heard for miles. When a mating takes place, the entire herd often takes part in a noisy melee known as the "mating

pandemonium." Females and calves mill, circle, wave their trunks and trumpet loudly for up to an hour. The gestation period is 21 months. Four babies have been born at Disney through artificial insemination and natural breeding—two males (2003 and 2008) and two females (2004 and 2005). When the program began, Disney baby-proofed its habitat by increasing its shade, closing gaps between boulders and installing a shallow backstage pool that allows calves to safely explore water and learn to swim.

FLAMINGO

These birds get their pink color from carotene-rich spirulina, an algae common in brackish lakes. The paler **greater flamingo** *(Kilimanjaro Safaris)* gets the algae indirectly by eating insects, shrimp and other small creatures that themselves have consumed the algae; the brilliant **lesser flamingo** *(Discovery Island)* eats it directly. *Spending much of their day with their heads upside down, flamingos stir up the mud with their webbed feet, then suck and filter the murky water through their bills. Like most wading birds, a flamingo is most comfortable while standing on one leg, and what appears to be its knee is actually its ankle.*

GIRAFFE

The world's tallest animal, the **reticulated giraffe** *(Kilimanjaro Safaris)* can stand up

Gray kangaroo, Discovery Island

to 19 feet tall. Its 6-foot legs support a 6-foot torso that's topped by a 6-foot neck and a foot-high head. It balances with help from an 8-foot tail (the longest of any land mammal) and rests on feet up to a foot wide. A giraffe has a stride of 15 feet and can run up to 45 mph; its tongue can be up to 20 inches long; its heart 2 feet wide; its lungs can hold 12 gallons of air; and its neck has only seven vertebrae, the same number as man. Females give birth standing up. Newborns drop head-first to the ground. Babies average 6 feet tall and grow an inch a day. Although generally quiet, giraffes are not mute. Calves bleat; adults can grunt, hiss, moo and snort. Unlike most grazing animals, a giraffe can't lower its head to the ground without splaying its legs.

GOAT

It's the devil! Well, actually it's an **African pygmy goat** (*Rafiki's Planet Watch*), but people have associated it and its relatives with Beelzebub since the animal was domesticated 10,000 years ago. For centuries Satan was thought to be able to transform himself into a goat at will, and is still often portrayed with the creature's hooves and horns. Some farmers once believed that owning a goat would protect them from the devil, or that when a goat could not be found it was meeting with him. Sailors once thought a goat on board would ensure a calm sea, which helped the 18-inch-tall African pygmy goat become common in North America. Its natural barrel shape makes it appear to always be pregnant.

GUINEA FOWL

The **Kenya crested guinea fowl** (*Discovery Island*) is a black bird covered in white polka dots that's known to take an occasional dust bath. It's a rare breed of the creature Egyptians domesticated in 2400 B.C. Renaissance traders often confused it with a turkey.

HIPPOPOTAMUS

A cross between a pig and a whale, a **Nile hippopotamus** (*Kilimanjaro Safaris, also Pangani Forest Exploration Trail*) spends its day in the water. With its ears, eyes and nose on top of its head, it can keep track of its surroundings while hiding its bulk under the surface. It has webbed feet, and can hold its breath for 12 minutes.

The hippo feeds after dark, eating land grasses, leaves and bark. With the largest mouth of any land mammal, it can eat up to 150 pounds of food a night. An aggressive, territorial animal, the hippo kills more humans than any other African creature. Over a short distance the 6,000-pound mammal can outrun a man.

Hippos were once thought to sweat blood. They ooze a pinkish oil that moisturizes their skin. Disney's herd is the largest in the country.

IBIS

Easily identified by its large spoon-shaped bill, the **African spoonbill** (*The Oasis*) fishes for its food by swinging its open bill in the water. The birds have an odd mating ritual. Males will offer a female sticks for her nest. When she accepts one (which isn't often) she has chosen her mate. The behavior can be seen with Disney's birds. The most common bird at Animal Kingdom, the **white ibis** is not one of Disney's creatures. Abundant in Florida, thousands of ibis have flown into the park and stayed for its lush habitat and plentiful food. Hundreds roost each evening in the trees along the Discovery River. The bird is easy to identify by its orange downcurved bill that's as long as its legs. It's the mascot of the University of Miami.

KANGAROOS

The only large mammal that hops, a kangaroo can jump 9 feet in the air, leap 40 feet and reach speeds of 30 mph. Tendons in the back legs act like giant springs. At full speed it can outpace a racehorse. At rest, a kangaroo's weight is supported by the tripod of its hind legs and tail.

A newborn resembles a jelly bean. An inch long, the hairless, still-developing "joey" has no back legs. It climbs into its mother's pouch, where it stays put for nine months. A mother produces different milk for different-aged joeys. In some species, a female can control the progress of her pregnancy so that each newborn has an open teat in her pouch. Gestation typically takes 35 days, but can be delayed for nearly a year. The world's largest marsupial, the **red kangaroo** (Discovery Island) can stand 6 and a half feet tall and weigh 200 pounds. It's color matches the red soil of the Australian desert outback. It can go without drinking as long as green grass is available. The small **swamp wallaby** (The Oasis) stands no more than 33 inches tall. The **western gray kangaroo** (Discovery Island) is the least common large kangaroo in American zoos. *Kangaroos cannot walk backwards. Males box each other to establish dominance. When it's hot, Disney's kangaroos lick their forearms to stay cool.*

KOMODO DRAGON

The world's largest lizard, the **Komodo dragon** (Maharajah Jungle Trek) can grow up to 10 feet long and weigh 250 pounds. Using its long, forked tongue as a nose, it picks up scents of animals up to 2 miles away. With a

Ring-tailed lemur, Discovery Island

burst of speed that can reach 15 mph, the dragon can kill its prey by simply biting it... then leisurely following it until it dies. The dragon's saliva contains so much lethal bacteria that death is inevitable. Living in the wild only on a few Indonesian islands, a wild Komodo eats deer, goats, pigs (and other Komodos) and can go six months without a meal. Because adult dragons cannibalize young ones, juveniles often roll in feces as a deterrent. Young dragons also conduct appeasement rituals, pacing around a feeding circle and lurching from side to side in a "circle of death." *To flee an attacker, a Komodo can vomit the contents of its stomach—which can hold 200 pounds of food—to increase its speed.*

LEMURS

The **collared lemur** (Discovery Island) sports reddish-blond muttonchops. Living in a group of up to 30 animals, the **ring-tailed lemur** (Discovery Island) uses its long tail as

Meerkats, Pangani Forest Exploration Trail

a flag—to tell others where it is or warn them of danger. Unlike most mammal groups, a lemur family is led by a female. A male will compete for her by rubbing his tail with an odor from his wrist glands, arching his tail over his back and shaking it at other males while baring his teeth—a competition that can last an hour. Found only on the island of Madagascar, the primitive primate is named for its big eyes and haunting howl; the word lemur is Latin for ghost.

LION

The King of Beasts, the **African lion** (*Kilimanjaro Safaris*) is the largest African carnivore. Its roar can be heard 5 miles away. Living in a pride of about 15 members, females do the hunting, slowly stalking their prey as a team before sprinting forward in a surprise attack. They can run up to 37 mph and leap up to 40 feet. Males defend the pride; their manes protect their necks in a battle. Lions sleep up to 20 hours a day.

LLAMA

Related to a camel, the **llama** (*Rafiki's Planet Watch*) is a domesticated pack animal. Tamed in the 16th century in the Andes mountains of South America, the sure-footed creature can carry up to 100 pounds. In the 2000 Disney film "The Emperor's New Groove," Emperor Kuzco (David Spade) was turned into a llama by his power-hungry advisor, Yzma (Eartha Kitt).

LUNGFISH

The **African lungfish** (*Pangani Forest Exploration Trail*) can breathe air and crawl. It has two swim bladders that take oxygen from the air when the animal surfaces. It lives in small pools of water that often evaporate, at which time it uses its long, fleshy fins to plod along in the mud. Its ancestors developed true limbs and evolved into early four-legged land animals.

MEERKAT

A type of mongoose, the **slender-tailed meerkat** (*Pangani Forest Exploration Trail*) works with others in organized multifamily communities of up to 30 individuals. The burrowing animals divide up jobs such as babysitting, food finding and sentry duty, a chore shared by rotating guards.

MONKEYS

One of the smallest monkeys, the **cotton-top tamarin** (*Discovery Island*) is about the size of a squirrel, but can still leap 10 feet. It's named for the puffy crest of white fur on top of its head. Living in Colombia, the creatures mate for life and live as a family. Older siblings help care for the infants. Active most of the day, Disney's tamarins usually take a nap about 4:30 p.m. The world's most colorful mammal and largest monkey, the **mandrill** (*Kilimanjaro Safaris*) is the inspiration for the character Rafiki in

Disney's 1994 film "The Lion King." The non-aggressive, social creature bares its teeth as a greeting. It makes a huge smile, with the corners of its mouth wide open, exposing its massive canines. The most colorful mandrills are males who have mated with many females. When upset it may energetically beat the ground.

NAKED MOLE RAT

The giant queen keeps a male harem and rules with brute force, shoving her soldiers and workers around to prod them into action. Everyone's naked, and blind, but all individuals have their own identity—a custom odor achieved by carefully rolling around in the community toilet. Such is the underground world of the **naked mole rat** *(Pangani Forest Exploration Trail),* the only mammal that organizes itself into ant-like colonies. The animal digs with four buck teeth but doesn't swallow dirt—the teeth are outside of its mouth in front of hairy lips and side skin folds that close completely. Neither mole nor rat but plenty naked, the pink, virtually hairless creature is related to a guinea pig.

Cotton-top tamarin, Discovery Island

OKAPI

The only mammal that can lick its ears and eyelids, the **okapi** *(Kilimanjaro Safaris, also Pangani Forest Exploration Trail)* uses its 14-inch tongue for grooming as well as eating. Its appearance combines the body and face of a stubby giraffe with the black-and-white legs and rump of a zebra. Its head is topped with the same skin-covered knobs of its giraffe relative and it walks in the same way: simultaneously stepping with the front and hind leg on the same side of its body. It sleeps five minutes a day. A solitary creature, it lives in the dense Ituri Forest of the Congo, an area so remote the species wasn't discovered until 1900.

OSTRICH

The world's largest bird, the **ostrich** *(Kilimanjaro Safaris)* has 2-inch-wide eyes, the largest of any land creature. Its eggs,

the largest of any living animal, can weigh nearly 2.5 pounds each. An ostrich doesn't fly but can run up to 45 mph—faster than any other two-legged animal. To stay cool the ostrich fans itself with its wings. An ostrich doesn't really stick its head in the sand. To hide, it lays its head on the ground.

OTTER

It's hard to leave the **Asian small-clawed otter** habitat *(Discovery Island)* when the animals play or feed. The world's smallest otters, they chase each other on the ground (at speeds to 18 mph) and in the water. They are especially cute when they wash up after a meal: their unique (for otters) non-webbed paws look like hands.

RHINOCEROS

It's been on earth for 60 million years, but today only 10,000 are left—less than 15

Asian tiger, Maharajah Jungle Trek

Trail) has a 14-inch bill and an 8.5-foot wingspan. Known as the world's ugliest bird, it has a pickax bill, two unsightly pouches and a naked cranium studded with scab-like spots. The carrion-eating bird communicates by clattering its bill; it has no voice box. The **painted stork** (Discovery Island) gets a bright pink patch on its back during breeding season. The male **saddle-billed stork** (Discovery Island, Kilimanjaro Safaris) has a yellow wattle; the female yellow eyes. The well-known **white stork** (Discovery Island) lives in African grasslands. The German legend about the bird bringing babies exists because for centuries it has migrated from Africa to nest on northern German chimneys and roofs in the spring, a time of many human births. Lifelong mates take turns incubating and feeding their young.

TAPIR

The world's largest tapir, the **Malayan tapir** (Maharajah Jungle Trek) can weigh up to 700 pounds. Looking like a fat black pig with a white saddle, it's actually related to both a horse and a rhino. Its front feet have four toes, but its back feet only have three.

percent of the number that roamed Africa as late as 1970. Why? Because poachers continually kill it for its horn—an alleged aphrodisiac in Chinese folk medicine despite the fact that it's really just a big toenail. Growing from the rhino's skin, it's made of the same material (keratin) as a human nail and grows back when you cut it. The nearly extinct **black rhino** (Kilimanjaro Safaris) is a solitary herbivore that uses its hooked lip like a finger to select leaves and twigs. It can live 40 years. The larger **white rhino** (Kilimanjaro Safaris) is a brownish-gray creature that gets its name from its wide upper lip—"white" is a mistranslation of "wijt," the Afrikaans word for "wide." Rhinos wallow in mud to protect their skin, which is sensitive to insects and sunburn. They can charge at 40 miles per hour.

STORKS

The world's largest stork, the 5-foot-tall **marabou stork** (Pangani Forest Exploration

TIGER

Each **Asian (Bengal) tiger** (Maharajah Jungle Trek) has its own stripe pattern, as well as large false eyes and white spots on the backs of its ears. The patterns are on both its fur and skin. Noted for its sheer power, it can drag up to 3,000 pounds, five times its own weight. The 8- to 10-foot animal can leap 30 feet and, thanks to its large webbed paws, swim easily. Its ears turn individually and can rotate 180 degrees. Disney's tigers often play in their fountain area after 4 p.m., especially during hot weather.

TORTOISE

The world's most primitive tortoise, the **Asian brown tortoise** (DinoLand U.S.A.) has heavy overlapping scales. The largest living tortoise, the 5-foot-long, 500-pound **Galapagos tortoise** (Discovery Island) lives only in the Galapagos archipelago, 600 miles west of Ecuador. It can live at least 150 years, but it's a slow life. The reptile's top speed is only 0.16 mph.

WARTHOG

Covered in wart-like growths of skin, the face of a male **common warthog** (Kilimanjaro Safaris) has two sharp 6-inch lower tusks and two curved upper tusks that can grow 2 feet. At breeding time a male performs a courtship chant of rhythmic grunts. The creature eats roots and, like other pigs, keeps cool by taking mud baths. The most famous warthog? Pumbaa, from Disney's "The Lion King."

ZEBRA

The unique stripes on every **Grant's zebra** (Kilimanjaro Safaris) serve as camouflage—the pattern blends right into tall grasses. Even in an open field, a single zebra's stripes break up its silhouette, making it less recognizable to predators, and a herd of complex stripes makes it tough to track any one animal. Because black absorbs heat more than white, the animal's black areas have an extra layer of protective fat. Zebras themselves are attracted to the pattern. Studies have shown that when stripes are painted on a wall, a zebra will walk over to it. Related more to an ass than a horse, a zebra has the same long ears, short mane, tufted tail and front-leg-only "chestnuts."

Tunis sheep, Rafiki's Planet Watch

Creatures great and small

Animal Kingdom has 1,500 animals, representing 250 species. Besides those listed in this guide, fascinating animals in The Oasis include the **yellow-bellied slider turtle** and **rhinoceros iguana** and many beautiful birds. Discovery Island has the toothy **tambaqui fish.** Kilimanjaro Safaris is home to **ankole cattle, greater kudu** and **scimitar-horned oryx.** Interesting birds in Africa include the **ground hornbill, pink-backed pelican** and, at the Pangani aviary, one of the largest flocks of **carmine bee-eaters** in North America. The Maharajah Jungle Trek aviary has the **New Guinea masked plover** (shown at right) and the world's largest pigeon. A variety of butterflies, scorpions, snakes, spiders and other small critters live at Rafiki's Planet Watch, including the world's most colorful amphibian, the Latin American **poison dart frog.** The petting zoo has **Tunis sheep** (above) and the rare **Sicilian miniature donkey.**

Animal guide field and library research by Micaela Neal

A teenager soaks up the
sun at Disney's Blizzard
Beach water park

Water Parks

Giggles, laughs and squeals fill the air. Close your eyes at either of these two water parks and you'll hear more happy people than anywhere else at Disney World. Why? Because it's just so much fun to ride a water slide, float down a lazy river or splash in a pool, especially when you're in such a fully realized fantasy atmosphere.

The U.S. has more than 1,000 water parks, but few offer the immersive theming of these two from Disney. Instead of plastic culverts and support columns, you see mountain streams and palms. Instead of rap and pop songs, you hear reggae tunes and Christmas ditties. And since these are Disney parks, everyone greets you with a smile, and everywhere you look is spic-and-span.

How do the two parks compare? Typhoon Lagoon offers more shade, unique snorkeling, face-first rides, bigger waves and more preschooler activities, while Blizzard Beach has more sun, longer and faster slides and the most for preteens and teens. The parks share a number of policies. Swimwear can't have rivets, buckles, or exposed metal. You can bring in small toys, towels, picnic coolers, food, strollers and wheelchairs, but not boogie boards, water toys, tubes (all tube rides have complimentary ones), glass containers or alcohol.

If bought separately, 2009 water park tickets are $40 for adults, $34 for children 3–9. When the water parks close for inclement weather, guests who have been inside less than three hours get complimentary rain checks (conditions apply).

To get the most of your day, arrive before a park opens. Do the slides before noon, the lazy rivers and playgrounds after lunch.

Blizzard Beach

It's a zany combination: a water park that looks like a ski resort. Disguised as ski slopes, water slides extend down the sides of Mt. Gushmore, a 90-foot snow-capped peak. Around it is a beach, wave pool, lazy river and children's areas. The 66-acre park sits east of Animal Kingdom.

Meals at three outdoor counter cafes feature hamburgers, hot dogs, sandwiches, salads and individual pizzas ($4–$7, at Lottawatta Lodge in the Alpine Village, the Warming Hut on the left side of Melt-Away Bay and Avalunch near the Ski Patrol Training Camp). Snack stands sell funnel cakes and cotton candy (Melt-Away Bay), ice cream treats ($4–$7, Sled Dog Expeditions, Ski Patrol Training Camp), yummy mini donuts (Alpine Village), nachos (Cooling Hut, Alpine Village) and snow cones (Snow Balls, near Ski Patrol Training Camp). Other stands offer coffee, tea and pastries (Frosty the Joe Man, Melt-Away Bay) and beer and specialty rum drinks (Frostbite Freddies at Alpine Village, Polar Pub at Melt-Away Bay).

As for shops, the Beach Haus (Alpine Village) has beachwear and swimming suits from Quiksilver, Roxy and Element. Across from

---

AS DISNEY TELLS IT, in early 1995 Central Florida experienced a freak winter snowstorm. Gazing at the flakes fall outside of their Disney World offices, the company's Imagineers had a brainstorm: "Let's build a ski resort!" Immediately they built a mountain, a ski jump, slalom courses, a chairlift and lodge. But just as they finished, the warm weather returned and the snow turned to slush. Reluctantly, the workers began to board things up. But then they spotted a lone alligator, blue from the cold but full of energy. Strapping on skis, he careened down the jump, flew through the air, landed in the women's restrooms, crashed into the gift shop... and emerged with a smile. Watching this "Ice Gator," as they named him, the Imagineers realized that their failed ski resort would make a great water park. The jump could be a body slide. The slalom, bobsled and sledding runs could be mat and tube rides. The slushy creek? A perfect lazy river. Basking in their genius, the Imagineers named their creation **Blizzard Beach** and proudly opened it to the public—on April Fools Day, 1995.

Though her boyfriend chickened out moments earlier, a teen girl still braves Typhoon Lagoon's Summit Plummet

the changing rooms, the Shade Shack has sunglasses, sandals, beach towels and disposable cameras. A branch of Hawaii-based Pearl Factory, North Pearl has farm-raised Japanese akoya pearls in oysters (6–9 mm, $15), settings ($9–$760) and pearl jewelry.

You enter the park through a re-creation of an alpine village, with buildings that include changing rooms, lockers, food stands and shops. There's an ATM at the ticket and Guest Relations booth, which also serves as Lost and Found. Inside the turnstiles is the Beach Haus shop, which rents lockers and towels and sells sunscreen. Around the corner, Snowless Joe's stand offers the same services and has complimentary lifejackets. The lockers themselves are in three places. Most are centrally located at Snowless Joe's. Other sit along the right side of the park near the Ski Patrol Training Camp preteen area, and along the left side next to the Downhill Double Dipper tube slide.

A First Aid station is to the right of the Beach Haus. Cast members take lost children to Snowless Joe's. Blizzard Beach parking is free. The Bizzard Beach telephone number is 407-560-3400.

Lazy river

CROSS COUNTRY CREEK Circling the park, this 3,000-foot stream has seven entry points, each with a stack of complimentary tubes. Lined with palms and evergreens, the river flows under bridges, over springs and through a cave with ice-cold dripping water. A round-trip journey takes about 25 minutes. The water is 2.5 feet deep.

Children's area

TIKES PEAK Gentle slides, rideable baby alligators and an ankle-deep squirting "ice" pond highlight this preschool playground. There's a fountain play area, a little waterfall, sand boxes, lawn chairs, chaise lounges and picnic tables. Kids should wear water shoes: the pavement can get hot. **Height restriction: Must be under 48 in.**

Preteen area

SKI PATROL TRAINING CAMP This inventive spot features Fahrenheit Drop, cabled T-bars that drop kids into an 8-foot pool; and the Thin Ice Training Course, slippery walks on floating "icebergs" with overhead rope grids for support. Also here: wide Snow Falls slides designed for a parent and child to ride together; Cool Runners, two short, bumpy tube slides; and Frozen Pipe Springs, a short, steep, covered body slide.

Body slides

SLUSH GUSHER Ninety feet above the beach, you start off slow and stay in control over the first drop. Then you get some airtime off the second drop, thanks to some playful Disney designers who followed the second lip with a steep drop. Heavier riders fly higher. The trip takes about 10 seconds; top speeds can reach 50 mph. The 250-foot flume has the look of a melting snow-banked gully. *Height restriction: 48 in.*

SUMMIT PLUMMET The tallest, fastest water slide in the country, this 350-foot chute has a 66-degree, 120-foot fall. A mock ski jump, the launch tower looms 30 feet above Mt. Gushmore. Lying down at the top of the ramp, you cross your arms, cross your feet and push yourself off this real Tower of Terror. There's a blur of sky and scenery as you fall, then a roar of water when you splash down. The impact can send much of your swimsuit where the sun never shines. Speeds can reach 60 mph. If you don't wear a T-shirt, the trip can sting your skin. In fact, the fall is so scary even some of its designers don't care for it. "I made the mistake when we were building it of going up the stairs and looking down," says Disney Imagineer Kathy Rogers. "I thought, 'There's no way I'd put my body in there!' I did it once and said, 'Done!'"

There are no exit stairs. If you chicken out you squeeze down the entrance steps doing what cast members call "the walk of shame." There's an observation deck as well as a viewing area at the end of the ride with a rider-speed display. *Height restriction: 48 in.*

Wave pool

MELT-AWAY BAY A one-acre spot nestled against the base of Mt. Gushmore, this swimming pool appears to be created by streams

Blizzard Beach tubers take it easy on the Cross Country Creek lazy river

of melting snow that wash down into it. Bobbing waves wash through the water for 45 minutes of every hour. Perfect for sunbathing, a sandy beach lines the shore.

Mat slides

TOBOGGAN RACERS Based on an amusement park gunnysack slide, this 8-lane, 250-foot mat slide has you race down its series of dips face first. Great for families, it's more fun than scary. To go fast, push off quickly then lift up the front of your mat slightly so it doesn't dig in the water. Regardless of technique, heavier riders usually win.

SNOW STORMERS When you were a kid, did you have a sled? If so, these three racing slides will bring back those memories. Lying face-first on a mat, you weave down a hill of S-curves dug into the ground like

Above: A chair lift takes Blizzard Beach riders to the top of Mt. Gushmore for easy access to Slush Gusher, Summit Plummet and Teamboat Springs. **Top:** Riders race each other on Downhill Double Dipper, Disney's scariest tube ride.

high-banked gullies. The 350-foot track is plenty fast, even a little scary — as you careen up the corners the splashing water

makes it tough to see. A horizontal line on the wall gives you a point of reference.

Want to win the race? Keep your elbows on the mat and your feet up. To be fair to your lighter-weight kids, give them a second or two head start.

Tube slides

DOWNHILL DOUBLE DIPPER This side-by-side racing run takes you through a tunnel with two steep drops before shooting you through a curtain of water at 25 mph. Your time is shown at a finish line. The 230-foot ride stands 50 feet high. Pull up on your tube handles just before the catch pool to fly across the water. *Height restriction: 48 in.*

RUNOFF RAPIDS You climb 127 steps to ride these three 600-foot flumes, but they're worth every huff and puff. Two allow two-person tubes, so friends or family members ride together. A third is like a watery Space Mountain, enclosed in darkness except for some pinlights. All three make you feel like a bobsledder, sliding you up on banked curves before shooting you into a catch pool.

TEAMBOAT SPRINGS All ages smile on this, the world's longest family raft ride. Sitting in a raft the size of a kiddie pool, you slide down a high-banked 1,200-foot-long course, spinning on tight curves which may toss you up on their steep walls. One thing's for sure: your rear end will get soaked. Thirty holes line each raft's bottom edge. A 200-

Braced for impact, a crowd at the Typhoon Lagoon surf pool awaits a breaking wave.

foot ride-out area takes you under a collapsing roof that's dripping with cool water. *There's often a minimum of four riders per tube, when smaller groups ride together.*

FUN FINDS ❶ An eclectic soundtrack mixes summertime tunes with Christmas ditties. ❷ Equipment from the Sunshine State Snow Making Co. sits along the Toboggan Racers queue and on the Cross Country Creek bank past Reindeer Landing. ❸ Barrels of equipment and "Instant Snow" from the Joe Blow Snow Co. sit along the walkways to Slush Gusher, Summit Plummet and Teamboat Springs. ❹ Snow is melting off a roof of a small building across from the Downhill Double Dipper entrance marked "Safe to Approach Unless Melting." ❺ Just after you enter the park, Ice Gator's ski tracks appear on the roof of the women's dressing room, behind a sign reading "Caution: Low Flying Gator." Directly across that walkway, his silhouette forms a hole in the side of the Beach Haus shop. ❻ "Ancient" drawings on the walls of the Cross Country Creek cave include a beach chair with umbrella, Ice Gator, a Yeti, people in tubes, people on skis and a skier with a leg cast. ❼ The Northern Lights shine through the cave's ceiling. ❽ "B-r-r-r-occoli" and "Sleet Corn" are planted in Ice Gator's garden alongside the creek, just past Manatee Landing. ❾ As you float by Ice Gator's house he often sneezes and says "Anybody got a hanky?"

Typhoon Lagoon

With an atmosphere that's one part Hawaii and two parts Gilligan's Island, this tropical park is an unsung Disney masterpiece. Like Magic Kingdom, its fun theme, passionate design and variety of things to do make it easy to have fun. Lushly landscaped, Typhoon Lagoon consists of four areas: a Harbor Village entrance, a central surf pool and lazy river, and two attraction zones that border the river. Across the street from Downtown Disney, the park covers 61 acres.

Three outdoor counter cafes offer hamburgers, hot dogs, sandwiches, salads and individual pizzas ($4–$7, at Leaning Palms, Harbor Village; Typhoon Tilly's, North Shore; and Lowtide Lou's, South Shore). Snack stands sell mini donuts (Harbor Village), funnel cakes and fried ice cream (Water Works), ice cream treats (Snack Shack, North Shore; Happy Landings, Harbor Village; Dippin' Dots cart, South Shore) and hot dogs and pretzels (Surf Doggies, surf pool). Other stands sell coffee, tea, pastries (Coffee Cappucino, surf pool) and beer and rum drinks (Let's Go Slurpin', surf pool).

For shopping, Singapore Sal's (Harbor Village) has beach and swimwear from Quiksilver, Roxy and Element, Disney beach towels and sundries. The Pearl Factory (Shark Reef, North Shore) sells farm-raised Japanese

Family float. Orlando's Rathbun family relaxes under the lush landscaping of Castaway Creek.

akoya pearls in their oysters (6–9 mm, $15), settings ($9–$760) and pearl jewelry.

Singapore Sal's rents lockers and towels, sells sunscreen and has an ATM. Most lockers are nearby; some are at Shark Reef. A photo stand offers complimentary lifejacket use. A First Aid station sits behind the Leaning Palms restaurant. Lost children are taken to High 'N Dry Towels. Lost and Found is at the Guest Relations kiosk. Parking is free. The park phone number is 407-560-7223.

Surf pool

It's not everyone's cup of chowder, but this giant wave pool is a perfect playground to many. Surf's up all day. Waves vary between bobbing 2-foot swells and body-surfable 6-foot breakers. Emerging with a "whoomph!" from two underwater doors, 80,000 gallons of water sweep down the pool every 90 seconds. Each wave is met by hundreds of people who swim into it, swim with it or get knocked down by it. A sign in front shows the wave schedule. Twice the size of a football field, the mushroom-shaped lagoon includes wading pools with kid-sized slides, infant-friendly bubbling tide pools with climb-on boats and a white sandy beach.

Lazy river

CASTAWAY CREEK This shady, palm-lined stream takes you on a tropical journey around the park. Along the way you'll be sprayed a few times by misters along the shore, drizzled on by the tank and pipes of a broken-down waterworks, and, as you're forced through a waterfall at a cave entrance, completely soaked. There's a lot to look at. You pass three crashed boats, travel along the kiddie playground and go under a suspension bridge. Once the river splits in two. The 2,100-foot waterway is 15 feet wide and 3 feet deep. It moseys along at 2 feet per second; a round trip takes about 25 minutes. There's never a wait, though the river can get crowded in the afternoon.

Children's area

KETCHAKIDDEE CREEK What was once, according to Disney, a no-man's land of volcanoes and geysers has become an elaborate tyke-sized water park with 18 activity spots. Your toddler will likely break into a huge grin as he or she splashes through the tube slide's three little dips toward the end of this palm-lined, 100-foot course. The surrounding area is filled with ankle-deep pools and creeks and low bubbly fountains. A 12-foot Blow Me Down boiler is topped with hoses that shake, shimmy and squirt. More adventurous kids will hurl themselves down the two slip 'n' slides — cushy 20-foot mats with 20-degree drops. Everyone has a blast at the S.S. Squirt. Using swiveling water cannons, you'll squirt each other with multiple streams of water as you take sides in a battle of oversized sand sculptures. To keep you soaked, a whistle shoots a continuous spray in the air. Many families build sandcastles. There are many shady chairs and picnic tables. *Height restriction: must be under 48 in. for slides.*

Body slides

HUMUNGA KOWABUNGA Like Splash Mountain without the boat, these zippity speed slides drop you 51 feet in just a couple of seconds. Three identical dark tubes sit at 60-degree angles and extend 214 feet. Speeds can reach 30 mph. Don't want to go? A waiting bench overlooks the catch pool. *Height restriction: 48 in.*

STORM SLIDES High-banked walls hug these three swooping flumes, which take you through rocky gulches on the shady side of Mount Mayday. Each slide is different: Rudder Buster (on the left as you stand at the boarding area) has a small tunnel; Stern Burner (in the middle) has a longer dark tunnel; Jib Jammer (on the right) has no tunnel. Top speed is 20 mph. The slides' average length is 300 feet.

Dads join in the water-cannon fun at Typhoon Lagoon's Ketchakiddee Creek children's area

BAY SLIDES Located in the calm left corner of the surf pool (an area called Blustery Bay), these two 35-foot slides are for kids too old for Ketchakiddee Creek but too young for the Storm Slides or Humunga Kowabunga. One is uncovered with a few gentle bumps; the other has a 4-foot tunnel. The walkway wanders out of your sight, but it's just 10 steps and leads only to the slides. Many parents wait in the water to catch their kids. *Must be under 60 in.*

Saltwater snorkeling

SHARK REEF Darth Vader lives! You hear nothing but your own breathing as you snorkel past "smiling" rainbow parrotfish and other tropical beauties—as well as passive rays and leopard and bonnethead sharks—in the crystal-clear water of this simulated reef. The fish usually swim away from you, but if you're very still one may come close. You can take as long as you want in the water, and even can take a break on a small center island. Use of masks, snorkels and vests is complimentary. You rinse off (beforehand and afterward) in an outdoor shower. Changing areas, lockers, showers and a picnic area are nearby.

Don't want to go? Portholes in an overturned, walk-through tanker let you watch your family as they swim by.

For a greater experience, an optional Supplied Air Snorkeling adventure introduces you to the basics of scuba diving. Run by the National Association of Underwater Instructors (NAUI), the 30-minute session ($20) includes use of a pony tank, mouthpiece (regulator), flippers and instruction.

You can't dive deep, but you get plenty of time in the pool. *Age restriction: 5 and older.*

Tube slides

KEELHAUL FALLS A big "C" curve, this gentle 400-foot slide slowly builds up speed. The ride ends just after you slide up on a bank.

MAYDAY FALLS This swervy, rippled flume simulates white-water rafting. A relatively long, fast course (460 feet at about 15 feet per second, lean back to go faster), it features a triple vortex that can turn you around. There's one small waterfall.

GANGPLANK FALLS The three- to five-passenger rafts on this short family adventure are plenty of fun. You brave waterfalls, dripping caves and squirting pipes as you twist past crates of fireworks on the banks. The 300-foot ride is over in about 30 seconds.

CRUSH 'N' GUSHER With both lifts and dips, this water-jet-powered ride gives you the experience of a roller coaster. Riding in either a two- or three-person tube, you're dropped by a conveyor belt into a flume, then thrust up a few lift hills. Lean back and a lip before each drop may get you airborne. Push your feet down to stay in control.

Three slides offer slightly different experiences. *Pineapple Plunger* offers the most air time, with two peaks and three medium-length tunnels. *Coconut Crusher* has one peak

Left: New Jersey's Amanda Mathus, 14, braces for the splash on the Stern Burner Storm Slide, which goes through a tunnel. **Below:** Shark Reef snorkelers swim past an shipwreck.

The Gangplank Falls tube slide has rafts that hold up to five people

and a long, short and medium tunnel. Banana Blaster has one peak, one long tunnel and two medium tunnels. It's the longest ride by a few seconds, but doesn't take three-person rafts. Each ride lasts about 30 seconds. The slides average 420 feet. Waiting lines are shaded.

The attraction is meant to be the remains of the Tropical Amity (say it slowly) fruit-packing plant. The flumes are said to have been wash spillways used to clean the fruit before it was shipped. Tucked behind the Typhoon Lagoon dressing rooms, the ride's remote 5-acre setting (Out of the Way Cay) also includes a small gradual-entry pool and many beach chairs and chaise lounges.

Height requirement for slides: 48 in.

FUN FINDS ❶ A message spelled out by the hanging nautical flags to the far right of the entrance turnstiles reads "Piranha in pool." ❷ The surf pool wall is a levee ready to burst. Water spits out between seams in the planks. ❸ An alligator totem stands under the clock tower, by Lagoona Gator's shack. ❹ Inside the shack are posters and flyers for The Beach Gators ("So cold blooded, they're hot!") and the film "Bikini Beach Blanket Muscle Party Bingo." A Surfin' Reptile magazine includes the article "How to Get a Golden Tan Without Being Turned into a Suitcase." ❺ At the Happy Landings snack bar, a rack of outboard motors lets you squirt water through their props. ❻ Ripped

open by a Great White, a supposedly "shark-proof" cage sits along the Shark Reef walkway, past the showers.

ONCE UPON A TIME there was a bayside village called the Placid Palms Resort, tucked into a valley next to a volcanic mountain in Florida. Over the years it had been subject to earthquakes and geothermal rumblings, but life remained tranquil. Even when cruise ships arrived, the Placid Palms stayed a quiet, thatch-roofed haven. Then came Hurricane Connie, in 1955. For an hour winds pounded the area. A boat blew through a building. A surfboard sliced through a tree. Crates of fireworks blew in from Mr. Pleasure's nearby island warehouses. A next-door fruit processing plant lost its walls but gained a tractor, which teetered on the roof. A small harbor had been cut off from the sea, trapping an overturned boat, thousands of fish and even a few sharks. Suffering the worst fate: a shrimp boat named Miss Tilly. Blown in from Safen Sound, Fla., it became impaled on the peak of Mt. Mayday. "No worries!" said the laid-back villagers. Sign paint in hand, they renamed the Placid Palms the Leaning Palms, the center of a new topsy-turvy tropical playground of pools, rapids, rivers and streams. They christened the spot **Typhoon Lagoon.**

A lonely Titan marches through the world of the Downtown Disney Cirque du Soleil spectacle La Nouba

Downtown Disney

Located near the eastern edge of the Disney property on the 43-acre Village Lake, this 120-acre commercial district is divided into three sections. The largest area, the 66-acre West Side, is the nightlife district. It includes an AMC movie theater, Cirque du Soleil theater, DisneyQuest and House of Blues. At the east end of the complex, the Downtown Disney Marketplace resembles a 1970s open-air mall. Originally known as the Walt Disney World Shopping Village, it has 25 shops and restaurants and various outdoor stands. A new outdoor stage will make it the primary venue for Disney's Magic Music Days amateur concerts. Water taxis shuttle guests between West Side and Marketplace.

Located between Marketplace and West Side, Pleasure Island was, until 2008, a nightclub area. Disney closed its clubs last September, but the area's shops and restaurants are still open.

Resources

West Side has two **ATMs:** at the House of Blues Company Store and Wetzel's Pretzels. Marketplace has three: near Summer Sands, next to the Ghirardelli Chocolate Shop and inside the World of Disney store.

Aspirin, Band-Aids and other **first-aid supplies** are available at World of Disney, Summer Sands, the Marketplace marina, Mickey's Groove, DisneyQuest and the Cirque du Soleil box office.

Downtown Disney has two **Guest Relations** offices, at the Marketplace (between Team Mickey and Arribas Brothers, 8:30am–11pm Sun–Thurs, to 11:30pm Fri–Sat) and at the West Side (across from Wetzel's Pretzels, 9am–11:45pm).

Rental **lockers** are located at the Marketplace marina near Cap'n Jack's Restaurant. **Strollers** ($15 day, $100 deposit) and **wheelchairs** ($10 day, $100 deposit) can be rented at the West Side DisneyQuest Emporium and at the Marketplace at Disney's Design-A-Tee Shop.

A **mailbox** sits next to the World of Disney fountain. Downtown Disney **parking** is free.

Entertainment
West Side

AMC THEATER ★★★★ Movie theater A $8–$10, C 2–12 $7, Sr. 60+ $8–$9. Digital 3-D movies $2 addl. Hours vary. 24 theaters, 18 w/ stadium seating, 2 3-story auditoriums with balconies. Audio: THX Surround Sound, Sony Dynamic Digital Sound. Listening devices avail. Guests may remain in wheelchairs, ECVs. Seats 5,390. Movie listings 407-298-4488.
This 110,000-square-foot complex is the only public movie theater on Disney property.

BONGOS CUBAN CAFE ★★★★ Live band, dancing. No cover. Live Latin traditional and pop music, dance floor, dancing starting at 10pm Fri, Sat. All ages. Created by pop star Gloria Estefan and her husband, Emilio. Seats 560. 407-828-0999.

DISNEYQUEST ★★★ Electronic games A $40, C $34. Admission inc. in Water Park Fun & More ticket upgrade, Premium Annual Pass. Sun–Thurs 11:30am–11pm, Fri–Sat to mid. Height restrict: 51 in. for CyberSpace Mountain virtual roller coaster, Buzz Lightyear's AstroBlaster; 48 in. Mighty Ducks Pinball Slam life-size pinball game; 35 in. Pirates of the Caribbean. Children under 10 must be accompanied by an adult. No strollers. Gift shop; 2 counter cafes. 407-828-4600.
Virtual reality experiences highlight this five-story arcade, which was state-of-the-art a few years ago. Evening crowds can create 30-minute waits for the most popular games. Those include **Pirates of the Caribbean: Battle for Buccaneer Gold**, which takes a crew of four into a 3-D world; **Aladdin's Magic Carpet Ride**, a virtual-reality hunt for a magic lamp; and **Buzz Lightyear's AstroBlaster**, where you battle other guests in cannon-firing bumper cars. Creative types will love the **Animation Academy**. Its 30-minute classes teach you how to draw a Disney character. Other rooms offer classic arcade games such as Donkey Kong, Frogger, Mario Bros., Pac-Man and Space Invaders. Like a ticket to a Disney theme park, the admission price includes unlimited experiences. DisneyQuest is least crowded on fair-weather weekdays from 4 to 6:30 p.m.

The five-story DisneyQuest building is one of the anchors of Downtown Disney West Side

HOUSE OF BLUES ★★★★ Music hall / restaurant $8–$95. Showtimes typ 7–9:30pm. General adm (restaurant diners get priority). Doors open 1 hr before showtime weekdays, 90 min early weekends. All ages. Capacity 2,000. 407-934-BLUE or hob.com. One of a handful of restaurant and music halls created by Hard Rock Cafe founder Isaac Tigrett and entertainer Dan Aykroyd, this two-story performance venue books a wide range of acts, but blues and rock dominate. First-come first-serve tables and stools seat 150; there's standing room for 1,850. Folk art, hardwood floors and quality sound and lighting add to the experience. The outside looks like a rusty, funky shack. The adjacent restaurant (no cover) has acoustic live entertainment on its Front Porch bar from 6 p.m. to 11 p.m., and a plugged-in show Thursdays–Saturdays from 10:30 p.m. to 2 a.m.

LA NOUBA ★★★★★ ✔ Musical European circus A $67–$117, C $54–$94. Showtimes Tues–Sat 6pm, 9pm. Arrive 30 min early. 90-min shows, no intermission. Best ages 4 and up. Gift shop; snack stand. Seats 1,671. Tickets avail 6 mos in advance. Info, tickets: 407-939-7600, www.cirquedusoleil.com or at the box office. With costumes, choreography, music and stagecraft that befit a Broadway extravaganza, this invigorating Cirque du Soleil spectacle fills you with delight. It blends the traditions of a European circus with modern acrobatics, dance and street entertainment. There are no animals, just humans—acrobats, dancers, clowns, gymnasts and others—putting on a show filled with action, color, whimsy and a quirky sense of humor. Designed for a Disney audience, it's performed on an Elizabethan stage.

Up high are tightrope walkers, trapeze artists and, in the show's most beautiful moment, hanging aerialists wrapped in huge red-silk ribbons. Onstage, performers cavort and somersault inside a pair of giant open wheels and jump, spin and twist on two BMX bikes. Four ever-smiling Asian girls dance, flip and climb on each other as they play Diabolo. A finale gymnastic ballet features power-track and trampoline performers. Their surreal diving into, and out of, windows looks like a film running backwards.

But there's so much more.

Sideshow characters—including a quartet of all-white simpletons and a flightless, envious Green Bird—participate sometimes as performers, sometimes as spectators. Each scene is presented as a figment of the imagination of a cleaning woman, a character who eventually becomes a princess. Childish clowns Balto and Serguei entertain between acts.

There's no master of ceremonies; instead the whole show is scored live. Hidden in

LA NOUBA BY CIRQUE DU SOLEIL® / © DISNEY

Cirque du Soleil's La Nouba begins with an invasion by the lock-step Urbanites

towers alongside the stage, the band's zesty mix of classical, jazz, hip hop, klezmer, techno and bluegrass adds an emotional accent to every performer. Some songs have vocalists—an androgynous male who performs at high alto registers and a spirited female who adds some Gospel soul. Both sing exclusively in words that sound vaguely French, but are nonsensical. Acoustics are crystal clear.

Though it doesn't tell a tale, La Nouba does have story elements. The opening is a meeting of two worlds, a modern urban society and an early 20th-century circus. Determined, de-personal and de-saturated, the Urbans march in lock step as they toe society's line. By contrast, the neon circus folk each march to their own beat. Movie buffs will find references to 1997's "The Fifth Element" (the odd music and warbling diva) and 1998's "Dark City" (the looming cityscapes and unexpectedly moving floors). Art lovers will sense Calder and Matisse.

The show's purpose, its producers say, is to "wake up the innocence in your heart." You'll be surprised how much it succeeds.

Every seat is good, but spending the money to sit down front does pay off—you'll see every costume and makeup detail, every smile and grimace, every tensed muscle. You'll hear the clowns squeak and grunt and the acrobats shout verbal cues. Catch the eye of a performer and he or she might wink back. Front-row center is Row 1, Section 103. Tickets go on sale six months in advance.

Pleasure Island

RAGLAN ROAD ★★★★★ ✓ Live band, dancer **No cover. Band plays 9pm–1:30am Mon–Sat, Irish table dancer every half hour. All ages. Seats 600.**
A cheerful crowd sings along to an Irish band, with occasional breaks for an Irish step-dancer at this gem of a spot, a favorite hangout of Disney cast members.

Brought over from the Emerald Isle, house band Tuskar Rock starts off with traditional ballads, jigs and reels such as "Whiskey in the Jar" and "Three Drunken Maidens." Later they slip in covers of U2, Cranberries, even a few Johnny Cash tunes. The four-piece band includes a guitarist, female fiddler and an accordion and mandolin player. The lead singer alternates between guitar and bodhran, the traditional Irish drum that added those infectious rhythms to the jigs performed in the 1997 movie "Titanic."

The dancer performs on a small table (an old parson's pulpit) in the middle of the room. Guests seated around her get an unforgettable up-close show.

A robotic octopus smothers the bar at the new T-Rex restaurant at Downtown Disney

Dining
West Side

BONGOS CUBAN CAFE ★★★ Cuban $$$$
L: $8–$17, 11am–4pm. D: $16–$33, 4–11pm Sun–Thurs, 4–mid Fri–Sat. Seats 560, inc 60 outside and 87 at the bar. Direct line for info: 407-828-0999.
Housed in a whimsical building dominated by a three-story adobe pineapple, this festive eatery offers Cuban standards as well as sandwiches and surf and turf. Good sides include yuca (a boiled root, similar in taste to a potato) and plantains. Bamboo bars and beautiful mosaic murals recall the B.C. (Before Castro) Cuba of the 1940s and 1950s. Ask to sit in the pineapple, where every booth is a different bold color, or on the second-story patio. An outside bar serves sandwiches, snacks, desserts and drinks. The restaurant was created by pop-star Gloria Estefan and her husband Emilio.

HOUSE OF BLUES ★★★★★ ✔ Southern $$$
L,D: $10–$27, 11:30am–11pm Sun–Mon, 11:30am–mid Tue–Wed, 11:30am–1:30am Thurs–Sat. Seats 578, inc 158 at outside tables and 36 at the outdoor bar. No reservations. Direct line for information: 407-934-BLUE. (Gospel brunch Sun. 10:30am, 1pm., in Music Hall, 250 seats. A: $33, C: $16.)
With good food and a comfy atmosphere, House of Blues is an ideal spot to refresh from too much Mickey. The tried-and-true Southern menu includes tender pork ribs and a soothing cornbread that melts in your mouth. Folk art covers the walls, ceilings, railings, window frames, lamps, even bathroom stalls. Kids will love the art and picking through the lobby's bucket of crayons to make their own. On Sundays the adjacent music hall holds a buffet brunch with live gospel music.

PLANET HOLLYWOOD ★ American $$$
L,D: $11–$27, 11am–1am; bar only until 2am. Seats 800. Direct line for information: 407-827-7827.
Shaped like a planet, this three-story cafe is filled with celebrity and movie memorabilia, including a blue gingham dress Judy Garland wore in 1939's "The Wizard of Oz." The menu is uninspired, the atmosphere loud, the service irritating.

WETZEL'S PRETZELS ★★★ ✔ Snacks $ $4–$7,
10:30am–11pm Sun–Thr, to mid Fri, Sat. 36 out. seats.
This indoor counter stand serves hot hand-rolled soft pretzels with a variety of coatings. There's also fresh-squeezed lemonade as well as Haagen-Dazs ice cream treats.

WOLFGANG PUCK CAFE ★★★★ ✔ Calif. Fusion
$$$$ L: $12–$25, 11:30am–4pm. D: $13–$29, Sun–Mon 4–10:30pm, Tue–Thurs till 11pm, Fri, Sat till 11:30pm. Weekend lunch serves dinner menu. Disney Annual Passholders save 20% at lunch, 10% at dinner. Take-out window. New private rm for groups. Seats 586,

inc 30 at sushi bar. Direct reservations: 407-938-WOLF.

Imaginative California dishes make up for the noisy atmosphere at this large lakeside dining room. The menu includes fish, hamburgers (lunch only), meats, pizza, salads, sandwiches, steak and sushi. Dinner adds Puck's famous veal weinerschnitzel. Best bets include the butternut squash soup and creamy mashed potato side dish. Make a reservation if you're coming after a La Nouba show; crowds can be thick. Creation of Puck's ex-wife Barbara Lazaroff, the original bold decor has been updated with new interior fixtures and furnishings.

WOLFGANG PUCK DINING ROOM ★★★★ Calif. Fusion $$$$ **D:** $25–$60, 6–9pm Sun–Thurs, 6–10pm Fri–Sat. Seats 120. Direct reservations: 407-938-WOLF.

No one can blend flavors like Mr. Wolfgang Puck, and this white-tablecloth eatery does its namesake proud. Entrees include chicken, fish, steak and veal dishes. For dessert, we get the banana beignets. Kid's choices range from chicken tenders to a 4-ounce filet. Located on the second floor of the Wolfgang Puck building at Downtown Disney, the room overlooks the Downtown Disney lakefront and, across the water, the Saratoga Springs resort. Dotted with celebrity caricatures, its orange walls are dominated by a gigantic ornamental hookah.

Marketplace

CAP'N JACK'S ★★★ Seafood/American $$$$ **L:** $9–$19, 11:30am–4pm. **D:** $15–$33, 4–10:30pm. Seats 113, inc 15 at bar. Direct reservations: 407-828-3971.

Though its worn wood decor is due for a makeover, this unpretentious 1970s throwback has good food. Lunch features a mozzarella crab cake melt. The dinner pot roast falls apart in your mouth. Both menus include white and red clam chowder; the kitchen will blend them on request.

EARL OF SANDWICH ★★★★★ ✔ American/British $ **B:** $2–$5, 8:30am–10:30am. **L,D:** $5–$6, 10:30am–11pm. Seats 190 inc 65 outside. 407-938-1762.

Tasty hot sandwiches make this counter-service restaurant a favorite of Disney locals. We usually get the Beef 'n' Bleu (roast

© GREAT IRISH PUBS FLORIDA

Creative presentations are part of Raglan Road's imaginative take on Irish Bistro cuisine

beef and bleu cheese); our daughter loves the Ultimate Grilled Cheese (bleu, brie and Swiss, with bacon and tomato). The crusty bread is baked all day; beef is roasted every morning. A good side dish: chunky cole slaw with touches of garlic and sour cream. The best deal: the $1.25 cup of steaming hot, creamy-orange tomato soup. Morning sandwiches include a Breakfast BLT. Owned by the ancestors of the fourth Earl of Sandwich.

FULTON'S CRAB HOUSE ★★ Seafood $$$$ **L:** $10–$18, 11:30am–3pm. **D:** $21–$55, 4–11pm. Seats 660, inc 24 outside. Direct reservations: 407-934-BOAT (2628).

OK for lunch but expensive for dinner, this white-tablecloth restaurant offers lots of crab dishes. The best is an appetizer: a filling bowl of crab-and-lobster bisque. You'd never guess this 20,000-square-foot replica paddlewheeler isn't the real thing. It looks just like an old riverboat from the outside, and inside its narrow halls, creaky floors and wooden ceilings suggest a long life on the water. Actually, it was built by Disney as a restaurant and, despite appearances, is not floating. Ask to sit on the lake side of the semicircular Constellation Room on the second deck. Its ceiling glows blue at night.

Downtown Disney's Wolfgang Puck building has a cafe downstairs, a dining room on top

GHIRARDELLI SODA FOUNTAIN ★★★ Ice cream $$ $3–$25, 10:30am–11pm Sun–Thurs, 10:30am–12pm Fri–Sat. Seats 88, inc 22 outside. Info: 407-934-8855. You can eat at a booth, table or bar at this busy ice-cream parlor, which has cones, waffle cones, banana splits, chocolate drinks, floats, milkshakes and specialty sundaes. The hot fudge sauce is made daily.

MCDONALD'S ★★ Fast food $ B: $2–$5, 8–10:30am. L,D: $5–$6, 10:30am–mid Sun–Thurs, till 1am Fri, Sat. Seats 254, inc 114 outside. 407-938-1762. The quietest tables are in back at this standard fast-food restaurant. There's a separate premium coffee and dessert bar.

PORTOBELLO ★★★★ Italian $$$$ L: $9–$16, 11:30am–3:45pm. D: $9–$40, 4–11pm. Seats 414, inc 86 outside. Direct reservations: 407-934-8888. A 2008 refurbishment shifted the theme of the former Portobello Yacht Club to that of a Tuscan country trattoria. A new chef from Wolfgang Puck brings lots of antipasti and entrees inspired by the dishes of Milan, Rome and Tuscany. Other changes include a nicer third outdoor dining space.

RAINFOREST CAFE ★★★ American $$$$ L,D: $11–$40, 11am–11pm Sun–Thurs, till mid Fri, Sat. Participates in Disney Dining Premium, Platinum plans only. Annual passholders save 10% off up to four entrees.

Seats 575. Reservations: 407-827-8500. No same-day reservations. A robotic rainforest filled with elephants, gorillas and other animated creatures comes to life every 20 minutes at this highly themed restaurant. A huge American menu offers many good choices, and portions generous. See our review in the Animal Kingdom theme park chapter.

T-REX ★★★★ ✔ American $$$$ L,D: $12–$30, 11am–11pm Sun–Thurs, till mid Fri, Sat. Participates in Disney Dining Premium, Platinum plans only. Annual passholders save 10% off up to four entrees. Small playground adjacent. Seats 626, inc 26 at the bar. Reservations: 407-828-TREX (8739). Imagine that you're on Animal Kingdom's Dinosaur ride, your vehicle stops, and out walks a waitress with a menu. That's what it would take to replicate the experience at this big, brash and very loud restaurant. A dinosaur-themed version of a Rainforest Cafe, T-Rex surrounds you with life-sized animated dinosaurs and other prehistoric creatures who live in dining areas that portray different environments. The loudest is the geothermal room, where a meteor shower hits every 21 minutes. Nearby is a glowing blue ice cave, where diners sit by a woolly mammoth mom and her infants. Dotted with large aquariums filled with real fish, a sea-life area is topped by swaying octopus tentacles that reach out 45 feet. Walls are embedded with real fossils.

Like Rainforest Cafe, T-Rex offers a huge American menu with a little of everything—chicken, hamburgers, pasta, sandwiches, salads, seafood, steak. The food is good and portions are generous. Our favorite item is the blackened mahi-mahi tacos, dry and spiced just right in soft corn tortillas. Sized for a family to share, desserts include the ridiculous Ice Age Indulgence, a slowly melting stack of whipped cream layered between ice cream sandwiches. Mixed drinks are highlighted by "Cotton-Tinis"—spirits served over candy candy.

Reservations are a must for dinner, when standby waits can exceed 90 minutes.

WOLFGANG PUCK EXPRESS ★★★★ ✔ Calif. Fusion $ B: $9–$11, 9a–11:30am. L,D: $10–$16, 11am–11pm. Seats 184, inc 96 outside. 407-828-0107.

The world's largest Pick-A-Brick wall at Downtown Disney's Lego Imagination Center

Remodeled in 2008 with hardwood tables, concrete floors and a much pricier menu, this indoor counter-service restaurant blares rock music down on its diners, an irritation that makes it tough to enjoy its first-rate food, an imaginative mix of pasta, pizza, salads, sandwiches and soups. Signature items include Crispy Cornflake French Toast and delicious butternut squash soup for lunch and dinner.

Pleasure Island

RAGLAN ROAD ★★★★★ ✔ Irish pub, restaurant $$$$
L: $10–$15, 11am–3pm. D: $13–$28, 3–11pm. "Pub Grub" 11pm–1:30am. Live band, table step-dancer after 9pm Mon.–Sat. 2 outdoor bars. Merchandise shop. Children welcome. Seats 600, inc 300 outside. Direct reservations: 407-938-0300.
Run by Irish proprietors and an Irish chef, this pretension-free bar and restaurant is the real thing. The food is a step beyond tradition—pub classics that have gone to cooking class. Tender meats are topped with subtle glazes, smooth mashed potatoes are covered in crispy braised cabbage. The creamy Rustic Chicken soup will warm your soul. Our daughter will vouch for the rich bread pudding, served with creamers of warm butterscotch and creme anglaise. There's a full selection of ales, stouts, lagers and whiskeys. Raglan Road was built using raw and recycled materials from Ireland, including antiques from Irish homes and two 130-year-old bars with traditional leaded-glass dividers. The restaurant is named after a street on the south side of Dublin immortalized in a 1960s folk song. The adjacent **Cooke's of Dublin** offers counter-service fish and chips, with fried candy bars for dessert.

Shopping
West Side

BONGOS Tucked into a corner of Bongos Cuban Cafe, this small shop has tropical shirts, T-shirts and hats as well as mugs, margarita glasses, maracas, even coffee.
CANDY CAULDRON This dungeon-style candy shop has lots of jellybeans. An open kitchen makes candied apples, chocolate-covered strawberries and other treats.
CIRQUE DU SOLEIL STORE Stunning Cirque-branded scarves, purses and fashion apparel mix leather, Italian prints and hand beading. Equally enticing: masks, figurines and circus caps. La Nouba goods include Diabolo games and soundtrack CDs.
DISNEYQUEST STORE This small shop sells Disney movie-related merchandise including plushies and DVDs.

The price of dreams. Bath bombs for sale at the Basin shop at Downtown Disney Marketplace.

SOSA FAMILY CIGARS This premium cigar shop often has hand-rolling demonstrations. Adults can smoke on the premises.

STARABILIAS Pricey memorabilia includes historical, movie, music and political items. Separate displays feature Elvis, the Beatles, Jimi Hendrix, Betty Boop and Harry Potter. Also for sale: apparel for all ages, bobbleheads, figurines, mugs and prints.

SUNGLASS ICON Sunglass brands include Ray-Ban, Maui Jim and Oakley.

VIRGIN MEGASTORE This 49,000-square-foot two-story store includes a good-sized trendy fashion shop with shirts, caps, purses and figurines, as well as a wide-ranging collection of DVDs and CDs. Upstairs is an eclectic selection of books, magazines and video games and the Coco Moka Cafe, with sweets, coffees and deli and panini sandwiches. Some of its 50 seats are on an outdoor balcony.

Marketplace

ARRIBAS BROTHERS Glassblowers work before your eyes in this dimly lit shop. The sparkly offerings include hand-cut crystal and hand-blown glass items, all of which can be engraved.

ART OF DISNEY Disney-themed oil paintings, animation cels, lithographs, theme-park attraction posters, Lenox china figurines, plates, vases and other quality art pieces fill the walls.

BASIN The intoxicating aroma of this all-natural skin-care store will cause you to linger longer than your credit card recommends. Indulge in massage and shampoo bars, bath bombs, body butters, lotions and salt and sea scrubs. Check out the make-your-own candle station.

DESIGN-A-TEE SHOP Personalize a T-shirt at this new Hanes store, located in the space of the former Disney's Wonderful World of Memories scrapbook shop.

DISNEY'S DAYS OF CHRISTMAS Disney World's largest Christmas shop, this Yuletide store is filled with ornaments. It also sells collectibles, figurines and Santa hats with Mickey ears. An embroidery and engraving area will personalize your find.

DISNEY'S PIN TRADERS This open-air shop doesn't have a tremendous selection of pins, but does have limited-edition versions, as well as albums, display sheets and carrying cases.

HOUSE OF BLUES COMPANY STORE This eclectic shop has blues CDs, cornbread mix, folk art, hot sauce and incense.

HOYPOLOI Uncommon home-accent pieces made of ceramic, glass, metal, stone and wood fill this gallery-style shop. The collection include candles, clocks, figurines, fountains, jewelry, lamps, paintings, pottery, puzzles, watches and windchimes.

MAGIC MASTERS Pick a trick from the menu board and a magician performs it at this neat little shop, which replicates Harry Houdini's private library and has a "secret" door. The tricks are for sale, as are books, DVDs and magic wands.

MAGNETRON A tiny shop filled with 50,000 quirky refrigerator magnets and silly knickknacks.

MICKEY'S GROOVE General Disney apparel and merchandise.

PLANET HOLLYWOOD ON LOCATION You guessed it: Planet Hollywood-themed attitude and fashion apparel.

POP GALLERY A bright collection of pop art includes signed paintings, three-dimensional wall hangings and some wild glass sculptures. There's a small champagne bar.

DISNEY TAILS Set within Pooh Corner, this pet-care and pampering nook has bandanas, clothes, toys, treats and collar-ID tags.

GHIRARDELLI CHOCOLATE SHOP A tempting aroma envelops this collection of chocolate candy squares. The store also offers its own brand of fudge sauce, baking cocoa and hot-chocolate mix.

GOOFY'S CANDY CO. Clerks top apples, cookies or marshmallows with your choice of crushed candy, nuts or chocolate drizzle. The jellybean and lollipop collection is huge; a coffee counter has lattes and cappuccinos. New for 2009: a private room for birthday parties.

LEGO IMAGINATION CENTER This bustling store offers dozens of Lego boxed sets as well as the world's largest Pick-A-Brick wall, where 320 bins let you buy individual pieces. Giant display creations include Brickley, a sea serpent outside in Village Lake. An outdoor play area lets children create their own masterpieces.

MCDONALD'S A glass case inside this fast-food restaurant sells McDonald's caps, coffee mugs, pins, puzzles, salt and pepper shakers and ties.

MICKEY'S MART Dozens of small items, all priced under $10.

MICKEY'S PANTRY This housewares shop stocks Mickey Mouse-styled small appliances and kitchen items, and non-Disney cooking supplies, tableware, even wine.

ONCE UPON A TOY This 16,000-square-foot toy store includes Disney theme-park items and Hasbro classics such as Lincoln Logs, Mr. Potato Head and Tinkertoys. The playful decor features a huge Game of Life spinner rotating upside down on the ceiling.

POOH CORNER The silly old bear and his friends adorn apparel, backpacks, pillows, plushies, toys and adorable infant onesies and dresses.

RAINFOREST CAFE STORE Next to the cafe, this shop sells Rainforest Cafe and animal-themed apparel, plushies and toys. Animated creatures come to life.

SUMMER SANDS This juniors shop features Roxy, Billabong, Hurley brands and similarly styled Disney Tinker Bell apparel.

TEAM MICKEY'S ATHLETIC CLUB Disney- and ESPN-themed sportswear and sporting goods include T-shirts, caps, jerseys, golf attire, baseballs, basketballs, footballs and soccer balls, as well as nice coats and sweatshirts in the winter. A Louisville Slugger corner sells custom-made bats.

T-REX DINO-STORE Disney World's best selection of dinosaur-themed children's apparel and toys fills this T-Rex restaurant store. Run by the Build-A-Bear Workshop folks, a Build-A-Dino area lets children create custom plushies. Kids search for faux fossils in an outdoor "sand" pit and sluice.

WORLD OF DISNEY This smartly organized department store has separate rooms for girls (here known as Princesses), Ladies and Juniors, Boys, Men, Infants, Hats and T-shirts, Housewares, Home Accessories, Jewelry and Pins, Candy and Snacks, and Souvenirs. The **Bibbidi Bobbidi Boutique** (10 chairs, 407-WDW-STYLE, reservations book quickly) is a makeover salon for young girls. Fairy Godmothers apply cosmetics and style hair.

Pleasure Island

CURL BY SAMMY DUVALL Created by the legendary water-skier, this beachwear shop offers teen fashion apparel, purses, hats, jewelry, sunglasses, as well as a few surf boards and skate boards.

FUEGO BY SOSA CIGARS Choose among 100 different hand-rolled premium smokes, and enjoy your selection with a cocktail in this intimate lounge. You must be 18 to smoke, 21 to drink.

ORLANDO HARLEY-DAVIDSON Everything Harley but the hogs: apparel for men, women and kids, collectibles, even pet products. Custom bikes are on display.

SHOP FOR IRELAND Irish merchandise includes fashion apparel, infantwear and mugs and cookbooks. Located at the Raglan Road restaurant.

DOWNTOWN DISNEY HIDDEN MICKEYS
Marketplace landscape: ❶ As a 20x20-foot arrangement of pavement squirters at the original Marketplace entrance, to the right of the Earl of Sandwich restaurant. ❷ The squirters themselves are small Mickeys. **Once Upon a Toy:** ❸ As robotic claws that hold toys, suspended from a hanging track. ❹ As blue support bars under stands that hold plushies. **World of Disney:** ❺ In a mural in the Women and Juniors room, as a red and white design on a blue flag to the left of the Queen of Hearts and as a gold design on Tweedledee's sumo cloth. ❻ As a design in a mural in the facing room, above the Chinese Theatre doors behind the floating Three Little Pigs. **DisneyQuest:** ❼ As ancient symbols in the carpets of Adventureport and the 5th-floor cafe. **Cirque du Soleil:** ❽ Outside the box office as black floor tiles inside both restroom doors.

A snowy version of Cinderella Castle highlights a hole at Disney's Winter Summerland miniature golf course

Sports and Rec

Bicycle and surrey rentals

Ten resorts rent **bicycles** ($8 hr, $22 day) and/or multi-seat **surreys** ($18–$22 30 min): the BoardWalk, Caribbean Beach, Coronado Springs, Fort Wilderness, Old Key West, Polynesian (surreys only), Port Orleans, Saratoga Springs, Wilderness Lodge and (bikes only) Yacht and Beach Club.

Boat charters

You'll cruise in style aboard the **Breathless II** (Ages 3 and up. 30 min ride: $85 per group. 90 min IllumiNations cruise: $250. Yacht Club marina. 407-WDW-PLAY), a 26-foot mahogany replica of a 1930s Chris-Craft inboard. You and up to nine friends can float Seven Seas Lagoon on a **pontoon boat** ($200–$250. 1 hr. Guide, snacks. 407-WDW-PLAY) to view Magic Kingdom's Wishes show or Epcot's IllumiNations. Wishes boats leave from the Contemporary, Grand Floridian and Wilderness Lodge docks; Epcot trips leave from the Yacht Club. You can cruise Seven Seas Lagoon or Bay Lake aboard the 45-foot Sea Ray **Grand 1** ($400 per hr, up to 13 people. Inc captain, deckhand. Food, butler opt. Leaves from Grand Floridian marina. 407-824-2682).

Boat rentals

With the world's largest rental-boat fleet and a variety of lakes, lagoons and canals, Disney offers nearly every way imaginable to get on the water. Boats vary by resort marina; call 407-WDW-PLAY (939-7529) for details. Your choices include two-seat **Sea Raycers** ($24 per 30 min, $38 per hr. Ages 12–15 may drive with a licensed driver. Min. height 60 in. Max. weight 320 lbs. per boat), **17-foot Boston Whaler Montauk** ($33 per 30 min), **21-foot SunTracker pontoon boats** ($42 per 30 min), **12-foot Sunfish sailboats** ($20 per hr), **13-foot Hobie Cats** ($25 per hr), **canoes** ($6.50 per 30 min) and **pedal boats** ($6.50 per 30 min). The Walt Disney World Swan and Dolphin has **swan pedal boats** ($12–$14 per 30 min).
At the Contemporary Resort, Sammy Duvall's Water Sports Centre has three-seat **Sea-Doo personal watercraft** (non-guided rides $75 per 30 min, $125 per hr. Morning group rides into Seven Seas Lagoon $125 per hr. Max. 3 riders per vehicle, max. combined weight 400 lbs. Operator must be 16 with valid driver's lic.; renters must be 18. 407-939-0754).

Campfire

It's free! Held at a small outdoor amphitheater, **Chip 'n Dale's Campfire Sing-a-Long** (Nightly. Fort Wilderness Resort & Campground. For schedule call 407-824-2727.) lets you bond with your kids without draining your bank account. You'll roast marshmallows in a fire pit, join in a 30-minute sing-a-long with the chipmunks, then watch a Disney movie on a large outdoor screen. There's a different film every night. A snack bar sells s'mores kits, packs of marshmallows and sticks, as well as hot dogs and beer. Sit on the benches to interact with the characters.

Carriage and wagon rides

Available at the Fort Wilderness Resort & Campground, Port Orleans Riverside Resort andthe Saratoga Springs Resort, **horse-drawn carriage rides** ($35. 25 min. 6–9:30 pm. Those under 18 must ride with an adult. Reservations accepted 90 days in adv at 407-939-PLAY (7529). Same-day availability info at 407-824-2832.) hold up to four adults or a small family. Fort Wilderness trips travel through natural areas. Night trips are romantic. Fort Wilderness also offers **wagon rides** ($8 A. $5 C 3–9. Under 3 free. 45 min. 7 p.m., 9:30 p.m. Fireworks rides often avail. Departs from Pioneer Hall. Children under 11 must ride with an adult. No reservations. Group rides with 24 hrs. notice, 407-824-2734.) down its trails. You ride with up to 32 other guests.

Diving and snorkeling

Certified divers can spend 40 minutes inside a 5.7-million-gallon saltwater aquarium at **Epcot DiveQuest** ($140, 40 min. in water, 3 hr experience. Includes gear, lockers, showers. Park adm not req. Ages 10 and up. Ages 10, 11 must dive with adult. 3

The authors' daughter holds one of many bass she caught on a morning Disney fishing trip

hrs. Open-water scuba cert. req. 407-WDW-TOUR), a guided tour at The Seas with Nemo & Friends pavilion at Epcot. You'll swim with more than 65 marine species, including non-aggressive sharks, rays, tropical fish and sea turtles. You suit up in waist-deep water and explore with up to 12 others. The program includes a presentation on marine life and an overview of the pavilion. The **Epcot Seas Aqua Tour** ($100, 30 min. in water, 2.5 hr experience. Inc instruction. Park adm not req. Ages 8 and up (under 18 must dive with adult). 407-WDW-TOUR) puts you in the tank with scuba-assisted snorkel (SAS) equipment. You also tour the aquarium and learn about the marine life you see. Proceeds from both experiences go to the Disney Wildlife Conservation Fund.

Dolphin encounter

You'll spend 30 minutes in knee-deep water with live bottlenose dolphins, learn about the anatomy and behavior of these mammals and watch biologists do dolphin research on a program called **Dolphins in Depth** ($150, 3 hrs. Includes use of wetsuit, T-shirt, photo of guest with dolphin, refreshments. No swim-

ming. Park adm not req. Ages 13 and up. Those under 18 must be with adult. 407-WDW-TOUR). No interaction is guaranteed, but then again you may get to feel a heartbeat. Trainers work with guests individually. Proceeds go to the Disney Wildlife Conservation Fund.

Wide World of Sports

Now officially known as the *ESPN* Wide World of Sports, this 220-acre compound includes a 9,500-seat baseball stadium, two large fieldhouses, a tennis compound with a stadium court, a 400-meter track and field center and many outdoor baseball, softball and soccer fields.

The complex is the leading venue for amateur and professional sports in the United States. It hosts more than 11,000 events each year—an average of 30 per day—in 50 sports with athletes from more than 70 countries. Held in February and March, Atlanta Braves Spring Training includes 15 exhibition games during its six-week season. During summer, the Tampa Bay Buccaneers NFL football team holds its training camp. Daily practices are free and open to the public. Other popular events include the AAU National Championships, Varsity All-Star Cheerleading competitions, Chelsea Football Club events and the Pop Warner Super Bowl. ESPN televised 20 sporting events from the complex in 2008.

A 100-lane bowling center will open in 2010. The United States Bowling Congress will stage 13 events there, with tournaments beginning in 2011.

The center draws 250,000 athletes and 1.2 million spectators a year. Spectators can attend amateur events for a nominal fee. Tickets for professional events are available through Ticketmaster outlets or at the ESPN Wide World of Sports box office. For information call 407-828-FANS (3267).

Fishing

Since all Disney fishing is catch-and-release and only a handful of anglers are on the water at any time, catching a large-mouth bass is almost guaranteed when you take a pontoon-boat **guided fishing excursions** ($200–$235, 2 hrs for up to 5 guests; $405 for 4 hrs, each add'l hr $100. Inc bait (shiners addl), guide, equipment, refreshments, digital camera. No license req. Trips on Bay Lake, Seven Seas Lagoon, Crescent

Lake, Village Lake and Lago Dorado at Disney's Coronado Resort. Leave early am, mid am, early pm. 407-WDW-BASS (939-2277). Reservations taken 2 wks in adv.). Guests routinely catch bass weighing 2 to 8 pounds. Most trips catch five to 10 fish; guests average 2.5 fish per hour. Bay Lake and Seven Seas Lagoon are teeming with bass; the largest fish (up to 14 lbs.) are in Crescent and Village lakes. The Bass Anglers Sportsman Society (BASS) runs the programs. You can **fish from the shore** (Cane poles $3.75 30 min, $8.50 day. Rods $5.25 30 min., $9.25 day. Bait addl. No lic. required. No reservations) at Fort Wilderness (407-824-2900) and Port Orleans Riverside (407-934-6000).

Golf

(Greens fees $35–$170 for 18-hole courses (req. cart rental inc); $38 for Oak Trail ($20 for under 18). Club, shoe rental avail. Proper golf attire req. 18-holes have putting greens, driving ranges. Free transportation from Disney-owned resorts. Reservations 90 days in advance for Disney resort guests, 30 days other players. Cancellations require 48 hrs notice. Fla resident Annual Golf Membership ($50) saves up to 60% (based on time of year) on greens fees after 10am for member, up to three guests; 20% on instruction. Disney Vacation Club members can buy a similar membership. Add'l summer savings. 407-WDW-GOLF, disneyworldgolf.com.)

Grouped into three facilities, Disney's five golf courses each offer a different experience. There's the long course, the short course, the flat course, the water course. And the kid-friendly 9-hole.

Home to deer, egrets, herons, otters, alligators and an occasional bald eagle, each course is designated as a wildlife sanctuary by the Audubon Cooperative Sanctuary System. All but the Lake Buena Vista course roam far from civilization. Best months to play are September, April and May, when the weather's nice and good tee times are easy to book. Build extra time into your round, as the pace may be slower than you expect.

How's that shoulder turn? It needs to be efficient on the long-game **Magnolia course** (Yardage: 5,232–7,516. Par: 72. Course rating: 69.4–76.5. Slope rating: 125–140. Designer: Joe Lee. Year open: 1971. Next to Shades of Green, across from the Polynesian Resort.), a rolling terrain that sits amid more than 1,500 magnolia trees. The Magnolia has elevated tees and greens and 97 bunkers, the most of any Disney course.

The 'mouse trap.' A bunker at the Magnolia's golf course's No. 6 green resembles Mickey Mouse.

And the greens are quick. Host to the final round of Disney's PGA Tour tournament stop since 1971, the course has tested pros from Jack Nicklaus to Tiger Woods.

Pretty palms. Ugly hazards. The **Palm course** (Yardage: 5,311–6,957. Par: 72. Course rating: 69.5–73.9. Slope rating: 126–138. Designer: Joe Lee. Year open: 1971. Next to Shades of Green, across from the Polynesian Resort) has them both. Water hazards line seven holes and cross six. The Palm is shorter and tighter than the Magnolia. Rated one of Golf Digest's Top 25 Resort Courses, it has a few long par 4s and a couple of par 5s that can be reached in two using a fairway wood. The large, elevated greens can be maneuvered with good lag putting. Save a sprinkle of pixie dust for hole No. 18. A long par 4, it has been rated as high as fourth toughest on the PGA Tour.

A 9-hole walking course, **Oak Trail** (Yardage: 2,532–2,913. Par: 36. Course rating: 64.6–68.2. Slope rating: 107–123. Designer: Ron Garl. Year open: 1980. Next to Shades of Green, across from the Polynesian Resort) is nice for a quick nine, practice, or letting the developing golfer learn the game. With small greens and two good par 5s, the course requires accuracy with short irons.

The longest hole, the 517-yard No. 5, features a double dogleg. Water hazards cross three fairways. Most greens and tees are elevated. The scorecard lists separate pars for children 11 and under and 12 and over.

Set within rolling Florida terrain, the beautiful **Osprey Ridge course** (Yardage: 5,402–7,101. Par: 72. Course rating: 69.5–74.4. Slope rating: 123–131. Designer: Tom Fazio. Year open: 1992. Just east of the Fort Wilderness Resort) winds through challenging dense vegetation, oak forests and moss hammocks. More than 70 bunkers, mounds and a meandering ridge provide obstacles, banking and elevation changes. Some tees and greens are 20 feet above their fairways. The course often has swirling winds. One bit of relief: fairway waste bunkers have hard sand, so you can play a shot out of one with a more-normal swing.

The least forgiving Disney course, the **Lake Buena Vista course** (Yardage: 5,204–6,802. Par: 72. Course rating: 68.6–73.0. Slope rating: 122–133. Designer: Joe Lee. Year open: 1972. Saratoga Springs) has narrow, tree-lined fairways and small greens. You tee off at the Saratoga Springs Resort, then weave through Old Key West. Play demands accuracy on the tee shot as well as the approach. Errant shots can hit windows. Signature hole No. 7 has an island green; No. 18 is a 438-yard dogleg to the right. Ten holes have water hazards.

All 18-hole greens have ultra-dwarf TifEagle turf, a short Bermuda grass that provides a truer, faster roll. Installation on the 9-hole Oak Trail is scheduled for 2009.

Disney's **Eagle Pines course** closed in 2007. In its place will be a Four Seasons resort.

PGA pros offer year-round **golf lessions** ($50–$150, 45 min. lesson for a single golfer $75. Shades of Green center. All ages, skill levels. Individual lessons, clinics: 407-WDW-GOLF (4653). Group lessons: 407-938-3870). Choose from one-on-one instruction focused on a specific skill, video swing analysis or on-course lessons that include course management and strategy, club selection and short-game skills.

Horseback riding

You ride on shady pine and palmetto trails inside Fort Wilderness on one of Disney's **guided horseback rides** ($42, 45 min. Daily starting at 8:30am. Ages 9 and up. Height min. 48 in. Max. weight 250 lbs. Closed-toe shoes req.; no sandals, flip-flops. No trotting. Reservations, required, can be made 30 days in advance at 407-WDW-PLAY). Rides start at the Tri-Circle D Livery. Go early and you'll likely see wildlife such as snakes and deer. Smaller kids can take a short **pony ride**

($4, cash only. Ages 2–8. Max. height 48 in. Max. weight 80 lbs. 10am–5 pm daily. 407-824-2788) at the petting farm. A parent walks the pony.

Jogging

A wooded 1.5-mile trail threads through the Fort Wilderness Resort. There's a bike path to it from Wilderness Lodge. Guests can take a 1-mile stroll on the Epcot Resorts promenade and continue jogging along the BoardWalk side to Disney's Hollywood Studios. A 1.4-mile walkway leads around a lake at Caribbean Beach. Two trails weave through the Port Orleans resorts (1-mile and .7-mile); a mile trek circles Lago Dorado at Coronado Springs. Shorter trails are at the Contemporary, Polynesian and Grand Floridian resorts.

Miniature golf

($12 A, $10 C. 10 am–11 pm. Gardens course at Fantasia Gardens closes 10:30 pm. Last tee time 30 min. before close. In-person same-day reservations accepted. 407-WDW-PLAY) Across the street from the Walt Disney World Swan and Dolphin, **Fantasia Gardens** (407-560-4753) is busy at night, when tee-time waits can be an hour. Splashing brooms and dancing-ostrich topiaries line the Gardens course, while the Fairways course replicates real links with bunkers, roughs, undulating and holes up to 103 feet long. Adjacent to Blizzard Beach, **Winter Summerland** (407-560-7161) is often deserted at night. Two whimsical courses are themed to the activities of elves who, as the story* goes, vacation here. Their tiny trailers dot the landscape. Getting a hole in one is easy, as the greens often funnel into the cups.

Spas

Signature treatments at the **Grand Floridian Spa** (407-824-2332, at the Grand Floridian Resort. Parking at Disney's Wedding Pavilion) include an aromatherapy massage and body wrap and citrus-zest facials, sugar scrubs and therapies. Couples can get massages together in a candle-lit room. The Asian-inspired **Mandara Spa** (407-934-4772, at the Walt Disney World Dolphin resort) retreat includes couples suites, a steam room and two indoor gar-

---

* Late one Christmas Eve as Santa was flying over Florida, he glanced down, saw snow (!), landed and purchased the spot as a vacation retreat for his elves. They built two golf courses: one for those members who enjoyed the snow, another for those who loved the Florida sun.

dens. It offers baking-soda micro-therapy, cellulite reductions, Glycolic facials; seaweed wraps, stone therapies and tooth whitening programs. Inspired by the spring waters of Saratoga Springs, New York, popular treatments at Disney's newest spa, **Saratoga Springs** (407-827-4455, at the Saratoga Springs Resort) include a maple sugar body polish, Adirondack stone therapy massage, a mineral springs hydrotherapy treatment and a rosemary spring therapeutic bath. The French whirlpool has 72 jets.

Stock car driving

(Rides $109. Drives $399–$1249 (8–30 laps). Hrs: 9 am.–4 pm. Duration: 30 min–1 hr for rides (3 min in car); 3–4 hrs for drives (10–15 min driving car). Gift cards available. Drives require reservations, include training. Cars reach speeds of 145 mph on ridealongs, which don't require reservations. Adj to Magic Kingdom parking lot. Must be 16 or older to ride, 18 or older

FUN FACTS ›› Once worn down, the foot-wide tires are sold for $5. **››** Nicknamed the "Mickyard," the one-mile tri-oval was built in 1995 by the Indy Racing League. Many pro races were held here, including five Indy 200s and some Craftsman Truck Series events. A large grandstand held over 51,000 fans. Racing stopped in 2000.

The Richard Petty Driving Experience puts you behind the wheel of a 630-horsepower stock car to drive. One-day Safe Driving Program (June, Dec) for drivers 15 to 25: $329–$399. Spectators welcome. 1-800-BE-PETTY, 1800bepetty.com.)

The engine rumbles. You tremble. Then you tear down a race track at over 100 mph, by yourself, driving a 630-horsepower stock car.

Held at the Walt Disney World Speedway, lessons at the Richard Petty Driving Experience start off with a training session that includes time out on the track. Then, wearing a fire cap, driving suit and helmet, you climb through the window, pop on the steering wheel and strap in.

Almost always in a turn, you tail your instructor who's in a car of his own. He watches you in a mirror, and drives as fast as you can handle. I (Julie) got up to 122 mph (fastest in my class!) and even passed a guy on Lap 7. Your NASCAR-style vehicle features a tube frame, huge V-8 and 4-speed clutch. The doors don't open, and the bodies are covered with logos.

Surfing lessons

Know how to swim? In shape? If so, then you are almost guaranteed to learn how to ride the crest of a wave at the **Craig Carroll Surfing School** ($140. Must be 8 yrs. or older, strong swimmer. Most students have never surfed. Days, hrs vary

A mom and daughter take off on a parasailing flight behind the Contemporary Resort

at the Grand Floridian ($8 hr., same-day reservations at 407-621-1991; parking at Disney's Wedding Pavilion). Some resorts reserve their courts for their own guests, though the BoardWalk, Contemporary, Fort Wilderness Campground and Yacht Club courts welcome guests from any Disney-owned resort. Organized programs for guests of all ages and abilities are offered on the two courts at the Grand Floridian. These include **private lessons** ($75 hr.), **hitting lessons** ("Play the Pro," $75 hr.) and **convention-style group tournaments** ($25 hr.) An adjacent **pro shop** (407-WDW-PLAY) rents rackets and ball machines and re-strings and re-grips guest rackets.

Tours

(No photography in backstage areas. Photo IDs req. To book any tour but a VIP outing call 407-WDW-TOUR).

Around the World at Epcot ($85, Epcot admission req. 2 hrs. Daily. Ages 16 and up. Max. weight 250 lbs.) Take a Segway Human Transporter through Epcot.

Backstage Magic ($199, lunch included, theme park admission not req. 7 hrs. Mon.–Fri. Ages 16 and up.) Takes you behind the scenes at Magic Kingdom, Epcot and Disney's Hollywood Studios. The longest Disney World tour.

Backstage Safari ($65, Animal Kingdom admission req. 3 hrs. Mon., Wed., Thr., Fri. Ages 16 and up.) Tours the vet hospital, elephant barn and other facilities of Disney's Animal Kingdom.

Behind the Seeds ($14, $10 ages 3–9., Epcot admission req. 45 min. Daily. All ages.) An inside look at the four greenhouses and fish farm at The Land pavilion.

Disney's Family Magic Tour ($27, Magic Kingdom admission req. 2 hrs. Daily. All ages.) A Magic Kingdom primer for first-time visitors with children; a skip (literally) through the park.

Keys to the Kingdom ($60, includes lunch at Columbia Harbour House. Magic Kingdom admission req. 4 hrs. Daily. Ages 16 and up.) Guides discuss the history and philosophies of Magic Kingdom. Goes backstage and spend time down in the Utilidor.

Mickey's Magical Milestones Tour ($25, Magic Kingdom admission req. 2 hrs. Mon., Wed., Fri. Ages 16 and under must be accompanied by an adult.) Visits Magic Kingdom attractions and locations that trace the career of Mickey Mouse.

The Magic Behind Our Steam Trains ($40, Magic Kingdom admission req. No cameras. 3 hrs. Mon., Tue., Wed., Thr., Sat. Ages 10 and up.) An inside

with season. 2.5-hr lesson has 30 min. on land, 2 hrs. in water. Surfboards provided. Spectators OK. Max. 12 students a day; classes sell out quickly. Reservations accepted 90 days early at 407-WDW-SURF.), held before park hours at the Typhoon Lagoon surf pool. Conducted on dry land, a step-by-step introductory lesson is easy to follow, then instructors plop in the water to demonstrate the technique. Once you're in the pool you get plenty of personal attention. After each attempt Carroll critiques you from the lifeguard stand, then an instructor in the water adds more tips. Waves average about 5 feet for adults; half that for kids.

Though about 70 percent of students succeed, Carroll says females do best. "Girls don't think as hard about it, and try to do exactly what you say," he explains. "Boys tend to think it's a macho thing."

A pro surfer since the 1970s, Carroll coached world-champion Kelly Slater and runs the Cocoa Beach Ron Jon Surf School.

Tennis

Walt Disney World has 34 **lighted courts.** All general court use is complimentary except

Learning to surf. Danielle Finke, 20, gets off her knees on her second attempt.

look at Magic Kingdom's Walt Disney World Railroad shows how trains are prepared for operation. Also discusses Walt Disney's love of steam trains.

Undiscovered Future World ($49, Epcot admission req. 4 hrs. Mon., Wed., Fri. Ages 16 and up.) Learn about Walt Disney's planned Experimental Prototype Community of Tomorrow, visit all Future World pavilions and glimpse backstage areas.

VIP Tours ($125 per hr., min. 6 hrs. Daily. All ages. 407-560-4033.) Guided custom tours based on your custom itinerary.

Wild by Design ($58, includes light breakfast. Animal Kingdom admission req. 3 hrs. Mon., Wed., Thr., Fri. Ages 14 and up. Guests under 16 must be accompanied by an adult.) Covers the art, architecture, story-telling and animal care at Disney's Animal Kingdom.

Wilderness Back Trail Adventure ($85. 2 hrs. Tue., Fri., Sat. at 8:30 and 11:30 a.m. Ages 16 and up. Max. weight 250 lbs. Starts from Mickey's Backyard BBQ pavilion. Same-day walk-up reservations at the Fort Wilderness marina.) Ride a Segway X2 through shady off-road trails of the Fort Wilderness Campground.

Yuletide Fantasy ($69, Late Nov.–Dec. only. No theme park admission req. 3 hrs. Mon.–Sat. Ages 16 and up.) Tours the holiday decorations of the Magic Kingdom, Epcot and a few resorts.

Wide World of Sports Guided Tour (Complimentary. 1 hr. All ages.) An inside look at the complex on selected days when sporting events are scheduled.

Water sports

Working out of the Contemporary Resort, Sammy Duvall's Water Sports Centre (407-939-0754) will take you parasailing, water-skiing or tube riding.

Parasailing (Single riders $95 for 8–10 min. at 450 ft. or $120 for 10–12 min. at 600 ft. Tandem riders $160 for 8–10 min. at 450 ft. or $185 for 10–12 min. at 600 ft. Min. weight per flight 130 lbs. Max weight 330 lbs.) will give you a birds-eye view of Walt Disney World. Hundreds of feet above the 450-acre Bay Lake, you can see everything from Animal Kingdom's Tree of Life to Typhoon Lagoon's Miss Tilly. Attached to an open parachute, you're pulled by a powerboat down below. You never get wet, as you take off and land on the back of the boat.

You can also **water-ski, tube, wakeboard or kneeboard** ($155 first hr., $125 per addl. hr. per boat. Up to 5 skiers. Inc equipment, driver, instruction. Extra charge if picked up from Fort Wilderness, Grand Floridian, Polynesian or Wilderness Lodge) behind a MasterCraft inboard. Instructors are friendly and patient, especially with kids.

A legendary skier himself, Duvall has won more than 80 pro championships.

Disney's All-Star Movies Resort is dominated by gigantic Disney characters, such as Pongo from 1961's "101 Dalmatians"

Accommodations

The Walt Disney company runs 19 resorts on its Florida property, which it divides into five categories. Motel-style **Value Resorts** have food courts, pizza delivery, pools, playgrounds and hourly luggage service. Most rooms sleep four. Large complexes, the **Moderate Resorts** add restaurants, limited room service, pools with slides, bellhops and some on-site recreation. Most rooms sleep four. **Deluxe Resorts** add full room service, club levels, fitness centers, kid's activities, child care and valet parking. Most rooms sleep five. Often available for nightly rentals, **Disney Vacation Club** (DVC) timeshare units have kitchens and sleep up to 12. A category of its own, the **Fort Wilderness Resort & Campground** is a wooded area with campsites, cabins and RV hookups, as well as a lakeside village that includes a restaurant, general store and unique activities. All resorts have shops, arcades, laundry services and free transportation to Disney theme and water parks and Downtown Disney. For reservations call 407-WDW-MAGIC (939-6244).

One oddity of Disney's resort categorization is it inadvertently segregates visitors by income. Typically, the Value resorts crowd includes guests who clearly can't afford to be there, while most of the Grand Floridian group looks like it just stepped out of a Lands' End catalog.

Benefits of Disney resorts

The themed architecture and decor, lush landscaping and, in most cases, quality restaurants at a Disney-owned resort immerse you in a vacation experience. Disney's reputation as a clean, family environment is well-deserved: grounds crews, maintenance workers and security guards seem to be everywhere. The convenient location makes it easy to take a midday break from theme-park or other adventures.

Complimentary Disney transportation (boats, buses and monorails) takes you to all theme and water parks, golf courses and Downtown Disney. In some cases, it takes just a few minutes to get from your hotel room to a theme park.

Each day one of the four theme parks opens one hour early, or stays open up to three hours late for Disney resort guests with theme-park tickets. Water parks also participate. These **Extra Magic Hours** offer you uncrowded time in the parks and make it easier to plan out your vacation.

A Disney resort I.D. (your **"Key to the World"**) lets you charge park food, merchandise and other services to your room. Disney's free package pickup and delivery service will take anything you buy from Disney and deliver it to your room.

Resort guests also get preferred tee times at Disney's five golf courses.

Disney's innovative **Magical Express** service offers complimentary shuttle and luggage delivery from the Orlando International Airport (OIA) to your Disney resort. In other words, you don't have to rent a car, you completely bypass baggage claim and your bags are automatically placed in your room. When it's time to return home, you check your luggage at your hotel (domestic flights only) and then hop on a bus back to the airport. If your flight departs late in the day, you can check out of the hotel, check your luggage at the desk nearby, then go off and still fully enjoy your last day at Disney.

The best part? There's no real catch. You have to book the Magical Express service at least 10 days in advance. Participating airlines for return luggage check-in include American, Continental, Delta, JetBlue, Northwest and United. The service is extraordinarily popular. On some days more than 10,000 people use it, and that's just on the incoming buses. The Walt Disney World Swan and Dolphin, Shades of Green and the Downtown Disney resorts are not included in the program. For details call Magical Express Guest Services at 866-599-0951.

Note: All Disney addresses in the following listings are in the city of Lake Buena Vista, ZIP code 32830. All phone numbers actually go to a central information center.

A giant megaphone disguises a stairway at the Hoops Hotel of the All-Star Sports resort.

All-Star Resorts

★★ $ **Rates** $82–$160, suites $184–$327. **Location** SW corner of WDW, near Animal Kingdom. **Distance to:** Magic Kingdom: 5 mi. Epcot: 5 mi. Hollywood Studios: 3 mi. Animal Kingdom: 1 mi. Blizzard Bch: 1 mi. Typh'n Lgn: 4 mi. Dwntwn Disney: 4 mi. WW of Sports: 3 mi. **Size** 5,740 rms, 298 suites, 246 ac. **Rooms** 260 sq. ft. Sleep 4. 2 dbl beds (1 king opt), table, coffeemkr. Internet access opt. Accessed by outdoor walkways. **Suites** Sleep 6. **Amenities** 2 swm pools, kiddie pool. Arcade, gift shop selling groceries, laundromat, laundry srvc, playground. **Transportation** Buses: Disney theme parks, water parks, Dwntwn Disney. **Check In** 3pm **Check Out** 11am **Telephone** Movies: 407-939-7000. Music: 407-939-6000. Sports: 407-939-5000. **Fax** Movies: 407-939-7111. Music: 407-939-7222. Sports: 407-939-7333. **Address** Movies: 1901 W. Buena Vista Dr. Music: 1801 W. Buena Vista Dr. Sports: 1701 W. Buena Vista Dr. **Parking** Free. **Disney Resort Category** Value.

Marching bands. Soccer teams. Large families. You'll find them all at these huge complexes, where low rates bring in everyone looking for a deal. When full, these side-by-side properties can hold 23,556 guests.

Each resort is laid out like a typical American motel, but on a giant scale. A central building holds the registration area, food court and gift shop, and fronts the main swimming pool. **Rooms** are spread out among detached, three-story rectangular buildings, many with adjacent parking lots.

Family suites (only at All-Star Music) are twice the size of a regular room. All rooms are accessed from outdoor walkways.

As for decorating ideas, they seem to be those of a 6-year-old. Themed to American pop culture, each building has been coated in what appears to be Day-Glo poster paint, then adorned with enormous garish props. All-Star Music has 40-foot guitars, huge cowboy boots and a walk-through neon juke box. All-Star Movies is dominated by gigantic Disney characters. All-Star Sports is defined by huge basketballs, football helmets, megaphones, surfboards and tennis rackets. Landscaping, for Disney, is relatively sparse.

Each resort has two themed **swimming pools**, a main one at its central hall and a second deeper within. The central pools have adjacent kiddie pools. No pool has a slide, but one at each resort has fountains that shoot water above your head. Each property also has a sandy **playground** with climbing areas, monkey bars and a slide.

Rooms at All-Star Music and All-Star Sports were renovated in 2007. The buildings closest to the buses, food courts, playgrounds and large swimming pools are Fantasia (All-Star Movies), Calypso (All-Star Music) and Surf's Up (All-Star Sports).

Each resort has a small gift shop with a standard mix of souvenirs and sundries.

From a practical standpoint, the resorts

differ in two ways. First, their food courts—the one at All-Star Movies has better food and a more comfortable atmosphere. Second, their position on the Disney bus route. As buses arrive to pick up guests, they stop first at All-Star Sports, then All-Star Music, then All-Star Movies. In other words, All-Star Movies guests have the shortest ride to the theme parks, while those at All-Star Sports have the fastest trip back.

Dining

None of the resorts has a restaurant, but all have a food court, bakery and convenience store, as well as a small bar open to the main swimming pool. As for room service, each food court delivers salads, pizzas and dessert from 4pm to midnight.
END ZONE All-Star Sports Resort **American food court.** B: 6–11am. L,D: 11am–12pm. Seats 550.
INTERMISSION All-Star Music Resort **American food court.** B: 6–11am. L: 11am–4pm. D: 5–12pm. Seats 550.
WORLD PREMIERE All-Star Movies Resort **American food court.** Lunch, dinner includes salmon, steak salads, deli sandwiches. B: 6:30–11am. L,D: 11am–12pm. Seats 550.

FUN FINDS

All-Star Movies: ❶ Vintage photographs on the back wall of the lobby include shots of Walt Disney and his team posing with Academy Awards. A 1938 panoramic image shows the entire Biltmore Bowl banquet hall as Shirley Temple and Frank Capra present Disney with a special eight-Oscar honor for the 1937 movie "Snow White and the Seven Dwarfs." ❷ A 1940s movie-theater projector sits in the back room of the food court. You can open its doors. **All-Star Music:** ❸ A lovely spot sits between the two buildings of the Jazz Inn: A 10-foot-tall weathered fountain is surrounded by benches, cobblestones and a wrought-iron fence with climbing roses. **All-Star Sports:** ❹ In the courtyard of the basketball buildings, palm trees are arranged to resemble a basketball team at a tip-off.

HIDDEN MICKEYS

All-Star Music: ❶ Around the Jazz Inn, the three-circle shape appears as a screw top on top of a cymbal. ❷ As beige designs on the front and back of the cowboy boots of the County Fair buildings. **All-Star Sports:** ❸ Between the lodging buildings, as a large round platform and two gray pavement ovals. ❹ As a pattern of a baseball and two white circles in the gift shop carpet.

Animal Kingdom Lodge

★★★★★ ✔ $$$$ **Rates** $240–$515, suites $345–$2920, villas $269–$2215. **Location** Southwest corner of WDW, west of Animal Kingdom. **Distance to:** Magic Kingdom: 6 mi. Epcot: 5 mi. Hollywood Studios: 3 mi. Animal Kingdom: <1 mi. Blizzard Bch: <1 mi. Typh'n Lgn: 5 mi. Dwntwn Disney: 5 mi. WW of Sports: 9 mi. **Size** 946 rms, 19 suites, 43 villas, 74 ac.. **Rooms** 340 sq. ft. Sleep 4. 2 qn beds (1 qn plus bunk beds opt.), table, sm refrig, coffeemkr. Internet opt. Hand-carved furniture. Balconies. Club lvl. **Suites** Sleep 6–8. Villas Sleep up to 9. **Amenities** 1 swm pool, 2 hot tubs. Arcade; childcare cntr; laundromat; laundry srvc; massage srvc; many comp. organized activities, inc wildlife programs. 33-acre savanna with over 200 African animals. **Transportation** Disney theme parks, water parks, Dwntwn Disney. **Check In** 3pm **Check Out** 11am **Telephone** 407-938-3000. **Fax** 407-938-4799. **Address** 2901 Osceola Pkwy. **Parking** Free. **Disney Resort Category** Deluxe. Adj. Disney Vacation Club resort opening in 2009.

A 33-acre savanna home to giraffes, flamingos, zebras, ostriches, gazelles and other non-aggressive species is the claim to fame of this family-focused resort. Nineteen interconnected lodging buildings arcs into the area, as does an interpretive walkway.

Topped by what appears to be a thatched roof, the lobby's four-story atrium has a look all its own. Chandeliers look like spears and shields; an indoor suspension bridge fronts a large window that overlooks the savanna. Glass cases hold real African artifacts, from ancient Sahara stone axes to modern Ghanaian gold-dust containers and Burkinan marriage baskets. A 16-foot Nigerian ceremonial mask stands in the corner.

The staff includes young adults from Botswana, Namibia and South Africa.

Dark wood furnishings handcrafted in Africa and multicolored fabrics give **rooms** an African feel. Bathrooms have marble-topped twin sinks and wider-than-usual bathtubs. Rooms above the first floor have balconies which extend about four feet; the few on the ground level have patios. Most overlook the wildlife savannas, though some face the pool or parking lot. Some suites have pool tables.

Open 24 hours, the lodge **swimming pool** is the largest at any Disney World resort. It includes a swerving 67-foot water slide and a "zero-entry" gradual ramp. Nearby are two isolated hot tubs, a nice kiddie pool and shady **playground.**

Cast members organize complimentary **children's and family activities** (9:30a–11p). Activi-

© DISNEY

Giraffes, antelope and other wildlife roam a zoo-like natural habitat at Animal Kingdom Lodge

ties range from African cultural lessons to after-dark animal spotting with night-vision goggles. A character from "The Lion King" (usually Rafiki) joins children in a **Bush Camp** ($30, ages 5–12, Sat. afternoons, 407-WDW-DINE) as they experience African culture through crafts, games and food. The **Wanyama Sunset Safari** ($210 adults, $160 children ages 8 and 9, 407-938-4755) takes guests out into the animal savannas in a truck, then to a meal at Jiko. For club-level guests, a **Sunrise Safari Breakfast Adventure** ($55 A, $28 C, inc meal; 407-938-4755) is an extended trip through the Animal Kingdom safari habitat.

There's only one store, but it's worth a stop. **Zawadi Marketplace** is divided into three sections—a convenience store, Disney gift shop and African art boutique. The latter features beaded animal figurines, wooden masks and statuettes, and drawings, paintings and sculptures by Nigerian artist Timothy Adebule. The Mara counter-service cafe has a small selection of groceries, bottled wine and swimming-pool merchandise.

The resort will almost double in size in 2009, as it adds Kidani Village, a Disney Vacation Club (timeshare) area with its own savanna and swimming pool area with a huge water-play area. Some rooms in the original buildings have become DVC properties as well.

Dining

BOMA—FLAVORS OF AFRICA ★★★★★ ✔
American/African buffet $$$ **B: $17 A, $10 C, 7:30–11am. D: $27 A, $13 C, 5–10pm. Seats 400.**
Outstanding food, ambience and value come together at this, the authors' favorite Disney restaurant. Breakfast is highlighted by a creamy sausage and biscuit skillet, pap (a white-cornmeal version of cream of wheat) and grilled tomatoes. Dinner appetizers include mulligatawny and seafood chowder, lavosh bread with three types of hummus and numerous salads. Entrees include prime rib and salmon. There's a standard-fare children's station at both meals, though most kids will love items like falafel (mashed chickpeas) and fufu (mashed white and sweet potatoes). Some foods are spiced with coriander and cumin, but none are very hot.

Boma's decor outshines anything in its class. Hanging light fixtures mix hand-cut tin with hand-blown glass. Wood tables have fabric inlays. Dining chairs have hand-carved, distressed or leather seatbacks. A concrete floor is colored to look like dirt. Stone walkways wind through it. Several seating areas sit under abstract thatched huts. The buffet itself resembles an outdoor market, with each serving station in its own hut or "makeshift" stand.

JIKO—THE COOKING PLACE ★★★★★ ✔
African fusion $$$$$ **D: $26–$39, 5:30–10pm. Seats 300.**
Disney Signature
Creative comfort food? You'll be surprised at the finds at this sophisticated jewel. The South African wine selection is the largest in the United States. Representing a sunset, the back wall of the dining room slowly changes color every 20 minutes. Another wall is a translucent piece of orange, green and yellow curved glass. Hanging from the ceiling are stylized kanu birds, flying over diners to bring them good luck.

THE MARA ✔ **American/African fast food B: 7–11am. L,D: 11am–11:30pm. Bakery 6am–11:30pm. Sm. food store has fruit, snacks, S African wines. Seats 250.** This counter-service cafe is spacious and relaxed. Cartoons play on televisions.

As for lounges, **Victoria Falls** hides above Boma with a dozen groupings of tables and chairs. It's noisy when Boma is bustling. The **Capetown Lounge and Wine Bar** offers the same African wines as the adjacent Jiko.

FUN FINDS
❶ Five abstract animal heads hang from the lobby's walkways. ❷ Metal antelopes leap along the railing of the fourth floor. ❸ Lion and giraffe faces hide in the railing that leads to the rear savanna. ❹ At the bottom of those steps, a lion face hides in plain sight. Ventilation vents form its eyes, a primitive ladder its nose, wall indentations its mouth.

HIDDEN MICKEYS
❶ Outside, as a design above the lower roof in the mouth of the second tall figure left of the motor lobby. ❷ As a yellow spot on the back of the right spotted creature just inside the entrance. ❸ As a design on the right middle lobby chandelier, facing the check-in counter. ❹ In back, as a leaf about two-thirds of the way up the left vine staircase. ❺ To the left of the pelican viewing area, as spots on the tallest giraffe in the stone carving. ❻ As dents in rock along that overlook's walkway, 4 feet off the ground. ❼ Behind the pool slide as three dents in a brown rock wall, 3 feet off the ground. ❽ As a small green shape right of a wall above the Mara snack bar. ❾ Inside Mara, as a hole in a painted leaf on a wall in front and above the wine selection and ❿ on the third leaf from the left tree on the upper left wall. ⓫ As three circles in the Jiko ceiling, formed by the tops of a column and two ovens alongside the show kitchen.

BoardWalk Inn & Villas

★★★★★ ✔ $$$$$ **Rates** Standard rms $335–$825, suites $630–$2715, villas $335–$2215. **Location** Centrally located on Disney property, between the Swan and Epcot. **Distance to:** Magic Kingdom: 4 mi. Epcot: 3 mi. Hollywood Studios: 2 mi. Animal Kingdom: 4 mi. Blizzard Bch: 2 mi. Typh'n Lgn: 2 mi. Dwntwn Disney: 2 mi. WW of Sports: 4 mi. **Size** 378 rms, 20 suites, 533 villas, 45 ac. **Rooms** 385 sq. ft. Sleep 5. 2 qn beds (1 king opt), daybed, table, sm refrig, coffeemkr. Ceiling fan. Internet opt. Balconies, patios. Club lvl. **Suites** Sleep 4–8. **Villas** Sleep up to 12. **Amenities** 3 swm pools, hot tubs. Arcade; bicycle, surrey rntls; biz cntr; laundromat; laundry srvc; tennis crts; walking tr. Conference cntr. **Transportation** Boats and walkways: Epcot, Hollywood Studios. Buses: Magic Kingdom, Animal Kingdom, water parks, Dwntwn Disney. **Check In** 3pm for Inn, 4pm for Villas. **Check Out** 11am **Telephone** 407-939-5100.. **Fax** 407-939-5150. **Address** 2101 N. Epcot Resorts Blvd. **Parking** Free. **Disney Resort Category** Deluxe.

This small village of buildings is surrounded by water on three sides. The grounds include a hotel, timeshare property, a boardwalk of shops and restaurants and a conference center. Both Epcot and Disney's Hollywood Studios are 15 minutes away via shuttle boat or walkway.

Meant to resemble a 1940s New Jersey oceanside resort, the BoardWalk has the look of a community that has grown over time. Mom-and-pop shops have tucked themselves into residential buildings. "Newer" structures appear unrelated to their older neighbors. Still, everything blends together. Noted architect Robert A.M. Stern restricted his palette to American looks common before World War II. The resort opened in 1995.

All BoardWalk **rooms** are getting a nice makeover this year. Though they still have a classic Atlantic City look, the new furnishings include plush mattresses on wood-framed beds, a small sleeper sofa, a 32-inch plasma television and a small work desk with a pull-out side table. There's also new carpet, marble bathroom sinks and wall treatments with scenes of a vintage Disney World that never was. Fabrics have a sunny palette of blues, greens and yellows.

The refurbishment is being done gradually throughout 2009. If you get an old room, it will have white brass beds, a daybed, a small table and chairs and duller fabrics.

Suites are being redone as well. Two-story garden suites each have an individual front lawns with a white picket fence. Inside is a master bedroom upstairs with a king bed

and private bath with a whirlpool tub; a sleeper sofa and standard bath downstairs.

Most rooms and suites are spread out among two semicircular arcs of interconnected buildings. Some overlook the lake, though most face landscaped areas or pools.

The **Luna Park swimming pool area** has the Keister Coaster, a 200-foot water slide with small dips and sweeping turns. It looks like a 1920s wooden roller coaster. Nearby is a kiddie pool, **playground** and sunny hot tub. **Two quiet pools** are less crowded. Nicely landscaped, the Villas swimming pool has some shady lounging spots as well as an adjacent hot tub and large barbecue grill. Over on the Inn side is a lesser version of the same thing—smaller pool, fewer trees, no grill. The resort has **lighted tennis courts** and **bicycle and surrey rentals**.

Cast members organize **children's and family activities** such as Giant Jenga games and poolside bingo. A pontoon-boat adventure, the **Albatross Treasure Cruise** ($30, inc lunch, ages 4–12, 407-WDW-DINE) sails to Epcot. Nightlife includes **midway games** as well as the **Atlantic Dance Hall** (adults only) and dueling-piano bar **Jellyrolls** ($10 cover, adults only). **Street performers** (no charge) often work the 'walk, too.

A **conference center** (9,600 sq ft ballrm, 12 breakout rms) is Disney's smallest, though cushy carpets and floral wallpaper help it rival the Grand Floridian's for luxury.

Just off the lobby, **Dundy's Sundries** stocks resort logo apparel and toiletries. Outside,

Wyland Galleries offers bronzes, giclees, Lucites and other fine art. Most are from marine-life artist Robert Wyland; also represented is former Disney animation background artist James Coleman. Along the boardwalk, interconnected stores have groceries and housewares **(Screen Door General Store)**; children's wear and toys **(Disney's Character Carnival)**; and Disney sportswear and dress wear **(Thimbles and Threads)**. There's an **ESPN shop** at the ESPN Club.

Dining

BIG RIVER GRILLE & BREWING WORKS
★★★★ ✔ American $$$ L,D: $9–$31, 11:30am–11pm. Seats 190, inc 50 outside.

Sporting Walt Disney World's only micro brewery, this classy little bar and grill offers down-to-earth food at decent prices. The menu offers meats, pasta, salads, soups, sandwiches and seafood. Best bets include the zingy beer cheese soup and ale-marinated dry-rubbed pork ribs. Six hand-crafted beers range from light lagers to malty ales. A modern decor features high cherry chairs and gunmetal tables, which makes the place noisy when it's crowded. With a pair of flat-screen televisions, the small bar can be a less-crowded alternative to the ESPN Club (see below).

ESPN CLUB ★★★ Sports Bar $$ L,D: $12–$15, 11:30am–11pm. Seats 450.
Two restaurants in one, the ESPN Club combines a sports bar with a second room that hosts radio talk shows. It has 123 television monitors. Weekends are packed. During a major football game fans of competing teams mix in a face-to-face ruckus.

FLYING FISH CAFE ★★★ Seafood $$$$ D: $26–$42, 5:30–10pm. Seats 193. *Disney Signature*
Cramped, crowded and loud, the atmosphere at this pricey nightspot can interfere with the enjoyment of its food. Sit in the back for the nicest experience. Our favorite entree is the potato-wrapped snapper, a chunk of comfort food doused in a thick wine sauce. Some fish comes from greenhouses at the Land pavilion in Epcot.

SPOODLES ★★★★ ✓ Mediterranean $$$ B: $8–$13, 7:30am–11am. D: $15–$23, 5–10pm. Seats 205.
Wood floors, planked tables and an open kitchen lend an inviting atmosphere to this pleasant place, though it can get noisy when crowded. For breakfast try the eggs-and-roasted-vegetable flatbread cooked in a wood-burning oven, or The Italian, which lays two poached eggs on toasted focaccia bread and surrounds them with a spicy casserole. Dinner choices include pan-roasted snapper, sausage-and-mushroom rigatoni and steak kabobs, Spoodle's most popular item. The restaurant sells pizza (whole and by the slice) from a takeout window.

Also outside are a bakery, sweet shop and, at night, three snack stands.

An intimate 1930s-style lounge, the **Belle Vue Room** (B: pastries, coffee. Evening: mixed drinks. Comp. board games.) is furnished with sofas, chairs and small tables. Big Band tunes and old radio shows waft through the air.

FUN FINDS
❶ An antique miniature carousel comes to life in the lobby every half hour. ❷ Working mutoscopes in the right hall include "Cat in the Bag" with Felix the Cat and "The Golfer" with W.C. Fields. ❸ Photos of Miss Americas hang on the Seashore Sweets walls. ❹ The shop also has a Miss America crown, scepter, trophy and robe. ❺ A trumpeting elephant hides in the Luna Park grounds.

HIDDEN MICKEYS
❶ In the foyer, as a spot on the neck of a white carrousel horse. ❷ As a second spot on its rump. ❸ On the sign for Seashore Sweets, as a cloud to the top right of the left woman. ❹ As repeating red berries in the carpet in front of many elevators.

Caribbean Beach Resort

★★★★ ✓ $$ **Rates** $149–$274. **Location** Centrally located, between Epcot and the Pop Century Resort. **Distance to** Magic Kingdom: 5 mi. Epcot: 4 mi. Hollywood Studios: 3 mi. Animal Kingdom: 5 mi. Blizzard Bch: 3 mi. Typh'n Lgn: 1 mi. Dwntwn Disney: 2 mi. WW of Sports: 3 mi. **Size** 2,112 rms, 200 ac. **Rooms** 314 sq. ft. Sleep 4. 2 dbl beds (1 king opt), table, sm refrig, coffeemkr. Internet opt. Caribbean-themed decor. Accessed by outdoor walkways. **Amenities** 7 swm pools, 1 kiddie pool. Arcade; beach; bicycle, surrey rntls; pedal-, power- and sailboat rntls; guided fishing trips; gift shop selling groceries; laundromat; laundry srvc; 4 playgrounds; volleyball crt; walking tr. **Transportation** Buses: Disney theme parks, water parks, Dwntwn Disney. A separate shuttle circles within the resort (signs will say "Internal Resort Shuttle.") **Check In** 3pm **Check Out** 11am **Telephone** 407-934-3400. **Fax** 407-934-3288. **Address** 900 Cayman Way. **Parking** Free. **Disney Resort Category** Moderate.

This 200-acre property consists of six lodging centers that wrap around a 42-acre lake. Three miles of roads circle the complex; a 1.4-mile walkway lines the lake. In the middle is Old Port Royale, a dining, shopping and recreation center. Registration is in a separate building near the entrance.

Rooms have tropical interiors with light oak furniture and muted pastel or tan fabrics. New for 2009, 384 rooms within the Trinidad South Village area have been remodeled with a pirate theme. Beds resemble ships, dressers look like old crates and drapes are tattered sails.

The main **swimming pool** appears to sit within a stone fort. Cannons spray swimmers as they pass; a small slide has a 90-degree turn. The area has a large kiddie pool and small (and very public) hot tub. Each village has its own small **quiet pool**. There are **playgrounds** at the Barbados, Jamaica, Trinidad and Old Port Royale areas, and **hammocks** around the lake.

Daily **children's and family activities** include a 15-minute indoor limbo street dance at the Centertown food court at 12:15 and 5 p.m. The **Islands of the Caribbean Adventure Cruise** ($30 inc lunch, 2 hrs, children only, ages 4–10, 407-WDW-DINE) is a pontoon-boat treasure hunt.

Dining

SHUTTERS ★★★ Caribbean American $$$$ D: $17–$25, 5–10pm. Seats 132.

Rooms at Disney's Value and Moderate resorts (such as Caribbean Beach, above) are located in two-story buildings with outside halls

Carved out of a corner of the Centertown food court, three small dining rooms offer entrees such as char-crusted strip steak, pasta with chorizo and goat cheese and pineapple chicken served on a black bean paste. Though still cursed with Disney's most generic decor—the restaurant's walls are dotted with stamped metal pieces that look like they came from a Pier One sidewalk sale—Shutters is comfortable, with big fat chairs and big wood tables.
CENTERTOWN FOOD COURT B: $2–$8, 6:30–11:30am. L, D: $6–$15, 11:30am–11pm. Sm food store sells fruit, snacks. Room delivery for salads, pizza, desserts (4pm–11:30pm). Seats 500.

FUN FINDS
❶ Centertown appears to be an outdoor market. Its two-story walls are building facades with balconies, shuttered windows and thatched roofs. The blue ceiling is a sky.
❷ Concrete alligators and turtles hide in the beach sand and on the island.

Contemporary Resort

★ ★ ★ ★ ✔ $$$$ **Rates** $280–$835, suites $910–$2885. **Location** NW corner of WDW, east of Magic Kingdom. **Distance to:** Magic Kingdom: <1 mi. Epcot: 4 mi. Hollywood Studios: 4 mi. Animal Kingdom: 7 mi. Blizzard Bch: 5 mi. Typh'n Lgn: 6 mi. Dwntwn Disney: 7 mi. WW of Sports: 7 mi. **Size** 632 rms, 23 suites, 295 villas, 55 ac. **Rooms** 394 sq. ft. Sleep 5. 2 qn beds (1

king opt), daybed, table, sm refrig, coffeemkr. Flat-screen TV, PC w/ Internet access. Modern, elegant decor. Balcony or patio. Club lvl. **Suites** Sleep up to 8. **Villas** Sleep up to 12. **Amenities** 2 swm pools, kiddie pool, 2 hot tubs. Arcade; beach; beach volleyball; powerboat rntls; guided fishing trips; fitness cntr; gift shops (one selling groceries); hair salon; laundromat; laundry srvc; marina; massage svcs; walking tr; water sports. 24-hr rm srvc. Convention cntr.. **Transportation** Monorail: Magic Kingdom, Epcot, Grand Floridian, Polynesian resorts. Boats: Wilderness Lodge, Fort Wilderness resorts. Buses: Hollywood Studios, Animal Kingdom, water parks, Dwntwn Disney. Walkway: Magic Kingdom. **Check In** 3pm **Check Out** 11am **Telephone** 407-824-1000. **Fax** 407-824-3539. **Address** 4600 N. World Drive. **Parking** Free. **Disney Resort Category** Deluxe.

Completely remodeled over the past few years, this 1971 landmark is within walking distance of Magic Kingdom and fronts Bay Lake. Grounds include a central 15-story A-frame, a three-story detached wing and a new timeshare tower that opens in September, 2009. The distinctive A-frame features an indoor monorail station. A curvilinear Bay Lake Tower is connected to the main building by an elevated covered walkway.

The **Electrical Water Pageant** passes the resort nightly at 10:05 p.m. A 120,000-square-foot **convention center** (4 ballrms, 33 breakout rms,

The author's daughter jumps backward into the Contemporary's main swimming pool.

1,600 sq ft stage) includes space in the A-frame as well as a connected building.

Rooms have Asian-inspired decor, with simple white lighting fixtures offset against tan fabrics and dark woods. Each comes with a computer. A small table holds a flat-screen monitor; a roll-out side table adds space. Though cramped, the bathrooms are attractive, with swing-out makeup mirrors and marble baths. Rooms on higher A-frame floors have spectacular views, though many balconies extend just a few feet.

Sitting above the atrium, 14th-floor suites serve as convention hospitality rooms. The size of three standard rooms, one-bedroom suites include a six-seat living area, a six-person dining table, two baths and three balconies, one with a large table. Scandinavian decors have abstract lithographs.

Bay Lake Tower has 295 two-bedroom-equivalent villas. Most have flat-screen TVs, full kitchens with granite countertops, modern artwork and washers and dryers.

The main **swimming pool** has a 17-foot-high spiraling slide, a large central fountain and a row of smaller sprays. A **second pool** sits next to the lake. It's round, and gets deeper in its center instead of its side. The complex also has a kiddie pool, two hot tubs and a beach volleyball court.

Three shops sit on the A-frame's open fourth floor. Expansive **Bay View Gifts** stocks adult apparel, artwork, character merchandise, housewares, jewelry, watches and re-frigerated chocolates and fudge. **Concourse Sundries & Spirits** carries books, liquor, magazines, newspapers and snacks. **Fantasia** offers children's apparel, plushies and toys.

Built between 1969 and 1971 by U.S. Steel, the hotel was an experiment in modular construction. While its steel skeleton was assembled at the site, its rooms were built at a specially constructed factory three miles away. As each room moved down an assembly line, workers added in its electrical and plumbing systems, air conditioning units, ceiling, floor, wall coverings, bathroom fixtures and even furniture. An average of 15 rooms were completed a day. Once finished, the nine-ton units were trucked to the resort site, lifted by crane and slid into the steel structure, much like an oversized set of dresser drawers. The result? A real budget-buster. Though each room had been forecast to cost about $17,000, the actual amount was more than five times that much.

The top floor was originally a supper club. During the 1970s, performers in what is today the California Grill restaurant included crooners Lou Rawls and Mel Torme.

In the resort's most infamous moment, President Nixon spoke to the press in one of its ballrooms on Nov. 17, 1973. As part of his address, he proclaimed his innocence in the Watergate cover-up, declaring "I am not a crook."

Reflecting the American Southwest, the eight-story atrium mural was created in 1971 by Mary Blair, the artist known for the abstract sets of the It's A Small World attraction as well as the vivid backgrounds of the Disney films "Cinderella" (1950) and "Alice in Wonderland" (1951).

Dining

CALIFORNIA GRILL ★★★★★ ✔ New American $$$$
D: $26–$41, 5:30–10pm. Seats 156. *Disney Signature* Superb fare is matched by an entertaining view at this Disney landmark, perched atop the A-frame tower. Two long-time favorites are the grilled pork tenderloin with goat-cheese polenta and zinfandel glaze, and an oak-fired beef filet that's so tender you don't get a steak knife. Sushi is prepared by Okinawa native Yoshie Cabral. She's famous for her imaginative sauces and use of fruit.

The view is better than you'd expect, since the land is so flat. Sit along the west windows and before the sun sets you'll see the steam of the Liberty Square Riverboat off in the distance. Diners along the south wall look down at Epcot's Spaceship Earth. You can watch Magic Kingdom's Wishes fireworks show from inside the restaurant or on one of two rooftop walkways. To beat the crowd head to the northwest terrace 10 minutes early. All areas pipe in the show's synchronized soundtrack. Book reservations three months in advance for prime dining times; six months for parties of six or more.

CHEF MICKEY'S ★★★ Character buffets $$$$ **Mickey, Minnie Mouse; Donald Duck; Goofy; Pluto. B: $23 A, $13 C, 7–11:30am. D: $30 A, $15 C, 5–9:30pm. Seats 405.** These character experiences aren't worth it. Often there's only one character in each room, dividing his or her time among up to 100 diners. On the plus side, the costumes are cute—Mickey is a chef, the others cooks—the huge buffets are kept fresh and their choices include such goodies as peanut-butter-and-jelly pizzas for breakfast, prime rib and salmon for dinner. For the best time, dine at an unpopular time, such as 11 a.m. Reserve your table a month early. Expect to be asked to pose for an optional souvenir photo package when you check in.

THE WAVE ★★★★ ✔ American $$$$ **B: $8–$18, 7:30–11am. L: $12–$21, noon–2pm. D: $18–$29, 5:30–10pm. Lounge: noon–mid. Buffet, private rooms avail. for groups. Opened 2008. Seats 222 plus 100 in lounge.** Healthy entrees highlight this near-Signature dining spot, which is ideal for conventioneers but too upscale for some families. Breakfast has specialties such as smoked salmon as well as egg and griddle dishes. Lunch offers salads and sandwiches; dinner features meats, pasta and seafood. House-made dessert flights are intense. The calm decor has wavy lines in its ceiling, chairs and carpet; cylindrical salt and pepper shakers look like stainless steel hockey pucks. Southern hemisphere wines have Stelvin caps.
CONTEMPO CAFE Quick-service. Unavailable for preview at press time.

The **California Grill Lounge** (5pm–2am) adjoins the 15th-floor restaurant and shares its view. No reservations are necessary. **The Outer Rim Lounge** (noon–mid.; appetizers 4–10pm) overlooks the pool and Bay Lake. Both lounges offers specialty drinks and light appetizers. In the lobby, **Contemporary Grounds** (coffee drinks, pastries, beer wine) has a wide-screen television with Disney cartoons.

FUN FIND
One of the goats in the atrium mural has five legs. It's facing the monorail tracks at the height of the seventh floor.

Coronado Springs Resort

★★★★ $$ **Rates** $149–$345, suites $350–$1290.
Location Next to WDW's Western Way entrance.
Distance to: Magic Kingdom: 4 mi. Epcot: 3 mi. Hollywood Studios: <1 mi. Animal Kingdom: 2 mi. Blizzard Bch: <1 mi. Typh'n Lgn: 3 mi. Dwntwn Disney: 4 mi. WW of Sports: 5 mi. **Size** 1,877 rms, 44 suites, 125 ac. **Rooms** 314 sq. ft. Sleep 4. 2 dbl beds (1 king opt), table, sm refrig, coffeemkr. Newer rooms 2 qn beds (1 king opt), desk, flat-screen TV. Internet opt. Colorful decor in blue, yellow, red. Mexican art. **Suites** Sleep 4–6. **Amenities** 4 swm pools, kiddie pool, hot tub. Two arcades; bicycle, surrey rntls; kayak, pedal- and powerboat rntls; fishing trips, biz cntr; gift shop selling groceries; hair salon; laundromat; laundry srvc; marina; playground; volleyball crt; walking tr. Rm srvc. 7am–11pm. Convention cntr (86,000 sq ft exhbt hall, 60,000 sq ft ballrm, 45 breakout rms). **Transportation** Buses: Disney theme parks, water parks, Dwntwn Disney. **Check In** 3pm **Check Out** 11am **Telephone** 407-939-1000. **Fax** 407-939-1001. **Address** 1000 Buena Vista Drive. **Parking** Free. **Disney Resort Category** Moderate.

This Spanish Colonial resort is anchored by its El Centro complex, which holds its registration, dining and shopping spots as well as the convention center. Lodging areas circle outward around a 15-acre lagoon. Detailing includes arched doorways and windows, tile roofs and mosaic accents.

The spacious Rancho section of Coronado Springs sits at the rear of the resort

Adjacent to the convention center are the Casitas, with rooms in three- and four-story buildings. Halfway around the lagoon, the spacious Ranchos are two- and three-story buildings in a sagebrush, cactus and gravel landscape. Finally come the Cabanas, on the northern shore of the lagoon. These two-story buildings are fronted by a white-sand beach dotted with palms, many with swaying hammocks underneath. All rooms are accessed by outdoor walkways.

Rooms are being refurbished in 2009 with queen beds, desks, and flat-screen televisions. Fabrics are blue, green and yellow. Business Club Level rooms include DVD players and access to a lounge with continental breakfast, midday snacks and evening wine and cheese.

The centrally located Dig Site recreation center has a large **swimming pool** with a long, twisting slide that goes under a spitting jaguar and an ivy-covered footbridge. A statue blows a stream of water into the pool, while a waterfall flows into it off a four-story pyramid. A soft-surfaced **playground** has swings and a sandbox with hidden faux artifacts, a kiddie fountain pool, a 22-person hot tub, a sand **volleyball court** and an indoor arcade. The area imagines Francisco Vasquez de Coronado's discovery of a lost Mayan kingdom. Smaller **quiet pools** are located in each lodging area. Organized **children's activities** (daily, some have a small fee) include arts and crafts and pool games.

Panchito's Gifts & Sundries stocks apparel, Disney merchandise, snacks, souvenirs and toys as well as Southwestern Native American handicrafts. The store is themed to the 1944 movie "The Three Caballeros."

Dining

MAYA GRILL ★★★ American/Latin $$$$ **B:** $17 A, $10 C, 7–11am. **D:** $20–$34, 5–10pm. Seats 220.
The most straightfoward of Disney's convention restaurants offers familiar food in a comfortable atmosphere. Entrees are an expense-account mix of steaks, seafood, chicken and duck, all with just a touch of Latin flavor. The wine list includes selections from Argentina, Chile and Spain. Breakfast is an American buffet. Tables have metal tops with wood trim. Chairs are wide and nicely upholstered. The room has a three-story open ceiling.

CAFE RIX Fast food, pastries, gelato. **B:** $5–$7, 6:30–11am. **L,D:** $7–$11, 11am–mid.

PEPPER MARKET American/Mexican food court. **B:** $3–$9, 6–10:30am. **L,D:** $6–$22, 11am–11pm. Seats 420. This indoor area looks like an outdoor market. Food counters sit under tents; tables under awnings and umbrellas. A waiter gets your drinks, which results in an automatic 10 percent tip.

Upscale **Rix Lounge** (Specialty drinks. Tapas-style appetizers. 5pm–2am. Nightly DJ, live band some evenings. Private rm avail. Seats 220) has a $15 cover charge. VIP tables seating up to 12 have a $500 minimum charge.

HIDDEN MICKEYS
❶ Jutting out from a bolt, a detailed Mickey face is on the top left of the left door of the main entrance. ❷ As impressions in the sidewalk near the lamppost closest to the resort's boat and bike rental.

Fort Wilderness Resort & Campground

★★★★ ✔ $ campsites, $$$$$ cabins **Rates** Campsites $43–$116 per night, cabins $265–$410. **Location** NW corner of WDW, southeast of Magic Kingdom. **Distance to** Magic Kingdom: 2 mi. Epcot: 4 mi. Hollywood Studios: 4 mi. Animal Kingdom: 6 mi. Blizzard Bch: 4 mi. Typh'n Lgn: 6 mi. Dwntwn Disney: 6 mi. WW of Sports: 6 mi. **Size** 784 campsites, 409 cabins, 740 ac. **Campsites:** Level, paved pads with electric, water and sewer hookups, charcoal grills, picnic tables. (Partial hookups provide electricity and water only.) **Cabins:** 504 sq. ft. Sleep 6. A/C, full bathroom, vaulted ceilings, outdoor grill, full kitchen, picnic table, private patio deck, TV, VCR. **Amenities** 2 swm pools. Archery instruction; arcade; basketball, horseshoes, tennis, tetherball, volleyball courts; bicycle, surrey rntls; beach; carriage, wagon and trail rides; comfort stations; cane-pole fishing; dog park; electric golf cart rentals; fishing trips; gift shop with camping supplies, groceries; laundromat; playgrounds; pony rides; horseback rides; Segway tour; walking tr; watercraft rentals. **Transportation** Boats: Magic Kingdom. Buses: Theme parks, water parks, Dwntwn Disney. Int. shuttles. Electric golf carts: Available for rent for transportation around the property. **Check In** 3pm **Check Out** 11am **Telephone** 407-824-2900. **Fax** 407-824-3508. **Address** 3520 N Ft. Wilderness Trail. **Parking** Free. **Disney Resort Category** Moderate.

Tucked in a thick pine forest, Fort Wilderness is a community all its own. The registration building, parking lot and riding stables are at the entrance. From there, three roads branch off into 28 loops, each lined with campsites or cabins. There's a centrally located swimming pool and recreation area and a commercial "Settlement" area in back, alongside Bay Lake.

Cabins are up front, just inside the entrance. Each has over 500 sq. ft. of air-conditioned living space, and comes with a full kitchen, bathroom, private patio deck with outdoor grill and picnic table, and daily housekeeping service. Located at the ex-

treme eastern and western edges of the resort, **tent sites** come with water and electric, a combination known as partial hook-up. If you don't have a tent, Disney will rent you one for $30 a night. Designed for **recreational vehicles,** campsites with full hook-up (water, electric and sewer) are located in the center of the resort, and surround the recreation area. Usually the choice of large RV owners, preferred campsites (water, electric, sewer, cable and Internet) take up the back quarter of the resort. All trailer and RV sites are sandy, crushed-shell pads. Each has an adjacent charcoal grill and picnic table. All sites have close access to air-conditioned comfort stations with private showers, ice dispensers, laundromats, telephones and vending machines. Fort Wilderness is the only Disney resort that takes pets. They're allowed at select campsites, but not in cabins. The surcharge is $5 per day.

Fort Wilderness is in the middle of a two-year refurbishment. Premium campsites are getting large concrete pads for big RVs; cabins are getting new furniture, carpeting, fixtures and paint. Cable TV and Internet service are being installed everywhere.

With many organized outdoor activities, the resort makes it easy to get back to nature. Horse lovers can get their fill with **guided horseback rides** ($42. 45 min. Ages 9 and up, max weight 250 lbs, min height 48 in. Closed-toe shoes. No trotting. Reservations 407-WDW-PLAY.) through the woods and **pony rides** (a parent walks the pony. $4, cash only. Ages 2–8, max weight 80 lbs, max height 48 in. 10am–5pm daily, 407-824-2788). Walk through a **stable** to see the draft horses that work in Magic Kingdom or catch a blacksmith fitting horses with shoes. Ride a Segway X2 on the **Wilderness Back Trail Adventure Tour** ($85, 2 hr. Tues, Fri, Sat at 8:30am, 11:30am. Ages 16 and up. Weight 100lbs–250lbs. Starts from Mickey's Backyard BBQ pavilion. Reservations 407-WDW-TOUR. Same-day walk-up reservations at the marina.) **The Archery Experience** ($25, 90 min. Thurs, Fri, Sat, 2:45pm–4:15. Ages 6 and up. At the Bike Barn. Reservations 407-WDW-PLAY up to 90 days in advance) includes instruction.

The main **swimming pool** is getting a water slide, hot tub and children's splash zone. A smaller **quiet pool** is closer to the resort entrance, beside the Wilderness Cabins. Scattered throughout the camping loops are complimentary **playgrounds; basketball, horseshoes, tetherball** and **volleyball courts.** Hammocks are set up on a beach along the shores of Bay Lake.

Dogs can run free at a new **dog park.** Leashed dogs are allowed on golf carts.

The nightly **Chip 'n Dale's Campfire Sing-a-Long** is a 30-minute songfest followed by a Disney movie shown on an outdoor screen. There's a different movie each night. Kids and adults alike roast marshmallows over a fire pit and make s'mores. A snack bar sells supplies including roasting sticks, as well as hot dogs and beer.

An **exercise trail** along a paved and sand path is nearly a mile long. A 3/4-mile **nature path** winds along Bay Lake. Disney's **Electrical Water Pageant** passes Ft. Wilderness nightly at 9:45 p.m.

Two stores—**Meadow Trading Post** and **Settlement Trading Post**—stock camping supplies, groceries and souvenirs.

Dining

TRAIL'S END RESTAURANT ★ ★ ★ American buffet $$$$ B: $23 A, $13 C, 7:30–11am. L: $23 A, $13 C, noon–2:30pm. D: $30 A, $15 C, 4:30pm–9:30pm Sun–Thurs, 4:30pm–10pm Fri–Sat. Takeout service 4:30pm–10pm. Seats 192, 6 at bar.
The food is exactly what you want it to be: simple and hearty. Lunch and dinner serve the same fried chicken as the Hoop-Dee-Doo Revue next door. You eat off of metal plates and drink from jelly jars. With trophy heads, wagon-wheel chandeliers and a ceiling of white acoustical tile, the dining room is straight out of a 1960s Route 66 tourist trap.

Crockett's Tavern is in Pioneer Hall near the Trail's End Restaurant.

Since Fort Wilderness doesn't allow automobile traffic, many guests get around in electric carts

Dinner shows

HOOP-DEE-DOO MUSICAL REVUE ★ ★ ★ ★ Saloon show $$$$$ $51–$59 A, $25–$31 C, 2-hr shows at 5, 7:15, 9:30pm. Tues–Sat. Seats 360. At Pioneer Hall.
The food's nothing special, yet everyone swears by it. The songs and skits, if you analyze them like a cold-hearted guidebook reviewer, are never that funny, yet the whole room keeps laughing. Why? Because the good-natured spirit of this thing is just so contagious. Kids in particular love the rootin', tootin' troupe of six Wild West performers, as well as their frequent forays into the audience. The food is all-you-can-eat fried chicken, ribs, mashed potatoes and, if you want, unlimited draft beer. The handsome heartthrob, the dumb blonde, "Call me butter! I'm on a roll!"—nothing's changed in decades. And why should it?

MICKEY'S BACKYARD BARBECUE ★ ★ ★ Character country show, buffet $$$$$ Mickey Mouse, Minnie Mouse, Goofy, Chip 'n Dale. $45 A, $27 C. 2-hr shows at 6:30pm, 9:30. Thurs, Sat except during Jan, Feb. Seats 300. At the Settlement's outdoor pavilion.
Hosted by live performers Tumbleweed and Sarsaparilla Sal, this corny country music celebration is an acquired taste, but if you've taken a cotton to line dancing and your kids want to meet Mickey you may love it. Held in an outdoor pavilion, it includes a live band and line-dance instruction. The buffet offers

The Grand Floridian Resort recalls the stately Florida seaside resorts of a hundred years ago

pork ribs, chicken, corn on the cob, watermelon and beer. You share a long table with other guests. Arrive early for a good seat.

FUN FIND
A tree with a push mower embedded in its trunk sits off the walkway between the marina and Pioneer Hall, 100 feet off the lake.

Grand Floridian Resort and Spa

★★★★★ $$$$$ **Rates** $385–$970, suites $670–$2795. **Location** NW corner of WDW, near Magic Kingdom. **Distance to** Magic Kingdom: <1 mi. Epcot: 4 mi. Hollywood Studios: 5 mi. Animal Kingdom: 7 mi. Blizzard Bch: 5 mi. Typh'n Lgn: 7 mi. Dwntwn Disney: 7 mi. WW of Sports: 7 mi. **Size** 842 rms, 25 suites, 40 ac. **Rooms** 440 sq. ft. Sleep 5. 2 qn beds (1 king opt), daybed, table, sm refrig, coffeemkr. Wireless Internet opt. Lux. Victorian decor. Terraces. Club lvl. **Suites** Sleep 2–8. **Amenities** 2 swm pools, hot tub. Arcade; beach; power-, sailboat-, yacht rntls. biz cntr; childcare cntr; fishing trips; laundromat; laundry srvc; hair salon; fine shps; full-srvc spa; tennis crts; walking tr. Convention cntr. **Transportation** Monorail: Magic Kingdom, Epcot, Contemporary, Polynesian resorts. Boats: Magic Kingdom. Buses: Hollywood Studios, Animal Kingdom, water parks, Dwntwn Disney. **Check In** 3pm **Check Out** 11am **Telephone** 407-824-3000. **Fax** 407-824-3186. **Address** 4401 Grand Floridian Way. **Parking** Free. **Disney Resort Category** Deluxe.

Expensive and elegant, Disney World's flagship resort reflects old-money affluence—the spare cash of Yankee tycoons of a hundred years ago, a time when a young Walt Disney was shoveling snow on a cold Missouri farm. With its gabled roofs, clapboard siding and miles of moldings, scrolls and turnposts, the Grand Floridian brings that era back to life. A five-story atrium, the lobby is topped with three illuminated stained-glass domes. An afternoon grand pianist and retro orchestra entertain.

Rooms are situated in four detached buildings. Victorian decor includes light woods and fabrics, ceiling fans and marble-topped sinks. Each room has live plants and special touches such as iPod docks in clock radios.

A calm **swimming pool** sits in a central courtyard, surrounded by a kiddie pool and hot tub. A second **beachside pool**, however, is the family favorite. It has a swerving 181-foot slide that takes 12 seconds to travel, as well as a 20-foot waterfall that pounds you into submission if you stand under it. A fountain play area keeps little ones entertained; a "zero-entry" side welcomes wheelchair guests. Disney's **Electrical Water Pageant** passes by nightly at 9:15 p.m.

Two clay **tennis courts** ($8 per person, per hr, 407-621-1991) require reservations; lessons are available. **Junior tennis clinics** ($25 per child, 4pm ages 6–8, 5pm ages 9–12) are held daily.

An elegant **convention center** (40,000 sq ft of flexible, functional space; 2 ballrms; 16 breakout rms) sits next door. Also a short walk away, the European **Grand Floridian Spa** (407-824-2332) offers aromatherapy, body treatments, facials, massages and similar services, including some for couples and children.

Cast members organize complimentary **children's and family activities.** Kids bake cookies and other treats in the **Grand Adventures in Cooking** (Mouseketeer Club childcare center, $28, ages 4–10.). Princess Aurora attends **My Disney Girl's Perfectly Princess Tea Party** (Garden View Lounge, $250 for one adult and one child ages 3–11; add'l adults $85, add'l children $165; mornings), a formal affair hosted by an operatic storyteller. Girls take home an elaborate doll and other merchandise. A pontoon boat takes children on a treasure hunt in the **Pirate Adventure** ($30, ages 4–10.). A **Wonderland Tea Party** (1900 Park Fare, $40, ages 4–10; afternoons.) is hosted by characters from Disney's 1951 movie "Alice in Wonderland."

Off the lobby, the **Sandy Cove** shop stocks home decor items, gifts, snacks, stamps and CDs from musicians who perform at the resort. **Summer Lace** offers upscale women's resortwear, swimsuits, fragrances and Grand Floridian logo items. On the second floor are **Basin White** (bath and beauty supplies), **Commander Porter's** (men's designer clothing and dress wear, golf apparel, fragrances) and **M. Mouse Mercantile** (Disney souvenirs, children's apparel, pins, plushies and toys).

Dining

1900 PARK FARE ★★★★★ ✔ Character buffets $$$$
"Supercalifragilistic Breakfast" (Mary Poppins, Winnie the Pooh, Tigger, Alice, Mad Hatter); $19 A, $11 C, 8–11:30am. "Cinderella's Gala Feast" dinner (Cinderella, friends); $30 A, $15 C, 4:30–8:30pm. Seats 270.
Face characters make these meals truly entertaining. At breakfast, Alice romps up to greet kids even if they're not quite sure who she is ("They call me Alison," she confides). At dinner, Cinderella chats with little clones of herself while Prince Charming makes women blush as he proposes table by table. The 40-item buffets include rich lobster Benedict for breakfast, terrific prime rib for dinner. Though reservations for either meal can be hard to come by, breakfast has many no-shows.

CITRICOS ★★★★★ ✔ Mediterranean $$$$$ D: $22–$39, 5:30–10pm. Seats 190. *Disney Signature*
This white-tablecloth restaurant can be noisy, but it hardly matters. Its imaginative takes on chicken, pork and seafood steal your attention. Lit with a soft yellow glow, Citricos is lined with windows that overlook the main pool and marina.

GRAND FLORIDIAN CAFE ★★★★ American $$$$ B: $5–$11, 7–11am. L: $10–$21, 11:45am–2pm. D: $17–$28, 5–9pm. Seats 326.
This nice sunroom offers quality dining in a relaxing atmosphere. Some items, such as signature Boursin club sandwich, are too rich for some tastes, but the varied menus offer plenty of choices. Tall ceilings and terrazzo tables keep things comfortable, though a blinding sun pours in at breakfast.

NARCOOSSEE'S ★★★★★ ✔ Seafood $$$$$ D: $20–$55, 5–10pm. Seats 270. *Disney Signature*
This cozy place knows how to make fish fancy, whether it's salmon, scallops or signature crab-crusted halibut. Equally great are the tartare appetizers. Wood floors and ceilings look nice but keep the noise level high. The circular building sits over the Seven Seas Lagoon; its view of Magic Kingdom's Wishes fireworks show includes beautiful reflections in the water.

VICTORIA & ALBERT'S ★★★★★ Gourmet $$$$$ D: $125, $185 w/wine pairings (Chef's Table $175, $245 w/pairings). Two seatings. Formal dress. Harpist. Women receive roses. Private restroom. No children. Seats 90, inc. 10 at Chef's Table.
This formal restaurant tries to provide the best meal you've ever had, and even hip foodies concede it knows what it's doing. A six-course dinner matches your personal tastes. A Chef's Table option includes more courses, a kitchen tour and chat with cooks.

GASPARILLA GRILL AND GAMES Fast food. 24 hrs. Seats 150. Diners sit in an arcade.

The **Garden View Tea Room** (L: $14–$25. 2–6pm) offers hot teas, specialty coffees and champagne to top off its delicate tea sandwiches, scones and tarts, served on flowery china in an elegant setting. Many choices include three courses. A cozy lounge overlooking the gardens, **Mizner's Lounge** (5pm–mid Wed–Sun.) has a carved marble bar.

FUN FINDS
❶ Housekeepers twirl their way to work in a Courtyard Parasol Parade at 8 a.m. ❷ An afternoon grand pianist and retro orchestra entertain in the lobby. ❸ Disney's venerable Electrical Water Pageant passes behind the resort nightly.

HIDDEN MICKEYS
❶ As tan border designs on the lobby staircase carpet. ❷ As a white pattern on the tan wallpaper. ❸ As a painted hot-air balloon on the ceiling of the convention center rotunda.

The **Old Key West** Conch Flats community hall includes a gift shop, restaurant and marina

Old Key West Resort

★★★★ $$$$$ **Rates** $295–$1690. **Location** Between Downtown Disney and Port Orleans French Quarter Resort, in the eastern part of WDW. **Distance to** Magic Kingdom: 4 mi. Epcot: 2 mi. Hollywood Studios: 3 mi. Animal Kingdom: 5 mi. Blizzard Bch: 4 mi. Typh'n Lgn: 2 mi. Dwntwn Disney: 2 mi. WW of Sports: 3 mi. **Size** 531 villas, 74 ac. **Studios** 376 sq ft, sleep 4. **1-bedroom** 942 sq ft, sleep 4. **2-bedroom** 1,333 sq ft, sleep 8. **3-bedroom** 2,202 sq ft (2-story), sleep 12. All units furnished with table and chairs, coffeemkr, high ceilings, kitchen facilities, wet bar. Internet opt. Key West decor. Accessed from outdoor walkways. **Amenities** 4 swm pools, kiddie pool, 4 hot tubs. 2 arcades; bicycle, surrey rntls; pedal-, power- and sailboat rentals; bsktbll, shfflboard, three lighted tennis, volleyball cts; DVD rntls; guided fishing trips; fitness cntr; gift shop selling groceries; laundromat; laundry srvc; marina; massage svcs; 4 playgrounds; walking tr. **Transportation** Boats: Dwntwn Disney, Port Orleans French Qtr, Port Orleans Riverside, Saratoga Springs. Buses: Disney theme parks, water parks, Dwntwn Disney. Int'l shuttle bus. **Check In** 4pm **Check Out** 11am **Telephone** 407-827-7700. **Fax** 407-827-7710. **Address** 1510 N. Cove Rd. **Parking** Free. **Disney Resort Category** Disney Vacation Club Resort.

You know you're in Florida at this sprawling resort, which is landscaped with palms, pines and other native plants. Inspired by the state's Tropical Victorian architecture, buildings combine tin roofs with clapboard siding and gingerbread accents. Like other Disney Vacation Club (DVC) timeshare properties, it offers nightly rentals to the public as owner bookings permit. Two- and three-story lodging buildings cluster into small groups. A central community hall contains a registration area, restaurant, gift shop and fitness center. Pontoon boats shuttle guests to Downtown Disney and the Port Orleans and Saratoga Springs resorts.

Accommodations range from studios to three-bedroom units. Some overlook the Lake Buena Vista golf course. Decor features wicker and upholstered furniture and a peach-and-green color scheme.

A **swimming pool** has a slide that looks like a giant sandcastle. Nearby is a kiddie pool, playground and hot tub. Three **quiet pools** are scattered among the villages. Cast members organize daily **children's and family activities** including sandcastle building.

Conch Flats General Store stocks books, Disney merchandise, groceries, liquor, sundries and Old Key West logo merchandise.

Dining

OLIVIA'S CAFE ★★★ American $$$ B: $9–$12, 7:30am–10:30am. L: $10–$17, 11:30am–5pm. D: $16–$23, 5pm–10pm. Seats 156, inc 22 outside.
Though it looks tropical, this restaurant believes that when it comes to meals, tour-

ists like to stick to the stuff they know. Steak and prime rib highlight dinner. Want to eat like a real Floridian? Try the key lime pie.

GOOD'S FOOD TO GO Burgers, salads, sandwiches, desserts. 7:30am–10pm. Pizza, salads and dessert delivery 4 p.m. to midnight.

A tiny bar next to Good's, **The Gurgling Suitcase** has a few seats indoors and more outside. The lounge got its name from the days of Prohibition, when travelers coming to the United States from Cuba carried alcohol in the fake bottoms of valises.

HIDDEN MICKEY

As three seashell imprints in a walkway from Building 36 to its parking spaces.

Polynesian Resort

★★★★★ ✔ $$$$$ **Rates** $355–$895, suites $815–$2910. **Location** NW corner of WDW, south of Magic Kingdom. **Distance to** Magic Kingdom: 1 mi. Epcot: 4 mi. Hollywood Studios: 4 mi. Animal Kingdom: 6 mi. Blizzard Bch: 5 mi. Typhn Lgn: 6 mi. Dwntwn Disney: 6 mi. WW of Sports: 7 mi. **Size** 853 rms, 5 suites, 39 ac. **Rooms** 415 sq. ft. Sleep 5. 2 qn beds (1 king opt), daybed, table, sm refrig, coffeemkr. Internet opt. Flatscreen TV. Balcony or patio. Concierge lvl. Suites Sleep 4–9. **Amenities** 2 swm pools, kiddie pool, 2 hot tubs. Arcade; beach; surrey rntls; power-, sailboat rntls; childcare cntr; fishing trips; gift shop selling groceries; laundromat; laundry srvc; playground; fine shps; walking tr. Rm srvc. 6:30am–midnight. **Transportation** Monorail: Magic Kingdom; Epcot; Contemporary, Grand Floridian resorts. Boats: Magic Kingdom. Buses: Hollywood Studios, Animal Kingdom, water parks, Dwntwn Disney. **Check In** 3pm **Check Out** 11am **Telephone** 407-824-2000. **Fax** 407-824-3174. **Address** 600 Seven Seas Drive. **Parking** Free. **Disney Resort Category** Deluxe.

This tropical resort offers large rooms, two nice pools, four child-friendly dining options and a location that's just a seven-minute monorail ride from Magic Kingdom. A laid-back attitude permeates everything.

Torch-lit walkways wander through lushly landscaped grounds. A 40-foot-tall atrium lobby includes a rocky waterfall. The 11 lodging buildings are standard 1960s-style hotel buildings disguised by an abundance of exposed dark wood beams and trim.

Refurbished in 2006 and 2007, **rooms** feature hand-carved furnishings and flatscreen televisions. Batik-print bedspreads and drapes enhance the tropical theme. All are accessed by interior hallways.

Nestled against a simulated volcano, the main **swimming pool** is centrally located behind the lobby. Kids love standing underneath its waterfall and taking repeat trips down its slide—a slippery two-story tunnel with squirting water and eerie colored lights. Listen closely to hear the pool's underwater music. One end is a "zero-entry" gradual ramp for disabled users. Nearby is a kiddie sprinkler area. Tucked in to a lodging area, the smaller **East pool** is less crowded. Hidden behind its lounge chairs are six shady open huts, each with its own table and ceiling fan.

Complimentary **children's activities** are offered in the lobby and at the main pool most afternoons. A 1.5-mile-long **walking trail** circles past the lodging buildings and continues to the Shades of Green resort.

Evening activities feature a torch-lighting ceremony with a fire-baton twirler. It's held just outside the front doors. Later, a musician entertains in the lobby. Disney's Electrical Water Pageant passes the resort nightly at 9 p.m.

Three shops line the lobby. Decorated with 1,000-lb. Balinese tiki statues, **BouTiki** has apparel and swimwear for men and women and souvenirs. **Trader Jack's** carries Disney merchandise, food, liquor, magazines, newspapers, snacks and toys. **Wyland Galleries** features bronzes, giclees, Lucite pieces and other pricey fine art. Most are from marine-life artist Robert Wyland.

Dining

KONA CAFE ★★★ Pan Pacific American $$$$ **B:** $9–$14, 7:30am–11:30am. L: $11–$17, Noon–3pm. D: $16–$25, 5pm–10pm. Seats 163.

Originally a coffee shop, this high-ceilinged, carpeted room is open to the lobby atrium. Dotted with wood tables and a few half-booths, it's been upgraded over the years to a full-service restaurant. It serves a Pan-Pacific-flavored breakfast, lunch and dinner and offers 100-percent Kona coffee as well as a full bar. The best meal is breakfast. With nuts in the batter and a topping made of crushed pineapple, brown sugar and butter, the Macadamia-Pineapple Pancakes are so flavorful you don't need syrup. Though it has its fans, we say skip the Cafe's Tonga Toast. Two slices of battered, deep-fried, sugar-coated sourdough bread stuffed with a banana, it's basically just a huge doughnut. Prepared in a small show kitchen, desserts include a pecan-pie-like Chocolate-Macadamia Nut Tart, a Kilauea Torte "brownie volcano" that's filled with warm liquid chocolate and the Kona Kone, a va-

The Polynesian Resort's quiet East pool is lined with palms

nilla-and-chocolate ice cream waffle cone that's surrounded by a base of cotton candy and topped with a chocolate Mickey stick.

'OHANA Mickey and Friends Character Breakfast: ★★★★ Character breakfast $$$ Lilo, Stitch, Mickey Mouse, Pluto. $19 A, $11 C. 7–11am. **Dinner:** ★★★★ Buffet $$$$ $27 A, $13 C. 5–10pm. Seats 300. The restaurant is well known for its fun Mickey and Friends character breakfast. One of Disney's most popular character meals, this meal is a memorable time. The reason: kids here *love* Lilo and Stitch. Mickey and Pluto are just as friendly, but they're definitely second fiddle. Characters are always on the floor. Every hour the characters come together to lead a maraca-shaking parade around the room. The fixed "family-style" menu (all-you-can-eat but brought to your table) includes fresh-baked coconut-pineapple bread as well as scrambled eggs, sausage and bacon. Note: After you check in, a cast member will direct you to stand in a line to pose for an optional photo package ($32). You can skip it if you like.

Carnivores, come hungry for dinner. Long skewers of Polynesian-flavored meats and seafood are grilled over an open fire pit and then continually brought to your table at this all-you-can-eat dinner. They're served with Hawaiian-style appetizers, homemade bread, salads and vegetables. Overlooking the resort's pool and marina areas, some tables offer a distant view of the Magic Kingdom's Cinderella Castle.

SPIRIT OF ALOHA ★★★ Dinner show with Polynesian music, dancing $$$$$ $51–60 A, $25–$31 C. 2-hr shows at 5:15, 8pm. Tues–Sat. Seats 420. A dancing, drumming and musical tour of Hawaii, New Zealand, Samoa, Tahiti and Togo, this venerable dinner show features skimpy costumes and lots of booty shaking. An odd first half has corny jokes and sitcom-style skits. Kids learn the hula. The meal is an all-you-can-eat feast of pork ribs, chicken and rice. If you go, splurge for the front-of-the-house seats. Folks who sit in back have a hard time hearing.

CAPTAIN COOK'S SNACK COMPANY Fast food. 6:30am–11pm. Offers standard American choices plus flatbread and stir-fry dishes, sushi. Pineapple Dole Whip dessert.

In the lobby, the **Kona Island Cafe Coffee Bar** (pastries, coffee. 6:30am–4pm) transforms into the **Kona Island Cafe Sushi Bar** (pastries, coffee drinks. 5–10pm). The nearby **Tambu Lounge** (1pm–mid, at 'Ohana) has a large-screen television.

FUN FINDS
❶ A volcanic stream behind the Grand Ceremonial House appears to flow into the main swimming pool. ❷ Known affectionately as Auntie Kaui, the diminutive Hawaiian woman stringing leis in the lobby has been at her job since the resort's opening day in 1971. Before that she worked at Disneyland. She's really friendly.

A **water-play area** sits in front of a 1960s-themed building at Disney's Pop Century Resort

Pop Century Resort

★★★ ✔ $ **Rates** $82–$160. **Location** Centrally located in WDW, near Hollywood Studios and Wide World of Sports. **Distance to** Magic Kingdom: 6 mi. Epcot: 5 mi. Hollywood Studios: 3 mi. Animal Kingdom: 4 mi. Blizzard Bch: 4 mi. Typhn Lgn: 2 mi. Dwntwn Disney: 3 mi. WW of Sports: 2 mi. **Size** 2,880 rms, 177 ac. **Rooms** 260 sq. ft. Sleep 4. 2 dbl beds (1 king opt), table, coffeemkr. Internet access opt. Hair dryer, iron, ironing board avail. from housekeeping. Accessed by outdoor walkways. Rooms in the 1960s section ($10 surcharge) are closest to the bus stand, food court and lobby. 1950s rooms (no extra charge) are almost as close. **Amenities** 2 swm pools, 2 adj. kiddie pools. Arcade; gift shop selling groceries; laundromat; laundry srvc; playground; walking trl. **Transportation** Buses: Disney theme parks, water parks, Dwntwn Disney. **Check In** 3pm **Check Out** 11am **Telephone** 407-938-4000. **Fax** 407-938-4040. **Address** 1901 W. Buena Vista Dr. **Parking** Free. **Disney Resort Category** Value.

This good-natured complex gets knocked for its small rooms and lack of a real restaurant, but it has a lot to offer. A collection of four-story motel-style buildings situated around a central registration area and food court, Pop Century is certainly more tacky than similarly priced hotels outside Walt Disney World property, but it's also cleaner, better maintained, much better landscaped and, for Disney vacationers, far more convenient.

Compared to Disney's other Value property, the All-Star Resorts, Pop Century is newer, cleaner, less wooded but more nicely landscaped. The food court and gift shop are much better.

One other benefit: Pop Century has the best Disney bus service of any Walt Disney World resort, with nonstop routes to nearly all theme and water parks. Routes to Disney's Animal Kingdom and Downtown Disney are direct, though each have a stop along the way.

A celebration of American pop culture, Pop Century is grouped into five areas, each representing a decade from the 1950s to the 1990s. Decked out in pop-art color, the buildings are adorned with huge, decade-appropriate catchphrases and dozens of gigantic props, such as 41-foot Rubik's Cubes and 65-foot bowling pins. The registration area features 51 display cases filled with hundreds of cultural artifacts, everything from a 1955 Lionel accessories catalog to a 1998 Spice Girls videotape.

So what happened to the rest of the century? Simple: it's not done yet. Only half of Pop Century is finished, its 1950s–1990s "Classic Years" section. On the other side of the resort's 33-acre lake are a few half-completed buildings of the 1900s–1940s Legendary Years development, which has been put on hold.

Guest rooms are identical except for their location. Rooms in the 1960s section are closest to the bus stand, food court and lobby, but come with a $10 surcharge. 1950s rooms are almost as close. Pop Century's rooms are cheery for an economy resort, with pop-culture artwork, colorful bedspreads, dark carpet and light furniture with inlaid woods.

None of the three **swimming pools** have slides, but all are themed. The best is the 1960s Hippy Dippy pool, where four giant metal flowers spray swimmers with water. There's also a 1950s pool shaped like a bowling pin, and a 1990s computer pool (a rectangle) with a spongy keyboard deck. All have adjacent kiddie pools; the 1960s pool has an outdoor bar.

Other amenities include a nice Memory Lane **walking trail**. It's lined with signs that identify significant events of each year from 1950 to 1999.

A cheery **Everything Pop!** shop carries a standard collection of Disney souvenirs, snacks and sundries.

Dining

EVERYTHING POP! ✔ Food court. B: 6:30–11am. L,D: 11am–mid. Sm. food store sells fruit, snacks. Sm. bar has beer, mixed drinks. Room delivery for salads, pizza, desserts (4pm–mid). Seats 650.
Though the signature items at this comfy food court (located behind the similarly named gift shop) are certainly noteworthy—they include a 1960s-style TV dinner, Twinkie tiramisu and tie-dyed cheesecake—we say go for the more serious items such as fresh made-to-order salads and flatbreads. A carpeted dining area has many comfortable booths; a catchy soundtrack of songs can segue Van McCoy's "Do the Hustle" into "Fire" by Jimi Hendrix.

FUN FINDS
❶ A sticker on the giant Big Wheel states that the trike can accommodate a rider that weighs up to 877 pounds. ❷ The 1960s kiddie pool has a flower shower. ❸ Bowling lanes line each side of the bowling-pin pool. ❹ The adjacent laundry building looks like a bowling-shoe bin. ❺ A 1990s service building appears to be a stack of floppy disks. ❻ Cast members join together to do the Hustle every evening at 6 p.m. in front of the resort's check-in counter. ❼ One of the signs along the Memory Lane walking trail has its fact wrong. The St. Louis Gateway Arch opened in 1966, not 1961.

Port Orleans Resorts

★★★★ ✔ $$ Rates $149–$249. **Location** Northeastern WDW, near Downtown Disney. **Distance to** Magic Kingdom: 4 mi. Epcot: 2 mi. Hollywood Studios: 4 mi. Animal Kingdom: 6 mi. Blizzard Bch: 4 mi. Typhn Lgn: 2 mi. Dwntwn Disney: 2 mi. WW of Sports: 4 mi. **Size** 3056 rms, 325 ac. **Rooms** 314 sq. ft. Sleep 4 (some in Alligator Bayou have trundle beds, sleep 5). 2 dbl beds (1 king opt), table, sm refrig, coffeemkr. Internet opt. Accessed from outdoor walkways. **Amenities** Riverside: 1 swm pool, kiddie pool, 5 quiet pools. Arcade; bike; surrey rntls; pedal-, powerboat rntls; carriage rides (same-day reservations 407-824-2832); cane-pole fishing for bluegill, sunfish; guided fishing trips; laundromat; laundry srvc; marina; playground. French Quarter: 1 swm pool, hot tub, arcade, laundromat; laundry srvc; playground. **Transportation** Boats: Dwntwn Dsny, Old Key West Resort, Saratoga Springs Resort. Buses: Disney theme parks, water parks, Dwntwn Dsny. **Check In** 3pm **Check Out** 11am **Telephone** French Quarter: 407-934-5000. Riverside: 407-934-6000. **Address** French Quarter: 2201 Orleans Dr. Riverside: 1251 Riverside Dr. **Address** French Quarter: 407-934-5353. Riverside: 407-934-6000. **Parking** Free. **Disney Resort Category** Moderate.

Divided into two sections—Port Orleans French Quarter and Port Orleans Riverside—this relaxed property is themed to the Old South. Riverside buildings reflect Cajun retreats in its Alligator Bayou area, as well as stately Mississippi plantation homes in a Magnolia Bend section. Nestled alongside a peaceful canal, a central recreation and dining complex resembles a riverboat landing.

French Quarter, of course, is themed to New Orleans. A much smaller complex, it has intimate garden areas and lots of wrought-iron railings. French Quarter has a nice swimming pool and playground (see below), but no table-service restaurant. French Quarter guests are encouraged to use the amenities of Riverside, as long as they don't mind the ten- to 20-minute walk.

Rooms in Riverside's Alligator Bayou have a backwoods feel, with hickory furnishings, quilted bedspreads and trundle beds. Magnolia Bend rooms are more dignified, with cherry woods and tapestries, in buildings with elevators. French Quarter rooms have cherry woods, pastel bedspreads and dark blue carpet.

At Riverside, parents and children alike will enjoy the centrally located Ol' Man Island **swimming pool**. Surrounded by trees, it's plenty relaxing, and also has the most wa-

terfalls of any Disney pool and a swerving slide that dribbles water on those who go down it. An elaborate playground is nearby. Five unguarded **quiet pools** are scattered throughout Riverside.

Bayou Pirate Adventure ($30 inc lunch, 2 hrs, children only, ages 4–10, 407-WDW-DINE) is a pontoon-boat scavenger hunt that tells the tale of John Lafitte.

French Quarter has few amenities, though its Doubloon Lagoon **swimming pool** is fun for families. A slide goes down the tongue of Scales, a giant parade serpent that, if you look closely, is swimming through the surrounding walkways. Frolicking nearby is a comical band of fiberglass Mardi Gras alligators. One plays a water-gushing clarinet, another squirts a sax for tots in a kiddie pool, a third holds an umbrella that provides its own rain.

Each resort has its own store that stocks resort logo apparel, Disney merchandise, snacks, sundries and toiletries. At French Quarter it's **Jackson Square Gifts & Desires.** Riverside's shop is **Fulton's General Store.**

Dining

BOATWRIGHT'S DINING HALL ★★★★ ✔
Southern American $$$$ B: $9–$12, 7:30am–11:30am. D: $16–$30, 5pm–10pm. Seats 206. Riverside.
One of Walt Disney World's most underappreciated restaurants, Boatwright's has the look of a 19th-century boat shop, where

Port Orleans French Quarter

unseen workers have just taken a break from building a 46-foot cotton lugger. Shipbuilding tools line the walls, and some tables sit underneath the boat's wooden frame. The menu includes choices Yankees rarely see. Breakfast has soothing sweet potato pancakes, served with a honey-pecan butter so tasty you don't need syrup. Dinner features crawfish cakes and a terrific blackened snapper served on grilled grits. Sides include "Southern Greens," a Disney name for collards. The pecan pie is homemade. Wood tables sit on tile floors.
RIVERSIDE MILL Food court. B: 6–11am. L,D: 11am–mid. Sm. store sells fruit, snacks. Room delivery of salads, pizza, desserts 4pm–mid. Seats 550. Riverside. Resembling a cotton mill, this spacious area has a large water wheel with working gears.
SASSAGOULA FLOATWORKS & FOOD FACTORY Food court. B: 6–11am. L,D: 11am–mid. Sm. food store sells fruit, snacks. Room delivery of salads, desserts 4pm–mid. Seats 550. Riverside. Varied lunch and dinner menus include salmon, steak salads and deli sandwiches.

Port Orleans Riverside's **River Roost Lounge** (large-screen television. Adj. to Boatwright's) looks like a cotton exchange. French Quarter's **Scat Cat's Lounge** (main lobby) specializes in Hurricane drinks.

HIDDEN MICKEY
As a design on a Native American's sandal in the food court.

Spacious Saratoga Springs resembles a luxurious condominium complex

Saratoga Springs Resort & Spa

★ ★ ★ $$$$$ **Rates** $295–$1690. **Location** North of Downtown Disney, in the eastern part of WDW. **Distance to** Magic Kingdom: 5 mi. Epcot: 3 mi. Hollywood Studios: 4 mi. Animal Kingdom: 6 mi. Blizzard Bch: 4 mi. Typhn Lgn: 2 mi. Dwntwn Disney: 2 mi. WW of Sports: 4 mi. **Size** 828 villas, 65 ac. **Studios** 365 sq ft, sleep 4. **1-bedroom villas** 714 sq ft, sleep 4. **2-bedroom villas** 1,075 sq ft, sleep 8. **3-bedroom villas** 2,113 sq ft, sleep 12. All units furnished with table and chairs, coffeemkr, kitchen facilities. Internet opt. All units accessed from outdoor walkways. **Amenities** 4 swm pools, kiddie play area, 4 hot tubs. Arcade; bicycle, surrey rntls; bsktbll, shffleboard, 3 lighted tennis, volleyball cts; DVD rntls; fitness cntr; gift shop w/groceries; Lake Buena Vista 18-hole golf course; laundromat; laundry srvc; 2 playgrounds; full-service spa; walking tr. No room srvc; opt. grocery delivery srvc. **Transportation** Boats: Dwntwn Disney, Port Orleans French Qtr, Port Orleans Riverside, Old Key West. Buses: Disney theme parks, water parks, Dwntwn Disney. Internal shuttle bus. **Check In** 4pm **Check Out** 11am **Telephone** 407-827-1100. **Fax** 407-827-1151. **Address** 1960 Broadway. **Parking** Free. **Disney Resort Category** Disney Vacation Club Resort.

This spacious upscale condo complex sits on the grounds of the former Disney Institute. Focusing more on adults than families, the grounds include a spa, the Lake Buena Vista golf course and a clubhouse restaurant. Nightly rentals are usually available.

Lodging buildings cluster into five sections that horseshoe around a registration and recreation center. **Accommodations** range from studio apartments to a four-bedroom Grand Villa. Studios include a queen bed and full-size sleeper sofa. Larger units have whirlpool tubs. Decor features large, masculine furniture. A new Treehouse Villas sections opens in the summer of 2009. Elevated ten feet off the ground, 60 stand-alone condos nestle in individual trees. Each has three bedrooms, two baths and can accommodate nine guests. Niceties include cathedral ceilings, granite countertops and flat-screen televisions.

Pontoon boats shuttle guests to Downtown Disney and the Port Orleans and Old Key West resorts.

The main **swimming pool** has a short, dark slide and an interactive fountain. It often shows Disney movies at night. Nearby is a kiddie pool, playground and hot tub. Three **quiet pools** are scattered in lodging areas. The **Saratoga Springs Spa** (407-827-4455) offers facials, manicures, massages, pedicures and many relaxing treatments. Its French whirlpool has 72 jets. Cast members organize daily **children's and family activities** at the Community Hall, such as arts and crafts sessions, bingo and ice-cream making.

The **Artist's Palette** gift shop stocks logo and resort apparel, books, Disney character merchandise, groceries, magazines, newspapers, plushies, souvenirs, snacks and sundries.

Dining

TURF CLUB BAR AND GRILL ★★★★ ✔ American $$$ B: $8–$13, 7:30am–11am. L: $8–$13, 11am–5pm. D: $15–$23, 5–9pm. Seats 146, inc 52 outside. Gourmet food at good prices makes this cozy country-club retreat worth seeking out. Lunch attracts golfers, as the restaurant is directly above the pro shop of the Lake Buena Vista course. Dinner has good steaks. The waiting area includes a walk-up bar (B pastries, coffee. Comp. board games) and billiards table. An outdoor balcony overlooks the golf course, a small lake and Downtown Disney.

THE ARTIST'S PALETTE ✔ Food court. B: 7:30am–11am. L,D: 11am–11pm. Store has fruit, snacks. Seats 112. This calm and comfortable eatery offers unusual items for a fast-food spot, including flatbreads for breakfast, lunch and dinner. Many items are made to order; to save time pay for your food while it's being prepared. A nice dining area has padded booths as well as drawing easels for children.

HIDDEN MICKEY
As a white design at the bottom of the signs outside of the spa.

Shades of Green

★★★★★ $ Rates $93–$141, suites $117–$275. **Location** NW corner of WDW, SW of Magic Kingdom. **Distance to** Magic Kingdom: <1 mi. Epcot: 4 mi. Hollywood Studios: 4 mi. Animal Kingdom: 7 mi. Blizzard Bch: 5 mi. Typh'n Lgn: 6 mi. Dwntwn Disney: 7 mi. WW of Sports: 7 mi. **Size** 575 rms, 11 suites, 29 ac. **Rooms** 455 sq. ft. Sleep 5. 2 qn beds (1 king opt), daybed, table, 4 chairs, sm refrig, coffeemkr. Internet opt. Balcony or patio. Light oak woods. Suites Sleep 6–8. **Amenities** 2 swm pools, kiddie pool, hot tub. 2 arcades; child-care cntr; fitness cntr; AAFES general store selling groceries; gift shop; laundromat; laundry srvc; Kodak photo-taking service; playground; remote-control boats; 2 tennis courts. Golf courses next door. 1,000 sq ft meeting space. Room service bkfast, dinner. **Transportation** Buses: Disney theme parks, water parks, Dwntwn Disney. **Check In** 3pm **Check Out** 11am **Telephone** 407-824-3600. **Fax** 407-824-3460. **Address** 1950 W. Magnolia Palm Drive **Parking** Free. **Resort Category** Armed Forces Recreation Center.

Exclusively for use by active and retired members of the U.S. military and their families, this relaxed resort is the only Armed Forces Recreation Center in the continental United States. Comparable in scope to a Disney Deluxe Resort, it features large rooms, full-service restaurants and a great location. Not far from Magic Kingdom, it sits directly across from Disney's Polynesian Resort and within Disney's main golf complex. Surrounding the resort are Disney's Palm, Magnolia and Oak Trail courses.

Room rates offer the best bargains in Walt Disney World. Though they're adjusted on a sliding scale, with prices increasing with rank and pay grade, even the highest rates are little more than those at Disney's Value Resorts. Eligible guests and their dependent spouses can each "sponsor" up to three rooms at a time, so groups of friends and family members can stay together.

Shades of Green has three restaurants—the **Garden Gallery** (Buffet, B $8–$14, D $10–$16), **Evergreens Sports Bar & Grill** (L,D $8–$14) and **Mangino's** (Northern Italian, D $13–$25). For counter service there's the **Express Cafe** and **America, The Ice Cream Parlour.** Cocktails are at the **Eagle's Lounge.** Room service is available for breakfast and dinner.

The resort offers discounted Walt Disney World park tickets to eligible members of the military, including those who don't stay at the property. Located to the right of the main lobby, the ticket office is open daily from 8 a.m. to 9 p.m. A special $55 golf rate is available for tee times after 10am that are booked at least 24 hours in advance.

Originally, Shades of Green was the Disney Golf Resort, a country club with no guest rooms. In 1993 Disney expanded the property and renamed it the Disney Inn. Disney sold the complex to the government in 1996. It was enlarged again in 2004. The name of the resort refers to that fact that, regardless of branch of service, all U.S. military standard uniforms have some shade of green.

FUN FIND
Near the back gazebo, a "Remember the Fun" walkway is lined with bricks engraved with the names and messages from previous guests. One brick is engraved with, of all things, the logo for Universal Studios Florida. Needless to say, it's the only Universal logo at Walt Disney World.

HIDDEN MICKEY
As the Millpond Pool.

Walt Disney World Swan & Dolphin Resort

★ ★ ★ ★ $$$$$ **Rates** $279–$555, suites $785–$3500. **Location** Centrally located, just north of Hollywood Studios. **Distance to** Magic Kingdom: 4 mi. Epcot: 3 mi. Hollywood Studios: 2 mi. Animal Kingdom: 4 mi. Blizzard Bch: 2 mi. Typhn Lgn: 2 mi. Dwntwn Disney: 3 mi. WW of Sports: 4 mi. **Size** 2,265 rooms, 191 suites on 87 acres. **Rooms** 360 sq. ft. Sleep 5. 2 dbl beds (Swan 2 queen) (1 king for handicapped accessible rooms), 32-in flat-panel LCD HDTV, desk w/work area, coffeemkr. Internet opt. "Heavenly" beds have pillow-top mattresses, white goose-down comforters. Club lvl. **Suites** Sleep 5–10. **Amenities** 5 swm pools, kiddie pool, 5 hot tubs. 2 arcades; basketball courts; beach; beach volleyball; biz cntr; pedal-boat rntls; child-care cntr; fitness cntr; hair salon; laundromat; laundry srvc; massage svcs; playground; fine shops; full-service spa; 4 tennis crts. 24-hr rm srvc. Miniature golf across street. 254,000 sq ft convention cntr. **Transportation** Boats: Epcot, Hollywood Studios. Buses: Magic Kingdom, Animal Kingdom, water parks, Dwntwn Disney. **Check In** 3pm **Check Out** 11am **Telephone** Dolphin: 407-934-4000 Swan: 407-934-4499. **Fax** Dolphin: 407-934-4884 Swan: 407-934-4710. **Address** Dolphin: 1500 Epcot Resorts Blvd. Swan: 1300 Epcot Resorts Blvd. **Parking** Self-parking $9 per day; valet parking $12 per day, $16 overnight plus tip **A Starwood resort**

These adjacent convention resorts are the signature properties of Starwood Hotels, a company that includes the Sheraton and Westin chains. Though both are popular with business travelers, the Swan is quiet and intimate while the Dolphin, with twice as many rooms and a large convention center, is often boisterous and impersonal.

Designed by Michael Graves, perhaps best known for his line of housewares sold at Target stores, the Swan and Dolphin feature one of the best known examples of postmodern "entertainment" architecture—a playful building style meant to stimulate the imagination through the use of details such as enormous statues and fountains. The tallest structure at Walt Disney World, the Dolphin's 27-story triangular tower sits between two wings topped with 20-foot tulip fountains and 56-foot statues of dolphinfish, or mahi mahi. In back, a nine-story waterfall cascades down giant clamshells.

The 12-story Swan has two seven-story wings crowned with 47-foot swan statues. Its wings have 20-foot clamshell spouts.

The buildings are connected by a palm-lined promenade that splits a lagoon.

Seen together, abstract designs on the buildings define the Dolphin as a tropical mountain surrounded by huge banana palms. Its waterfall splashes into the lagoon and onto the Swan, a huge sand dune.

Rooms feature pale woods, muted floral carpeting and pastel drapes. Maple bureaus have frosted glass accents. The rooms are especially well-lit.

An elaborate **swimming area** stretches in an arc between the two resorts. Its meandering Grotto pool features a huge waterfall and a decent slide. A row of tiny waterfalls splashes near a volleyball net that extends over a narrow area. During the summer, the pool shows a Disney movie every Saturday night, and hands out tubes for guests to float on as they watch it. The area also includes a spring pool, kiddie pool and two lap pools. A circus-themed beach area includes two volleyball nets, a basketball court, and a boat-like playground piece with covered slides. Kids will love finding the statue of a seal that sprays water out of its nose.

The resorts turn off their fountain and statue lights during Epcot's IllumiNations fireworks (nightly 9pm), which is visible from the walkway between the resorts.

The Dolphin's Asian-inspired **Mandara Spa** specializes in Balinese massage and includes a hair and nail salon. Two serene interior gardens help spa guests relax before treatments.

The Swan has a Disney store, **Disney's Cabanas**, with character merchandise, apparel and souvenirs.

The Dolphin has seven shops. A poolside beach kiosk, the **Cabana Beach Hut** stocks sunscreen and other pool essentials. Similar to Disney's Cabana's, **Daisy's Garden** is the Dolphin's Disney store, as well as the place to buy postage stamps. **Galleria Sottil** displays pricey original paintings and sculptures, many by artist Luis Sottil. **Lamont's** carries ladies resortwear, Ralph Lauren swimwear and Brighton accessories. **Mandara Spa** sells professional spa products and salon accessories such as curling irons. Candy store **Sugar3** tempts with chocolates and other sweets, many sold by weight.

The **Picabu** restaurant (see below) includes a small 24-hour convenience store with light groceries, medications, snacks and toiletries.

The Dolphin's **convention center** (254,000 sq ft convention/exhibit space, 4 ballrooms, 9,600 sq ft ballrm, 84 breakout rms) is Disney's largest.

The Swan and Dolphin (above) are world-famous examples of fanciful "entertainment" architecture

Dining

FRESH MEDITERRANEAN MARKET ★★★
American/Mediterranean $$$ **B: $18 A, $11 C, 7:30am–11am.
L: $14–$24, 11am–3pm. Seats 264. Dolphin.**
Try the gray stuff; it's delicious! A fresh juice bar mixes up a gray-colored Wheatgrass juice for breakfast that really does taste great. A breakfast buffet has roasted meats, griddle items, pastries and hot cereals. Lunch is a la carte, with a limited variety of Mediterranean-inspired salads, sandwiches, chicken, fish and pasta. For a peaceful dining spot ask to sit in the back verandah.

GARDEN GROVE CAFE ★ American $$$$ **B
weekdays: $17 A, $11 C, 6:30am–11am. B weekends:
$19 A, $12 C, 6:30am–11am. Characters come out at
8am. L: $11–$22, 11am–3pm. D: $29 A, $13 C, 5:30–
10pm. Seats 150. Swan.**
A circular dining room places you under a huge rotunda, surrounded by green walls dotted with murals of apple trees. Some tables tuck under a central tree. But though it is pretty, this is the worst table-service restaurant on Disney property. We always leave disappointed. Weekend breakfasts and all dinners have Disney characters. On Saturday mornings Goofy and Pluto appear; on Sundays Chip 'n Dale join them. Rafiki and Timon greet guests Monday and Friday evenings; Goofy and Pluto on other nights. Though the characters are sweet, the buffets still generate more customer complaints than any other Swan or Dolphin meal.

IL MULINO NEW YORK TRATTORIA ★★★★
Italian $$$$$ **D: $16–$45, 5–10pm. Seats 224. Swan.**
Many New Yorkers consider the original Il Mulino the best Italian restaurant in New York City, and this branch is right with it. A variety of Abruzzi entrees are highlighted by creamy risottos and good seafood. Unlike the original, this Il Mulino has a relaxing atmosphere and attentive service.

KIMONOS ★★★★ ✔ Sushi bar $$ **D: $4–$24, 5pm–
mid. Seats 105. Swan.**
More bar than restaurant, this friendly, dark little spot combines karaoke sing-a-longs with hot and cold sake, plum wines, Japanese beers and over 50 sushi and sashimi creations. There's also red-bean and green-tea ice cream. Additional options are available for children. Colorful kimonos hang from the ceiling.

SHULA'S STEAK HOUSE ★★ Steakhouse $$$$$
D: $23–$75, 5–10pm. Seats 215. Dolphin.
Big steaks for big bucks, for big hats with no cattle. This testosterone-fueled spot suckers in guys willing to spend madly for anything to make them feel manly. As you arrive you're greeted by a young babe in a short black dress, who, if you want her to, will sell you an autographed Don Shula football for $400. The dames disappear once you're seated. Ridiculously overpriced, steaks are good but not at the level of the less expensive Yachtsman Steakhouse at

Disney's Yacht Club Resort, just a short walk away. The clubby decor commemorates Shula's 1972 undefeated season as coach of the Miami Dolphins.

TODD ENGLISH'S BLUEZOO ★★★★ Seafood $$$$$ D: $27–$60, 5–10pm. **Seats 400. Dolphin.**
This high-style nightspot is all about the show. Designed to look as if it's underwater, a beautiful dining room has glass "bubbles" hanging overhead, animated ambient blue lights and throbbing techno music. Buried under it all is a coastal cuisine that unfortunately suffers from a style-over-substance mindset. Desserts are the same chocolate and fruit creations you'll find at any upscale restaurant. Many appetizers, however, are outstanding, rivaling those of Narcoossee's at Disney's Grand Floridian Resort.

THE FOUNTAIN ★★ Soda shop $$ L,D: $7–$15, 11am–11pm. **Seats 58. Dolphin.**
This classy soda fountain offers an uninspired menu of sandwiches, salads and ice cream. Service can be slow.

CABANA BAR AND BEACH CLUB Daytime grill, nighttime bar. Dolphin.
Featuring an illuminated bar, this new sophisticated spot next to the Dolphin lap pool offers everything from seared tuna to hot dogs. Exotic woods and billowing wall coverings frame intimate seating areas.

PICABU ✔ Cafeteria. B: 6:30am–11am (noon Sun). **L,D: 11am–1:30am. 24 hrs. Seats 140. Dolphin.**
Hidden behind Fresh Mediterranean Market, this nice cafeteria offers honest food and attentive service, in a clean, comfortable atmosphere that's surprisingly artistic. Columns are trimmed with figures of dancing men who have huge holes where their hearts should be, while back walls portray a trail of tail feathers left by a small bird who flew down from the ceiling. As you ponder what it all means, eclectic tunes from artists such as David Bowie and Lou Reed fill the air.

The Swan has one cocktail spot **(Il Mulino Lounge)**; the Dolphin three. A **Lobby Lounge** serves coffee and pastries in the morning, a full bar in the evening. **Shula's Lounge** has lots of leather armchairs and plenty of sports coverage on its large-screen TVs. **Todd English's bluezoo Lounge** offers a signature Zooberry martini—fresh blueberries are steeped for three days, then infused into vodka with a splashes of fresh lemon juice and rock candy syrup.

FUN FIND
A fiber-optic shooting star traces its path in the curved ceiling of the Dolphin foyer.

Wilderness Lodge

★★★★★ ✔ $$$$ **Rates** $240–$620, suites $525–$1405, villas $325–$1155. **Location** NW corner of WDW, southeast of Magic Kingdom. **Distance to** Magic Kingdom: 1 mi. Epcot: 3 mi. Hollywood Studios: 4 mi. Animal Kingdom: 6 mi. Blizzard Bch: 5 mi. Typhn Lgn: 5 mi. Dwntwn Disney: 5 mi. WW of Sports: 7 mi. **Size** 701 rms, 27 suites, 136 villas, 65 ac. **Rooms** 344 sq. ft. Sleep 4. 2 qn beds (1 king opt), daybed, table, sm refrig, coffeemkr, flat-screen TV. Internet opt. Balcony or patio. Club lvl. **Suites** Sleep 4. Villas Sleep 4–8. **Amenities** 2 swm pools, kiddie pool, 3 hot tubs. Arcade; beach; bicycle, surrey rntls; pedal-, power-, sailboat rntls; child-care cntr; guided fishing trips; fitness cntr; shop w/ groceries; laundromat; laundry srvc; playground; walking tr. Rm srvc. 7am–11am; 4pm–mid. Meeting room. **Transportation** Boats: Magic Kingdom, Contemporary Resort, Fort Wilderness. Buses: Theme parks, water parks, Dwntwn Disney. **Check In** 3pm for Lodge, 4pm for Villas. **Check Out** 11am **Telephone** Lodge: 407-824-3200, Villas: 407-938-4300. **Fax** 407-824-3232. **Address** 901 Timberland Drive. **Parking** Free. **Disney Resort Category** Deluxe.

This 'Faithful homage to American Western lodges is isolated yet convenient, a child favorite yet romantic, luxurious yet pomposity free. Nestled in a forest along the shores of 450-acre Bay Lake, the four-building complex consists of a central eight-story lodge and three guest wings, one of which is a Disney Vacation Club timeshare property.

Re-creating the geysers, tall timber and Lincoln-Log-like retreats of the American West, the property recalls in particular the Old Faithful Inn at Yellowstone National Park. A towering lobby atrium is dominated by four 60-foot bundled log columns which appear to support a wood truss. Viewed from bottom to top, the layers of a three-sided stone fireplace illustrate the geological history of the Grand Canyon.

Refurbished in 2006, **rooms** are decorated with vibrant quilts, plaid drapes, mission-style furniture and handcrafted embellishments. Native American and wildlife motifs accentuate a log-cabin ambience. Bathrooms have separate vanities with double sinks. An adjacent five-story tower houses the timeshare units, available to the public as owner use permits. They include studios, one- and two-bedroom units.

Portrayed as part of a mountain stream, a large **swimming pool** features a curving slide that sprays riders with mist. Nearby are two hot tubs, as well as a geyser that erupts on the hour. The Villas has a smaller **quiet pool** with four bubbling "springs" and an adja-

The Wilderness Lodge swimming pool sits behind the Lincoln Log-style resort

cent 15-person whirlpool. A wooded .75-mile **walking trail** leads to Fort Wilderness.

Cast members hold complimentary children's and family craft activities from 2:30–4 p.m. at the Cub's Den child-care center. Disney's Electrical Water Pageant passes the resort nightly at 9:35 p.m.

Just off the lobby, **Wilderness Lodge Mercantile** stocks resort logo apparel and merchandise, sundries, toiletries and toys. Twelve-inch souvenir totems replicate the 12-foot pole that stands in front of the store. Its figures include Mickey Mouse, Donald Duck, Goofy and the rarely seen 1950s Disney character Humphrey the Bear.

Dining

ARTIST POINT ★★★★ ✔ Pacific Northwest $$$$$ **D:** $26–$50, 5:30–10pm. **Seats 225.** *Disney Signature*
This pretension-free dining room specializes in creative offerings that never get too trendy. Entrees are seriously Northwestern, but so well-prepared that anyone will find something to love. The wine list has bottles from Washington State and Oregon. The L-shaped dining room mixes landscape murals with blond and cherry woods. Chairs are upholstered.

WHISPERING CANYON CAFE ★★★★ ✔ American barbecue $$$ **B:** $8–$14, 7:30–11am. **L:** $10–$16, noon–3pm. **D:** $14–$25, 5–10pm. **Seats 281.**
All-you-can-eat skillets are a specialty at this rowdy family favorite. During busy times the servers' hijinks become a free floor show. When my husband once scarfed one of our daughter's french fries, our cowgirl server yelled "Everyone! Repeat after me: 'Hey dad! Eat your own stinkin' food!'"

ROARING FORK SNACKS American fast food with grill, pizza, salads, sandwiches. **B:** 7–11am. **L,D:** 11am–11pm. 24 hrs. **Seats 250.**

Next to Artist Point, the **Territory Lounge** (4:30–11:30pm) features microbrewed beers.

FUN FINDS

❶ Hoof prints are embedded into most of the sidewalks. Buffalo prints lead to the front lawn's buffalo topiaries. ❷ The fourth-floor balcony has a few rarely used sitting areas, as well as a front and back porch. The fifth floor has a small back balcony.

HIDDEN MICKEYS

❶ As three stones above and to the right of the lobby fireplace. ❷ Behind the main building, as lumps of earth about a third of the way up a stream that flows from the geyser by the pool. ❸ As nuts in a small bulletin board at the entrance to Roaring Fork Snacks. ❹ As leaves in the wallpaper in the guest room hallways. ❺ As dents in the wood on a beam to the right of the exit to the Boat and Bike Rental. ❻ As dents in the wood on the second closest post to room 4035 and ❼ on the post closest to room 5066.

Yacht & Beach Club

★ ★ ★ ★ ★ ✔ $$$$$ **Rates** $335–$780, suites $580–$2725, villas $335–$1175. **Location** Centrally located at WDW, east of Epcot. **Distance to** Magic Kingdom: 5 mi. Epcot: 4 mi. Hollywood Studios: 2 mi. Animal Kingdom: 5 mi. Blizzard Bch: 3 mi. Typh'n Lgn: 3 mi. Dwntwn Disney: 3 mi. WW of Sports: 5 mi. **Size** 1197 rms, 112 suites, 208 villas. **Rooms** 381 sq. ft. Sleep 5. 2 qn beds (1 king opt), some have daybeds, table, sm refrig, coffeemkr. Internet opt. Club lvl. **Suites** Sleep 4–8. Villas Sleep 4–8. **Amenities** 3-acre swimming area, 2 kiddie pools. Arcade; beach volleyball; powerboat rntls; biz cntr; child-care cntr; guided fishing trips; hair salon; laundromat; laundry srvc; marina; massage svcs; fine shops; lighted tennis crt, croquet crt; walking tr. 24-hr rm srvc. Convention cntr. **Transportation** Boats, walkway: Epcot, Hollywood Studios. Buses: Magic Kingdom, Animal Kingdom, water parks, Dwntwn Disney. **Check In** 3pm **Check Out** 11am **Telephone** Beach Club Inn: 407-934-8000. Beach Club Villas: 407-934-2175. Yacht Club: 407-934-7000. **Fax** Beach Club: 407-934-3850. Yacht Club: 407-934-3450. **Address** Beach Club: 1800 Epcot Resorts Blvd. Yacht Club: 1700 Epcot Resorts Blvd. **Parking** Free. **Disney Resort Category** Deluxe.

This two-in-one resort has a great location on Crescent Lake, within walking distance of Epcot. Disney's Hollywood Studios is only a boat ride away, as are the BoardWalk and Swan and Dolphin resorts.

From the outside the resorts look similar. Five-story, nautical-themed compounds with clapboard trim, both are meant to evoke summer homes of an 1870s Martha's Vineyard and Nantucket. The stately Yacht Club is trimmed with heirloom statues, gold-fringed drapes and red-white-and-blue carpet that seems straight from the Hall of Presidents. The Beach Club, by contrast, is cool and relaxed. It looks like the cover of a magazine—specifically, Coastal Living.

Rooms have nautical motifs, with ceiling fans and white furniture. Yacht Club rooms are navy blue and white; those in the Beach Club have muted greens and blues. Bathrooms include separate vanities with double sinks. Beach Club Villas (Disney Vacation Club timeshare properties, often available to the general public) range from studio apartments to large suites.

The best **swimming area** at any Walt Disney World resort, Stormalong Bay is a miniature water park. Situated between the two resorts, it includes a meandering central pool, lazy river, shallow inlet with a real sandbar, a shady hot tub and an assortment of bubbling fountains, waterfalls and bridges. A spiral staircase on a life-sized shipwreck leads to a 300-foot slide. Starting off in a dark tunnel (the inside of a fallen mast) it plummets into daylight at a rocky outcropping. Riders get showered by two waterfalls before splashing into the central pool. A kiddie pool ("Guppie Bay") with overhead sprinklers has an adjacent sandy play spot, while back on the pirate ship is a second kiddie pool with its own tiny slide. Designed so it appears to flow into the lake, the 2 1/2-acre complex is themed to be a Nantucket lagoon. Constantly re-filtering 750,000 gallons of water, it's the largest sand-bottomed chlorinated swimming area in the world.

Epcot's IllumiNations fireworks are visible nightly at 9 p.m.

The marina offers rides in the **Breathless II** (30-min ride $85 per group. 90-min IllumiNations cruise $250. Ages 3 and up, 407-WDW-PLAY), a 26-foot Hacker Craft inboard that's a replica of a 1920s mahogany Chris-Craft. For children, the **Albatross Treasure Cruise** ($30 inc lunch, 2 hrs, children only, ages 4–10, 407-WDW-DINE) pontoonboat scavenger hunt travels to the Swan and Dolphin and BoardWalk resorts as well as the Canada and Mexico pavilions in Epcot.

Fittings & Fairings Clothes and Notions stocks resort logo apparel, books, Disney merchandise, snacks, swimwear, sundries and toiletries, topped with a gelato bar and prepackaged food. The Beach Club has a similar store: **Beach Club Marketplace**.

Dining

BEACHES & CREAM ★ ★ ★ ★ ✔ Soda shop $$ **L,D:** $6–$22, 11am–11pm. Takeout counter. Seats 48. Next to Stormalong Bay.

Clog those arteries! Gigantic sundaes are the draw at this tiny spot, where the treats are so tempting absolutely no one is thinking about their health. Guilty pleasures include the No Way José (scoops of vanilla and chocolate in a bed of peanut butter, topped with hot fudge), though the claim-to-fame is the ridiculous Kitchen Sink sundae that's served, literally, in a kitchen sink. There are good burgers and sandwiches, too. A tin ceiling has a tray center with elaborate moldings. With only three booths and six small tables, the place is usually packed.

CAPE MAY CAFE Goofy's Beach Club Breakfast: ★ ★ ★ ★ ✔ Character buffet $$$ **Goofy, Minnie Mouse, Donald Duck.** $20 A, $12 C. 7:30–11am. Dinner: ★ ★ ★ Buffet $$$$ **$27 A, $13 C.** 5:30–9:30pm. Seats 234. Beach Club.

The only Disney-operated character meal not in a theme park or on the monorail loop,

The Yacht Club (above) and Beach Club recall the looks of 19th-century Nantucket Island.

this breakfast buffet is calm and relaxed. Screaming kids are rare, as children are a mix of ages. Narrow aisles continually put the characters right up next to your table. Five buffet lines are well attended. The background music is a mix of Disney and beach tunes. Listen closely and you'll hear Annette Funicello's 1965 duet with the Beach Boys, "The Monkey's Uncle." Small parties can often get in without a reservation.

Though the dinner buffet is billed as a clambake, the advertised clams, mussels, corn-on-the-cob and potatoes are here, of course, but they take up just four feet of the 52-foot buffet line. The standout is a carved-to-order top sirloin. Subdued lighting and soothing background music (occasionally with sounds of sea gulls) make it a perfect place to recover from a day in the parks.

CAPTAIN'S GRILLE ★★★ American $$$$ B: $9–$16, 7–11am. L: $10–$18, 11:30am–2pm. D: $15–$28, 5:30–9:30pm. Seats 280. Yacht Club.

This generic cafe is sort of like a Perkins Pancake House–the food is fine but the atmosphere is not memorable. Breakfast features a heat-lamp buffet. Lunch offers salads and sandwiches, while dinner has steaks, chicken, fish and seafood.

YACHTSMAN STEAKHOUSE ★★★★★ ✔ Steakhouse $$$$$ D: $27–$44, 5:30–10pm. Seats 286. Yacht Club. *Disney Signature*

The best Disney steakhouse, this white-tablecloth restaurant offers the same top-quality cuts found in any fine steakhouse,

but here they're more than just plated pieces of meat. The New York strip is brushed in a peppercorn brandy sauce. The prime rib comes with a savory bread pudding. The restaurant will hand-cut custom sizes of any steak but the porterhouse. Half of the restaurant is on a wood floor, the other half is carpeted. From November through January, about a third of the crowd is conventioneers.

BEACH CLUB MARKETPLACE American fast food with pastries, salads, sandwiches, soups. Sm. food store sells fruit, snacks. B: 7–11am. L,D: 11am–10pm. Seats 16 outside. Beach Club.

As for lounges, **Martha's Vineyard** adjoins Cape May Cafe, **Crew's Cup Lounge** is next to Yachtsman Steakhouse and **Ale and Compass** (B: pastries, coffee) is in the Yacht Club lobby.

HIDDEN MICKEYS

❶ On the wallpaper in the guest room halls, as repeating white designs on a tan background. In the entrance hall to the Solarium, as wheels of trunk-mounted tires of ❷ the far left yellow car and ❸ the far right blue car in the first painting to the left (Mickey faces). ❹ In that same painting, as the hood ornament on the right red car and right blue car. ❺ As a cloud in the second painting to the left (a detailed face). ❻ As a red balloon held by a girl at the right of the third painting on the left wall. ❼ As a yellow balloon held by the girl next to her.

Downtown Disney Resorts

Located at the east end of the Disney property, these hotels are run by outside companies but offer many Disney amenities, including free theme-park shuttles and discounts at Disney golf courses. Developed in the early 1970s as Disney's Hotel Plaza, the area was extensively renovated after the 2004 hurricane season.

BEST WESTERN LAKE BUENA VISTA ★★★ $$ 321 rms, 4 suites. 2 restaurants. Play area, fitness cntr. 18 stories. 2000 Hotel Plaza Blvd. 32830. 407-828-2424.

BUENA VISTA PALACE AND SPA ★★★★ $$ 1,012 rms. 7 restaurants inc. Disney character breakfast. Concierge; convention cntr; fitness cntr; salon; tennis; volleyball cts. Spa (407-827-3200). 27 stories. On 27 ac. 1900 Buena Vista Dr. 32830. 407-827-2727.

DOUBLETREE GUEST SUITES ★★★ $$ 229 suites. Restaurant. Fitness center; playground; tennis ct. Sweet Dreams bedding. The only all-suite hotel on Disney property. 7 stories. Renovated 2006, 2007. 2305 Hotel Plaza Blvd. 32830. 407-934-1000.

HILTON ★★★★ $$ 704 rms, 110 suites. Six restaurants inc Benihana, Disney character breakfast Sun. Concierge, cyber cafe, golf pro shop, salon, health club. The only Downtown Disney hotel that offers Disney's Extra Magic Hours benefit. 10 stories. Renovated 2008. 1751 Hotel Plaza Blvd. 32830. 407-827-4000.

HOLIDAY INN 323 rms, 1 suite. 32-inch HDTVs, pillow-top mattresses, work desks. Atrium restaurant. Grab & Go food shop. Kids Eat Free program (2–12 yrs.) Biz cntr, concierge, health club, "zero-entry" swimming pool w/ whirlpool. Wireless, wired Internet srvc. 11,000-sq-ft meeting space. 1805 Hotel Plaza Blvd. 32830. 407-828-8888. Scheduled to re-open in late 2009. Rates unavailable at press time.

ROYAL PLAZA ★★★ $$$ 394 rms. Large rms, separate sitting areas, some kitchenettes, wet bars, whirlpool tubs. Restaurants, fitness cntr, tennis cts. 17 stories. 1905 Hotel Plaza Blvd. 32830. 407-828-2828.

REGAL SUN ★★★ $$ 619 rms, 7 suites. Restaurant, English pub, Sat. murder-mystery dinner show, Disney character breakfast Tue., Thur., Sat. Basketball, shuffleboard, tennis, volleyball cts; health club. 19-story tower, 2 wings. On 13 ac. Renovated 2007. Formerly Grosvenor. 1850 Hotel Plaza Blvd. 32830. 407-828-4444.

Outside Disney

BUENA VISTA SUITES ★★★★ $$ World Center Dr: Restaurant. Free breakfast buffet. 8203 World Center Dr. 32821. 800-537-7737. Free mall and WDW shuttle. WDW 2 mi.

CARIBE ROYALE ★★★★ $$$ World Center Dr: All suites. Restaurants, pool with slide, waterfall. 24-hr. rm service. 8101 World Center Dr. 32821. 800-823-8300. Free shuttle. WDW 2 mi.

CELEBRATION HOTEL ★★★★ $$$ Celebration: Restaurants. 700 Bloom St. 34747. 888-499-3800. Free shuttle. WDW 4 mi.

COUNTRY INN & SUITES ★★★ $ Kitchenettes. Free continental breakfast. **U.S. 192 area:** 5001 Calypso Cay Way 34746. 407-997-1400. Fee for pets. Free shuttle. WDW 5 mi. **Int'l. Dr. area:** 7701 Universal Blvd. 32819. 407-313-4200. Free shuttle. WDW 8 mi. **Lake Buena Vista:** 12191 S. Apopka-Vineland Rd. 32830. 407-239-1115. Free shuttle. WDW 1 mi.

COURTYARD BY MARRIOTT ★★★ $ Breakfast restaurant. **Lake Buena Vista:** 8501 Palm Pkwy. 32836. 407-239-6900. Free shuttle to outlet mall, WDW. WDW 1 mi. **Little Lake Bryan area:** 8623 Vineland Ave. (Marriott Village) 32821. 877-682-8552. Shuttle for $5 roundtrip. WDW 1 mi.

EMBASSY SUITES ★★★ $$ 2-rm suites with work table, 2 TVs, refrigerator, microwave, coffeemaker. Restaurant(s). Free cooked-to-order breakfast. Evening Mgrs Reception. Business srvcs. **Airport:** 5835 T.G. Lee Blvd. 32822. 407-888-9339. Free airport shuttle. WDW 15 mi. **Downtown Orlando:** 191 East Pine St. 32801. 407-841-1000. WDW 14 mi. **Int'l. Dr.:** 8978 Int'l. Dr. 32819. 407-352-1400. Free shuttle. WDW 5 mi. Also: 8250 Jamaican Ct. 32819. 407-345-8250. WDW 6 mi. **Lake Buena Vista:** 8100 Lake Ave. 32836. 407-239-1144. Free shuttle. WDW 3 mi.

FLORIDAYS ORLANDO ★★★ $$$ SeaWorld area: All suites. Restaurant, kitchens, balconies. 2-person jetted tubs. 12550 Floridays Resort Dr. 32821. 866-797-0022. Free shuttle to Epcot. WDW 3 mi.

GAYLORD PALMS ★★★★ $$ Adjacent to WDW: Restaurants, convention space, spa, hair salon. 5-ac tropical atrium with alligators, koi, snakes, other live animals. 6000 W. Osceola Pkwy. 34746. 877-677-9352. Free shuttle. WDW 1 mi.

GRAND BEACH ★★★ $$$ Little Lake Bryan area: 1- to 3-bedrm condos. Kitchens, lakefront, water sports. Whirlpool jet tubs. 8317 Lake Bryan Beach Blvd., 32821. 407-238-2500. WDW 2 mi.

HAWTHORN SUITES ★★★ $ Lake Buena Vista: Kitchens. Free breakfast. 8303 Palm Pkwy. 32836. 407-597-5000. Free shuttle to Epcot. WDW 1 mi.

HILTON GARDEN INN ★★★ $$ Refrigerator, microwave, coffeemaker. Garden Sleep System, HDTV. Restaurant. **Airport:** 7300 Augusta National Dr. 32822. 407-240-3725. WDW 15 mi. **SeaWorld area:** 6850 Westwood Blvd. 32821. 407-354-1500. WDW 4 mi. **Universal Studios area:** 5877 American Way 32819. 407-363-9332. WDW 9 mi.

HILTON ORLANDO BONNET CREEK ★★★★ $$$$ Adjacent to WDW: Largest Hilton in mainland U.S. 3 restaurants. Pool with water slide, tennis ct, golf course, spa. 14100 Bonnet Creek Resort Ln. 32831. 407-597-3600. Opens Nov. 1, 2009. WDW 1 mi.

HOMEWOOD SUITES ★★★ $$ Studio, 1- and 2-bedrm suites. Kitchens, microwave, dishwasher. Free hot breakfast; free light meal and beverages Mon.–Thurs. evenings. Business srvcs. **Int'l. Dr. area:** 8745 Int'l. Dr.

32819. 407-248-2232. WDW 5 mi. Free shuttle. **Universal Studios area:** 5893 American Way 32819. 407-226-0669. WDW 9 mi.

HYATT REGENCY ★★★★ $$$ **Airport:** Multiple restaurants, health club, beauty salon, spa, convention services. Atop airport. 9300 Airport Blvd. 32827. 800-233-1234. WDW 16 mi. **Lake Buena Vista:** Hyatt Regency Grand Cypress. Restaurants, convention space, lake with beach, 2 golf courses, spa, equestrian cntr, nature trails, complimentary boat, canoe use. One Grand Cypress Blvd. 32836. 407-239-1234. Free shuttle. WDW 1 mi.

MARRIOTT ★★★ $$$ **Airport:** Orlando Airport Marriott. Restaurants, free continental breakfast, indoor/outdoor pool, sauna. 7499 Augusta National Dr. 32822. 407-851-9000. Free shuttle to airport. WDW 16 mi. **Downtown Orlando:** Adjoins Amway Arena. 400 W. Livingston St. 32801. 407-843-6664. WDW 16 mi. **Lake Buena Vista:** Marriott Cypress Harbor: Pools, sauna, kitchens, washer/dryers, lake, water sports. 2 bed./2 ba. villas. 11251 Harbour Villa Rd. 32821. 800-845-5279. WDW 4 mi. **SeaWorld area:** Marriott Grande Vista: Lake, some kitchens and kitchenettes, sauna. 5925 Avenida Vista 32821. 407-238-7676. WDW 5 mi. Also: JW Marriott Grande Lakes. Restaurants, pool with lazy river, large spa, sauna, Greg Norman-designed golf course. 4040 Central Florida Pkwy. 32837. 800-576-5750. WDW 7 mi. **World Center Dr. area:** Orlando World Center Marriott. Restaurants, pools (waterfalls, slides), spa, sauna, golf course, meeting rooms. 8701 World Center Dr. 32821. 800-228-9290. WDW 2 mi. Also: Marriott Royal Palm. Next to Orlando World Center Marriott; free access to its amenities. Lakefront, kitchens, washer/dryers. 8404 Vacation Way 32821. 407-238-6200. WDW 2 mi.

MONA LISA ★★★★ $$ **Celebration:** 1, 2-bedroom suites. Kitchens, washers/dryers. Restaurant. 225 Celebration Place 34747. 888-783-3408. Free WDW shuttle. WDW 2 mi.

MONUMENTAL HOTEL ★★★ $ **Int'l. Dr. area:** Restaurant. 12000 Int'l. Dr. 32821. 407-239-1222. Formerly Crown Plaza. WDW 4 mi.

NICKELODEON FAMILY SUITES ★★★★ $$ **World Center Dr. area:** Restaurants, salon. Cartoon decor, wacky pools, activities, character breakfast. Run by Holiday Inn. 14500 Continental Gateway 32821. 877-387-5437. Free shuttle. WDW 1 mi.

OMNI CHAMPIONSGATE ★★★★ $$$ **West of WDW:** Restaurants, pool w/lazy river, water slides. 2 golf courses, golf academy, spa, steam rm. Free shuttle. 1500 Masters Blvd. 33896. 407-390-6664. WDW 7 mi.

PEABODY ORLANDO ★★★★ $$$ **Orlando Convention Cntr:** Restaurants, beauty salon, spa, convention space. Mallard march at fountain twice daily. 9801 Int'l. Dr. 32819. 800-732-2639. WDW 6 mi.

RADISSON ★★★ $ Restaurant. **U.S. 192 area:** 3011 Maingate Ln. 34747. 407-396-1400. Free shuttle. WDW 1 mi. Also: 2900 Parkway Blvd. 34747. 800-634-4774. Free shuttle. WDW 2 mi.

RENAISSANCE ORLANDO ★★★★ $$ **Airport:** Restaurant, meeting space. 5445 Forbes Pl. 32812. 407-

240-1000. Airport 1 mi. WDW 16 mi. Free shuttle to airport. **SeaWorld area:** Restaurants, sushi bar, convention space, spa. Across street from SeaWorld. 6677 Sea Harbor Dr. 32821. 800-327-6677. WDW 4 mi.

RESIDENCE INN BY MARRIOTT ★★★ $$$ Studios, suites. Kitchens. Free breakfast. Fee for pets. **Int'l. Dr. area:** 8800 Universal Blvd. 32819. 407-226-0288. Free shuttle. WDW 7 mi. **Lake Buena Vista:** 11450 Marbella Palm Ct. 32836. 407-465-0075. Free shuttle to Epcot. WDW 1 mi. **SeaWorld area:** 11000 Westwood Blvd. 32821. 800-889-9728. Free shuttle. WDW 4 mi.

RITZ-CARLTON GRANDE LAKES ★★★★★ $$$$ **SeaWorld area:** Restaurants, pool, spa w/salon, convention space, Greg Norman-designed golf course, concierge floors. Life-size chess board. 4012 Central Florida Pkwy. 32837. 800-576-5760. WDW 7 mi.

ROSEN CENTRE ★★★★ $$$$ **Orlando Convention Cntr:** Restaurants, spa, salon, convention space, concierge floors. 9840 Int'l. Dr. 32819. 800-204-7234. WDW 6 mi.

ROSEN PLAZA ★★★★ $$ **Orlando Convention Cntr:** Restaurants, meeting space. Nightclub. 9700 Int'l. Dr. 32819. 800-627-8258. WDW 6 mi.

ROSEN SHINGLE CREEK ★★★★★ $$$ **Orlando Convention Cntr:** Restaurants, outdoor pools, spa, salon, convention space, golf course. 9939 Universal Blvd. 32819. 866-996-9939. WDW 7 mi.

SHERATON ★★★ $$ **Lake Buena Vista:** Sheraton Safari. Restaurants, meeting space. African theme. 12205 S. Apopka-Vineland Rd. 32836. 407-239-0444. Free shuttle. WDW 1 mi. **SeaWorld area:** Sheraton Vistana Villages. All suites w/kitchens. Restaurants. 8800 Vistana Centre Dr. 32821. 407-239-3100. Free shuttle. WDW 4 mi.

SPRINGHILL SUITES ★★★ $$ **Convention Center:** Sauna. Free continental breakfast. 8623 Universal Blvd., 32819. 407-938-9001. WDW 7 mi.

STAYBRIDGE SUITES ★★★ $$$ Kitchens. Free cont'l breakfast. **Int'l. Dr. area:** 8480 Int'l. Dr. 32819. 800-238-8000. WDW 7 mi. **Lake Buena Vista:** 8751 Suiteside Dr. 32836. 800-238-8000. Free shuttle. WDW 1 mi.

VILLAS OF GRAND CYPRESS ★★★★ $$$$ **Lake Buena Vista:** Restaurants, convention space, lake with beach, 2 golf courses, spa, equestrian cntr, nature trails, complimentary boat, canoe use. 1 N. Jacaranda St. 32836. 800-835-7377. Free shuttle. WDW 4 mi.

WALDORF ASTORIA ORLANDO $$$$ **Bonnet Creek:** 3 restaurants. Golf course, spa. 14200 Bonnet Creek Resort Ln. 32831. 407-597-5500. Opens Nov. 1, 2009. WDW 1 mi.

WESTIN GRAND BOHEMIAN ★★ $$$ **Downtown Orlando:** Restaurant. Art gallery. 325 S. Orange Ave. 32801. 407-313-9000. WDW 14 mi.

WORLDQUEST ★★★★ $$$ **World Center Dr. area:** All suites. Condo rentals. Free breakfast. 8849 Worldquest Blvd. 32821. 877-987-8378. WDW 2 mi.

WYNDHAM ORLANDO ★★★★ $$ **Int'l. Dr. area:** Restaurants, sauna. Family suites have bunk beds, play areas. Fee for pets. 8001 Int'l. Dr. 32819. 407-351-2420. WDW 8 mi.

Bounty hunter Aurra Sing roams the
Backlot of Disney's Hollywood
Studios during Star Wars Weekends

Special Events

Winter

MARATHON WEEKEND

Jan 8–11. Entry fees: $125 (26.2), $115 (13.1), $40 (5K). Disabled runners welcome. Advance registration required; entry deadline is typically early Nov. but events can reach capacity much earlier. Details at 407-939-7810 or disneysports.com.

A pair of running events—a 26.2-mile full marathon and a 13.1-mile half marathon—highlight this January weekend. Typically more than 30,000 athletes compete; the route goes through theme parks. There's also a 5K run for families and children and a health and fitness expo at the host complex, the ESPN Wide World of Sports center. Note: A Minnie Marathon Weekend women's endurance event (15K, 5K and kids' races) follows in early May.

SPRING TRAINING

Feb–March. Training sessions $12, games $15–$24. Tickets on sale Jan 10. Info, tickets: 407-939-1500, 407-839-3900 (Ticketmaster) or disneysports.com.

The Atlanta Braves Major League Baseball club hold its Spring Training at ESPN Wide World of Sports. Workouts start in February. More than a dozen Grapefruit League exhibition games follow in March.

Spring

ESPN: THE WEEKEND

Early March

Legendary athletes join popular ESPN broadcasters during this no-extra-charge fan-fest at Disney's Hollywood Studios. The events include Q&A sessions, celebrity motorcades, interactive sports activities and live telecasts. Many fathers visit with their sons. Coincides with Atlanta Braves Spring Training.

ST. PATRICK'S DAY

Tuesday, March 17

Two Disney World locations mark the Irish holiday with special events: The Raglan Road restaurant at Downtown Disney's Pleasure Island, and the U.K. pavilion at Epcot's World Showcase.

EPCOT INTERNATIONAL FLOWER AND GARDEN FESTIVAL

March 18–May 31. No extra charge. Info: 407-W-DISNEY (934-7639).

Disney's most elaborate one-park promotion, this 75-day garden party includes hands-on seminars, demonstrations and celebrity guest speakers, as well as character topiaries, floating water gardens and 30 million flowers. A walk-through butterfly garden often includes a live caterpillar/chrysalis exhibit. Themed weekends celebrate art, bugs and Mother's Day. Nightly concerts feature "Flower Power" acts from the 1960s and 1970s, such as Monkees singer Davy Jones. Vendor booths line the main walkways. For 2009, the front entrance topiary features a "Cinderellabration" of Disney princesses.

EASTER

Sunday, April 12

The Magic Kingdom Easter Day parade includes the Easter Bunny and the colorful Azalea Trail Maids from Mobile, Ala.

STAR WARS WEEKENDS

May–June. No extra charge. Info: 407-W-DISNEY (934-7639).

This fan-fest includes autograph booths featuring actors who have appeared in the "Star Wars" film series. Other highlights: roving characters, special motorcades, question-and-answer sessions, trivia games and children's activities. Merchandise includes an incredibly popular Darth Mickey plushie. Many guests dress up. Get there when the park opens to take advantage of all of the activities.

GAY DAYS

First weekend in June. Info: 407-896-8431 or at gaydays.com.

Tens of thousands of gay adults come to Walt Disney World (especially Magic King-

Mr. and Mrs. Easter Bunny appear at Magic Kingdom during Easter weekend

dom) during the first weekend in June, most wearing red shirts in a sign of solidarity. Straight parents can be uncomfortable (a very few guests are flamboyant), but the experience does show children that even some old folks and yes, parents, are gay. There is, naturally, less demand for strollers as well as shorter lines at Fantasyland attractions. Disney does not sponsor the event but doesn't interfere with it.

Summer

SOUNDS LIKE SUMMER CONCERT SERIES
June–Aug
Cover bands offer their renditions of timeless tunes from crowd favorites such as U2, Elton John and The Supremes. The shows take place three times a night at the 1,950-seat America Gardens amphitheater.

INDEPENDENCE DAY
July 4
Usually the most crowded day of the year at Walt Disney World, Independence Day features a Magic Kingdom fireworks show that surrounds guests watching from Main Street U.S.A. Historic characters visit Epcot's American Adventure pavilion to share their stories. Disney's Hollywood Studios presents a special fireworks show at 9 p.m., with skyrockets and patriotic music.

PIRATE & PRINCESS PARTY
Aug–Sept. $46 adults; $40 children 3-9. Apx. a dozen evenings. Info and tickets: 407-W-DISNEY (934-7639).
Popular with young singles as well as families, these nighttime events feature a unique parade and one of Disney's most spectacular fireworks shows. Interactive events for children include a treasure hunt for a bibbidi-bobbidi-booty of beads and candy. Most major attractions are open, and lines are short. Many guests dress up. Though the parties officially run from 7 p.m. to midnight, partygoers can arrive as early as 4 p.m., which makes the price a bargain.

DISNEY STEP CLASSIC
Sept. 4, 5. Adv. tickets $25, $45 for two nights. ESPN Wide World of Sports
High school and collegiate step teams battle in a two-day competition and show. Portions of the 2008 event were aired on ESPN2.

DISNEY'S ROYAL QUINCEAÑERA WEEKEND
Late Aug–early Sept. $283. Info at 321-939-4555.
Epcot hosts this celebration of the passage of young Latinas into womanhood as they turn 15. A private viewing of IllumiNations follows a ball. Packages include stays at the Coronado Springs Resort and park tickets.

NIGHT OF JOY

Early Sept. Adv. tickets $45, $76 for two nights. Day of event $5 more. Often sells out. Info and tickets: 407-827-7200.

Concerts by at least a dozen Contemporary Christian artists highlight this long-time event, now held at Disney's Hollywood Studios. Most attractions are open.

Fall

MICKEY'S NOT-SO-SCARY HALLOWEEN PARTY

Sept–Oct. $56 adults; $50 children 3–9. Many dates offer $7 advance savings. Friday events near Halloween, and the holiday itself, often sell out. Info and tickets: 407-827-7200.

There's nothing but fun during these charming Magic Kingdom evenings, which include a terrific parade—it starts with a galloping headless horseman—a spectacular fireworks show and many free-candy stations. Most attractions are not crowded. Many families wear home-made costumes.

INTERNATIONAL FOOD AND WINE FESTIVAL

Sept–Nov. Info: 407-WDW-FEST (939-3378). Demonstrations, seminars and entertainment included in Epcot admission.

Dozens of booths around Epcot's World Showcase feature low-cost food and wine samples from Spain, India, Italy, Turkey, Ireland, Poland and other locales during this six-week festival. Special events include cooking demonstrations and pricey gourmet dinners and wine seminars. Nightly free concerts feature classic pop acts such as Kool & The Gang and David Cassidy.

CHILDREN'S MIRACLE NETWORK GOLF CLASSIC PRESENTED BY WAL-MART

Oct.–Nov. $20 for any one day, $30 for a weekly badge. Proceeds benefit local Children's Miracle Network hospitals. Food packages avail. Info and tickets: 407-824-2250.

You'll be just a few feet away from the top names in men's golf with a pass to this PGA Tour tournament, held on Disney's Magno-

Tweedledum appears in costume as part of the parade at Mickey's Not-So-Scary Halloween Party

lia and Palm golf courses. Tiger Woods often participates.

FESTIVAL OF THE MASTERS

Nov. No charge. Info: 407-824-4321.

One of the top art festivals in the United States, this Downtown Disney event features over 150 artists, each of whom has won a primary award at a juried art show within the past three years. Works include paintings, photographs, sculptures and jewelry. Even more interesting are the pieces at the adjacent House of Blues folk-art festival, which features self-taught creators. Cirque du Soleil artists perform in front of their theater each afternoon. Chalk artists cover 6,000 square feet at the Marketplace. Held annually since 1975.

Toy soldiers from 1961's "Babes in Toyland" march in the Magic Kingdom Christmas parade

Christmas

Even the most determined Scrooge will warm up to Walt Disney World in the weeks between Thanksgiving and Christmas. The mood is most contagious at Magic Kingdom, which salutes the spirit of the American secular holiday with festive decorations, four special shows, a Santa Claus parade and an amazing fireworks display. Here's a guide to everything Disney has to offer:

Decorations

MAGIC KINGDOM

Disney World's signature park focuses its decor on **Main Street U.S.A.** Thick garlands hang over the street, adorned with fruit, pine cones, poinsettias, giant plaid bows, bells and candles. Poinsettias hang from lampposts. Some second-story windows display Menorahs. The horse trolley has bows along its roof, and one on its horse's bridle. Inside the stores, garland embellishments often match the nearby merchandise. A 65-foot-tall Christmas tree stands in the center of Town Square. The spruce is so thoroughly decorated most guests don't notice that it's artificial. A toy train circles its base.

Just down the road, **Cinderella Castle** is wrapped in a transparent net of 200,000 tiny white "Castle Dreamlights." A twilight cer-

emony (Cinderella's Holiday Wish, pg. 320) turns them on. Elsewhere, 18-inch bulbs trim Mickey's Country House and Minnie's Country House at **Mickey's Toontown Fair.**

EPCOT

After sunset, an archway over the walkway between the Future World and World Showcase sections of the park becomes the **Lights of Winter.** Its lights flash rhythmically to holiday music as well as the sprays of a large nearby fountain. The lights lead to Epcot's signature holiday tree, decorated in a world motif. Also lovely at night, the courtyard of the World Showcase **Germany** pavilion is decked out with trees, wreaths and garlands. Its miniature train village has its own decorations and a tiny tree lot. Inside the snack bar of the U.S. pavilion (the **American Adventure**), a life-size gingerbread house sells cider and hot chocolate.

DISNEY'S HOLLYWOOD STUDIOS

Straight out of a 1940s holiday musical, silver strands form garlands above **Hollywood Boulevard** while red and silver stars hang from **Sunset Boulevard** lampposts. Out front is period-perfect 65-foot-tall tree.

Each storefront window, balcony and brownstone along the **Streets of America** is decorated to reflect the life of its tenant. One celebrates Hanukkah. Pizza Planet is decked out with oversized bulbs; a giant Santa climbs a nearby fire escape. At night thousands of lights cover the facades in the **Osborne Family Spectacle of Dancing Lights.** Hanging from the rooftops in huge nets, they flash rhythmically to holiday tunes. Displays above include a spinning carousel and rotating globe. Rope-light angels fly over a town square; others pray to a creche. Disney sprays snow-like soap bubbles from overhead spouts. The spectacle was created by Little Rock, Ark., business tycoon Jennings Osborne during the 1980s for his 6-year-old daughter. To the dismay of many of Osborne's neighbors, it covered his home and yard, and drew throngs of traffic. The Osborne lights use 800,000 watts of power and 12 miles of extension cords.

DISNEY'S ANIMAL KINGDOM

Entrance areas and hub walkways display natural decorations. A 65-foot-tall Christmas tree is adorned with primitive metal and wood animals; gift-shop garlands are filled with berries, flowers, grain stalks and straw. At **Dinoland U.S.A.,** the tongue-in-cheek Dino-Rama carnival is trimmed with shredded-plastic trees, candy canes and a huge cheesy snowman. The Dinosaur Treasures gift shop has plastic Santas and Santa heads and a tree with pink flamingos and Styrofoam snowmen. Meanwhile, each tree at **Camp Minnie-Mickey** belongs, on close inspection, to a Disney character. The ornaments on Lilo's tree include her handmade doll and Elvis records.

The park's **ambient music** features nice flute-and-drum renditions of traditionals such as "Silent Night" in the entrance area,

Epcot's Lights of Winter archway choreographs its flashing lights to holiday music

and obscure ditties such as Spike Jones' 1956 "My Birthday Comes on Christmas" and Augie Rios' 1958 "Donde Esta Santa Claus?" at Dinoland U.S.A.

RESORTS

All Disney-owned lodging complexes are decorated for the holidays. The largest **Christmas trees** are at the Contemporary (75 feet tall, with 77,000 lights), Wilderness Lodge (50 feet, 52,000 lights) and Grand Floridian (45 feet, 45,000 lights). Many resorts have **confectionery displays.** A 16-foot-tall gingerbread house sits in the Grand Floridian lobby; a concoction of honey, sugar, egg whites and apricot glaze covers its wood frame. There are miniature villages at Animal Kingdom Lodge and the Contemporary

---

FUN FACTS ›› Walt Disney World displays more than 1,500 Christmas trees, 15 miles of garland and over 300,000 yards of ribbon. ›› Disney's signature theme-park trees weigh at least 28,000 pounds each.

The Osborne Family Spectacle of Dancing Lights lights up Disney's Hollywood Studios

Resort, a complete Santa's workshop at the BoardWalk, a carousel at the Beach Club and a sugary mountain at the Yacht Club.

Attractions

MAGIC KINGDOM

CELEBRATE THE SEASON ★★★★ ✔ Outdoor stage show **Mickey Mouse, Minnie Mouse, Donald Duck, Chip 'n Dale, Pluto, Santa Goofy. 20 min. Cinderella Castle forecourt. Times vary.**
Remember when your neighbors got together for holiday sing-a-longs? When carolers came to your door? When your town held its Santa Claus parade? No? Well Disney does, and brings it back with this campy revue of dancing reindeer, hoofing horses and very merry elves. Evening spotlights add theatrical flair.

MICKEY'S 'TWAS THE NIGHT BEFORE CHRISTMAS ★★★★ Outdoor stage show **Mickey Mouse, Minnie Mouse, Santa Goofy. 20 min. Galaxy Palace Theater, Tomorrowland. Times vary.**
A tongue-in-cheek take on the poem, this musical revue features the hippos from Disney's 1940 "Fantasia." Minnie sings "Santa Baby." Live orchestra.

CINDERELLA'S HOLIDAY WISH ★★★ Outdoor stage show **Cinderella, Fairy Godmother, Mickey Mouse. 20 min. Cinderella Castle forecourt. 5:45 p.m.**
When Cinderella wants her home to sparkle for the holidays, her Fairy Godmother waves her wand, and suddenly the castle is covered with 200,000 twinkling lights.

BELLE'S ENCHANTED CHRISTMAS ★★★★ Outdoor stage show **16 min. Fairytale Garden, Fantasyland. Times vary. Arrive 30 min. early.**
The princess uses audience members to retell the tale of her first Christmas in the Beast's castle (from the 1997 video "Beauty and the Beast: The Enchanted Christmas"). Sit by the stage steps and your child may be chosen to be in the show.

COUNTRY BEARS CHRISTMAS SPECIAL ★ Robotic country music revue **18 min. Frontierland. Continuous shows.**
"When the snow begins a'fallin' and your blood begins to freeze, it's time to stomp and holler and slap your hairy knees." Silly lyrics—most of which are not as funny as that one—rule at this hokey revue, where doofus-faced mechanical bears sing countrified novelties. Way past its prime, with poor sound.

MICKEY'S ONCE UPON A CHRISTMAS PARADE ★★★★★ ✔ Santa Claus parade **15 min. Times vary. Starts in Frontierland, to Liberty Square, down Main Street U.S.A. Find seats 45 min. early.**
This lively procession includes horse-drawn sleighs; marching toy soldiers; dancing reindeer, snowflakes and gingerbread men; elves; plenty of Disney characters; and, of course, Mr. Santa.

HOLIDAY WISHES ★★★★★ ✔
Fireworks show **15 min. Times vary. Arrive 15 min. early.**

Fireworks form Christmas images in the sky while projected images decorate Cinderella Castle in this synchronized pyrotechnic show. During "O Christmas Tree" the castle becomes a Christmas tree: a star explodes above it while flood lights turn it green. The best viewing spot is on Main Street U.S.A., on the cusp of the bridge in front of the castle hub.

EPCOT

HOLIDAYS AROUND THE WORLD STORYTELLERS ★★★★★ Cultural storytellers **20 min. World Showcase pavilions. Hourly noon–dusk.**

Sharing the seasonal legends and traditions of cultures from throughout the world, these actors perform to small crowds outside each World Showcase pavilion. **Canada:** Comic lumberjack Nowell describes Boxing Day, the Inuit's impish Nalyuks and the legend of "people who come to homes dressed in strange outfits. We call them... relatives!" **United Kingdom:** Father Christmas tells how holiday cards and decorating with holly and mistletoe began in his countries. **France:** Pére Noël comically explains how children leave shoes on their doorsteps for him to put presents in. **Morocco:** A drummer describes the Festival of Ashura, which gives presents to children who behave well. **Japan:** A vendor ex-

Winnie the Pooh and his friends appear in the Magic Kingdom Christmas parade

plains Daruma dolls, pupil-free charms that children paint eyes on as they make wishes. **The American Adventure:** One storyteller

Backstage at Disney's Holiday Crafts Shop

Decking the halls of Walt Disney World is a full-time job for 26 employees, who toil backstage at a 70,000-square-foot Holiday Services warehouse 12 months of the year. When I stop by one fall afternoon, each cast member is hard at work. Some scurry past me pushing shrink-wrapped wardrobe carts, each tagged with its ID number ("MK 035"), contents ("Checked and Fluffed Garland") and destination ("Main Street Train Station 2nd Floor"). Others drive forklifts loaded with crates of ornaments, or use long poles to remove giant 3-D stars from the building's rafters.

Outside, electricians test out what appears to be a utility pole. "This is the guts of the Main Street unit," one says, explaining that the contraption is the electrical transformer of Magic Kingdom's signature Christmas tree. Nearby sit six circular sections of greenery, some more than 10 feet tall. In a few days everything will be trucked over to the park, where crane operators will stack it together like a giant ring-toss game. The six-hour job will be done overnight so guests don't see it. Similar operations take place at the other theme parks. Each tree is used up to five years.

And yes, managing Walt Disney World's holiday trimmings is a 12-month job. In the spring the staff cleans and repairs the decorations. In the summer it designs new ones. In the fall the group prepares for installation; after Christmas it puts everything away.

Dancers 'Celebrate the Season' in front of the Magic Kingdom's Cinderella Castle

Norway: Farm girl Sigrid is sure Gnome Julenissen doesn't exist, though you can see him easily. The strangest, and most fun, Holiday Storyteller skit. **Mexico:** The Three Kings explain the customs of Posada.

CANDLELIGHT PROCESSIONAL
★★★★★ ✔ Religious Christmas pageant **60 min. Three times nightly at the America Gardens amphitheater, American Adventure pavilion.**
This inspirational religious pageant recounts the birth of Jesus Christ with a 50-piece orchestra, 400 singers and a celebrity narrator. Though free with park admission, the Processional is so popular that on peak evenings the only guaranteed way to see it is to buy a Candlelight Processional Dinner Package (407-939-3463), which includes dinner at an Epcot restaurant. Otherwise you wait in a line for up to two hours.

DISNEY'S HOLLYWOOD STUDIOS
CITIZENS OF HOLLYWOOD
★★★★★ ✔ Street characters **20 min. Hollywood Blvd., Sunset Blvd. Times available at Guest Relations.**
Portraying directors, starlets, script girls and wanna-bes, these improvisational actors perform holiday street skits with audience participation. Appearing as the Hollywood Glee Club, they sing the lyrics to "Jingle Bells" to the music of "Joy to the World."

DISNEY'S ANIMAL KINGDOM
MICKEY'S JINGLE JUNGLE PARADE
★★★★ ✔ Character parade **15 min. Circles Discovery Island. Starts, exits in Africa, at gate between Tusker House and Kilimanjaro Safaris. Choose a viewing spot 30 min. early to get a shady seat.**
A reworking of the theme park's regular safari-themed Mickey's Jammin' Jungle Parade, this 12-minute procession finds Mickey Mouse and Rafiki (the mandrill in

explains Hanukkah, another describes the principles of Kwanzaa. **Italy:** Good witch La Befana, who slides down chimneys to leave treats, explains why she travels on the anniversary of the day the Three Kings came to Bethlehem. **Germany:** St. Nicholas fills you in about the first Christmas tree and Nutcracker as well as the Christmas pickle, a hidden tree ornament that rewards its finder with an extra present. **China:** The Monkey King spins a tale of how he defeated a monster and found a magic stick.

On Tape with Regis and Kelly
Though ABC-TV implies that it airs the Walt Disney World Christmas parade live on Christmas Day, the event is actually taped during the first weekend in December. Hosted by Regis Philbin and Kelly Ripa, the production fills Main Street U.S.A. and the Cinderella Castle stage with cameras, crews and celebrities. Miley Cyrus starred in the 2008 parade. The work moves at a snail's pace. Hang out for awhile and you'll see stars painstakingly perform take after take of the same few-second sequence. Want to be on camera? Come early, be happy and wear festive clothes without advertising slogans. Special access may be available at www.lightshiptv.com.

1994's "The Lion King") leading Minnie Mouse, Donald Duck and Goofy in an SUV parade that's headed out for a rustic holiday adventure. You can smell the chocolate when candy-making Minnie passes by in her truck; Donald's vehicle will spray you with artificial snow. Giant mechanical puppets include a partridge in a pear tree. Selected at random each day, up to 25 guests ride in the parade in giant rickshaws and open-top trailers.

CAMPFIRE CAROLERS ★★★★ A cappella singing group **20 min. Show times vary. Camp Minnie-Mickey.** This youthful a cappella group isn't above cracking a few jokes as they belt out holiday pop tunes. When one sings that she wants an "opotamus" for Christmas, the others correct her. "You must mean a hippopotamus!" "No, he doesn't have to be very cool." Crowds are small; you'll sit, or stand, just a few feet from the performers.

Avoiding the holiday crush

The week between Christmas and New Year's is Magic Kingdom's most crowded of the year, and not, frankly, the best time to visit. Not only does the park often close (reach its 80,000-person capacity) around lunchtime, the throng is largely made up of people who appear to have IQs somewhere south of Goofy's. They clog the rides, crowd the restaurants and wander the park aimlessly. We've even seen guests drunk.

The other theme parks can be almost as bad, and service at the resorts suffers as well. If you must visit Magic Kingdom during this week, arrive at the park by 7:30 a.m. Use the morning for attractions, see the noon parade, then leave for a long lunch, time in a pool, or nap. Return after dark for the castle show, Holiday Wishes and, after the crowd is gone, more attractions.

The week *before* Christmas is much better. All the holiday events are happening but the monster crowd isn't here yet.

An easy way to enjoy the Magic Kingdom fun is Mickey's Very Merry Christmas Party (7 pm–mid. $49 A, $43 C 3–9 adv; $7 more day of show). Held every few nights from Thanksgiving through a few days before Christmas, these events have crowds of only 10,000 to 25,000 but give you all the park's holiday events, plus cookies and hot chocolate. All major rides are open, and lines are short. For the best time arrive before 6:30 p.m. and see the less-crowded second parade. The least crowded party is the one on the Sunday after Thanksgiving; those on December Fridays and Saturday nights sell out early.

Holiday Hits

Walt Disney World's holiday celebration is filled with the vintage pop songs of the American Christmas experience. A hit for The Carpenters in 1978, **"The Christmas Waltz"** was written in 1954 for Frank Sinatra. Its music comes from a finger-exercising routine for piano players... **"Deck the Halls"** sets American lyrics to a 17th-century Welsh tune... Gene Autry was billed as the main draw of a 1946 Hollywood, Calif., Christmas parade, but during it noticed that children in the crowd were far more focused on the guy behind him, and kept yelling **"Here Comes Santa Claus"** instead of looking at him. The cowboy star responded by writing that 1947 classic... 1963's **"It's the Most Wonderful Time of the Year"** was penned by George Wyle, who later wrote the theme to the television series "Gilligan's Island"... First published in 1840 as "One Horse Open Sleigh," **"Jingle Bells"** is a tribute to sleigh races that once took place down in Medford, Mass.... 1955's **"Mr. Santa"** is a knockoff of the 1954 Chordettes hit, "Mr. Sandman"... **"Must Be Santa"** debuted on the "Sing Along with Mitch [Miller]" television show in 1961... **"The Nutcracker Suite"** is a medley the Russian composer Tchaikovsky created from his own Nutcracker ballet. First performed in 1892, it includes the tale of a family whose Christmas presents include two life-sized dolls, each of which takes a turn to dance... **"O Christmas Tree"** is an English take of the 16th-century German carol, "Oh Tannenbaum" ("Oh fir tree")... Based on a character that appeared in a 1939 Montgomery Ward newspaper ad, Autry's 1949 **"Rudolph the Red-Nosed Reindeer"** is the best-selling single in the history of Columbia Records... 1950s Christmas hits include **"Run, Run, Rudolph"** (1958, Chuck Berry), **"Santa Baby"** (1953, Eartha Kitt) and **"There's No Place Like Home for the Holidays"** (1954, Perry Como)... **"We Wish You A Merry Christmas"** is a 16th-century English Christmas carol... Published in 1934, "Winter Wonderland" was released in 1946 by both Perry Como and the Andrews Sisters. Each version sold a million copies.

Walt Disney (left) poses with famed rocket pioneer Dr. Wernher von Braun, 1954

Walt Disney

A tycoon with the mind of a farm boy. A storyteller who didn't finish high school. An artist who thought like an engineer. A visionary who loved the past. A mix of contradictory characters, Walt Disney was the personification of the American dream. He received hundreds of accolades, including 32 Academy Awards. But just as he started his grandest dream... he died.

The namesake of Walt Disney World was born in Chicago on Dec. 5, 1901. He had three older brothers and a younger sister.

Between the ages of 4 and 10, from 1905 to 1911, Disney was raised on a 45-acre farm near Marceline, Mo. Clad in overalls, the young boy spent much of his time playing with animals, swimming in a pond, picking apples, or daydreaming under a tree. He often ignored his homework to doodle animal pictures. While still in grade school, Disney sold cigars, gum and soda pop to passengers at the town's railroad depot. His uncle was a train engineer. Free to roam, the boy came to know an elderly Civil War veteran who told him dramatic old stories.

After his family moved to Kansas City, Disney impersonated Charlie Chaplin in skits with other neighborhood kids. When the family moved back to Chicago, Disney attended high school for just one year, contributing cartoons and photos to the school paper. He took night courses at Chicago's Academy of Fine Arts.

At 16 Disney dropped out of high school and left home. Germany had just signed an armistice ending World War I, but he still tried to enlist in the Army. Rejected because of his age, Disney instead snuck into the Red Cross, which sent him to France to drive an ambulance. He took up smoking.

Returning to Kansas City at age 20, Disney formed his first business. Using a borrowed camera and working in a shed, he made "Laugh-O-Gram" cartoons of a live little girl in an animated world. When his distributor went under, Disney paid the bills by producing a dental-health film ("Tommy Tucker's Tooth"), but soon he had to close shop, too. Raising train fare by photographing babies door-to-door, Disney soon headed to Hollywood. His brother Roy was already there.

Carrying a print of his last Kansas City cartoon, an unfinished extravaganza called "Alice's Wonderland," Disney applied at every major studio. Finally, a New York distributor agreed to market his work. He was in business again. Forming the Disney Bros. Studio, Walt and Roy set up shop in the rear of a real estate office. Running the money side of the operation, Roy insisted its name be changed to the Walt Disney Studio, today's Walt Disney Company.

The new business prospered. Disney celebrated by buying a Moon roadster, growing a mustache and, in 1925, marrying a woman who inked and painted his celluloids, Lillian Bounds. The couple later raised two daughters, Diane and the adopted Sharon.

In 1927 Disney created a new character: Oswald the Lucky Rabbit. He produced 26 Oswald cartoons. Distributed by Universal, they spawned an Oswald candy bar and some merchandise. But a year later, on a trip to New York to renew his contract, Disney learned of a clause in his deal that gave Universal ownership of the character. Devastated, on the train ride back to California he realized he needed a star he owned outright. Remembering a mouse that used to climb up on his desk in Kansas City, Disney turned to his wife, Lillian, and said "I think it will be a mouse, and I think I'll call him Mortimer." "Mortimer?" she asked. "I don't like it. What about Mickey?"

Using many of the visual cues of Oswald, Disney and partner Ub Iwerks designed the new mouse and cranked out two cartoons. Inspired by the fame of Charles Lindbergh, the first was the gag-filled "Plane Crazy." The second, "The Gallopin' Gaucho," cast Mickey as an Argentine outlaw. Neither sold.

Disney's solution? Make one with sound. To raise cash, Disney sold his roadster. He figured that, with the recent success of "The Jazz Singer," distributors would want a cartoon with sound, too.

He was wrong. Again and again, distributors still said no. When a New York promoter offered to run the cartoon for free just for the publicity value, Disney, with no other options, reluctantly agreed. The first synchronized sound cartoon, "Steamboat Willie" premiered at New York's Colony Theatre on Nov. 18, 1928. The public loved it, but only one distributor showed interest: Universal. Walt said no.

Finally, Disney did strike a distribution deal. With a sound-machine salesman.

As his Mickey cartoons took the country by storm, Disney put his profits back into his company. To ensure his artists were skilled, he paid for them to attend art school and later set up an in-house training center. Disney introduced Technicolor to animation with the 1932 Silly Symphonies cartoon "Flowers and Trees." In 1937 he released "The Old Mill," which used a multiplane camera to add realistic depth to animation.

All of that, however, was a warm-up for Disney's next idea: an animated feature film. The idea had been tried in Europe (with "Lotte Reiniger's Adventures of Prince Achmed") but never in the States. Disney knew he had the story, a dramatic, romantic, sympathetic fairy tale he had seen as a kid as a silent film: "Snow White." Though Hollywood scoffed at the idea, dubbing it "Walt's Folly," Disney mortgaged his home to help cover expenses.

The gamble paid off. Premiering December 21, 1937, "Snow White and the Seven Dwarfs" was such a smash that within six months the Disney company had millions in the bank. The film went on to gross $8 million, at a time when a child's movie ticket was just 10 cents.

Not interested in making a sequel, Disney instead created 1940's imaginative "Fantasia" and "Pinocchio," 1941's "Dumbo" and 1942's "Bambi." All lost money. None of the films could break even without the European market, which had disappeared after the outbreak of World War II.

There was more trouble. Rumors spread throughout the studio that major salary cuts and layoffs were coming. Soon, union organizers appeared at the studio, and on May 29, 1941, many of the company's animators went on strike. The walkout ended in just a few weeks, but Disney firmly believed the strike was inspired by communists. In 1947 he testified before the House Un-American Activities Committee that there was a threat of Communism in the motion-picture industry, though he added "I don't think they have gotten very far, and I think the industry is made up of good Americans, just like in my plant—good, solid Americans."

For awhile it seemed Disney couldn't catch a break. "Dumbo" was scheduled to appear on the cover of Time magazine the first week of December, 1941, until Japan bombed Pearl Harbor. During the war the U.S. military took over the studio in an effort to protect a nearby Lockheed aircraft plant, an act which essentially shut down Disney's commercial business for years.

By now Disney was a chain smoker. Studio workers could tell if he was coming down the hall by listening for his cough.

Disney's golden touch returned in the 1950s. Animated films included 1950's "Cinderella," 1951's "Alice in Wonderland" and 1953's "Peter Pan." The 1954 movie "20,000 Leagues Under the Sea" was the company's first live-action film and the first to have major stars, in this case Kirk Douglas, James Mason and Peter Lorre. Unlike many studio chiefs, Disney embraced television. He found success with shows such as "The Mickey Mouse Club" and "Zorro."

During the decade Disney also created a series of shorts on science and technology. Broadcasts of the "Disneyland" television show included three films produced with rocket designer Dr. Wernher von Braun. A 1957 episode of the show featured "Our Friend the Atom," a collaboration with the U.S. government designed to enhance the image of nuclear energy.

Back during the war, Disney would take his daughters to the carousel at Hollywood's Griffith Park, 10 miles from his home. A "As I'd sit there," he later recalled, "I felt there should be something built where the parents and the children could have fun together." In 1951 he visited Copenhagen's Tivoli Gardens, a lushly landscaped park with fireworks, parades, a railroad and exotic buildings, many with little white lights. "Now this is what an amusement place should be," Disney told his wife.

Two years later Disney bought 160 acres near Anaheim. Gathering some of his best motion-picture talent, he set about building Disneyland, the world's first theme park. Disney decided its central attraction would be a castle, and that its entrance would be a re-creation of a turn-of-the-century small town. As budgets increased Disney hocked his life insurance to get more cash. Construction began in July of 1954, and the park opened just one year later. It was a huge hit.

Success continued in the 1960s. In 1961 "One Hundred and One Dalmatians" was the year's No. 1 movie, and Disney's "Wonderful World of Color" was among the first color television programs.

Walt and Roy even entered the field of education. They provided the funds to merge the Los Angeles Conservatory of Music with the Chouinard Art Institute (where Disney had earlier sent his animators) to create the California Institute of the Arts. It would be the nation's first art institute to grant undergraduate and graduate degrees. Of Cal Arts, Walt once said, "It's the principal thing I hope to leave when I move on to greener pastures. If I can help provide a place to develop the talent of the future, I think I will have accomplished something." The campus is located in the city of Valencia, 32 miles northeast of downtown Los Angeles.

Everything came together in 1964. The New York World's Fair opened in April, and Disney's contributions, including Carousel of Progress, Great Moments with Mr. Lincoln and It's a Small World, became its top attractions. In August "Mary Poppins" premiered at Grauman's Chinese Theatre and soon became the studio's biggest hit ever.

In September President Johnson invited Disney to the White House to receive the Presidential Medal of Freedom, the nation's highest civilian honor. The man who 40 years earlier was bankrupt was now not only rich, but also a national hero.

Then 62 years old, Disney had one dream left: to fix America's cities. In 1965, Disney turned his attention toward the problem of

FUN FACTS » Married in 1888 in Acron, Florida, 40 miles north of today's Walt Disney World, Walt Disney's parents later grew oranges and ran a hotel in nearby Kissimmee. **»** The Disney company regained the rights to Oswald in 2006. Universal gave the bunny back in exchange for sportscaster Al Michaels. Really. **»** In 1949 Walt Disney built a scale-model live-steam railway in his backyard. The half-mile layout included a 46-foot-long trestle, overpasses and a 90-foot tunnel underneath his wife's flower beds. **»** Walt Disney's favorite meal was chili and beans with tomato juice.

improving urban life in America. His idea: Combine the money he made from "Mary Poppins" with corporate sponsorships, and then—using 43 square miles of land he had secretly purchased in Florida—build an experimental city. Filled with technological advancements, it would demonstrate how communities could solve their problems of housing, pollution and transportation. Disney called it the Experimental Prototype Community of Tomorrow. "EPCOT" for short.

"I don't believe there is a challenge anywhere in the world that is more important than finding the solution to the problems of our cities," he said. "We think the need is for starting from scratch on virgin land and building a community that will become a prototype for the future. EPCOT will be a community of tomorrow that will never be completed, but will always be introducing and testing and demonstrating new materials and new systems."

The design called for a 50-acre town center enclosed in a dome, an internationally themed shopping area, a 30-story hotel and convention complex, office space, apartments, single-family homes, monorail and PeopleMover systems, an airport, underground roads for cars and trucks, even a nuclear power plant. To make money he'd have a theme park, too, a larger version of Disneyland. Disney planned to finish the project by 1985. On Nov. 15, 1965, Walt and Roy held a press conference in Orlando to announce the project. "I'm very excited about it," Walt said to the media, "because I've been storing these things up over the years. I like to create new things."

But less than a year later, he got sick. The smoking had caught up with him.

In November 1966 doctors found a tumor the size of a walnut in Disney's left lung. But when they operated, they discovered the cancer had spread through the lung, and the entire organ had to be removed. Afterward Disney checked out of the hospital and went back to work, but he had to check back in just two weeks later. His body wasn't recovering.

On the night of December 14, Disney lay in his hospital bed and discussed his Florida project with Roy. Using the acoustical tiles on the ceiling above, Walt showed Roy his detailed, if imaginary, vision of the undertaking—the roads, airport, everything.

The next morning, Walt Disney died.

Some called Walt Disney too naive, a boy who never became an adult. But, to him, that was the point. "The American child is

SOURCES FOR THIS ARTICLE INCLUDE "WALT DISNEY: AN AMERICAN ORIGINAL" BY BOB THOMAS AND "WALT DISNEY AND THE QUEST FOR COMMUNITY" BY STEVE MANNHEIM

sensitive, humorous, open-minded, eager to learn, and has a strong sense of excitement, energy, and curiosity about the world in which he lives," he wrote in 1963. "Lucky indeed is the grown-up who manages to carry these same characteristics into adult life. That's the real trouble with the world. Too many people grow up."

Had he not smoked, Disney may have lived long enough to finish his EPCOT city. One of his brothers lived until age 98; his sister died at 92.

Disney's Fab Five

Since his debut in 1928's "Steamboat Willie," **Mickey Mouse** has been an American pop-culture icon. Modeled in part on silent-film star Charlie Chaplin, Mickey was an underdog who dreamed big, a character everyone could root for. In the 1930s his optimistic attitude was the perfect antidote to the Great Depression. During World War II he become symbolic of the can-do attitude of the United States. During the 1960s Mickey was embraced by the counterculture, a symbol of mischievous rebellion.

Today Mickey Mouse is still enormously popular, the most recognized and celebrated cartoon character in history. Sure he's a corporate symbol, but he's also an honest, pure piece of Americana.

When Mickey Mouse cartoons debuted in the late 1920s, an opening short had been a common feature at movie theaters for more than a decade. But these cartoons were different. Not only did they have sound, a newfangled novelty at the time, but Mickey had a strong personality, a happy-go-lucky approach to life that was said to be Walt Disney's alter ego. At many theaters, the name "Mickey Mouse" would be the largest on the marquee. In 1933 Mickey received 800,000 fan letters, the most of any Hollywood star. "Mickey Mouse is an international hero," Fortune magazine wrote in 1934, "better known than Roosevelt." Perhaps wondering what all the fuss was about, the president himself began showing Mickey Mouse cartoons at the White House.

During World War II, the password of the Allied forces on D-Day was "Mickey Mouse." Mickey was banned in Nazi Germany in 1933, the Soviet Union in 1936, Yugoslavia in 1937, Italy in 1938 and East Germany in 1954.

After World War II Mickey became so popular with children artists found it difficult to give him interesting behaviors. If he misbehaved, parents would complain.

Minnie Mouse is Mickey's girlfriend. She's always around to flatter, giggle at and swoon over her main squeeze. Still, she does have her own life. Quick-witted and energetic, she loves animals, cooking and gardening, and can play the harmonica, guitar and piano.

She also gets mad. After Mickey forces her to kiss him in 1928's "Plane Crazy," Minnie slaps him, then jumps out of their open-cockpit airplane. She smashes a lamp on Mickey's head when he pulls her nose in 1930's "The Cactus Kid." And when she mistakenly thinks Mickey has given her a bone for a present in 1933's "Puppy Love," she kicks him out of her house and sobs "I hate him! I hate all men!"

As portrayed in the 1928 cartoon "The Gallopin' Gaucho," the couple first laid eyes on each other in a bar in Argentina. When Minnie, a flirty dancer, bats her eyes at Mickey, a cigarette-smoking outlaw, he watches her perform, chugs a beer, then grabs her for a tango. Minnie has an old flame (suave, tap-dancing Mortimer) in the 1936 cartoon "Mickey's Rival." In 1933's "Mickey's Steam Roller," she has kids.

Walt Disney originally did the voices for both Mickey and Minnie.

He's rude, he's crude, he doesn't wear pants. He shouts, pouts and loses his temper at the drop of a pin. He often just likes to be mean. Yet who doesn't love **Donald Duck,** who responds to life the way we are tempted to, but rarely dare.

Created in 1934 as a foil for the then-gentlemanly Mickey, Donald soon emerged as Disney's most popular star. Besides his personality, Donald is famous for his nearly unintelligible voice, originally done by bird impressionist Clarence "Ducky" Nash. The "duck with all the bad luck" is also known for his "hopping mad" boxing stance, a leaning, jumping posture with one arm straight and the other twirling like a windmill.

A good-hearted simpleton, **Goofy** appeals to your inner idiot. He's clumsy and gullible, has a hard time concentrating and seldom finishes what he starts—just like, ahem, many husbands. He has bad posture, his clothes don't fit, his stomach is too big, yet he always mugs for a camera. First known as Dippy Dog, Goofy made his debut in 1930. He later became the host of a series of "How To" sports parodies. In the 1950s Disney transformed Goofy into George Geef, a suburban everyman often drawn without ears. As for the eternal question—man or dog?—the answer is... both! Unlike Pluto, Goofy is an upright talking character, but he has physical characteristics of a dog, including floppy ears and a snout.

One of the greatest dogs in Hollywood history, gangly yellow hounddog **Pluto** is only Five Fab character who doesn't speak or walk upright (except at the theme parks). Instead, Mickey's pet licks, sniffs, romps and runs in a fashion instantly recognizable to dog lovers everywhere. Always thinking, Pluto is known for his vivid expressions.

He once spoke. In the 1931 short "The Moose Hunt," Pluto got down on his knees and, doing his best impersonation of Al Jolson, proclaimed "Mammy!" Moments later, he looked into Mickey's eyes and whispered "Kiss me!"

'Cinderella'

The classic rags-to-riches tale, "Cinderella" began as a Chinese fable. In the 9th-century "Yeh-Shen," a stepmother and two daughters humiliate a hard-working girl. But when a 10-foot fish gives her food, a beautiful dress and tiny slippers*, she gains confidence.

Often sweeping the fireplace, the girl gets so covered in ash her stepsisters call her Cinderella ("cinder girl") in Charles Perrault's French version, written to entertain the 17th-century court of Louis XIV. When a king wants his son to wed, he has the prince invite all the land's maidens to a two-night ball. Cinderella's stepmom won't let her go, but then her fairy godmother (the spirit of her real mom) appears. Waving a magic wand, she turns a pumpkin into a coach, mice into horses, rats and lizards to footmen, and the girl's ragged dress into a ball gown, with glass slippers. Cinderella can go to the ball, the godmother says, but the magic wears off at midnight. The first night the girl mesmerizes the prince and leaves on time, but the next night she stays until the moment the clock strikes twelve. Rushing out, she loses a slipper, which the prince recovers. Determined to find her, he orders his Grand Duke (chief of staff) to test the shoe on every girl in the kingdom. On Cinderella's foot it slides on perfectly.

* In ancient China tiny feet were a status symbol. The practice of foot binding started with palace dancers, but was soon used by wealthy parents to fashion their daughters for marriage. The painful process began when a girl was about 5 years old. Each foot was wrapped in a long bandage (compressing her arches and bending under all of her smaller toes) then jammed in a shoe far too small. As the girl grew, her feet could not. Eventually they would deform into hoof-like clubs just a few inches long.

The story got bloody when Germany's Brothers Grimm published their version, "Aschenputtel," in 1812. When the slipper won't fit the stepsisters, their mom has them slice off their heels and toes and try again. During Cinderella's wedding, birds peck out the sisters' eyes.

Disney's 1950 film gave Perrault's tale new life. It cleaned up the plot, added a supporting animal cast and catchy songs, and beefed up the finale. Disney's stepmother locks Cinderella in her room when the Grand Duke arrives. The girl's mice pals unlock it, but then the stepmom trips the Duke, causing him to drop the slipper and break it. Cinderella, however, reaches into her pocket and pulls out the mate.

Walt Disney produced the first animated Cinderella in 1922, when his Laugh-O-Grams Co. produced an "Alice" silent cartoon based on the tale. Betty Boop danced her way through 1934's "Poor Cinderella." Rodgers and Hammerstein's 1957 musical "Cinderella" is still the most popular television special ever. Starring Julie Andrews, it drew 71 percent of all Americans with a TV set. The production was remade with Lesley Ann Warren in 1965, and with Brandy in 1997. Jerry Lewis learns geeks, too, have charms in 1960's "Cinderfella" when a Disney-like Cinderella pops out of the past to flirt with him: "If I weren't a married woman," she purrs, "Grrrr!"

Hollywood ignored the fable for decades, but in the '90s Cindy was back and always in charge. In 1998's "Ever After," the princess-to-be (Drew Barrymore) escapes her step family and enlightens the prince about social policy. A feisty "Ella" breaks out into Queen's "Somebody to Love" in the 2004 musical "Ella Enchanted." And she's no passive patsy in 2004's "A Cinderella Story." After dressing as Cinderella for a high-school ball, Hilary Duff gains the courage to simply walk out on her step family and her princely quarterback, until he decides to join her. Then they're off to their dream college: Princeton.

'Beauty and the Beast'

"Beauty and the Beast" got its start in Roman mythology. In "Cupid and Psyche," philosopher Lucius Apuleius told the tale of Psyche, the youngest of three mortal sisters. Incredibly pretty, Psyche earns the envy of Venus, the goddess of beauty. But when Venus orders her son, Cupid, to make the girl fall in love with a castle-dwelling snake, Cupid himself falls in love with her, and secretly turns himself into the snake. Cupid gives Psyche a great life in the castle, including invisible servants who prepare her food, and eventually turns himself back to a man.

The story spreads as societies became mobile, and eventually over 200 Eurasian folk tales have a similar plot: a beautiful girl with two mean sisters finds herself living with a beast, who becomes human once she cares for him. A Chinese version makes a few changes — including a "golden shoe" — and becomes the first "Cinderella."

The love of a good woman turns a pig into a prince in the first published beauty-and-beast fable. Produced soon after printing presses became widespread in 1553, "The Pig King" was one of many folk tales transcribed by Italian novelist Giovanni Straparola. This beast marries all three sisters, one at a time. He kills the oldest two because they don't like him "climbing into bed stinking with filthy paws and snout."

The Beast is a snake again in 1650, when the story becomes a popular parlor tale among French aristocrats. In this, the first story named "Beauty and the Beast," a king has three daughters, and one day he leaves to get them each a gift. When he comes upon a deserted castle he plucks a rose for his youngest, named Beauty. "Who said you could take my flower?" a voice asks. "I will kill you for that, unless you bring me one of your girls." Beauty volunteers. She doesn't see anyone when she arrives at the castle, but the next morning wakes up to find a serpent in her lap. "You must marry me," it hisses. Beauty says no, but the snake persists. It orders its servants to starve her, and each day repeats its demand. Finally, she gives in. "I won't marry a serpent," she says, "but I will marry a man." The snake turns itself into a handsome prince.

Oodles of *oo-lá-lá* come into the Beauty and the Beast story once French blueblood Gabrielle de Villeneuve gets hold of it in 1740. Writing for the pleasure of her salon friends, she turns her prince into a beast after he refuses a promiscuous fairy. When Beauty arrives, he doesn't ask "Will you marry me?" but "Will you go to bed with me?" He stays a beast until after the wedding night.

The story becomes a child's fable 16 years later. In 1756, French tutor Jeanne-Marie Leprince de Beaumont publishes her version, a tale she had written to prepare her young charges (girls ages 5–13) for arranged marriages. She bases her story on the earlier serpent tale, but makes the Beast a humble, gentle mammal. Wanting her girls to believe that love can make any man princely, Beaumont contrasted Beauty's beastly fate with that of the girl's two sisters: The first is matched with a handsome man who thinks only of himself. The second gets a smart man who belittles his bride. "Many women," this Beauty ponders, "are made to marry men far more beastly than mine." Beaumont's own arranged marriage had been annulled when her philandering husband contracted a venereal disease. To encourage girls to read, Beaumont makes Beauty a book lover. Her story becomes the definitive "Beauty" fairy tale.

The love of a beauty rescues the soul of a bloodthirsty beast in the first "Beauty and the Beast" movie, a 1947 French film by avant-garde artist Jean Cocteau. The adult melodrama grows tedious in its second act (40 minutes of little more than the Beast bellowing "Belle!") but its surreal images (living busts and candelabras, and a disembodied arm that pours wine) make it an art-house favorite. Its Beauty is no role model. She faints when she first sees the Beast and shudders ecstatically when she sees him again. A remake of the film appears in 1983 as an episode of the Showtime television series "Faerie Tale Theatre." Directed by French auteur Roger Vadim, it stars a blond Susan Sarandon.

Can a man sleep in a sewer and still hook up with a society gal? That's the premise of the 1987–1990 CBS television series "Beauty and the Beast." Linda Hamilton plays Catherine Chandler, a wealthy New Yorker who wants more out of life. Ron Perlman is Vincent, her beasty boy beneath the streets.

It's no wonder that Disney's animated "Beauty and the Beast" was nominated for a Best Picture Oscar. Packed with life, humor and music, it also has a great message: A girl can be herself, speak her mind and still end up with a prince of a hubby. Smart, gutsy and with plans for her life, this Belle is no pushover. The villagers say she's a "most peculiar mademoiselle" but she couldn't care less; while street tarts swoon for the town hunk she pushes him off. And when the Beast yells at her, she yells back.

Disney keeps the meat of Beaumont's tale but cuts the fat, eliminating the sisters and downplaying the dad. And it adds a villain: the handsome Gaston, who grows beastly as the Beast grows human.

BOOKS

Anderson, Philip Longfellow. "The Gospel in Disney: Christian Values in the Early Animated Classics." Augsburg Books, 2004.

"The Annotated Classic Fairy Tales" edited by Marie Tatar. W.W. Norton & Company Ltd., 2002.

Appelbaum, Stanley. "The New York World's Fair 1939/1940." Dover Publications, 1977.

Bacher, Hans. "Dream Worlds: Production Design for Animation." Focal Press, 2007.

Barrie, J. M. "Peter Pan." Charles Scribner's Sons, 1911, 1985.

Barrier, Michael. "The Animated Man: A Life of Walt Disney." University of California Press, 2008.

Borgenicht, David. "The Classic Tales of Brer Rabbit." Running Press, 1995.

Brode, Douglas. "From Walt to Woodstock: How Disney Created the Counterculture." University of Texas Press, 2004.

Canemaker, John. "The Art and Flair of Mary Blair: An Appreciation." Disney Editions, 2003.

Canemaker, John. "Walt Disney's Nine Old Men and the Art of Animation." Disney Editions, 2001.

Capodagli, Bill. "The Disney Way, Revised Edition." McGraw-Hill, 2006.

Connellan, Tom. "Inside the Magic Kingdom." Bard Press, 1997.

Corey, Melinda and Ochoa, George. "The American Film Institute Desk Reference." Stonesong Press, 2002.

Davis, Stephen. "Walk This Way: The Autobiography of Aerosmith." Harper Paperbacks, 2003.

Dunlop, Beth. "Building a Dream: The Art of Disney Architecture." Harry N. Abrams, 1996.

"E.Encyclopedia Animal." DK, 2005.

Eisner, Michael. "Work in Progress." Random House, 1998.

Finch, Christopher. "The Art of Walt Disney." Harry N. Abrams, 2004.

Finch, Christopher. "Jim Henson: The Works: The Art, the Magic, the Imagination." Random House, 1993.

Finch, Christopher. "Walt Disney's America." Abbeville Press, 1978.

Fjellman, Stephen M. "Vinyl Leaves: Walt Disney World and America." Westview Press, 1992.

Flower, Joe. "Prince of the Magic Kingdom: Michael Eisner and the Re-making of Disney." Wiley, 1991.

Gabler, Neal. "Walt Disney: The Triumph of the American Imagination." Vintage, 2007.

Griswold, Jerry. "The Meanings of 'Beauty and the Beast,' a Handbook." Broadview Press, 2004.

Grover, Ron. "The Disney Touch: Disney, ABC and The Quest for the World's Greatest Media Empire." McGraw-Hill Trade, 1996.

Hahn, Don. "Disney's Animation Magic." Disney Press, 1996.

Harris, Joel Chandler. "The Complete Tales of Uncle Remus." Houghton Mifflin Company, 1955.

Heide, Robert and Gilman, John. "Mickey Mouse: The Evolution, the Legend, the Phenomenon!" Disney Editions, 2001.

Hench, John. "Designing Disney: Imagineering and the Art of the Show." Disney Editions, 2003.

"The Imagineering Field Guide to Disney's Animal Kingdom at Walt Disney World." Disney Editions, 2005.

"The Imagineering Field Guide to Epcot at Walt Disney World." Disney Editions, 2005.

"The Imagineering Field Guide to the Magic Kingdom at Walt Disney World." Disney Editions, 2005.

Kinney, Jack. "Walt Disney and Assorted Other Characters." Harmony, 1988.

Koenig, David. "Realityland: True-Life Adventures at Walt Disney World." Bonaventure Press, 2007.

Kurtti, Jeff. "Since the World Began: Walt Disney World's First 25 Years." Hyperion, 1996.

Kurtti, Jeff. "Walt Disney's Legends of Imagineering and the Genesis of the Disney Theme Park." Disney Editions, 2008.

Lamb, Bob. "Field Guide to Disney's Animal Kingdom Theme Park." Roundtable Press, 2000.

Lambert, Pierre. "Mickey Mouse." Hyperion, 1998.

Lane, Jack. "A Gallery of Stars: The Story of the Hollywood Brown Derby Wall of Fame." Luminary Press, 2005.

Lester, Julius. "Tales of Uncle Remus: The Adventures of Brer Rabbit." Puffin, 2006.

Malmberg, Melody. "The Making of Disney's Animal Kingdom Theme Park." Hyperion 1998.

Maltin, Leonard. "The Disney Films." Disney Editions, 1995, 2000.

Maltin, Leonard. "Of Mice and Magic: A History of American Animated Cartoons." Penguin Books, 1987.

Mannheim, Steve. "Walt Disney and the Quest for Community." Ashgate Publishing, 2002.

Marling, Karal Ann. "Designing Disney's Theme Parks: The Architecture of Reassurance." Hyperion, 1997.

Milne, A.A. "Winnie-the-Pooh." Puffin Books, 1926, 1992.

Mosley, Leonard. "Disney's World." Scarborough House, 1990.

Neary, Kevin and Smith, Dave. "The Ultimate Disney Trivia Book Vols. 1–3." Hyperion, 1992, 1994, 1997.

"Official Guide: New York World's Fair 1964/1965." Time Inc., 1964.

Paik, Karen. "To Infinity and Beyond!: The Story of Pixar Animation Studios." Chronicle Books, 2007.

Philip, Neil. "The Complete Fairy Tales of Charles Perrault." Albion, 1993.

Philip, Neil. "The Illustrated Book of Myths: Tales and Legends of the World." DK, 1995.

Pinsky, Mark I. "The Gospel According to Disney: Faith, Trust, and Pixie Dust." Westminster John Knox Press, 2004.

Price, David. A. "The Pixar Touch: The Making of a Company," Knopf, 2008.

Price, Harrison "Buzz." "Walt's Revolution! By the Numbers." Ripley Entertainment, 2004.

Rafferty, Kevin. "Walt Disney Imagineering." Disney Editions, 1996.

Ridgway, Charles. "Spinning Disney's World: Memories of a Magic Kingdom Press Agent." Intrepid Traveler, 2007.

Samuelson, Dale. "The American Amusement Park." MBI, 2001.

Schickel, Richard. "The Disney Version: The Life, Times, and Commerce of Walt Disney." Simon & Schuster, 1968, 1985, 1997.

Schroeder, Russell K. "Disney: The Ultimate Visual Guide." Dorling Kindersley Ltd., 2002.

Schroeder, Russell. "Walt Disney: His Life in Pictures." Disney Press, 1996.

Smith, Dave. "Disney A to Z: The Official Encyclopedia." Hyperion, 1998, 2006.

Smith, Dave. "The Quotable Walt Disney." Disney Editions, 2001.

Smith, Dave and Clark, Steven. "Disney: The First 100 Years." Hyperion, 1999.

Stewart, James B. "Disney War." Simon & Schuster, 2005.

Surrell, Jason. "The Disney Mountains: Imagineering At Its Peak." Disney Editions, 2007.

Surrell, Jason. "The Haunted Mansion: From the Magic Kingdom to the Movies." Disney Editions, 2003.

Surrell, Jason. "Pirates of the Caribbean: From the Magic Kingdom to the Movies." Disney Editions, 2005.

Taylor, John. "Storming the Magic Kingdom." Knopf, 1987.

Telotte, J.P. "The Mouse Machine: Disney and Technology." University of Illinois Press, 2008.

Thomas, Bob. "Building a Company: Roy O. Disney and the Creation of an Entertainment Empire." Hyperion, 1998.

Thomas, Bob. "Walt Disney: An American Original." Hyperion, 1994.

Thomas, Frank and Johnston, Ollie.

"The Illusion of Life: Disney Animation." Disney Editions, 1995.

Tieman, Robert. "The Disney Keepsakes." Disney Editions, 2005.

Tieman, Robert. "The Disney Treasures." Disney Editions, 2003.

Tieman, Robert. "The Mickey Mouse Treasures." Disney Editions, 2007.

Tieman, Robert. "Quintessential Disney." Disney Editions, 2007.

Twain, Mark. "The Adventures of Tom Sawyer." Fine Creative Media, 2003.

"25 Years of Walt Disney World." Disney's Kingdom Editions, 1996.

"Walt Disney Animation Studios The Archive Series: Story." Disney Editions, 2008.

"Walt Disney Imagineering: A Behind the Dreams Look at Making the Magic Real." Hyperion, 1996.

"Walt Disney Resort: A Magical Year-By-Year Journey." Hyperion, 1998.

Watts, Steven. "The Magic Kingdom: Walt Disney and the American Way of Life." Houghton Mifflin, 1997.

Zipes, Jack. "The Complete Fairy Tales of the Brothers Grimm." Bantam, 1992.

VIDEO

"101 Dalmatians (Two-Disc Platinum Edition)." Walt Disney Studios Home Entertainment (WDSHE), 2008.

"A Bug's Life (Two-Disc Collector's Edition)." WDSHE, 2004.

"Alice in Wonderland (Masterpiece Edition)." WDSHE, 2004.

"Aladdin (Disney Special Platinum Edition)." WDSHE, 2004.

"The Aristocats (Special Edition)." WDSHE, 2008.

"Bambi (2-Disc Special Platinum Edition)." WDSHE, 2005.

"Beauty and the Beast." WDSHE, 2002.

"Cars (Widescreen Edition)." WDSHE, 2006.

"The Chronicles of Narnia - The Lion, the Witch and the Wardrobe." WDSHE, 2005.

"Cinderella (Two-Disc Special Edition)." WDSHE, 2005.

"Dinosaur." WDSHE, 2001.

"Dumbo (Big Top Edition)." WDSHE, 2006.

"Ella Enchanted (Widescreen Edition)." Miramax, 2004.

"Enchanted (Widescreen Edition)." WDSHE, 2008.

"Fantasia (Special 60th Anniversary Edition)." WDSHE, 2000.

"Finding Nemo (Two-Disc Collector's Edition)." WDSHE, 2003.

"Hercules (Disney Gold Classic Collection)" WDSHE, 2000.

"High School Musical (Encore Edition)." WDSHE, 2006.

"High School Musical 2 (Extended Edition)." WDSHE, 2007.

"High School Musical 3: Senior Year." WDSHE, 2009.

"The Incredibles (Two-Disc Collector's Edition)." WDSHE, 2005.

"Indiana Jones - The Adventure Collection." Paramount, 2008.

"The Jungle Book (40th Anniversary Platinum Edition)." WDSHE, 2007.

"Lady and the Tramp (50th Anniversary Edition)." WDSHE, 2006.

"Lilo & Stitch." WDSHE, 2002.

"The Lion King (Disney Special Platinum Edition)." WDSHE, 2003.

"The Little Mermaid (Two-Disc Platinum Edition)." WDSHE, 2004.

"The Little Mermaid Trilogy." WDSHE, 2008.

"The Many Adventures of Winnie the Pooh (The Friendship Edition)." WDSHE, 2007.

"Mary Poppins (45th Anniversary Edition)." WDSHE, 2009.

"Meet the Robinsons." WDSHE, 2007.

"Modern Marvels: Walt Disney World," A&E Home Video, 2006.

"Monsters, Inc. (Two-Disc Collector's Edition)." WDSHE, 2002.

"Mulan (Special Edition)." WDSHE, 2004.

"The Muppet Show - Season One (Special Edition)." WDSHE, 2005.

"The Muppet Show - Season Two." WDSHE, 2007.

"The Muppet Show - The Complete Third Season." WDSHE, 2008.

"The Nightmare Before Christmas (2-Disc Collector's Edition)." WDSHE, 2008.

"Peter Pan (2-Disc Platinum Edition)." WDSHE, 2008.

"Peter Pan (Widescreen Edition)." Universal Studios, 2004.

"Pinocchio (2-Disc Special Platinum Edition)." WDSHE, 2009.

"Pirates of the Caribbean - The Curse of the Black Pearl (Two-Disc Collector's Edition)." WDSHE, 2003.

"Pirates of the Caribbean - Dead Man's Chest (Two-Disc Collector's Edition)." WDSHE, 2006.

"Pirates of the Caribbean - At World's End (Two-Disc Collector's Edition)." WDSHE, 2007.

"Pixar Short Films Collection - Volume 1." WDSHE, 2007.

"Pocahontas (10th Anniversary Edition)." WDSHE, 2005.

"Ratatouille." WDSHE, 2007.

"Robin Hood (Most Wanted Edition)." WDSHE, 2006.

"Saludos Amigos / Three Caballeros." WDSHE, 2008.

"Sleeping Beauty (Two-Disc Platinum Edition)." WDSHE, 2008.

"Snow White and the Seven Dwarfs (Disney Special Platinum Edition)." WDSHE, 2001.

"Star Wars Trilogy (Widescreen Edition with Bonus Disc)." 20th Century Fox, 2004.

"Swiss Family Robinson (Vault Disney Collection)." WDSHE, 2002.

"Tinker Bell" WDSHE, 2008.

"The Sword in the Stone (45th Anniversary Special Edition)" WDSHE, 2008.

"Toy Story (10th Anniversary Edition)." WDSHE, 2005.

"Toy Story 2 (Two-Disc Special Edition)." WDSHE, 2005.

"Wall-E (Widescreen Single-Disc Edition)" WDSHE, 2008.

"Walt: The Man Behind the Myth." WDSHE, 2004.

"Walt Disney Legacy Collection - True Life Adventures, Vol. 3." WDSHE, 2006.

"Walt Disney Treasures" series, WDSHE, 2002-2008.

"Who Framed Roger Rabbit (Vista Series)" WDSHE, 2003.

"The Wizard of Oz (Three-Disc Collector's Edition." Warner Home Video, 2005.

Acknowledgments Our thanks to Jonathan Frontado, Jason Lasecki, Dave Herbst, Juliana Cadiz, Liz Benz, Darrell Fry, David Hillstrom and Bebee Frost at Walt Disney World Public Relations for providing a variety of assistance. We also thank everyone else who supplied information and resources, including: Rosa Acosta, Ross Adams, Craig Albert, Ngonba Anadou, Odalys Aponte, Stephen Ashley, Ron Asimos, Karen Aulino, Kevin Baker, Jasmine Barczyk, Jane Berry, David Brady, Theresa Broderick, William Burke, Shawn Cannon, Shelly Carter, Chrissy Chamberlain, Jody Chase, John Chenciner, Steve Christ, the Cleary family and their beautiful princesses, Lee Cockerell, Egg Man Extraordinaire Greg Collins, the Connells (Matthew, Sherri, Anna), Brian Cotten, Elise Cottle, Amy and Mitch Crews, Megan DeVries, Karen Derose, Princess Becky DeSenti (Uncle Tony's favorite niece), the Dix family, Jason Dobbins, Jamie Entwistle, Catherine Ewer, Aiden Feeback, Andrea Finger, Eric Jacobson, Keith Gimbel, Michelle Ginesin, Lorraine Gorham, Aurélie Grand, Jeff Green, Barbara Gross, Charlie Hall, Dana Hall, Liz Hall, Robert Hargrove, Barbara Harris, Laura Hatch, Lonnie Hicks, Tonia Hill, Mark Hoevenaars, Trina Hofreiter, Roger Isako, Bob Iske, Jennifer Jacobsen, Eric Jacobson, Kristie A. Jones, Kristine Jones, Traci Kennedy, Mary Kenny, Azhar Khan, Tommy King, Kelly Knowlen, Daniel Lahr, Jeff Lindberg, Josh Little, Kathy Mangum, Tony Marotta, Roberto Martinez, Carrie Matlack, Amanda Maure, Jennifer McKay, Suzan Meaux, Sherri Mercer, Albert Miller, Bob Miller, Bo Morris, Doobie and Rebekah Moseley, Nenette Mputu, Laura Murphy, Kim and Diane Nelson, NFFC World Chapter members, Zakee Nichols, Theresa Nieves, David Njoroge, Sanja Novakovich, Sandra OShields, Tina Pankow, Sunni Petty, Thabo Pheto, Brian Piasecki, Brenda Porter, Ernie Porterfield, Honor Rasch-Gush, Jodi Rauer, Michelle Reeves, Frank Reifsnyder, Mark Renfro, Kevin Renzi, Alfonso Ribeiro, Laura Richeson, Charles Ridgway, Joe Rindler, Wally Robinson, Todd Roby, Kathy Rogers, Joe Rohde, Catherine Roth, Hanns-Claudius and Monika Scharff, Steve Schussler, Shannon Shelton, Brandon Sims, Theron Skees, Jennifer Smith, Lynne Smith, Courtney and Jerry Soares, Brian Spitler, Jason Surrell, Rheo Tan, Gary Terry, Dikeledi Tlhako, Kendra Trahan, the Turners (Jeff, Anna, Laura, Michael, Andrew), Michelle Valle, Kim Veon, Jon Wagner-Holtz, Jenn Wakelin, Robin Walker, Andy Warren, Christopher White, Dave Williams, George Willis, Consuelo Wint, Herb and Debbie Wright and all the various Disney resort managers and park duty managers.

INDEX

Tweedledum takes a call at Magic Kingdom

Phone directory

DISNEY RESORTS
Reservations:
407-934-7639
All-Star Movies:
407-939-7000
All-Star Music:
407-939-6000
All-Star Sports:
407-939-5000
Animal Kingdom Lodge:
407-938-3000
Beach Club:
407-934-8000
Best Western:
407-828-2424
BoardWalk:
407-939-5100
Buena Vista Palace:
407-827-2727
Caribbean Beach:
407-934-3400
Contemporary:
407-824-1000
Coronado Springs:
407-939-1000
DoubleTree Suites:
407-934-1000
Fort Wilderness:
407-824-2900
Grand Floridian:
407-824-3000
Hilton:
407-827-4000
Holiday Inn:
407-828-8888
Old Key West:
407-827-7700

Polynesian:
407-824-2000
Pop Century:
407-938-4000
Port Orleans French Quarter:
407-934-5000
Port Orleans Riverside:
407-934-6000
Regal Sun:
407-828-4444
Royal Plaza:
407-828-2828
Saratoga Springs:
407-827-1100
Wilderness Lodge:
407-824-3200
Yacht Club:
407-934-7000
Shades of Green:
407-824-3600
WDW Dolphin:
407-934-4000
WDW Swan:
407-934-3000
GENERAL
Birthday parties:
407-939-2329
Carriage rides:
407-939-7529
Disney Institute:
407-566-2620
Disney operator:
407-824-2222
Foreign language assistance:
407-824-2222

Florist:
407-827-3505
Merchandise:
407-363-6200
Post office:
Lake Buena Vista:
407-238-0223
Scooters, strollers and wheelchairs:
EZ Street Rentals:
866-394-1115
SunTrust Bank:
407-828-6103
Tours:
407-939-8687
Travel packages:
407-934-7639
VIP Tours:
407-560-4033
Weather:
407-824-4104
LOST AND FOUND
Animal Kingdom:
407-938-2785
Downtown Disney:
407-828-3150
Blizzard Beach:
407-560-5408
Hollywood Studios:
407-560-3720
Epcot:
407-560-6646
Magic Kingdom:
407-824-4521
Typhoon Lagoon:
407-560-6296
After 24 hours:
407-824-4245
MEDICAL CARE
Florida Hospital Emergency Dept:
407-303-4034

Centra Care Walk-In Clinic:
407-239-6463
In-Room Care:
407-238-2000
Turner Pharmacy:
407-828-8125
RECREATION
General reservations:
407-939-7529
Boat rentals:
407-939-7529
ESPN Wide World of Sports:
407-828-3267
Fishing excursions:
407-939-2277
Golf reservations:
407-939-4653
Horseback riding:
407-824-2900
Miniature golf:
Fantasia Gardens
407-560-4753
Winter Summerland:
407-560-7161
Pony rides:
407-824-2788
Richard Petty Driving Experience:
1-800-237-3889
Surfing lessons:
407-939-7873
Tennis:
407-939-7529
Water Sports:
407-939-0754
RESTAURANTS
Reservations:
407-939-3463
TRANSPORTATION
Car Care Center:
407-824-0976
After-hours:
407-824-4777
Alamo Rent A Car:
407-824-3470
Hess Express:
Magic Kingdom:
407-938-0143
Epcot Resort Area:
407-938-0151
Downtown Disney:
407-938-0160
Magical Express:
866-599-0951
Mears (cabs, etc.):
407-423-5566